"The Ideal Place . . . for the
Establishment of a Great Law School"

"THE IDEAL PLACE . . .
FOR THE ESTABLISHMENT
OF A GREAT LAW SCHOOL"

History of Washburn Law School,
1903–2003

JAMES M. CONCANNON
Distinguished Professor of Law

To John Reynolds -
Best wishes.
Jim Concannon
10/10/12

Washburn University School of Law Alumni Association
Topeka, Kansas · 2012

Cataloging-in-Publication Data
Concannon, James M.
"The ideal place...for the establishment of a great law school" : history of Washburn Law School, 1903-2003 / James M. Concannon.
p. cm.
Includes bibliographical references and index.
ISBN 978-0-615-60187-8 (alk. paper)
1. Washburn University of Topeka. School of Law–History. 2. Law schools–Kansas–History. 3. Law–Study and teaching (Graduate)–Kansas–History. I. Title
KF292.W284C66 2012
340.071'1781
Library of Congress Control Number: 2012933264

Book design by Ashley Muehlbauer
Printed in the United States of America by Thomson-Shore

Printed on 50# Natures Book Natural paper, which is certified by the Forest Stewardship Council. FSC certification ensures the environmentally responsible, socially acceptable, and economically viable use of well-managed forests.

CONTENTS

ILLUSTRATIONS

View these photographs, and others related to the history of
Washburn Law School, online at washburnlaw.edu/history/

PREFACE

Books commonly are published to celebrate the centennial of an institution. I was the logical person to write that book about Washburn Law School. I learned much about its history during my years on the faculty and thirteen years as Dean. In addition, research for my article about other law schools of early day Kansas broadened my understanding of the legal profession and legal education in Kansas near the time the Law School opened. Still, this project has taken far longer than I anticipated, and I am amazed how much of this history I did not know.

A history of the Law School was written more than forty years ago by Ellen Sue McLane, a non-lawyer staff member for the Washburn Alumni Association. It was published as a special issue of the University's alumni magazine, *The Washburn Alumnus,* in September 1969, coinciding with the dedication of the new law building constructed after the 1966 tornado. Its title was "A Home at Last: A History of Washburn School of Law." It was only seventeen pages long, including many photographs. Thus, it was short on detail and it emphasized the positive. It is clear from the text that Ms. McLane solicited written recollections from graduates of early classes and may have interviewed some of them personally. Efforts to locate the source materials Ms. McLane compiled have failed. Sadly, they likely were not preserved.

There are many wonderful stories here that will make Law School graduates proud of their school and help faculty members, present and future, appreciate what a unique institution it is. However, this book is not a selective puff piece that focuses only on the school's successes. Times of struggle and times when the school's survival was in doubt are integral to its history. I have attempted to tell the full story, challenges and all. Of course, there are a few stories that prudence dictates not be told yet, but there aren't many. I urge readers who know stories that should be in this book but are not to send them to me so they can be included in a subsequent history of the school.

I was a member of the faculty for the last thirty of the school's first 100 years. The chapters covering those years are longer than earlier chapters, in part because I was a witness to many of the events I describe but also because we had so many more students and so many more faculty members doing so much more than in earlier years.

I am grateful to many readers of preliminary drafts for the corrections they made, the omissions they identified, and the improvements they suggested, both substantive and editorial. I particularly thank Margaret Carkhuff, Jalen O'Neil Lowry '87, Jim Sloan '52, Tim Belsan '09, and Roy Bird for reading the full manuscript and providing extensive feedback. Others who provided valuable input to one or more chapters include Professors William Harvey and Keith Hey, the late Dean John Howe, Joseph W. Morris '47, Bill Bunten '56, Winton Hinkle '68, Tom Loftus '80, Lynn McCreary '94, Christina Apperson '97, Kathy Webb '83, Sabrina Standifer '99, Ken Morse '80, and Paul Hoferer '75, and my faculty colleagues Bill Rich, Linda Elrod '72, Alex Glashausser, David Pierce '77, Sheila Reynolds, and Carl Monk. I also am grateful to Martin Wisneski, Assistant Director of the Law Library, Carol Duffy McDowell '75, former Alumni Director Carolyn Barnes, and university archivist Martha Imparato for their work in evaluating publication options and identifying sources of information and photographs to include. Carolyn's and Martin's efforts were indispensable in coordinating publication. In addition, I thank library staff members Sarah Tenfelde-Dubois for her meticulous work preparing the index, Dee Barker, and Janet Todwong for scanning and preparing photographs. Thanks, too to my administrative assistant for much of the project, Carol Rhodes, and her successor, Monice Crawford.

Any profits from this book will go to the Washburn University School of Law Alumni Association for the benefit of the school and I thank the alumni Board of Governors for underwriting publication costs.

Chapter 1 reprints, with minor modifications, my article about the early years of the Law School in the Centennial Issue of the *Washburn Law Journal*. Unless noted otherwise, unpublished material cited in the footnotes is on file at Washburn Law Library or in administrative files of Washburn Law School.

James M. Concannon
March, 2012

FOREWORD

With eloquence and candor, former Dean James Concannon has compiled a historical piece about Washburn University School of Law that only he can deliver. His nearly 40 years of experience teaching and leading the law school as dean uniquely qualify him for a task of this magnitude.

Rarely will you find an organization that produces a detailed account of its history without gently "refining" the rough edges. Dean Concannon himself acknowledges that his book, however, is not a watered-down version of the law school's history, or as he puts it, "This book is not a selective puff piece that focuses only on the school's successes." Thank goodness, for it's this type of storytelling that intrigues and hooks the reader until the final period.

What you are about to read are authentic accounts of the law school's storied life. Most revealing among the recollections of the devoted professors, staff members, students, and friends of the law school are the accounts of relationships forged during both turmoil and triumph, including the devastation and subsequent revitalization of the law school following the 1966 Topeka tornado that killed 16 and injured more than 500 residents. The tornado's violent winds, estimated at 300 mph, damaged every building on the Washburn campus, totally destroying many of them. From the rubble, the dedicated individuals you will hear from built bonds for life while constructing a remarkable future for Washburn Law.

Like an archeologist carefully excavating a significant historical site, Dean Concannon has found rare nuggets of information from peers, former students, staff members, and friends of the law school. He delves beyond the bedrock to uncover the substance of relationships, including political strife within the law school walls.

As Dean Concannon points out, throughout changes in leadership and location, Washburn Law's main focus always has been and always will be on its students. In its 100-plus years of educating some of the brightest and most dedicated individuals ever to write a brief or argue a case, Washburn University School of Law has maintained its core values of respect for students, emphasis on student learning, faculty collegiality and camaraderie, and providing a caring atmosphere. I'm grateful for Dean Concannon's perseverance in compiling this comprehensive history of Washburn Law and for demonstrating how the law school's core values have created the cornerstone on which we continue to build.

Thomas J. Romig
Dean and Professor of Law
Washburn University School of Law

"The Ideal Place . . . for the
Establishment of a Great Law School"

1

THE EARLY YEARS (1903–1922)

When Washburn College hired Norman Plass in 1902 to be its new president, it was a private school, affiliated with the Congregational Church. It had only three departments, a College of Liberal Arts, a School of Music, and a preparatory school called the Washburn Academy. While Washburn had offered classes since 1866 and attendance was not limited to church members, enrollment the previous year totaled only 328 students.

President Plass was dynamic and entrepreneurial and quickly set about expanding the size and prestige of the College. Washburn had agreed in 1902 to merge with the twelve-year old Kansas Medical College, located at Twelfth and Tyler Streets, and offered classes there during Plass' first year. Plass completed a merger with the Reid-Stone Art School, forming a Department of Fine Arts. During the six-year Plass presidency, enrollment reached 800 students in six departments. Justice David Brewer, a member of the College's Board of Trustees and the only Kansas lawyer ever to sit on the United States Supreme Court, helped Plass persuade Andrew Carnegie to donate $40,000 for a new library. Carnegie Library as well as Crane Hall and Observatory were completed during the Plass years and construction started on Thomas Gymnasium.

A principle guiding Plass' plan for growth was that the College should meet community needs. During his inaugural address on October 7, 1902, Plass announced that the Board of Trustees that afternoon in a special session had authorized the College's Executive Committee to investigate the feasibility of adding a dental college[1] and a law school and, if appropriate, to open them both

---

1. The dental college never opened.

in 1903. Plass believed there were educational advantages in Topeka that were not available in other cities and that resources in the city's legal community could be used to reduce the costs for faculty and for a law library that a small college like Washburn otherwise might not be able to afford:

> Topeka is the ideal place for such a school. We have here the United States District Court and Circuit Courts, and the Bankruptcy Referee; the Supreme Court of the State, with its seven judges; the District Court and the Probate Court, in constant session; and the City and Police Courts. We have also in Topeka a large proportion of the leading lawyers of the State. We have the headquarters of the great railroads, with their special attorneys. We have the State Law Library, with its 50,000 volumes, which men come hundreds of miles to consult. It is manifest beyond doubt that this is the one place in Kansas for the establishment of a great Law School.[2]

Plass asked local lawyer Robert Stone to chair a committee to form a law school. Stone's "high ideals of law and his success in fund-raising activities made him the perfect candidate. Stone immediately began working on the idea."[3] The Secretary of the College Board of Trustees, L.H. Greenwood, another local lawyer, was one of the most active members of the committee and his "untiring efforts" were credited for much of the school's early success.[4] The school's mission would be "to furnish facilities for legal training and preparation for the practice of law as a profession, equal to those offered anywhere, and to encourage the systematic study of general jurisprudence, legal history, and the fundamental principles of government."[5]

Understanding the challenges Stone's committee faced requires understanding of the status of law schools and the ways lawyers were trained at the turn of the twentieth century. Attendance at a law school had not been the predominant method of preparation for the practice of law. As of 1900, more than half of America's lawyers not only had not attended law school but had

---

2. WASHBURN COLL. BULLETIN 9–10 (Nov. 1902).

3. Ellen Sue McLane, *A Home at Last: A History of Washburn School of Law,* WASHBURN ALUMNUS 1, 4 (Sept. 1969).

4. 3 KANSAS: A CYCLOPEDIA OF KANSAS HISTORY 641 (Frank W. Blackmar ed., 1912).

5. WASHBURN COLL. SCH. OF LAW BULLETIN 5 (June 1903).

not attended so much as one year of college.[6] Until 1897, applicants for admission to the bar in Kansas were required to show only that they had "read law for two years, the last of which must be in the office of a regularly practicing attorney."[7] There was no requirement of even a high school diploma. Graduation from a law school not only was not required, it was not alone sufficient to satisfy the training requirement. There was no statewide bar examination. Applicants who satisfied any district court that they possessed the requisite learning were admitted to practice in all district and inferior courts, and then could be admitted on motion to practice before the Kansas Supreme Court. The examinations administered by the district judges, or by committees of local lawyers appointed by them, often were oral and in many districts lacked rigor.[8] Lax standards for admission to the bar, of course, made it difficult for law schools to attract students. Those seeking the easy way saw no need to endure the rigor of law school when there was no rigorous test to pass to become a lawyer. In 1897, the legislature enacted a diploma privilege, requiring district courts to admit without examination graduates of the law school at the University of Kansas (KU), but the legislation had little impact on the prevalence of study in an office.

By the mid-1890s, the Kansas Bar Association regularly urged that education requirements for admission to the bar be increased and that admission by district be abolished. Finally, in the spring of 1903, as Washburn was preparing to open its law school, the legislature transferred responsibility for admission to the bar from the district courts to the Supreme Court,[9] which in turn created a Board of Law Examiners to administer a written examination to qualified applicants. The statute further required applicants either to have read the law for two years in the office of a practicing attorney or to be a graduate of the law school of the University of Kansas "or some other law school of equal requirements and reputation." The diploma privilege was repealed.

---

6. Paul R. Carrington, *Legal Education for the People: Populism and Civic Virtue*, 43 KAN. L. REV. 1, 26 (1994).

7. GEN. STAT. KAN. 1868, ch. 11, §2.

8. Paul E. Wilson, *Centennial Footnotes*, 27 KAN. L. REV. vii, at ix (1979); N.H. Loomis, *Report of Special Committee on Admission to the Bar*, in BAR ASS'N. OF THE STATE OF KANSAS, PROCEEDINGS OF THE 12TH ANNUAL MEETING 17 (1895).

9. 1903 Kan. Sess. Laws, ch. 64, §1.

KU began in 1900 to require graduates to complete a three-year course of study. Two small law schools operating in Kansas at the time, one at Campbell College in Holton that opened in 1897, and one at Bethany College in Lindsborg that opened in 1902, both offered two-year courses of study.[10] The national trend was toward a three-year program but by 1904, only sixty-five of 111 law schools required it. Washburn opted from the outset to require three years of study. By 1904, the new Board of Law Examiners announced it would not recognize "as a standard law school any institution that does not require a three years' course."[11] This literal interpretation of the statute as mandating a length of program equal to that at KU created, temporarily, an anomaly in bar admission requirements. An applicant who attended law school had to complete three years but an applicant who studied in a law office could take the bar examination after only two years. This disparity disfavored the law schools. The legislature in 1905 increased the requirement for law office study to three years.

ADMISSION REQUIREMENTS

No one today questions that an applicant to law school needs the broad general education a college degree provides. It was not always so. At the turn of the century, only three schools, Harvard, Columbia, and the University of Chicago, required a college degree before admission to law study. Indeed, as late as 1896, only seven law schools required applicants to have completed a high school course,[12] and even in 1904 less than half, fifty-one, did so. There were schools that had no minimum age for admission and required no more than an eighth grade education. Reflecting the populist views of its dean, James W. Green, the law school at the University of Kansas for many years resisted imposition of strict admission requirements.[13] Green discounted the need for a college education, writing:

10. James M. Concannon, *The Other Law Schools of Early Day Kansas*, 65 J. KAN. B. ASS'N. 24, 30 (Nov. 1996).

11. *Id.* at 25.

12. James Barr Ames, *Address to the Section of Legal Education of the American Bar Association*, 1 AM. L. SCH. REV. 265, 266 (1904).

13. Carrington, *supra* note 6; Green wrote, "This school is supported by a tax levied upon all the property of the State. Each property holder is compelled to

I believe the man with a good English education, who has spent three or four years in active commercial life, where he has met his fellow man and learned their way of doing things, and the ways of the business world, has had a better preparation, and is better fitted to enter a law school than the man who has spent the same time in acquiring a collegiate education.[14]

By 1903, KU required applicants to have a diploma from a high school or academy or otherwise to meet requirements for admission to the university, but, if they did not, they could be admitted upon passing an entrance examination demonstrating equivalent preparation. However, there were no economic incentives to grade that examination rigorously and few applicants, if any, were turned away.

Not surprisingly, Washburn adopted similar admission requirements. While it urged applicants to "preface their legal study with a college course wherever practicable," it was

not deemed advisable to require a college degree for admission, as such requirement excludes many who are abundantly qualified to pursue the study of law and to become practitioners, who cannot afford to spend the time and money required to complete the college course before beginning their professional study. It is deemed wise, however, that a thorough elementary preparation be required before entering upon the study of a learned profession.[15]

Applicants for the degree program were required to be eighteen years of age and were admitted without examination if they were graduates of a high school course covering four years, or, if it covered less than four years, if they had completed the subjects required for admission to Washburn College. These subjects included three years of English, three years of Latin, two-and-one-half years of mathematics, one year of physics, one year of history, one-half year of

---

contribute to its support, whether he will it or not. It is maintained for the benefit it may be to the State. Should its doors not be thrown wide open, with as little restriction as possible, to all the young men and women of the State who may desire to enter therein?" James W. Green, *The History and Future Policy of the School of Law*, 4 GRADUATE MAGAZINE, No. 2, 45 at 57 (Nov. 1905).

14. Green, *supra* note 13, at 59.

15. WASHBURN COLL. SCH. OF LAW BULLETIN 5 (June 1903).

additional science, plus three additional units of specified electives.[16] Applicants could be admitted conditionally if they lacked no more than one-and-one-half of the required credits, provided they later made up the missing credits in the Washburn Academy. Applicants lacking these credentials were admitted if they passed an examination covering the required subjects. In addition, like KU and many other law schools, Washburn provided for admission without examination of "special students" who were not seeking a law degree. Special students had to be nineteen years old and "of adequate maturity and scholarship." It was thought this category would attract those "engaged in mercantile pursuits," who would benefit from business law courses, and others wishing to dabble in the law. Special students could convert to degree-seeking status after one or more years by meeting the requirements of those entering the regular course. Practicing lawyers could take courses as special students too. In addition, lawyers admitted after reading law in an office for two years who wanted a more formal legal education and better credentials could be admitted as regular students with advanced standing upon passing examinations on the subjects of the first year or of the first and second years. Applicants who had read law for one year could attempt to pass examinations in first-year subjects and also be admitted with advanced standing.

PRELIMINARY STEPS

Stone's committee began recruiting local lawyers and judges to teach one or more courses as Lecturers, without pay, to help the school get started. Many would not be needed until after the first year, but the list of twenty-five volunteer lawyers read like a *Who's Who* of the Topeka Bar. It included four Justices of the Kansas Supreme Court (William R. Smith, John C. Pollock, Rousseau A. Burch and Henry F. Mason), former Chief Justice Frank Doster, Kansas Court of Appeals Judge Theodore Garver, District Judge Lee Monroe, Judge of the Court of Topeka and Washburn Trustee Arthur J. McCabe, and Judge of the Police Court Clad Hamilton. For reasons that are not clear, three of the part-time faculty were given the title Professor of Law: J.G. Slonecker; George H. Whitcomb; and William H. Rossington. They taught no more than other part-time faculty members and less than some. Slonecker was then President

---

16. *Id.* at 10–13.

of the Kansas Bar Association and later would be Referee in Bankruptcy. He previously taught part-time at KU. Whitcomb later would be District Judge in Topeka and taught Sales for many years. Rossington was one of the best-known lawyers in the state.

While organizers planned to rely principally on the State Law Library for research materials, the new school did need to have a working library on site. Prospects for starting the school received a boost in February 1903 with the donation by Colonel T.W. Harrison of Topeka of an "excellent set" of law books valued at $5,000.[17] It included the Kansas statutes and digests, the Kansas and United States Supreme Court reports, the Kansas Court of Appeals reports, *American Law Reports*, the Supreme Court reports of several other states, plus digests and treatises on various topics. The books arrived in March. Because quarters for the school were not yet available, they were stored in the College's mechanical drawing room.

By May, a dean had been hired and he came to Topeka to confer with Stone's committee. Ernest Bancroft Conant became Dean just five years after he received his law degree from Harvard. He was thirty-three years old. His pre-legal education was at Phillips Exeter Academy and Harvard. He practiced law in Boston from 1898 through 1902 and taught classes in the evening law program of the Boston Y.M.C.A. In January 1903, Conant moved to Chicago where he practiced law and taught Torts and Damages at the Illinois College of Law.

> Conant was a very personable young bachelor with a splendid baritone voice that set many young Topeka hearts to palpitating. I remember one of his recitals where he sang a beautiful arrangement of the Rubaiyat. He was younger than many of his students but he handled the job well...[18]

---

17. *More Books*, WASHBURN REV., Feb. 20, 1903, at 3.

18. McLane, *supra* note 3, at 5. McLane states Washburn "obtained the services of Conant from a branch of the old Boston family of educators." *Id.* An Ernest L. Conant was a member of the Harvard Law School faculty in 1894 and 1895 and a James Bryant Conant was President of Harvard University from 1933 through 1953. However, it does not appear that Dean Conant was related to either of them. Harvard's comprehensive listing of its alumni indicates Dean Conant's father was a woolen mill overseer. CHARLES WARREN, 3 HISTORY OF THE HARVARD LAW SCHOOL AND OF EARLY LEGAL CONDITIONS IN AMERICA 253 (1999). Conant was born and raised in Enfield, New Hampshire. JAMES L. KING, HISTORY OF SHAWNEE COUNTY, KANSAS AND REPRESENTATIVE CITIZENS (1905).

1. Ernest B. Conant, Dean 1903–1907

Students had to be recruited. A twenty-page catalogue was issued in June, announcing that the school would open for academic year 1903–04, listing faculty, describing admission requirements, the course of instruction, and requirements for a degree, and generally promoting the advantages of the school. Tuition was a seemingly modest fifty dollars per year but that was twice the tuition for Kansas residents at KU's law school, where tuition had been free to Kansas residents as late as 1901–02. Expenses for room and board, plus books and laundry, were estimated to range from $123 to $254 for the college year.

The College rented facilities for the law school at 118 West Eighth. Washburn had roots downtown, having opened in 1865 as Lincoln College at the corner of Tenth and Jackson and only later moving to its current campus. Locating College programs downtown was consistent with Plass' community-based vision. The Kansas Medical College continued to hold its classes downtown after its merger with Washburn. The school's location not only provided students with access to the State Law Library, the courts, and downtown employment

2. 118 West 8th Street, first home of the Law School, 1903–1911

opportunities, but it also was convenient for part-time faculty who might have been unwilling to travel to the campus to teach. The school occupied the top floor of the three-story building, above Dougherty's Shorthand School. The quarters were described as "more than could be desired for the purpose. The rooms are high-studded and excellently lighted."[19] There were three lecture rooms, a large reading room and library, coat rooms, toilet rooms, and offices. Before the school's second year, the three lecture rooms were remodeled and turned into two larger classrooms. Another window was added. Like the school's two later homes downtown, the building still stands. The top floors were not used for many years. Currently, the building is the site of the Celtic Fox Pub and Restaurant and loft apartments on the upper floors.

Registration for the first semester was held September 15, 1903. Entrance examinations for those lacking high school diplomas were administered that day and the next. Classes began September 17. Classes were scheduled to accommodate students who worked but the schedule caused both students and Dean Conant to have long days. Conant taught three classes during the fall

19. *The New Law School*, WASHBURN REV., Aug. 20, 1903, at 13.

term: Contracts each day at 8:00 a.m., Evidence at 5:00 p.m. each day except Wednesday, and Torts on Tuesday from 7:15–9:15 p.m. Students in Torts were split for an additional class, with one group meeting on Friday evening and the other on Thursday and Friday afternoons at 2:00. Harry G. Larimer taught Bills and Notes at 1:00 p.m. A.W. Dana taught Real Property in the Monday evening slot and L.H. Greenwood offered Personal Property and Bailments on Thursday evening.

Dean Conant thereafter taught three, and occasionally even four, courses each semester in addition to administering the school. His other subjects included Common Law Pleading, Suretyship and Guaranty, Quasi-Contracts, Trusts, and Municipal Corporations. Occasionally, he taught part of the courses in International Law and Private Corporations.

To receive the Bachelor of Laws degree, students had to complete "the required course of instruction and have passed the regular examinations in all subjects."[20] The content of the "required course of instruction" clearly varied from year to year. Not until March 1911 did the catalogue make specific reference to a number of credit hours required for a degree. A total of seventy-two credit hours apparently was required and this was made explicit in the March 1913 catalogue. The normal semester load was twelve hours, the maximum load allowed was fourteen hours, and third-year students were required to take at least ten hours each semester to assure compliance with the Association of American Law Schools' requirement that they complete three full years of study. The 1913 catalogue also was the first one to explain explicitly the grading system: A, B, C, D or E. E was a failure and the student was required to retake the course. D also was a failure, later called a condition, but the student was required only to retake the next examination in the course. This system had one advantage over later grading systems: students had to demonstrate minimal competence in every subject to graduate.

THE FIRST STUDENTS

Forty-one students took law classes during the school's first year. Eighteen were classified as regular students and twenty-three were special students. Students at the College who enrolled in a law class were assigned this classifica-

---

20. WASHBURN COLL. SCH. OF LAW BULLETIN 18 (June 1903).

tion, as was a student who transferred to Washburn after taking his first year of law school at KU, Chauncey Brown. Eight students already were lawyers, and five of them completed the course of study and received degrees at the school's first commencement three years later: John S. Dawson, William H. England, Ross B. Gilluly, Ernest R. Simon, and William H. Vernon.[21] Dawson, for example, already was thirty-four years old when he enrolled. A native of Scotland, he had been admitted to the bar in 1898 in Wakeeney after reading law in a lawyer's office in Hill City. He came to Topeka in 1899 to be Bond Clerk in the State Treasurer's office and in 1903 was named Chief Clerk in the Attorney General's office. He was admitted on motion to practice before the Kansas Supreme Court on May 4, 1904.[22] He continued to attend as a special student even after he was named Assistant Attorney General, although he did not enroll in classes in the fall of 1904 because of political responsibilities during the election.

Fifteen of the regular 1Ls continued law classes after the first year and ten ultimately received degrees, nine as members of the initial graduating class. Only eight of the special students continued. Five graduated with the 1906 class while a sixth, Herbert Clayton, took classes for nine years before completing his law degree in 1912.[23] Three women enrolled as special students that first year but did not enroll for the second year.[24]

The class was augmented in the fall of 1904 by three students who entered with advanced standing. Edward R. Sloan and John W. Wilson had received LL.B. degrees that spring from Campbell College after completing its two-year course of instruction. They withdrew their applications to take the bar examination when the Board of Law Examiners enforced its decision that only applicants who had completed a three-year course met the statutory requirement for admission based on law school study.[25] Washburn encour-

---

21. *Attorneys Admitted Upon Motion*, 72 Kan. ix, xiii–xvii (1906).

22. *Attorneys Admitted to Practice Before the Supreme Court of the State of Kansas, From Earliest History of State To July 1, 1935*, 140 Kan. xli, at lii (1935).

23. Clayton worked in the State Law Library while attending classes and ultimately became Law Librarian at McGeorge Law School in California.

24. Two other women took at least one class that year. The history of women students at Washburn is described in detail in Chapter 10 and in Linda D. Elrod, *Washburn Law School Celebrates a Century of Welcoming Women*, 42 WASHBURN L.J. 853 (2004).

25. Concannon, *supra* note 10, at 30–31.

aged enrollment by those who had received law degrees at two-year schools by offering them advanced standing.[26] Sloan and Wilson thus chose to enroll at Washburn. That November, Sloan was elected Sheridan County Attorney. He named the opponent he defeated as his deputy to act as County Attorney until Sloan was eligible to practice law. Sloan soon told his classmates, "The questions put to a county attorney are not like those we get in school—they expect a fellow to know the statutes from cover to cover."[27] Sloan and Wilson were permitted to take the June 1905 bar examination, based on their combined three years of study at Campbell and Washburn. They formed a law firm in Hoxie and Sloan assumed full responsibility as County Attorney. They returned to the school periodically the following year and were members of the first graduating class.

The class of 1906 numbered seventeen graduates, a number not matched until 1912 and not exceeded until 1914. Each paid a five dollar diploma fee. Seven members of the class already had been admitted to practice. "By intention or accident," two or three members of the class wore street clothes at the ceremonies on June 2.[28] The class adapted a motto from Shakespeare: "A fee! A fee! My advice for a fee!"[29] Perhaps in response, the graduation speaker, part-time professor William Rossington, told them what one might tell a graduate entering solo practice today:

> I presume that you all intend to make the law the business and chief concern of your lives or you would not have gone to the trouble, labor and the expense of this course of preparation. I need not tell you that, like young bears, you have all your troubles ahead of you. To begin with, you will have to wait....It is one thing to express a willingness to practice law and to assert your fitness to undertake its...responsibilities by hiring a small office and hanging out a sign; and another thing to bear with a cheerful heart the seeming unwillingness of clients with cases to mount your stairs and intrust you with business. If you are depending upon the law for your living from day to day, you may soon be discouraged. If you have certain versatility of talents, you may still

---

26. WASHBURN COLL. SCH. OF LAW BULLETIN 12–14 (May 1904).
27. *Law School*, WASHBURN REV., Feb. 28, 1905, at 7.
28. *Lawyers Who Were "Made in Topeka,"* TOPEKA DAILY CAP., June 3, 1906.
29. THE KAW 46 (1906).

adhere to your purpose and retain your connection with the law until you can tide over this period.[30]

All members of the first graduating class passed the bar examination and a Washburn graduate was the only one of fifty-seven takers singled out for special commendation.[31] "The showing surpassed the record of any other school in Kansas," the 1907 *Kaw* gloated. In fact, no Washburn graduate failed the Kansas bar exam through at least 1915. As late as 1921, the school touted that only one of its graduates had ever failed the test. Students took delight in pointing out that graduates of the state's other law school were not as uniformly successful in passing it.[32] Even Chief Justice William A. Johnston would point to Washburn's successful record on the bar exam when telling those attending the school's tenth anniversary banquet, "The best test of the school is its product....Washburn College and the Law School are the proudest possession in Topeka."[33]

The class of 1906 was remarkable in many ways. Two of its members, Dawson and Sloan, would serve together on the Kansas Supreme Court. Dawson was the unquestioned intellectual leader of the class and gave remarks on its behalf at graduation. William W. Harvey, who taught Insurance Law to the group in its third year and later would sit with Dawson on the Kansas Supreme Court, remembered him as "an unusually intelligent, hard-working student, eager to be confronted with legal principles new to him, to search their source and the reasons for them, and to become familiar with their use. Actually, we studied the subject together—I am sure I learned as much from him as he did from me."[34] It was said that Dawson was the law school's "de facto instructor in Latin...When in doubt, ask him. He knows."[35] When the John Marshall Club that was formed during the school's first semester argued a moot court appeal, *Grief v. Strychnine*, Dawson sat as Chief Justice.[36]

Dawson achieved prominence almost immediately. He became personal secretary to Governor W.R. Stubbs for six months in 1909 before becoming attorney for the State Railroad Commission. In 1910, he was elected Attorney

30. *Lawyers Who Were "Made in Topeka,"* supra note 28.
31. THE KAW 52 (1907).
32. *Law School Notes*, WASHBURN REV., Mar. 1, 1916.
33. *Washburn City's Best Possession*, TOPEKA DAILY CAP., May 27, 1913.
34. *Dawson Encomium*, 159 Kan. iv, xvi (1945).
35. *Notes from the Law School*, WASHBURN REV., Oct. 23, 1903, at 12.
36. *Notes from the Law School*, WASHBURN REV., Dec, 21, 1903, at 14.

General of Kansas. In 1914, just eight years after receiving his law degree from Washburn, and after only sixteen years as a lawyer, he was elected to the Kansas Supreme Court. He was the first graduate of any Kansas law school to sit on the Court.[37] He was a member of the Court for thirty years, then the third longest term in Kansas history, and for the last eight years was Chief Justice. For ten more years he was Pardon and Parole Attorney for four governors, concluding a state record of fifty-six years working in the State Capitol.

Edward R. Sloan was elected or appointed to six public offices, including three terms in the Kansas House of Representatives. In March 1931, Governor Harry Woodring appointed him to fill a vacancy on the Supreme Court. He served the remaining twenty-one months of the term but opted not to seek election for a full term. He later was appointed to the Kansas Corporation Commission and in 1947 was appointed Referee in Bankruptcy.

Other members of the class achieved success. All but two practiced law. Llewellyn J. Graham became Kansas Supreme Court Reporter after having worked in the office while attending law school. He published the first Kansas advance sheets. His untimely death in 1911 was noted in the Kansas Reports, an unusual honor for one who did not serve on the Court.[38] George A. Kline became District Judge in Shawnee County in 1928, serving until 1948, and Hugh McFarland was Probate Judge there for four years.[39] Class President William H. Vernon initially was selected as law clerk to Justice Henry Mason, one of his instructors, and he and Ernest R. Simon were asked to be Lecturers at the Law School the year following their graduation. Vernon moved to Larned,

---

37. Thomas A. Lee, *What Washburn Law School Does for Kansas*, WASHBURN COLL. SCH. OF LAW BULLETIN 14 (Mar. 1917). The memorial for Justice Judson S. West, 144 Kan. iii (1936), states he "attended" law school at KU, but he is not listed among KU graduates. The number of early Justices was small since there were only three members of the Supreme Court until 1901. The early Justices either read law in an office or graduated from out-of-state law schools. Three Washburn graduates became Justices before the first KU graduate joined on the Court in 1933, Walter G. Thiele.

38. 84 Kan. vi (1911).

39. Photographs in THE KAW and lists of students printed in the WASHBURN COLL. SCH. OF LAW BULLETIN confirm that when he entered law school, Hugh McFarland spelled his name MacFarland but changed the spelling after his first year. His great-granddaughter Kelly McDonald '06 was a member of the centennial entering class in 2003.

became Pawnee County Attorney, and later served four terms in the Kansas House of Representatives, beginning in 1927. When he was elected Speaker of the Kansas House in 1933, the legislative directory reported that he was the first Kansan elected to the position by acclamation. Simon was elected Judge of the Court of Topeka in the spring of 1907 and then was Shawnee County Attorney. He became President of the Law School Alumni Association and was largely responsible for its decision, starting in 1909, to underwrite fifty-dollar annual scholarships to the top students in the first- and second-year classes. He taught part-time until 1914, when he was offered a full-time teaching position. He opted instead to move to California to practice law. According to one student, "There is no more popular man connected with the Law School than Judge Simon. Brilliant, thoroughly charged with his subject and with the 'smile that won't come off,' he holds his classes from start to finish."[40] Another member of the class, Benjamin Scandrett, taught Evidence during the 1909–10 academic year and later became general attorney for the Union Pacific Railroad.

CHARTING DIFFERENT PATHS

At the turn of the century, the law school at the University of Kansas had three full-time faculty members and a modest number of part-time lecturers for selected courses. Because of the small size of the bar in Lawrence, many of the lecturers were recruited from nearby communities. Coinciding with the opening of Washburn, KU expanded its full-time faculty to four professors and eliminated part-time teaching positions, "owing to the inability of the several persons who held these positions to fulfill their engagements at the times fixed" because of demands of their practices.[41] The four full-time faculty members, including Dean Green, taught all the regular courses and had astonishing course loads of ten or eleven courses each during the academic year.[42] KU's catalogue took a competitive shot at Washburn's plan to rely heavily on part-time lecturers: "It is believed to be proved by experience that to be

---

40. *Law Notes*, WASHBURN REV., Nov. 16, 1910, at 3.

41. Green, *supra* note 13, at 50. Ten of the twelve Special Lecturers listed in the school's 1904–05 bulletin were from distant communities like Wichita, Anthony, Minneapolis, St. Louis, and Kansas City, Missouri, suggesting that they gave only occasional lectures and did not teach entire courses.

42. UNIV. OF KAN. SCH. OF LAW BULLETIN (1904–05).

thoroughly efficient, instructional training in law courses must be given by resident teachers who give their whole time to instruction."[43]

However, Washburn's model of reliance on part-time lecturers was followed by many schools and resulted in a practical approach that played well with members of the bench and bar. Just four months after the school opened, the Committee on Legal Education of the Kansas Bar Association reported, "There are two well equipped schools of legal education in the state of Kansas.... Your committee believes that this school gives promise of becoming one of the most important factors in legal education to be found anywhere."[44] One year later, the committee "heartily endorse[d] the work" of the school, noting that "students have peculiar advantages in being able to witness the actual trial of cases in State and Federal courts and listening to arguments in the State Supreme Court." It concluded, "This law school, like that of the University of Kansas, gives advantages to students seeking a legal education equal to those given in many of the old schools of national reputation."[45]

TEXTS VERSUS CASES

The two Kansas schools soon emphasized different methods of instruction. The traditional method was to require students to read text books that summarized the law as the basis for class recitations and lectures. Dean Green at KU was steadfastly devoted to the text method and it was used almost exclusively in first year courses there until after World War I and Dean Green's death.[46] Green believed, "The average student, in the beginning of his study of the law, is not prepared to discover the rule laid down in a case, not to decide, from the mass of irrelevant matter it contains, whether the decision is good or bad in principle, or whether it should or should not be recognized as law."[47] The

---

43. *Id.* at 27.

44. BAR ASS'N OF THE STATE OF KAN., PROCEEDINGS OF THE 21ST ANNUAL MEETING 26, 28 (1904).

45. BAR ASS'N OF THE STATE OF KAN., PROCEEDINGS OF THE 22ND ANNUAL MEETING 7, 9 (1905).

46. UNIV. OF KAN. SCH. OF LAW BULLETIN 27 (1904–05); Bruce A. Kimball, *The Proliferation of Case Method Teaching in American Law Schools: Mr. Langdell's Emblematic "Abomination," 1890–1915*, 46 HIST. EDUC. QUALITY 192, 233–234 (Summer 2006).

47. Green, *supra* note 13, at 57.

only rational way for students to master the principle, he thought, was to "go to the works of some learned writer who has, after an examination of the cases, developed the principle and clearly stated it," before considering cases from which the rule is deduced.[48]

The competing case method, instituted at Harvard, began to spread to other schools in the 1890s but its merits were the subject of sharp debate among legal educators at the turn of the century. By 1904, the case method was used in varying degrees by a majority of member schools of the Association of American Law Schools but in less than half of all law schools.[49] During Washburn's first academic year, the text method predominated. In the class on Bills and Notes, students first studied a textbook but by December were studying "special cases."[50] Not surprisingly, the Harvard-trained Dean Conant pushed for greater use of the case method in the school's second year. Instead of using *Harriman on Contracts*, a book only one inch thick, a casebook of two volumes was used, costing ten dollars. A similar switch was made in Common Law Pleading. A student wrote, "The plan of work is harder but more profitable. Those who do not like hard work complain some but it is hoped we all may be benefitted by the change."[51]

In an address to the Kansas Bar Association in 1906, Conant set forth the virtues of the case method while diplomatically acknowledging that the state's two law schools, like most schools, used it to varying degrees:

> I do not understand that any law school has officially indorsed any one system of instruction to the exclusion of all others, although four or five schools may be using the system exclusively. Much depends upon the personality of the individual instructor in charge of each particular course or subject. A method of instruction that one man might find adapted to his needs and personality might not do at all for another. It may not be well to adopt any one method to the exclusion of all others. The instructor should choose as the basis of his work that system which he knows himself to be most qualified to use and which he considers

---

48. *Id.*

49. Ames, *supra* note 12, at 268.

50. *Notes from the Law School*, WASHBURN REV., Dec. 14, 1903, at 16.

51. *Notes from the Law School*, WASHBURN REV., Oct. 23, 1903, at 12.

best adapted to the work he has at hand, and every instructor should be allowed absolute freedom of choice in his methods of teaching.[52]

Regardless whether the instructor used a text or a casebook, the work was more challenging than some students expected:

> We find that one must grow into a lawyer. He must eat with the law, talk with the law, smoke with the law, break the Sabbath for it, go to bed with it and get up with it. He must meditate upon it day and night. 'Truly the law is a jealous mistress!' One has to be vaccinated for the law, and it must *take*. Shades of Coke and Parke! watch the score of our embryonic jurists roosting on desks and chairs in every conceivable fashion with their number-ten feet propped up higher than their heads and their noses buried in Ames's Cases on Common Law Pleading, tearing their hair because some fractious gearing in their heads won't work smoothly on the niceties of *replication de injuria sua propria absque tali causa*.[53]

However, the tone was not always serious. A history of the law school published in 1969 included the recollection of a former student of Conant who was not identified but whose reference to the absence of "any feminine students" suggests he must have enrolled near the end of Conant's four years at Washburn. "Conant's classroom," he wrote, "was frequently organized as a bull session and would hardly have been pleasant even to our more sophisticated coeds."[54]

JOINING THE ASSOCIATION OF AMERICAN LAW SCHOOLS

No decision made during Washburn Law School's first year was more important to its future than the decision to apply for membership in the Association of American Law Schools. The AALS was formed in 1900, at the encouragement of the Section on Legal Education of the American Bar Association. Its principal purposes included raising the quality of legal education and improving the preparatory training of entering students. Its initial requirements for membership were only that member schools: (1) require a two-year course

---

52. Ernest B. Conant, *The Case System*, BAR ASS'N OF THE STATE OF KAN., PROCEEDINGS OF THE 23RD ANNUAL MEETING 53, 65 (1906).

53. THE KAW 54 (1905).

54. McLane, *supra* note 3, at 5.

of law study, which increased to three years effective in 1905; (2) require applicants to have completed a high school course "or its equivalent;" and (3) have a library containing at least the reports of the state and the United States Supreme Court. Yet, many American law schools did not meet even these minimal requirements. When Washburn was admitted to membership, only thirty-seven law schools were members and as late as 1920 only forty-seven of 150 American law schools were members.

Washburn's application was considered by the AALS Executive Committee in May 1904 and was continued for a year, no doubt because the school had not even completed its first year. Washburn was admitted to membership on August 22, 1905, at the Association's annual meeting at Narragansett Pier, Rhode Island. Dean Conant and J.G. Slonecker represented the school. Other law schools admitted that year were those at the University of Nebraska and at Trinity College in North Carolina, which later became Duke Law School. It is not clear that the school's leaders at first fully appreciated the importance of AALS membership. It was not even mentioned in the catalogue until March 1911 and was not touted in the text until the catalogue of June 1923. The AALS periodically increased its membership requirements and the need to comply with those requirements to maintain Washburn's membership would provide the law school leverage many times when the College's central administration sought to use recurrent financial problems to justify providing the law school insufficient resources to maintain quality.

SKILLS TRAINING IN THE EARLY YEARS

A feature of law office study that allowed it to compete with law schools was the opportunity it provided to learn the nuts and bolts of daily practice and to draft documents for actual cases. The first catalogue addressed the issue directly:

> In the course in Code Pleading the students will receive instruction and be given practice in the preparation of pleadings, petitions and motions. The object will be to duplicate as far as possible the routine work of the law office in a systematic manner through the whole field of practice. The papers will be read and criticised and returned to the student....The students will thus be given...practical training that will enable them to

3. The Blackstone Club

go directly from the Law School into active practice without obtaining any experience in a law office with a regular practitioner.[55]

The school also conducted Practice Court, in which students prepared and conducted mock trials of jury cases. When the same mock cases were used during the school's second year which had been used in the first, student interest and performance predictably declined.

At the turn of the century, many lawyers relied on oral advocacy skills to compensate for the limited general education they possessed. Thus, by December of the school's first year, students formed two clubs, the Blackstone Club and the John Marshall Club, to help develop these skills. Club members discussed legal questions at weekly meetings and presented appellate arguments of mock cases. Students sat in panels as judges and issued written opinions, although sometimes after much delay. Some decisions were even held over until the following academic year. Interest in these clubs varied from year to year and the Blackstone Club outlasted the Marshall Club.

In the fall of the school's second year, Professor Orwell Bradley Towne from the College taught a special oratorical course. Among questions the class debated was the advisability of abolishing the requirement of unanimous verdicts in

---

55. WASHBURN COLL. SCH. OF LAW BULLETIN 17 (June 1903).

THE JOHN MARSHALL CLUB.

HUGH MC FARLAND.   R. A. MAXWELL.   W. H. VERNON.   F. M. LEACH.
J. G. STEWART.   C. R. DODGE.   L. J. GRAHAM.   B. W. SCANDRETT.

4. The John Marshall Club

civil cases. The College was known among colleges in Kansas for its success in debate and oratory competitions and had active literary and debating societies for both men and women. Several law students elected to participate in the Prize and Inter-Society Debates on the main campus. "This is some evidence to show a mixture of the departments, which will probably be a benefit all around."[56] However, the next year, law students decided to form their own debating society, called the Forensics Club. There had been adverse reaction on the campus to participation in the College societies by those the student newspaper described as "the Laws." Plus, there were advantages to have a separate society since it "would serve to unify and harmonize the student body"[57] and allow students to discuss legal, ethical and political questions of importance to them but of little interest to students in other departments. Professor Slonecker offered a prize of twenty-five dollars for the winner of a law school oratorical contest and Henry G. Larimer put up a second prize of fifteen dollars. During academic year 1906–07, the College made law students eligible to represent

56. *Law School*, WASHBURN REV., Nov 1, 1904, at 5.
57. *Laws to Debate*, WASHBURN REV., Sept. 26, 1905, at 11.

Washburn in intercollegiate debates, realizing that tapping their special skills might help win more competitions. John W. Huntsberger '08 promptly became Washburn's top debater in its annual debate with Baker University.

There were other attempts to blend in with the College. Wilber Greer, Professor of Latin at the College, taught Roman Law. Justice Rousseau Burch's course in International Law in the spring of the school's first year was opened as an elective for students in the College and any student entering law school who already had taken the course at the College was granted credit for it toward the law degree. The College accepted enough law courses as electives that students could earn both a Bachelor of Arts degree and a Bachelor of Laws degree in six, rather than seven, years.

During the school's second year, the College faculty made students at the Law and Medical Schools eligible to join Greek letter societies if they met the requirements of membership for College students. The following year, the Laws were permitted to try out for the baseball team. They soon became important members of the College football team. In those years, Washburn annually competed with KU and often played the University of Missouri and Kansas State Agricultural College in Manhattan. In 1907, Washburn's team was undefeated, beating both KU and the University of Oklahoma. By 1912, there was a chapter of the Alpha Kappa Phi legal fraternity, one of three legal fraternities that later combined to form Delta Theta Phi law fraternity.[58]

Law students sometimes complained of "being ostracized and looked down upon by the people out on the Hill.... [T]he Laws are slighted by the Arts students."[59] After the first annual Law School edition of the student newspaper was published in early 1911, the editor, a liberal arts major, admitted that "a good many of the college students hardly realized that we have an active and efficient law school as one of the integral parts of the institution."[60] Later, when more students entered the law school after completing one or more years of college, interaction increased. One year, half the football lettermen were Laws.

---

58. *Alpha Kappa Phi Frat Installed at Law School*, WASHBURN REV., Mar. 20, 1912, at 1.

59. *Editorial*, WASHBURN REV., Nov. 30, 1910, at 5.

60. WASHBURN REV., Feb. 1, 1911, at 4.

All captains of the men's debating teams, half the debaters, and two of the College orators were Laws. However, some law students felt they gave more than they received when building bridges to the College:

> The Laws sacrificed their opportunity for developing a Law School football team in order that they might unite with the College. They refused the challenge of other law schools to debate in order that they might assist the College in fulfilling its heavy debate schedule. The hope and ambition of the Blackstone club has been sacrificed for the College literary societies.[61]

From the school's first days, there was both love and hate in the relationship between the Law School and the College. Law students declined to make pledges to President Parley Womer's endowment campaign, the so-called "$100 idea," citing various grievances.[62] A year later, future Congressman Clifford R. Hope '17 offered this perspective:

> The Washburn Law School might be compared to a boisterous youth that has strayed away from home and sometimes does things that shock its staid and dignified mother. However, a fourteen-year-old could not be expected to behave with all the discretion of its fifty-two-year-old parent.... Our environment is perhaps not one to especially uplift and inspire us.

> [T]he Law School occupies much the same relation to the College proper that Australia does to England. They are from the same stock and are ready to fight for the mother country, even though separated by a barrier of water. The Law School is separated from the College by a gulf of distance that renders it impossible to take part in all the activities which it desires. It is willing to do all that it can, however, to help out any college enterprise.[63]

Law students made the most of their downtown location. There was a favorite gathering place:

> Not only in faculty and student body were we blessed, there was Augustin Alba. Augustin had been a high ranking officer in the Mexican army, a graduate of Chapultapec Academy, the Mexican West Point. He bet on

---

61. *"Laws" in Athletics*, WASHBURN REV., May 13, 1914, at 3.

62. WASHBURN REV., Jan. 26, 1916, at 2.

63. *Law School*, WASHBURN REVIEW, Feb. 14, 1917.

the wrong horse in one of the revolutions which plagued that unfortunate nation in the first years of this century and was lucky to make it out with his life. The only thing he could do to make a living was cook. So on the ground floor of the law school building he opened the town's first Chili Parlour. It was a first experience for most of the students. But in those days American hard money was really worth face value. Most of us boys were making a large part of our own way. And Augustin was a Godsend. There at the crowded tables you could get a bowl of chili (about two cups) and hot as the dew of hell plus another bowl full of oyster crackers and 'dippin' rights in a big bowl of chopped onion for the sum of one nickel 5¢ no more. We all got the big end of our proteins out of Augustin's chili.[64]

There also were social events. However, law school parties were not quite what they are today. At a stag party organized by the freshman class, "music, games and storytelling kept the company entertained. At a suitable hour, refreshments of doughnuts, pumpkin pie, apples and cider were served."[65] One year, students even formed a Mandolin Club. The school held a banquet at the National Hotel to celebrate completion of the school's second year. Four students and two faculty members made remarks and gave toasts. The banquet became an annual event.

Almost all law students in the early years worked. Many found employment in offices at the State Capitol.[66] Thirteen of the sixteen seniors in 1913 were described as self-supporting. Four were stenographers, four worked in lawyers' offices, two delivered newspapers, one was a collector, one was a mail clerk, and one worked in the Santa Fe shops.

A LOYAL PART-TIME FACULTY

Initially, only the Dean taught full-time. Even when the full-time faculty briefly was at its peak size of three during the School's first sixteen years, full-time

---

64. McLane, *supra* note 3, at 5. The TOPEKA CITY DIRECTORY lists the address for Alba's restaurant in 1905 as 810 Kansas Avenue and as 1009 Kansas Avenue by 1912. Throughout the time the Law School was at 118 West Eighth, it lists Jordan Electric Co. as occupying the ground floor.

65. *Law Notes*, WASHBURN REV., Nov. 23, 1910, at 3.

66. *Washburn Law News*, WASHBURN REV., Feb. 12, 1908, at 8.

faculty taught no more than 60% of the courses. The extraordinary commitment of local judges and lawyers to the school's success was indispensable, particularly as leadership at the school changed frequently during its first two decades. No less than twelve Justices of the Kansas Supreme Court and one Judge of the Kansas Court of Appeals taught classes during the school's first thirteen years and their presence on the faculty list added luster to the school. Two of the original adjunct faculty members, Justice Henry Mason, who taught Constitutional Law, and George H. Whitcomb, who became Judge of the Third Judicial District in 1911 and taught Sales, taught for twenty-three and twenty-nine years, respectively. Among other members of the original faculty, Henry G. Gottlieb taught for sixteen years and was Judge of the Practice Court for many of them, John G. Slonecker taught for fourteen years, and Robert Stone, District Judge Lee Monroe, Clad Hamilton, Bennett Wheeler, John Switzer, and John Rosen all taught for twelve years. Several other lawyers who joined the adjunct faculty during the school's years downtown also taught for many years. William C. Ralston taught fourteen different courses over twenty-two years beginning in 1909 and often taught more than one class each year. Clinton J. Evans taught for twenty years starting in 1912 and Thomas Amory Lee taught for more than a quarter century starting in 1916.

Part-time faculty members participated in setting academic policy. They attended faculty meetings, made motions, and voted. The earliest minutes that survive are from 1920. Even after the school moved to the main campus, meetings ordinarily were held downtown, at the Chamber of Commerce office, to make it convenient for practitioners and judges to attend.

Practitioners and judges brought "real world" cases into the classroom. Justice Mason frequently presented cases that were before the Kansas Supreme Court to his class in Constitutional Law.

> I remember one such case where Judge Mason, in commenting on one of the answers I had written, remarked "You haven't decided the case as the court now has but you get an A anyway because your reasoning was clear and would have been usable by us.".[67]

One drawback of heavy reliance on part-time faculty, of course, was the frequency with which they canceled classes because of other commitments.

---

67. McLane, *supra* note 3, at 5.

When Fred S. Jackson was a candidate for Attorney General in 1906, for ex-ample, his Criminal Law class often did not meet. "Competition is the life of trade; but irregularity of classes is death to the school," one student wrote in 1904.[68]

Barely half of the initial part-time faculty members had themselves gradu-ated from law school. Six had neither college nor law degrees. Thus, there was a grain of truth in the tongue-in-cheek comments of one of the first graduates:

> The school has been of immense value to the members of the local bar who have served upon its faculty. Those who have essayed to teach the embryo legal minds have often learned points and principles which in many particulars within the knowledge of the writer has redounded to the advantage of their clients. The direct fruition of their able work is now exemplified in the graduating class of 1906, the members of which will at all times be ready and willing to give their old-time profs legal advice and counsel, and, if need be, take full charge of their practice (and fees).[69]

CHANGE AND GROWTH

Annual enrollment in law school courses remained constant, ranging from 39–45 students, during the school's first six years. The number of regular students grew to about thirty per year, as 1Ls became 2Ls, 2Ls became 3Ls, and special students became regular students. The number of special students declined to an average of ten per year. One consequence of the school's small size was that many courses were offered every other year. 1Ls could find themselves taking an upper level class like Sales with 2Ls.[70] While the number of law graduates was small, they constituted a significant percentage of the graduates of the College. In 1908, Laws numbered nine of 68 graduates.

The school's first black student, Samuel E. Cary '10, enrolled in 1907. He came to Washburn from Providence, Kentucky. He joined the practice of a renowned black trial lawyer, W.L. Sayers, in Hill City. Later, he moved to Colo-rado.[71] Washburn's second black graduate, Frederick C. Helm '12, began his law

---

68. *Law School*, WASHBURN REV., Oct. 14, 1904, at 6.

69. THE KAW 38 (1906).

70. *Law School*, WASHBURN REV., Feb. 14, 1905, at 12.

71. In 1971, a new organization in Denver, formed to instill professionalism

studies during Cary's senior year. Helm was well-regarded by his classmates, who elected him as an officer of the first-year class, Sargent-at-Arms, and Vice-President of the first-year Arthur Debating Club.[72] He showed a talent for trial work in Practice Court. After graduation, Helm opened a law office in Wichita. The third black graduate, legendary trial lawyer Elisha Scott '16, received a law dictionary for winning the Special Prize Debate as a beginning student in 1910. He was "heralded with much applause among the students as the advocate of their cause" when they were assigned the role of the criminal defendant in cases he defended in Practice Court.[73] He and Helm conducted mock trials and debates in local black churches.

Helm's election as a class officer at the same time the only woman in the class, Jessie Nye '12, was elected Secretary-Treasurer is some evidence that law students then were progressive on issues of diversity. Reverend Nathan A. Mitchell, a native of Jamaica who enrolled in the spring semester 1911, "came to Topeka in preference to attending law school in Louisville because here, he says, he has found no race prejudice. When he applied for entrance in a college in Illinois, he found a sentiment among the students, which he interpreted as unfriendly."[74]

The school offered summer classes for the first time in 1907. That summer, Dean Conant resigned to become Professor of Law at the University of Nebraska. The College administration named a member of the part-time faculty to be "Acting Dean" until a permanent dean could be hired. Edward Delahay Osborn was thirty-six years old and had been a Lecturer since 1905, co-teaching the course in Wills and Administration of Estates with former Kansas Supreme Court Chief Justice Frank Doster. Osborn was a native Kansan whose grandfather, Mark Delahay, was the second United States District Judge for the District of Kansas, and whose father, Thomas Osborn, was Governor of Kansas from 1873 until 1877. He spent a large part of his boyhood days in Brazil and Chile where his father served by presidential appointment as U.S. Minister. He attended Washburn Academy, then attended Williams College from 1890 through 1893. He is the only dean and one of only two members of

---

among African-American lawyers, was named the Samuel Cary Bar Association in his honor.

72. *School of Law*, WASHBURN REV., Oct. 20, 1909, at 6; *School of Law*, WASH-BURN REV., Dec. 15, 1909, at 9.

73. *Law School*, WASHBURN REV., May 17, 1916.

74. *Legal Atmosphere Is A Drawing Card*, WASHBURN REV., May 1, 1912.

5. Edward D. Osborn, Acting Dean 1907–
1909, Professor 1907–1913 and 1930–1941

the full-time faculty who never graduated from law school. He studied in the offices of Rossington, Smith & Dallas in Topeka before being admitted to the bar in 1895. He practiced law in Topeka with Alex M. Harvey and was retained as an attorney for the Missouri-Pacific Railroad.[75]

Though he only held the title "Acting Dean," Osborn nevertheless made significant changes. He inaugurated in each course a moot court in which at least four cases were argued each term. He expanded Practice Court, inviting various lawyers, primarily those who had served as judges, to preside over trials before juries composed of members of the student body.[76]

Osborn served as Dean for two years. President Frank Sanders, in his annual report for 1908–09, reported oddly that Osborn "felt compelled by weakening

75. 3 KANSAS: A CYCLOPEDIA OF KANSAS HISTORY 697 (Frank W. Blackmar ed., 1912).

76. *Law News*, WASHBURN REV., Nov. 20, 1907, at 8.

eyesight to ask to be relieved of so many hours of work and of administration,"[77] but had agreed to remain as professor and the new Dean's associate. Sanders explained that the school "has come to a parting of the ways. The services of one permanent instructor have been inadequate."[78] Although the school generated a profit of only $18.29 that year, Sanders believed increased attendance would justify the change. Osborn thereafter devoted substantially all his time to teaching, although he did keep an office downtown. On November 9, 1911, Osborn argued before the United States Supreme Court for the only time in his career.[79] He represented a landowner challenging the railroad's claim of right-of-way. The Court affirmed the ruling of the Eighth Circuit Court of Appeals against Osborn's client.

The College selected William Reed Arthur to become Dean in academic year 1909–10. He was only thirty-one years old and had received his law degree from Northwestern University just one year earlier, but Sanders described him as "a man of teaching ability, aggressiveness and administrative power." Arthur came to Topeka from Chicago but had roots both in Kansas and at Washburn. His family had moved to Kansas from Pennsylvania when he was a child. He started college at Emporia but received his bachelor's degree at Washburn in 1899. He was an instructor at Kinsley High School and principal of the Logan schools during six years in which he saved money to attend law school. After receiving his LL.B., Arthur worked as Assistant Librarian at the Chicago Law Institute and traveled to several cities to study card cataloguing.

Arthur's challenge was to increase the size of the school. There was said to be talk of discontinuing the school because of low enrollment.[80] Indeed, College Secretary L.H. Greenwood postponed any "definite arrangement" for Arthur's salary for his second year "until some estimate could be made on how the law department was going to show up this year." Arthur was forced to alert President Sanders late in the academic year about the "oversight in relation to my salary" and to explain he had "delayed taking the matter up,

---

77. Frank Sanders, President's Annual Report FY 1909, at 3 (June 2, 1909) (on file in Mabee Library).

78. *Id.* at 7.

79. *Kindred v. Union Pac. R.R.*, 225 U.S. 582 (1912).

80. *Ex-Washburn Law Dean Dies*, TOPEKA CAP., Nov. 4, 1963, at 1.

6. William R. Arthur, Dean 1909–1915,
Visiting Professor 1946–1947

thinking that possibly at the end of the first six months the allowance would be made."[81]

Arthur quickly implemented new recruitment strategies. He sent circulars to all teachers in the city inviting them to enroll in Justice Henry Mason's class on Constitutional Law. He encouraged students who formerly were teachers to invite their friends to visit the school when they attended the meeting of the state teachers' association in Topeka. He invited prospective students to attend the school's annual spring banquet. At least two of Arthur's relatives even enrolled and his brother John Arthur graduated as a member of the class of 1912. To make it possible for those holding full-time jobs to complete a law degree, Arthur created a separate night school program, commencing

---

81. Letter from William R. Arthur to Frank Sanders (April 24, 1911) (on file in Mabee Library).

its operations November 1, 1909. He received no extra pay for the extra work. Classes were taught by the same instructors who taught in the day program. Initially, classes were held three nights each week for two hours. By the spring semester, night classes were extended to three hours each, starting at 7:00 p.m. "Students will not be permitted to use stimulants during the session," the student newspaper reported.[82] As soon as the night school opened, day students reorganized the Blackstone Club and night students organized the Kent Club. The day students challenged the night students to a debate. Night school classes continued throughout the summer.

Arthur understood the importance of rallying support from alumni and members of the bar. "[T]o judge by the little talks he made in introducing the speakers at the Booster Lunch last Saturday noon, everybody that ever even saw the school is 'a loyal supporter,' 'a backbone,' 'an old friend' or some other kind of a helping hand."[83] In his third year, Arthur sent a letter to all former students who had not graduated, asking them to join alumni in establishing scholarships.

Arthur's efforts worked. Enrollment increased by 75% during 1909–10. Arthur set a goal to reach 100 students and this goal was achieved by the spring of 1911. A "Century Jubilee" was held to celebrate.[84] One student later wrote, "[E]veryone remarked about the 'swell eats' for a small price but a couple of years later, it leaked out that the Dean had noticed beforehand the scanty menu and had dug down in his pocket and added 'two bits' to each plate."[85]

The school benefitted from broader publicity. An article in the February 1911 issue of *Case & Comment* about John Dawson's election as Attorney General noted that he received his law degree at Washburn, "[l]ike others of the younger men in Kansas politics."[86] Later that spring, students learned of a favorable article about the Law School in the *Chicago Record Herald*.[87] The following year, enrollment passed 120, although many of the students were not pursuing a degree. In the fall of 1912, Arthur offered lectures on law for business people, giving away 100 free tickets to the first lecture by Professor Osborn,

---

82. *School of Law*, WASHBURN REV., Mar. 10, 1910, at 6.
83. *"At Least 100 Students Next Year,"* WASHBURN REV., Mar. 30, 1910.
84. *Law School Has Big Celebration*, WASHBURN REV., Mar. 1, 1911, at 6.
85. *Law Banquet*, WASHBURN REV., Mar. 26, 1915.
86. *The Editor's Comments*, 17 CASE & COMMENT 481 (1911).
87. *Law Notes*, WASHBURN REV., May 24, 1911, at 9.

and forty people attended.[88] The following spring, twenty-six people enrolled in a special class for business people.[89] Arthur devised a plan to distribute the catalogue directly to high school graduates. The fall of 1913 saw the largest first year class yet, and there were twenty students in the night school.

For the only time in the school's history, its tuition relative to that at the College helped student recruitment. Although law tuition had risen to $60 per year, tuition at the College was $65 per year and students "on the hill" also paid gymnasium and other fees law students did not have to pay. Ray Hugh Garvey '15, who was taking classes both at the College and the Law School, exhibited the acumen that would lead him to success in the business world. He observed the price differential, realized that law students were free to take classes at the College, and promptly switched his enrollment to the Law School.[90]

Besides recruiting students, Arthur sought to enhance academics. Not surprisingly, given his background in the law library in Chicago, Arthur immediately added to the curriculum a course in "Brief Drawing" that he taught himself. It was a course about "where and how to find the law" and included brief-writing exercises. In 1912, a course was added focusing on the enactment and interpretation of statutes, as was a practical course on Kansas practice and procedure. The school established a second division of the Practice Court during the spring semester in 1914 so students could gain more trial experience. Juniors practiced in the second division, seniors in the first division. Starting in academic year 1913–14, first-year students were given weekly exams in all subjects. The increase in enrollment meant more classes were offered and 1Ls did not have to be mixed with upper level students. The number of class sessions held each week reached fifty-eight by 1915, double the number when Arthur arrived.[91]

On April 5, 1913, two teams from Washburn, selected by the Blackstone Club, debated two teams from the Kansas City Law School, one debate being held at Washburn and one in Kansas City. It was the school's first intermural competition. The students debated whether the government should own and operate interstate railroads. Washburn's representatives included future

---

88. *Law Notes*, WASHBURN REV., Oct. 12, 1912, at 14.

89. *Law Notes*, WASHBURN REV., Feb. 19, 1913, at 12.

90. OLIVE WHITE GARVEY, THE OBSTACLE RACE: THE STORY OF RAY HUGH GARVEY 27 (1970).

91. TOPEKA DAILY CAP., July 31, 1915, at 4.

Dean Antrim Hambleton '14, future long-time member of the adjunct faculty Edward Rooney '14, future Congressman Harold C. McGugin ex-'15, Harry Logan ex-15, for whom an endowed lecture series is named, and future Newton lawyer J. Sidney Nye '15. McGugin and Logan enrolled with members of the class of 1915 but did not complete requirements for a degree after they were permitted to take the bar examination based on a combination of law school courses and law office study.

Arthur was the student's friend. In 1913, a student considered quitting school because of gambling losses. "How much money will you need to finish the year?" Arthur asked. When the student quoted a figure of $400, Arthur said, "Come up to my office tomorrow and I'll have the money for you."[92] The student later became a District Judge in western Kansas. Arthur later estimated he loaned more than $10,000 to students, and signed notes for many more, over his forty-year teaching career. The second Washburn graduate to serve on the Kansas Supreme Court, William A. Smith '14, believed he owed his legal career to Arthur:

> Smith had delivered the Topeka Capital one year while attending college, and ended up owing the paper about $100. The next fall he enrolled in the law school. The college authorities told him he could not attend unless he made settlement with the Capital. "[Arthur] heard about this," Smith said, "and unsolicited by me got in touch with Arthur Capper. The result was that the newspaper gave me an afternoon job, with arrangements whereby I applied one-half of my pay to the paper bill and the other one-half to live on. I have often wondered what would have been my fate if a man of less human characteristics had happened to be dean of the law school at that time."[93]

MOVING AROUND DOWNTOWN

Predictably, growth in enrollment taxed the capacity of the school's rented facilities on Eighth Street. By the spring of 1911, Supreme Court Justice Clark Smith elected to meet his class in Extraordinary Legal Remedies in his cham-

---

92. *William Reed Arthur Is "Pop" to Judges and Others He Helped Through School,* KAN. CITY TIMES, May 14, 1949.

93. *Id.*

bers at the State Capitol to relieve the congestion a bit. Even before the enrollment spike, the school's quarters were not optimal. Custodial service and
maintenance were irregular and students sometimes undertook these tasks
themselves. It would be May 1909 before "the lives of law students [would be]
made more secure by the construction of good substantial fire escapes."[94] A
student visiting the school from another department described the scene in
bleak terms late in 1908:

> [O]ne must abruptly climb three flights of dark, narrow stairs, and
> upon reaching the top, find as gloomy a scene as can well be imagined.
> The rooms are not only dark and dingy, but the walls are smoky and
> covered with pencil works, the desks and chairs cut up, and broken,
> and the outlook from the grimy windows as discouraging as the rooms
> themselves. Every year when the Washburn Campus is being improved
> and made more beautiful, why must this other division in the college not
> share in the benefits received, nor obtain some of the cleaner, pleasanter
> quarters we of the Arts Course have profited from?[95]

It did not help matters that the 1903 Kansas Legislature had appropriated
$50,000 for construction of a new law building at the University of Kansas,
which was occupied in 1905. As early as 1906, President Plass included a goal of
$40,000 for a law building in his plan to raise endowments through a Million
Dollar Club, but he made no progress toward this goal during the remainder
of his presidency.

Coinciding with Arthur's arrival in 1909, the rooms were cleaned and the
walls were repaired. Lighting was fixed in the library and classrooms. Sec-
ond- and third-year students on their own initiative papered the lounge and
purchased mission furniture for it. Still, there were problems. In December,
instructors and students were unable to study in the library because of the
cold. By the spring, Arthur was fueling talk of a new building.[96] A committee
was formed to search for a new location that retained the school's advantage
of proximity to the State Law Library and the courts. Regret was expressed
that the original location of Lincoln College could not be obtained. By the
end of 1910, the committee started to raise the funds that would be needed.

94. *Law Notes*, WASHBURN REV., May 26, 1909, at 6.
95. *Law Notes*, WASHBURN REV., Dec. 9, 1908.
96. *Greater Washburn Law School in Sight*, WASHBURN REV., Mar. 9, 1910.

However, the need to alleviate overcrowding could not wait for the committee to complete its work.

The College leased larger quarters in the double building at 725–727 Kansas Avenue, while the search for a permanent home continued. The school occupied the third floor over the Mills Dry Goods Store. The move to the new quarters was sufficiently completed so that classes could begin on time for the fall semester 1911, although the move continued into the next month and some students spent several Saturdays helping to put the facilities into usable shape. There were two large lecture rooms and two library rooms, plus an office for the Dean, a faculty office, a cloak room, and a student reception room. To returning students it was "a wonderful improvement over the cramped space" on Eighth Street and gave the school "an air of prosperity" not possible before.[97] However, it was not ideal. Roy Painter '16 later described it as "an old warren," observing that "with its rheumatic stairs and splintered seats, dingy rooms and broken plaster, and its isolation from the college, the dreamer needed heroism to discover the great law school."[98] The building was the school's home for only two years. Many years later, alums Mike Jackson '80 and Chris Woolery '80 opened law offices on another floor of the same building.

Increased enrollment and larger facilities meant more support services were needed. There were no funds to hire a secretary, so Arthur handled "the continual and ever increasing mass of petty yet necessary details"[99] himself. At the start of the spring semester in 1912, Antrim Hambleton '14, a future Dean, agreed to stay in the building all day "to keep the microbes cleaned out" in addition to being in charge of the library during the afternoon.[100] Students serving as librarian received a scholarship. A year later future Kansas Supreme Court Justice William A. Smith '14 had the job. Finally, in 1914, Emily Sanford Platt was hired as Secretary. She was the widow of a minister and was supporting her two young daughters. According to one student, she had "a happy little way that promotes acquaintanceship."[101] She would be the law school's anchor for more than twenty-six years and lived with one daughter

97. *Legal Atmosphere Is a Drawing Card*, WASHBURN REV., May 1, 1912.
98. *A Word from "Grads,"* WASHBURN REV., Apr. 4, 1917.
99. *Dean Arthur*, WASHBURN REV., Jan. 25, 1911, at 4.
100. *Law Notes*, WASHBURN REV., Feb. 14, 1912, at 11.
101. *Law School Notes*, WASHBURN REV., Mar. 24, 1915, at 4.

7. 725 South Kansas Avenue as it looks in 2011

in Whiting Hall on the campus at the time she retired in 1941.[102] She had a "strong and loyal personality" that was a "fine influence in all the college life. She has been a friend and counselor to all the faculty and students," and, in particular, "mothered" the small group of women students with "wisdom and affection."[103] Mrs. Platt kept track of student attendance, standing "silently at the front of the classroom, spotting the empty chairs—if there are any."[104] The speed with which she learned the names of freshmen "was always a matter of great astonishment to them."[105] She attended all faculty meetings and prepared the minutes of the meetings.

The trustees of the College decided to close the Medical Department at the end of the academic year in 1913, due to rising costs and declining enrollments. They resolved, however, to strengthen the remaining downtown department, the Law School. The trustees appointed a subcommittee, composed of the three lawyer members of the board, Robert Stone, James W. Gleed, and A.A. Godard, to secure a permanent home for the school. By December 1912, the committee announced that it had negotiated a contract to purchase the Bell Telephone building at 211 West Sixth Street. It became available because the company was moving to a larger building following a merger. Trustee Gleed was credited with securing favorable terms since he also was a director of the telephone company.[106] The cost was approximately $20,000, 80% of which was pledged or already paid when the deal was announced.

> The money has been raised by solicitation among the lawyers of Topeka but more especially among the lecturers and instructors in the school who have put their interest in the school before everything else and made large contributions toward the fund for purchasing the building.[107]

Additional funds were required for renovation. Mrs. Lewis H. Greenwood made a significant contribution and the library in the new building was named for

---

102. Current faculty member Bill Rich is related to Platt. He describes her as his aunt's husband's aunt.

103. THE KAW (1941), at 54.

104. *Only Secretary of Law School Retires July 1*, TOPKEA ST. J., May 21, 1941.

105. Eulogy to Emily Sanford Platt, 1951 (on file in Washburn Law Library).

106. *New Law Building Washburn College*, WASHBURN REV., Mar. 26, 1913.

107. *Law School Will Have a New Home*, WASHBURN REV., Dec. 3, 1912.

8. 211 West 6th Street, the Law School's third location downtown, 1913–1918

her husband, the long-time Secretary of the Board of Trustees and Lecturer on Domestic Relations, who had died nearly two years earlier.

The building measured 25 feet by 125 feet, stood two-and-one-half stories high and was constructed of pressed brick. Remodeling of the first floor created offices and three lecture rooms, one for each of the three classes, with seniors assigned the room closest to the front door and freshmen assigned the one in the rear of the building. The moot court room was on the second floor, along with the library and reading rooms. The basement was used for lockers and storage. Future expansion to a lot at the rear of the building, which the College also owned, would be possible.

Renovation of the building took longer than expected. Hopes of having classes in the new building some time during the spring semester of 1913 evaporated and it was necessary to cancel the summer session for lack of classrooms in which to teach them. Moving the library books from Kansas Avenue nevertheless commenced in April and a "Decennial New Building Jubilee Banquet" was held at the Throop Hotel on May 26. New furniture was

9. Students marched from downtown Topeka to Washburn's
campus to celebrate new law building in 1914

purchased. The building opened with much fanfare in September 1913. The following spring, on April 20, the entire student body "marched—complete with drums and flags—from West Sixth to the campus to celebrate 'one of the finest law buildings in the West'."[108]

Marching was fine for one day, but it was not a desirable solution to the need for transportation daily between the campus and downtown.

> Many of the law students, especially freshmen, still lived on the hill. It was the early days of the jitney buses. Sardines in a can are not better packed than we were on that jitney. We had one which would deviate from its regular route early in the morning and fill up with law students from close by 17th and College and we would go non-stop to the law school and be there in time for the first class.[109]

Many students congregated between classes at Percy Walker's nearby drug store and were prone to arrive back late for class. Thus, when a system of electric bells was installed in the classrooms early in 1915, Arthur placed a bell on the same circuit at the drug store and rang it a minute or two before classes began.[110]

---

108. McLane, *supra* note 3, at 7.

109. *Id.* at 8.

110. Law School Notes, WASHBURN REV., Mar. 3, 1915; *William Reed Arthur Is "Pop" to Judges and Others He Helped Through School*, KAN. CITY TIMES, May 14, 1949.

FACULTY TURNOVER

Growth in enrollment led to a need not only for larger facilities but also for more full-time faculty. Arthur and Osborn were the only full-time teachers until 1911. However, attempts to increase the number of faculty were frustrated by sudden departures. Arthur recruited Shelby L. Large to become the third full-time professor in the fall of 1911. Large had just graduated from Arthur's law school, Northwestern. Large had started law school at Stanford and worked briefly for the Legal Aid Society of Chicago before moving to Topeka. He stayed just one semester, however, before returning to Illinois, where he practiced in Rockford until his retirement. No replacement was hired. Before the new building opened in 1913, KU enticed Osborn away to fill a vacancy on its full-time law faculty caused by a death. Arthur persuaded local lawyer Clinton J. Evans, who had been a Lecturer on Wills and Corporations the previous two years, to devote a substantial part of his time that year to teaching. Besides Arthur, he was the only member of the faculty who taught courses to all three classes of the Law School plus the night school. In addition, Paul H. Dodge was added as Professor of Law. He received his J.D. from the University of Chicago and studied law at Oxford for a year. He had practiced in New York City and had taught at Stetson College of Law in Florida the previous year. Dodge offered prizes in his Contracts and Equity classes for the best brief of assigned cases. The prizes consisted of "ten rules of practice" which he valued at one hundred dollars.[111] Perhaps not surprisingly, only one student submitted a brief. Dodge left the faculty at the end of the year.

Limited financial resources no doubt made retention of full-time faculty difficult. The College was operating at a deficit, and College President Frank Sanders took an unpaid leave of absence during the 1913–14 academic year. Expenditures at the Law School for 1911–12 totaled only $2,591.37, barely more than $2,000 of which went for salaries. When Large was not replaced, salaries fell to only $1,725 the next academic year. By 1915, a local newspaper reported there were four faculty members on salary, including the Dean,[112] suggesting the school did allocate some funds to pay local lawyers like Clinton Evans

111. *Law Notes*, WASHBURN REV., Oct. 29, 1913.

112. *Dean W.R. Arthur Quits Washburn Law School*, TOPEKA DAILY CAP., July 31, 1915.

who devoted a substantial part of their time to teaching. There were token honoraria for other Lecturers but many continued to donate their time.

Ernest R. Simon '06 initially agreed to devote full-time to law teaching in the fall of 1914. He taught his initial classes but left abruptly to accept a position practicing law in California. Arthur again invoked his ties to Northwestern and persuaded William Cullen Burns on short notice to leave his practice in Chicago to replace Simon for one semester. It was a financial sacrifice for Burns but he had Kansas ties. He had grown up in Oswego, was admitted to practice in 1899 after reading law in an office, then practiced law in Oswego and served four years as Labette County Probate Judge before moving to Chicago to attend Northwestern. He completed an LL.B., then was the first student to earn an LL.M. from Northwestern. Burns had taught as a Lecturer in Chicago at Illinois College of Law. He was popular with students who appreciated the amusing anecdotes he told in class, his experience in public life, the fact he knew every student's name by the second week, and "his earnest desire to share what he knew with students."[113]

Burns decided to return to Chicago after the fall semester. As luck would have it, at least for Washburn, one of the most respected lawyers and judges in Kansas, Justice Alfred Washburn Benson, was unexpectedly defeated for re-election to the Kansas Supreme Court in November 1914. "Such a misfortune may always happen wherever judges are elected by the people," the student newspaper astutely observed.[114] Benson had been a Lecturer on Code Pleading for six years. He agreed to replace Burns as a full-time faculty member for "an almost nominal remuneration" but refused to discuss school matters until his term expired because "my time belongs to the state until January 11, 1915."[115]

Benson was a Civil War veteran. His fifty-year career as a lawyer included twelve years as District Judge in Ottawa and Lawrence, where he taught law classes at KU. He served terms in the Kansas House of Representatives and Kansas Senate and was appointed to fill an unexpired term in the United States Senate. Finally, in 1907, he was appointed to fill a vacancy on the Kansas Supreme Court. That appointment led Benson to teach part-time at Washburn. In his first semester as a full-time professor, Benson taught ten credit hours in five subjects, Quasi-Contracts, Mortgages, Domestic Relations, Criminal

---

113. *Honor W. Burns*, WASHBURN REV., Feb. 3, 1915.
114. *Albert Washburn Benson Memorial*, WASHBURN REV., Feb. 16, 1916.
115. *Id.*

Pleading, and Damages. In addition, he made himself available in the library for one hour each afternoon to advise students informally on any legal questions they wished to ask him. From the outset, students

> responded to the intense interest this veteran of the law has taken in their training. No lapse of years has dimmed the youthful outlook of his mind for the years to come; no firmly settled habits of life have prevented him from adapting himself wholly to the new work; no bitterness or pessimism have chilled the natural enthusiasm and ardor of his scholars; no lagging interest in his work that was, to say the least, different to him, has permitted any student an excuse for his own disinterest…[116]

So large was Benson's legend that the school's chapter of Phi Alpha Delta law fraternity was named in his memory even though it was not formed until six years after his death. He threw himself into the whole of academic life, leading law students on several marches out to the main campus and in various school parades. Benson began compiling his own casebook on Damages as the first step in a broader publishing project that had been discussed at the school for several years.

> A demand for books of this type has been felt by western law schools because the eastern institutions nearly control the law book publishing. Owing to an important divergence in the code law of the eastern states, many leading cases in New York and Massachusetts cannot be made to apply in Kansas and it is to supplement these cases and their holdings with western decisions that the Topeka school is undertaking this work.[117]

Spurred by reports that the cost of educating a doctor at the University of Kansas was $3,000, members of the 1915 Kansas Legislature asked Washburn to determine the cost of educating a lawyer. Arthur's "carefully tabulated results showed that each diploma, on average, cost the school $312.50."[118] Arthur acknowledged that a graduate paid only $165 in tuition plus a $5 diploma fee for

---

116. *Former Justice A.W. Benson, Now Washburn Law Instructor*, WASHBURN REV., May 26, 1915.

117. *Washburn Law Books*, TOPEKA ST. J., Mar. 1, 1915.

118. *Full Fledged Washburn Law Grad Costs $312.50*, TOPEKA DAILY CAP., Apr. 4, 1915, at 10B.

the three-year course but explained the school nevertheless was self-supporting because of the tuition payments of those who commenced law studies but failed to "reach the final goal." He also cited the willingness of several members of the part-time faculty to teach without pay as a factor keeping costs down.

Dean Arthur was justifiably praised for his remarkable success in increasing enrollment and strengthening the school. The 1914 College yearbook was dedicated to him. At the school's annual banquet that year, James Coleman lauded Arthur as "a tireless worker… who had dreamed a dream which he was able to put into reality, in the placing [o]f the Washburn Law School on an equal with all other law schools of this country."[119] Arthur's abilities were noticed elsewhere. In 1913, KU recruited Arthur, before it ultimately hired Osborn, but he declined the offer because he felt he needed more time to solidify the school's future.[120] Later, he rejected an offer to join a California law firm for the same reason. In 1914, he was invited to judge a debate between the law schools at Creighton University and the University of South Dakota and to present a series of lectures at the John Marshall Law School in Chicago. Finally, during the summer of 1915, the University of Colorado offered him a professorship in real property law, funded by a new endowment that paid almost double his Washburn salary. Arthur accepted and resigned the deanship.[121]

Public announcement of Arthur's departure was delayed so that candidates to replace him could be recruited.[122] Justice Benson was urged by some to become a candidate, but he expressed hesitancy. William Cullen Burns, who taught at Washburn the previous fall, applied. C. Martin Alsager of the University of Chicago also applied, even though he had rejected an offer for a full-time faculty position the prior year. Dean D.E. McDugan of St. Louis University asked to be considered.

The person selected was Thomas Welburn Hughes. Unlike the first three deans, Hughes already had built a reputation as a legal educator. He was fifty-seven years old and had taught for twenty-two years at four major law schools, most recently while serving for three years as Dean at the University of Florida. He was born in the province of Ontario, Canada, and began teaching in the

119. *Annual Banquet*, WASHBURN REV., May 27, 1914, at 14.

120. *Dean W. R. Arthur Quits Washburn Law School*, TOPEKA DAILY CAP., July 31, 1915.

121. *Id.*

122. *Id.*

10. Thomas W. Hughes, Dean 1915–1917
and 1919–1920, Professor 1915–1928

common schools there at age seventeen. He also taught in Manitoba before
entering the University of Michigan School of Law when he was nearly thirty
years of age.[123] He received his LL.B. in 1891 and stayed to complete an LL.M. in
1892. He did such high quality work that he was invited to remain at Michigan
after graduation and taught law there for six years. He then taught for twelve
years at the University of Illinois College of Law and for two years at Louisiana
State University before accepting the deanship at Florida. It was reported that
his decision to move from Florida to Washburn was because "the climate in
Florida and his health do not agree."[124] In addition, he was moving to a school
with higher standards. Florida required only two years of high school for
matriculation when he arrived there, a requirement he raised to four years

123. *Life of Service*, TOPEKA ST. J., Apr. 9, 1927, at 9.
124. *Florida Man to Be Law Dean*, TOPEKA DAILY CAP., Aug. 5, 1915, at 1.

during his deanship, but it remained a two-year law program until the year after his departure.

Hughes was a nationally recognized scholar. His treatise, *Hughes on Evidence* (1906), was being used in more than twenty law schools, including for the past eight years at KU, where Dean James Green called it "the best work on this subject for class instruction that is in print. It brings the rules of evidence out with great clearness and precision." It had been recommended by Professor John C. Gray, Jr. of Harvard and the instructor who used it at Buffalo Law School also praised it: "I know of no clearer definitions anywhere in any work on evidence than those of Mr. Hughes....I know of no work on evidence that puts more that is modern and practical into the same number of pages."[125] There were 5,000 copies in print by 1917. The treatise later was cited by the United States Supreme Court which referred to Hughes as an "author of repute."[126] He also had published *Hughes on Commercial Law* (1909), *Hughes on Criminal Pleading and Practice* (1910), and *Hughes on Criminal Law* (1913). After arriving at Washburn, he published a shorter *Hughes Pocket Digest of Evidence* (1917), for use primarily by lawyers and judges, and a new casebook, *Hughes Cases on Criminal Law and Procedure* (1919).

Hughes was described as one who "takes a deep interest in good citizenship and in the moral welfare of the community."[127] While he was teaching at Illinois, a proposal was submitted to voters in Urbana and Champaign to ban saloons in those cities. Hughes spoke in churches and public halls in support of the proposal, and his efforts helped anti-saloon forces win majorities in both cities.

Curiously, in light of Hughes' credentials, the announcement of his appointment described him only as Acting Dean,[128] and he was described the same way in the catalogue. There was public speculation that the trustees still hoped to entice Arthur to return as Dean.[129] Understandably, Arthur was a hard act to follow, and Hughes had a difficult first semester. Justice Benson died on December 15. A Harvard-educated lawyer who had recently arrived in

---

125. William C. Ralston, *Dean Hughes*, WASHBURN COLL. SCH. OF LAW BULLETIN, No. 6 (Mar. 1917).

126. *Clark v. United States*, 289 U.S. 1, 13 (1933).

127. Ralston, *supra* note 125.

128. *Florida Man to Be Law Dean*, *supra* note 124.

129. *Arthur May Come Back*, TOPEKA DAILY CAP., Jan. 29, 1916, at 12.

Topeka, Thomas Amory Lee, agreed to take over Benson's classes in Contracts, Code Pleading and Mortgages, teaching nearly full-time. Students complained that examinations given by an unidentified professor, apparently not Hughes, "were so vague and indefinite that it was impossible to answer them, and that as a result grades were unfairly low." Students asked local lawyers to review the questions and the lawyers "were unanimous in branding them unfair and unjust."[130] A local newspaper reported there was talk of a strike and that some students threatened not to take any work from the professor if he was retained for the following semester. It also reported that Dean Hughes had been severely criticized by several students. The student body reacted, passing a resolution that the article "did not express the sentiments of the school at all" and voicing "our confidence in and appreciation of Dean Hughes and his work for the institution. His teaching is satisfactory to us and his administration of the affairs of the school is of a high order."[131] An editorial in the campus newspaper a week later also offered support. "Handicapped though he has been by the tremendous popularity of his immediate predecessor, and by the death of the great Benson—Kansas' incomparable jurist, teacher and man—Dean Hughes has more than justified expectations."[132]

Hughes did not act like an Acting Dean. He continued to expand student recruitment, ordering 400 copies of the law edition of the student newspaper to mail to high schools that had a four-year course and mailing a copy of the new catalogue to every lawyer in the state along with a cover letter touting the school's advantages. He re-wrote the catalogue's statement of the Law School's purpose so that it included not only knowledge of court procedure and fundamental principles of law and equity but also "legal methods of reasoning and legal habits of thought; intellectual power and acumen; and a high sense of honor and professional duty."[133] His desire for quality rather than quantity was greater than that of his predecessor.[134] Near the end of his first year, the faculty "decided that a few of the lower classmen should be requested to withdraw from school owing to unsatisfactory work."[135] Good grades were

---

130. *Questions Peeve Embryo Lawyers*, TOPEKA DAILY CAP. Jan. 16, 1916, at 12.

131. *Law School Resolution*, WASHBURN REV., Feb. 9, 1916.

132. *Editorials*, WASHBURN REV., Feb. 16, 1916.

133. WASHBURN COLL. SCH. OF LAW BULLETIN 5 (June 1916).

134. *Letter from Dean Hughes*, WASHBURN REV., Oct. 25, 1916.

135. *Law Faculty Meets*, WASHBURN REV., Apr. 5, 1916.

harder to make and a few students who did not make them the following fall threatened to attend Kansas City Law School.[136]

Hughes added a full semester one-hour course on Legal Ethics, teaching it himself, and later increased the number of credits to two. Previously, the topic had been the subject only of special lectures. He inserted into the catalogue for the first time a lengthy statement about the ethics of the legal profession. "The Dean is a man of lofty ideals," wrote a part-time faculty member. "His moral impress upon the student is of the best. He stands for the highest ethical standards of the profession. He is thorough and painstaking in his methods of instruction. He takes a deep personal interest in his students. He likes his work. He enjoys association with students."[137] He had "a remarkable power of setting forth in a simple form the difficult problems and principles of law."[138] Students quickly grew fond of Hughes. One student wrote:

> The law school to a man would put its money on Dean Hughes against any one in the state of Kansas in his grasp of the principles underlying every branch of the law....And he makes it interesting. When it comes to livening up a dull subject Dean Hughes could make Topeka on a Sunday afternoon look like San Francisco on New Year's night.[139]

An earlier history of the school called Hughes a "colorful teacher," and included recollections of Hughes' students:

> When he would come to the point in a long discussion, he would say, "Now gentlemen, that is the milk of the coconut." There was a standing reward of five dollars to anyone who dared to put glue in the top of his hat so his toupee ("an early day one and a horrible fit") would come off when he removed his hat; but "we all loved him so that we didn't pay much attention to it except to note what a poor imitation it was for real hair."[140]

During his second year as Dean, Hughes was the only full-time teacher, although William Chalmers Ralston carried nearly a full-time load. Ralston

136. *Law School,* WASHBURN REV., Jan. 31, 1917.
137. Ralston, *supra* note 125.
138. *New Law Book Out,* TOPEKA ST. J., July 7, 1917, at 10.
139. *Our Dean,* WASHBURN REV., Apr. 4, 1917.
140. McLane, *supra* note 3, at 9.

then was in private practice after serving six years as City Attorney and would not become Assistant Attorney General until 1921. He had been a Lecturer since 1909. Evans, Lee, and Otis Hungate also carried heavier teaching loads than most part-time faculty members.

RAISING STANDARDS

While requirements for admission to Washburn Law School's first classes seem modest from a modern perspective, they exceeded those of many law schools nationally. In Kansas, it was not until 1921 that the Supreme Court required applicants for admission to the bar to have completed one year of college, effective at the 1924 bar examination. Of course, nothing prevented law schools from imposing requirements of pre-legal education higher than those for admission to the bar. However, there were practical limitations to consider. As a fledgling department at a small college, Washburn Law School needed to attract students to survive. When KU in 1912 instituted a requirement of thirty hours of college credit, its junior class reportedly dropped from 125 to 47.[141] If a law school's requirements were too far in excess of the Court's requirements for bar admission, prospective law students, instead of taking the additional preparatory work, could go elsewhere. Law office study remained an available option for them, and the Supeme Court did not begin to tighten regulation of that option until 1926. Alternatively, they could enroll in a nearby state in a law school whose admission requirements merely matched those of the Kansas Supreme Court, and they would be eligible upon graduation to take the Kansas bar exam.

The ability to admit "special students" was a wild card in the admissions process. By requiring only completion of a high school course "or its equivalent," the AALS membership standards contemplated the occasional admission of special students and almost all member schools had them. When done too routinely, however, admission of special students could mean a school's pre-legal education requirements were merely published ones, not real ones. The presence of too many under-prepared students also could diminish the quality of classroom discussion. Washburn did not always do a thorough

141. William A. Kelly, *The University of Kansas School of Law, in* REQUISITE LEARNING AND GOOD MORAL CHARACTER: A HISTORY OF THE KANSAS BENCH AND BAR 107, 115 (Robert W. Richmond ed., 1982).

job of documenting in its records what it deemed "special" about the special students it admitted, something AALS regulations required. Of course, the ultimate check on laxity in standards was performance on the bar examination, and here Washburn's early performance was extraordinary.

Dean Hughes began to reform admission of special students. "From its inception," he wrote after assessing the reality of admission requirements, the Law School "has been handicapped by lack of funds to meet its operating expenses. In consequence of this misfortune, and founded upon necessity, many students, not qualified to matriculate, have been enrolled. Some of these students were not even qualified to enter the higher grades in the ward schools." He reduced the number of special students from twenty-eight the year before he arrived to fourteen in 1915 and to four in 1916. "It is not the policy of the Law School totally to eliminate special students. Its policy, however, is to reduce the number to a minimum. No first-class law school has more than a few special students. Some have none at all."[142] Having persuaded Washburn President Parley P. Womer to support this change of policy, regardless of its consequence for tuition revenue, Hughes publicly called Washburn fortunate to have a President "who possesses keen foresight and excellent judgment."[143] The change was made not a moment too soon, since the 1917 AALS inspection report concluded that the former practice of admitting students "deficient in entrance requirements" violated the Association's membership requirements.

Nearly half the members of the entering class in 1916 had at least one year of college training, and the student newspaper noted the faculty's "pleasure and satisfaction in teaching students whose preliminary training has fitted them to study law."[144] By November, the faculty recommended to the trustees a requirement of one year of college work for all students, subject to continued discretion in the Dean to admit occasional special students. The change was approved, effective for the entering class in 1918, although the effective date later was postponed one year due to World War I. Still, this was two years before the Kansas Supreme Court adopted this requirement and well before the AALS in 1923 required all its member schools to impose it. Hughes' work to increase standards "made him liked and respected by every Washburn supporter."[145]

142. *Letter from Dean Hughes, supra* note 134.
143. *Id.*
144. *Law School,* WASHBURN REV., Oct 4, 1916
145. *Dr. Hughes Writes Book on Evidence,* WASHBURN REV., May 4, 1921.

The school devised a four-year course to which students who had not completed one year of college could be admitted. The only law course these students took in the first year was Torts. They took Introduction to Economics in the second year along with law courses. The four-year plan gave the school control of the content of students' pre-legal education it did not have with students who completed a year of college work on their own. American History, British Constitutional History, History of the British Empire, Composition and Literary Types, Principles and Practice of Modern Free States, and Public Speaking all were included in the first year, along with one College elective each semester.

THE AALS REQUIREMENT FOR LIBRARY BOOKS

The school's founders assumed it could avoid major expenditures for a library because the proximity of the State Law Library gave law students ready access to the largest collection of legal materials in the state. The 1905 legislature by statute directed the State Law Librarian to supply Washburn Law School with a free set of the *Kansas Reports*, the *Kansas Court of Appeals Reports* and *Dassler's Kansas Digest*, along with new volumes as they were issued.[146] This may have been the first public funding the College ever received. Donations were a principal source of growth of the collection from the school's inception. Rarely would more than a few months pass without announcement of a donation of books. For example, U. S. Senator and future Vice President of the United States Charles Curtis of Topeka gave the school 700 volumes of Senate and House Reports. Mrs. L. H. Greenwood contributed a valuable set of *Cyclopedia of Law and Procedure*. In 1912, however, the AALS adopted a requirement that member schools must own a library of at least 5,000 volumes. Easy access was not the test; ownership was. Funds were not available to add to the collection the number of books needed. James W. Clark '09, then a part-time Lecturer, attended a meeting at which Dean Arthur outlined the problem:

> I left Dean Arthur in full contemplation of certain ruin; but on my way back to my office downtown, I stopped in at one of the city's leading firms of lawyers. They told me the group had many books in their library which were of no value to them but could be a great help to the school

146. 1905 Kan. Sess. Laws, ch. 485, § 1.

aside from meeting the Association's demand. I called upon several law firms, meeting the same cordial and generous reception. All promised to deliver the books.[147]

Local lawyers donated 1500 books.[148] The problem with reliance on donations for collection development, of course, was that it lacked planning and purpose. Many of the materials received were outdated or not very useful. Only by happenstance were they books essential to a good core collection.

Washburn was by no means the only member school with a collection that was too small. The AALS made it clear schools would have a reasonable time to come into compliance. The first AALS membership inspection after the requirement went into effect was in April 1917 and the library was found deficient. The disruption of legal education caused by World War I bought the school some additional time. The AALS canceled the 1917 annual meeting, to which a Washburn representative had been summoned to respond to the deficiency. However, when the school moved to the campus during the war, the loss of easy access to the State Law Library made the issue more critical. President Womer represented in a letter to the AALS Executive Committee before the 1918 meeting that Washburn was taking "active steps" to meet the library deficiency but asked for more time because of the "abnormal conditions" produced by the war.

Womer appeared before the Executive Committee on December 29, 1919, explaining that the library had been overhauled, that much obsolete material had been eliminated, and that the library had 4,500 volumes and would reach the required 5,000 volumes in one and one-half years. The Executive Committee ordered a follow-up inspection in 1920. The AALS inspector, H.C. Horack from Iowa, found gaping holes in the collection. In January 1921, the Executive Committee took the extreme step of specifying by name sets of books the school must acquire before the 1921–22 academic year to retain its Association membership. The required books included the *First Decennial Digest* and all missing volumes of the National Reporter System and its *Shepard's Citators*. At its December 1921 meeting the Executive Committee found there was substantial compliance with its acquisition requirements, although some items remained to be purchased. However, when Horack inspected the school again

147. McLane, *supra* note 3, at 7.
148. *Among the Lawyers*, WASHBURN REV., Oct. 8, 1913, at 3.

in the fall of 1922, he disagreed with the school's volume count, reporting that only 3,600 volumes were on the shelves, and recommended that Washburn be excluded from the Association.[149] President Womer, new Dean Harry K. Allen, and Chief Justice William Johnston appeared before the Executive Committee on December 29, 1922. They claimed Horack had miscounted the collection but acknowledged there were only 4,300 volumes on the shelves after further weeding of obsolete materials when the school moved to new quarters. They reported that 1,400 books had been ordered and would be on the shelves within two weeks. The issue at last was resolved.

THE IMPACT OF WAR

Foreign conflicts affected the school. When Mexican bandit Pancho Villa began his raids into New Mexico, two first-year law students were members of the Kansas National Guard battery that was sent to the Mexican border in 1916 to mobilize for the Punitive Expedition.[150] Other law students were eager to help. A 1L at the time later recalled:

> We decided to declare a holiday and march out to the campus to recruit men to go to Mexico and help. I was quite willing to go myself. But Dean O.D. McEachron [Vice-President and Dean of the College] marched out to meet us and stopped us before we ever got to the campus. The holiday came to an immediate end.[151]

The next conflict was more serious. The United States entered World War I in April 1917. Graduating seniors who were scheduled to attend Officer Candidate School in May were granted their degrees early and were admitted to the bar based on what one graduate remembered to be a one-question oral exam.[152]

Despite the uncertain times, Albert J. Harno agreed to leave law practice in Los Angeles to become the new Dean. Enrollment throughout the College

---

149. The recommendation also was based on Horack's finding that the school lacked the required three full-time faculty because new Dean Harry K. Allen spent afternoons in a downtown law office examining abstracts.

150. *Law Notes*, WASHBURN REV., Mar. 29, 1916, at 3.

151. McLane, *supra* note 3, at 8.

152. CLIFFORD HOPE, JR., QUIET COURAGE: KANSAS CONGRESSMAN CLIFFORD R. HOPE 22 (1997).

plummeted in the fall of 1917 from 900 to 400. In the Law School, the decline was 37%. The separate night school was abandoned. Of forty-three students who began law studies in 1916–17, only three graduated within the normal three years time. Imposition of the requirement for admission of one year of college was deferred until 1919. Harno sought to shore up enrollment by persuading students who did not plan to practice law to take law courses. The College accepted as electives up to twenty-six hours in law courses, and Harno argued in the student newspaper that the "study of law should be regarded as part of a liberal education" that would be "of incalculable value to you in your business or profession."[153]

Some law schools suspended operations during the war. Washburn fared better than most. The Government Committee on Education and Special Training selected Washburn to participate in the Student Army Training Corps program. Law students between eighteen and forty-five years of age who had registered for the draft could be inducted into S.A.T.C. and take classes toward a law degree. The weekly schedule included eleven hours of practical military training plus sixteen classroom hours. However, it was not the traditional law school curriculum. S.A.T.C. students took a two-credit course in International Law, a three-credit course in Military Law, and five credits split between war issues and theoretical military instruction, but that left six hours for electives in standard law courses.[154] Harno spent the summer of 1918 at Fort Sheridan, training to teach in this revamped program.[155] Given the attractive option of S.A.T.C., a large number of the new students who registered at the College for 1918–19 elected the law course, and the Law School had the two largest freshman classes in its history in 1918 and 1919. Few of the new students completed the degree program but for the first time Washburn's law enrollment exceeded that at KU, which saw enrollment decline to only twelve students. Indeed, Washburn touted a Carnegie Foundation study showing it had the highest enrollment of all strictly day law schools in the country, two more than Harvard.[156]

---

153. *The Study of Law and Its Non-Professional Value*, WASHBURN REV., Oct. 17, 1917, at 1, 3.

154. *Washburn Law School Moves to Campus*, WASHBURN REV., Oct. 2, 1918, at 1.

155. *Law School*, WASHBURN REV., Aug. 20, 1918.

156. *Law School Enrollment*, WASHBURN REV., Mar. 5, 1919.

There were other firsts in these uncertain times. During the spring semester of 1919, the Student Bar Association elected its first woman president, Ruth Miller Kaster '21.

MOVING TO THE CAMPUS

The new building on Sixth Street initially was hailed as "a home for all time."[157] However, the luster wore off quickly as students came to take for granted having their classes on the ground floor for the first time. The student newspaper commented

> It is generally conceded that the present location is inappropriate. Facing on Sixth Street, with a brick paved alley on the west, the noise and confusion is frequently so great that classes have to be discontinued. Street cars, racing autos and delivery wagons blast all powers of concentration. The building itself is inadequate and unfitted to the needs of a modern law school. The class rooms are poorly lighted and absolutely without suitable means of ventilation. In the brief intermission between classes the windows are thrown open while the budding lawyers with coat collars turned up and their hands in their "own" pockets stamp about to keep their blood from congealing—only later to sit and breathe, rebreathe and breathe again the fast depreciating ozone ... The building as it greets the prospective student is unattractive and even repulsive and many a good man is lured away to another school of a more prepossessing appearance.[158]

As early as the second year of Hughes' deanship, there was talk of a new building, to be financed in part by the sale of the current building as well as the old Medical College building.[159] World War I would resolve the issue. When it became clear that a majority of the law students in 1918–19 would be members of S.A.T.C., and thus would have to be on the main campus for military training each day, the College arranged for law classes to be held in the basement of Crane Observatory, with offices on the main floor of the building.

---

157. THE KAW 71 (1913).

158. *A New Law Building Is the Dream of Dean Hughes*, WASHBURN REV., Apr. 4, 1917.

159. *Law School—New Building for Laws?*, WASHBURN REV., Nov. 22, 1916.

The move was thought to be a temporary one but there were advantages to having the Law School on campus. It was easier for students in the College to take courses in the Law School and visa versa. Greater cooperation between the departments was possible. By the spring, it was decided the Law School would stay on the campus and, in April, the library was moved from the downtown location to Crane Observatory. The building on Sixth Street ultimately was sold for $12,000. The building most recently has been home to an insurance agency and a firm producing business forms.

Starting in 1919, three consecutive catalogues proclaimed, "Plans are laid which give every reasonable assurance that in another year the law school will be located in a new home equipped for its exclusive use." Indeed, the College agreed that Holbrook Hall, which was one of the earliest buildings on campus and had been a dormitory since 1885, would be remodeled for the Law School to use once a new dormitory was completed. However, the new dormitory was not completed until 1922, and the Law School remained in the Observatory for four years. President Womer attributed the delay to "uncertain conditions of the present day and high cost of material and labor."[160]

The Observatory was not designed to meet the needs of a law school. "It could accommodate only a crowded 124; there was no special courtroom for moot court—'furniture was rearranged and imagination was brought into play.'"[161] There were not sufficient reading rooms in the library. When the full-time faculty reached three in 1920, faculty too lacked adequate quarters. In January 1921, the AALS ordered the College to provide adequate temporary facilities before the fall semester, pending renovation of Holbrook Hall, and that permanent quarters had to be provided by the fall of 1922.

CHAPEL EXERCISES

Because of Washburn College's religious affiliation, it held mandatory weekly chapel exercises in MacVicar Chapel, at 1:00 p.m. on Mondays. Part of the time was set aside for devotions but during the rest of the time there were speakers and meetings. Law students were exempt from having to attend when the school was downtown. When the Laws moved to campus, the question was

---

160. Minutes, Washburn Coll. Sch. of Law faculty meeting (Jan. 22, 1921).
161. McLane, *supra* note 3, at 9.

whether their exemption would continue. As long as the move to campus was thought to be temporary, law classes were not scheduled during the chapel hour so that students could attend, but attendance was not mandatory. When the move was made permanent, the College administration believed it imperative that law students be required to attend. There was a battle of wills. At a law student assembly, one of the students made a motion that the Laws refuse to go to chapel. When the chairman called for the vote the "ayes" were given with such force that some of the residents of College Avenue wondered if the football season had started. The Laws then voted that any Law man caught attending chapel would be treated the same as the timid Freshman who forgets to wear his little blue cap.[162]

Submission of the dispute to the full faculty of the College produced the predictable result. Dean Hughes issued a notice: "Students of the Law School are required to attend chapel the same as other students. All excuses heretofore granted to law students for absences from chapel exercises, for the future are hereby revoked."[163] Before long, the Law School was allowed to conduct its own chapel exercises, inviting speakers of interest to its students, and the controversy went out of the issue.

THE FIRST SIX DEANS

In Washburn Law School's first nineteen years, there were six different deans. The dean was the only full-time member of the faculty during the school's first six years and in five other years the dean and a former dean were the only full-time faculty members. Four of the first six deans held their first full-time faculty positions at Washburn, and three had been lawyers for five years or less. Washburn made remarkable choices, however. The available evidence suggests they were talented teachers and administrators. Other law schools lured five of the six away from Washburn with more lucrative offers. All six early deans had long and distinguished careers in legal education and three of them served as deans at other law schools.

After resigning as Dean in 1907, Ernest Conant taught at the University of Nebraska for six years. He then spent four years as Professor of Law at the

---

162. *Laws Elect Officers,* WASHBURN REV., Oct. 1, 1919, at 3.
163. *Laws Required to Attend Chapel,* WASHBURN REV., Jan. 7, 1920, at 1.

University of the Philippines, a law school with 240 students, and represented that school at meetings of the Association of American Law Schools. Finally, he became Professor of Law at Washington University in St. Louis, teaching full time from 1917 through 1935 and thereafter as Professor Emeritus. He was named Madill Professor of Law there. Throughout his career he maintained a strong interest in the school he helped to start, visiting several times while he taught at Nebraska and returning to describe the early history of the Law School at its twenty-fifth anniversary celebration.

Upon leaving Washburn in 1913, Edward Osborn taught at KU full time until the start of World War I. He served in France in 1918 with the American Red Cross. He chose to leave teaching after the war, practicing law in New York City for four years, then returned to Paris where he practiced law for six years.[164] He rejoined the Washburn faculty in 1930 and continued to teach until his retirement in 1941 at age sixty-nine. Beginning in 1932, he wrote a number of articles as part of Washburn's contribution to the initial four volumes of the *Journal of the Kansas Bar Association.*

Osborn was described as "thorough and fair to everyone," and as one "who looks through all the frills and fantastics of a fellow and sees the real man and then he deals with the real man rather than any disguise he may try to assume."[165] In his later years, he "was affectionately known as 'Daddy' Osborn."[166]

Coincidentally, Osborn's successor later would be known as "Pop" Arthur. At Colorado, he was named the Charles Ingles Thomson Professor. An additional attraction of the position at Colorado was that it provided more time for legal writing than Arthur had at Washburn, where he found time only to write legal guides for township officers and police officers and to publish compiled Kansas election laws. By the end of his career, he had authored five other books, the best known being multiple editions of *The Law of Newspapers* and *The Law of Drugs and Druggists*, the latter of which was used in nearly every pharmacy school in the country, and one edition of *The Law of Dentists and Dentistry*. When he retired at Colorado in 1946, an issue of his school's journal was dedicated to him[167] and he was named Professor Emeritus.

---

164. E.D. Orborne[sic], *Instrumental in Founding Law School, Returns to Teach,* WASHBURN REV., Sept. 15, 1930.

165. *A Tribute,* WASHBURN REV., Mar. 26, 1913.

166. THE KAW 54 (1941).

167. *Dedication,* 18 ROCKY MTN. L. REV. insert after 344 (1946).

Arthur continued his association with Washburn Law School through the years. In 1935, he taught at Washburn during the second summer session, trading places with Dean Harry K. Allen, who taught at Colorado.[168] When the school was flooded with new students after World War II, Arthur spent the 1946–47 academic year, his first year of retirement, as Visiting Professor of Law at Washburn.[169]

After two years as Dean, Thomas Hughes continued teaching at Washburn for more than eleven years until he retired in 1928 at age seventy. When his successor in the deanship, Albert Harno, left on short notice after only two years, Hughes agreed in 1919 to serve as Acting Dean but within six months announced he would serve only one year. His administrative duties interfered too much with his real love, writing law books. He was under contract with Callaghan and Company to write a casebook on Evidence but had been unable to make any progress on that work. Not only were administrative duties time consuming, they kept him in the law building and away from the State Law Library downtown, which was the only place he could conduct his research since Washburn's law library was inadequate for that purpose.

Hughes's love for writing was enhanced by its financial rewards. The student newspaper observed, "The additional compensation for performing the executive duties pertaining to the law school is a mere trifle as compared to the remuneration for writing law books; and Dean Hughes has made a considerable financial sacrifice this year in having to abandon the writing of his case book on Evidence."[170] It was said when he arrived in 1915 that annual royalties on his popular treatise on Evidence, at 20% of sales, were about $1200 per year. *Hughes Cases on Evidence* was published in 1921 and soon was selected for use at NYU and Georgetown, among other schools.[171] The next year, he completed a casebook on Criminal Law and Procedure. Although his early works were treatises, he now believed that students should be taught by "use of case books in the main, and text books for references only."[172] Unlike many

---

168. *New Summer School Ideas*, WASHBURN REV., Mar. 29, 1935.

169. The next two years he visited at Kansas City Law School, then taught in Florida at Stetson College Law School. He still was teaching as a Visiting Professor at St. Louis University School of Law as late as the 1952–53 academic year.

170. *Law Dean Requests to Be Relieved*, WASHBURN REV., Jan. 21, 1920.

171. *To Use Topekan's Book*, TOPEKA ST. J., Mar. 27, 1922, at 3.

172. *Dr. Hughes Writes Book on Evidence*, WASHBURN REV., Mar. 22, 1922.

casebook authors, Hughes edited cases closely, so that students would not have to read useless material to find the main point.[173] He continued to write and, shortly before he retired, completed his first book not designed for use in law schools or by practitioners, *Was Jesus Guilty?*[174]

When Hughes announced plans to retire from teaching due to impaired hearing, students called a special assembly. They unanimously passed a resolution urging the president and trustees of the College to grant him an appropriate lifetime pension.[175]

When Albert J. Harno succeeded Hughes as Dean in 1917, he was only twenty-eight years old and had been a lawyer for only three years. Thus, no one could have anticipated he would become one of the leading figures in the history of American legal education. He was a native of South Dakota and received his B.S. from Dakota Wesleyan University in 1911. He had stellar academic credentials, earning his LL.B. *magna cum laude* from Yale in 1914. He received Yale's Foster Prize as the graduate with the highest grade average, twice won the Wayland Prize in competitive debates, and was an editor of the *Yale Law Journal* during his final two years. Following graduation, Harno joined the Los Angeles firm of Bennett, Turnbull & Thompson but left within a year to practice on his own before coming to Washburn.

It was said that Harno had "a keen legal mind and is very industrious. He is a good mixer, has a very sunny disposition, is very approachable and is an exceedingly likable young man. He is a firm believer in the case method of teaching law and stands for quality…"[176] He taught Persons, Property I, II, and III, Wills and Administration, and Suretyship, and one year taught Common Law Pleading and the next year co-taught Torts. While at Washburn, he published in the *Kentucky Law Review* the first of many articles he would author during his career[177] and accepted an invitation to become an Alumni Contributing Editor of the *Yale Law Journal.*

On June 30, 1919, Harno resigned as Dean to become Professor of Law at the University of Kansas, filling Osborn's vacancy when Osborn opted to practice

---

173. *Id.*

174. *Review by Dr. T.W. Hughes*, TOPEKA ST. J., Apr. 27, 1927, at 9.

175. *Hughes to Retire*, TOPEKA ST. J., Mar. 26, 1927, at 2.

176. *Albert J. Harno*, WASHBURN REV., Apr. 17, 1918, at 1.

177. Albert J. Harno, *Revocability of Licenses as Applied to Property in Land*, 7 KY. L.J. 1 (1919).

11. Albert J. Harno, Dean 1917–1919

in New York after the war. It was the third time in just six years KU tried to lure away a member of Washburn's faculty, and the second time it succeeded. Washburn's President Parley Womer was happy to see Harno leave. The campus was then in an uproar over Womer's dismissal, without hearing or formal charges, of Dr. J. E. Kirkpatrick, the popular head of the Department of History and Political Science. Kirkpatrick had been critical of the administration and urged its reorganization.[178] Harno sided with Kirkpatrick and was among faculty members who applied to charter a Washburn local of the American Federation of Teachers, a union affiliated with the American Federation of Labor. As a parting shot in an interview the day before his resignation, Harno charged that the current system of administration was unfair.

> "I candidly believe that under this system the college cannot have a wholesome growth," he declared last night. "The strength of the col-

---

178. ROY BIRD, WASHBURN THROUGH THE YEARS 75 (1997).

lege lies primarily in its faculty, with the proper co-ordinated heads of the departments. Any college administration which regards its heads of departments and faculty members as mere hirelings is building on false premises."[179]

Harno stayed at KU only for two years before becoming a professor at the University of Illinois College of Law. He was named Dean there one year later and held the position, remarkably, for thirty-five years. For thirteen of those years, beginning in 1931, he also served as Provost. He would be a leader in almost all of the national legal organizations of his era, serving terms as President of the National Conference of Commissioners on Uniform State Laws, the Order of the Coif, and the American Judicature Society, as chair of the Council of the American Law Institute, and as a member of the ABA Board of Governors.[180] Harno was recognized as a "prime mover" in raising standards for legal education through the AALS and the ABA.[181] He published four editions of a widely used casebook on Criminal Law and Procedure.

In 1916, the AALS adopted a requirement that member schools have at least three faculty members "who devote substantially all of their time" to the work of the school. Only for one semester during 1911 had Washburn had three full-time teachers. Washburn was not unique among AALS members in its reliance on part-time faculty. The AALS requirement was made effective for the 1919–20 academic year, to give schools time to come into compliance. However, with Harno's sudden departure, Thomas Hughes was the only full-time teacher for 1919–20. Washburn President Parley Womer's preference was still to operate the Law School on the cheap, but he concluded that "on the whole

---

179. *Union at College!*, TOPEKA ST. J., June 30, 1919, at 1.

180. Harno also served on the executive committee and then in 1932 as President of the Association of American Law Schools. He was President of the Order of the Coif from 1934 through 1937. He was chair of the Council of the Section on Legal Education of the American Bar Association from 1942 until 1945 and was a member of the ABA Board of Governors from 1950 through 1953. He was selected as a member of the Council of the American Law Institute in 1947. He became a Commissioner from Illinois to the National Conference of Commissioners on Uniform State Laws in 1934 and served as President from 1947 until 1949. He was chair of the Board of Directors of the American Judicature Society from 1945 through 1951 and was its President from 1953 until 1956.

181. Roy R. Bartlett, *Heritage of Excellence*, WASHBURN ALUMNUS 1, 2 (Oct. 1960).

Standing—Evans, Allen, McBride, Lee, Mason, Hughes
Seated—Raines, Platt, Womer, Whitcomb, Carpenter, Ralston

12. The full-time faculty reached three in 1920. Seven part-time Instructors
join President Womer, Dean Carpenter, Professors McBride and Hughes,
and Law School Secretary Emily Sanford Platt in a photo

it will be better for us to make a supreme effort to meet" the requirement "and
retain our place in the association."[182] Dean Hughes praised Womer's "excellent
judgment," observing that AALS membership "gives Washburn Law School
considerable prestige which it cannot afford to lose" and that having three
full-time faculty "will add greatly to the value of the instruction."[183] Washburn
came into compliance in 1920 when new Dean Charles E. Carpenter and Assistant Professor James R. McBride, who had just earned his LL.B. from the
University of Chicago, joined Hughes as full-time faculty members.

Expanding the law faculty to three full-time members while at the same time
seeking to comply with the AALS requirement of 5,000 library volumes taxed
the limited resources of the College. That Womer decided "on the whole" to

---

182. *Law School to Raise Standards*, WASHBURN REV., Jan. 14, 1920.
183. *Id.*

do so suggests he saw the options as closely balanced. He received unsolicited advice from an unexpected source. The Dean of the Graduate School at the University of Kansas, Frank W. Blackmar, wrote Womer to suggest "that you could best solve your present difficulties by discontinuing your Law School"[184] and by seeking to make Washburn an elite undergraduate liberal arts college. Blackmar acknowledged he was open to attack because his "interest in the Law School at the University of Kansas is paramount," but claimed he based his suggestion entirely on his experience, his observation of "ideal administration," and his belief there should be only one law school in the state. In the elite liberal arts college Blackmar envisioned for Washburn, "all professional schools of whatever sort should be eliminated because wherever they exist, they have a tendancy (sic) to dominate the college and rob it of its funds, power and ability to develop as it should....Professional schools attached to small colleges breed trouble as the sparks fly upward." No record of Womer's response, if any, exists.

Charles Carpenter became the Law School's sixth Dean in 1920 at the age of forty-two. He received his LL.B. from Harvard in 1908 and practiced for a year in Boston. He then taught at the University of North Dakota for five years, initially as Assistant Professor and then as Professor of Law. The next four years, he was Professor of Law at the University of Illinois College of Law. He already had begun to establish a reputation as a productive scholar, having published two articles in the *Harvard Law Review* and one in the *Columbia Law Review*.[185] He left teaching during the war to serve with the Y.M.C.A. in France. For reasons that are not clear, he did not return to Illinois after the war but instead came to Washburn for the 1919–20 academic year. A partial explanation is that he had Kansas ties, having earned his A.B. degree in 1903 and his M.A. degree in 1904 from the University of Kansas. Curiously, given that Hughes was the only full-time law faculty member that year, he was hired to teach not in the Law School but in the embattled Department of History

---

184. Letter from Frank W. Blackmar to President P.T. [sic] Womer (Jan. 5, 1921) (on file in Mabee Library). Blackmar had visited the campus in the course of determining that graduates of Washburn College would continue to be admitted to the Graduate School without question.

185. Charles E. Carpenter, *DeFacto Corporations*, 25 HARV. L. REV. 623 (1912); Charles E. Carpenter, *Court Decisions and the Common Law*, 31 COLUMBIA L. REV. 593 (1917); Charles E. Carpenter, *Jurisdiction Over Debts for the Purpose of Administration, Garnishment and Taxation*, 31 HARV. L. REV. 905 (1918).

13. Charles E. Carpenter, Dean 1920–1922

and Political Science.[186] However, he was "eager to get back into law work, where his interest lies."[187] His resumé in later years would not acknowledge his year teaching non-law subjects. In fact, Carpenter's entry in the annual AALS directory claimed he was Dean and Professor at Washburn Law School from 1918 through 1922.[188] Among the courses Carpenter taught as Dean were Torts, Contracts, Legal Liability, Suretyship, Trusts and Conflict of Laws.

Carpenter experienced a difficult start to his deanship. There were reports of "a grave feeling of unrest among the students of the law school," and Hughes felt obliged to tell students who invited him to speak at their pep meeting that he "would not accept the Deanship of the [S]chool of [L]aw under any circumstances."[189] However, Carpenter earned praise by the AALS Executive

---

186. *Law School on Improved Basis*, WASHBURN REV., Sept. 22, 1920.
187. *Id.*
188. *See, e.g.,* AALS DIRECTORY OF LAW TEACHERS 17 (1927).
189. *Quality Rather Than Quantity Is Creed of Prof. Hughes*, WASHBURN REV.,

Committee when it found the school had achieved substantial compliance with AALS requirements for the library.

Carpenter instituted the Juris Doctoris degree for work beyond that required for the LL.B. It was awarded to graduates who held a Bachelor of Arts or of Science, completed their law courses with "distinguished excellence," apparently meaning *cum laude*, and also produced a thesis on a subject approved by the Dean. The thesis had to be between 2,000 and 10,000 words and had to "exhaust the cases decided during the period covered by the thesis."[190] It could be returned for revision or rejected altogether if unsatisfactory. The J.D. also was available to those who earned an LL.B. at Washburn or another law school "of recognized standing," but without "distinguished excellence," if they held the A.B or B.S. degree and completed the thesis and a fourth year of courses at Washburn. Roscoe W. Graves '21 and Ruth Miller Kaster '21 were the first graduates to earn the J.D., but there were not as many candidates for the degree as Carpenter may have expected, as only five J.D.s were awarded in the next seven years.

A stricter grading system was adopted in 1921 after a report compiled by Mrs. Platt showed a large percentage of A's were given by most instructors the prior year. Dean Carpenter discussed plans suggested by Professors Horack of Iowa and Eugene A. Gilmore of Wisconsin, then submitted his own "Suggested Distribution of Grades" for faculty approval:[191]

A (85–100)	5–10%
B (75–84)	15–20%
C (65–74)	40–50%
D (60–64)	10–20%
E (below 60)	5–10%

A memorandum distributed to faculty explained that the guideline "does not mean that the distribution of grades should follow rigidly the schedule submitted but the grader should feel that if through a series of years his standard did not approach the standard here submitted he is at fault." It also noted that a larger proportion of lower grades normally would be given in lower-level classes than in upper-level classes.

Nov. 24, 1920.

190. WASHBURN COLL. SCH. OF LAW BULLETIN 17 (Apr. 1921).

191. Minutes, Washburn Coll. Sch. of Law faculty meeting (Jan. 15, 1921).

One of Carpenter's changes did not last long. Beginning in 1921, each student was required "to keep a satisfactory note book embracing an abstract of the cases and notes on the lectures in each course, except practice courses, as a condition precedent to his receiving a grade in such course."[192] Students were not amused. In November, a committee selected at a student assembly met with Carpenter and argued that "the value of abstracting every case, did not compensate for the time necessary to abstract them." Four of the students, including future Supreme Court Commissioner Earl Hatcher '23, were invited to present their objections to the full faculty. They reported that notes often were copied from other students, that abstracts often were copied from opinions without real abstracting, and that students often delayed preparing the notebooks until the day before they were due and were forced to neglect preparing for the following day's classes. Dean Carpenter sought to preserve compulsory abstracts in first-year classes, but the faculty voted to terminate compulsory abstracts altogether and to leave the matter to the discretion of each instructor.[193]

In 1922, Carpenter left to join the law faculty of the University of Oregon. Like Harno, he would become a major figure in legal education. After five years of full-time teaching at Oregon, Carpenter served four years as Dean there, from 1927 until 1931. He then accepted a position at the University of Southern California Law School and later was named the Henry W. Bruce Professor of Law, a position he held until 1947. He became one of the country's leading authorities on Torts, writing numerous law review articles on that subject as well as Constitutional Law. He engaged in a four-part debate with Professor Prosser about *res ipsa loquitur*[194] and authored a series of nine articles on proximate cause, published between 1940 and 1942 in the *Southern California Law Review*. He also wrote two books as a "crusader" to preserve private enterprise, *A Real New Deal* and *Private Enterprise and Democracy*, which brought him in touch with numerous industrial and political leaders.[195]

---

192. WASHBURN COLL. SCH. OF LAW BULLETIN 17 (Apr. 1921).

193. *No More Abstracts*, WASHBURN REV., Nov. 9, 1921; Minutes, Washburn Coll. Sch. of Law faculty meeting (Nov. 5, 1921).

194. Charles E. Carpenter, *The Doctrine of Res Ipsa Loquitur in California*, 10 S. CAL. L. REV. 166 (1937); Charles E. Carpenter, *Res Ipsa Loquitur: A Rejoinder to Professor Prosser*, 10 S. CAL. L. REV. 467 (1937).

195. ASS'N OF AM. LAW SCHS, 1948 handbook 241–242 (1949).

CONCLUSION

From today's perspective, Washburn President Norman Plass' proposal in 1902 that his private, church-affiliated college of 328 students start a law school should have been doomed to failure. Insufficient financial resources was a recurring issue for the College as a whole and limited the Law School's ability, both during its first two decades and later, to expand the full-time faculty, build an adequate library, and have facilities conducive to quality legal education. Other Kansas law schools affiliated with small colleges had struggled financially. A law department that opened in Wichita in 1888 at Garfield University, a school affiliated with the Christian Churches, lasted only two years before financial problems forced the entire University to close. The law schools at Campbell College in Holton and Bethany College in Lindsborg closed shortly after Washburn's opened. Plass nevertheless may have been correct in his inaugural address in describing Topeka as "the ideal place" in Kansas for a law school. Members of the bench and local bar were devoted to the school, and many of them freely gave their time to assure that the school would succeed despite limited resources.

The Law School's second decade closed in academic year 1922–23 with its move to its fifth location, the remodeled Holbrook Hall, and with the appointment of its seventh Dean, Harry K. Allen. There was greater stability during the next chapter of the school's history than in the school's early years. The Law School would remain in Holbook Hall for seventeen years, and Allen would serve as Dean longer than anyone in the school's history, more than fourteen years.

2

THE ALLEN YEARS (1922–1937)

Harry K. Allen was forty-nine years old when he became Dean of Washburn Law School. Born in Missouri, he graduated from Gallatin High School, then read law in the office of Joshua Alexander, a future member of Congress and Secretary of Commerce under President Woodrow Wilson. Allen was admitted to the bar, then in 1894 enrolled in the law school at Washington University in St. Louis. He was admitted to the senior year after passing an examination on the subjects of the first year. By taking extra courses, he completed his LL.B. in only one year. Allen returned to Gallatin to practice with Alexander, became City Attorney, and in 1900 was elected County Prosecutor. He soon moved to Kansas City to examine land titles for a large real estate firm operated by his brother. Reading the fine print weakened his eyesight, so in 1903 he moved to the Oklahoma Territory, where the government was opening the Chickasaw country to settlement, to open a law office with a classmate from Washington University. When the government land office moved to Ardmore, Allen did too and worked to develop his expertise in land title law. In 1909, he was elected to the State Senate of Oklahoma's first legislature, serving one term. His knowledge about Indian land titles was one of the qualifications that led to his election. Allen returned to Kansas City in 1913, practicing law and working in the land title business. His final move was in 1916 to Topeka, where he began a practice examining Missouri land titles for mortgage loans for Prudential Life Insurance Company's subsidiary, the Davis-Welcome Mortgage Company.

In 1918, Allen was invited to teach Property part-time at Washburn Law School. Soon, he was teaching all three Property courses plus Conveyancing

14. Harry K. Allen, Dean, 1922–1936

and Abstracts of Title. When the faculty created an executive committee during academic year 1921–22, Allen was one of two part-time instructors selected to join the three full-time faculty members on the committee.[196] He later admitted, "I had been one of the most active kidders of the teaching profession anyone ever knew. I held teachers up to ridicule and kidded them every time I had the chance. Then I went out to the Washburn Law School and found I liked teaching."[197] When he was introduced to students as the new Dean in 1922, Allen told them of the Missouri Supreme Court Justice who declined to run for re-election, even unopposed, and instead became Dean at Allen's alma mater "because he believed it a bigger and higher mission to instruct the future lawyers of the country."[198]

196. Minutes, Washburn Coll. Sch. of Law faculty meeting (Feb. 4, 1922).

197. *Dean Harry K. Allen's Dream Comes True with Suddenness*, KAN. CITY STAR, Nov. 6, 1936.

198. *Laws in Assembly*, WASHBURN REV., Sept. 20, 1922.

Compliance with the AALS rule requiring three full-time faculty members became an issue during Dean Allen's first year. Allen spent each afternoon in the offices of the Topeka firm Wheeler, Brewster and Hunt, continuing to examine Missouri land titles. He examined as many as 100 per month. Allen paid no rent and received a salary from which he hired a young attorney to relieve him of much of the work. Allen's position was that he should be treated as a full-time teacher since he taught a full load of eight hours of classes and, although he went downtown to be available to consult the young attorney on title questions, he was able to use most of his time preparing for his classes. The AALS did not agree and, before academic year 1923–24, Allen terminated his relationship with the Wheeler firm.

Dean Allen's first year coincided with the school's move to Holbrook Hall, which had been remodeled at a total cost of $25,000. It would be Washburn Law School's home for seventeen years. Those who originally thought the Law School would have a home of its own were badly mistaken. The University's administrative offices, including President Womer's, occupied all of the first floor and part of the basement. The rest of the basement was used for general College purposes, including the College bookstore and classrooms. The University Registrar's office was on the second floor. The Law School had only the third floor to itself. The Dean and Mrs. Platt had their offices there and the library and courtroom occupied the rest of the floor. For the first time, there was a full-time Librarian, Ruth Inez Emch, wife of an instructor in the engineering department. Professors Hughes and McBride had their offices on the second floor, where there were three classrooms the Law School used but shared with the College when law courses weren't scheduled. At the insistence of the AALS, an additional room soon was assigned to the law library as a reading room, by converting a second floor classroom into offices for the Dean and Secretary. President Womer was not otherwise inclined to give the Law School more space. In 1927, the student newspaper asked, "Why is it, that when new classrooms are added in Holbrook Hall, they go to the college? As compared with the amount of space the college has, that occupied by the law school is woefully inadequate."[199]

Allen smoked a pipe, carrying tobacco loose in his pocket,[200] but was happy with cigars and cigarettes as well. He soon was stopped as he walked outside

199. *The Law School*, WASHBURN REV., Sept. 28, 1927.
200. McLane, *supra* note 3, at 9.

15. Student body and faculty at Holbrook Hall, home of the Law School 1922–1939

Holbrook Hall smoking his pipe, unaware that smoking had been prohibited on campus.

> The dean was liberal, but law-abiding. Between classes he would walk with his students out to 17th street, just off the campus, where they would stand chatting and smoking. He early won their respect and affection.[201]

According to Roy Bartlett '49, Allen's "ability to make steadfast friends was almost legendary. His leadership furnished the vital human inspiration that gave Washburn lawyers an esprit de corps and a sense of pride in their school that has become traditional with them."[202] He also was an inspiring teacher. Thirty-four years after his graduation, Joseph W. Morris '47 still recalled the profound effect Allen had on his life:

> Without any doubt whatsoever, Judge Allen—early in my life—inspired me more in my love for the law than any other man. Unbelievable as it may seem to some, he set me on fire with an unending flame of enthusiasm for the law and, as a law student, especially for the law of future interests. I shall always be indebted to him.[203]

201. *Supreme Court Election Only Incidental in Jurist's Career*, TOPEKA CAP., Feb. 15, 1953.

202. Roy L. Bartlett, *Heritage of Excellence*, WASHBURN ALUMNUS 1 (Oct. 1960).

203. *Commencement Speaker Recalls History to Guide Future*, THE CIRCUIT

Another student recalled:

> He would frequently take decisions of the Kansas Supreme Court involving property questions and analyze them in the classroom. He would tell us what was good or bad about the decision. If he agreed with them, he would explain why; if he did not, he would tell what he thought the court had missed in considering the case.… One of his favorite expressions was, "In order to understand a legal question, you have to be able to see it first."[204]

Understanding the Allen years requires appreciation not only of Allen's remarkable rapport with students but also of his wife Florence's involvement with them. They always went "to the parties, dinners and other affairs of the students. If the boys had a smoker, Dean Allen was there. If the girls had a slumber party, Mrs. Allen was there. Thus was built up much closer friendships than ordinarily develop from the contacts of teacher and student."[205] Topeka columnist Peggy Greene wrote of the Allens:

> Both liked young people and every student knew the warm friendliness of the Allen home at 1247 Clay.…Students took their problems to the Allens and found sympathy and wise counsel. They were helped to find jobs and the discouraged were heartened.
>
> During the depression three students, all of them later prominent lawyers, shared one room in order to stay in school, and slept together in one bed. Sunday morning breakfasts of biscuits and strawberry jam at the Allen home were grand occasions for the trio.[206]

Allen believed that a law school "should train the student not only in all the technical branches of the law, but to give him a broad background of culture that will make him a leader in the community in which he lives."[207] Schuyler Jackson saw tangible evidence of that belief. "The library in his home was

---

204. McLane, *supra* note 3, at 10.

205. *Dean Harry K. Allen's Dream Comes True with Suddenness*, *supra* note 197.

206. *Supreme Court Election Only Incidental in Jurist's Career*, TOPEKA CAP., Feb. 15, 1953.

207. TOPEKA ST. J., Feb. 7, 1931.

filled with books that covered the walls. The great writers of English literature and poetry shouldered Blackstone and Coke for room on the shelves."[208]
Allen was known as "a square shooter. Once he dismissed seven law school
students for failure to live up to the code of ethics of the bar. A lawyer must
first be a gentleman," he said.[209] He also was open to expanding opportunity
for law study. He inserted into the first catalogue he prepared a new section
specifically encouraging enrollment by women.

RAISING STANDARDS

During the early years of the twentieth century, members of the bar and legal
educators frequently debated the question of what pre-legal education to
require. The factors considered in setting entry standards did not all push in
the same direction. Most leaders of the bar urged that standards be raised, to
reduce the number of lawyers, particularly inept lawyers. "We have enough
ignorant, ill-bred, half-baked lawyers now. Any supply exceeds the demand,"
the Chair of the Committee on Legal Education told the 1900 annual meeting of the Kansas Bar Association.[210] The Bar Association regularly lobbied
the Legislature to eliminate the option of study in a law office and lobbied
the Supreme Court both to regulate law office study more tightly and to increase requirements for pre-legal education. However, there were dissenters,
including those who felt their own study in a law office prepared them well,
without attending college or law school, and those who feared that requiring
attendance at law school and imposing a prerequisite of college study would
unfairly restrict entry into the legal profession by all except the well-to-do elite.

While the Kansas Supreme Court consistently was a leader nationally in
increasing educational requirements for admission to the bar, it nevertheless
moved cautiously, and far slower than urged by the Kansas Bar Association.
In 1921, an American Bar Association resolution urged state Supreme Courts
to require bar applicants to have graduated from a law school that required
two years of pre-legal college education before enrollment. The next year
the Kansas Supreme Court mandated that applicants have completed one

---

208. In Memoriam, 187 Kan. xxiii, xxv.

209. *Dean Harry K. Allen's Dream Comes True with Suddenness, supra* note 197.

210. BAR ASSOCIATION OF KANSAS, PROCEEDINGS OF THE 17TH ANNUAL
MEETING 26 (1900).

year of college, effective at the June 1924 bar exam, increasing to two years of college at the June 1925 exam. There still was no requirement that the college work be completed prior to starting law studies and law office study still was permitted in lieu of attendance at a law school. Nevertheless, the Carnegie Foundation for the Advancement of Teaching had high praise: "Kansas may now fairly claim the distinction of having the highest requirements of general education in the country and of having in this respect led rather than followed the action of the American Bar Association."

Students entering in the fall of 1922 would be the first graduates covered by the two-year rule. Washburn conformed to the Court's new rule by requiring matriculants that year to complete two years of college work as a prerequisite to receipt of the LL.B. For the transition year, it developed a five-year course for those entering directly from high school. It modified the four-year course so that it applied to applicants who had completed one year of college work. Of course, from the school's founding there had been a six-year course, in which the first year of law school could be counted also as the fourth year of a bachelor's degree. In 1923, Washburn went beyond the Court's requirement, making completion of two years of college a prerequisite to enrollment. Fear that this change would result in a decline in enrollment long-term proved unfounded, although there was a one-year dip, to seventy-three students in the fall of 1923 from 105 the prior fall, while about thirty students remained in the College taking pre-legal work.[211] Washburn's actions led it to be included on the first list of ABA approved schools, issued in 1923. The Carnegie Foundation included Washburn and KU among thirty-eight "first class" law schools, and only eleven schools were of higher rank than the two Kansas schools.[212]

In 1928, only sixteen of sixty-two AALS member schools required three or more years of college work. At its December 11 meeting that year, the faculty recommended that Washburn's Board of Trustees adopt the three-year requirement as a prerequisite for admission, effective with the entering class of 1931. Implementation later was postponed until 1932. Dean Allen described this increase in standards, put in place twenty years before it was required of all AALS schools, as giving Washburn "the prestige that comes from being in

---

211. BAR ASSOCIATION OF KANSAS, PROCEEDINGS OF THE 40TH ANNUAL MEETING 83 (1923).

212. *Id.*

this select group of schools with a three year requirement."[213] Not everyone supported the change. Shortly before it went into effect, the faculty passed a motion, made by part-time instructor William C. Ralston, permitting applicants over twenty-one years of age and of high scholastic standing to be admitted after two years of college, on a vote of the faculty.[214] The minutes of faculty meetings that survive do not reflect exercise by the faculty of this authority, and if done at all it surely was done rarely. The Kansas Supreme Court in 1931 made three years of college a prerequisite for the 1936 bar exam.

Raising standards involved more than just raising the credentials of the entering class. In 1914, the school increased the number of credit hours required for graduation from seventy-two to seventy-eight. Under Dean Hughes, the number was raised again in 1916 to eighty. For reasons that are not clear, the requirement was scaled back to seventy-six hours in 1920. However, they were full credit hours. Although AALS members schools only had to require ninety weeks of resident study and 1,080 hours of classroom instruction, Washburn in 1927 touted its higher requirements of 108 weeks in residence and 1,368 hours of instruction.[215] The number of credit hours required was increased back to eighty in 1935.[216]

Allen had high standards of academics. He believed a law school should "give every man, who is qualified, the opportunity to enter the profession and at the same time eliminate the unworthy and unfit."[217] During Dean Allen's second year, he told students "he was willing to make concessions upon anything except scholarship, but that he would not grant one jot there."[218] That became particularly clear in 1931 when a bill was introduced in the Kansas legislature to exempt graduates of the Washburn and KU law schools from the requirement to take the bar examination. Two Washburn students helped draft the bill and the House Judiciary Committee recommended passage by the full House. Dean Allen felt compelled to issue a statement opposing the bill as "a backward step" that was contrary to efforts by the ABA and AALS "to elevate the bar," in part through

---

213. Annual Report for 1929–30 of Dean Harry K. Allen (on file in Mabee Library).

214. Minutes, Washburn Coll. Sch. of Law faculty meeting (Feb. 6, 1932).

215. WASHBURN COLL. SCH. OF LAW BULLETIN (Mar. 1927).

216. *Raise Law Standards*, WASHBURN REV., Apr. 5, 1935, at 1.

217. TOPEKA ST. J., Feb. 7, 1941.

218. *President Talks at Law School Chapel*, WASHBURN REV., Feb. 6, 1924.

examination of the applicant by the state itself. The lawyer is a member of the court and a public official and the state should not delegate this authority to the school. The bill, if passed, would have no special effect on the Washburn Law school except a possible tendency for the student to let down, in his strenuous work in mastering the profession.[219]

Class attendance was a problem in the early years. The school's solutions to the problem are humorous in their specificity. It started benignly enough in the catalogue issued in 1912 with the clear statement, "All students of the school are required to be in actual attendance. The law work cannot be done by a non-resident student. The faculty reserves the right to sever the student's connection with the School for irregular attendance, poor class work or for conduct which annoys or impedes school work." The next catalogue added teeth to the statement: "Any student who has not been present 85 per cent of the number of lectures given, will not be permitted to take examination in such courses. Coming in tardy and leaving classes are not permitted." The minimum attendance was relaxed to 80% of classes in 1916. However, the policy adopted under Dean Carpenter and announced in the 1921 catalogue would make drafters of the tax code proud:

I.   All students are required to be present during the regular classroom discussions and to attend all special lectures. Students who are absent during more than one-fifth of the regular class periods of a subject are excluded from the final examination in that subject.

II. If in a course requiring five hours per week a student is absent from more than eight recitations, or, in a course requiring four hours per week a student is absent from more than seven recitations, or, in a course requiring three hours per week a student is absent from more than six recitations, or, in a course requiring two hours per week a student is absent more than four recitations the student will be required to take a special examination, in order to obtain credit for the course in which the absence occurred, for which a fee of one dollar ($1.00) will be charged.

III. The Secretary shall deduct from each student's final grade that proportion of one-hundred percent which the number of his or her unexcused

---

219. *Dean Allen Not in Favor of Bar Bill*, WASHBURN REV., Mar. 9, 1931, at 1.

absences bears to the total number of hours in the course in which the absence occurred.

Under Rule III, excuses for absences must be presented to the Secretary for record and determination before or immediately after the absence occurs. Delay in presenting an excuse will bar its consideration.

The 1922 catalogue added still more detail. Absences immediately before or after a regular holiday counted as two absences; three instances of tardiness counted as one absence; late enrolling students were counted absent on the class days before they enrolled; and when combined absences in all courses reached eighteen, a credit hour was forfeited.

The Law School inserted the College policy on penalties into its catalogue published in 1923: "For six to nine unexcused absences one semester hour of credit is forfeited; for ten to fourteen absences two semester hours of credit are forfeited; fifteen unexcused absences result in the student's suspension from school." Many students allowed credit hours to be forfeited under this policy, perhaps because, at the end of the day, the faculty usually waived the forfeitures. The prevailing sentiment was that if students' grades showed they understood the subject, the hours should be restored. However, much time at faculty meetings was spent passing on requests to restore lost hours by students who otherwise satisfied graduation requirements. Finally, in 1941, the faculty adopted a rule that purportedly would not be waived.

CURRICULAR INNOVATION

Allen led the faculty to modernize the curriculum, once using the curricula of fifteen leading law schools as the basis of discussion.[220] In 1923, a three-hour required course in Criminology was added to the first semester. The catalogue explained:

> A course which exemplifies the progressive spirit of the Washburn Law School is that in Criminology, taught by Dr. Karl A. Menninger, an eminent specialist in nervous and mental diseases. In it are studied scientifically the kinds of conduct usually called criminal, their causes, and, so far as possible in an elementary course, their treatment.

220. Minutes, Washburn Coll. Sch. of Law faculty meeting (Dec. 19, 1935).

...John H. Wigmore, in his report to the Association of American Law Schools, 1921, criticises [sic] the generality of law schools as unprogressive for their failure to include this, and similar courses, in their curricula.

Before publication of this report, Washburn Law School took the stand that the understanding and cooperation of lawyers is essential to improvement in the methods by which society handles its so-called criminals. Recognizing that the medical profession had advanced furthest in the study of criminology, it procured the services on its faculty of a medical expert in this field.[221]

Dr. Menninger was only thirty years old when he first taught the Criminology class. He and his father had founded the Menninger Diagnostic Clinic less than four years earlier. Menninger's class opened students' eyes. "Each semester he took us through the State Hospital so we could have some understanding of the conditions and methods used to treat them. It was a rather startling experience that none of us ever forgot."[222] The course was scaled back to a one-hour course in 1928, and the next year Dr. Menninger no longer had time to teach it. He published the book that launched his national celebrity, *The Human Mind,* in 1930. However, a relationship was thus started with Dr. Menninger and the Menninger Clinic that was renewed frequently for nearly eighty years, in various ways that benefitted law students and enhanced the school's reputation.

Wigmore had identified twelve "modern" subjects law schools should teach. Only four of fifty schools he examined taught six of them and more than half taught two or less. Allen committed himself to add as many of Wigmore's suggested subjects as he could.[223] As of 1923, Washburn taught three of them, Legal Bibliography, International Law, and Criminology; a fourth, Public Speaking, was part of the pre-requisite college training. A new course in Professional Ethics was offered in the spring semester of 1926, after a five-year absence from the curriculum, and it became a required course. Allen taught it himself the next year and moved it into the first-year curriculum. Later, consistent with Wigmore's view, he renamed the course Legal History and Ethics.

Other innovations included the addition to the first-year curriculum in 1925 of a one-hour course on Study of Cases, an early recognition of the

---

221. WASHBURN COLL. SCH. OF LAW BULLETIN 9–10 (June 1923).

222. McLane, *supra* note 3, at 10.

223. WASHBURN COLL. SCH. OF LAW BULLETIN 16 (Nov. 1922).

need for instruction on legal methods. It was taught by Earl Hatcher '23. In 1928, Allen hired the first woman to be a part-time faculty member, to teach Common Law Pleading. Marie Russell '25 was a *cum laude* graduate who had completed the additional work required to earn the J.D. A few years later, she began teaching Conflict of Laws also.

Not all of Allen's innovations look good in hindsight. One year, for example, he required students using books in the library to sign slips showing the time the books were borrowed and returned. Allen hoped "to establish the relation between the amount of time a student spends in the library and the grades he makes in his courses."[224]

As early as 1921–22, the faculty endorsed a suggestion to promote the school through publication of a law review or bulletin,[225] but nothing came of the suggestion. Several years before 1932, there were discussions between representatives of the Kansas Bar Association and the deans of the two law schools about publishing a state bar journal. However, it became evident that the schools did not feel "able to venture to take separately or jointly the responsibility of starting and keeping up a law journal in Kansas, though very willing to aid if the state bar or others will assume the burden and look out for the support needed to pay or assure printers' bills.[226]

In January 1932, Dean Harry K. Allen published a twelve-page *Washburn Law School Bulletin*, containing summaries of cases and critiques he wrote during his preliminary work to compile Kansas annotations for the *Restatement of the Law, Property*. What Dean Allen described as "[f]avorable comment from the bar throughout the state" about the first issue "encouraged the continuance of the project."[227] The *Bulletin* would be restricted to "calm, dispassionate, and frank" comments on Kansas law and suggestions to improve it.[228] The second issue was dated June 1, 1932, but was distributed in advance of the annual meeting of the Kansas Bar Association on May 27–28. This issue expanded to

---

224. *Lawyers to Sign for Books*, WASHBURN REV., Sept. 28, 1931, at 1.

225. Minutes, Washburn Coll. Sch. of Law faculty meeting (Sept. 24, 1921) and (May 13, 1922).

226. Report of Committee on Tentative Plan for Kansas Law Journal, *Report of the Proceedings of the Fiftieth Annual Meeting of the Bar Association of the State of Kansas*, 1 J. KAN. B. ASS'N. 49, 81 (1932).

227. 1 WASHBURN L. S. BULL., No. 2, 1 (1932).

228. *Id.*

twenty-eight pages. Advertising sold to law book publishers and trust companies underwrote printing costs. In addition to Allen's analysis of property cases, it also included the first part of what was to be a two-part article on torts by Professor Edward Osborn.

Publication of the *Bulletin* was one factor that spurred the KBA to publish its own journal. At the 1932 annual meeting, the chair of the bar's study committee moved that the Executive Committee be authorized to publish a quarterly journal. The committee's report noted Allen's publication of the *Bulletin* and observed that other issues might follow, "especially if no organ is provided by and for the state bar association."[229] The Secretary of the KBA urged that the decision be postponed for a year, allowing time to explore whether faculty members at the law schools would accept editorial responsibility or whether the journal could be combined with the *Kansas Judicial Council Bulletin*, which had been published for the first time in May that year.[230] A. Harry Crane '25 responded by noting that Washburn's *Bulletin,* already "an entrance in this field,…gotten out for the first two issues, you will see, is very well gotten out."[231] He successfully urged members to authorize the Executive Committee to proceed, if it saw fit, before the next annual meeting.

The first issue of the KBA *Journal* appeared in August 1932. The law schools agreed to cooperate and the KBA agreed to publish student notes and comments along with articles by faculty members. Dean Allen contributed case comments to volumes 2 and 3. He included in volume 2 three case summaries John P. Davis '35 had prepared as class papers. James W. Taylor '36 published a freestanding case note in volume 3. Volume 4 included four student pieces. There were notes by Edgar K. Thiel '36 on the privilege against self-incrimination and William C. Attwater '36 on the doctrine of election of remedies and case comments by William Tinker, Jr. '37 and W. Jay Esco '36. During academic year 1935–36, each law school created a student editorial board "to create an even greater interest than exists in both of the law schools" in publishing in the *Journal.*[232] This was thought to be "another step forward in insuring the

---

229. Report of Committee on Tentative Plan for Kansas Law Journal, *supra* note 226, at 81.

230. *Id.* at 83.

231. *Id.* at 84.

232. Report of Committee on State Bar Journal, *Report of the Proceedings the Fifty-Third Annual Meeting of the Bar Association of the State of Kansas*, 4 J. KAN. B.

permanency of this publication."[233] Washburn announced it would award one hour of credit to a student whose work was accepted for publication. One woman, Lorraine McMullen '36, was a member of the first editorial board. Ten Washburn students each semester through 1939–40 served on the "Law Review Board." For reasons that are unclear, the *Journal* discontinued the student boards in 1940,[234] but it continued to publish student works.

Practice Court was made more interesting by using "real" witnesses. The student newspaper explained how it was done:

> Before the startled eyes of some 200 or more fellow students, J. Charles Tillotson, Washburn cheer-leader, last Friday morning shot and killed Harry R. Elliott, editor of the Washburn Review.
>
> That states the facts in a murder case which will be tried in the senior division of the Washburn school of law Wednesday night, November 13. Tillotson's preliminary hearing will be Wednesday, November 6.
>
> Every year, the student lawyers enact a drama in an effort to gain evidence and facts for a trial. This year they chose a murder for consideration. It effectively was staged in the Ichabod Inn last Friday morning, at 11:30 o'clock, and a huge crowd of students gazed in horror at the tragedy enacted before them. After the shot was fired, however, the students realized it was all part of a play—a play forming the basis of a law school trial.[235]

Even trials to the court could be interesting. In one case, the State sought an injunction restraining the Alpha Delta house from selling liquor. Arriving for the trial, students

> found a huge still, with an eight-gallon crock, copper tank, 'n everything, all set up and ready for operation, reposing on the court room floor....

ASS'N. 35, 65 (1935).

233. *Id.*

234. Report of the Editor of the Journal, *Proceedings of the Sixty-Sixth Annual Session of the Bar Association of the State of Kansas*, 17 J. KAN. B. ASS'N. 37, 52 (1948).

235. *Ichabod Inn Murder Case Throws Huge Scare Into Bystanders Who Watched as Student Was Killed*, WASHBURN REV., Oct. 30, 1929.

Harold Hauser and Eldon Sloan, lawyers for the state, further appealed to the spectators by producing two quart bottles of genuine beer. When the corks were pulled off a veritable fountain of the brown beverage cascaded onto the table. Judge Raines was offered a taste of the 'stuff' to prove its pre-war genuineness, but, being a good Kansas prohibitionist, he resisted the temptation.

Ward Martin and Stuart McAlister, defense attorneys, spurned the suggestion that good respectable college boys would even look at such a nasty, vile concoction as beer. They appealed to the higher motives of human life as proof of the innocence of the accused parties.

After due deliberation, Judge Raines, unconvinced of the "genuineness" of the beverage, denied the injunction. Immediately after the trial, the whole of the large crowd gathered around the table to inspect the bottle. Strangely enough, when the crowd had cleared away, the bottles were empty. Evidently, in their haste to "view" the beer, the lawyers had "spilled" the contents from the bottle. The still also mysteriously disappeared.[236]

CAMPUS LIFE

Because of the Law School's physical separation from the downtown legal community, Allen felt it was important to create opportunities for students to mix with members of the bar. There was an annual smoker, featuring "talks by prominent lawyers and judges, plenty of smokes, refreshments, high class vaudeville entertainment and an evening of general good fellowship."[237] In 1927, biweekly luncheons were held at the Chocolate Shop to discuss legal questions. The idea was said to be "patterned after the old English custom of maintaining Inns of Court to which the prospective barristers were compelled to go to gain their knowledge of the law from the old practitioners who discussed questions of practical jurisprudence there."[238] When the Kansas Bar Association met in Topeka, the school hosted a reception at Holbrook Hall

---

236. *Law Seniors Bring Injunction Suit Against Alpha Deltas*, WASHBURN REV., Nov. 18, 1932.

237. *Law School to Have Smoker for Barristers*, WASHBURN REV., Nov. 24, 1926, at 1.

238. *Gleanings from the Law School*, WASHBURN REV., Dec. 6, 1928, at 4.

and Allen persuaded Dean Harry M. Bates of the University of Michigan Law School, who was in town to address the bar meeting, to come to campus for an address to students. When the state bar meeting was in Kansas City in 1923, about twenty students attended, including four women students, long before the Bar Association admitted women as members.

Allen appears to have realized that he needed strong advocacy by the alumni to support the Law School when College leaders were unwilling to provide needed resources. An alumni association once again was organized informally in 1927. Ralph Glenn '26 served as Secretary and recalled that he "even had fancy stationery—it was all pretty heady for a kid fresh out of law school."[239] Then, in March 1930, alumni leaders meeting at the Chamber of Commerce adopted a formal constitution for the Washburn Law School Association and elected officers. The preamble identified the organization's purposes as "forming a closer bond among ourselves for concerted and united action in promoting the best interests of the school" and helping the school maintain "high standards of faculty, facilities, number of students, membership in the Association of American Law Schools and compliance with its requirements and with requirements of the American Bar association."[240]

Allen organized a celebration of the Law School's 25th anniversary, held on April 18, 1929. Faculty from all departments of the College opened the morning ceremonies with a processional from the Library to MacVicar Chapel. Dean Roscoe Pound of Harvard Law School delivered the principal address. It was Pound's second visit to Washburn.[241] "Great ages have been ages of liberalism," he said, "of people striving for the highest development of the powers of each by an organization of society which left a maximum scope for free individual development."[242] Honorary Degrees were awarded to Judge George T. McDermott of the United States District Court, a long-time Lecturer, and to Kansas Supreme Court Justice Rousseau A. Burch. The school's first Dean,

---

239. McLane, *supra* note 3, at 11.

240. *Law School Alumni Organize*, WASHBURN REV., Mar. 12, 1930.

241. He had made a special presentation to students in 1910, when he was on the faculty at the University of Chicago and was in Topeka to address the annual meeting of the Kansas Bar Association. WASHBURN REV., Feb. 2, 1910. His topic, "English Tenures Up to the Statute of Uses," may have been a bit tedious for a Friday evening presentation.

242. *Deplores the Great Lack of Individualism*, WASHBURN REV., Apr. 25, 1929.

Ernest B. Conant, returned for the celebration and made remarks at a $1.25 per plate evening banquet, as did Dean Pound.

Soon, law students, like everyone else, had to cope with the Great Depression. One graduate from the 1930s recalled:

> We had many going to law school taking only a few hours and working at any kind of job they could get. We collected accounts, worked in filling stations, anything. Some had to quit because they just could not make it. It was just as hard to find jobs even after graduation. You might find yourself working in a filling station with an LL.B. degree just because there weren't any law positions open.[243]

Nevertheless, the school saw a modest spike in enrollment in 1931 and 1932, in part traceable to an unexpected source. At least nine students who had started law studies at KU transferred to Washburn.[244] Some of them publicly attributed their departures to the condition of the KU school.[245] A new dean who arrived there from Idaho in 1929 made unpopular changes in the faculty, tightened grading standards, and irritated students in other ways. Student protests there included distribution at the 1931 homecoming football game of handbills attacking the dean and seeking reinstatement of the former faculty members.[246] The resulting flow of law students from Lawrence to Topeka even merited the attention of a Lawrence newspaper.

The admission requirement of three years of college work, implemented in 1932, was expected to cause applications to decline. In addition, the school announced it would, for the first time, limit enrollment to forty 1Ls, to secure "a select group of law students and to eliminate the unfit."[247] Criteria for selection included the applicant's character, general background and grades, plus the intellectual content of the applicant's college work. The number of 1Ls in fact declined some from the seventy new students who enrolled in 1931, but only to fifty new students. During the eight years that the entering class was advertised as being limited to forty, the average number of new students was

243. McLane, *supra* note 3, at 11.

244. *K.U. Loses Six Law Students*, WASHBURN REV., Oct. 12, 1931; DOUGLAS CO. REPUBLICAN, Feb. 11, 1932.

245. DOUGLAS CO. REPUBLICAN, Feb. 11, 1932.

246. Kelly, *supra* note 141, at 117.

247. WASHBURN COLL. SCH. OF LAW BULLETIN 9 (May 1932).

forty-eight and the target was exceeded seven times. In the spring semester 1933, a total of 140 students enrolled, up from 115 the prior spring, when law students comprised almost 17% of the College's enrollment. The graduating class of 1934 was the largest in the school's history, with fifty-three students receiving degrees. The proportion of law graduates among all graduates of the College was much higher than the Law School's percentage of enrolled students. In 1935, fifty-one of Washburn's 128 graduates were from the Law School, 40% of the total. The Law School in 1939 accounted for fifty-one of 151 graduates, 34%.

CAMPUS POLITICS

When the Law School was downtown, student participation in campus life was limited, although some law students were members of the literary societies, the debate and athletic teams, the glee club, the social fraternities, and the staff of the student newspaper. Although law students were eligible to vote for representatives in student government as members of the sophomore, junior and senior classes, few did so and there was no separate Law School representation on the student council.

Once the Law School relocated onto the campus, issues about how the Law School and the College would relate loomed larger. The Law School stayed aloof for a while. It opted to have a separate representative to the student government, in preference to voting in elections for individual class representatives. Soon, however, the competitiveness and aptitude for leadership that characterize those pursuing a career in law could not be restrained. By November 1923, a headline in the *Washburn Coll. Sch. of Law Bulletin* proclaimed "Poo-Bahs of The Entire Campus Are Students From Law School." The "poo-bahs" included student council president Olin Buck '24 and president of the Y.W.C.A. Isabel Obee '24, plus the editor and business manager of the newspaper. In addition, A. Harry Crane '25 was the College's only nominee for the Rhodes Scholarship that year.

Though law students constituted only 10–15% of Washburn's students, with increasingly frequency they were elected as president of the student council and to other offices. Members of Phi Alpha Delta law fraternity partnered with undergraduate Greek letter houses to form the Kagpadat Party that won the majority of campus elections for a decade. Other law students were leaders of rival parties. More than once, law students were the candidates of each of the two principal campus political parties. In 1930, Jay Kyle '31 defeated Warren Shaw '31 for the presidency. In 1929, the *Topeka State Journal* reported "considerable dissatisfaction" among College students "owing to the supremacy of the legal students" in leadership:

> "In Washburn college the tail wags the dog," said one member of the college faculty recently. He was referring to the relations between the college and the law school.
>
> Of late, many of the upperclassmen in the college of liberal arts and sciences have come to the same conclusion. The law school leads—and like meek little lambs—the college follows along....
>
> The student body, rather than choose its leaders from the senior class, chooses law school men. Political campaigns are managed by the law school. Publications are usually subsidized by the lawyers. And those in the college of liberal arts and sciences bow their heads to what to them seems the inevitable. Thus, "the tail wags the dog".[248]

Despite their dominance of student government, law students insisted on independence in many matters, due to their status as professionals. Apparently because AALS regulations required fewer class days each year than the American Association of Colleges, law students each year voted to take three vacation days while classes still met in the rest of the College. When the Law School declared Armistice Day a holiday in 1929, there was dissension among College students forced to attend classes. The faculty council determined that, under the bylaws of the student association, declaring special vacation days at any department required advance approval by the student council and then by the faculty council. Because law students were members of the student association, they were bound by these procedures.[249] The sentiment of some law students was to withdraw from the student association and to adopt a separate constitution for the Laws. Instead, the strategy adopted was to argue that the custom of allowing the Law School to declare three extra holidays

---

248. *State Journal Writer Tells of Dissatisfaction at Washburn on Account of Supremacy of Laws*, reprinted in WASHBURN REV., Nov. 20, 1929.

249. *Students of Law Consider Forming Their Own Council*, WASHBURN REV., Dec. 18, 1929.

was sufficient precedent to make them "official" holidays exempt from the approval process. President Womer brokered a compromise, codifying the precedent of three law-only holidays but imposing a "double cut" penalty for observing any other holidays without obtaining the required approval.[250]

Law students thus remained part of the student association. One and one-half years later, however, law students passed a resolution declaring the Law School independent "of the regulations of" the College student council.[251] Total secession was viewed as undesirable but exemption from the regulations was necessary to permit the newly-elected President of the Student Bar Association to serve, since he was not enrolled in the eight credit hours the College student association constitution required for one to hold a student office. It was help-ful to the Law School side of the issue that the student council president was James Erwin '33, who had defeated fellow law student William Schnatterly '34 in the campus elections. The student newspaper was outraged:

> Now, no one has any objections to the Law school students' considering themselves independent of the Student association. But the lawyers want it fixed so they can consider themselves independent when it suits them, and consider themselves a part of the student government at election time. They want to eat their cake and keep it, too.
>
> The lawyers are using the typical politicians' club, political patronage. "If we are kicked out of the Student council," they say to their various affiliated groups (sororities and fraternities) 'where will your party be in the next election. Where will your offices go?'
>
> …The issue is clearly whether the Law school should be allowed to remain in the Student Association, since it has declared its independence. It is The College and the Music school vs. the Law school.[252]

Despite this protest, law students remained in the student association and the next three student council presidents all were from the Law School: Auburn Light '34; Duke Cheney '34; and Drew Hartnett '37. After law students for years complained about having to pay a campus-wide student activity fee while the

---

250. *Committee Seeks Compromise Plan on Law Holidays*, WASHBURN REV., Jan. 15, 1930.

251. *Strong Is Law School President*, WASHBURN REV., Oct. 5, 1931, at 1.

252. *The College vs. Law School*, WASHBURN REV., Oct. 12, 1931.

Student Bar Association received no funding from it, the student council in 1938 began allocating $100 annually for the Student Bar's activities.

LOOKING INWARD FOR FACULTY

The faculty remained intact during Dean Allen's first four years, with Allen, Hughes and James McBride teaching full-time. McBride taught a variety of courses, Agency, Bankruptcy, Bills and Notes, Conflict of Laws, Insurance, Personal Property, Quasi-Contracts and Trade Regulation. He left in 1926 to practice law in Pittsburgh, Pennsylvania, but will always be the answer to a Washburn Law School trivia question. It was at his urging that senior students adopted the tradition of carrying canes whenever they left the law building, to distinguish themselves from other students on campus. The practice started after a class vote on October 2, 1923. At the same meeting, seniors also voted to wear wing collars, to which McBride was partial, and polka dot ties each Monday, but enthusiasm for that tradition quickly faded. However, seniors carried canes during more than four decades, with only occasional lapses of the tradition. In a number of years, the practice persisted only for two or three weeks, but the class of 1935 committed to "brandishing the implements all year." In the fall of 1938, the senior class voted to fine any senior who "dares show himself without cane" a jitney.[253] In later years, the penalty was having to buy coffee for classmates. Predictably, classrooms often were filled "with the intermittent crashes of canes sliding or dropping to the floor," agitating professors both intentionally and accidentally.[254]

Norman F. Arterburn was hired as Assistant Professor to replace McBride for the 1926–27 academic year. He had been admitted to practice in 1923 and had just earned a J.D. from the University of Chicago. His record of publication that year, articles in the Michigan, Illinois and Pennsylvania law reviews,[255]

---

253. *Seniors Must Have Canes or Forfeit One Jitney*, WASHBURN REV., Oct. 28, 1938.

254. *Senior Barristers Again Wear Canes, Trouble Profs*, WASHBURN REV., Oct. 21, 1939.

255. Norman F. Arterburn, *The Early Liability of a Bailee*, 25 MICH. L. REV. 479 (1927); Norman F. Arterburn, *The Origin and First Test of Public Callings*, 75 U. PA. L. REV. 411 (1927); Norman F. Arterburn, *Liability for Breach of Gratuitous Promise*, 22 ILL. L. REV. 479 (1927).

suggested a bright future in legal education. However, he stayed only one year before leaving for Indiana to practice in Vincennes. He did teach again, at Indiana University in 1949 and in 1953–54. In 1955, he was appointed to the Indiana Supreme Court, serving for twenty-two years. He served twice as Chief Justice, including a four-year term as the first permanent Chief Justice when Indiana abandoned its former practice of rotating Justices in the position.

Washburn graduate Antrim M. Hambleton '14 was hired to replace Arterburn. Thomas Hughes was persuaded to delay his retirement. Nevertheless the shortage of full-time faculty took its toll. The student newspaper reported that Dean Allen taught five classes in the fall of 1927, in addition to his administrative duties, and Hughes taught four.[256]

The inability, or unwillingness, of the College to compete with salaries offered by other schools and in private practice made recruiting and retaining faculty from elsewhere difficult. An honors graduate from the 1928 graduating class, Howard Jones, was hired to replace Hughes. He was called out of class during his third year by the Law School's Secretary, Mrs. Platt, who told him the Dean wanted to see him. "The guys got a big laugh out of that, thinking I was in trouble," Jones recalled. "The Dean asked me to teach the next fall. I had no experience, of course and was quite taken by surprise....I made $2,000 the first year; $2,100 the second."[257]

Both Hambleton and Jones would teach, at least part-time, for more than three decades, and both later would serve substantial periods as Acting Dean. Hambleton was forty-eight years old when he was hired and had practiced for thirteen years with the Topeka firm of Blair, MaGaw & Lillard and its successors. He had been an educator for seven years before starting law school, first as a high school science teacher and principal in Ohio, then as principal of schools in LeRoy, Kansas. He received his Ph.B. in 1903 from Ohio University and his A.M. in 1907 from the University of Kansas. Jones taught full-time for only two years before leaving in 1930 to begin private practice, but he continued to teach part-time. Allen recruited former faculty member Edward Osborn to fill the full-time vacancy Jones created. Having spent many years in Paris, Osborn caught students off guard when he pronounced "cestui que trust" in proper French.

---

256. *Stone to Lecture on Constitutional Law*, WASHBURN REV., Sept. 14, 1927.

257. *Alumni Profiles*, THE CIRCUIT RIDER 12, 14 (Fall 1989).

Allen argued that a fourth full-time faculty member was needed, but it was not until the AALS amended its membership requirement in 1932 to mandate a minimum faculty size of four that President Womer gave Allen hiring authority. The new professor was Thomas A. Larremore, a 1916 Columbia law graduate who had been on the faculty of KU's law school from 1922 until 1929, had taught before that at the law schools at Stanford, Oregon, and Tulane and, in 1928–29 was a Visiting Professor at the University of Pennsylvania. Interestingly, the year he moved from Tulane to Kansas, 1922, Larremore had been a member of the AALS Executive Committee when it gave Washburn a final chance to meet its membership requirements of 5,000 library volumes and three full-time faculty. He had directed men's glee clubs when he was at Stanford and Tulane and in 1929 interrupted his career to earn a bachelor's degree in Music and a master's degree in Sacred Music. He resumed his full-time law teaching career at Washburn and also became director of the Chapel choir. He taught from his 1928 textbook, *A Selection of Cases on Personal Property,* in a fall class. Larremore took a leave of absence in the spring of 1933. The next year, he was the first full-time dean, for one year, of the newly-accredited Hartford College of Law, which ultimately became part of the University of Connecticut. Later, he taught at George Washington.

When Larremore's departed in January 1933, Washburn again looked inward, hiring recent graduate Kenneth Wagner '32, who would teach full-time for ten years. Wagner was a native of western Kansas. He spent his early years in Russell Springs, went to high school in Wakeeney, and graduated from Kansas State Teachers College in Hays. He attended KU for his first year of law school before transferring to Washburn. After graduation, he opened a law office in Gove. As a faculty member, he was "far more interested in the average student and the student who might be having scholastic difficulties than he was in the exceptional student."[258]

There were no further changes in the full-time faculty during Allen's deanship. It consisted of two Washburn graduates, Hambleton and Wagner, and two lawyers who had practiced in Topeka, Allen and Osborn. The increased in-breeding of the faculty can be explained, in part, by the economic problems the entire country faced during the Great Depression. However, there were economic factors unique to Washburn that contributed to the school's

---

258. WAGNER: FAMILY HISTORY 34.

inability to offer competitive salaries. "Every year for sixteen years," President Womer wrote to the AALS in 1930, "the administration of Washburn has been obliged to provide for a deficit in current expense income that has ranged from $10,000 to $50,000, and besides this to assume the burden of developing endowment funds, and providing new buildings and equipment."[259] Without "contributing constituents" the College would not have remained afloat. The Depression compounded the burden of interest payments on indebtedness undertaken during the peak years of the 1920s to support building construction and program development. In the spring of 1932, faculty throughout the College voted for a voluntary 10% reduction in their wages to help balance the books[260] but a one-week fundraising campaign to raise $50,000 for operating expenses still was necessary the next spring.[261] Womer emphasized at a law faculty meeting that the prosperity of the Law School was tied to the advancement of the entire school.[262]

Allen was concerned about the proportionate allocation of resources to the school. At the same faculty meeting, after Womer gave figures "showing the expense necessary for the Law School," Allen felt compelled to call Womer's attention to AALS rules "that a law school should not be expected to be self supporting."[263] Rarely were law schools affiliated with such small institutions. Allen observed in 1928 that of sixty-two AALS members, sixty were located at large universities; in 1930 he found that of seventy-one ABA approved schools, Washburn was the only one attached to a college.

The 1930 AALS inspection report expressed concern that the salary scale "seemed to be entirely inadequate." The report speculated that the cause of the inadequacy was "that the college authorities are waiting for the faculty of

---

259. Letter from Parley P. Womer to AALS President Edson Sunderland (Dec. 2, 1930) (on file in Mabee Library).

260. *Law Standards Made Higher*, washburn rev., May 2, 1932.

261. *Washburn to Conduct Campaign*, washburn rev., Feb. 24, 1933, at 1. Dean Allen chaired the Law sub-committee with Earl Hatcher '23, Wendell Garlinghouse '31, Margaret McGurnaghan '27, Beryl Johnson, Hall Smith '26 and student St. Elmo Else '35 as members. Early in the week, the Law committee had raised $3,100 of the total of $17,319 raised college-wide. Among committee members, McGurnaghan had raised the most. *Campaign Money Is Increasing*, washburn rev., Mar. 3, 1933, at 1.

262. Minutes, Washburn Coll. Sch. of Law faculty meeting (Oct. 2, 1929).

263. *Id.*

the law school to bring about a larger attendance as a condition precedent to increasing salary disbursements." There is evidence casting doubt on that speculation. Washburn consistently had been ahead of many law schools in raising admission standards, which inevitably impacts enrollment and tuition revenue negatively. It already had determined that three years of college work would be required for admission, effective in 1932. In addition, the College administration supported Allen's proposal to limit the number of 1Ls admitted in 1932 to forty. The more likely explanation, then, is that the College's administration sought generally to operate on the cheap and resisted giving the Law School more than the minimum necessary.

Even before the Depression, the College had failed to provide the Law School essential resources, and not solely in the areas of faculty size and salaries. Although the library book budget during Dean Allen's first three years averaged more than $3,100 annually, it barely averaged $1,000 annually the next three years. It was less than $1,500 in 1929–30. The necessity to share Holbrook Hall caused problems too. Allen wrote in his 1929–30 annual report:

> Our library room is small and crowded. We do not have sufficient tables and chairs to accommodate our students. As the library increases, additional space will be required. We could use the entire top floor of the building for library and reading room. The modern law school, to be effective, must compel the student to use and dig into the books. We are doing the best we can with our present equipment. Any plans for the future should take that into account.

AALS President Edson Sunderland of the University of Michigan, who conducted the 1930 membership inspection, had many of the concerns Allen already had expressed. "The library, it would appear, contains somewhat more than the required number of volumes but it is not 'housed and administered as to be readily available for use by students and faculty,' and a most serious deficiency exists in the matter of legal periodicals," Sunderland wrote to President Womer, inviting him to appear before the Executive Committee to address that concern and the concern that salaries were not competitive. By coincidence, former Dean Albert Harno was a member of the Executive Committee, ex-officio, while serving as the Association's Secretary-Treasurer.

Womer was in poor health, on leave from the campus, and unable to travel to the meeting. Philip C. King already had been identified as Womer's successor

16. Holbrook Hall, Library, 1935

and was then serving as Assistant President, in essence Chief Operating Officer, while Womer continued to hold the title of President. In a handwritten note, Womer urged King to attend the Executive Committee meeting:

> I think I should tell you confidentially the report bears unmistakable evidence that Dean Allen in giving the information for the report has not been very fair to his institution. I have suspected for some time that Dean Allen was using the Executive Com of the Ass. in order to force the hand of the College with respect to various matters. This report, I think, confirms that suspicion....
>
> I do not believe that you will have much difficulty in staving off action on the Report by the Executive Com. of the Association. However if you find that adverse action is likely to be taken it would be better for us to withdraw from the Association. I am inclined to believe that little harm would come to our Law School by a withdrawal from the Association.[264]

While Womer is not the only president in Washburn's history to misapprehend the needs of quality legal education, it is doubtful that any made a worse assessment of the value of being part of the national legal education community. Happily, King took a less hostile approach.

The College gave the Law School more space. The Practice Court was moved from the third floor to another room in Holbrook Hall so that space for the

---

264. Note from Parley Womer to Philip C. King (on file in Mabee Library).

library nearly doubled. The Law School now had exclusive use of the second floor as well as the third. However, one class had to be held in Crane Observatory. The Little Theater in the Mulvane Art Museum was used for assemblies.[265] Even this fix was short-term. When the fourth full-time faculty member was added in 1932, an additional office had to be created on Holbrook Hall's second floor. Soon, only two classrooms were available in Holbrook Hall. While the classrooms in Holbrook were of adequate size, scheduling difficulties were exacerbated by the Law School's policy of offering all classes between 8:00 a.m. and 12:30 p.m. All first-year classes had to be held in another building. Once again, law students found themselves in the basement classroom in Crane Observatory, a block away.

> [I]t was necessary during a considerable part of this winter for students and instructor to wear their overcoats during recitations. It…is equipped with a variety of chairs of varying ages and patterns with arms attached for note taking. If physically comfortable as to temperature, it would be a dismal place for the pursuit of any kind of educational endeavor.[266]

Even Holbrook had its problems. Sets of large iron rods had to be run completely through the building and walls at opposite points because of doubt about safety due to the weight of books on the third floor that the building was not designed to carry.[267] One estimate was that the books weighed twenty-seven tons.[268] Once again, there was clamor for the Law School to have a home of its own. By 1935, the administration talked about remodeling a nearby building but three years passed without plans being finalized.

THE BIG SWITCH

Allen had served as Dean for thirteen years when the College honored his extraordinary service by awarding him the honorary degree LL.D. in 1935. He surely could have remained Dean until his retirement. From his earliest days of practice, however, Allen had the ambition to sit on his state's Supreme

---

265. *Changes in Library,* WASHBURN REV., Sept. 21, 1931.
266. AALS Report on Inspection of Washburn College School of Law (Mar. 24, 1936) (on file in Mabee Library).
267. *Id.*
268. TOPEKA ST. J., Feb. 24, 1939.

Court. During the summer of 1936, friends invited him to a meeting at a local lawyer's office. Several other lawyers were there and they all urged him to seek the Democrat Party nomination for Justice of the Kansas Supreme Court. The odds were long. No Democrat had ever won election to the Court in strongly Republican Kansas.[269] Worse yet, they wanted him to challenge the longest serving member of the Court, Rousseau A. Burch, who by seniority had been Chief Justice since July 1935. Burch was a highly respected jurist, was a member of the Council of the American Law Institute, and had been active in the development of the *Restatement of the Law* of both Torts and Property. It had been on Burch's recommendation that Allen had been named by the Bar Association as annotator of Kansas citations for the *Restatement of Property*. However, labor unions remained angry about Burch's dissents in decisions in the early 1920s which would have restricted the scope of the industrial court law in Kansas and found a broader scope to be unconstitutional.

Allen discussed the matter overnight with Florence. "It is one chance to gratify my ambition," he told her.[270] She urged him to try it. He filed his candidacy the next day. In the primary election, he defeated W.E. Langmade of Oberlin by nearly a 2–1 margin. For one with such a longstanding ambition and such a formidable general election opponent as Burch, Allen's campaign strategy was surprisingly low key. He made only three political speeches during the campaign, one to students at Baker University, one to a law fraternity at KU, and one short talk in Ottawa. However, he did make speeches about the Constitution before civic clubs and local bar associations. During those speeches, he never mentioned his candidacy or asked anyone to vote for him. Nevertheless, he was elected. The labor unions were one factor in his victory. The more than 500 graduates of Washburn Law School during Allen's years as Dean were another. The *Kansas City Star* reported that the

> factor of the law school students may have been larger in its effects than that of labor. In the eighteen years Dean Allen has been a teacher and

---

269. Two Democrats had served on the Court by appointment to fill mid-term vacancies. Theodore A. Hurd served from April 23 until December 1, 1884, and Washburn graduate Edward R. Sloan '06 served from April 6, 1931, until January 9, 1933. Sloan did not seek election to a full term.

270. *Dean Harry K. Allen's Dream Comes True with Suddenness*, KAN. CITY STAR, Nov. 6, 1936.

dean of the law school, he has turned out lawyers who now are located in ninety counties of the state....In some fifteen or twenty counties Washburn law students are county attorneys or were candidates for county attorneys or probate judges or other offices. Most of them were Republicans.

But Republicans or Democrats, Socialists or anything else, most of these boys and girls who studied law under Dean Allen were for Dean Allen for justice of the supreme court. And those not running for office also were for Dean Allen.

When he entered the campaign Dean Allen wrote to every Washburn law school graduate and asked him to send him a list of Democrats and Republicans to whom he might send literature. He never asked a graduate to vote for him or work for him. But it would appear that almost every one of them not only voted for Dean Allen, but got out and hustled among his relatives and friends and persuaded them to vote for Allen also.

Just one instance of this unusual loyalty to Dean Allen. He went to a Kansas town one day and met a law school graduate on the street. Dean Allen was not in town on political business.

"Watcha doin', Dean?" the lawyer said.

Allen told him why he was in town.

"Stay over until tomorrow noon and we'll put on a party for you," the lawyer said. "All the boys would be glad to see you again."

Dean Allen agreed to stay. The next day he went to the luncheon. There were twenty-seven Washburn graduates in the group. Only one was a Democrat. Yet before the luncheon was over the group had divided the town, the county and even other counties into sections, each one took a section and agreed to "work his head off" for Dean Allen. The five counties in which these young men worked all went for Allen just as effective work was done in many other counties by Washburn graduates.

W.P. Lambertson, member of Congress from the first district, has a daughter who was graduated last year and admitted to the bar. Lambertson is a dyed-in-the-wool Republican and has served many terms in the state legislature and in congress as a Republican. Yet his daughter was one of the active Allen supporters in Northeastern Kansas. There wasn't a thing her father could do about it. She was for Dean Allen.[271]

The same article described the efforts of one of the school's black graduates who organized the black community in his town to vote for Allen and then went to other towns to do the same. To become a lawyer, he had to work his way through school. "Dean Allen found work for him. The boy raked the leaves of the Allen lawn. He did all sorts of odd jobs and Dean and Mrs. Allen saw to it that he had employment most of the time."[272]

Kansas law required a lawyer to have been in the active practice of law for four years before election as a judge. After the election, a newspaper reported that some lawyers had questioned whether teaching law classes constituted the active practice of law, but no one formally challenged whether Allen met the statutory qualification.

Washburn had only two months between the November election and the swearing-in ceremonies in January to find a new dean. A distinguished lawyer and jurist was available—Justice Burch. After several conferences with prominent Topeka lawyers and President King, he accepted the position and joined the school for the spring semester 1937. It was known as "the big switch."

Allen let it be known that he was willing to continue teaching part-time. Perhaps not surprisingly, Burch did not invite his election opponent to do so. Allen did not take the slight well, writing a stinging letter to King. He circulated it widely to trustees and alumni and the local paper published its full text. He wrote, in part:

> I have before me a copy of the catalogue of the Washburn Law School for 1937–1938. I believe it is the first time my name has not appeared as a member of the faculty of the law school since I taught my first class in 1918.
>
> Having given the best years of my life to the Washburn law school, I have, of course, a deep and abiding interest in the welfare and progress of the school. However, without a word of any kind to me, my name has been

271. *Id.*
272. *Id.*

dropped from the faculty. I assume, under the circumstances, for me to continue to act as chairman of the committee on wills and trusts would be a source of embarrassment to you. Will you therefore be good enough to accept my resignation as chairman of this committee?

If at any time or place I may be of service to you or to the school, please command me.

The two years from 1937 through 1939 would be the only ones between 1918 and 1956 in which Allen did not teach at least one class at the school. Allen served only one six-year term on the Court. He was defeated for re-election in 1942 by popular Republican Attorney General Jay S. Parker. Allen's Property I class met the morning following the election. Joseph W. Morris '47 described the moment:

> We all knew what the results of the election were when we came to class the morning after his defeat. We were all very, very sad, although many of us, including myself, were "died-in-the-wool" Republicans.
>
> He walked into that class at 8:00 a.m. He laid his case book down on the podium and opened it. He raised his eyes and looked out at the class and he had a smile on his face. He said: "You look worse than they do down at the Democratic Headquarters." We felt worse too. We loved him.[273]

Allen opened a law office in the New England Building. For a time he also served on the board of legal examiners for the U.S. Civil Service Commission for Kansas. In November 1945, The Associated Press reported he was being considered for appointment to the United States District Court of Kansas. He continued teaching part-time into his 80s, for as long as he maintained his office, and he and Florence attended law school and law student events with nearly the frequency they had when he was Dean. His advanced age added to his legend:

> In cold weather, he wore a buffalo-robe coat that probably weighed as much as he did. Coming across campus, like the hour hand on a watched-clock, he gave a fine imitation of being a stationary moving object. He called the class to attention with the feeble cry, "Children."[274]

273. Letter from Joseph W. Morris to James M. Concannon, dated Oct. 21, 2003 (on file in Washburn Law Library).

274. Duane A. Bybee '53, Class Notes, Washburn School of Law Alumni Weekend,

Just before New Year's Day, 1956, a committee of former students announced the start of fundraising for an endowment in Allen's name "so he will know while alive how much we honor him."[275] He died in July 1959 after an extended illness. In remarks on behalf of the Supreme Court, Justice Schuyler Jackson noted the various titles Allen held: Senator, Doctor, Justice, and Dean. "Since his hundreds of friends agree that of all his positions his work as Dean of a school of law was the summit of his accomplishments, he shall be referred to in this memorial as Dean Allen."[276]

Aug. 21–22, 1998.

275. *Washburn Alumni to Honor Ex-Dean Harry K. Allen,* TOPEKA ST. J., Dec. 27, 1955.

276. In Memoriam, 187 Kan. xxiii, xxiv.

3

GOING PUBLIC AND GOING TO WAR (1937–1945)

Rousseau A. Burch taught International Law during Washburn Law School's first year but was listed as a Lecturer only that year and the next. He was a "special lecturer" in 1921–22. However, he was well known by legal educators nationally. He frequently taught summer classes at such law schools as Northwestern, Michigan, Wisconsin, and Minnesota. The practice of the AALS was to invite a leading American jurist to address its annual meeting and Burch was chosen to speak in 1931. His topic was "The Spirit and Method of Legal Research."

Burch's family had moved to Salina, Kansas in 1869, and he returned there to practice law in 1885, the year he graduated from the University of Michigan law school. His brother later joined him in a partnership. He was appointed to a vacancy on the Kansas Supreme Court in 1902 and his tenure lasted thirty-four years. A colleague observed that he "had a brilliant legal mind, was a thorough student and wrote in a trenchant style which attracted attention and appealed to his readers. No justice of this court has had a wider reputation with the bench and bar of the United States."[277] Wigmore called him one of the five best writers of judicial opinions in the country.[278] His alma mater awarded him an honorary degree LL.D. in 1924. Washburn College conferred the honorary Litt.D. on him in 1929.

---

277. Memorial, 160 Kan. v, vii (1945).
278. *Id.*

17. Rousseau A. Burch, Dean 1937–1938

Burch's high standards and tendency to be "sharp" with lawyers "when they were negligent or sloppy"[279] led authors of a thorough student note about Burch to conclude that he "evidently was not popular with many Kansas attorneys."[280] Eulogies by contemporaries imply as much. C.A. Magaw of the Topeka bar praised Burch as one who "acquired knowledge day and night and gave the world the benefit of it," but noted that as a result he "was a man who did not care to associate with any but the most intelligent and scholarly of people. He was like a great many other scientists and scholars, rather exclusive and in that

---

279. Telephone interview with Howard Harper '40, quoted in Jalen O'Neil and Curtis Waugh, *Style and Substance: Kansas Supreme Court Justice Rousseau Angelus Burch*, 26 WASHBURN L.J. 297, 315 (1987). This note received the GNIP GNOP Award as the outstanding student note that year.

280. *Id.* at 314.

way he was cut off from the public to a large extent."[281] Justice Walter Thiele put it this way:

> Those who came to know Justice Burch well know that while he was brusque in manner, and impatient with those pretending learning they did not possess, he was a highly educated, cultured gentleman who listened to the problems which others found difficult, and gave generously of his own time and ability in order that a proper solution might be reached.[282]

Burch was seventy-three years old when he became Dean on February 2, 1937. At an inauguration ceremony, Burch quoted works of his favorite poet, Robert Browning. "The reporter covering the event admired the address as 'truly literary' and described it as 'concise and expressive' but added rather lamely, '[T]he full purport of [the speech] could not be gotten from a first hearing.'"[283]

Burch persuaded the faculty to change the grading system, stating that his purpose was to promote higher standards of educational achievement. Effective for the fall of 1938, the lowest A was 93, rather than 85, the lowest B was 85, rather than 75, and the lowest C was 77, rather than 65. The minimum passing grade was 70. Previously, passing scores received a grade of C, while a D was a condition and an E was a failure. Now, scores between 70–76 were Ds, but passing. However, a cumulative GPA of 75 was required to graduate. Scores between 60–69 received a grade of E, a condition, and anything lower received a new grade of F. Students who did not make passing scores in 40% of their work were, as before, suspended for one semester. Burch added a provision placing students on probation if in any two semesters they had barely passing, i.e. D, or worse grades in 50% of their work. However, neither of these rules was enforced strictly enough to lead to the early exclusion of a significant number of students because of unsatisfactory work. The faculty had voted in 1935 that students entering after June 1935 could only count toward graduation thirty credit hours in which they had received barely passing, then C, grades. As students who entered that year neared graduation, however, the faculty voted not to enforce the rule.[284]

---

281. C.A. Magaw, *Chief Justice Rousseau A. Burch*, J. KAN. B. ASS'N 41 (1994).

282. Memorial, 160 Kan. v (1945).

283. Jalen O'Neil and Curtis Waugh, *supra* note 279, at 320, n. 188 (1987), quoting TOPEKA ST. J., Feb. 5, 1937, at 1.

284. Minutes, Washburn Coll. Sch. of Law faculty meeting (Apr. 1938).

When he wrote an earlier short history of Washburn Law School, Phil Lewis '35 observed that Burch was "not enamored" with the deanship.[285] During the summer of 1938, Burch was involved in an automobile accident in Canada and his injuries prevented him from resuming his duties in the fall. He announced his resignation on October 24.[286] Students took the news hard. Future law professor Arthur White '39 wrote of their

> sudden sense of loss and realization…that they no longer have direct contact with this brilliant and learned man. Judge Burch is said by Dean Wigmore…to be one of the five leading jurists in the United States but to us he was our Dean, the man to whom we brought our problems and sought advice…the man to whom we looked for guidance. His opinions rank among the highest, his learning and knowledge is sought by the great legal minds of the nation, yet he was our teacher, patiently working to instill into us a truer understanding of legal principles, guiding us carefully thru the maze of problems confronting a student of the law. Let others pay tribute to his achievements, but we shall always remember him as our Dean, our teacher, and for that we owe him a debt of gratitude which cannot be paid.[287]

Students sent him a bouquet of red roses. Burch thanked them in a letter to the student newspaper. "I was deeply moved by the gracious letter which accompanied the bouquet.…My association with the law students at Washburn college was one of the most gratifying of my varied enthusiasms."[288]

TIGHT FINANCES

Tight finances continued to present problems. In October 1938, just two weeks before Burch resigned, Professor Wagner advised President King he would resign effective at the end of the semester if his salary was not raised to that of other

285. Philip Lewis, *Washburn University School of Law*, in REQUISITE LEARNING AND GOOD MORAL CHARACTER: A HISTORY OF THE KANSAS BENCH AND BAR 124, 128 (Robert Richmond ed. 1982).

286. *R.A. Burch, Noted Jurist, Quits as Dean*, TOPEKA DAILY CAP., Oct. 25, 1938.

287. *A Great Man Bids Farewell*, WASHBURN REV., Oct. 28, 1938.

288. *Justice Burch Expresses Appreciation to Students*, WASHBURN REV., Nov. 11, 1938.

full-time faculty members. He wrote that while he wanted to continue teaching, he felt "it is my duty to take graduate work in the near future, not only for my personal gain but to aid the law school in its academic standing,"[289] but he could not afford to do so. Wagner somehow was persuaded to remain on the faculty.

Students had to be creative to meet their own financial challenges. Floyd Taylor '46, one of the few black students who attended during the 1930s, took ten years after enrolling in 1936 to complete his degree, with two lengthy periods of absence. The local paper reported that he "worked and talked his way along in a dozen different jobs, and used every student fund in the Washburn catalog, and some that weren't."[290] Even so, when it was time to take examinations at the end of his second year, "he lacked having paid his tuition by $4 and was threatened with disqualification. But a fellow student learned about the situation and took up a collection to pay the debt, and again Taylor squeezed thru."[291] Taylor's most important benefactor, though, was the ventriloquist's dummy named "Ashes Woodson" that he brought with him to Topeka. Once, when he was "down to his last nickel," Topeka's Park Commissioner hired him for an engagement and he got another at the Best Theater. He composed a new dialogue for Ashes and was swamped with requests for appearances, leading to more than fifty performances one year before civic clubs, Greek letter organizations on Washburn's campus, and other groups. Taylor and Ashes continued to perform even while he studied for the bar exam.

AN INTERNAL OR EXTERNAL DEAN?

Antrim Hambleton '14 was named Acting Dean when Burch resigned. Hambleton had Washburn Law School in his blood. As a 1L, he was the law librarian, part-time. He won the Freshman Prize Debate, receiving a law dictionary. In his second year, he won a place on the Blackstone Club's team that represented Washburn in its first debate with another law school, the Kansas City Law School. As a sideline while also working part-time in the Probate Judge's office,

---

289. Letter from Kenneth Wagner to Dr. Philip C. King, President (Oct. 11, 1938) (on file in Mabee Library).

290. *'Ashes' Won't Get the Law Degree, But Floyd Taylor Is Ready to Give Him the Credit*, undated 1946 newspaper article glued to Floyd Taylor's transcript at Washburn Law School.

291. *Id.*

18. Antrim Hambleton '14, Acting Dean 1938–1939
and 1943–1946, Professor 1927–1950

he used his experience as a high school teacher to help special students make up missing credits. His classmates elected him President of his class.

When Hambleton joined the faculty, he became a revered friend of students, not only at the law school but throughout the campus. He also served as tennis coach for the College and was Washburn's faculty representative to the Missouri Valley Conference. One of his students described him this way:

> Hambleton was rather a strict disciplinarian but once the students got to know him, they liked him. He didn't look like a lawyer—he was a big man and vigorous, interested in athletics. His specialty was contracts. He was so very thorough-going a teacher that he never missed any point. He was pleasant, kind and comfortable in life; it was obvious he enjoyed what he was doing.[292]

292. McLane, *supra* note 3, at 11.

Another student recalled, "Hambleton was sort of a legend around the school. And how he loved to dance! His wife couldn't dance, so he would dance with all the girls. When it came to the last dance and everyone joined his own partner so all the girls were taken, he would go out in the middle of the floor and dance with a chair."[293]

Hambleton believed that a "great amount" of the Law School's success was

> due to the fact that Washburn Law School is a personal-contact school. By this I mean the faculty is not only interested in the law but is also interested in the student of the law. This is manifested in class room discussions, in office room interviews, and wherever the student and teacher meet. These discussions extend outside of the field of law into the personal problems of the individual student.[294]

Hambleton's main tasks as Acting Dean were to lobby the administration for more spacious and more appropriately equipped quarters and then to prepare for the move that was planned for the beginning of the fall term, 1939. He pushed to limit eligibility for the J.D. to those who completed one year of graduate study, an additional twenty-seven credit hours, after receiving the LL.B. It is not clear what prompted this change since only four students during the previous decade earned J.D.s the alternate way while completing just the three-year LL.B. curriculum: Philip H. Lewis, Francis C. Clark and C. Harold Hughes, all in 1935; and Karl Ahlborn, Jr. in 1938. Only one J.D. was awarded based on Hambleton's preferred method of graduate study, to Jay Kyle '31 in 1938, years after he received his LL.B.

The school launched a search for a new dean. President Philip C. King attended the AALS annual meeting in Chicago to seek suggestions. In January 1939, he appointed an advisory committee both to provide assistance in the search and also to act as a sounding board on law school policy. The committee included Robert Stone, still active with the school thirty-six years after he helped start it, Judge Roy McCue '24, Judge Warren Shaw '31, Irving Platt '08, A. Harry Crane '25, and four other lawyers who were not law alumni but were active supporters of the College. King sent a letter to all law school graduates seeking comments on the problems and possibilities of the school.

293. *Id.*

294. Undated memorandum from Antrim Hambleton to President Philip King, 1939 (on file in Mabee Library).

Hambleton applied to be the permanent dean. Karl Ahlborn, Jr. '38 wrote to support him, saying he "has the respect and admiration of all the students who have come in contact with him."[295] Former Dean William R. Arthur also wrote to support Hambleton, who had been one of his students. Robert Stone responded to Arthur's letter, "We all of us feel very friendly toward Professor Hambleton, but felt a little doubtful whether he had that aggressive spirit" that was needed.[296] An additional obstacle for Hambleton arose when King sought advice from Herschel W. Arant, who then was Dean at Ohio State and President of the AALS. Arant was familiar with Washburn both because he had conducted the school's 1936 AALS inspection and from previously having been Dean at KU. Arant urged that a dean be hired from outside Washburn to reduce the inbreeding of the faculty.

King received a second letter from Arant shortly after the AALS meeting. Arant recommended Lester W. Feezer and indicated he had reason to believe Washburn could interest Feezer in the position, even though Feezer had joined the University of Arizona law faculty just that year. Feezer had been Visiting Professor at Ohio State and Arant described him as in "the very prime of life" with "that maturity of scholarship and personality" one wants in a dean. Feezer, forty-nine years old, was a Harvard Law School graduate and member of the Order of the Coif. For nine years he was a legal assistant with the New York, Massachusetts, and Minnesota State Health Departments. He then was a member of the law faculty at the University of South Dakota for fifteen years, the last eleven as both a professor and librarian. During that time, he spent one year as Visiting Professor at the University of Missouri and taught one summer at Northwestern. He had published articles in eight different law reviews and bar journals. A member of President King's advisory committee, Frank Quail '29, conducted an initial interview with Feezer in Arizona and soon Feezer was invited to interview on campus. Salary negotiations were difficult. Feezer somehow knew that Harry K. Allen had received $5,000 per year. King offered him $4,000. Feezer asked for more. King replied that was not possible in light of the College's tight finances but he did offer $200 for moving expenses. Feezer's desire to become a dean apparently was strong enough that he accepted that offer. King announced his appointment on May 10, 1939.

295. Letter from Karl Ahlborn (Feb. 17, 1939) (on file in Mabee Library).
296. Letter from Robert Stone to William R. Arthur (Jan. 20, 1939) (on file in Mabee Library).

19. Lester W. Feezer, Dean 1939–1940

A NEW OLD BUILDING

The announcement of Feezer's appointment also informed alumni of the
Board of Trustees' decision to move the Law School to Boswell Hall. Boswell
housed the College library prior to construction of Carnegie Library and since
then had been home to the School of Music. For the first time since it moved
from downtown twenty-one years earlier, the Law School would occupy an
entire building. Substantial renovation and remodeling were required, at an
estimated cost of $9,000. King announced that three Board members had
made contingent gifts totaling $2,000 but urged alumni to contribute the
remaining $7,000 needed "to fulfill this long-felt need for the Law School."
When Feezer's arrived, the school's new home was ready for him to help with
the move. Predictably, in light of the experience in Holbrook Hall, the library
and reading room occupied the lowest floor, rather than an upper floor. The
collection now numbered 15,000 volumes. The administrative offices, a student

20. Boswell Hall, home of the Law School 1939–1956

lounge, and one classroom occupied the second floor. Two classrooms and faculty offices were on the third floor.

Formal dedication ceremonies were held at 8:00 p.m. on November 3, 1939. A plaque was unveiled during the ceremony, recognizing the names of 380 alumni donors to the renovation. Feezer urged guests to "observe the conveniences which have been provided—new chairs, new tables, new book stacks, and especially new lighting. In the reading room we have not just lights, but the kind of lights which afford artificial daylight." Judge Orie Phillips of the United States Court of Appeals for the Tenth Circuit gave the principal address, entitled "Lawyer's Place in Modern Society." The looming war in Europe preoccupied the American mind and Judge Phillips, perhaps surprisingly, weighed in on the central issue of the day. "If we treasure our individual liberty, our system of representative government, our free enterprise, our American way of life, if we want to remain free men, we must keep America out of this European conflict."[297] He feared participation in another European war might lead America to some form of totalitarianism that would eliminate lawyers and destroy the law's critical role in American society.

297. Text of remarks by Judge Orie Phillips, Boswell Hall Dedication file.

[O]ur legal system is based on justice and practical common sense. It opposes reason to passion, accepted principles to unbridled discretion, and the requirements of fair play to the favoritism of tyranny of power. It has not been ideal. The law has lacked sufficient clarity. Procedure has been unnecessarily complex. Lawyers have sometimes employed its processes for delay, rather than for the speedy attainment of justice. Judges are not always competent, honest and impartial. But these defects are gradually being eliminated through the efforts of the organized bar, through the restoration of the rule-making power to the courts, through the better training of lawyers, and through a response to the increasing demand that judges shall be independent, impartial and competent. So that our judicial system stands today as the embodiment of a sincere desire of our people to be just, each to the other, and to afford to all equal justice under law.[298]

At the end of the academic year, Feezer expressed appreciation to President King for the conveniences and efficient arrangement of the new building. However, he cautioned that normal library growth would in very few years "make it necessary to consider how the additional books are to be shelved." He pointed out that even then a number of infrequently used older books "that should be shelved and accessible" were being stored in the basement of Benton Hall.[299]

DEANS FEEZER AND PRICE AND THE MUNICIPAL PLAN

One of Feezer's first acts, long before arriving in Topeka, was to urge Harry K. Allen to rejoin the faculty as a part-time instructor. Allen readily agreed. Another new grading policy was put in place, responding further to criticism during the 1936 AALS inspection that grades were higher than at other schools. For the first time, grades were expressed as grade points, on a 3.0 scale. At Feezer's urging, the faculty adopted new rules for the exclusion of students for poor grades, and for their exclusion earlier in the course of study. A student whose cumulative GPA after one year was less than .75 or who did not pass 50% of the work in any one semester was not permitted to continue. Eighty credit hours and eighty grade points were required for graduation. Requirements

---

298. *Id.*

299. Annual report of Lester W. Feezer, 1939–40 (on file in Mabee Library).

for academic honors were quantified and remained unchanged for sixty-one years: *cum laude* 2.4; *magna cum laude* 2.6; and *summa cum laude* 2.9.

Feezer's preferred response to another AALS criticism, that an excessive percentage of classes were taught by part-time faculty, was to hire more full-time faculty. However, that response was not available due to budget restraints. The solution he implemented was to reduce the number of courses offered. The work of both the first and second years was made required. The number of credit hours offered annually dropped from 107 to 95. This solution had the additional advantages of stemming what had been ad hoc growth of the curriculum and adding coherence through pruning of offerings. A happy by-product was that a few hundred dollars previously paid to part-time faculty were freed up to address in small part the problem of inadequate salaries for full-time faculty.[300] The school continued to require more weeks of study than the AALS minimum standard but reduced the number of class hours each student had each week so they could do better work, particularly when they were employed part-time.

Feezer continued his own scholarly activities, publishing two book reviews in the *Texas Law Review* and an article in the *Minnesota Law Review*.[301] He used a classroom technique that became popular decades later, staging a fight in his Torts class to demonstrate how the recollections of witnesses to such an event differ.[302] In the spring, Feezer and Frank Oberg '40, President of the Student Bar Association, visited alumni in ten central Kansas cities seeking assistance in student recruitment and graduate placement. The Kansas Bar Association appropriated $300 to the school for student research assistants, Jack Campbell '40, Kenneth Wilke '41, and James McClain '41, to help Professors Wagner, Hambleton, and Osborn prepare Kansas annotations for the Restatements of Property, Contracts, and Restitution.[303]

---

300. *Id.*

301. Lester W. Feezer, *Book Review: The Judicial Process in Torts Cases 2d by Leon Green*, 18 TEX. L. REV. 116 (1939); Lester W. Feezer, *Book Review: Cases on Creditor's Rights 3d by John Hanna and James McLaughlin*, 18 TEX. L. REV. 246 (1940); Lester W. Feezer, *Intervening Crime and Liability for Negligence*, 24 MINN. L. REV. 635 (1940).

302. Robert Stone Johnson '48, Class Notes, Washburn School of Law Alumni Weekend, Aug. 21–22, 1998.

303. *Law Students Work on Law Restatement*, WASHBURN REV., Mar. 29, 1940.

A prolonged attack of arthritis early in 1940 partially incapacitated Feezer.[304] By late October, he announced he would resign as Dean at the end of the fall semester and return to his former position as Professor of Law at Arizona. He continued to teach there until retirement. His departure was attributed to health reasons,[305] but it could have been because of the College's financial health more than his own. Although the College reported in the fall of 1938 that its finances were the best in many years,[306] only in relative terms could the statement be viewed as accurate. By February 1940, President King warned of "a heavy budget deficit this year" and a tight budget for the next.[307] Although Feezer had negotiated an increase in summer teaching salaries, as urged in the AALS inspection report, from $45 to $70 per credit hour, when summer enrollment was lower than expected, the administration *ex post facto* reduced the summer teaching rate to $45 per credit hour. Feezer was irate, placing his objection "of record" prior to the next AALS inspection and vowing to President King, "I cannot approve or consent to the operation of a summer session hereafter while I am connected with the school unless a definite appropriation for the purpose is made in advance."[308] The Law School's budget for 1940–41 totaled $17,604 and included only a $100 salary increase for Feezer.

A week after Feezer's resignation, King announced his own resignation, due to the College's poor finances, but by December he was persuaded to withdraw it. After years of having to cover operating deficits by fundraising, College trustees concluded they could not produce a balanced budget except by cutting faculty salaries or reducing the quality of education, neither of which they were willing to do. "Rather than operate on an unsound basis, until resources were gone" and the College's various accreditations lost, the trustees determined "it would be better to face the issue frankly while Washburn is a going concern."[309] Less than a year after celebrating the College's 75th anniversary, trustees voted

---

304. Letter from Lester W. Feezer (Feb. 23, 1940) (on file in Mabee Library).

305. THE KAW 53 (1941).

306. TOPEKA DAILY CAP., Oct. 18, 1938.

307. Memorandum from President Philip C. King to Lester M. Feezer (Feb. 27, 1940) (on file in Mabee Library).

308. Letter from Lester W. Feezer to President Philip C. King (Aug. 12, 1940) (on file in Mabee Library).

309. Letter from President Philip C. King to AALS Secretary and President-Elect Harold Shepherd (Nov. 22, 1940) (on file in Mabee Library).

not to open the College in the fall of 1941. They appointed a committee to explore other options, principally merger with another institution or turning Washburn into a municipal institution, but the option of becoming a junior college was at least discussed and likely would have meant the end of the Law School. The trustees advised College faculty that there was no assurance they would have positions beyond the current year. Rumors were rampant and King was forced to issue a statement in late November emphasizing that "The college is not 'broke,'" asserting that the "college resources are actually larger today than they were ten years ago," and assuring students "there will be no change in the college program for the rest of this year."[310]

King reported these developments in detail to Harold Shepherd of Duke University, the Secretary and President-elect of the AALS. While King suggested the Board believed its action was "the best way of arousing the forces necessary to assure Washburn's continuance under some other type of organization," he acknowledged that "the uncertainty as to Washburn's future puts us in a very difficult position in the matter of filling the vacancies which will exist for the second semester in our full-time law school faculty. It is exceedingly doubtful whether any definite assurance as to the future of the program can be given before well along in the second semester."[311] Shepherd responded that the Association would be glad to assist the school to reorganize so that "it can continue to comply with our requirements." However, he suggested that "if a reorganization under proper auspices is not shortly made, it might save embarrassment all around if the school were voluntarily to withdraw from the Association."[312]

It is remarkable that in these difficult circumstances King was able to name Feezer's successor quickly. Within days of Feezer's resignation, King had asked Shepherd to suggest candidates[313] and Shepherd recommended James F. Price, who was then Professor of Law at the University of San Francisco. Price had Kansas ties. His father was a faculty member in the Department of History and Government at Kansas State College in Manhattan and Price received his

310. *The Washburn Situation—A Statement by Dr. Philip C. King*, WASHBURN REV., Nov. 22, 1940.

311. Letter from Philip C. King to Mr. Harold Shepherd, *supra* note 309.

312. Letter from Harold Shepherd to President Philip C. King (Nov. 29, 1940) (on file in Mabee Library).

313. Letter from President Philip C. King to Harold Shepherd (Oct. 29, 1940) (on file in Mabee Library).

DEAN JAMES F. PRICE
Dean Law School

21. James F. Price, Dean 1940–1943

bachelor's degree there after attending Swarthmore College. He received his law degree from Stanford in 1930. For two years, Price was legal counsel to the Raven Trust Company in Shanghai, China, helping to introduce the active trust business there, establishing accounting procedures, drafting documents, and coordinating advertising campaigns.[314] He was present when Japan bombed Shanghai in 1931. From 1932 until 1935, Price was managing partner of the security and commodity brokerage firm of Hedges and Price, which had seats on the New York Stock Exchange, the Cotton Exchange, the Commodity Exchange, and the New York Board of Trade.[315] He then became head of the Social Science and Commerce Department at Menlo Junior College while pursuing an LL.M. at Stanford, which he completed in 1937. He continued his work at Menlo Junior College and was a part-time Instructor at the University of San Francisco Law School before his appointment as Professor there in 1939.

---

314. *Law School Executive New Head of K.I.D.C.*, KAN. BUS. MAG. 10 (June 1942).
315. *The New President of K.S.T.C., Emporia*, 51 KANSAS TEACHER 31 (May 1943).

Price performed due diligence about the school, talking with representatives of the faculty, alumni, students, Washburn trustees, and the state Board of Regents, and with the President at Kansas State, the Chancellor at KU, the Dean of KU's law school, the President and the Secretary of the AALS, and the Chair and the Secretary of the ABA's Committee on Legal Education. He accepted the position just before Christmas. He sent President King a detailed analysis of his findings, dated Christmas Day, 1940, and an equally detailed follow-up report dated January 4, 1941.

Price's discussions with Topekans persuaded him that Washburn's "municipal plan" would succeed. He found no sentiment that Kansas should have only one law school, only that Washburn's could continue only if it was an "A" grade school. Yet, there was fear that Topekans might object to being taxed to support a law school that was training many students from outside the city. The objection might not arise initially, since many Topekans believed the school was self-supporting, but later when demands were made to increase the budget. There was fear that the new board of a municipal school would make undergraduate work its primary focus, "and the law School would only come in for what is left, if any." In addition, the new board might be involved in city politics "which might have an adverse effect upon the Law School unless the Law School was financially independent." Thus, Price summarized the dilemma:

> How can provision be made to assure the students, the alumni, the citizens of Topeka, and the Association of American Law Schools (and I should add the American Bar Association) that the Washburn Law School can and will continue as an A grade law school, remaining a part of the College, and yet not be a burden to the Topeka tax payer?[316]

Price heard three chief criticisms of the school: too many students were spending too much of their time in part-time employment; inadequate faculty salaries made it difficult to keep capable full-time faculty or to hire replacements who were experienced, rather than recent graduates; and the school's inability to more than barely meet AALS membership requirements.

Price proposed to address the first criticism by starting a four- or even five-year part-time program, to improve performance by those who had to work.

---

316. Letter from James F. Price to President Philip C. King (Dec. 25, 1940) (on file in Mabee Library).

However, in his view all three criticisms related principally to resources. He compared Washburn Law School's $17,500 budget with the national average of $43,000 and with KU's budget of $60,000. He realized Washburn's budget could not be increased to the national average but concluded $30,000 was the minimum needed to provide an "A" grade law school. His minimum was hardly overstated, since it included only $1,000 more for library books and an increase in faculty salaries that was so modest it would leave Washburn's average salary $300 below the starting figure at KU. However, it would provide a fifth full-time faculty member and $2,000 for scholarships and loans that not only would permit students to work less but also would help attract "some of the most able scholars in the Middle West" who would help raise the school's standards.[317] Based on his discussions with ABA and AALS officials, Price was convinced a "concrete plan must be made to assure an adequate budget. At the present time these organizations believe that the presumption is against the possibility of the Washburn Law School obtaining an adequate budget. This presumption must be overcome."[318]

Price's proposed solution was to obtain commitments that law tuition revenue would be earmarked for the school and that income from the $500,000 of the University's endowment which would remain after payment of the College's $200,000 indebtedness and a $400,000 annuity obligation would be allocated to cover the difference between law tuition revenue and budgeted expenditures. Under Price's plan, upon municipal affiliation, title to all land, buildings, and equipment would pass to the City, which would become responsible for the operating expenses of the other units of the College. The Law School, by using the earnings of the endowment, would become essentially self-supporting. The only option Price saw, if it was not possible to set aside $500,000 from the present endowment, was "to take immediate steps" to raise the needed funds. The proposal to relinquish its endowment did not appeal to the College and it never was pursued far enough for technical issues to be resolved, such as whether the Law School would be charged a pro rata share of maintenance as overhead.

Because of existing commitments at San Francisco, and no doubt in part to keep his options open in case the municipal plan failed and the College actually closed, Price did not move to Topeka until May. He did attend a faculty

---

317. *Id.*

318. Letter from James F. Price to President Philip C. King (Jan. 4, 1941) (on file in Mabee Library).

meeting on January 9 and was introduced, along with Ralph Rice, a new faculty member from Washington, D.C., at an assembly at which students presented Dean Feezer with a desk set and florescent light as a going away gift. Despite all the challenges, Price wrote after returning to California, "The more I analyze the matter the more enthusiastic I become over the future possibilities of the Washburn Law School."[319] Price's appointment was formally effective February 4, but until he arrived in May the school was run by a faculty committee chaired by Professor Wagner.[320]

On New Year's Day, 1941, Washburn announced formation of the Committee of One Hundred to lead the push to become a municipal school. Justices John Dawson '06 and Homer Hoch '09 and Mrs. Harry K. Allen were among Topeka leaders named to the Committee. State law required the signatures of 3,500 voters to place the Washburn question on the ballot for the city elections, scheduled ominously for April Fool's Day. Existing law, passed when Wichita took over Fairmont College, also required a municipal university to bear only the name of its city. Thus, a special bill was hurried through the Kansas Legislature permitting voters to create "Washburn Municipal University of Topeka."[321]

The decision of the College's trustees not to open the school in the fall had raised the stakes sufficiently to get voters' attention. Students at the time perceived little threat that either the College or the Law School would close.[322] Topekans voted to make the College the Municipal University by a strong margin of 17,825 to 4,481.

Immediately after the election, the question whether the Law School would continue as part of the University or be maintained as a separate entity was said to be a decision entirely for the University's new Board of Regents.[323] Not unexpectedly, the new board decided to keep the Law School as part of the College. While undergraduate students benefitted from a 45–60% reduction in tuition, to $75 annually for Topeka residents and $100 annually for others, law tuition remained unchanged at $180 annually because it was a graduate

319. Letter from James F. Price to President Philip C. King (Jan. 26, 1941) (on file in Mabee Library).

320. THE KAW 53 (1941).

321. THE KAW 24–25 (1941).

322. Telephone conversation with Hon. Harold Herd '42 on July 22, 2002.

323. *Municipal Issue Through with 4 to 1 Margin*, WASHBURN REV., Apr. 4, 1941.

professional school. None of the College endowment was reallocated to the Law School. Not much changed. However, the school's greater financial security and the reduction in faculty in-breeding pleased the AALS. After his inspection in the fall of 1941, Bernard C. Gavitt of Indiana University School of Law reported that his evaluation "was wholly favorable and the committee concurred in my judgment that your school was in excellent condition. We all agreed that you were to be congratulated on the present condition of the school and that we have every confidence in its maintenance on a high plane."[324]

When Price arrived on campus in early May 1941, Charles Davis, Jr. '43 described him in the student newspaper as a "tall and dark newcomer…the six foot 'Greek god'" who would "pass for a movie star in front of anybody's camera."[325] He was only thirty-four years old. Davis reported Price was "full of initiative and energy" but also was "one of the boys" who, when asked to say a few words at the Phi Delta Theta house, broke into one of the fraternity's songs he had sung in college, asking, "Don't you remember this one?" Price initially taught Equity, Constitutional Law, and Labor Law.

THE WAR YEARS

Price may have thought his greatest challenges would be improving the school's finances and managing the transition to a municipal university. Of course, they were not, because of World War II. Even before the attack on Pearl Harbor, enrollment fell to fifty-six in the fall of 1941 from ninety-two the previous year, as men were called to the Army or other defense work.[326]

On Friday, December 12, five days after Pearl Harbor was bombed, the Kansas Supreme Court adopted a special rule that students who were sufficiently advanced in their studies that they could complete the educational prerequisites to be eligible to take the bar examination by September 1, 1942, and who before that date were called or volunteered for military service or joined the F.B.I., would be admitted on motion, without taking the exam. At a meeting the following Monday, the faculty determined that students would be eligible to invoke the rule if they had completed fifty-five hours by the end of the fall

324. THE KAW 123 (1942).

325. *Dean Price's Cosmopolitan History and His Informality Mislead Coeds Passing Law School*, WASHBURN REV., May 9, 1941

326. *Enrollment 119 Over Last Year*, WASHBURN REV., Sept. 26, 1941, at 1.

semester. The faculty deferred for later consideration the question whether the LL.B. should be awarded to students who were admitted to the bar under the rule but had not completed all hours required for the degree, no doubt because of accreditation issues that would arise. Faculty urged students who received a draft notice to notify the school immediately so that the instructor could provide for a special examination or make some other arrangement for credit depending on the individual case.

The AALS adopted an emergency rule permitting students called into the armed forces to receive credit for an entire semester's work if they had completed half the course and passed an examination over that work. Mid-semester examinations were administered for the first time during the first week of April 1942.[327] At a dinner on April 3, held in connection with the Shawnee County bar meeting and with several hundred in attendance, eligible students "were inducted into the practice and given diplomas."[328] Two six-week summer sessions were planned during which students could complete as many as twelve credit hours. Then, the school moved to a schedule with three, 16-week trimesters, starting in July, November, and March. The school undertook other heroic efforts to help students nearing graduation to complete their degrees before leaving for the armed forces. Some students facing induction were allowed to take additional hours, and in at least one instance to take a total of twenty hours in a single semester, to complete graduation requirements early. Shortly before the war, the faculty had toughened the absence rule by prohibiting students from taking examinations if they had ten absences in a three-hour course or seven absences in a two-hour course. Students with seven to nine absences in a three-hour class or six absences in a two-hour class had to achieve a C on the exam to receive credit. After the war started, the matter was made discretionary with the instructor.

Some students remembered extraordinary accommodations beyond official ones reflected in surviving records. Most of the remaining members of Ray S. Schulz's '43 entering class were married and had been classified 3A by their draft boards but they suddenly were reclassified 1A.

> I and the others were facing a call from the draft board but we still had one and a half years to complete to graduate.... Professor Kennie Wagner

327. *Departing Men Get Present—Early Exams*, WASHBURN REV., Mar. 20, 1942.
328. R.S. Barnett, *Hash, Country Style*, 10 J. KAN. B. ASS'N 439, 441 (1942).

{Bless his heart} announced to the remaining five that he would teach enough hours in courses we needed for us to earn a full semester by starting classes at 5:30 A.M. running to 10:30 A.M. all week long. The thing I am proud of was his willingness to do this and our willingness to accomplish it....Washburn law school would credit any of us who went to war before we could finish our last semester as having satisfied the requirement for graduation.[329]

Glenn Archer '46 recalled completing Suretyship Law, with an 1,100-page textbook, in just one month.[330]

The Supreme Court in 1939 adopted a rule requiring applicants for the bar in June 1943 to have completed a bachelor's degree prior to starting law school. Washburn announced it would apply that rule as an admission requirement for student entering in September 1941 and prohibit new students from pursuing the six-year program in which the first year of law school could be counted as the last year of the bachelor's degree program. The faculty expressed the view that three years of college and four years of law study would be preferable for a seven-year program. Such a program would comply with the Supreme Court's new rule since the University could treat the first of the four years of law study as the last year of the bachelor's degree, so that students could start the three years required for the law degree after completing the bachelor's degree. Price speculated that other Kansas universities might be persuaded to count Washburn law hours toward their bachelor's degrees on the theory that a plan permitting students to study more law in Kansas than elsewhere might persuade Kansans to remain in Kansas who otherwise would select out-of-state law schools and never return.[331] The issue was not resolved because six weeks after the attack on Pearl Harbor, the Court withdrew the new rule and reverted to the rule that became effective in 1940, still requiring bar applicants to have both bachelor's and law degrees but permitting the six-year course.

Price's background was in business. Not surprisingly, then, he agreed to collaborate with Washburn's Department of Economics to allow its students to take relevant law courses to equip them "to meet today's business conditions."[332]

---

329. E-mail from Ray S. Schulz to James Concannon (Apr. 27, 2002).
330. *Special Feature*, THE CIRCUIT RIDER 16 (Spring 1989).
331. Minutes, Washburn Coll. Sch. of Law faculty meeting (July 21, 1941).
332. *Law Classes Aid Economics*, WASHBURN REV., Feb. 6, 1942.

For example, students specializing in accounting were authorized to take such courses as Contracts, Bills and Notes, Private Corporations, and Federal Taxation. Professor Hugh G. Wales, head of the Department of Economics, claimed Washburn was the only school in the Midwest "that has worked out law courses in collaboration with fields of business and enterprise."[333] Price likewise encouraged political science students to take law courses.

Despite these efforts to expand the base of students, enrollment declined dramatically. The school reduced the number of classes. Resources diminished. Ralph S. Rice had joined the faculty in January 1941, replacing Edward Osborn who had been forced by ill health to give up his teaching duties in the middle of the fall semester. By March 1942, Rice added to his Washburn teaching responsibilities work as Law Clerk for United States District Judge Walter Huxman, whose former clerk John Shamberg '37 was leaving for induction into the Army. Immediately before coming to Washburn, Rice had been a lawyer for the Reconstruction Finance Corporation and the National Labor Relations Board. He received his LL.B. in 1932 at the University of South Dakota, where he was a student under Lester Feezer. He then practiced in South Dakota for seven years, first in private practice and then as Assistant Attorney General. He received an LL.M. from Harvard in 1940. Rice's place in Washburn's history is that, in the fall of 1941, he offered the school's first separate course in Legal Writing. He published an extensive article on the Wagner Act.[334] The war interrupted his promising teaching career and before the fall term in 1942, Rice was granted a leave of absence to work in the Alien Property Custodian's Division in Washington, D.C. He did not return to Washburn. After the war, he resumed law teaching in 1947 at the University of Cincinnati, with taxation as his primary teaching and research interest, then in 1952 joined the faculty at U.C.L.A. Law School, where he was named Connell Professor of Law in 1964.

A number of law schools suspended operations until the end of the war because there were so few students. President Byron Stoffer decided to keep Washburn Law School open, saying "Altho Washburn cannot operate its law department without a large deficit I feel that we must make the sacrifice in order to maintain its continuity."[335] For the 1942–43 academic year, Dorothy

---

333. *Economics, Law Classes to Integrate*, WASHBURN REV., Feb. 13, 1942.

334. Ralph S. Rice, *The Wagner Act: Its Legislative History and Its Relation to National Defense*, 8 OHIO ST. L. J. 17 (1941).

335. TOPEKA ST. J., Mar. 17, 1942.

22. Dean Price with Dorothy Tyner '41, first full-time woman faculty member

Davidson Tyner '41 was appointed as Instructor of Law, replacing Rice. She was the first woman to be a full-time law professor in Kansas, and was among the earliest women nationally to hold such a position. That year, Tyner taught Domestic Relations, Legal Bibliography, and Property II and co-taught Federal Taxation with Dean Price. She had graduated sixth in her class and became Law Librarian for 1941–42. She had performed extra duties as Secretary during the second semester when Mrs. Platt's successor as Secretary resigned after only one and one-half years.

There were only thirty-two students in the fall of 1942, including six unclassified students, apparently from other departments. Price began to look for other things to do. In the summer of 1942, Governor Payne Ratner named him Director-Secretary of the Kansas Industrial Development Board. Washburn's Regents decided to retain Price as Dean while he held this seemingly full-time position. They announced that Professor Wagner would be "in more active charge of the school instruction and daily administration."[336] In February 1943,

336. TOPEKA ST. J., June 4, 1942.

Price was named one of twenty-four members of a five-state regional War Labor Relations Board. On March 12, he agreed to become the next President of Kansas State Teachers College in Emporia, starting in the summer. Public announcement of his appointment was delayed two weeks, awaiting formal action by Emporia's governing board. He stayed at Emporia for just two years before moving to Denver in 1945, a move attributed to his wife's health issues.[337] He immediately became dean of the University of Denver Schools of Law and Business. In September 1947, Price was appointed Acting Chancellor of the University and in April 1948 was named Chancellor. However, he left the position abruptly in October, just seven months later, upon the discovery of an affair with a faculty member in a University department.[338] He moved to La Jolla, California, to open a law practice. At age 80, he still was active as a trust advisor for California firm. He died in 1994, at age 88.

The plan for 1943–44 was to have two full-time faculty members, Hambleton and Tyner. Professor Wagner accepted a position as Assistant General Counsel for the Kansas Corporation Commission, although he continued to teach one course each term. He entered the Navy in 1944. He returned to the K.C.C. after the war and again taught part-time before moving to Washington, D.C. in January 1947 to become an attorney for the Federal Power Commission. In 1951, he joined the legal department of Natural Gas Pipeline Company in Chicago and in 1956 became a partner with a large Chicago firm, Ross & O'Keefe, a position he held until his death from cancer in 1964 at age 55.

Schedules were issued showing Tyner would teach State Taxation, Introductory Law, Torts I, Torts II, Constitutional Law and Domestic Relations during 1943–44. However, she left just before the start of the fall term to join the legal

---

337. *Three Kansas State Schools*, KANSAS HISTORICAL QUARTERLY 101, at 109–112 (1946) (address by Price's father as President at the annual meeting of the Kansas State Historical Society).

338. Telephone conversation on October 6, 2009, with Steven Fisher, Archivist, Penrose Library, University of Denver, after he reviewed materials in Volume 14 of *University of Denver Historical Sketches* in the Leslie W. Scofield Collection, including a letter dated May 11, 1950, from Caleb F. Gates, Professor of History to President Arthur G. Coons of Occidental College, entitled "James F. Price—Concerning His Leaving the University of Denver," and "James F. Price: Chancellor of the University of Denver, 1947–48" by Leslie Scofield. Price's telegram of resignation blamed ill health and the need for complete rest. *Price Quits As U. Of Denver Chancellor; Health, Need for Complete Rest Blamed*, DENVER POST, Oct. 22, 1948, at 1.

staff of the War Production Board in Kansas City.[339] It is unclear whether she was encouraged to leave as a cost-cutting measure to address sharply declining enrollment. Tyner recalled in an oral history that she "didn't care much for the new Dean," so that when she received an offer from the War Production Board, she "got out of the teaching job."[340] After the war, Tyner settled in Anchorage, Alaska, and throughout the 1970s was a state court district judge there.

When Price announced his departure, there was speculation Harry K. Allen would return as Dean, since his term on the Supreme Court had ended less than three months earlier. Due to low enrollment, however, the issue of naming Price's successor was put on hold. Antrim Hambleton now was the only full-time faculty member and by default was Acting Dean. Allen and Howard Jones '28, an experienced former full-time faculty member, agreed to teach additional classes to fill gaps left by the departures of Tyner and part-time faculty members called to war. Hambleton did what he could to maintain as much normalcy as possible. The annual spring picnic with the local bar was scheduled as usual on May 30, 1944.

The entire College switched to a trimester system of 16-week semesters to permit full participation in the Navy's College V-12 Program, but regular summer sessions with concentrated classes were held at the same time. The Navy used the old Theta house as a barracks and complained about the lounge furniture there, noting that there was nice furniture in the Law School lounge, four divans and two chairs, that wasn't being used. The furniture had been purchased with Student Bar Association funds but Hambleton reluctantly agreed to loan it to the Navy when President Stoffer explained that cooperating with the Navy would increase the chance of retaining the V-12 program and that if the V-12 program were not retained "the chances of keeping the law school open would be greatly decreased."[341]

339. *New Semester Finds Many New Faculty, Changes*, WASHBURN REV., Nov. 5, 1943.

340. Transcript of oral history interview with Tyner conducted for the Alaska Bar Association, at 4.

341. *Memo In Re Law School Lounge Furniture* signed by Bryan S. Stoffer and A.M. Hambleton, dated Feb. 18, 1944. ROY BIRD, WASHBURN THROUGH THE YEARS 98 (1997), states that students protested the attempt to commandeer the furniture "so the administration decided not to bother." The memorandum contradicts this statement, reciting that the furniture had been moved at 1:15 p.m. the day before, following Stoffer's visit to the Dean's office at 9:50 a.m.

4

THE POST-WAR YEARS (1945–1959)

When the war ended, students whose law studies it interrupted began to return to school. The G.I. Bill made it possible for veterans in large numbers to attend both college and law school. In the fall of 1945, there were seventy veterans on campus, including sixteen in the Law School. Lack of housing for married veterans was a major problem. By January 1946, enrollment campus-wide ballooned to 804 students, forty in the law school. A month later, the Law School was the College's most rapidly expanding department and had ninety students, more than seventy of them veterans.

Even though it was mid-academic year, the school desperately needed another full-time teacher. Richard C. Donnelly, a Washburn graduate who received a Ph.B. in 1936 and an LL.B. in 1938, had just been discharged from the service and was hired with the title Instructor of Law. He had been a lawyer with the Federal Land Bank in Wichita before the war.

That spring and the following year were spent re-starting not only academic but also social life. Delta Theta Phi reactivated with returning veteran John Hayes '46 as its only carry-over active member. The holiday formal dinner/dance was held in December at the Roof Garden of the Jawhawk Hotel. A Law School team played intramural basketball. The Student Bar Association started an annual tradition of adopting a family for Christmas and later voted that law students would be permanent volunteer donors for the Topeka Blood Bank. Reverting to pre-war patterns, a law student was elected student body president that year and two of the next three years as well. The seniors' custom of carrying canes, which was abandoned during the war due to lack

23. Senior cane rack

of enrollment, was resumed in the fall of 1946 when the Phi Alpha Delta law fraternity presented a cane rack to the school.[342] It had spaces for thirty-four canes, including permanent ones for Deans Hambleton and Allen. Stickball games ensued outside Boswell Hall, using canes and pine cones.[343]

Still, the veterans' experiences in war affected their approach to their studies. One veteran observed:

> For the most part, we were of a different frame of mind than the undergraduates and non-veterans. There were few of us who could have afforded the legal education without the GI Bill of Rights. We were out there for business. There wasn't a great deal of coke drinking or bridge playing. If we were on campus we were in class or studying.[344]

Senator Bob Dole '52 later put it this way:

> I wasn't interested in hanging out at the student union or going to campus parties. Like most of the men and women who had been in the war and were now in school, I had a new seriousness about my education. I wanted to learn more than mere keys to success. I was searching for meaning. I had a new appreciation for the American way of law, justice, and government. I had seen firsthand in the bombed-out villages and the shredded, mangled bodies where less noble forms of government could lead. Somehow, these memories removed the study of the rule of law from the realm of the purely pedantic and philosophical, and put real faces on it.[345]

The school retained for a time the innovation of two six-week summer sessions but soon abandoned the accelerated trimester system and returned to offering two regular eighteen-week semesters. More faculty were needed, since enrollment for 1946–47 would grow to 144 students, 80% of them ex-servicemen. Former Dean William R. Arthur agreed to be Visiting Professor for a year after being named Professor Emeritus at Colorado. Professor Frank V. Flaska was a graduate of the University of Illinois College of Law and practiced

342. *P.A.D.'s Present Cane Rack to Law School*, WASHBURN REV., Sept. 27, 1946.

343. James W. Scoville '50, Class Notes, Washburn School of Law Alumni Weekend, Aug. 25–26, 1995.

344. McLane, *supra* note 3, at 13.

345. BOB DOLE, ONE SOLDIER'S STORY 262–63 (2005).

in Illinois from 1934 until he entered the Army in 1943. Earl T. Crawford was hired with the rank of Instructor. He practiced in Sedalia, Missouri, after receiving his LL.B. in 1928 from Washington University in St. Louis but always had an interest in academic life. He took time out from practice to earn an LL.M. in 1935 at Northwestern. He was the author of seven articles, the most recent one in the *Cornell Law Review*, and two books, *The Law of Group Insurance* (1936) and *Statutory Construction* (1940). Mindful of the disruption caused by the war, the catalogue soon stated that "in normal times," there would be five full-time faculty.

Hambleton continued as Acting Dean for the fourth consecutive year, and the fifth since he joined the faculty. When the Board of Regents on February 26, 1947, confirmed that Glenn L. Archer '46 would become Dean on July 1, it also, in a fitting gesture of appreciation for Hambleton's sacrifice and service in difficult times, struck the word "Acting" from his title and made him the Dean he had hoped to be a decade earlier. A luncheon in his honor at the Jayhawk Hotel in May drew 230 students, alumni, and faculty. Sixty SBA members presented Hambleton an executive desk. Seniors presented a portrait of him to be hung in the school.

Archer, like Dean Arthur before him, surely is one of few individuals in the history of legal education to be named Dean within only one year of graduation from law school. When Archer started his legal studies, however, he already was thirty-eight years old and was a prominent Kansan. He had been a public school teacher and administrator after graduating from college in 1927, holding positions as superintendent of schools in Almena and county superintendent in Norton County. Along the way he earned an M.A. from the University of Colorado and a journalism degree from the University of Iowa. In 1936, he assisted Governor Alf Landon's campaign for President, drafting a speech on educational policy. In 1939, he became Administrative Assistant to Governor Payne Ratner, for whom he had worked during the election campaign. A gifted orator, Archer frequently traveled the state to give speeches for the Governor. There was talk he one day would be the Republican nominee for Governor himself. He served as President of the Kansas Native Sons and gave the annual toast to Kansas. When Governor Ratner's term ended, Archer became Director of Professional Relations for the Kansas State Teachers Association. Later, he combined that position with work as Associate Director of the Legislative Division of the National Education Association, maintaining an office part-

Glenn L. Archer
Dean, School of Law

24. Glenn L. Archer '46,
Dean 1947–1948

time in Washington. Archer was co-chair of the 1944 White House Conference on Rural Education, held in the East Room of the White House with President Franklin Roosevelt as keynote speaker.

Even though Archer already held three degrees and was offered the position of Director of the Legislative Division of N.E.A., he decided to "embark on a mid-life career change that encompassed the arduous tasks of obtaining a law degree—something I had always wanted to do."[346] He enrolled in August 1944 and completed law school in twenty-two months under the accelerated plan then in effect. He graduated *magna cum laude* while still managing operations of family farms in Norton totaling 5,000 acres and serving as a member of the Kansas State Board of Education. He was president of the Student Bar Association during his final semester. According to Archer's autobiography, Washburn's President

---

346. GLENN L. ARCHER, THE DREAM LIVES ON 55 (1982).

Bryan Stoffer approached him while he was still a student about becoming Dean immediately upon his graduation,[347] but Archer felt he should defer the opportunity for a year to gain experience. Instead, he joined the Topeka firm of Allen and Ascough.[348] "Allen," of course, was Harry K. Allen. Before becoming Dean, Archer took graduate courses at Northwestern Law School.

Archer taught Torts and Corporations. He persuaded Hambleton to continue teaching full-time, foregoing his announced plan to retire at the conclusion of his time as Dean. Richard Donnelly left in 1947 to be a Sterling Fellow at Yale while pursuing an S.J.D. He then taught for two years at the University of Virginia's law school before becoming Professor of Law at Yale. Donnelly is the only Washburn graduate who has taught at either of these schools.

Schuyler W. Jackson replaced Donnelly, teaching procedure courses and International Law. A 1930 Harvard Law School graduate, Jackson had been a part-time Lecturer on International Law the previous two years while serving as Reporter for the Kansas Supreme Court, a position he held for nearly six years. Before that, he had been a research attorney for the Court for three years. His initial position after law school had been with the Topeka firm founded by his father, Fred S. Jackson, a former Attorney General of Kansas, member of Congress, and part-time Lecturer at Washburn between 1915 and 1920. The new professor had just won second prize in the 1947 Ross Essay Contest sponsored by the American Bar Association.[349] Most years, only the winning essay was published in the ABA's *Journal*. That year, the editors published both essays "because Mr. Jackson's essay was a competent and thoughtful exposition on a subject of increasing importance," international legislation.

Enrollment reached 195 for 1947–48. Monthly luncheons with the Topeka Bar Association were re-started. Governor Frank Carlson and Attorney General Ed Arn were among the speakers. The student editorial board for the *Journal of the Bar Association of Kansas* was reactivated and for the first time a student was named Editor-in-Chief, Derbert Scott '48.

Archer used his public speaking skills to increase the Law School's visibility. He agreed to be commencement speaker at high school graduations throughout

---

347. *Id.* at 66.

348. *Glenn Archer to Topeka Law Firm*, undated newspaper article attached to Archer's unofficial transcript (on file in Washburn Law School).

349. Schuyler W. Jackson, *International Legislation—Discussions of Methods for Its Improvement*, 34 AM. B. ASS'N J. 206 (1948).

the state. In May 1948, Archer flew to Washington to attend the annual meeting of the American Law Institute. A representative of the executive committee of a new organization, Protestants and Other Americans United for the Separation of Church and State, contacted him there. The committee wanted Archer to be its first Executive Director. After three months of soul searching, Archer accepted the position and submitted his resignation as Dean in early August. He continued as Executive Director of Americans United for twenty-eight years until retiring in 1976, lobbying Congress frequently, helping to shape the country's church/state policy, and becoming a first-name acquaintance of the country's leaders. In 1992, Washburn awarded him the Honorary Doctor of Education degree and in 1993 the Washburn Law School Association presented him with its Distinguished Service Award.

Hambleton, now holding the formal title Dean Emeritus as did Harry K. Allen, served briefly, for a third time, as Acting Dean until the Regents could name a new dean.[350] Hambleton continued to teach full-time through 1950 and part-time through the next decade until he was almost eighty. He still "was able, in a special way, to communicate the law as a living system to his students" and they called him "The Grand Old Man of Contracts."[351] When he died in 1967, Professor Jim Ahrens aptly wrote of him:

> Dean Hambleton was great in the tradition of men who are great because they form the cement of society. Not particularly noted on a casual inspection, they are the ones who hold the social structure together and impart to it the cohesiveness necessary for its survival.[352]

THE JACKSON YEARS

On September 15, 1948, the Regents selected Schuyler Jackson as Dean. He was forty-four years old. Howard Jones '28, who combined the perspectives of full-time professor, practitioner and Acting Dean, later described Jackson's appointment as

---

350. *Dean Jackson Heads Largest Washburn Law School; 275 Overflow Classes,* WASHBURN REV., Sept. 24, 1948.

351. James R. Ahrens, *In Memoriam,* 7 WASHBURN L. J. 283, 284 (1968).

352. *Id.*

25. Schuyler Jackson, Dean 1948–1958,
Professor 1947–1958

a recognition of his scholarly achievements and of his fine character. He was endowed with an even temperament, and known by all for his honesty, integrity, humility and kindness. He was always the same. Never up in the clouds or down in the dumps. All who knew him admired and respected him for his intellect and fine sense of values. Perhaps his greatest qualifications for his position as Dean were his studious spirit, and his knowledge of what constitutes proper legal training to prepare young people for the practice of law—a qualification sometimes overlooked by those imbued with academic rank and trappings.[353]

Mel Poland ’49, one of Jackson’s students and later his faculty colleague, used similar words to describe him. “Jackson would be considered by many as a man of small physical stature,” he wrote, “but to everyone who was privi-

353. Memorial to Justice Schuyler W. Jackson, 197 Kan. xvi, xviii (1966).

leged to know him, he was a giant in the things that count most in this walk through life—honesty, integrity, humility, kindness, service…without thought of personal reward." Poland added, "His youthful outlook and attitude, his faith in youth, his enthusiasm for the law and his discriminating mind made him an interesting and inspiring teacher."[354]

However, he could have his stern side. "As aptly as of any man," Justice Alfred Schroeder remarked, it could be said of Jackson "that in his work as a judge, and in all his going out and coming in as a lawyer, teacher and citizen, he feared God and nobody else!"[355]

Jackson emphasized the lawyer's role as writer. In 1954, he opined that a student "should learn English—not only spoken English but English composition. Great lawyers, such as Cardozo, Holmes and Learned Hand were men who knew literature. It is important for a lawyer to be able to express his own thoughts, but equally important to be able to grasp the thoughts of others."[356] However, Jackson was not enamored of some of the formality of academic legal writing. In one article, his only footnote read as follows:

> We are using sparingly the academic affectation, the footnote, which is so much in vogue in most of the law reviews of the country. Our reasons for not using it, are: We hope that members of the Bar, who happen to read this article will let their eyes run over the citations made herein, and that they may do so without putting down their pipes for the purpose of using a finger on each hand to trace the citation which goes with a particular point. Further, we dislike to make the printer unnecessary work in setting up an article thus, perhaps increasing printing costs. Lastly, we have a pet aversion to footnotes, especially when they are used, as they often are, to split a citation in two. It has been painful to note that both the Washburn and Kansas University sections of this Journal have, within the last two years, taken up this asinine footnote practice.[357]

Enrollment during Dean Jackson's first year reached 275, the largest number in the school's history. With classrooms overflowing, MacVicar Chapel was

354. Melvin C. Poland, *In Memoriam*, 4 WASHBURN L.J. 176 (1965).

355. Memorial to Justice Schuyler W. Jackson, *supra* note 353.

356. *Id.*

357. Schuyler W. Jackson, *More To Do About Master Brown and Missie Gong*, 20 J. KAN. B. ASS'N 288 (1952).

used as a scheduled classroom for the first time, for Ed Rooney's Criminal Law class of 130 students. There were three vacancies on a five-person faculty. Not only did Archer depart, Earl Crawford left to be a Visiting Professor for one year at the University of Kansas City and the following year at KU, and Frank Flaska returned to private practice. Due to Archer's distraction and the shortage of other faculty members, President Stoffer became involved in faculty recruitment. During the summer of 1948, Stoffer planned a trip back to the University of Chicago campus where he had received his Ph.D. He asked the law dean there to recommend recent graduates who might be interested in law teaching. He interviewed several of those suggested, including James R. Ahrens. Ahrens had taken the Illinois bar exam in 1947 and was admitted to the bar before completing requirements for his law degree in May 1948. He then was a special assistant for the U.S. Treasury Department. Not long after the interview, Ahrens received a letter from Stoffer extending to him an offer to join the faculty. Ahrens accepted without even discussing the position with any member of the law faculty, although he was familiar with Topeka from serving as a briefing officer at Forbes Air Force Base during the war. Ahrens would be a member of the full-time faculty longer than anyone else in the school's history, forty years.

A second new instructor, Lloyd Hall, also had just graduated in 1948 from the University of Nebraska. He taught full-time at Washburn for only three years before entering practice in Topeka and becoming a part-time Lecturer. The third new faculty member, Marvin Larson '40, taught full-time for eleven years. He had been Republic County Attorney for four years, was attorney and general manager of a bus line, then practiced in Topeka with John Dean before becoming attorney for the State Board of Social Welfare in 1946.[358]

Soon, there would be other changes in the faculty. In 1950, when Hambleton stopped teaching full-time, Robert J. Fowks was named Associate Professor. Fowks had moved to Topeka two years earlier and was a part-time Lecturer in 1949 while he was in private practice. He was a 1942 law graduate of the University of Missouri, where he was Note Editor of the law review. He earned an M.B.A. from Harvard in 1943 before leaving for military service and was Assistant Professor of Economics at Missouri after the war before coming to Topeka.

---

358. *Dean Jackson Heads Largest Washburn Law School; 275 Overflow Classes,* WASHBURN REV., Sept. 24, 1948.

26. Roy R. Bartlett '49, Professor 1950–1959 and 1973–1982

Fowks returned to Missouri to practice in Joplin after one year at Washburn but rejoined the faculty in 1953, remaining until his retirement in 1981. Also in 1950, Roy R. Bartlett '49 replaced Elizabeth Bowers '48 as full-time Law Librarian and part-time teacher, initially with the rank of Instructor and later Assistant Professor. He would remain in that dual position until 1958, when he became a full-time classroom teacher for academic year 1958–59. Bartlett was called to military service just before the 1951–52 academic year. Professor Ahrens, who had been on leave due to illness the prior year, took his place as Law Librarian and taught only part-time that year. John Bohannon '52 was the Law Librarian the next year until Bartlett returned from the service in mid-year.

The school added two faculty members in 1951, the year Lloyd Hall resigned. One was a Washburn graduate, Melvin C. Poland '49. He had completed an LL.M. in 1950 at the University of Michigan, then clerked for a year for Judge Walter Huxman of the United States Court of Appeals for the Tenth Circuit. The other new faculty member was an experienced professor, Chester James

Antieau. He had taught at Creighton Law School during academic year 1946–47 and for the next four years at his alma mater, Detroit College of Law. Antieau just had received an LL.M. from Michigan, and he completed requirements for the S.J.D. during his first year at Washburn. Antieau got the attention of students quickly, making it clear that slacking off would not be permitted. He locked the classroom door as soon as the class bell rang so that latecomers could not attend. Students got even one day when Antieau was late for class. They locked him out. Antieau stormed to the Dean's office and demanded that Dean Jackson do something about it, but the Dean responded only with uncontrolled laughter.[359] Professor Ahrens picked up Antieau's practice too, but the Fire Marshal soon forced both of them to abandon it.

With a new dean and so many new faculty members, there was a predictable reexamination of the curriculum. Several courses were combined into "more general courses to give students a broader picture of the different phases of the law."[360] There were four year-long courses in the first year, Civil Procedure, Torts, Contracts, and Property, plus Criminal Law and Criminal Procedure. By 1952, twenty-nine upper level hours were required, unless waived, in Evidence, Bills and Notes, Business Associations, Constitutional Law, Wills, Trusts, Conflict of Laws, and Taxation. In 1954, the one-hour course in Legal Ethics once again became required. By prescribing sixty of the eighty-two hours needed for graduation, Washburn had more required hours than most law schools and emphasis on required courses remained a hallmark of the curriculum for thirty years. Semesters were lengthened so that the 96 weeks of instruction required in 1946 grew to 99 weeks in 1951 and to 108 weeks in 1952, the same number that had been required in the 1920s and far more than required by AALS and ABA standards or by KU. The faculty simply "decided to go our own way."[361]

The post-war influx of students taxed faculty resources and, as enrollment neared 300, the capacity of Boswell Hall. The graduating class of 1949 had seventy-eight members, including the 1,000th graduate. Because students received diplomas in alphabetical order, Harry W. Saums was identified as that graduate.[362] The class of 1950, with 117 graduates, was the largest in the school's

359. Conversation with Hon. Fred Jackson '60, Dean Jackson's son.
360. WASHBURN U. SCH. OF LAW BULLETIN (Apr. 1949).
361. Minutes, Washburn U. Sch. of Law faculty meeting (Mar. 20, 1952).
362. WASHBURN UNIVERSITY BULLETIN (Nov. 1949).

history and remained the largest until 1973. Mirroring national trends resulting from the war, the number of law graduates at Washburn actually declined to 304 in the decade of the 1940s, from 385 in the 1930s, even though population nationally increased by thirty million. The rapid rise in enrollment after the war nevertheless worried some lawyers and non-lawyers. Dean Jackson's response was remarkably similar to what deans would say fifty years later:

> The fear of laymen and some lawyers that the bar was becoming overcrowded, may need to be revised. Especially is this true, when it is remembered that the increased complexity of government during the last twenty years has increased rather than decreased the need of the country for lawyers.[363]

While 15% of the students came from outside Kansas, Washburn was still overwhelmingly a Kansas school. The school started an informal placement service, relying heavily on alumni both in private practice and with corporations to help graduates find employment. An alumni directory, *Who's Where*, was published to encourage graduates, particularly more recent ones, to cooperate in their practices.

Student interest in publishing in the KBA *Journal* varied from year to year, and in some years more students from one Kansas law school published than from the other school. In November 1949, a student from each school submitted a case note on the same Ohio case. The *Journal* published both notes, adding an editor's note referring to the similar note in the other school's section.[364] Ordinarily, Washburn's Editor-in-Chief served only one semester, although a single student served for two semesters in three instances between 1947 and 1960[365] and a different student was appointed just for the summer semester in 1950 and 1951. The burden on the Law Review Board did not approximate the burden a board of editors faces today. For example, the staff for 1948–49 was responsible for only fifty-eight pages of the *Journal*, spread over four issues, and the next year's staff produced just thirty-nine pages. Some members of

---

363. Schuyler Jackson, "Annual Report of the Dean, 1951–52."

364. The Washburn student's case note was Olin M. Stansbury, Jr., *Torts—Prenatal Injuries—Right of an Infant to Sue*, 18 J. KAN. B. ASS'N 159 (1958).

365. They were James L. Berlin '53 in the spring and fall of 1952, Gene A. Powell '55 during academic year 1954–55, and William L. Parker, Jr. '57 during academic year 1956–57.

the bar complained that allocating even that number of pages to the schools was excessive.[366] However, there were many substantial student pieces. Joseph W. Morris '47 had the distinction not merely of having his student article selected for publication in the *Journal* but also of having it published as the lead article. His discussion of the ability to transfer property to the grantor and another as joint tenants was prefaced by a rare editor's note that it "covers a very timely subject in Kansas and it is believed that it will prove of considerable value to the members of the Bar," perhaps becoming the subject of proposed legislation.[367] A 1948 comment by Roy O. Sage '49 prompted an amendment to the Kansas escheat statute.[368]

In the fall of 1949, Editor-in-Chief Dean Gibson and Associate Editor Thomas Hurst '50 attended the first national conference of editors of law reviews in Chicago. Dean Jackson appointed a faculty committee in November 1951 to investigate publication of a law review, either alone or jointly with KU, but KU already was planning to commence publishing a separate review in 1952. The idea surfaced again the next academic year, but it would be 1960 before the first issue of Volume 1 of a separate *Washburn Law Journal* would appear.

In 1950, the Association of the Bar of the City of New York sponsored the first National Moot Court Competition. Washburn entered a team for the first time in 1951 and it reached the regional semi-finals. Team members were Robert Groff '52, James Berlin '53, and Rolland Cox '52. The Topeka Bar Association and the Student Bar Association provided funding to cover travel costs to the competition in St. Louis. H. M. Ives and Sons printed the briefs for free. The following year, sixty-two teams competed nationally. Washburn's team of Thomas Wood '54 and Charles McCarter '53 finished second in the regional competition, defeating KU and Lincoln University of Missouri be-

---

366. Report of the Editor of the Bar Journal, *Report of the Proceedings of the Sixty-Ninth Annual Meeting of the Bar Association of the State of Kansas*, 20 J. KAN. B. ASS'N 31, 38 (1951). The utility of the law school sections was defended, in part, on the ground they made students more aware of the bar association and thus more likely to become active members after graduation.

367. Joseph W. Morris, *May a Grantor Convey Property Directly to Himself and Another as Joint Tenants in Kansas?*, 15 J. KAN. B. ASS'N 241 (1947).

368. Roy O. Sage, *A New Escheat Statute or a Legislative Oversight (G.S. 1947 Supp. 58–508)?*, 17 J. KAN. B. ASS'N 102 (1948). Report of the Editor of the Bar Journal, *supra* note 366, at 38, credits the comment with prompting amendment of the statute.

fore losing in the finals to Vanderbilt. In the early rounds, teams were allotted thirty-five minutes to argue; in the finals, judges questioned the students for three hours. Because of the number of teams in the region, both finalists qualified to compete among fifteen teams in the national final rounds. Wood and McCarter went to New York, where they tied for third place with Vanderbilt, losing in the semi-final round to the ultimate winner, Georgetown. They defeated Southern Methodist in the quarter-finals. The issue argued that year was the constitutionality of a state alien land law that denied those not eligible for citizenship the right to own land and escheated to the state all land transferred to them. McCarter wrote that the team's performance "marked the school as a national institution and able to rate successfully with other schools throughout the country. It increased the pride of the student body in their institution, and it educated the law student in the practical application of legal theory."[369]

Wood competed again the following year, teamed with John Carlson '55. The team did not return to New York but tied for third among seventeen teams in the region, losing to host Washington University in St. Louis in the semi-finals. The issue that year was timely, whether a college professor could be fired for refusing to state whether he was a Communist. Washburn's team came to be chosen in a competition held as part of fall Law Day homecoming activities. Routinely, three Justices of the Kansas Supreme Court judged the competition.

In 1950–51, an informal legal assistance program was started to assist patients at the Winter V.A. Hospital. It introduced students to the lawyer's pro bono obligation to "meet a social need,"[370] but the volume of requests for assistance was small. In the fall of 1952, the Law School cooperated with the Topeka Bar Association in opening a Legal Aid Bureau downtown to provide legal services to those who could not afford a lawyer and to give law students "what they said they yearned for, namely 'a live client with a live case.'"[371] Initially, the office was open one day each week in the offices of Topeka Family Service at Fourth and Jackson. Students worked under the supervision of lawyers on a

---

369. Charles C. McCarter, *Washburn Goes to New York*, 21 J. KAN. B. ASS'N 286, 288 (1953).

370. WASHBURN UNIVERSITY BULLETIN 115 (Apr. 1952).

371. Raymond Briman, *Legal Aid in Topeka*, KAN. JUD. COUNCIL BULL. 10 (July 1954).

special TBA committee and sometimes full-time faculty. Senior law students observed the initial interview with the applicant for legal aid, then discussed the case with the lawyer, conducted legal research and fact investigation, and sometimes prepared pleadings. Dick Hite '53 was the first student participant.[372] Later, seniors and freshmen worked together as teams, primarily through the office of Topeka lawyer Ray Briman.[373]

Dr. Karl Menninger again was involved with the school, addressing occasional classes, annual banquets, and other events on topics such as the relation of psychiatry to criminal law and its use in the courts,[374] the need to improve penal institutions,[375] and insanity and criminal responsibility.[376]

Washburn's Student Bar Association became a charter member of the American Law Students Association and sent representatives to its annual meeting. Bill Tincher '53 served as National Secretary in 1951–52. The following year Lee Banks '54 was a national Vice-President while serving as President of the Tenth Circuit Association. Washburn was an active participant in regional ALSA meetings. Fourteen students attended the 1951 regional meeting in Albuquerque and, as a result, Washburn was chosen to host the 1953 meeting of ten regional schools. Washburn was host again in 1956.

A ROLE IN PUBLIC AFFAIRS

Law students who served their country in war understood when they returned home the importance of being heard on public issues. Three weeks before the general election in 1948, the Student Bar Association passed by a vote of 101–57 a resolution urging the people of Kansas to repeal the Prohibition Amendment of the Kansas Constitution that kept Kansas a "dry" state even after repeal of the Eighteenth Amendment of the United States Constitution.[377]

---

372. *Bar Briefs*, WASHBURN REV., Oct. 5, 1952.

373. *Legal Aid Bureau Into Fall Session*, WASHBURN REV., Nov. 18, 1955, at 6; Minutes, Washburn U. Sch. of Law faculty meeting (Nov. 11, 1957).

374. *Law Students Tour Penal Institutions*, WASHBURN REV., Nov. 21, 1952.

375. *Bar Members Hear Talk*, WASHBURN REV., Feb. 18, 1955, at 4.

376. *Karl Menninger Speaks to Moot Court and Law Students*, WASHBURN REV., Nov. 9, 1956, at 1.

377. *Bar Association Endorses Repeal By 101–57 Vote*, WASHBURN REV., Oct. 29, 1948.

Other monumental events were going on in the world outside the Law School. In 1951, three black lawyers trained at the Law School, Charles Scott, Sr. '48, John Scott '47, and Charles Bledsoe ex-'37, filed the landmark case of *Brown v. Board of Education* in the United States District Court of Kansas, challenging the maintenance of segregated elementary schools in Topeka. Washburn lawyers were on both sides of the case. Lester Goodell '25 was counsel for the school board, along with George Brewster '29. A three-judge panel of the District Court, relying on precedent beginning with *Plessy v. Ferguson,* upheld the constitutionality of segregated schools. Before the case was briefed before the United States Supreme Court, three Washburn professors engaged in a spirited exchange in the pages of the *Journal of the Bar Association of Kansas* about the merits of the District Court's opinion.

In the November issue, Professor Antieau identified nine reasons supporting his conclusion the District Court had "erred grievously," including that its opinion had misunderstood precedent, was contrary to the United Nations Charter, and was "not only legally wrong and indefensible, but morally evil and sociologically and economically pernicious to the welfare of this nation."[378] Antieau's strong language led some to suggest that he was questioning the integrity of the court and its judges.[379]

In the following issue, Dean Jackson asserted he would have submitted a companion piece for the November issue "[h]ad we read the final copy of the article before the same appeared in print." He pulled no punches. "Our colleague's article is volatile, one might say effervescent—a quality quite admirable in champagne. His exuberance often endears him as a friend, but we fear it has, in this matter, led him to adopt a non-judicial attitude and to overlook the specific facts and *ratio decidendi* of many of the cases."[380] Jackson acknowledged that the District Court's "revolutionary finding" of fact that segregation leads to a sense of inferiority and affects motivation to learn might undermine *Plessy* and its progeny. However, in Jackson's view, the District Court had reached the result required by precedent and only the Supreme Court, not a District

---

378. Chester J. Antieau, *The Ghost of Gong,* 20 J. KAN. B. ASS'N 211 (1951).

379. Melvin C. Poland, *Grievous Error,* 20 J. KAN. B. ASS'N 294, 295 (1952). Poland expressed confidence that Antieau did not have that intent but called Antieau's "loose choice of words" unfortunate.

380. Schuyler W. Jackson, *More To Do About Master Brown and Missie Gong,* 20 J. KAN. B. ASS'N 288 (1952).

Court, could overrule it. "Only a missionary-minded zealot," Jackson wrote of Antieau, "would allow the enthusiasm for his theories to so blind him that he would intimate that a trial court which made" such a revolutionary finding "might be lacking in courage, and might fear chastisement by having its judgment reversed."

Professor Poland, who had clerked for the author of the District Court's opinion, Judge Huxman, concurred with Dean Jackson, arguing that a lower court was not free to depart from binding precedent based on its view of what was morally justified. "The application of such a non-legal theological approach to the determination of legal questions, whether they be constitutional questions or other, would open the door for decisions based on the moral predilections of the particular judge, a highly undesirable if not intolerable result."[381] The Jackson and Poland articles provided little comfort for Washburn graduate Paul E. Wilson '40, the Assistant Attorney General assigned to brief and argue the case before the United States Supreme Court. Poland made it clear, "I do not wish to be understood as favoring the separate but equal doctrine and least of all its application to segregation within our public school systems. I fully agree with Professor Antieau that such a practice is morally evil as well as sociologically and economically pernicious."[382] His, and Jackson's, disagreement with Antieau was about whether any court other than the Supreme Court could overturn the separate but equal doctrine.

Yet another Washburn professor had a role in the *Brown* case. When the case was set for re-argument, Attorney General Harold Fatzer '33 and Wilson asked Professor Jim Ahrens, whom Wilson described in his book about the case as "an able and respected scholar,"[383] to research two questions: first, what was the historical evidence that Congress in submitting the Fourteenth Amendment, and the states in ratifying it, did or did not understand that it would abolish segregation in the public schools; and a second related question, whether Congress had power under section 5 of the Amendment to abolish segregation. The exhaustive paper Ahrens prepared was used extensively by Wilson in his brief.

---

381. Poland, *supra* note 379.

382. *Id.* at 304.

383. PAUL E. WILSON, A TIME TO LOSE: REPRESENTING KANSAS IN *BROWN V. BOARD OF EDUCATION* 165 (1995); *see also* Paul E. Wilson, *A Time to Lose*, J. S. CT. HISTORY 1, at 178 (1999).

STUDENT LIFE AND STABLE TIMES

Enrollment by women declined from pre-war levels. While thirteen women graduated in the five years from 1939 through 1943, it took twelve years for thirteen more women to graduate from 1947 through 1958, and there were none in the five years after that. In 1955, Dean Jackson instituted a separate graduation ceremony for "seniors" in the Washburn Law Wives Association that was formed that academic year, presenting them with P.H.T. degrees—for Putting Hubby Through. The organization continued until the mid-1970s, supporting its members and also supporting the school through service projects and fundraisers for special items like the Law School's silver service.

There were extracurricular diversions. In the spring of 1951, Gerald Michaud '51 and Bradley Post '53, then a junior in the college, won the National Intercollegiate Bridge Tournament held in Chicago. Post competed in the national finals again the following year as a 1L. Ping-pong also was popular. In the spring of 1952, Ted Morgan '56 defeated Jim Benfer '53 to win the Women's Council Ping-Pong Tournament. The game, with its name spelled backwards, inspired nine post-war alums to form the Free Society of GNIP GNOP, Inc., a group that still meets annually and later created GNIP GNOP awards to encourage outstanding student writing in the *Washburn Law Journal*.[384] In the spring of 1954, Robert J. Roth '55 and Cecil Merkel '55, as officers of Benson Chapter of Phi Alpha Delta, were invited to the Governor's office for a photo session with Vice President of the United States and fellow P.A.D., Richard M. Nixon, and the state's two Senators, Frank Carlson and Andrew Schoeppel. The photograph later appeared on the cover of the fraternity's national magazine.

The veterans who flooded the law school were part of what Tom Brokaw called the "greatest generation." It was indeed a time when future giants of the profession walked Boswell's halls. During their law school years, the forty-two members of the Class of 1952 not only studied with Bob Dole '52, a future majority leader of the United States Senate and Republican nominee

---

384. Regina Cassell, *Friends for Life*, WASHBURN ALUMNUS 10 (Spring 2001). According to Joseph W. Morris '47, the group picked the name when limited finances forced them to feature affordable distractions such as ping pong and horseshoes at their first meetings. *Id.* When their finances became more secure and they decided to contribute to the school, they initially chose to honor a professor with the "Goode Boy Award." When that professor left Washburn shortly thereafter, they ultimately chose to support the *Law Journal* instead.

for President, but also with future Chief Justice of the Kansas Supreme Court Richard Holmes '53, two United States District Judges, Sam A. Crow '52 and Patrick Kelly '53, Chief Judge of the United States Court of Military Appeals Albert Fletcher '51, leaders of the corporate world such as Ronald K. Richey '51, C.E.O. for Fortune 500 company Torchmark, Inc., and Dan Pinick '52, vice president of Boeing Corporation, as well as nationally-known trial lawyers including Gerald L. Michaud '51, Charles Fisher, Jr. '51, Bradley Post '53, and Richard C. Hite '53, who served as President of the National Conference of Commissioners on Uniform State Laws, to name only a few of the graduates of the period who achieved significant distinction.

The decency and comradery that long have characterized Washburn faculty and law students was clearly evident during these years and caused many applicants to choose Washburn. Chief Justice Holmes recalled the reception he received from Dean Jackson, Professor Fowks, and Secretary Christine Johnson when he contacted the Dean about attending Washburn. "I had just been brushed off an hour earlier by the Dean of [KU] who didn't seem to care whether I attended his law school or not. Dean Jackson rolled out the red carpet, including lunch, and my mind was made up."[385] Another student, Stan Sager, '57, had contracted polio while serving as a naval officer during the Korean War and was confined to a wheelchair when he wanted to attend law school. He wrote to KU, where he earned his bachelor's degree.

> The full response, which I still remember, was "You need not apply. We can not accommodate wheelchair students. Very truly yours..." It was signed by the then Dean.

> I wrote a similar letter to Washburn Law School. The response was an enthusiastic invitation. I applied and was accepted.

> On the day of my enrollment, I wheeled up to the front door of Boswell Hall and found to my absolute surprise that the array of steps was far longer, steeper, and more intimidating than anything I had seen in front of Green Hall at K.U. However, Dean Jackson was waiting for me. On seeing me, he emerged from the front door, whistled over his shoulder, then bounded down the steps followed by three students.

---

385. Class Notes, Washburn School of Law Alumni Weekend, Aug. 21–22, 1998.

The four carried me into the building. The Dean decided I was skinnier than the other student then attending in a wheelchair, so I was assigned to classrooms on the second floor since there was only one first floor classroom. Classroom assignments were juggled so that the heavier student could use the first floor classroom and the burden on the student body which carried both of us in and out, without reward, would be reduced.

The students and faculty carried me into the building and up to the second floor until I was able to get out of the wheelchair and propel myself on crutches by the end of my second year.[386]

The sensitivity of students to the needs of students like Sager was rooted in the school's environment. Two faculty members had overcome obvious disabilities. Professor Larson had a crippled left arm resulting from poor care by a country doctor but, as Professor Ahrens put it, "he taught his one hand to do the work of two." Dean Jackson's handicap was a speech impediment. "What people admired about him," one student recalled, "was that despite his handicap...he accomplished so much. That itself inspired others to have confidence in themselves."[387] Jackson's handicap also made his classroom tirades memorable. Wright Crummett '57 recalled Jackson "roaring at some hapless and deserving law student...'God Damath! If you canth thinkth like a lawyer, at leasth acth like a lawyer, and if you canth acth like a lawyer, at leasth lookth like a lawyer.'"[388] His students never forgot the definition of a demurrer: "Whath the hell?"[389]

Not surprisingly, veterans who had fought in World War II or in Korea were not overly intimidated by their professors. One day in Clyde Christey's '56 Property class,

A stray dog wandered into the third floor classroom, and "Professor" Poland decided he didn't want to share the podium with a dog, so he

---

386. Letter from Stanley C. Sager to W. Terrence Kilroy, dated March 30, 1993, reprinted in THE CIRCUIT RIDER 2 (Summer 1993).

387. McLane, *supra* note 3, at 13.

388. Class Notes, Washburn School of Law Alumni Weekend, Aug. 22–23, 1997.

389. James M. Caplinger '53, Class Notes, Washburn School of Law Alumni Weekend, Aug. 21–22, 1998.

27. Melvin C. Poland '49, Professor 1951–1966

took the dog by the collar and was going to oust him from the room. The dog was heels down, Mr. Al Phipps stated pretty loud, "Professor Poland, I believe you'll find that if you start your lecture, the dog will leave."[390]

Essentially open enrollment of course meant there were some law students who shouldn't become lawyers. In the early years after the war, there were problems with cheating. The faculty's response sometimes was subtle. Rules distributed for the fall 1948 exams concluded, "5. Law students in taking the examinations shall conduct themselves in such a manner as to comply with Julius Caesar's rule for his wife."[391] By spring semester 1950, the faculty was

---

390. Clyde Christey '56, Class Notes, Washburn School of Law Alumni Weekend, June 7–8, 1996. John Dekker '55 recalled the same incident but believed Ed Wheeler '55 made the comment. Class Notes, Washburn School of Law Alumni Weekend, Aug. 25–26, 1995.

391. Minutes, Washburn U. Sch. of Law faculty meeting (Jan. 6, 1949).

more direct, sending a letter to the Student Bar Association "regarding the prevalence of cheating," asking it to appoint a committee to work with the faculty "in improving the present system."[392] The faculty ultimately adopted a proctor system and thereafter faculty members were assigned to monitor each examination room, a practice that continued into the 1970s. Later, the faculty discussed the possibility of an Honor Code but decided to consider one only if a proposal was initiated by the Student Bar Association.[393]

An incident at the P.A.D. formal in April 1957 went beyond cheating. Professor Bartlett and Lloyd Hall, then a part-time teacher, attended with their wives. They left their coats, stoles and bags on their table while they danced. While the music played, a law student who had insulted them when they arrived pushed their table under a curtain. Hall reached for his things and told the student "in effect, 'Leave our things alone.' [The student] then became very hostile and profane and slapped Mr. Hall on the side of the head."[394] Other P.A.D.s grabbed the student and led him out, and the faculty members left. At a faculty meeting three days later, the student was permitted to withdraw with prejudice. The Justice of P.A.D., Ray Stewart '57, admitted that the fraternity failed to police for members who had too much to drink and should have intervened with the student sooner. He asked that the fraternity "as a whole bear part of the blame and that the punishment be directed at the fraternity." The faculty was unable to agree on a sanction for the fraternity.

Jackson recognized that benefits under the G.I. Bill would not sustain the Law School's larger enrollment forever, once the demand of veterans for legal education was fully met. He also was concerned that some current students would exhaust their eligibility for benefits before they completed their legal education. He feared that when the loss of federal financing was combined with the greater number of years of pre-legal education required at Washburn and by the Kansas Supreme Court, it might in time "limit the prospective students for the Bar to sons and daughters of the rich."[395] Only one small fund, known as the "Judges Fund," was designated for scholarships. It consisted of salaries returned by part-time Lecturers who were judges who taught without

---

392. Minutes, Washburn U. Sch. of Law faculty meeting (Mar. 4, 1950).
393. Minutes, Washburn U. Sch. of Law faculty meeting (Oct. 9, 1958).
394. Minutes, Washburn U. Sch. of Law faculty meeting (Apr. 15, 1957).
395. *Jackson States Law Problem*, WASHBURN UNIV. BULLETIN 2 (Nov. 1949).

compensation. Jackson saw an urgent need to increase student financial aid, through both scholarships and loans. "For the good of the school and the profession," he wrote to President Stoffer, "some provision should be made for the student who is on his own and who has the making of a good lawyer."[396] Stoffer printed Jackson's plea in the University's alumni newsletter and urged alumni to contribute to scholarship funds. However, the University did not allocate any of its general scholarship money to law students.[397] Jackson ultimately had to warn the law alumni board that contributions to the Washburn Alumni Association had to be earmarked specifically for the Law School or they would be used for college students.

In 1951, a new Washburn Law School Association was formed with Irving Platt '08 of Junction City as President. President Stoffer urged the group to see that the Law School in the years to come had scholarships, lecture series, and endowed chairs.[398] In January 1953, the Association was reorganized as a tax-exempt charitable organization and a Board of Governors was selected.

The law faculty was small but its members had strong personalities and issues often were decided on close votes. The strongest personality surely belonged to Chester J. Antieau. On February 14, 1953, he circulated a memorandum to his colleagues indicating that he planned at the next faculty meeting to make ten motions on a wide range of issues that he listed on a crowded legal-size page. He did so "[f]eeling that it may be unjust to the institution to any longer remain reticent about advancing proposals for the advancement of this Law School." He went so far as to suggest by name faculty members to chair for some of the committees he proposed. He asked that a committee refine admission criteria and consider the desirability of using a law school aptitude or entrance examination. He asked that another committee again investigate initiation of a law review, an idea first suggested in the fall of 1951,[399] and that another committee be responsible for organizing one or more institutes to offer continuing legal education. Each of these proposals would

---

396. *Id.*

397. Report of Dean Schuyler Jackson 1954–55 to the Washburn Law School Association.

398. TOPEKA DAILY CAP., Nov. 4, 1951.

399. Minutes, Washburn U. School of Law faculty meeting (Nov. 11, 1951). The faculty committee appointed that year was directed also to consider a joint law review with KU.

be implemented in less than a decade but Antieau was ahead of his time. He proposed raising the GPA required to remain in school after a student had attempted twenty-four credit hours from .75 to .90 and that standards of grading be made more uniform. He asked that seniors be required to spend one afternoon at the Legal Aid Office. One proposal went to the issue of faculty governance:

> That the committee on curriculum be instructed to bring in a report before the end of the present semester specifically recommending what courses are to be offered during the summer and fall semesters; and that the vote of said committee be free from any veto.

Dean Jackson, a strong personality himself, claimed authority to veto changes in curriculum or policy passed by the faculty. The minutes of faculty meetings specifically record only one instance of its use, when in 1951 Jackson vetoed the faculty's decision to make participation in a moot court club mandatory.[400] Nevertheless, when Jackson called a faculty meeting to consider Antieau's memorandum, he circulated his own memorandum commenting on three proposals, including the governance issue:

> As I read the by-laws of the university, the dean is charged by the Board of Regents and the President with the duty of adopting a curriculum and school policy with the help and approval of the faculty. Certainly, the approval of the dean is necessary in such things. If not, he is a janitor indeed....One might just as well say, that the faculty could adopt a policy in disregard of the directions of the Board of Regents, which is in fact, what it would be doing if it disregarded the By-laws of the Board. Certainly, no one would accept the position of dean, if he could be compelled to carry out policies which he deemed to be detrimental to the school, to legal education or which would keep the school from being "progressive."

The faculty met four days after Antieau circulated his memorandum. The potential for fireworks was real. However, Professor Larson, noting that all faculty had read the two memoranda and that "undoubtedly all members had already formed their own opinions," made a motion to table, which passed by

---

400. Minutes, Washburn U. Sch. of Law faculty meeting (Nov. 15, 1951).

a 3–2 vote, with Dean Jackson abstaining and Professors Poland and Antieau voting against the motion.[401]

Antieau resigned from the faculty at the end of that year, after two years at Washburn, and returned to teach again at his alma mater, Detroit College of Law. Despite his brief tenure, Antieau had an impact on his Washburn students. The Law Journal Board published a tribute lamenting his departure and describing study under Antieau as "a rich and rewarding experience . . . . The enthusiasm which he possesses for the law, as well as his superior achievements in legal teaching and practice, have given us a zeal for legal knowledge which otherwise we might never have attained."[402] After five years at Detroit, he was Professor of Law at Georgetown for twenty years before becoming Professor Emeritus. He became a prolific scholar in the fields of Municipal Corporations, the Federal Civil Rights Acts, and Constitutional Law, authoring multi-volume treatises on each subject. While at Washburn, he completed most of the work for the first edition of his treatise on municipal corporations that was published in 1955. Antieau remained an active scholar well into his 80s. He returned to Washburn and worked from an office in the Law School during the summer of 1994 while visiting a daughter who had moved to northeast Kansas. That summer he became acquainted with, and grew to respect, Washburn Constitutional Law Professor Bill Rich. Antieau invited Rich to collaborate on a new edition of one of his treatises and the result, published by Westgroup, was Chester J. Antieau and William R. Rich, *Modern Constitutional Law 3d* (1997).

Antieau's departure led to Bob Fowks' return to the faculty, and the faculty then remained unchanged through the final five years of Jackson's deanship. Fowks had remained in close contact with the school after leaving in 1951, returning to teach two summer school courses as Visiting Professor in 1952.

The Law School celebrated its 50th anniversary on October 9–10, 1953, and offered two continuing legal education programs. The entire first day was an institute on marriage and divorce, in cooperation with the Menninger Foundation. Judge Paul Alexander of the Family Court of Toledo and Professor Max Reinstein of the University of Chicago were the featured presenters. The following morning the topic was whether the Kansas Code of Civil Procedure

---

401. Minutes, Washburn U. Sch. of Law faculty meeting (Feb. 18, 1953).
402. *Chester James Antieau*, 21 J. KAN. B. ASS'N 384 (1953).

28. Faculty Grow Beards for 1954 Topeka Centennial

should be amended to conform to the Federal Rules. At an evening banquet, United States District Judge Delmas Hill '29 presented the principal address, "The Meaning of 50 Years of Washburn Law School."[403]

During 1949–50, the Kansas Bar Association's Committee on Legal Education, including both Dean Jackson and KU Dean Fred Moreau as members, urged the Supreme Court to require that applicants to take the Kansas bar exam complete seven years of post-high school study, a requirement the Court previously adopted but then deferred because of World War II. The two faculties solidly supported a seven-year requirement but disagreed somewhat on whether it should contain four years of college and three years of law, three years of college and four years of law, as a majority of KU's current faculty and Washburn's wholly different pre-war faculty favored or three and one-half years of each.[404] The Korean War once again stalled momentum for the

403. *Law School Plans Homecoming Fetes*, WASHBURN REV., Oct. 2, 1953.
404. *Report of the Committee on Admission to the Bar and Legal Education*, 20 J. KAN. B. ASS'N 100, 101 (1951).

seven-year proposal. The schools were reluctant to adopt the change on their own after the war, without the Court making the requirement a general one for admission to the bar, since that might drive students to schools in surrounding states that still awarded both degrees in six years, or might lead to the opening of a new Kansas school that did so.[405]

Thus, the traditional LL.B. continued to be awarded to graduates who earned both degrees in six years, using the first year of law studies as electives toward their college degrees. Nevertheless, Washburn created incentives for students to complete seven years of study. In April 1953, the school reinstated the Juris Doctor degree, awarding it to graduates who devoted fourteen semesters to earning both college and law degrees. There were two ways to earn the J.D. A student who had a bachelor's degree before starting law school had to complete the required eighty-two credit hours of law studies with "distinguished excellence" and prepare a thesis. The determination of what constituted "distinguished excellence" was ad hoc, based on review by the full faculty of an application and the student's transcript. As an alternative, the required standard of work was only "general competence" and the thesis was excused if the student completed 15–30 credit hours of law courses and used them to complete the bachelor's degree before taking 82 more law credits, in effect studying law for three and one-half or four years. However, the students also had to complete three of the following courses: International Law, Trade Regulation, Comparative Law, Administrative Law, Legal Writing, and Legislation. "General competence" for this alternative was defined four years later as a 1.5 Grade Point Average on a 3.0 scale.

Finally, in December 1954, the Supreme Court by rule provided that applicants for the summer 1960 bar exam must have completed fourteen semesters while earning both college and law degrees, leaving it to individual schools to determine the content of those semesters so long as six were in law and six were in college studies. The change impacted applicants entering during the 1957–58 academic year.

A new issue emerged in the fall of 1954 that would occupy the University for the remainder of the century and would impact the Law School in varying ways. Of 1,591 students campus-wide that year, 36% were from outside

---

405. *Report of Committee on Legal Education and Admissions*, 22 J. KAN. B. ASS'N 31, 32 (1953).

Shawnee County and another 9% were from Shawnee County but outside the
school's property tax base in Topeka. Washburn University and the University
of Wichita for the first time proposed legislation to provide state assistance
to meet the growing need for funding at both schools, in recognition of their
roles in educating students from throughout the state.

ANOTHER NEW HOME

Boswell Hall was not designed for classes as large as those that enrolled after the
war, or for the larger number of faculty hired to teach them. Professors Ahrens,
Larson and Hall were forced to share a single faculty office beginning in 1948
and never had private offices in Boswell. Needed growth in the library was
not possible because available shelf space capped the volume count at around
20,000 volumes.[406] The reading room in the library could accommodate no
more than 32–40 students, providing far less seating than the required standard of one-third of the student body. In the fall of 1948, the school's crowded
conditions and facilities were topics at a meeting of Phi Alpha Delta. Students
proposed a comparative study of law schools of similar size and standing.[407]
As early as April 1950, the catalogue declared that "under present University
building plans" Carnegie Library is "soon to become" the new home of the
Law School.[408] The same statement would appear in six catalogues. President
Stoffer told alumni in 1951 that the move to Carnegie would occur when a
new central building was completed.[409] However, because of financial issues,
it would be 1954 before the University administration even began to move
forward with a building plan that would re-house the Law School and the
move would not occur until 1956.

The years before the move were particularly difficult ones for the library.
When he became Law Librarian in 1950, Roy Bartlett arranged for the school to
use storage space in the basement of Benton Hall and immediately moved 1,500
books there. These books were duplicates, nearly obsolete, or in poor condition.
Benton had capacity to hold 4,000 books and Bartlett expressed the belief that
the shelf space freed up at Boswell could accommodate collection growth for

406. *Carnegie to House Law School Library*, WASHBURN REV., Nov. 12, 1954.
407. *P.A.D. Plans Early Study of Law Schools*, WASHBURN REV., Oct. 22, 1948.
408. WASHBURN UNIV. BULLETIN 113 (Apr. 1950).
409. TOPEKA DAILY CAP., Nov. 4, 1951.

29. Carnegie Hall, home of the Law School 1956–1966

up to five years. By then, he assumed, the Law School would have moved to Carnegie.[410] He was overly optimistic and by 1953 reported there was only room for one more year of growth. This was not because of lavish spending on books. The acquisitions budget for books and periodicals in 1951 was just $3,230 and did not exceed $5,000 until after the move to Carnegie. The ratio of funds pre-obligated for continuations as compared to discretionary new purchases rose to 19:1, far above the 2:1 standard for libraries. Much of the increase in the size of the collection came from gifts from lawyers, which Bartlett attributed to the fact that the cost of office space at $1.50 to $3.00 per foot made maintenance of a private library too expensive for some firms.[411] Of course, many of the donated materials were duplicates but they were stored for use as replacements, traded to book dealers for materials that were needed, or sold.

The library's location in Boswell's basement led to other problems. In 1954, Bartlett reported there had been bug and worm infestation of the books that required complete fumigation of the library the prior December. It had to be

410. Roy L. Bartlett, "Annual Report of the Law Librarian 1950–51."
411. Roy L. Bartlett, "Annual Report of the Law Librarian 1954–55."

30. Carnegie Hall Library

done twice annually thereafter. Summers were particularly bad. From mid-May through September, student patronage "declined almost to the vanishing point, coinciding with the time the air conditioning is turned on at the Topeka Public Library."[412]

Carnegie Library was built shortly after the Law School opened downtown. Finally, the University library would be relocated to newly-completed Morgan Hall to make room for the Law School. Substantial renovation was needed, costing more than $40,000. Plans were developed for the Law Review Board and the Legal Aid Bureau to have private offices for the first time, and there were private offices for each faculty member[413] and the Law Librarian. "Special features" included a student lounge, newly furnished library space with shelf capacity for twice the number of books possible at Boswell, plus two large reading rooms with a total of 104 seats and a "browsing corner" complete with "comfortable overstuffed furniture"[414] that seated twelve more. The library had capacity for 36,000 books which, with what proved to be excess optimism, led Bartlett to believe the "margin of growth should be adequate for fifteen to twenty years to

---

412. *Id.*

413. *Carnegie to House Law School Library*, WASHBURN REV., Nov. 11, 1954.

414. *Law Day and Dedication of Law Building*, 25 J. KAN. B. ASS'N 197 (1956).

come,"[415] even assuming a substantial increase in the rate of acquisitions. The building had a new heating system and new classroom furnishings, though still no air conditioning. The four main classrooms were named for former Deans Allen, Arthur, Hambleton and Conant.[416] Two were on the lower level and the other two were on the top level, along with faculty offices.

Construction at Morgan and Carnegie Halls took longer than expected and even when the Law School moved into Carnegie at the start of the fall semester in 1956, the work there was not yet complete. Materials from the Boswell Library were efficiently moved in just three days but the nearly 4,000 books that had been stored in Benton Hall could not be moved until late November. The electric bell system had not been installed yet so the Secretary, Christine Johnson, rang her father's old school bell by hand to dismiss classes. It proved not to be loud enough so Blaine Schoolcraft brought a huge 100-year-old bell for Mrs. Johnson to use.[417]

Dedication ceremonies were held October 12–13. Chief Justice William A. Smith '14 and United States District Judge Delmas Hill '29 recalled what the Law School had been like forty and twenty-five years earlier. The principal speaker was Chief Judge Sam Bratton of the United States Court of Appeals for the Tenth Circuit. He observed that the value of the new building "does not lie in the beauty or quality of the materials. The intrinsic value of the edifice lies in the contribution which will be made within its portals to the education of the young men and women who come this way…for useful service in the field of law." He urged students to follow the model of lawyers who "in successive periods of history have raised their voices with greater strength than that of the bayonet or the cannon when liberty was in peril or urgent need existed for the vindication of the rights of the public."[418] He praised the practice of states that had adopted the Federal Rules of Civil Procedure, described efforts to reduce delay in judicial proceedings, and opposed photographing or televising trials.

The dedication included a continuing education program, chaired by Michael Barbara '53, and it was so successful that it was made an annual event.

---

415. Roy L. Bartlett, "Annual Report of the Law Librarian 1955–56."

416. *Law Dedication Set for October*, WASHBURN REV., Sept. 21, 1956, at 5.

417. *Law School Gets 100 Year Old Bell*, WASHBURN REV., Oct. 5, 1956, at 5.

418. Hon. Sam G. Bratton, *Address Delivered at Convocation*, 25 J. KAN. B. ASS'N 197, 198, 199 (1956).

The next fall, Washburn, partnering with the Topeka Bar Association and what then was called the Kansas Association of Plaintiff's Attorneys, offered a full-day Law Institute on medico-legal issues. There was an afternoon trial demonstration and it became a feature of the annual Institute for many years to come. Judge Jean Breitenstein, an appointee to the United States Court of Appeals earlier that year, and Judge Walter Huxman were banquet speakers. The following year the institute for the first time was sponsored solely by Washburn and the Topeka Bar Association.

Student life during the first year at Carnegie was typical of most years. For the fall student elections, the Independent Party used a model-T Ford to reinforce its slogan "Old, reliable, tried and true" while the Equitable Party used a Chevrolet Corvette to represent progress.[419] In mid-April, students complained that grades from the fall course in Wills still had not been posted. A motion was made before the Student Bar Association to give an award each year to the lowest ranked member of the graduating class. "In his usual eloquence, Dick McGrath helped defeat the motion by stating, 'Generally I don't mind being laughed at, but I certainly hate to be laughed at with pomp and circumstance.'"[420] Law student teams participated, often successfully, in intramural sports. The following year, the Law School even built a homecoming float, featuring a briefcase and cane.

On top of all that, there was The Phantom:

> The Phantom recorded all the idiosyncrasies of staff and student in his notorious cartoons. "On some unsuspecting day, a cartoon would appear on the bulletin board—complete with true-to-life caricatures of the staff and an occasional student—and signed 'The Phantom.' For several months we were unsure who our accomplished cartoonist was but finally the news leaked out. It was none other than Hal Des Jardins. Despite his identity leak, the cartoons continued, much to the students pleasure."[421]

The 1956 catalogue announced a new admission requirement. Applicants had to take what initially was called the Princeton Legal Aptitude Test.[422] The

---

419. *Law School Elections Held Last Wednesday*, WASHBURN REV., Oct. 19, 1956.
420. *Legal Briefs*, WASHBURN REV., Apr. 12, 1957.
421. McLane, *supra* note 3, at 14.
422. Minutes, Washburn U. Sch. of Law faculty meeting (Nov. 14, 1955).

faculty did not foresee the commercial opportunities the test later would spawn. "No special preparation is required for the law aptitude test. It is designed to measure the mental abilities and aptitudes which are closely related to success in legal studies. It is not a test of the candidate's knowledge of subject matter in academic fields. The test should be therefore taken in stride, without cramming and without undue concern."[423] The test score was not a significant factor in an era of essentially open admission and, for at least several years, some students were permitted to take the test after starting law classes. By the time the first entering class that was required to take the test was about to graduate, three students still had not taken it. The faculty voted to force them to take the test, treating it as a prerequisite for graduation even though the test result would not be used in any way.[424]

ANOTHER DEAN BECOMES A JUSTICE

On the morning of April 7, 1958, Justice Fred Hall submitted his resignation from the Kansas Supreme Court so that he could seek election for a second time as Governor of Kansas. That same morning, Governor George Docking, a Democrat, appointed Dean Jackson to replace Hall.[425] The Court was hearing arguments that week. Jackson was sworn in immediately in the office of Chief Justice Jay Parker, in the presence of the other Justices, Jackson's family, and members of the Washburn law faculty. He sat with the Court that afternoon, having borrowed Hall's robe.[426] The suddenness of the appointment caused some disruption. Jackson continued teaching his classes until the end of the semester but Civil Procedure was moved from 11:00 a.m. to 7:00 a.m. and International Law was moved to Monday evening, for three hours starting at 6:30 p.m.

Fred Hall had been involved fifteen months earlier in the infamous "triple play," in which he resigned as Governor with only eleven days left in his term, after losing his bid for re-nomination in the Republican primary to Warren Shaw '31, then was appointed to the Supreme Court by the Lieutenant Governor who succeeded him as Governor. Hall filled a vacancy William A. Smith '14 created for Hall's benefit by resigning as Chief Justice. Docking

---

423. WASHBURN UNIV. BULLETIN 127 (Apr. 1956).
424. Minutes, Washburn U. Sch. of Law faculty meeting (Apr. 11, 1959).
425. TOPEKA DAILY CAP., Apr. 8, 1958.
426. *Id.*

31. Dean Jackson is sworn in as Justice of the Kansas Supreme
Court with Professors Ahrens and Bartlett in attendance.

touted Jackson's appointment as "one of our moves to take the court out of
politics and administer the law as the people desire,"[427] but acknowledged that
he first offered the appointment to state Democrat Party Chair Frank Theis,
later a United States District Judge. The triple play in major part prompted
Kansans in November 1958 to approve a constitutional amendment providing
for non-partisan selection of Supreme Court Justices, subject only to votes
for or against retention. However, partisan elections still were held that year.
Jackson filed to run for a full term but, given his party affiliation, his election
was hardly certain. Only one other Democrat, Dean Allen, had won election
to the Court. Jackson, in fact, was given a formal leave of absence by Washburn
to serve on the Court,[428] so that he could return as Dean if he lost the election.
Former full-time faculty member and long-time Adjunct Professor Howard

427. KAN. CITY STAR, Apr. 7, 1958.
428. *Howard Jones Is Appointed Dean of Law*, WASHBURN REV., Apr. 18, 1958, at 1.

32. Howard Jones '28, Acting Dean 1958–1959,
Professor 1928–1930

A. Jones '28 agreed to be Acting Dean through the election, while continuing his practice with the firm Addington, Jones, Davis and Haney.

Democrats fared unusually well in Kansas elections that year and, as had been the case when Dean Allen was a candidate, Washburn graduates through-out the state, Republicans as well as Democrats, worked hard for Jackson's election. He won by a large margin, defeating John McCall of Chanute. Jones assured a smooth transition by agreeing to continue as Acting Dean through a national dean search. In all, Jones served fourteen months as Acting Dean until John E. Howe arrived to become the new Dean in June 1959.

Jackson's departure for the Court meant more than the loss of the Dean. Once his election victory assured him a full term, Christine Ash Johnson an-nounced she would leave her position as Secretary to follow Jackson to the Court, although she agreed to stay until the transition to a new dean was complete, to provide continuity. She had been the glue of the school since becoming

Secretary in 1943, after a year as assistant librarian. She did not remain in the position as long as the school's first Secretary, Emily Sanford Platt, but she was equally revered by students. In 1947, she was made an honorary member of the Student Bar Association and presented with her own cane.[429] Her son, David Ash Johnson '49, graduated on her watch.

Sadly, Justice Jackson did not serve a full term. In January 1962, he fell on glazed ice while leaving his home for work and broke his hip. After two surgeries, deteriorating health forced him to resign from the Court two years later and he died in December 1964 at age sixty. Jackson was highly respected as a jurist but Chief Justice Parker said in his eulogy:

> It was as Dean of the Washburn University School of Law that he made his greatest impact on the jurisprudence of this state. The love, gratitude and respect which he kindled in the hearts of all the students of law who studied under him has stimulated and preserved high ideals that will be passed on. This is the rich heritage he has left the legal profession.[430]

There were two other departures from the faculty the year after Jackson's appointment to the Court. Roy Bartlett '49 left at the end of the academic year 1958–59 to become legal officer for the Kansas State Selective Service System. He remained involved with the school, serving as Secretary for the alumni Board of Governors and immediately proposing a plan to increase the number of dues-paying members of the Association. His effort produced a sharp increase to more than 300 paid members. The importance of this increase in alumni involvement would become readily apparent after the 1966 tornado.

Marvin Larson also left the faculty in 1959, to return to the State Department of Social Welfare as Director. Then, in 1970, he became State Director of Vocational Rehabilitation for four years. Larson was, according to Professor Ahrens, "a civil libertarian long before being one was fashionable. Marvin was a man who liked and respected women. He hated injustices to minorities, the welfare client and the mentally ill." He thought a fourth year should be added to law school and used to "acquaint law students with the kind of problems that should be solved by the healing and helping professions rather

---

429. *Law School Party*, WASHBURN REV., Nov. 7, 1947.

430. *In Memoriam*, 4 WASHBURN L.J. 175 (1965). This appears to be a reprint of Chief Justice Parker's eulogy. See Memorial to Justice Schuyler W. Jackson, 197 Kan. xvi, xx (1966)

33. Marvin Larson '40, Professor 1948–1959

than through the adversary process."[431] During the spring semester of 1958, Larson collaborated with Dr. Joseph Satten, staff psychiatrist at the Menninger Clinic, to teach for the first time a new course on Medical Evidence. Washburn was one of only twelve law schools offering the course.[432] The course focused on the use of medical expert witnesses and the relationship of psychiatrists and physicians with lawyers.

No student who had a class with him could forget him. Ahrens described Larson as "complex and brilliant," sensitive and caring, but also as "earthy."

> He was a man who raised swearing to a minor art form. He usually swore with a twinkle in his eyes, unless it was at persons like Senator Joe

431. James R. Ahrens, *Marvin Larson: A Personal Remembrance*, THE CIRCUIT RIDER 10 (Winter 1987).

432. Library Talk—Larson Speaks of New Course in Law School, WASHBURN REV., Feb. 14, 1958.

McCarthy. Once when his mother-in-law commented that she couldn't get over how much Josephine (his wife) was swearing, Marvin replied, "I know, and do you know, she's got me doing it too."[433]

Larson enjoyed telling a story about one of the few times he became nonplussed. Toward the end of one class, Jerry Ann Foster '58 raised her hand and Larson called on her. "Professor," she asked matter-of-factly, "I didn't get the citation to the last God damn case. Would you repeat it?"[434]

ONCE MORE TO NEW YORK

Washburn returned to the finals of the National Moot Court Competition for a second time in 1958–59. The arguments that year involved the Federal Corrupt Practices Act. Raymond Spring '59 and Dan Dibble '59 earned the right to compete in New York by placing second in the regional competition. They defeated Washington University in St. Louis and South Dakota before losing in the regional final round to a team from KU. It was the first time since Washburn entered the competition in 1951 that its team had lost a round to KU.[435] Rutgers defeated Washburn in New York but the trip was memorable for the conversation Spring and Dibble had with United States Supreme Court Justice Charles Whittaker, a native Kansan and Kansas City, Missouri lawyer, who served on the Eighth Circuit Court of Appeals before appointment to the Supreme Court.[436] Dibble also remembered the trip for the tight budget the team had. Faculty advisor Jim Ahrens ordered only soup and rolls for the team's dinner, to save money, and objected when the waiter added a 15% service charge. "We nearly got thrown out of the hotel," Dibble recalled, "but Jim finally paid it."

---

433. Ahrens, *supra* note 431.

434. Conversation with Hon. Fred Jackson '60, Dean Jackson's son.

435. WU Moot Court Team Plans St. Louis Trip, WASHBURN REV., Nov. 7, 1958, at 1.

436. *Lawyers Return from New York*, WASHBURN REV., Jan. 6, 1959, at 1.

5

THE HOWE YEARS AND
THE TORNADO (1959–1970)

Because of the possibility Justice Jackson might return as Dean, no effort was
made to search for his successor until after the November 1958 election. During
December, the faculty forwarded to University administrators its specification
of qualifications for the new dean.

John E. Howe was in his fourth year as Assistant Dean at St. Louis University, in charge of admissions, scheduling, and budget. Howe learned of the
Washburn vacancy at the AALS annual meeting in December from former
Washburn faculty member Chester J. Antieau. Howe and Antieau had taught
together during Howe's first year in law teaching at Creighton in 1946. Antieau
introduced Howe to Professor Poland, who encouraged Howe to apply.

It had been nineteen years since the school had even searched other than
locally for a dean and no current member of the full-time faculty had ever
taught elsewhere. Thus, it is not surprising that there was considerable discussion "of the merits and demerits of having a local or out-of-state man as
Dean" or that there was diversity of opinion.[437] Howe and Grissim Walker, the
Dean at Cumberland Law School, then located in Tennessee, were invited to
interview and the faculty unanimously made Howe the top choice. The Dean
at St. Louis sought to keep him there by offering to resign and arrange for
Howe to become Dean, but Howe declined.[438]

437. Minutes, Washburn U. Sch. of Law faculty meeting (Feb. 5, 1959).
438. *The Importance of Adjunct Professors*, 43 WASHBURN LAWYER 5 (Summer
2005).

34. John E. Howe, Dean 1959–1970,
Professor 1959–1978

Howe brought much-needed experience of teaching at other law schools, as well as a more national perspective on issues. Howe had been a professor at St. Louis University since 1952. In addition to teaching at Creighton, he also had taught as Visiting Professor during summer sessions at the University of Missouri-Columbia and at the University of Kentucky, from which he had received his LL.B. in 1943. Immediately after graduation, he completed an LL.M. at the University of Michigan, then entered private practice in Mt. Sterling, Kentucky. He was aptly described in a 1969 publication as "an easy-going individual, generous to a fault and gifted with a droll sense of humor."[439]

Following the 1955 ABA/AALS accreditation inspection, Dean Jackson had stubbornly defended the school's practice of not scheduling afternoon classes against criticism that the practice facilitated excessive work by students and

---

439. McLane, *supra* note 3, at 15.

called into question whether Washburn's program could be characterized as "full-time." Jackson's stubbornness had led to difficulty with the accreditation agencies. As part of his due diligence before accepting the deanship, Howe called his friend, John Hervey, Adviser to the ABA Section on Legal Education. Hervey urged Howe to decline the offer, saying he was scheduled to make a follow-up inspection that fall and feared he would be unable to recommend continued accreditation as a full-time program. Howe nevertheless accepted the job and persuaded Hervey to postpone the inspection for a year.

Professor Bill Harvey believes that Dean Jackson "keenly understood" that the ABA/AALS definition of a full-time program institutionalized the "college-campus law school program...available to students who could afford to attend law school on a college campus without being employed," and disadvantaged students who needed access to schools in municipal areas where they could work "to pay for law school and their expanding families."[440] While these students often had "an academic and economic history quite different from the college-campus law students," their differences in perspective nevertheless "produced excellent students and fully engaged student bodies," and Professor Harvey believes Dean Jackson's objection to the ABA/AALS definition of "full-time" was that it meant that "economics rather than aptitude or ability would determine one's availability and admission to a law school."[441]

However principled, defiance of an accrediting agency usually is a losing strategy. By the fall of 1960, Howe had scheduled five upper-division electives and one required first-year course in the afternoons. Students who worked excessive hours were required to take reduced loads. The school attempted to control outside employment and found not more than 3% of students worked more than twenty hours per week. These steps were sufficient to satisfy Hervey, whose 1960 inspection report observed: "Three separate counts at afternoon hours showed not less than thirty students using the library. While the amount of outside employment appears to be heavy it is materially less than it was at the time of the previous inspection."

Howe was only 40 years old when he became Dean. Only three faculty members that year, Bob Fowks, Jim Ahrens, and Mel Poland, returned from the prior year. Four new arrivals, including Howe, constituted a majority. Everyone

---

440. *Memories and Comments*, letter from Professor William F. Harvey to James Concannon, August, 2007 (on file in Washburn Law Library).

441. *Id.*

35. John Howe, who was only 40 when selected as dean, rides a motorcycle to work

was young, with Fowks, at age 43, the oldest. Howe reported at an early faculty meeting that rumors had reached him expressing concern about the extent of faculty turnover. He commented that there might be a public relations problem and urged faculty to use every opportunity to dispel concerns.[442]

With the departures of Marvin Larson and Roy Bartlett, there were two new full-time teachers. Walter D. Navin, Jr., age 34, and Richard C. Allen, age 33, replaced them. Their hiring eliminated growing concern about inbreeding of the full-time faculty with the school's own graduates. Navin's J.D. was from the University of Iowa and Allen was a graduate of Washington University in St. Louis. Still, they had local or regional practice connections. Navin was in practice with Brewer, Myers, and Branton in Kansas City, while Allen was a partner in Cray and Allen in Topeka and was serving as area counsel for Southwestern Bell, for whom Allen previously worked full-time

---

442. Minutes, Washburn U. Sch. of Law faculty meeting (Sept. 3, 1959).

in St. Louis. Allen assumed Larson's role co-teaching the course on Medical Evidence, continuing the Law School's collaboration with Menninger and Dr. Joseph Satten.

There also was a new Librarian. Miles Mustain '58, who held the position for most of the year after his graduation when Roy Bartlett became a full-time teacher, left to enter private practice. Howe hired Eleanore Blue, his former student and a 1957 graduate of St. Louis University. She was the first Librarian also to hold a bachelor's degree in library science. She stayed only one year before becoming Librarian at the University of Kansas City, where she stayed and became Professor Emeritus in 1977.

No less important vacancy was that of Secretary, which arose because of Christine Johnson's plan to join Justice Jackson at the Supreme Court as soon as the transition was complete. Dorothy Swecker was hired to be the "person of all trades" the position required, and she was that person for thirteen years. Only near the end of Howe's deanship was a half-time secretary hired to help her. Before that, she had only ever-changing student assistants, and if she was ill for a day, Mrs. Howe had to fill in. "Dean" Swecker, as students came to call her, followed in the tradition of Emily Sanford Platt and Christine Johnson. "Her concern was always for the school and the students," Ray Spring later wrote. "Neither hour of the day nor day of the week had meaning for her; if there was work to be done, she was there to do it."[443] Swecker "spoke in a rather flat, monotonic voice," another faculty member observed, "because she did not show or reflect distress, regardless of the crisis of the moment. In short, in addition to her talent she lived in peace and brought it to her office."[444]

MAKING CHANGES; SOLVING PROBLEMS

Howe quickly set about invigorating the school. Legal writing was a primary focus. In part because of the opportunity students had to publish in the KBA *Journal*, the two Kansas law schools were latecomers as publishers of their own scholarly journals. Seventy-seven of 107 AALS member schools already were publishing a journal when the *Kansas Law Review* first appeared during academic year 1952–53. When the first issue of the *Washburn Law Journal* was

443. Raymond L. Spring, *The Dean's Report to the Bar*, 12 WASHBURN L.J. 262, 264 (1973).

444. *Memories and Comments, supra* note 440.

published, Washburn became the ninety-second of 108 AALS member schools to publish a journal. In late September 1959, the Law Review Board reported that it planned to produce an intramural journal that would be mimeographed. The school's budget for academic year 1959–60 already was set and there was no line item to cover a more expensive form of publication. That was fine with the faculty, which insisted there be procedures in place to assure any publication bearing the school's name was a quality product. Robert L. Roberts '61 credits Professors Navin and Allen for backing his and other students' initiative to publish a journal.[445] For the start-up year, the faculty mandated that the journal be distributed only within the school and that the volume not be numbered.[446] The Law Journal Board, with David Wheeler '60 and Roberts as Editor-in-Chief for one semester each, produced two issues, in addition to material for the KBA *Journal*. Subsequently, the two issues were spiral bound with a cover and Editors' Comment as Volume 0 of the *Washburn Law Journal*. The fall issue of thirty-eight pages included notes on movie censorship and conflicts between a general verdict and special questions, completed by 1959 graduates Frank Rice and Raymond Spring, plus an additional note and a case comment by current students. The spring issue of seventy-seven pages also included two case comments, a note by a December graduate, and a lead article discussing *Erie v. Tompkins* by Professor James Ahrens.[447] The article was reprinted, in a slightly expanded form and with a new title, in the more widely-distributed third issue of volume 1.[448]

Dean Howe's budget for academic year 1960–61 included funding to print the journal professionally. Professor Walter Navin was the faculty advisor. A Law Journal Advisory Committee, chaired by William Treadway and composed of five attorneys and two judges, including Kansas Supreme Court Justice Alfred Schroeder, provided guidance. Lowell Hahn '61 was named Editor-in-Chief. That year's Board of Editors published the first two issues of volume 1, covering 325 pages.

---

445. Telephone conversation between James M. Concannon and Robert L. Roberts, Feb. 14, 2011.

446. Minutes, Washburn U. Sch. of Law faculty meeting (Sept. 28, 1959).

447. James R. Ahrens, *Erie v. Tompkins—The Brooding Omnipresence*, 0 WASHBURN L.J. No. 2, 1 (1960).

448. James R. Ahrens, *Erie v. Tompkins—The Not So Common Law*, 1 WASHBURN L.J. 343 (1961).

36. First issue of the *Washburn Law Journal*

Volume 1 ultimately included four issues, published over two years by successive staffs. The issues published during academic year 1961–62 included 308 pages, plus an index. Thereafter, until 1966, two issues each year comprised a volume. The first issue of volume 1 began with a nine-page "Dean's Report to the Bar."[449] The report would be an annual feature in the *Journal* through volume 20. There were articles by two Kansas practitioners. One was adapted from a paper on depositions John Shamberg '37 presented at the Washburn-Topeka Bar Association Annual Law Institute in October 1960.[450] The other, by recent graduate Frank Rice '59, was the first part of a two-part article on mental competency to stand trial under federal criminal procedure.[451] The is-

449. John E. Howe, *The Dean's Report to the Bar*, 1 WASHBURN L.J. 1, 5 (1960).

450. John E. Shamberg, *The Deposition—A Discovery Instrument in Kansas Civil Practice*, 1 WASHBURN L.J. 10 (1960).

451. Frank M. Rice, *Mental Competency to Stand Trial Under Federal Criminal*

sue included a major article by Professor Calvin Kuenzel of Stetson University College of Law, discussing jurisdiction over courts-martial.[452] There were two student notes and two case comments. The lead article in issue two by Professor Samuel Fahr of the University of Iowa, discussing dissatisfaction by lawyers with the social sciences,[453] prompted a response in issue four[454] Professor Navin also published an article.[455] This issue included four student notes, including one by Editor-in-Chief Lowell Hahn, and eight case comments.

There were two editors-in-chief during the *Journal's* second year. Zerne P. Haning '62 served during the fall semester, until his graduation. Gerald Letourneau '62 succeeded him in the spring semester.[456] The final two issues of volume 1 included six student notes and eleven case comments. Article authors included Justice Gordon Sloan '35 of the Oregon Supreme Court, Washburn Professor William Harvey, and former professor Roy Bartlett. Issue four included book reviews for the first time, by Professors Navin and Allen. The *Journal* received requests to reprint in other legal publications one lead article and five student works from the first three issues of volume 1.[457]

The subscription price was $4 per year. For issue one, 750 copies were printed. Circulation grew to 1300 copies by volume 5. The *Journal* was typeset and printed locally, and that created problems. Reports of delays in publication appeared as early as volumes 3 and 4 and periodically through volume 12, the last volume published locally.[458] To become a member of the Board of Editors,

---

Procedure, 1 WASHBURN L.J. 91 (1960). Part two was published in issue 2. Frank M. Rice, *Mental Competency to Stand Trial In Federal Criminal Procedure. Part II: The Constitutional Issues*, 1 WASHBURN L.J. 176 (1961).

452. Calvin A. Kuenzel, *Federal Court Jurisdiction Over Courts-Martial*, 1 WASH-BURN L.J. 25 (1960).

453. Samuel M. Fahr, *Why Lawyers Are Dissatified with the Social Sciences*, 1 WASHBURN L.J. 161 (1961).

454. Gilbert Geis, *The Social Sciences and the Law*, 1 WASHBURN L.J. 569 (1962).

455. Walter D. Navin, Jr., *State Criminal Jurisdiction Over Federally Controlled Lands*, 1 WASHBURN L.J. 200 (1961).

456. Stanley E. Antrim '65 served as Editor-in-Chief for volume 4 for the spring semester after first semester Editor-in-Chief William J. Hunsaker '65 graduated at mid-year. Since then, the need for continuity has led to the selection of students to be Editor-in-Chief only if they would be on campus for the full academic year.

457. *Obiter Dictum*, 1 WASHBURN L.J. 515 (1962); *Washburn Law Journal Beginning Its Third Season Of Publication*, WASHBURN REV., Oct. 17, 1962.

458. Publishing delays in volume 12 were so severe that the *Journal* published

students had to have a 1.5 GPA on the then applicable 3.0 scale, be in the top one-third of the class, and complete either one Note or two case Comments. Members who thereafter completed an additional Note or two Comments received a Certificate of Achievement.

Publication of the *Journal* had the desired effect of stimulating student interest in research. "Our library tables are loaded with books," Dean Howe observed in the spring of 1961, "and I like to believe that it is because the students are working, and not because we have a messy librarian. The Journal editor tells me that he now has some twenty-five students that are engaged in working on case comments and case notes. This is quite a change from two years ago."[459] Washburn became an active participant in the National Conference of Law Reviews. By volume 3, Washburn was elected to a two-year term on the National Committee of Planning and Organization.

The faculty determined that enhanced training in legal writing was needed for all students, not just those on the journal staff. Dean Howe described the problem in terms similar to those still found in faculty committee reports and heard at bar meetings:

> One constant complaint of law teachers, prospective employers and appellate judges has been the inability of the average law student to express himself in written form. In the law school we place the blame on the college English department. They in turn contend that the high schools have failed to fulfill their obligation in this matter. The high school points the finger at the elementary school, and for lack of a better excuse, the elementary school contends that it is a product of what the public desires, and that the blame must therefore rest with that public.[460]

---

an apology to a student author. *Obiter Dictum*, 12 WASHBURN L.J. iv (1973) (issue three). The student completed a note in which the student argued how an unsettled question should be resolved. While publication was delayed, the Kansas Supreme Court decided the issue in a different way. The student's note still was published but there was no opportunity for the student to revise the note in light of the decision. The next year, the *Journal* commissioned a national publisher of law journals. Also, for the first time, the school provided permanent secretarial services for the *Journal*.

459. Letter from John E. Howe to John G. Hervey, Adviser, Section of Legal Education and Admission to the Bar (Mar. 22, 1961).

460. John E. Howe, *The Dean's Report to the Bar*, 1 WASHBURN L.J. 1, 5 (1960).

In 1959, the only required research course was Legal Bibliography, a one-hour course. The faculty adopted a new graduation requirement in 1960 that students complete at least one course involving research and the preparation of a written paper. Three separate courses were added to the curriculum, each structured to satisfy the requirement. Law Journal Note Editing was open to members of the journal staff, who already had to produce an article of publishable quality. A basic course, Legal Research & Writing, required preparation of a legal memorandum and similar papers. Enrollment was limited to ten students each semester to "enable the instructor to do a thorough job in constructively criticizing the papers that are prepared."[461] The third new course, Appellate Practice, included instruction in appellate procedure and students were required to write an appellate brief. Appeals were taken from cases tried in Practice Court and were based on transcripts prepared by students who were training to become court reporters.[462]

The faculty continued to tinker with the writing requirement throughout the decade. It soon concluded that having the only required writing project in courses most students completed in the third year gave faculty too little time to correct major deficiencies. Thus, an additional requirement was added in 1962. All entering students were assigned an advisor and were required to submit for the advisor's review during their first semester a memorandum brief or other simple research paper.[463] Students exhibiting difficulty in writing were required to complete additional projects during the second semester. By 1965, the faculty made Appellate Practice a required upper level course for all students. It eliminated the upper level Legal Research & Writing course and incorporated writing projects into the first-year course in Legal Bibliography. All faculty members participated in teaching this course and senior students were used to supervise mechanical aspects. For unknown reasons, in May 1964, the faculty voted no longer to give academic credit for work on the law journal. However, it reversed itself in 1966 and voted to award two hours of credit to provide "additional incentive" for the best students to join the journal staff.[464]

Howe persuaded the University to provide additional resources to help close gaps in the library collection and to make faculty salaries more competitive, at

---

461. *Id.*

462. WASHBURN UNIV. OF TOPEKA CATALOGUE (1959).

463. Minutes, Washburn U. Sch. of Law faculty meeting (May 3, 1962).

464. Minutes, Washburn U. Sch. of Law faculty meeting (Mar. 1, 1966).

least regionally. However, he was frequently surprised to learn how limited his resources were. One morning shortly after he arrived, he asked Mrs. Johnson to mimeograph a memorandum and distribute it that afternoon. She informed him it would take two days, because she had to send it across campus to be run on the mimeograph machine in the dean's office at the College. Howe asked what was wrong with the Law School's machine and learned the school didn't have one. Dean Engelbert of the College controlled allocation of the limited equipment budget campus-wide and the Law School didn't receive much of it. Howe immediately purchased a used mimeograph machine with his own money and loaned it to the Law School until funds were budgeted to buy a new one.

When Howe arrived, there was no concern nationally that too many students were seeking to become lawyers. Rather, professional schools were concerned that too few talented students were seeking graduate degrees. The number of applicants to Washburn Law School had remained relatively constant for several years and Dean Howe foresaw no "difficulty in providing an opportunity for a legal education to those who are qualified and motivated to that end."[465] Almost every applicant was admitted. There were seventy-six applicants for academic year 1959, at least seventy were accepted, and fifty-nine enrolled. The following fall, there were sixty applicants, fifty-nine were accepted, and thirty-nine enrolled. However, performance requirements for students increased, in part in response to criticism in the 1955 accreditation inspection report. The legendary admonition to entering students became reality at Washburn: "Look to your left, look to your right, one of you won't be here next year." The first-year attrition rate for academic year 1959–60 was 33% and continued at that level well into the 1960s. In the fall of 1961, a faculty committee, chaired by Professor Fowks, for the first time focused on student recruitment. It concluded the school should be proactive in seeking students with superior credentials rather than rely essentially on word-of-mouth to bring Washburn to their attention. The Committee suggested inviting pre-law advisors to campus for a program and having faculty visit Kansas colleges, focusing on Kansas State and Wichita.[466] A pre-law advisors' conference ultimately was held in the fall of 1963.

The faculty also established a placement committee. While there were only thirty-six graduates in 1960, an insufficient number "to take advantage of the

---

465. Howe, *supra* note 460, at 3.
466. Minutes, Washburn U. Sch. of Law faculty meeting (Nov. 11, 1961).

openings that are brought to our attention," the perceived problem was that there were graduates who would be "excellent… for a particular type of locality, or a certain phase of work, and we are unable to find the right place for him."[467] The Student Bar Association already published annually a brochure containing pictures of each anticipated graduate, descriptions of their backgrounds, and listings of their preferred employment.

The school expanded its role in continuing legal education. The afternoon trial program of the third annual Washburn Law School-Topeka Bar Association Law Institute in October 1959 featured University of Chicago Professor Harry Kalven, Jr., reporting the findings of his pathbreaking empirical study of the jury system. The following summer, the Law School hosted a two-day national conference on traffic courts, in cooperation with the American Bar Association, the Kansas Bar Association, and numerous other groups.

Howe sought to address the 1955 ABA/AALS inspection report's criticism about excessive student employment in part through scholarships. Barely two months into his first semester, Howe reported to the Board of Regents that the school needed a scholarship program "so that more top notch students will have time for extra activities such as moot court and the law journal instead of working outside." He expressed concern that many married students "were not getting the education they were capable of" because of their reliance on outside employment.[468] A campaign to fund a scholarship honoring Harry K. Allen had been discussed for years and a $200,000 goal was set after Allen's death in July 1959. If that ambitious goal could be met, the school could award annually five $500 scholarships continuing for all three years of study. A. Harry Crane '25 was chair of the fundraising committee, which assigned alumni to solicit graduates in their geographic areas and also assigned class representatives to solicit classmates who resided outside areas where graduates were concentrated.[469] Contributions to the Allen Fund ultimately totaled $44,000. However, as late as 1964, the Allen Fund and a small fund in memory of Ray Hugh Garvey '15 were the Law School's only endowments. Earnings from those funds and from a portion of one University endowed fund, plus an unendowed cash gift, provided a scholarship budget of approximately

---

467. Howe, *supra* note 460, at 7.

468. *Howe Cites Need for Law Scholarships*, WASHBURN REV., Nov. 17, 1959.

469. *$200,000 Drive Started for Law Fellowship Aid*, WASHBURN REV., Sept. 23, 1960.

$5,000 that year. It was used to make five one-year awards of $500 to entering students. The remainder was awarded to upper level students who served as editor of the law journal and faculty research fellows.[470] A bequest of $129,000 from George A. Kline '06 and Mabel Kline significantly increased funding for scholarships. By the end of the decade there was a fourth endowed scholarship, created by J. Robert Wilson '39. The amount awarded for scholarships grew to $8,465 by academic year 1968–69, benefitting sixteen students.

Howe's early efforts to improve the school earned high praise after the joint ABA/AALS accreditation inspection in October 1960. ABA Adviser Hervey wrote, "The tone and atmosphere of the place have been altered for the good."[471] He and the AALS representative, Dean Page Keeton of the University of Texas, reported that Howe "impresses one as an alert, competent, and knowledge-able dean" and that "a new day has dawned at Washburn under Dean Howe. Except for the location, the Adviser would not have known that it was the same institution which he had inspected five years earlier."[472]

MORE MOOT COURT SUCCESS

Washburn competed in the final rounds of the National Moot Court Compe-tition in New York four times in seven years between 1958 and 1964, and did so again in 1968. As early as 1959, students bragged that only Georgetown and Virginia had better records in the history of the national competition[473] and that certainly was true by the mid-1960s. The 1960 team of L.D. Klenda '61, Royce Wallace '62, and Charles Cline, Jr. '62 qualified for the national finals by finishing second in the regional competition, defeating the University of Kansas City, University of Nebraska, and St. Louis University before losing to Washington University of St. Louis in the finals. The problem involved al-legations of unfair labor practices. The school's success made moot court a prestigious activity and the number of students competing in the intramural competition increased significantly in 1961. The 1962 team of Steve Flood '63,

---

470. Minutes, Washburn U. Sch. of Law faculty meeting (Feb. 14, 1964).

471. Letter from John G. Hervey to John E. Howe (Nov. 28, 1960).

472. Inspection Report, Washburn University of Topeka School of Law, October 5–7, 1960.

473. *W.U. Lawyers Rank High in Moot Court Competition*, WASHBURN REV., Nov. 10, 1959.

Arnold Mize '64, Rich Enochs '63, and Fred Phelps '64 again was runner-up in the region, defeating KU, University of Kansas City, and St. Louis University before losing to the University of Nebraska. The issue was the extent of the right to counsel at preliminary stages of a criminal trial.

The 1964 team of Bill Kurtis '66, Stewart Entz '65, and John Prather '65 was Washburn's first to win the regional competition. Washburn defeated the University of Nebraska in the finals. The team received the top brief award and Kurtis won the American Trial Lawyers Association Award as Top Oralist. In New York, Washburn lost to the eventual winner of the competition, Ohio State University. Kurtis competed again in the fall of his senior year but the Washburn team was eliminated by the team from the University of Kentucky that won the regional final. Kurtis' practice was to go to the podium without a single note in hand. Faculty advisor Ray Spring overheard Nebraska's coach at the 1965 regionals telling his team, "Did you see what he just did—go up there without a note? I don't ever want to see you do that—unless your name is Bill Kurtis."

The 1968 competition involved the timely issue of the legality of the Vietnam war. Washburn's team of Robert Vohs '69, Mike Jarvis '69, and Ron Wilson '69 won the right to compete in New York by finishing second in the regional competition.

ACTIVE STUDENTS AND GREATER VISIBILITY

Students were active in a number of extracurricular activities, combining community service with valuable experience. In 1961, the Student Bar Association established a juvenile probation program, collaborating with the Probate Court of Shawnee County, which faced a shortage of paid workers. Law students agreed to serve, without pay or academic credit, as assistant juvenile probation officers. Each student spent several hours each week with an assigned offender and thereby learned firsthand the practical and policy issues arising in juvenile proceedings. The program was popular and continued with high levels of student participation throughout the decade. Thirty-six students participated the first year. Some worked at the Boys Industrial School, at Menninger Foundation's Southard School, at hospitals, and at family guidance centers. In 1963, thirty-eight students worked with seventeen children. *The*

37. Kerry McQueen '65 is counsel in Practice Court

Kaw reported in 1970 that the program had served more than 500 juveniles.[474] Starting in 1965, the school offered an elective course on Juvenile Court Problems to complement the student activity.

In the spring of 1962, students formed the Advocates Club with the goal of expanding public understanding of the legal process. Students performed a mock trial for various civic groups. Their innovation was integrating into the program an explanation of each step in the trial process. In the spring of 1964, the Student Bar Association initiated a program with the Shawnee County District Court in which students did research for judges on pending cases, thereby bringing students "into greater participation in the active work of the courts."[475]

WSBA also undertook several tasks that the Law School administration could not perform because of inadequate staffing, such as coordinating publication of the placement brochure. In 1960, it started an orientation program for new students. WSBA provided funds to help students attend the National Moot Court Competition. In October 1959, it began publishing a student

---

474. THE KAW 191 (1970).
475. *Bar Association Initiates Program*, WASHBURN REV., Jan. 8, 1964.

newspaper called *Case and Cane*. The paper was discontinued during the 1962–63 academic year and was not restarted until March 1967. Until 1971, the publication was mimeographed. The reason for the pause in publication is not clear but an article in the October 1962 issue was discussed at a faculty meeting at which the faculty voted 4–3 to require the editor to produce facts supporting the article or print a retraction.[476]

The law fraternities were at the core of the school's social life. Both of the school's law fraternities achieved distinction. Washburn's Ingalls Senate of Delta Theta Phi ranked first in scholastic achievement for academic year 1958–59 among the fraternity's 58 chapters nationally and took possession of the forty-inch-tall national traveling scholarship trophy at a banquet in September 1960. The local chapter donated a permanent trophy case to the Law School and it housed the trophy that year. In the fall of 1964, Washburn senior Stewart L. Entz '65 was named Outstanding National Student of the Year by Delta Theta Phi.

The same year Delta Theta Phi received its national trophy, the Benson Chapter of Phi Alpha Delta was named the outstanding chapter in the Midwest and ranked second nationally for its professional program. A group photograph of P.A.D. members behind Benson Chapter's banner with former President Harry Truman on the steps of Carnegie Hall appeared in the fraternity's national magazine. Truman had delivered a lecture on the Washburn campus on April 1, 1960, then held an informal session with faculty and students at the Law School. Truman himself was a P.A.D. and Jack Focht '60 recalled that "our then Justice, Bill Tomlinson, had the guts of a Tyson chicken and asked him" to visit the P.A.D. house. "As I recall we had dinner at the PAD house and visited."[477]

Throughout the decade, P.A.D. members enjoyed an unusual benefit after graduation. The faculty in 1958 declined a request from students to offer a bar review. In 1960, Judge Alex Hotchkiss '27 of Lyndon offered a bar review course exclusively for Benson Chapter members, at no cost. Hotchkiss was a devoted P.A.D. and served as Justice of the national fraternity in 1967. The notion that a single lecturer could cover all bar exam topics is foreign to today's students but Hotchkiss was one of several one-man shows around the country in those days. He started the review the year his son Bruce graduated, driving from

476. Minutes, Washburn U. Sch. of Law faculty meeting (Oct. 10, 1962). Neither the October or November issues are in the archives maintained by the library.

477. Email from Jack Focht '60 to James Concannon (Oct. 19, 2001).

Lyndon to teach in the library in the attic of the P.A.D. house at 1612 College. He emphasized recent cases in the advance sheets. In later years, graduates drove to Lyndon and the Judge lectured for several hours each afternoon at the Osage County Courthouse. The courtroom wasn't air conditioned and the drive was inconvenient but it was worth it. The success rate on the bar exam for those completing Judge Hotchkiss' course was unsurpassed. He was called the "Oracle of Lyndon." By 1964, Delta Theta Phi started a separate bar review that was open to anyone, including graduates of other schools. It was taught by practicing lawyers who covered one subject each. It attracted graduates of KU, where a separate bar review was not organized until 1971.

The fascination with ranking law schools first reached the Midwest in the 1960s. A *Denver Post* survey in 1963 listed Washburn, along with Colorado and Denver, as the top law schools among sixteen schools in the region.[478]

THE END OF OPEN ENROLLMENT

There were 159 students enrolled in 1960. Most were married, and many of them lived on campus in married student housing units on the southeast corner of the campus. They developed a close-knit social community. In later years, graduates described these units with remarkable consistency as "thin-walled."

Predictions at the beginning of the decade for flat or declining applications to law school proved unfounded. 1L enrollment for academic year 1962–63 increased by 35%, pushing total enrollment to 181, the highest number in ten years. When summer school was reorganized in 1962 into two separate six-week sessions, 1L classes were offered each session so that new students could start in the summer as well as during the fall and spring semesters. In academic year 1963–64, enrollment reached 217 and Dean Howe's annual report for the first time observed that the maximum capacity of Carnegie Hall was approximately 250 students.

The Law School Admissions Test still was a minor factor in admission and as late as 1961 two students enrolled who had not taken it yet. The school preferred essentially an open admission policy, giving all applicants who met minimum requirements a chance to prove their worth but achieving quality

478. TOPEKA ST. J., Apr. 27, 1963.

by rigorous grading and high attrition. Dean Howe reported in 1962 that the faculty was "engaged in a study to determine if we can find some sound basis for entrance standards that will insure our having an entering class with high potential for success. Our preliminary findings—based upon a study of our own students—causes us to have doubts as to the validity of any present system of evaluation."[479] Applicants with a B grade average were admitted regardless of their LSAT score, those with a lower GPA were admitted if the LSAT score was above a specified threshold, and the remainder were reviewed by a committee chaired by Dean Howe.

The flood of applications continued and enrollment for 1964–65 reached 259. Having reached the law building's capacity, not to mention that of its faculty, and with applications projected to reach 350 for academic year 1965–66, Washburn was forced to adopt a more selective admission policy. The change was made reluctantly. "We know of no infallible test that will enable us to select only those students that can complete successfully the program of studies in the School of Law," Dean Howe wrote, "but we are hopeful that a method of selection can be devised that will lower our present attrition rate. At the same time we will make every effort to admit any student that we believe has the potential to become an asset to the profession."[480] The new admission policy succeeded in holding enrollment to 263 but there was a longing to meet the larger demand for legal education. There was consensus that with an expanded library, larger classrooms, and additional faculty, enrollment could reach 500 within five years. The faculty was "hopeful that we will, in the near future, be able to obtain a greatly expanded physical plant."[481]

Required courses consumed sixty-two credit hours for students entering in 1965. Having predominantly a prescribed curriculum could be justified in the era of open enrollment by the desire to assure that all graduates achieved basic competence, particularly since most of them were training for general practice. Even after open enrollment ended, Washburn's position was that all graduates should have a "liberal arts" training, with exposure to a wide range of core topics. That position surely was influenced by pragmatic factors. There was no practical alternative to large section classes when the school had a growing number of students and a faculty that was not growing as fast. The

---

479. John E. Howe, *The Dean's Report to the Bar*, 2 WASHBURN L.J. 9, 10 (1962).
480. John E. Howe, *The Dean's Report to the Bar*, 4 WASHBURN L.J. 178 (1965).
481. John E. Howe, *The Dean's Report to the Bar*, 5 WASHBURN L.J 169, 171 (1966).

only way to assure a large section was to make the class required. The faculty had the power to waive required courses and much time at faculty meetings was devoted to petitions for waiver. Some made perfect sense, such as the waiver of Appellate Practice for regional moot court competition top oralist Bill Kurtis '66. Some were necessitated by the fact that students, particularly those entering in February, were out of phase in the curriculum and were not able to enroll in a particular required course. Students presented other reasons for waivers, good and bad, and there was no harm in asking. It was not until 1969 that initial consideration of requests for waivers and to take hours in excess of the normal limit for a single semester was delegated to the Curriculum Committee. At the same time initial consideration of petitions for readmission by students with academic deficiency was delegated to the Admissions Committee.[482]

TALENTED NEW PROFESSORS RECRUITED
BY OTHER LAW SCHOOLS

New professors energized the school during Howe's early years. Most were new to law teaching.

Richard Allen was an activist. He was an early advocate of inter-disciplinary approaches to law, stressing the importance for law of drawing on the learning of the behavioral sciences. "If the future lawyer and future psychiatrist can achieve a greater understanding of the important role of psychiatry in law," he said, "both disciplines can progress in their helping roles."[483] He spoke frequently before civic and campus groups about mental illness and criminal punishment and was described as having a "humorous and lively style."[484] He submitted articles on these topics to the undergraduate journal of opinion, *Hemlock*, and the University's alumni magazine. Allen joined with Professor Ahrens to represent death row inmate Lowell Lee Andrews in his habeas corpus challenge to his conviction, unsuccessfully urging the Kansas Supreme Court to abandon the M'Naghten test for the insanity defense.[485] According

---

482. Minutes, Washburn U. Sch. of Law faculty meeting (May 27, 1969).

483. *Allen to Address Open Meeting March 28*, WASHBURN REV., Mar. 27, 1962.

484. *New Light Is Thrown on Law and Sociology*, WASHBURN REV., Apr. 3, 1962, at 1.

485. *Andrews v. Hand*, 190 Kan. 109, 372 P.2d 559 (1962).

to a colleague, Allen was "enthralled with all schools of psychiatry and psychoanalysis" and "extended this enthusiasm to everything…If others did not share his enthusiasm," he viewed them as too traditional.[486] He told the student newspaper, "I am appalled by the trend toward conformity which many of today's under-graduates manifest. This is not the time of life to be a conformist, but rather a time to question, to doubt, and thereby to learn. The world in which we live cannot afford a generation of unquestioning accepters of the status quo."[487] He was determined that law students would not be subject to the same criticism.

In addition to his classes at the Law School, Allen taught both Law and Psychiatry and Criminology at the Menninger School of Psychiatry. He and Dr. Satten developed a proposal for a joint Menninger-Washburn program in law and psychiatry that would provide academic, clinical, and research training for students, plus graduate study for practicing lawyers. Allen and Satten assured the Board of Regents that much of the estimated cost, $50,000 per year, could be covered at least initially by grants, such as the Ford Foundation's initiative to improve internship programs in law schools through the National Council on Legal Clinics.[488] However, a number of faculty members opposed the project and the Regents declined to approve it, citing uncertainty regarding future funding.

Walter Navin became the faculty advisor for volume 1 of the new law journal and collaborated with Dean Howe, first in evaluating a proposal to adopt the Uniform Commercial Code in Kansas and then in writing comments about it for *Vernon's Kansas Statutes Annotated* upon its adoption.

Dean Howe persuaded the University to fund an additional faculty position in 1961 and the school hired William Harvey that fall. Harvey had both LL.B. and LL.M. degrees from Georgetown, completing the latter during a clerkship with Judge James A. Danaher of the D.C. Circuit Court of Appeals. By agreement with Judge Danaher, Harvey had worked overtime as a part-time clerk for Judge (later Chief Justice) Warren E. Burger on several cases and subjects.[489] Harvey and Bob Fowks undertook a study of the proposed Kansas Code of

---

486. *Memories and Comments, supra* note 440.

487. *WU Law Professor Has Many Interests*, WASHBURN REV., Oct. 17, 1961.

488. TOPEKA DAILY CAP., Mar. 10, 1961.

489. William F. Harvey, *The Judiciary: An Appointment to the Supreme Court*, CHRONICLES 43 (June 2005).

Civil Procedure and, upon its adoption, produced a six-volume analysis for *Vernon's Kansas Statutes Annotated.*[490] Harvey soon became faculty advisor for the Collegiate Young Republicans and in 1965 would be the first chair of the new Washburn faculty senate.

Improvement of resources was short-lived. President Stoffer retired in 1961. Viewed charitably, the focus of Stoffer's successors—Harold Sponberg and John Henderson, Sponberg's successor in 1965—simply was on the undergraduate school. In the less charitable view of some law faculty members, however, they exhibited "lacerating disdain" for the Law School.[491] They were influenced by the University's long-time Treasurer Richard Vogel, who served many administrations. Howe once described him as not understanding law schools and being "totally unaware of the difference between the law school and the department of business administration."[492] The result was "a strong tendency at Washburn University to compare law faculty senior professors' salaries with those of administrative officials in the Liberal Arts School and officials in the University rather than to compare them with salaries of senior law professors in other schools of the middle west having a similar student population and prestige."[493] Law school tuition rose in 1960 from $10 per credit hour to $12 per credit hour, but then remained constant for four years, only one dollar more than undergraduate tuition. By 1965, Howe told the alumni Board of Governors that the Law School "was receiving less in the overall University budget allocation than had been the case when he first became Dean."[494] Senior faculty were paid $4,000 less on average than senior faculty at KU and other law schools in the region. Washburn's salaries would have had to increase by one-third to achieve parity. The disparity became greater as the decade progressed and salaries for senior faculty were among the nation's lowest.

Not surprisingly, there was faculty turnover. During the decade of the

---

490. Leonard Thomas is listed as a co-author. His role was limited to reviewing manuscripts Fowks and Harvey prepared. However, the publisher believed that having a practitioner as a co-author would enhance marketability. *Memories and Comments, supra* note 440.

491. *Id.*

492. Letter from John E. Howe to Melvin C. Poland. (Nov. 28, 1966).

493. Minutes, Washburn U. Sch. of Law faculty meeting (June 23, 1967).

494. Minutes, Washburn U. Sch. of Law faculty meeting (Nov. 19, 1965).

1960s, five faculty members who began their teaching careers at Washburn were lured to higher paying positions at other schools, including three who would become deans. Richard Allen was granted leave for academic year 1962–63 to pursue graduate study at the University of Michigan. He accepted a position the following year at Georgetown Law School, where in 1965 he became Director of its Institute of Law, Psychiatry, and Criminology. In 1976, he became Dean of Hamline Law School in Minnesota. Navin was a Ford Fellow at New York University's law school for academic year 1963–64. He returned for one year, but then significantly higher compensation and greater institutional support for research led him to join the faculty at the University of North Carolina. Mel Poland, after sixteen years on Washburn's faculty, joined Navin at North Carolina as Visiting Professor in 1966, and remained there in a permanent position in 1967. Bill Harvey left Washburn in 1968 to join the faculty at the University of Indiana-Indianapolis. He served as Dean there from 1973 until 1979, was Chair of the Board of Directors of Legal Services Corporation in 1982, and once was nominated for a position on the United States Court of Appeals for the Seventh Circuit. He retired as holder of the Carl M. Gray Chair at Indiana. In 1969, when Poland left North Carolina, he joined Harvey at Indiana-Indianapolis and became Cleon H. Foust Professor in 1983.

One group of alums tried to help reduce faculty attrition. Nine graduates from the late 1940s and early 1950s, all of whom were members of the Phi Delta Theta college fraternity, had formed the Free Society of GNIP GNOP, Inc. (FSOGG) and met annually at different locations. GNIP GNOP spells backward the name of the game members frequently played for inexpensive amusement before success in law practice and business made more costly entertainment feasible. At the 1967 meeting, members decided to memorialize their "esteem" for Washburn's law faculty, from which they had "taken comfort" and "benefitted in great measure," by establishing an annual honorarium for a faculty member recipient of the "FSOGG GOODE BOY! AWARD." Funding for the stipend was generated by annual assessments of $50 on each GNIP GNOP member who attended the group's annual meeting and $100 on members who did not attend. Members selected the recipient by majority vote, considering skills of classroom pedagogy, "scholarly things done," contributions to the "GOODE NAME" of the school, and "such other habits of personality, proclivities, idiosyncrasies, RIGHT THINKING WAYS, and achievements that, to FSOGG in its absolute

38. 1963–1964 law faculty

discretions, comport with habits of GOODE! BOYS everywhere."[495] Members selected Bill Harvey to receive the first award. When he left the Washburn faculty at the end of the ensuing academic year, members discontinued the award. In time, members used similar annual assessments for awards each year to students the members determined had written the best Notes and Comments in the *Washburn Law Journal.*

Either two or three new full-time faculty were hired each academic year beginning in 1964, primarily because of frequent turnover. The size of the full-time faculty grew by only three positions during Howe's eleven-year deanship, even though enrollment quickly shot up by 100 students and had increased by 140 students by his final year. The school was comfortable with its traditional heavy reliance on part-time faculty, many of whom had been talented and dedicated teachers for many years. Howe once described the need for additional full-time teachers as "not acute."[496]

However, limited resources made it difficult for the school to compete for experienced teachers to fill vacancies. Three times, those hired were not even

495. Resolution of the Free Society of GNIP GNOP, Inc., adopted Aug. 20, 1967, at Shangri La Lodge, Afton, Oklahoma (on file in Washburn Law Library). GNIP GNOP members were Robert A. Anderson '47, Richard C. Byrd '47, John F. Hayes '46, Joseph W. Morris '47, Melvin R. Quinlan '49, Ronald K. Richey '51, John N. Sherman, Jr. '49, Edwin M. Wheeler '55, and Paul M. Wise '47.

496. John E. Howe, *The Dean's Report to the Bar*, 2 WASHBURN L.J. 9, 15 (1962).

experienced lawyers, as the school occasionally was forced to solicit applications from graduating seniors at other schools in the region. Some succeeded and some did not. In the former category was Keith Hey, who joined the faculty in the fall of 1963, immediately following his graduation from Creighton Law School, to fill the vacancy created by Allen's departure. Hey returned to Omaha at the end of that year to enter private practice and was replaced for one year by Don Stimmel, who had just graduated from the University of Colorado. Hey rejoined the Washburn faculty in 1965, when Navin departed for North Carolina. Hey stayed just three years, received a leave of absence for graduate study and teaching at Georgetown for the 1968–69 academic year, then was recruited to a better paying position at Temple. He later taught at Dayton before becoming Dean for two years at Thomas Cooley Law School in Michigan in 1980. He remains a member of the faculty there.

Larry Deemer, hired as Visiting Professor in 1966 when Mel Poland was on leave at North Carolina, also came from within the region. He received his LL.B. from Tulane in 1963 but spent three years in practice in Omaha before coming to Washburn. When Poland remained at North Carolina in 1967, Deemer remained on his permanent faculty line. He stayed for two years before pursuing an LL.M. at Columbia Law School as part of a two-year fellowship. He later taught at the University of Montana. He was "well-intended and worked very hard"[497] but students perceived him a "young and very nervous professor who repeated everything." Professor Fowks, whose sense of humor led him to devise pet names for colleagues and even some students, referred to him as Larry Larry Deemer Deemer and students picked up on it. "The story was that if he said something three times, you could be sure it would be on his final exam."[498] In 1967, for the third time in five years, another faculty member was hired who had just graduated from law school. J. Scott Brown was a top student at the University of Oklahoma but was a law teacher for only two years before returning to practice in Oklahoma City.

Students did not accept docilely the negative effects of faculty turnover. The journal's Editor-in-Chief, Winton Hinkle '68, published a remarkable "open letter" in *Case and Cane* as his graduation day neared, addressing this topic

---

497. *Memories and Comments, supra* note 440.

498. Sandy Vogel, *Down Memory Lane with Class of '69*, THE CIRCUIT RIDER 27, 28 (Summer 1994).

and many others.[499] He wrote with "not one shred of bitterness," acknowledging that the "dedicated men and women on the faculty have had a profound impact upon me," and that "[t]hree years here have altered the course of my life, and all for the good." However, he warned that if improvements were not made immediately, "degeneration and decline will immediately set in." Using the University's financial shortages as an excuse and continuing to compare the Law School budget to the undergraduate school's budget would sound "the death knell for this School of Law as a first-class center for legal training." He conceded, "I've taught no law classes, I've wrestled with no budgetary problems, and I've recruited no new professors." On the other hand, "I've been in the classes, and I've been the victim of budgetary problems, and I've been the student of new professors." Thus, he felt qualified to observe:

1. The faculty is too small. It is manifest that unless the full-time faculty of the school is enlarged, and soon, to around double its present size, the entire school, and all of its graduates...are seriously jeopardized. The part-time faculty members make valuable contributions...but wholesale reliance upon them (and I think this is demonstrably now the case) is intolerable.

2. The faculty is underpaid....Are we blind to the fact that able men are refusing to come to Washburn Law School, and that able men are leaving as well, for this very reason?...[500]

Hinkle traced limited curricular offerings and the lack of extracurricular programs that were "so long asked for by our students" to the "understaffed faculty."

The lack of resources caused the Law School once again to look locally for faculty. Edward Robinson, at age 59, became a full-time faculty member in 1964. His personal resources meant Washburn's lower than market level compensation did not deter him from teaching. He was a 1930 graduate of

---

499. Winton Hinkle, PARTING SHOT—*An Open Letter Address to the Faculty, Students, and Friends of Washburn Law School*, CASE AND CANE (May 1968). He also discussed such matters as the problem extensive part-time employment caused for extracurricular programs and a perception that clear standards did not govern decisions by the faculty and administration on student petitions for readmission, waiver of required courses, or other relief.

500. *Id.*

39. Dorothea Warren '42, Law Librarian, 1967–1979,
Professor 1967–1984

the University of Michigan Law School and had practiced law in Iowa and in Omaha before moving to Topeka. He had taught part-time starting in the spring of 1963. Washburn graduate Raymond L. Spring '59 replaced Stimmel in 1965. In 1966, Virginia Creitz Martin '54 became a full-time classroom teacher, six years after she left practice in Wichita to succeed Eleanore Blue as Law Librarian. Martin taught full-time for only one year. She planned to follow her husband to the location of his new employment, but she died from a tragic illness in 1967 before she could do so. Washburn graduate Dorothea Warren '52 left her position as Assistant State Law Librarian to become Law Librarian in 1967. She replaced Maurice "Bud" Michel, who left after just one year to become Law Librarian at the University of Montana. He was unnerved by the tornado that struck the Law School days after he arrived in Topeka and by the overwhelming task of reassembling the library. Yet another graduate, David L. Ryan '65, was hired as Visiting Professor in 1968 during Keith Hey's

40. Otto Kratochvil, Professor 1969–1978

leave of absence for graduate study, then remained full-time when Hey did not return the following year.

There was one source of faculty members for whom Washburn's low salary scale was less of an impediment: retiring military lawyers. When Bill Harvey left in 1968, Washburn hired J. Elwood Slover, who was completing seventeen years as a Judge Advocate for the Air Force. His law degree was from the University of Texas and he had earned an LL.M. at George Washington during his military service. A second retiree from the Air Force, Otto Kratochvil, came on board the following year. Kratochvil had been a professor at the Air Force Academy for four years. He also earned an LL.M. at George Washington after joining the service following completion of his J.D. in 1950 at Louisiana State University. Kratochvil taught for nine years and Slover taught for fifteen years, including six years as Assistant Dean for Dean Ray Spring.

IMPROVING CARNEGIE

Lack of ventilation meant the library was largely unused in the late spring and summer months until central air conditioning was installed in Carnegie Hall in 1964, at a cost of $45,000. Carnegie was the fourth campus building to be air-conditioned. That fall, the school was a beneficiary of construction of a new Shawnee County Courthouse. Law faculty persuaded the Board of County Commissioners to donate the judge's bench, jury chairs, and other courtroom equipment from one of the four courtrooms in the old courthouse that was to be razed. The donated items were installed in the basement of Carnegie Hall to create a long-needed courtroom and lecture hall. That same year, Dean Howe announced the acquisition of audio-visual aids, including a sound movie projector, a slide projector, and a tape recorder and reported that the faculty "is also being encouraged to take advantage of any help that can be gained through this method of instruction."[501]

However, there were limits on what could be done in the building. As enrollment grew, the faculty in 1962 proposed reconfiguring Allen Hall so that it could accommodate 100 students but was told it was not feasible in light of code requirements. The law journal staff occupied a back portion of the library and the library periodically was used for non-library purposes, such as the annual Law Institute and student bar election campaigns. There were frequent complaints of excessive noise. A report of the Library Committee in 1965 put matters succinctly: "Major Problems: too few books, too little money and too little storage space."[502] The acquisitions budget was approximately $13,500, with $12,000 of that committed to continuations. The cost of acquiring legal periodicals was kept manageable by having agreements with 80 law schools to exchange journals.

The annual Washburn Law School-Topeka Bar Association Institute in October 1965 offered special programs as part of the University's centennial celebration. Professors Alfred Conard of Michigan and Harry Kalven of the University of Chicago collaborated for a presentation on automobile accident litigation and the Institute offered the premiere showing of the ABA's new film on revocable trusts. Chief Judge Alfred Murrah of the United States Court of Appeals for the Tenth Circuit was featured speaker at the evening banquet.

---

501. John E. Howe, *The Dean's Report to the Bar*, 4 WASHBURN L.J. 178, 182 (1965).

502. Minutes, Washburn U. Sch. of Law faculty meeting (Dec. 6, 1965).

The University's centennial year brought a new University President, John Henderson. He almost immediately rankled law students, not on an academic matter but on one sometimes more important to them: alcohol. University regulations prohibited alcohol at University functions and parties. Henderson announced the ban applied to events held in private rooms of public places off campus when there was no mingling with the general public. Law and graduate students argued they should be excepted from the regulation because they all were over twenty-one years old. Henderson responded that "if the faculty are under the same restrictions as the undergraduates, then why should law and graduate students who are younger than the faculty not be included also?"[503]

THE TWO LAW SCHOOL ISSUE

The Kansas Supreme Court always had occupied the third floor of the State Capitol. However, some leaders of the Kansas legal community envisioned a separate Kansas Legal Center in Topeka housing not only the Court but also the office of the Attorney General, the two law schools, and the law school libraries merged with the State Law Library. An op-ed piece in the state bar journal in 1960 outlined the concept and predicted economic benefits from the elimination of duplicate resources, greater diversification and specialization in curriculum, freeing of needed space in the Capitol and at the two Universities, greater service to the bar and public, and other benefits.[504] Another op-ed piece in the bar journal two issues later endorsed the concept, adding that it would facilitate graduate programs in law and law-related education and suggesting the Center should also house the Kansas Bar Association headquarters.[505]

Apart from the Law Center concept, the question whether Kansas should have two law schools, or where they should be located, never arose when Washburn was a private school, or even when its only source of public funding was local taxes. The issue surfaced only after the University sought an appropriation of state funds and finally succeeded in 1961. Legislators discussed the two law school issue even though Washburn sought credit hour aid only

---

503. *A Touchy Issue: Drinking Policy Parallels Law*, WASHBURN REV., Jan. 6, 1966, at 2, 6.

504. Fred L. Connor, *A Kansas Legal Center*, 29 J. KAN. B. ASS'N 200 (1960).

505. Kenneth E. Peery, *For a Kansas Legal Center*, 29 J. KAN. B. ASS'N 304 (1960).

for freshman and sophomore students. Focus on the issue heightened when, in the midst of the 1963 legislative session, Rep. Ralph Skoog '59 proposed to include Washburn in a bill to make the Municipal University of Wichita a state university, a proposal Washburn's Regents quickly opposed.[506]

Further attention was brought to the two law school issue on October 19, 1964, when an editorial in the *Topeka Capital Journal* embraced the Law Center concept and urged its construction in Topeka. WIBW-TV editorially endorsed this proposal. One county bar association distributed a resolution calling for study of the idea.[507] To many, the time seemed ripe, since construction of new facilities was on the wish lists of both law schools. Dean James K. Logan of KU had made clear in his 1964 Dean's report that his school needed a new building, and Dean Howe as early as 1962 had argued Washburn needed either an addition or a new building, based on the need for additional space for the law journal staff and the library, as well as for new space for student offices, seminar rooms, a moot courtroom, and additional staff.[508] In May 1965, John Shamberg '37, upon his election as President of the Washburn Law School Association, told a reporter he would "push for plans to construct a new law school building" when his term began in July.[509]

There was sufficient discussion of the Law Center idea, and an assumption that any Law Center would be located in Topeka, that it became a turf issue. KU's Dean Logan in October 1965 devoted the first sixteen pages of his annual Dean's report to the proposal, which he attributed principally to "Topekans and supporters and alumni of the Washburn Law School."[510] Logan did so at the request of KU Chancellor W. Clarke Wescoe, who approved the article before its publication.[511] Logan argued that various projected cost savings from a merger were illusory and noted that the optimal size of a law school was 500 students, not the 700–1000 students a combined school would serve. The previous year, he had surveyed deans of law schools separated

506. *Regents Opposed to WU Becoming State School*, WASHBURN REV., Feb 13, 1963.

507. James K. Logan, *Law School Dean's Report*, 14 KAN. L. REV. 1 (1965).

508. John E. Howe, *The Dean's Report to the Bar*, 2 WASHBURN L.J. 9, 15 (1962).

509. TOPEKA CAP.-J., May 30, 1965.

510. *Id.*

511. Letter from James K. Logan to Henry Bubb (on file in Mabee Library, John W. Henderson Office Files).

from the main campuses of their universities and used their responses to argue that many of the perceived benefits of locating a law school in a State Capitol complex were unlikely to be achieved in reality. However, Logan's most basic argument was that any joint law center should be located on the KU campus in Lawrence, rather than in Topeka, and certainly not on the Washburn campus. "As a practical matter," Logan further argued, "Washburn University can be forced to give up its law school if the legislature so determines. That university is dependent upon state aid now. While no aid is being given directly to its law school, if the state legislature should declare that it would be desirable to have only one law school in the state, Washburn would not be in a position to lay down demands or conditions as to location or status."[512]

The article created a firestorm that was fueled by press reports of Dean Howe's response. In its October 19 issue, the *Kansas City Star* summarized Logan's arguments for location of the Law Center in Lawrence, then reported that "Dean Logan and John Howell [sic], Washburn law school dean, agreed last weekend in principal [sic] to a consolidation sponsored by their students."[513] The reporter apparently meant to say "at a joint appearance sponsored by their students." *The Washburn Review* on October 27 reported as fact that "discussion is underway for a proposed merger" of the two law schools and referred to an earlier report on KEWI radio that Dean Howe had said the "merger would cost less than the current expenditure of both schools."[514] It did suggest most signs pointed to a Topeka location for the merged schools.

Faculty members were concerned. At a meeting on October, the faculty voted unanimously to express "its continued unequivocal position that the Washburn Law School remain in separate existence for the purpose of legal education, with improvements in faculty, salaries, library and buildings with urgent expedition."[515] Another meeting was held November 2, with President Henderson present. The faculty stated its position on merger and Henderson "indicated that he did not intend to see Washburn lose the law school."[516] He authorized faculty members to advise students in classes of their position

512. James K. Logan, *Law School Dean's Report*, 14 KAN. L. REV. 1, 2 (1965).
513. *Would Unify Law Schools in State*, KANSAS CITY STAR, Oct. 19, 1965.
514. *Law School Merger Under Discussion*, WASHBURN REV., Oct. 27, 1965.
515. Minutes, Washburn U. Sch. of Law faculty meeting (Oct. 26, 1965).
516. Minutes, Washburn U. Sch. of Law faculty meeting (Nov. 2, 1965).

and that he had been consulted, but referred the faculty's request to write to alumni on a mass basis to Washburn's Board of Regents.

At a secret meeting on November 11, the Regents considered that request without action but informally agreed to oppose any severance of the school. However, the merger issue was discussed at length at the November 24 public meeting of the Kansas Board of Regents when it approved a fee increase for KU's law school. Several regents spoke favorably about a merger, believing it would be cheaper to operate one physical plant rather than two. One regent suggested the only question was where one law school should be located.[517]

It was hard to put the genie back into the bottle. Alumni were upset. Dean Howe explained to the alumni board that he had been misquoted by a student reporter for the *Star*, that he and Logan merely had participated in a public discussion of the issue, and that they had only agreed on some of the problems.[518] Howe tried to quiet campus rumors by granting an interview to the *Review*, but it quoted him as saying the proposed merger "is so far only in the planning stage" and that "discussion so far has not looked at any of the fundamental questions such as location or size." The article attributed to Howe the observation, "Although the law school as such is not directly connected to Washburn's undergraduate school, there would be some repercussions if we just 'packed up in the middle of the night and stole away.'"[519] Howe felt compelled to respond and used a letter to the editor to do so, assuring that his words could not be mischaracterized by a reporter. He explained that he merely had said there had been discussion that could involve a merger. "There is a tremendous difference between discussion and planning," he wrote. "And, neither I, nor any other person I know is doing any planning that would lead to a merger of the two law schools."[520] He further disclaimed the ability to pack up the law school and steal away in the night. "My authority is such that my right to dispose of a used file cabinet is extremely limited." What limited faculty discussion there had been of a merger had been generated by the various newspaper reports, he wrote, and "faculty discussion has centered around the expansion of our present school," not a merger. Nature, however, would change the focus of discussion.

517. TOPEKA CAP.-J., Dec. 5, 1965.
518. Minutes, Washburn L. Sch. Ass'n Board of Governors (Nov. 19, 1965).
519. *WU Dean Comments on Possible Merger*, WASHBURN REV., Nov. 10, 1965.
520. *Law Merger Denied by Dean*, WASHBURN REV., Dec. 1, 1965.

THE TORNADO

The University's 1966 commencement originally was scheduled for Wednesday, June 8. Early in the spring, however, the date was changed to the prior weekend, June 5. Robert Sarnoff, president of R.C.A., was the speaker. The Law School planned an ambitious summer schedule, offering eighteen credit hours in the first session and thirteen hours in the second session, with only one class taught by a part-time faculty member. Of course, things did not go quite as planned.

In the days following commencement the campus was quiet, since summer classes would not start for a week. When President Henderson left on June 7 for a trip to Iowa, the Provost and the Treasurer also were out of town, so he placed Dean Howe in charge of the University. According to Dean Howe, "I told him, 'Okay John, I'll take care of it. You'll never know this place when you return.' He didn't."[521]

Recent law graduates were among the few users of the campus as they prepared for the bar exam later that month. A study group including Bill Kurtis '66 met on June 8 in the basement of Carnegie Hall, anticipating a routine evening. Kurtis had been a radio broadcaster in his home town of Independence before starting law school and while at Washburn was on the staff of WIBW-TV. He worked there part-time while studying for the bar exam and left the study group so he could start work at 6:30 p.m. Kurtis recalled:

> At 6:30 we received word that a storm was on its way through Manhattan—tearing off roofs....Never having seen a tornado, I believed the old Indian legend that Burnett's Mound would protect the city from tornados. I decided to go live on the air at 7:00—a 26-year-old in shirt and tie—'a front moving our way, high winds coming.' Out of the corner of my eye I saw someone waving a note at me, which was momentarily handed to me. It said, 'A tornado approaching Burnett's Mound.' About 45 seconds later we received word that the Huntington Apartment Complex had been wiped out. It was a new 200 unit building. I could feel an inner hysteria welling up.[522]

---

521. Patti Slider, *Once upon a time on a warm summer evening...*, 35 THE CIRCUIT RIDER 31, 32 (Fall 1996).

522. *Id.* at 32–33.

41. Bill Kurtis '66 prepares
for a moot court argument

The words Kurtis chose to get viewers' attention, "For God's sake, take cover!" have been credited with saving lives that night. He stayed on the air all night, not even taking time to call his wife at their married student apartment in the barracks on campus. The tornado hit the campus at 7:21 p.m. Nearly two hours later, Judge E. Newton Vickers '50 arrived at WIBW studios to report, "Washburn University is gone." In an act he later described as "reckless," Professor Harvey drove the two blocks from his house south of the campus to see the law building as soon as the tornado passed Washburn. "We were certain that all persons in the Law School were killed."[523]

D. Keith Anderson '67 was on campus throughout the ordeal. He first noticed the sky was "a sickening greenish color and it felt like something was wrong." When he turned on the television in his campus apartment, he heard Kurtis's initial report that a tornado was on the ground and headed toward Topeka.

523. *Memories and Comments, supra* note 440.

I gathered my wife Carmen and our only child four-year-old Don, in the only new car we ever owned, and drove to Stoffer Science Hall, our assigned place of shelter. We laid on the basement floor along with Helen Kurtis and her baby and about 200 other people. When the tornado hit the building, sand from the cigarette ash can blew all over us, and Helen and her baby were sucked up against the elevator door.

When the concrete floor under us started shaking, I assumed the building would come down on us. I remember getting angry for not being smart enough to get us up next to a wall where we might have made it.

When the storm was over and we hadn't died, I supposed it was really no big deal after all. As we started up the stairs, I was struck by the shape of the steel doors at the bottom of the stairs. They were bent outward at the bottom by the force of the vacuum. The security officer had held the handles during the storm keeping the doors closed—protecting us. When we got outside, the scene was such that my mind couldn't completely wrap around it. The old rock building just to the west, built before the era of structural steel, with rock walls at the bottom five feet thick or more, looked like London after the blitz. Its three stories had been reduced to little more than one.

As we looked around at the electric lines sparking in the water and wondering where we'd stay that night (it appearing all the barrack housing was gone), I spotted our new car roughly at the bottom of a pile of 50 or so cars that had been parked in the Stoffer parking lot. The day before, I'd have been real upset about a scratched fender. Today, happy we were alive and watching bloody people crawling out of the crumbled building to the west, it didn't matter anymore.[524]

The experience was equally harrowing for those who rode out the storm in Carnegie Hall. Leon Taylor '66 was attending the bar review class in the basement when the sirens went off.

About 15–20 of us went outside for a look-see. I remember that it was incredibly still, which was surprising since it had been storming so hard. Suddenly someone yelled and pointed and we could see this huge black

---

524. Slider, *supra* note 521, at 34–35.

funnel. It seemed like it was some distance away. Then it seemed to change directions and head straight for us. I could see lots of paper and boxes floating on the edge of it. I guess I was mesmerized by the majesty and power of it. Everyone else went to the basement, but I stayed on the law school steps and watched it come closer.

The funnel must have hit a gas pump or something, because there was an explosion in the cloud. I could see roofs and other debris flying around. Mostly I remember the noise; it sounded like 10,000 freight trains. The funnel was almost on me when I came to my senses and ran back into the basement. Just as I got to the bottom of the stairs, the funnel hit the building. A heavy Coke machine was simply picked up and carried off. Windows were sucked in and glass flew everywhere and some fragments hit me in the back and legs. I grabbed hold of the first solid thing I could find and held on firmly.

The whole thing was over in a matter of seconds. It got real quiet except for the tinkling of glass. I can still remember choking and spluttering from the huge clouds of dust from the broken masonry. Several of us climbed out of a basement window and the extent of the damage was breathtaking. Trees were uprooted and electric lines had broken loose and were popping. In the parking area just north of Crane Observatory, cars had been picked up and piled together. It looked like a Dairy Queen of twisted metal.[525]

Jim Roth '66 also was in the basement before the storm hit. One of the cars in that parking area was his.

We could hear the sirens and several of us went to the back door in the southwest part of the building. We could see the tornado clearly and watched it approach. I wasn't particularly concerned, since I was in the basement of a stone building. Suddenly the twister was on top of us. There was an old-fashioned wall vault in the basement of Carnegie. I held on to the door handle and several people hung on to me. I remember clearly that I had to keep my eyes tightly shut because the wind was filled with small particles of gravel and dirt that peppered my face. When the

---

525. *Id.*

tornado passed, several of us crawled out of a basement window. The devastation was incredible. My old Volkswagen bug that was parked in the lot behind Crane Observatory wound up in a tree about six foot above the ground. The running boards had curled up over the doors so they couldn't open"[526]

The path of the tornado was twenty-two miles long and it was on the ground for twenty minutes. It cut a swath through the city, southwest to northeast, and directly across the campus. Eight campus buildings were destroyed beyond repair, including Rice, MacVicar, Crane and Boswell Halls and Thomas Gymnasium. Every other building was damaged and more than 600 trees were uprooted. Damage to the campus ultimately was estimated at $8 million. Dean Howe lived just three and one-half blocks from the campus but was far enough away to be outside the tornado's path:

> We sat and listened to TV. The tornado was on continuously. We heard about damage but nothing about Washburn....My son came in...and said, "Dad, have you seen your law school?... It's pretty well gone. Your office is completely torn off."[527]

Howe and his neighbor, University Treasurer Richard Vogel, walked to the campus. Carnegie Hall was in shambles. The roof was gone and the west portion of the third floor had collapsed. Rich Hayse '69 was a 1L and his first reaction was, "I couldn't imagine what they were going to do, how they were going to continue. It seemed to me like it was a hopeless task at that point."[528]

The back wall caved in, rather than out, and fell across library stacks, preventing many volumes from blowing away. They were still at risk, however, if it rained, so work started immediately the next morning to move the books "even while the engineers were debating whether or not it was safe to go into the wreckage."[529] It was obvious to Lloyd Durow, Director of the University's Building and Grounds Department, that moving all the books would take more than two 14-hour days.

---

526. *Id.*

527. Washburn University School of Law Tornado Video (1996).

528. *Id.*

529. *Dean Howe Reports Restoration Progress and Future Plans for WU's Law School*, WASHBURN REV., Oct. 5, 1966.

42. Carnegie Hall, the Law School's home, after the 1966 tornado

43. Tarps protect the contents of Carnegie Hall

The contractor...reported to me there was no way possible to build a protective cover for the books in the building. I asked him if he had thought of renting a large circus tent. His next report to me was that a tent was not available, but that he was having a large tarpaulin made at a tent company. This tarpaulin was supported at the center by a cable stretched between two telephone poles located on two sides of the building—it worked...[530]

"They said it couldn't be done," Howe wrote to alumni, "but...our Physical Plant doesn't know the meaning of the word 'can't.'"[531]

Though his contract did not commence until July 1, the new librarian Maurice "Bud" Michel started working immediately, on June 9. Adjunct Professor William Treadway, a member of the Topeka Public Library board, arranged for the school to use space in the Public Library's basement. On June 10 and

---

530. Lloyd Durow, *How a Catastrophe Affects a Physical Plant Department* 5–6 (on file in Mabee Library).

531. *Dean Howe Reports Restoration Progress and Future Plans for WU's Law School, supra* note 529.

11, volunteers moved all of the books. Because of the lack of a work room in which to sort and inventory the collection, the books were moved again, beginning July 5, to a warehouse at the Topeka Air Force Depot across from Forbes Field. Both times, professors drove rented trucks back and forth to move the books. "'I kept telling Howe there was no place in my contract where driving a truck was covered,' one professor joked."[532] During the move to Forbes Field, Dean Howe made sure there was a small reward: "We could only move at night from five til ten. Two trucks. We'd load the last load usually before ten then it would be midnight before unloading. Then came the highlight—going over to my house and having a big pitcher of martinis. It was the only good thing to come out of the tornado."[533]

Of course, transporting the books to Forbes Field was only the first step. The books that were piled on the floor had to be cleaned and sorted, for example, into units of the National Reporter system. Librarian Bud Michel "was an unsung 'hero.'... He worked about eighteen hours a day in the hot A.F.B. hanger.... 'Bud' did this every day, the entire summer."[534]

Many people volunteered to help. Kansas Supreme Court Justice Harold Fatzer '33 joined students and others in sorting through the debris on campus. Dean Howe expressed appreciation:

> The law school students have been most helpful in this time of disaster. Immediately after the tornado the students that were still in town offered their services for any work that had to be done. Many of the law wives volunteered to help clean the library books, and I know that in some cases they worked at a regular job during the day and then gave their time at night to assist in the work that we had to do.[535]

The herculean effort of students, faculty, and friends paid off. While some 9,000 volumes had to be re-bound, fewer than 3,000 of more than 30,000 volumes in the collection were lost. Books were mailed back to the school from St. Joseph, Missouri, and from small towns in Iowa to which the storm carried them. The school received numerous donations to replace books that were lost.

---

532. McLane, *supra* note 3, at 15.

533. Slider, *supra* note 521, at 32.

534. *Memories and Comments*, *supra* note 440.

535. John E. Howe, *The Dean's Report to the Bar*, 6 WASHBURN L.J. 413, 414 (1967).

New impacts of the tornado were realized each day. A rumor began to circulate among students that the Supreme Court would waive the bar examination for Washburn graduates and admit them all on motion. It proved merely to be wishful thinking.

Some impacts were individual ones. For Bill Kurtis it was a twister of fate. He already had accepted employment in Wichita with John Frank '39 and Pat Kelly '53 and planned a career as a trial lawyer. However, his non-stop coverage of the tornado led to his national debut with a report on CBS-TV the day after the storm. His performance caught the attention of the news director at WBBM-TV in Chicago, who soon offered him a job. For Kurtis, "The tornado was like a big sign from God saying, 'You idiot, I told you broadcasting!'"[536] Shortly after passing the bar exam he moved to Chicago and launched a broadcasting career, in which he would rely on his legal training repeatedly, that would take him to be anchor of the CBS Morning News and host of A&E network programs such as American Justice and Investigative Reports.

There were many institutional impacts. The spring examination period had just concluded but most exams had not been graded. Part-time faculty had their papers off campus but exams stored in faculty offices blew away and students had to be given ungraded credit. Professor Ahrens had taken his blue books home, "which I regretted later because I had to grade them," and years later he believed he was the only person who graded papers,[537] although in fact he was not. A recurring legend of the school, which should be true if it isn't, is that Professor Fowks, having also taken his papers home to grade, was observed on campus in the dim light of the evening following the tornado heaving blue books into the air.

More than just exam papers went blowing in the wind. Dean Howe and Keith Hey were in the final stages of preparing the Kansas Comments to the recently adopted Uniform Commercial Code. Their draft and also their research notes were spread throughout the county and there were no back-up disks as one might have had decades later. They had to begin the project anew. As Hey described it, "What had been a demanding project the first time around became almost a nightmare the second time. To this day I wonder how we ever got through that time period."[538] Bill Harvey had the same experience with

536. Slider, *supra* note 521, at 33.

537. *Id.* at 31.

538. Email from Keith Hey to James Concannon (Aug. 14, 2007) (on file in

volume 5 of *Vernon's Kansas Statutes Annotated, Code of Civil Procedure*. He had completed the volume the day before the tornado, and the 4" x 6" color-coded cards the publisher required authors to use sat in three boxes, each one-yard in length, on his office floor, ready for shipping.[539]

The morning after the tornado, Dean Howe wanted to retrieve file cabinets from his office but was told that portion of the building was too unsafe. The Physical Plant used a crane to lift the file cabinets through Carnegie's open roof and moved them to Howe's carport. Kansas Supreme Court Justice John Fontron soon appeared at the carport. He said he was "reporting for duty" and was put to work removing mud from the exteriors of the file cabinets. When Howe unlocked one of the file cabinets, he was amazed to find a huge clump of dirt inside. Most of the equipment from the old building was saved from the wreckage.

There were some surprises in the wreckage too. The winds deposited in Carnegie a massive whale bone that had been on display in the natural sciences building. Dean Howe kept it in his basement as a souvenir and presented it to Ray Spring as a symbol of the transfer of power when Spring succeeded Howe as Dean. Spring in turn presented it to his two successors, Carl Monk and Jim Concannon.[540]

Within two days of the tornado, Howe turned the basement of his home at 1346 Wayne into the Law School's administrative office for the summer, "complete with desks, typewriters, mimeograph machine and 'people tramping through Mrs. Howe's back door at all hours of the day.'"[541] Two secretaries took over one corner of the converted family room. Marggy Howe hand-painted a plywood sign and placed it in the Howes' front yard: "Office Washburn Law School—Rear Entrance."[542]

Something had to be done immediately about summer school classes. Dean Logan at KU volunteered the use of Green Hall in Lawrence but the recent merger controversy made that option seem unwise. The University arranged

Washburn Law School).

539. *Memories and Comments, supra* note 440.

540. Primarily due to lack of storage space at the time but in part to further good relations on campus, I returned the bone to its home in the natural sciences building.

541. McLane, *supra* note 3, at 15.

542. *WU Law School Gets New Home*, TOPEKA DAILY CAP., July 8, 1966.

for all summer classes, including those of the Law School, to be held at Topeka West High School. A few law classes met downtown. Space in the Shawnee County Courthouse was made available for the summer to the law journal staff.[543] Registration was delayed by only one day.

Speculation was rampant about the long term. Five days after the tornado, President Henderson publicly "squelched a rumor spreading across the campus that the law school would be moved from the campus," and vowed that "under no circumstances will it be removed from the campus in the fall."[544] Nevertheless, that rumor, and worse ones, reached alumni. At the July 14 meeting of the alumni Board of Governors, President Henderson was asked about rumors the University was "pulling the rug out from under the law school."[545] Although Henderson was emphatic that the administration was giving no thought to a merger, board member and Senator Jack Quinlan '51 reported there was talk among legislators about a "unified" school. There still was such talk when the 1967 legislative session began.

There was only limited time to make arrangements for fall classes, scheduled to start September 12. The federal Office of Emergency Planning agreed to loan the University, at no cost, mobile units to be used for classes and other functions. Each "white box" was air conditioned and heated, had paneled walls, restroom facilities, windows, tile floors, and drapes. A single unit held a class of 34–36 students and units could be combined to form a double unit accommodating 70–75 students. There was concern they would not be ready in time. The Law School did not occupy its new quarters until the day before fall registration. "We were jittery; there was absolutely nothing on the ground. But three weeks later, they came to pour the concrete pilings; by evening the buildings—complete with curtains—were setting there."[546] In all, there were 41 mobile units on campus, organized into five villages: Law, Boswell, Crane, MacVicar and Air Force. Law Village comprised eight units, located south of Benton Hall and east of sorority row. A claim that Washburn had "the only law school in the country with a complex of eight buildings"[547] may be one of the earliest examples of the modern-day practice of "spin." Three units

---

543. *Obiter Dictum*, 6 WASHBURN L.J. 11 (1966).

544. TOPEKA ST. J., June 13, 1966.

545. Minutes, Washburn L. Sch. Ass'n Board of Governors (July 14, 1966).

546. McLane, *supra* note 3, at 16.

547. *Id.*

44: Law Village in the trailers

45: Grades posted on The Wailing Wall

46. Students confer between classes in the Law Village

were used for classrooms, three for the library, one for faculty and one as the administrative office. The library units could accommodate only a working library of about 20,000 volumes and, when the lease of the warehouse at Forbes Field expired in November, the remaining books were placed in storage to await a new building.

There usually are two sides to every story and the Library Committee told the other one in a report to the faculty dated October 10. Once all the books were at the warehouse in early July, the Librarian, three student librarians and one paid non-student worker, without any assistance from the University, commenced sorting the more than 30,000 surviving books. The student librarians worked three forty-hour weeks but, because their contracts limited them to working twenty hours per week, they were unable to work the next three weeks, leaving the Librarian without help in compiling an inventory. A newspaper column solicited volunteers and their help was welcomed, but their lack of legal or library training led to predictable errors. At the same time, a private firm was hired to clean the books but it did what the committee called "a very bad job," leaving sand and plaster particles in the books that would shorten their life by one-third. Eventually, 500 cardboard boxes were filled with state and federal reports, A.L.R., encyclopedias, and *Shepard's Citations.* Commercial movers delivered them to Building 6 when it was ready. The time-consuming task of unloading and shelving the books and sending the boxes back to the warehouse to be refilled fell on the Librarian and the three student assistants. In mid-September, funds were available to hire students at $1.10 per hour to box books at the warehouse. "Students worked three hours one afternoon and then abandoned the project."[548] As of October 10, Building 7 was not yet available and shelving that was to be installed in Building 8 lay unassembled for three weeks because the University's maintenance department was "working on the Art Building." There still were 15,000 volumes at the warehouse and the lease was to expire November 7. Faculty members agreed to meet at the warehouse on October 15 to help sort books.

In the Library Committee's view, the library was "in desperate condition. At this time, the Washburn Law School is a case-book law school. There are no adequate facilities for either student study, or student and faculty research."[549] The report stated that "shelving constructed in buildings 6 and 7 is in a dangerous condition, and the Committee herewith gives notice to the faculty and the University of this opinion on condition. The weight limitations for the floor have been greatly exceeded."

THE LONG ROAD TO A NEW BUILDING

Upon learning about the tornado, President Henderson hurried back from Iowa to the campus. He first saw Dean Howe and several professors as they were digging in the wreckage. "I knew you wanted that new building," Henderson told Howe, "but did you have to go this far?"[550] The University had insurance on campus buildings but it only covered repair costs. If the remains of Carnegie were razed, insurers would pay "only the cash value of the old building, less depreciation."[551] Henderson asked Howe whether the Law School wanted to return to a repaired Carnegie Hall and said he needed to know by the next morning. Howe called an emergency faculty meeting in his basement that evening. Faculty sentiment unanimously favored a new building. Carnegie contained only 14,000 square feet and needs for well more than 30,000 square

---

548. "Report of the Library Committee on the Condition of the Washburn Law Library," Minutes, Washburn U. Sch. of Law special faculty meeting (Oct. 10, 1966).

549. *Id.*

550. McLane, *supra* note 3, at 16.

551. Minutes, Washburn L. Sch. Ass'n Board of Governors (July 14, 1966).

feet previously had been identified. The University elected to repair the Carnegie building for other uses and that work proceeded rapidly. Renovation was completed by spring semester 1967, when it opened as the new home of the Department of Education.

Nine days after the tornado, the Regents, seeking to reassure all constituencies that the University would survive, announced plans for a modern campus. One Regent urged that an architectural planner be commissioned to develop a master plan for campus facilities.[552] President Henderson assured the law alumni Board of Governors at its July 14 meeting that a new law building was part of the plan for rebuilding but qualified that assurance when he commented that "the big question remaining was whether we could raise the money for it." Insurance proceeds and federal funds would not be enough. Henderson had sent 6200 letters seeking contributions to the University-wide rebuilding fund but they had yielded only about $40,000 so far and Henderson reported that no one he had solicited was prepared to make a large capital gift.

The University's public face was positive but the financial uncertainty made matters more difficult behind the scenes. Two members of the Regents were opposed even to planning for a law building at that time, and they blocked a proposal to do so for at least two meetings. According to John Howe, "We had quite a bit of pressure put on, and Henderson helped in this respect. Finally, we obtained the vote"[553] authorizing planning to begin.

It took far longer for University officials to organize the fundraising effort than law alumni anticipated. Repeated delays, plus concerns about whether funds were being allocated properly to the Law School, created a rift between law alumni leaders and the University's central administration that persisted for many years after the new building opened. Ultimately, it was law alumni themselves who made sure the Law School would survive the crisis.

Some of the University's initial steps seemed innocent enough. On July 30, six law alumni board members, Dean Howe, and President Henderson heard presentations about a potential capital campaign for the Law School by three fundraising consultants. Regent Phil Lewis '35 told this group that insurance proceeds plus federal funds might total $700,000. The estimated cost of construction was $1,000,000, leaving a minimum of $300,000 to be raised, plus

552. ROY BIRD, WASHBURN THROUGH THE YEARS 126 (1997).

553. Letter from John E. Howe to Melvin C. Poland (Nov. 28, 1966).

additional amounts if an endowment fund was sought for faculty salaries and the like. The alumni group was most impressed by the presentation by the firm Marts and Lundy. It suggested that a fund raising goal of $500,000 likely was too small and that even a $1 million goal might be small. President Henderson asked about the feasibility of a much larger campaign on behalf of both the University and the Law School.

By the September 17, 1966 Board of Governors meeting, the University had received total insurance proceeds of $1,451,000 for campus-wide losses and $1,250,000 remained after commitments for the repair of the Carnegie building. Phil Lewis '35 told the Board that $500,000 of that amount was being allocated for a new law building. The student newspaper confidently, but erroneously, reported that construction of the new law building would "begin in late spring."[554] University administrators proposed a joint feasibility study for fundraising not only for the law building and law endowment but also for the University as a whole, to replace classroom space that was destroyed. Justice Harold Fatzer '33, then president of the University alumni association, reported it had committed up to $2,000 toward the cost of the study and the Board of Governors agreed to underwrite the remaining cost, up to $3,500.

An architect for the law building was named in November and completion was said to be expected in time for fall semester classes in 1968.[555] However, by the January Board of Governors meeting, the conversion from a free-standing campaign for a new law building and law endowment to a University-wide campaign for $5 million, of which a Law School campaign for $1.5 million was merely a discrete part, was complete. Marts and Lundy would be paid $4,500 per month for sixteen months to conduct the University-wide campaign.

The shift in focus of fundraising efforts unnerved some Board members:

> President Henderson, wishing a free hand in dealing with the delicate problem of news releases and their possible impact on individuals and on the legislature (in re the fund raising campaign) asked the Board of Governors to give him a vote of confidence in advance on his conduct of press releases and announcements, which, he stated, might necessarily embrace a combined University fund drive without any specific reference

---

554. *President Outlines Future of Washburn*, WASHBURN REV., Sept. 21, 1966, at 1.
555. *Architects Named for Law School*, WASHBURN REV., Dec. 7, 1966; TOPEKA CAP.-J., Nov. 18, 1966.

being made to the Law School's inclusion in this drive. President Henderson assured the Board that any such omission as to the Law School's role would be dictated by the politics of the contemporary situation only and would not in any case reflect any lesser role or share in the building or fund-raising program that the Law School would actually play. He emphasized that he would keep faith with the Law School and its alumni on the distribution of campaign funds. President Shamberg remonstrated that with only five officers and Governors of the Association (of a total of thirteen) present, he felt it would be unfair to the others to enter into such a thorough commitment at this time.[556]

Near the end of the meeting, however, after Henderson's departure, a feeling "manifested itself that both courtesy and expediency called for some kind of response." The Board endorsed the request to support the campaign, with the understanding that the goal for Law School funds would be $1.5 million and that donors would have the privilege of designating gifts solely for the Law School.

The University's Board of Regents approved plans for the new building, now estimated to cost $1.2 million, on March 20, 1967. It would contain 42,000 square feet, accommodate up to 500 students, and have thirteen faculty offices. The building was to be constructed to permit a future addition of 10,000 square feet to the library when the size of the collection required it. A grant program of the U.S. Office of Education would pay one-third of the total cost of the building and the University committed itself to spend $800,000 in matching funds to qualify for $400,000 in federal funds. Insurance proceeds and gifts after the tornado represented $500,000 of the University's commitment and it expected reimbursement from private fund raising for the rest. There was a separate $30,000 federal grant application for additional library books, with no University match required. The last week of March, President Lyndon Johnson signed legislation earmarking $1.7 million for campus reconstruction that was used for other campus priorities.

At the April 7 Board of Governors meeting, Judge Delmas Hill '29 expressed to the Marts and Lundy representative his concern "that a great deal of delay had been occasioned already and expressed the hope that the fund-raising drive would swing into high gear with all possible speed." There were broader concerns about the joint fundraising effort:

---

556. Minutes, Washburn L. Sch. Ass'n Board of Governors (Jan. 20, 1967).

The question was raised as to just what unequivocal commitment of funds to the Law School had been made by the University from insurance and other funds on hand which could be used for the Law School regardless of the amount of money raised in the forthcoming drive (i.e., assuming that the drive were successful in raising $1,500,000, would the Law School still receive $500,000 from the University insurance proceeds?) but nobody was able to furnish the answer to this question with complete assurance.[557]

The Board received informal assurance on the issue at its June 23 meeting, based on its Treasurer's conversation with Regent Phil Lewis '35. It also learned that estimated costs had risen to $1,293,000, with corresponding increases in the size of the federal grant and of the University's matching commitment. However, the informal assurance was undercut during the presentation by the Marts and Lundy representative. He initially reported that, as a result of the feasibility study, the University-wide fundraising goal had been revised downward to $1.7 million, of which $931,000 would be earmarked for the Law School and of that amount $431,000 would be spent on the building and associated costs, leaving $500,000 for endowment. Then, "in an apparent amendment to earlier figures furnished," he indicated that just $712,000 of the amount raised would be set aside for the Law School, of which $462,000 would be spent for the building, leaving $250,000 for endowment. President Shamberg "expressed some feeling of disappointment in that no members or officers of the Board of Governors of the Law School Association were on the fund raising executive committee for the Law School nor had they been consulted in determining the campaign goal."[558] The estimated time of completion was pushed back again, to the spring semester of 1969.[559] There were two bits of good news. One was that the Mabee Foundation, at the urging of Don Moyers '34, a member of its board, had made a $100,000 challenge grant for the building, contingent on $200,000 being raised from one or two large donations. The other good news was that, due to the need for continuity, John Shamberg reluctantly agreed to serve a second two-year term as President of the alumni Board.

---

557. Minutes, Washburn L. Sch. Ass'n Board of Governors (Apr. 7, 1967).
558. Minutes, Washburn L. Sch. Ass'n Board of Governors (June 23, 1967).
559. TOPEKA DAILY CAP., June 16, 1967.

As months passed and little progress seemed to be made, alumni frustration grew. Groundbreaking for the new building, scheduled for November 1967, was postponed. By the December 15 Board of Governors meeting, the University had received just $405,000 in pledges, only $94,000 of them for law. The University's campaign thus far had focused on the Topeka area and only on the general University campaign, with no separate drive in Topeka for the Law School. Significant efforts had not yet started in Wichita or Kansas City, except for a special committee that raised $1,200 for the Law School in Wichita. Locations outside the three Kansas metropolitan areas, and outside Kansas where law graduates predominated over undergraduates, had not been targeted. The University terminated the services of Marts and Lundy and assigned Gerald Barker, Assistant to the President, to take charge of the university-wide campaign.

Various Board of Governors members expressed concern about the effect of the delay and some wanted to have a campaign separate from the University. Dean Howe expressed the disappointment of the faculty and students about the delay in the groundbreaking, finding it quite difficult to explain to the faculty and students why the project has not started and what action is being taken to get it started. He further stated there is a possibility that he may lose a faculty member not because of salary reasons particularly but because of uncertainty as to the future of the law school. He is concerned also about what effect this uncertainty may have on future enrollment"[560]

The deadline for meeting the Mabee Foundation $100,000 challenge grant was December 31 and no prospects for doing so were in sight. Don Moyers expressed willingness to seek an extension of the deadline and a change in the terms so that multiple small gifts could meet the challenge, but Moyers worried the challenge might be withdrawn.

The Board of Governors' response to the crisis was to adopt unanimously and deliver to University Regents and administrators a resolution asking that, if the Mabee Foundation challenge was not met by its deadline two weeks later, the Board of Governors be assigned responsibility for conducting the fundraising effort for the new building. It pledged to organize law alums and, if advisable, independently to employ professional assistance.

The University administration quickly agreed to the proposed transfer of responsibility for the campaign and a special meeting of the Board of Gover-

---

560. Minutes, Washburn L. Sch. Ass'n Board of Governors (Dec. 15, 1967).

nors was held on January 15, 1968, to begin planning. Kansas Supreme Court Commissioner Earl Hatcher '23 agreed to be General Campaign Chair. Much of the meeting was spent dividing Kansas in six areas, in addition to the three metropolitan areas, and selecting area chairs who would, in turn, select district chairs. Organizing the out-of-Kansas campaign was deferred until the next meeting. President Henderson announced that pledges plus cash in hand had risen to $185,000 but the estimated cost of construction also had risen $100,000 to $1,393,000. The Board still hoped to raise $250,000 for endowment in addition to the construction costs. The Board clashed with Henderson on the question how to publicize the takeover and launch of the building campaign by the Association. The Board discussed issuing news releases announcing the kickoff of the drive. Henderson was strongly opposed to any general publicity about the campaign and wanted to restrict the announcement to a letter to law graduates. Resolution of the dispute was deferred, but some news coverage subsequently appeared.

No one will ever know whether the fundraising effort would have succeeded if judicial ethics rules regarding charitable solicitations by judges were then what they are today. According to John Shamberg, the morning after the Board meeting, Commissioner Hatcher, "with his usual drive," went to his chambers at the Supreme Court

> and dictated a letter to all the living alumni of the Law School whom he could locate, directing them to appear at an emergency fund raising campaign organization meeting in the Union Building on the Washburn campus on Saturday, February 3, 1968, at 11:00 a.m. At that time, there were about 1,550 graduates of the Law School since its beginning…As expected, there was a big turn out at that organizational meeting since Earl's letter was more a command than an invitation!…From that point on, we went into high gear.[561]

Hatcher's many years of teaching at the school gave him "a wide acquaintance with the alumni of the law school" and contributed "in a substantial manner" to the fund drive.[562] He, Supreme Court Justice Harold Fatzer '33, and Tenth Circuit Judge Delmas C. Hill '29, traveled the state, sat in the offices of alums and asked

---

561. Slider, *supra* note 521, at 34.
562. Hon. Harold R. Fatzer, *Dedication*, 11 WASHBURN L.J. v, viii (1971).

them to contribute. Hill invited Wichita alums to his chambers and handed them pledge cards to fill out. The area and district captains did their jobs as well. The head of the campus Air Force R.O.T.C. program made his personal airplane available to fly Howe and others to district alumni meetings around the state. The extended Mabee Foundation challenge was met. The campaign succeeded, as Shamberg later reflected, "beyond our wildest expectations." The number of $500 pledges was remarkable, many of them from recent graduates.

Hatcher worked tirelessly throughout the fund drive and was awarded an Honorary Doctor of Laws degree in recognition of his efforts. Even non-alums recognized those efforts. When Hatcher retired from the Supreme Court, Justice John Fontron included the following in an eight stanza poem commemorating the occasion:

> Emerging from a Kansas farm
> That lay in Graham County
> He came to sample Washburn's charm
> And savor of her bounty.
>
> This noble school right well he served
> As student, prof and proctor,
> Until at last, as was deserved.
> They made of him a doctor.
>
> But most fame came, so say his chums,
> To this illustrious scholar
> Through separating old alums
> From many hard-earned dollars.[563]

Favorable bids for construction were opened in February and the delayed groundbreaking took place in late March. By the June 29, 1968, Board of Governors meeting, Gerald Barker, now the University's Vice President for Development, reported total contributions as of that date were $784,787. While the Board suggested "that Commissioner Hatcher and Mr. Barker meet in the near future to reconcile their figures," the Board had the luxury to discuss potential uses of the funds raised in excess of those needed for construction. Ultimately, a scholarship fund was endowed and the principal reached $360,000.

---

563. *Id.*

NOT QUITE BUSINESS AS USUAL

Immediately after the tornado, there were natural concerns that current students might transfer and admitted students might not enroll in the fall. By the end of July, however, Howe wrote to alums, "I do not know of any student who has transferred as a result of the tornado. Furthermore, all facts at hand indicate that our prospective students are not being influenced as a result of the disaster."[564] In fact, 276 students enrolled for the fall semester of 1966, an increase of thirteen over the prior year. The trailers were at maximum capacity and enrollment was limited to a similar number the following two years, despite increases in applications.

Life in the trailers was hardly ideal. Between classes, there were only "open air halls"[565] available for students. "When it got cold or was raining," Judge Fred Lorentz '69 recalled, "we went out to our cars and turned on the heater."[566] Dean Howe summarized the problems:

> We have no area other than the library units that can serve as a place for students to meet outside of class. We believe that this is somewhat of a handicap as a chance to meet and discuss problems is one phase of a student's education. The units afford little privacy; and in the classrooms the noise of the air circulation unit is a distraction, especially to students that are in the back of the room.[567]

Students tended to come for classes and then leave the campus, and as a result some student traditions died. The longstanding practice of seniors carrying canes was discontinued. Although a cane rack was built into the "pit" area of the new building, the practice was not revived. Other traditions did continue. Elections of officers of the Student Bar Association were as raucous as ever, with the traditional parades, signs, speeches, heckling, and jeering, plus high voter turnout. The student newspaper, *Case and Cane*, reappeared in mimeographed format in March 1967.

---

564. *Dean Howe Reports Restoration Progress and Future Plans for WU's Law School*, WASHBURN REV., Oct. 5, 1966.

565. *Ceremony Dedicates School; Host of Dignitaries Present*, WASHBURN REV., Sept. 17, 1969.

566. Sandy Vogel, *Down Memory Lane with Class of '69*, 33 THE CIRCUIT RIDER 27 (Summer 1994).

567. John E. Howe, *The Dean's Report to the Bar*, 6 WASHBURN L.J. 413 (1967).

47. Student elections at
the law school

It was important to maintain comradery and morale. The Law Day Banquet was held again, at the Ramada Inn. Professor Ahrens "read a play depicting the enterance [sic] of a typical freshman law student as members laughed to each eneundox [sic]," graduating seniors performed impersonations of faculty, and students presented Professor Robinson with a mod bathrobe.[568] Faculty had their own bizarre fun, too. To commemorate the storm's first anniversary, they had a "Tornado Twister" party, which was repeated for several years thereafter, underwritten by Professor Robinson. An appearance of continuity in the community was important too. The Washburn-Topeka Bar Association annual CLE Institute was held as scheduled in the fall of 1966.

In February 1967, 150 law students attended an all-day program on trial techniques, presented by an American Trial Lawyers Association panel that included renowned trial lawyers Moe Levine and William F.X. Goeghan from New York and Abner Sission from Boston. Levine soon sent an unsolicited contribution to the building campaign and his name appears on the plaque in the Law School honoring donors of $500 or more.

It was vital that the school maintain, and even expand, both its academic program and its academic reputation while it occupied the trailers. Preliminary planning for a third issue of the *Washburn Law Journal* had begun with the volume 5 staff and the volume 6 staff implemented the plan. It was a symposium on medical-legal issues and included nine articles. For the first time, the issue did not include student notes or comments. The next two volumes had symposium issues too. The topic in volume 7 was International Law and Affairs, a topic covered rarely at the time, if at all, in journals published by Midwestern law schools. Editor-in-Chief Winton Hinkle acknowledged that "it must be fairly said, this issue of the *Journal* contains nothing that will be of immediate and practical value to our readers in the practice of law."[569] However, he argued, the topics were "of immediate and practical value to every concerned citizen."[570] The symposium included six articles. The *Journal* published articles by foreign lawyers and judges in volumes 6 and 8 as well. The six-article symposium topic in volume 8 was Civil Rights.

Faculty Advisor Bill Harvey persuaded then-Circuit Judge Warren E. Burger, for whom he had clerked, to permit the *Journal* to publish in volume 7 the

---

568. *Federal Grants Given Washburn, K-State*, WASHBURN REV., May 3, 1967.
569. *Obiter Dictum*, 7 WASHBURN L.J. 151 (1968).
570. *Id.*

address on "Trial Advocacy" Burger presented to the American College of Trial Lawyers earlier that year.[571] There were unique student pieces both before and after the tornado, such as one George E. Erickson, Jr. '66 prepared on the 1945–49 Navy war crimes trials that involved charges of cannibalism, solely as acts of vengeance, by Japanese soldiers on the island of Chichi Jima, Bonin Islands.[572] Erickson's uncle had been the commanding Admiral and convening authority for those trials, so Erickson had access to the original records and transcripts.[573] The *Journal's* innovation was recognized in 1967 when it was rated the best journal published by any of the universities of the Big Eight Mid-West Conference in a national survey of attorneys, judges, and academics conducted by the University of Denver.[574] Washburn's journal tied for 53rd among 102 journals nationwide, so the focus on "Big Eight Mid-West Conference" schools made the results seem better than they were. Still, it was a significant achievement for such a young journal.

Professor Harvey believes the academic credibility the *Journal* gave not merely Washburn Law School but the University as a whole was an important factor in the Law School's survival following the tornado when senior University administrators seemed ambivalent about the school's future. "The Law Journal gave John Howe an 'internal academic club' with which he could 'negotiate' with a Harold Sponberg or a John Henderson and their ilk or kindred spirits in Washburn's central administration.... [S]everal years later John Howe said to me, 'Bill, that was a major internal effect the Law Journal had.'"[575]

National and even international publicity about the Law School that brought the University uncommon academic recognition helped too. M. Martin (Max) Halley '66 practiced thoracic surgery while he attended law school. Successful completion of the first heart transplant by Dr. Christiaan Barnard prompted widespread debate about the definition of death. The May 6, 1968, issue of

---

571. Hon. Warren E. Burger, *Remarks on Trial Advocacy: A Proposition*, 7 WASHBURN L.J. 15 (1967).

572. George E. Erickson, Jr., *Note: United States Navy War Crimes Trials (1945–1949)*, 5 WASHBURN L.J. 89 (1965).

573. *Memories and Comments, supra* note 440.

574. TOPEKA ST. J., Oct. 23, 1967, quoting a recent article in THE DENVER POST. These articles appear to be based on results reported in Lowell J. Noteboom and Timothy R. Walker, *The Law Review—Is It Meeting the Needs of the Legal Community?*, 44 DENVER L.J. 426, 430 (1967).

575. *Memories and Comments, supra* note 440.

the *Journal of The American Medical Association* featured Dr. Halley's article, which Professor Harvey joined as co-author, comparing medical and legal definitions of death.[576] Requests for reprints were received from throughout the world, including fifteen from countries behind the Iron Curtain.[577] Four days after the article was published, a story in the *Wall Street Journal* discussed at length the insights of the "two medical-legal experts…of Washburn University School of Law in Topeka, Kan."[578] Then, a column by Howard A. Rusk, M.D., for the Sunday *New York Times* likewise identified Washburn Law School in its analysis of the definition Halley and Harvey proposed.[579] That article was reprinted in the Paris edition of the *New York Herald Tribune.*

Believing that "an understanding of international relations and problems is beneficial to every student,"[580] the school broadened its offerings in international and comparative law beyond articles in the *Law Journal.* In February 1967, Honorable Maynard Golt, Q.C., from Montreal, Quebec, was guest speaker at a student program. In December, a former Justice of the Supreme Court of Victoria, Australia, who then was Australian Consul-General in New York, delivered an address.[581] In the spring of 1968, Washburn students competed for the first time in the Philip Jessup International Law Moot Court Competition. Arguments involved the dispute between the Republic of Israel and the United Arab Republic regarding the international character of the Gulf of Aqaba and the Straits of Tiran. In the fall of 1968, students organized the International Law Society. At its first meeting, Phil Lewis '35 discussed the World Peace Through Law Conference. The next semester Brigadier General Martin Menter, chair of the Space Law Committee of the ABA's International and Comparative Law Section, addressed the group.

In the summer of 1968, Washburn became one of the first Midwestern law schools to offer a foreign summer program. Partial funding of $20,000 came

576. *Medical vs Legal Definitions of Death,* 204 J. AM. MED. ASS'N 423 (May 6, 1968).

577. *Memories and Comments, supra* note 440.

578. *Life-Saving Advances Are Seen Forcing New Definition of Death,* WALL ST. J., May 10, 1968, at 14.

579. Howard A. Rusk, M.D., *Definition of Death,* N.Y. TIMES, May 19, 1968, at 78.

580. John E. Howe, *The Dean's Report to the Bar,* 7 WASHBURN L.J. 287, 289 (1968).

581. The Hon. Sir Reginald Sholl, *The Australian Legal System, and Extended Remarks,* 7 WASHBURN L.J. 195 (1968).

from the Department of Foreign Studies of the Department of Health, Education, and Welfare and covered about half the cost. As he did so often, Professor Robinson quietly contributed the remaining funds so that the program could go forward.[582] Washburn's proposal was one of the few by a law school to be approved. Twenty-two students spent eight weeks studying abroad, two weeks in England at University College of London, four weeks in Yugoslavia, and one week each in Paris, France, and in Bonn and Dusseldorf, Germany.[583] Students thus studied the civil law system, the socialist legal system, a system without a written constitution, and the English roots of the American common law system. Professors Hey and Deemer were, respectively, Director and Associate Director of the program. Students received seven hours of academic credit. They attended lectures by local scholars, judges, and practitioners, had follow-up discussions with Washburn faculty, visited courts, and sat in on several trials.

The Institute of Comparative Law in Belgrade served as headquarters in Yugoslavia, but students also traveled to other cities to learn about the socialist system in greater depth. Professor Ahrens made contacts to set up this part of the program the prior summer while he studied in Europe as the first recipient of the new Kline Summer Sabbatical. The Paris part of the program was arranged by Dr. Philip Whitcomb, who had been an international correspondent and editor there for thirty years. Whitcomb was a graduate of Washburn College and the son of a member of the initial part-time law faculty, Judge George Whitcomb. The President of the Paris Bar Association received the students in his private chambers and they met with noted international lawyer Dr. Rene de Chambrun. The highlight of the week in Germany was a lecture by Baron Franz Von Papen, who defended his father in the Nuremberg trials. Of course, there were social highlights too, including a hydrofoil trip up the Danube River. A welcome by-product of contacts made while arranging the program was that Yugoslav lawyer Kosta Hadzi, from Novi Sad, enrolled the following fall at Washburn. He graduated in 1972 before returning to his homeland. The Law School hoped to repeat the program in 1969 but the grant was not renewed. Efforts to offer a summer program at London College in 1970 also were unsuccessful.

---

582. Email from Keith Hey to James Concannon (Aug. 14, 2007).

583. The description of the program is drawn from John E. Howe, *The Dean's Report to the Bar*, 7 WASHBURN L.J. 287, 289 (1968); WASHBURN REV., Oct. 30, 1968; WASHBURN REV., Apr. 10, 1968.

The school's awkward facilities did not thwart student achievement. Washburn's Benson Chapter of Phi Alpha Delta received the 1968 award as the most outstanding chapter in the nation. Kathleen Powell '71 received the first place award in 1968 in a national essay contest sponsored by the *Women Lawyers Journal*, which published her winning essay on civil rights and underwrote an all expenses paid trip to England for three weeks. She had the opportunity to work for a week in the office of a solicitor or barrister, visited an Inn of Court, Parliament, and the courts, and met with former Attorney General and Home Secretary Right Hon. Lord Stow Hill.

LOOKING AHEAD

Once funding for the new building finally was assured and it was targeted for completion in the summer of 1969, Dean Howe decided its opening would be a good time for a change in leadership. In the fall of 1968, he submitted his resignation to the Personnel Committee of the Board of Regents, effective at the end of the academic year. The Committee asked him to withdraw it until at least January 1970, to assure a smooth transition to the new building. Before responding to the Committee, Howe told President Henderson that if he remained that long, he should serve the full academic year until July. He confided to a colleague that he had "a fear that I will have my neck in the noose a year longer than I want."[584]

In 1968, Ray Spring became the first faculty member formally to hold the title Assistant Dean. He had been *de facto* Assistant Dean since 1966, when he received a twelve-month contract so he could help Howe with growing administrative responsibilities. Later, as Dean, he would write, "it is the work of the faculty to think and teach and of the Dean to travel and speak. The Assistant Dean's function is to keep the Dean from thinking and the faculty from speaking."[585]

Having mobilized and been energized by the building crisis, the Law School Association turned its attention in October 1968 to the school's other needs. One committee, chaired by Earl Hatcher '23, developed strategies for enlarging the library collection, and another, chaired by Stanley Garrity '27,

---

584. Letter from John E. Howe to Keith Hey (Nov. 25, 1968).

585. Raymond L. Spring, *The Dean's Report to the Bar*, 12 WASHBURN L.J. 262, 264 (1973).

examined faculty issues, including faculty turnover caused by non-competitive faculty salaries. As a short term solution, the Board of Governors adopted a resolution at its January 1969 meeting calling on the Board of Regents to increase tuition by $5 per credit hour, effective the next academic year. The increase increased the hourly rate only to $27.50 but it was a 22% increase. The Board of Governors correctly predicted the increase would not harm enrollment, because of the steady increase in applications the school was experiencing. Board members continued to solicit alumni who had not been reached during the building campaign and committed up to $15,000 to salary improvements over three years. For a longer-term solution, the Board recommended creation of four Chairs, although it recognized fundraising could not start in earnest for four years, when outstanding building pledges would be paid off. While the Chair in Natural Resources the Board recommended made sense, other subject areas recommended for Chairs were unusual for a school in a landlocked agricultural state with a right-to-work law: Labor, Management, and Industrial Relations; Public Utilities; and International and Space Law, later changed to Oceanography and Space Law. This long-term plan never got off the ground, in part because an addition to the building became a higher priority.

A HOME OF ITS OWN

The Class of 1969 spent its entire three years in the trailers. Yet, it publicly displayed a positive attitude. The senior placement brochure began as follows:

> The Class of 1969 feels fortunate to be the only class that will complete its entire law school career in the portable classrooms that now house Washburn School of Law. The rebuilding of an entire law school takes time and our class takes pride in the fact that in such a short time the law school has been able to relocate in permanent facilities.

> We wish to extend our gratitude to the Law School Alumni and friends that have made contributions to our new building. Although we will never know the new building as our law school home, we appreciate the efforts of the many who have made our new building possible, because we know the Washburn School of Law can continue to provide quality legal education to the people of Kansas and the Nation.

Dean Howe expressed pride in the students' attitude and noted the contrast between Washburn and those campuses where student protests about the war in Vietnam were rampant:

> On some campuses a minority of students have been able to suspend the educational operations by destroying the buildings and forcefully preventing the holding of classes. This has not been the rule in the law schools, and it is quite refreshing to know that our own students, even though operating under a handicap of inferior facilities, adopt a constructive, mature approach rather than the infantile, destructive philosophy that has been advanced at some schools.[586]

The new building was the first ever constructed for the use of the Law School. The faculty initially thought a two-level "ranch" style building would be more appropriate than a three-story "skyscraper" style,[587] but in January 1967 approved a three-story design in preference to a T-shaped two-story design.[588] A site on the northwest corner of the campus was selected over at least two other options, although this meant the building would need its own utilities because tying it into the existing steam tunnels on campus would be too expensive.

The first classes were held in the new building during the summer of 1969. The transition was completed in the fall, when a record enrollment of 300 students enjoyed the spacious new quarters. The Law School's volunteer-in-chief, Mrs. Howe, oversaw selection of furniture for the pit area and creation of a small kitchen area on the lower level.

> The older students, not quite used to waiting between classes without a steady wind whistling through their hair, have been shuffling nervously through the anti-septic looking halls, breathing the unfamiliar air-conditioned climate; while the freshmen, having younger and more flexible minds have more readily assumed the roles dictated by their new home. To them, lounge furniture is no stranger and a university under roof is no novelty.[589]

---

586. John E. Howe, *The Dean's Report to the Bar*, 8 WASHBURN L.J. 277 (1969).

587. Minutes, Washburn U. Sch. of Law faculty meeting (Dec. 14, 1966).

588. Minutes, Washburn U. Sch. of Law faculty meeting (Jan. 27, 1967).

589. *Environmental Shift Effects [sic] WU Students At New School of Law*, WASH-

Students wondered "why the building was not given a name instead of being left to face the world known only by the mundane title of 'The Law Building.'"[590] However, no donor contributed the $500,000 required to name the building. Professor Robinson offered to fund construction of either a fountain or a sculpture outside the building. The faculty preferred a sculpture and commissioned a design. The sculptor submitted a model depicting clasped arms emerging from a base, raising a bar that held a balanced scales of justice. The sculpture omitted the chains connecting the bar to the scales. Some faculty thought it was too stark. The minutes of a faculty meeting politely recited that, "The question was raised as to whether a 'massive outside' structure was feasible, or whether a statue should instead be placed inside the building."[591] Robinson purchased the model and the project was abandoned. When Bill Rich became Associate Dean, he found the model in storage and displayed it in his office. It remained there through two transitions of Associate Deans. Today, it is displayed on a table in the Clinic library.

The Law Journal Lamp that had been erected outside Building 8, which housed the law journal office, was mounted on a plaque and placed in May 1970 outside the journal office in Room 106. The inscription notes, "Tradition has it that the lamp sheds the light of knowledge and insight upon all those who labor earnestly within." One monument was placed outside the building, just west of the student lounge, as a tribute to the students who attended the school after the tornado. It was a pillar that supported one of the mobile units in Law Village. Sadly, it had to be removed to make way for the 1992 addition.

Initially, it was assumed dedication of the building would coincide with commencement in 1969. Regent Phil Lewis '35 first suggested a separate event in the fall. His reasoning was surprising, but percipient. He wanted to emphasize that the Law School was a professional school separate from the College:

> It is a little difficult for many of the old timers to realize the importance of this emphasis since they went to school during periods when undergraduate and law school were reasonably merged. This is no longer true, and will not be true in the future. By far the largest percentage of

BURN REV., Sept. 17, 1969.

590. *'The Law Building' Again Calm; Mickey Mouse Is Alive and Well*, WASHBURN REV., Oct. 8, 1969.

591. Minutes, Washburn U. Sch. of Law faculty meeting (Nov. 5, 1969).

our law school graduates currently and in the future will come from undergraduate schools other than Washburn. This makes it extremely important that these graduates be able to identify with the School of Law at Washburn University without having to make a choice between it and their undergraduate school to whom they basically owe their collegiate allegiance.[592]

The formal dedication was held Saturday, September 27, 1969, culminating a three-day celebration. An all-school reunion was held on Thursday. On Friday, a panel of the United States Court of Appeals for the Tenth Circuit, with Chief Judge Alfred Murrah presiding, heard arguments in four appeals in the magnificent new Robinson Courtroom that was a gift from Professor Robinson. It was the first time the Court convened in Topeka. Closed-circuit television allowed an overflow crowd to observe the arguments. United States District Judge George Templar '27 spoke at a luncheon at Whiting Fieldhouse, reviewing the school's history and connections to the courts. Chief Judge Murrah was the speaker that evening at a celebratory banquet at the Municipal Auditorium. His remarks were entitled, "The 7 Lamps of Advocacy." Following the banquet, the law fraternities sponsored "After Glow" sessions.

The dedication was at 10:00 a.m. on Saturday and clouds cleared just before the ceremony started. A crowd of approximately 1,200 alumni, students, and friends attended. The eight trailers that formerly housed the school "stood a few hundred yards to the south, mute evidence of the school's endurance for three years" following the tornado.[593] Following a band concert, a processional of more than 100 persons in academic regalia made its way from the new fine arts building to the new law building. Professor Robinson, an accomplished musician, composed a special processional march for the Washburn band to play and that march would be used at Law School commencement ceremonies for more than thirty years. Representatives of twenty-five American law schools attended, including seven deans. President Henderson, Professor Ahrens and Bruce Kent '70, president of the Student Bar Association, made remarks. Justice Byron R. White of the United States Supreme Court gave the principal address. "I am impressed with what I have seen here at Washburn,"

592. Letter from Philip H. Lewis to John W. Henderson, dated June 17, 1968 (on file in Washburn Law School).

593. TOPEKA ST. J., Sept. 27, 1969.

the Justice said. "Only energy and vision could have produced this building and those same qualities, I am sure, will be powerful support for sustaining a relevant and vital educational enterprise in this beautiful structure."[594] Honorary Doctor of Laws degrees were presented to Justice White, Senator Robert Dole '52, and Commissioner Earl Hatcher '23. The Student Bar Association surprised Dean Howe with a plaque recognizing his efforts and it continues to be displayed on the school's first floor.

In many ways, the celebration lasted all year. The new Robinson Courtroom permitted Washburn for the first time to host the regional round of the National Moot Court Competition. Washburn's team lost in the semi-finals to eventual winner Oklahoma but overcame unusual obstacles to get that far. Team member Jerry Pickerill '70 was involved in a two-car collision while driving home from the library the evening before the competition and co-counsel David McLane '70 competed while his wife was in the hospital awaiting the birth of their child. Participating schools "were happy enough with their surroundings" that they invited Washburn to host the event again the following year, when Retired Justice Charles Whittaker of the United States Supreme Court was one of the judges for the final round.[595] Robinson Courtroom also was the site, in March 1970, of the regional round of the Jessup International Law Moot Court Competition.

Howe wrote to Moe Levine, inviting him to speak again to the student body and offering to pay his expenses. Levine agreed to come. Students who had heard him speak in 1967 who were still enrolled spread the word that the lecture was not to be missed. Robinson Courtroom was packed. Levine began speaking at 10:00 a.m. and planned to conclude at 11:00 a.m. but students urged him to share more of his experiences. When he stopped at noon, students shouted "More!" but he told them "Moe is just too tired." When Dean Howe gave him a check for expenses, Levine endorsed it and gave it back to Howe, telling him to use it for anything the school needed.

A special Law Day Convocation was held May 1, 1970, at which Richard J. Farrell, vice president and general counsel of Standard Oil Company of Indiana, was the principal speaker and received an honorary degree. He presented the University with a pledge for $25,000 over five years from his company's

---

594. Hon. Byron R. White, *Dedicatory Address*, 9 WASHBURN L.J. 173, 178 (1970).
595. *Moot Court Three-Day Event At Washburn*, WASHBURN REV., Dec. 3, 1969.

Foundation, to be used to enhance law faculty salaries. During the ceremony in White Concert Hall, more than 300 alumni who upon graduation had received a Bachelor of Laws (LL.B.) degree took advantage of the opportunity to receive, retroactively, the Juris Doctor (J.D.) degree. Washburn had begun awarding the J.D. to all of its graduates, not just rare students completing special requirements, in 1965. The change was consistent with requirements that each student complete an undergraduate degree before starting law school, engage in academic research and writing while in law school, and complete three years of study after receiving a bachelor's degree. Upgrading the degree had been endorsed by the A.B.A.'s Section on Legal Education and Admission to the Bar. By 1964, the change already had been made by eleven of the thirteen law schools in Kansas and surrounding states. Many other schools had offered graduates from earlier years a similar opportunity to upgrade their degrees retroactively. An additional ceremony to confer the J.D. was held during the annual Law Institute in October 1970.

Professor Robinson received one perquisite in appreciation for his extraordinary contribution for the courtroom, a personalized parking space in the faculty row on the north side of the building, the third space west from Plass Avenue. He drove a black Cadillac and defended his perquisite vigorously. If he arrived at the Law School and found that a late arriving student had parked in his space, he would park his Cadillac perpendicular to the rear of the student's car, blocking it from backing up. The student would have to go to Professor Robinson's office and sheepishly apologize before Robinson would relent and move his car. Once, to avoid the Professor's wrath, a student gunned his car forward to get over the curb, then drove across the lawn and over another curb to get away.

Howe's extra year as Dean was not merely a caretaker year. Professor Warren, who had struggled alone to maintain the library until the new building could be occupied, finally was allowed to hire a law-trained Assistant Librarian, Ruth Gough. The alumni association published the first issue of a quarterly alumni newsletter, *The Circuit Rider*. The school agreed informally to coordinate more closely with the University of Kansas School of Law and the Kansas Bar Association in presenting continuing legal education programs statewide, with the Bar Association taking the lead.[596]

---

596. John E. Howe, *The Dean's Report to the Bar,* 9 WASHBURN L.J. 309, 313

Curricular revision continued, to accommodate new elective courses such as Government Contracts and Water Law without significant increases in the teaching staff. The school for several years had been combining existing courses and reducing the number of credit hours awarded, although not necessarily reducing the number of topics considered. For example, separate three-hour courses in Bills and Notes and Sales had been combined into Commercial Law I and II courses that awarded five hours of credit but also covered secured transactions and documents of title. Combining separate courses in Equity and Damages into a single course in Remedies saved two credit hours.

There was progress on other fronts. Mary Senner '70 was the first woman selected as Editor-in-Chief of the *Washburn Law Journal*, for Volume 9. Having a woman in the position was enough of a novelty that the female reporter for the University newspaper chose to begin an article about Senner by writing, "The striking blond was all business as she explained the obstacles she and her staff work with…" Senner refused to be a novelty. "Being a woman in the seeming man's world of the Law School has no effect on Mary. As she puts it, 'there's not a problem being a woman because you are judged by the work you DO.'"[597]

Howe's decision to retire as Dean and resume full-time teaching was announced publicly after Thanksgiving, 1969. Among other projects, he planned to develop the new course in Water Law. His final seven months as Dean were hardly uneventful. President Nixon's decision to invade Cambodia led to campus protests nationwide that increased after the death of four students at Kent State University. Law students at KU joined undergraduates there in demanding that classes be canceled in protest and that final examinations be made optional. Students there who elected not to take finals received full credit for the semester. Students at Washburn did not protest in the same way but law students presented to the May 12 faculty meeting a petition to make finals optional for graduating seniors to prevent them from suffering disadvantage vis-a-vis KU students in studying for the bar examination. The petition was denied unanimously, 9–0.[598]

Students immediately speculated that Assistant Dean Ray Spring would become Dean and, in response to a request by President Henderson for sugges-

(1970).

597. *Woman Edits Law Journal*, WASHBURN REV., Apr. 29, 1970.
598. Minutes, Washburn U. Sch. of Law faculty meeting (May 12, 1970).

48. Mary Senner, Editor-in-Chief, and the volume 9 Board of Editors

tions, the faculty on December 9 unanimously recommended Spring.[599] However, he was only in his fifth year as a legal educator. Some alumni questioned
whether a more experienced person was needed. A dean search started early
in the spring semester. Letters were sent to leading legal educators requesting
nominations. A committee of the Board of Governors forwarded to President
Henderson nearly a dozen names of potential candidates from throughout the
country. Three external candidates were invited to the campus but one was
eliminated during his interview. Alumni, faculty and student representatives
interviewed the other two candidates. Ray Spring also was being considered
but not all the constituent groups were scheduled for formal interviews with
him. Then, the one external candidate who received positive evaluations from
all constituent groups withdrew from consideration. Spring was named Acting
Dean for one year.

Alumni leaders were upset, not so much with the outcome but with the
way the University administration handled the process. The seeds of distrust
President Henderson had sewn during fundraising for the new building grew.
The Board of Governors demanded to know if its suggested candidates had

---

599. Minutes, Washburn U. Sch. of Law faculty meeting (Dec. 9, 1969).

even been contacted. Phil Lewis '35 and two Board members investigated. Lewis summarized their findings:

> Unfortunately, there was a lack of communication in advising interested groups of what was being done. While follow-ups were made, the Committee making the suggestions were not notified of this fact. Particularly unfortunate was the absence of understanding as to whether Ray Spring was or was not under consideration as the Dean. This misunderstanding probably contributed more than anything else to the emotional unhappiness which occurred.[600]

However, Acting Dean Spring soon earned the confidence of the school's varied constituencies. The Regents confirmed him as the permanent Dean on February 16, 1971.

---

600. Letter from Phil H. Lewis to Hon. Delmas C. Hill, dated Oct. 14, 1970, attached as exhibit to Minutes, Washburn L. Sch. Ass'n Board of Governors (Oct. 30, 1970).

6

THE SPRING YEARS (1970–1978)

Raymond L. Spring '59 was the third Washburn graduate to serve as Dean. The serendipity of military service brought him to Topeka, assigned to Forbes Air Force Base as a B-29 pilot after he volunteered during the Korean War. He remained in Topeka on his discharge in 1956 to complete his final years of undergraduate study and his law degree. Meeting and marrying Lois Stratton, sister of Wayne Stratton '58, helped keep him in Topeka after graduation. He entered practice with the firm for which he clerked during law school, Crane, Martin, Claussen & Ashworth. For three of the next six years, he primarily tried condemnation cases, spending two weeks each month in Council Grove.

An article in the student newspaper, *Case and Cane*, described the new Dean as "a dapper, distinguished looking man of 38" whose "contagious idealism of a youthful teacher combines with a no-nonsense astuteness of an old guru to reveal a purposive, singularly inner-directed person, with many interests but one goal, to make Washburn the finest of law schools....A tang of Dale Carnegie enthusiasm flavors his voice."[601]

Spring's eight-year deanship was marked by unprecedented growth in enrollment, the size of the faculty, clinical education, the library collection, and the size of the building.

---

601. Jim Parrish, *New Law Dean Looks to the Future*, CASE AND CANE (May 1971).

49. Raymond L. Spring '59, Dean 1970–1978,
Professor 1965–2001

RECORD ENROLLMENT

Because the new building was designed to accommodate 500 students, the school increased the size of the entering class, with a target of 175 students. Total enrollment grew rapidly, to 335 in 1970 and 440 in 1971, when 217 entering students exceeded the target by forty-two. A higher percentage of students accepted offers of admission than in prior years. The student population was 35% higher than at any time in the school's history. The number of applicants shot up, exceeding 1,100 for the 1972 class. The school for the first time charged an application fee to cover the added staff cost of processing applications and required an acceptance deposit to better gauge the probable size of the entering class. The school discontinued spring and summer admission and limited matriculation to the fall semester. The change was prompted not only by the increased workload of the admission process but also because students starting in the spring and summer experienced difficulty enrolling in courses in an effective sequence and lacked background required for classes they were forced to take with upper level students. Without fanfare, the target for admission shifted upward, to 220 new students, and soon total enrollment exceeded the planned capacity of the building. There were 517 students in 1972 and 593 in 1973, when Washburn was larger than KU by more than 125 students. Enrollment remained at approximately the same level for the remainder of the decade, peaking in 1975 at 620 students.

The Law School was the only unit on campus that limited enrollment. The University administration, seeing lost revenue potential in the applicants being turned away, urged the Law School to consider starting a separate night program. A faculty committee in December 1971 recommended resoundingly against the idea, concluding such programs are feasible only in larger urban areas, do not enhance a law school's reputation, and either strain limited faculty resources or require large expenditures for new faculty.

Admission decisions became more complex as the number of applications rose. LSAT scores and undergraduate grades, with special emphasis on grades during the junior and senior years, were used to screen applicants, but the school took pride that it used individual factors to select from the large middle of the applicant pool those applicants most likely to become good lawyers. Dean Spring acknowledged that schools that based admission decisions solely on LSAT scores and GPAs assured that students had glittering entering credentials, but he thought that approach "loses sight of ultimate objectives." In his view, "the two questions—'What makes a good student?' and 'What makes a good lawyer?'—may not, probably don't, lead to the same answer. Thus a law school must not lose sight of the fact that the quality of the student body is *not* the objective. The making of good lawyers *is*."[602]

Responding to reports of unmet needs for legal services in smaller communities where many graduates were unwilling to accept positions, Washburn considered an applicant's geographic origin and the likelihood the applicant would return to practice in a small home town.[603] There was some preference for Kansas residents, even before resident law credit hours became eligible for state aid, and Kansans frequently comprised 85% of entering students. Washburn undergraduates were said to have a slight advantage

---

602. Raymond L. Spring, *Turning the Corner: The Dean's Report to the Bar*, 14 WASHBURN L.J. 429, 431 (1975).

603. Raymond L. Spring, *The Dean's Corner*, 2 THE CIRCUIT RIDER 4 (June 1971).

in the admission process, but only if there were two equal applicants for a single seat.[604]

When there were no black students in the 1968 or 1969 entering classes, recruitment of minority students became a priority for the first time. The impediment was thought primarily to be financial. In 1970, a Minorities in Legal Education (MILE) scholarship was endowed in a joint project with the Topeka Bar Association. The alumni Board of Governors voted to contribute $1,500 of Association funds to it.[605] However, in 1972, one black graduate who helped establish the MILE scholarship, Charles S. Scott '48, publicly faulted the school for not having a formal, on-going program to increase the number of minorities in the applicant pool.[606] An Ad Hoc Committee on Minority and Disadvantaged Students was appointed that fall and the faculty adopted a policy statement that "every reasonable effort will be made to admit and retain disadvantaged persons" with each case being considered "on an individual basis, with all relevant factors being considered."[607] Applicants could be considered disadvantaged because of race, national origin, having a native tongue other than English, or station in life such as poverty. The policy rejected any specific standard for admission for such applicants.

The policy did not treat women as being disadvantaged solely because they were under-represented in the legal profession. However, women began to enroll in greater numbers even without a concerted recruitment effort. In Assistant Dean El Slover's view, the reason simply was that more women were deciding on their own to apply.[608] The editor of *Case and Cane*, in discussing current issues in legal education nationally, posed the question:

> Should law schools seek out women in favor of the traditional "bread-winner"? There are studies which indicate that women are making good use of their degrees and finding a place in the legal community while other research shows that most will marry and raise children without ever using the education practically.[609]

---

604. *Id.*

605. *M.I.L.E. Scholarship Fund for Minorities*, THE CIRCUIT RIDER 2 (July 1970).

606. *WU Law School Students Stress Need for Minority Recruitment*, WASHBURN REV., Apr. 19, 1972.

607. Minutes, Washburn U. Sch. of Law faculty meeting (Nov. 8, 1972).

608. *Law School Selection Underway*, WASHBURN REV., Feb. 4, 1976, at 3.

609. *Editorially Speaking*, CASE AND CANE (Mar. 1972).

Women chose to come despite such questions by some of their classmates. By 1977, the catalogue's section on the Washburn Law Wives organization reflected a name change to Washburn Law Partners.

There were many consequences of the flood of applications and of students. For example, as admission decisions became highly selective, the rate of academic attrition declined sharply. More students withdrew for personal reasons than for bad grades. Classes were so large that the faculty concluded the traditional grading system did not sufficiently differentiate student performance, so in 1975 it added B+, C+, and D+ grades, each worth .5 grade points more than the grade without the plus.

Faculty and students faced the challenge of "working together in a setting much different than the small-school community once so familiar to us."[610] The increase in students changed the pace of classroom discussions and required faculty to spend more time in counseling and grading. To Dean Spring,

> The great risk…was in student anonymity, with decreasing student-faculty rapport, increasing communications failure and continuing frustration from the many complexities of too few attempting to deal with too many in too diverse ways. Apathy and disinterest might have set in; so might intolerance and negativism.[611]

In Spring's view, none of these results occurred, and he credited "a revival of student activism." At a time when for many administrators nationally student activism was something to be quelled, Spring wrote in the student newspaper, "The watchword of your activism has largely been responsibility and responsible action—whatever the result—almost invariably provides a positive contribution to any situation." He acknowledged that students had called to the faculty's attention "matters of concern to you which are in need of at least an explanation, or in some cases, change." He expressed appreciation that students had "shown the interest and responsibility to take hold in a fluid situation and work in a cohesive way for the best interest of our school."[612]

The experience of Phil Knighton '71 shows it was more than just student activism that helped preserve small-school community values. As a 3L, he worked

---

610. Raymond L. Spring, *The Dean's Report to the Bar*, 11 WASHBURN L.J. 331, 334 (1972).

611. *The Dean's Column*, CASE AND CANE (Apr. 1972).

612. *Id.*

50. J. Elwood Slover, Professor 1968–1983,
Assistant Dean 1970–1976

five jobs: making coffee in the student lounge at 5:00 a.m. weekdays; being student coordinator in the Law Clinic during the day; inspecting pier borings at construction sites late afternoons; teaching evening geology courses to under-graduates; and working weekends at the State Highway Department Research Lab. Still, he determined he would be short $700–$900 needed to finish the year. He inquired whether there was an emergency loan fund that could help him make it until graduation. Professor Howe advised him there was "an ad hoc 'slush fund'" and that he should contact Assistant Dean Elwood Slover.

The Washburn Law School Association maintained an emergency loan fund. A report as of April 30, 1969, showed that twenty-three students had loans totaling $6,801.25.[613] However, the average loan was under $300. The day after Slover informed Knighton that the "committee" would consider his

---

613. Minutes, Washburn L. Sch. Ass'n Board of Governors (June 21, 1969).

request, Slover handed him a cashier's check for the requested amount. Slover explained that it was "a non-interest-bearing loan. No papers were signed; it was conditioned verbally on honor to pay it back at his earliest opportunity."[614] The fall after graduation, Knighton returned to the campus from Wichita for a seminar and went to Slover's office to repay "the committee." When he asked to whom the check should be made payable, "Slover replied, 'Oh, just make it out to Elwood Slover.'" That is when it first dawned on Knighton that Slover had made this loan personally.[615]

At its May 7, 1971, meeting, just before Knighton graduated, the Association's Board of Governors increased its emergency loan fund by transferring $5,000 into it from the Life Membership Endowment. Loans were interest free until one year after graduation, when the student's note came due. In October, Association President Warren Shaw '31 appointed a three-person committee to pass on loans requests, with the proviso that one committee member had to interview each loan applicant. Later, the loan fund was transferred to a University agency account, to simplify administration and expedite distribution of funds. The maximum loan was $500 and the maximum duration was ninety days. In 2009, Knighton created a new loan fund, named in honor of Dean Slover, to assist 3Ls with emergency needs on the same basis as the one he received, with repayment resting solely on the recipient's sense of honor.

RECRUITING A FACULTY FOR THE FUTURE

Doubling enrollment in only four years from 1969 to 1973 would have taxed the resources of any faculty. Faculty size grew by only half during these years, exacerbating the difficulties. The student-faculty ratio ballooned to 39.5:1 by the fall of 1973, and, if the Dean, Assistant Dean, and Librarian were excluded from the faculty count as they are today, the ratio would have been 49.4:1. What kept the school functioning was that it continued to prescribe for graduation one of the highest numbers of required courses of any American law school, and the required courses could be divided into two large sections of 110 students each. The number of required hours grew from 59 hours among the 85 hours required in 1965 to a peak of 64 hours among 90 hours required in 1971.

---

614. *Elwood Slover Law Emergency Fund*, 47 THE WASHBURN LAWYER 29 (Fall 2009).

615. *Id.*

A recommendation by the Curriculum Committee in 1973 that all upper-level courses besides Legal Ethics be made electives was not adopted. The number of required hours remained at 60–61 until 1979. Continued reliance on part-time faculty also helped the school cope with the volume of students.

Many new faculty members added during these years became fixtures at the Law School. The 1970–71 academic year brought Donald F. Rowland '59 to be Director of the new Washburn Law Clinic and David Dale to teach courses in Property, Environmental Law, and Oil and Gas. Rowland had been Probate Judge in Hays. Dale had practiced for ten years with Vinson, Elkins, Searls and Connally after his graduation in 1957 from the University of Texas School of Law. He came to Washburn from the legal department of Quintana Petroleum Company.

The following year, Professor Robinson took Emeritus status, although he continued to teach part-time. His replacement, Bruce Levine, was the first newly-hired faculty member who had taught full-time at another law school since John Howe arrived twelve years earlier. Levine taught the previous three years at South Texas College of Law in Houston. He was a graduate of Brooklyn Law School, had an LL.M. from NYU, was a C.P.A., and had practiced for five years before entering law teaching.

That same year, William Treadway accepted appointment as Visiting Professor of Law when he retired as General Attorney for the Santa Fe Railway. Happily, it became an extended visit. He had lectured part-time for many years and his credentials for teaching were impeccable. He earned his first law degree in 1927 from George Washington and completed an S.J.D. at Michigan in 1933. Treadway was a model of professionalism. Once, while on railroad business in Colorado the day before he was to teach a class as an Adjunct Professor, his scheduled passenger train to Topeka was not permitted to run through a flooded area. Elwin Cabbage '56 recalled:

> Bill rode in a caboose on a freight train from La Junta, Colorado, to meet his 8:00 a.m. class. Having asked the Dean's secretary to "hold the class in place," Bill strode in about 8:15 a.m. After taking his seat at the lecture table, he remarked "Even the best are not on time all the time," and proceeded to call for the first case discussion.[616]

---

616. Elwin Cabbage, Class Notes, Washburn School of Law Alumni Weekend 1996, June 7–8, 1996.

51. William Treadway, first recipient of William O. Douglas
Outstanding Professor Award

When senior students initiated the William O. Douglas Outstanding Professor Award in 1976, they elected Treadway as the first recipient. Students described him as a model of "a scholar and a gentleman" and wrote:

> He has made the Socratic search for an understanding of agency and corporate law principles an exciting and inquisitive pilgrimage. Moreover, he has suggested his students find more in the law than merely a suitable livelihood; challenging them to consider their professional careers charged with public responsibilities beyond the pale of ethical codes and regulatory rules. For all this and more we are grateful.[617]

Lack of resources continued to make faculty recruitment and retention challenging. Dean Spring opined in 1972 that, because of rapid growth at some

---

617. *Dedication*, 16 WASHBURN L.J. *ix* (1976).

law schools and the opening of new ones, "there are more law faculty positions available than there are qualified candidates."[618] By 1973–74, Washburn's median salary ranked 143rd among 148 accredited schools. The five-year grant from the Standard Oil of Indiana Foundation was designated in 1970–71 for salary supplements for three Distinguished Professors of Law, Professors Ahrens, Fowks, and Howe, but the school's highest 1973 salary still ranked only 121st, limiting the school's ability to recruit experienced teachers. Nine of ten faculty members hired from 1972–74 were new to full-time teaching. The lone exception was Roy Bartlett '49, who returned to full-time teaching in 1973 after fourteen years as a lawyer with the Selective Service System, ultimately as its Chief Counsel.

Given the "very unfavorable" salary situation, the team conducting the spring 1972 ABA/AALS site evaluation seemed almost surprised to find faculty members were competent and even was "impressed by the quality of instruction." Further, the inspectors concluded the curriculum was "entirely adequate" and that "Washburn compares favorably with other law schools in its curriculum." Still, they warned that the school's ability to compete for faculty in the future would be compromised if resource issues were not addressed quickly.

Indeed, there were misses as well as hits in faculty recruitment. Ridgeley Scott had been a lawyer for just two years when he came to Washburn after completing an LL.M. at the University of Miami and working for the I.R.S. in Washington D.C. A magazine article published thirty years after Scott's departure from Washburn described him as "the rare person whose name actually matches his personality: Ridgeley Scott is rigid.... [H]e is decidedly not warm and cuddly.... [H]e can be brutally direct and anything but politically correct."[619] A student who had immigrated to the United States from Cuba vividly recalls that early in Scott's next-to-last semester at Washburn, Scott told the student that he was going to fail Scott's course. Scott in fact gave the student an F. After the faculty determined the grade was given arbitrarily, the faculty voted to correct it.[620] The incident led to a proposal from the WSBA to assume responsibility for issuing and decoding exam numbers "to instill a greater degree of faith"

618. Raymond L. Spring, *The Dean's Report to the Bar*, 11 WASHBURN L.J. 331, 333 (1972).

619. Bob Calandra, *Without a Trace*, PHILADELPHIA MAGAZINE (Oct. 2003) (article about the disappearance of Scott's heiress wife).

620. Minutes, Washburn U. Sch. of Law faculty meeting (Aug. 21, 1972).

that "exams will be graded objectively on the content of the paper alone." The faculty declined to delegate the responsibility but adopted an anonymous grading policy prohibiting release to the professor of the names of students until raw scores on the examination had been determined, and then only for the purpose of adding points, as the student proposal contemplated as well, for class participation, papers, and other components of the final grade besides the examination.[621] Scott's three-year stay at Washburn ended that year, in 1972. Scott remained in law teaching, first at Stetson in Florida and then at Widener in Delaware, where he became a full professor in 1978. Curiously, however, in 1988 his title was changed back to Associate Professor.[622] After 1997–98, he no longer was in law teaching and he subsequently taught history part-time at Delaware County Community College in Pennsylvania.[623]

When Kurt Morgan replaced Scott in 1972, he likewise had been out of law school for only two years and had spent one of those years completing an LL.M. at SMU. Morgan's heart did not appear to be in teaching. Students nicknamed him "Sparky" and once reported seeing him on a golf course on a day he canceled class because of illness. No doubt sensing limited long-term prospects at Washburn, Morgan resigned at the start of orientation for the fall semester of 1975 and moved to California to open a foosball franchise.[624] It was too late to hire a replacement and he was scheduled to teach two large classes. Dean Spring combined Morgan's section of Criminal Law with his own and taught all 220 students in Room 100 in the Henderson building, since no room in the Law School was large enough. John Howe agreed to teach Morgan's section of Contracts. Although Howe was an experienced Contracts teacher, he recently had concentrated on commercial law courses and Water Law. Assuming he would not teach Contracts again before he retired, Howe had discarded his teaching notes for Contracts the summer before Morgan left.

Dennis Stewart was, in contrast, a hit, even though he was a member of the faculty for only one year, 1972–73. He had spent three years after graduation from UMKC as Law Clerk for a United States District Judge in the Western

---

621. Minutes, Washburn U. Sch. of Law faculty meeting (Apr. 5, 1972).

622. Association of American Law Schools, DIRECTORY OF LAW TEACHERS 849 (1996–97).

623. Calandra, *supra* note 619.

624. Since at least 1990, Morgan has been counsel to the Oklahoma Alcoholic Beverage Laws Enforcement Commission.

District of Missouri and then one year as Assistant General Counsel for the University of Missouri-Columbia. Stewart was a workaholic. While teaching both Contracts and Evidence for the first time, he prepared massive outlines of the topics, with extensive case annotations, and distributed mimeographed copies to his students. In addition, he completed text for inclusion in the influential *Manual on Complex and Multi-District Litigation* for the federal courts and an article for the *Washburn Law Journal*. Stewart left Washburn to accept appointment as United States Magistrate in the Western District of Missouri. He later was Chief Judge of the Bankruptcy Court there.

Had Stewart not departed, it is doubtful that his replacement, Jim Concannon, would have become a full-time teacher. That the school was hampered in recruiting nationally by limited resources surely was a factor as well. I[625] was completing my second year of a clerkship with Kansas Supreme Court Justice Alex Fromme, after graduating from KU's law school in 1971. I taught Conflict of Laws as a Lecturer during the summer of 1972. Dean Spring had mentioned in a hallway conversation in April with a student, my friend State Representative David Heinemann '73, that he was having difficulty finding someone to teach the course. When Heinemann told him I might be willing to do it, Dean Spring called me the same day and, sight unseen, asked me to teach that summer. Student reviews in the huge class were positive and I was asked to teach Appellate Practice during the fall semester. I had no thought of full-time teaching. I was planning to move to Lawrence to be an Assistant County Attorney when Ed Collister won election that November as County Attorney, and also to join his private firm. Collister unexpectedly was defeated in the election and his private practice was not large enough yet to support a full-time associate. My letter to Dean Spring expressing interest in a full-time teaching position was on his desk when he learned Stewart would be appointed as United States Magistrate and, by December, I was hired.

The Law School's limited resources in the 1970s reflected the central administration's treatment of it as a "cash cow" relative to other departments. Although tuition for law students remained constant at $30 per credit hour from 1970 through 1974, the huge increase in enrollment meant the Law School was generating much more new revenue than it received in new budget allocations.

---

625. Because it is awkward to refer to oneself in the third person, I will write in the first person even though this book is not meant to be a personal memoir.

While tuition accounted for 46% of revenues University-wide, the Law School's tuition revenue exceeded its operating budget by about $35,000 in 1973–74. Dean Spring did not object to the Law School contributing to indirect costs at this level, or even higher, but as early as October 1971 he proposed tuition increases of $7.50 per credit hour over three years contingent on the proceeds being dedicated to additional faculty and staff positions and other Law School needs. An editorial in the student newspaper already had commented that a number of students supported a tuition increase for these purposes and that "it is exceptionally difficult to obtain experienced professors with the low salaries our law school offers."[626]

Spring also attempted to use the 1972 accreditation team's concern about non-competitive salaries and its conclusion that "the University should respond to this situation immediately" to gain new resources for faculty. President Henderson expressed sympathy for the problem but was concerned how favoring the law faculty would be received elsewhere on campus. Besides, the Nixon administration's wage-price controls precluded significant action. Spring devised a stop-gap measure that was ingenious. Converting law faculty from academic year contracts to twelve-month contracts met both concerns, since law faculty then had different obligations from undergraduate faculty and the wage-price controls permitted additional compensation for additional work. The increase in compensation was more than faculty members traditionally earned from summer teaching. Faculty members remained on twelve-month contracts through academic year 1978–79.

The 1974 legislature increased state aid to Washburn by, for the first time, making law and graduate hours eligible for state payment of $10 per credit hour for Kansas resident students, $4 less per hour than the State paid for resident undergraduate hours. This increased the revenue generated by the Law School by about 30%, or $150,000, but Henderson indicated it would merely be "absorbed" into the following year's budget since the Legislature's action took place so late in the University's budget cycle.[627]

However, even before the increase in state aid, Dean Spring persuaded the University administration to permit the Law School to hire five new faculty members in 1974 to reduce the excessive student-faculty ratio. A $4 per credit

626. *Editorially Speaking*, CASE AND CANE (Mar. 1971).

627. *State Aid for Grad Hours Upped; AA Degree Delayed*, WASHBURN REV., Mar. 27, 1974, at 1.

52. Linda D. Elrod '72, Richard Righter Distinguished
Professor of Law, 1974–present

hour increase in tuition and grant funding for two positions in the Law Clinic
made the Law School's case more persuasive. Not surprisingly, the two clinic
positions were filled by local lawyers, Joel Meinecke '69 and Randall Jones,
and a classroom position was as well, by Linda Henry Elrod '72.

Elrod's path into law teaching was strikingly similar to my own. After graduation, she was Research Attorney for the Kansas Judicial Council. Dennis
Stewart's selection as U.S. Magistrate Judge meant he was unable to teach
Creditors' Rights as planned during the summer of 1973. In early May, just
two weeks before the class was to start, Dean Spring asked Elrod to teach the
class. She had not taken the class as a law student, but, exhibiting the utter
fearlessness that characterizes her, she accepted Spring's offer. In those two
weeks, she read three textbooks, interviewed lawyers who practiced in the area
and was ready to go.[628] Student reaction was so positive that Dean Spring asked

---

628. Linda Diane Henry Elrod, *Washburn Law School Celebrates a Century of*

her to teach Legal Methods the following fall and Legal Research and Writing the following spring. That spring, in March, David Dale became ill and could not complete his classes. Dean Spring called Elrod once again, on a Friday, and she agreed to take over Dale's four-hour class in Property for the remainder of the semester, starting on Monday. It did not matter that she was then seven months pregnant with her first child. Not surprisingly, the faculty one week later extended an offer to Elrod to fill one of the new full-time positions, starting in the second summer session just six weeks after her son was born. She has maintained the same astonishing energy level and ability to multi-task throughout her teaching career. For example, when her daughter was due to be born several days after Thanksgiving in 1976, she refused to ask substitute teachers to cover three classes after the holiday that she thought she would miss. Instead, she videotaped lectures for them. When her daughter arrived several days earlier than expected, she came back to teach live the three classes she had taped.

Even though Washburn's median salary for 1974–75 would be the sixth lowest among all ABA schools, Spring was determined to fill the other two 1974 positions from the national market. He had to rely on intangible substitutes for the high salaries Washburn was unable to offer. Carl C. Monk was practicing with Simpson, Thacher & Bartlett in New York City when he interviewed with Washburn and some thirty other schools during the AALS annual convention at the Fairmont Hotel in New Orleans. Carl stopped by the hotel bar for a nightcap sometime between midnight and 1 a.m. at the end of the last long day of interviews. Ray and Lois Spring were there and invited Carl and his wife Trish to join them. The four of them ultimately closed the bar—and bars don't close early in New Orleans. Monk later attributed his decision to cast his lot with Washburn and to reject higher paying offers from other schools to the appreciation he gained in those hours for Spring's humanity, decency, and integrity. Clearly, the appreciation he gained from finding a dean who not only could but also would close the bar with him was a factor too.

Hiring Carl Monk led Washburn to hire John F. Kuether for the final vacancy that year, and without having to compete with other schools. Like Monk, Kuether was an associate at Simpson, Thacher & Bartlett. He had thought about law teaching, but only at some future time, so he had not attended

Welcoming Women, 42 WASHBURN L.J. 853, 887 (2004).

the AALS annual meeting. When Monk told Kuether he planned to teach at Washburn and that there was an additional vacancy, Kuether applied to fill it. Monk recommended him and he ultimately received an offer. Both Monk and Kuether were 1971 law school graduates, Monk from Howard and Kuether from Virginia.

Having hired ten new faculty members in three years, Dean Spring worried, "Should this group begin to disintegrate in the next year or two, the credibility of our faculty would suffer an impairment difficult, if not impossible, to overcome."[629] Only after President Henderson was summoned during the summer of 1974 to appear with Dean Spring and the Chair of Washburn's Board of Regents before the Council of the ABA's Section of Legal Education was a genuine effort made to achieve competitive salaries. Significant improvements were made in the 1975–76 budget, although they were not paid for from the newly instituted payments of state aid but instead from tuition increases of $8 per credit hour for Kansas residents and a whopping $22 per credit hour for non-residents, a 65% increase. It was felt that non-resident tuition should be at least $10 more per hour than resident tuition, to reflect the state aid differential.

Dean Spring held two meetings with students to explain the tuition increase. The University student newspaper found it curious that law students "don't seem to have much animosity" about the increase, other than the fact it was late April before it was announced. The "general reaction seemed to be a shrug of the shoulders"[630] since it would help keep and attract faculty. Even though the tuition increase exceeded the increase in the budget, Dean Spring happily reported the outcome to alumni:

> For the first time in many years we will be in a situation where no member of the faculty should be susceptible to being attracted away by salary alone. Indeed, as we look to faculty additions in the future, we should no longer have to draw from those moving for the first time into the ranks of law teachers. We can expect to do what others too often have done at our expense—bring in faculty of established competence, that we may gain the benefit of their most productive years.[631]

---

629. Raymond L. Spring, *Turning the Corner: The Dean's Report to the Bar*, 14 WASHBURN L.J. 429, 430 (1975).

630. *Students Shrug Off Hike*, WASHBURN REV., Apr. 30, 1975, at 9.

631. *Id.*

Change was not limited to the faculty. Dorothy Swecker retired as the Dean's assistant in the spring of 1973. WSBA declared "Dean Swecker Day" on March 9 and presented gifts to her at a reception. Swecker's replacement, Betty Webb, held the position until 1981.

WASHBURN LAW CLINIC

The academic hallmark of Spring's deanship was the development of a curriculum for clinical legal education as extensive as that offered at any law school. Of course, the concept that the law school should increase experiential training was not a new one. As early as 1938, Antrim Hambleton included it among his dreams for the school in his unsuccessful application to be dean. "I am in favor of further investigating the advisability of a legal clinic for the senior class students," he wrote. "This need not encroach on the business of the local bar."

By the mid-1950s, some members of the Kansas Bar Association's Committee on Legal Education and Admissions urged that a system of apprenticeships be established. In 1961, the Law School's alumni Board of Governors endorsed student internships in law offices. Dean John Howe was concerned that the concept sounded good in theory but would not have the expected benefits in practice. "Many states, and an even larger number of schools, have tried to formulate a workable plan to bring to the law student an opportunity to have an internship program," he acknowledged in his 1961 Dean's report. "To date, it is doubtful that such plans have met with any degree of success.... We do not have any present plans to inaugurate an internship program at Washburn. However, we are interested in this possibility, and if some workable system can be devised we will be more than willing to make it a part of the curriculum."[632] Howe likewise was lukewarm about a formal program for credit for students working in external legal aid programs for those unable to afford counsel. "[T]he number and types of cases that come to the legal aid clinic leave something to be desired, and student participation without controlled supervision, from the standpoint of the clinic being a teaching tool, leaves much to be desired."[633]

---

632. John E. Howe, *The Dean's Report to the Bar*, 1 WASHBURN L. J. 335, 339 (1961).
633. *Id.*

By 1966, however, the school cooperated with the Topeka Legal Aid Society in a volunteer program that Dean Howe described positively as giving students an opportunity to obtain "valuable experience" while also providing valuable service to society.[634] Finally, beginning in 1969, students participating in the Juvenile Probation Program and those working with the Legal Aid Society could earn one hour of academic credit. Professors Ryan and Kratochvil helped supervise the probation program, which included a special series of lectures, and Professors Ahrens and Spring supervised the legal aid program.

Two developments provided impetus for an expanded clinical program. First, the Kansas Supreme Court in 1969 adopted a student practice rule, Rule 213, authorizing third-year students to practice before Kansas courts, with appropriate supervision, when they represented state agencies or clients who could not afford to hire lawyers. By permitting students to appear in actual cases, rather than merely be law clerks, the student practice rule "provided the access to real clients necessary to work that was truly clinical in nature."[635] Second, grant funding became available to offset a significant portion of the costs that deterred law schools from offering quality clinical training. The Council on Legal Education for Professional Responsibility (CLEPR) was created in 1968. It was funded by a $6 million grant over five years from the Ford Foundation, which was concerned that the rights of the poor were not being protected adequately. CLEPR began awarding grants to support establishment of meaningful university-based clinical programs.

As Assistant Dean during John Howe's final year as Dean, Ray Spring drafted a CLEPR grant application and negotiated its details. In April 1970, CLEPR approved a $35,500 three-year grant to establish Washburn's clinical program, covering part of the cost of a clinical director, a secretary, and expenses in the first year for travel to observe other clinical programs.

The grant application contemplated that supervision of the existing Juvenile Probation and Legal Assistance programs would come under the Clinic umbrella, with continued involvement by WSBA. The grant's innovation was that students would represent clients directly, both in external placements that were developed during the grant's first year in the District Attorney and

---

634. John E. Howe, *The Dean's Report to the Bar*, 5 WASHBURN L. J. 169, 171 (1966).

635. Raymond L. Spring and Donald F. Rowland, *On the Visibility of the Legal Clinic*, VI CLEPR NEWSLETTER No. 10, 1, 2 (Mar. 1974).

City Attorney offices and at Topeka Legal Aid and also in-house under the supervision of a full-time member of the law faculty. An in-house program was thought to assure a better and more uniform educational experience than students could have in external placements, plus cases could be selected for their educational value. Students in the Washburn Law Clinic initially enrolled for one credit hour per semester and the focus of students in the in-house program was defense of misdemeanor cases.

In many law clinics being established at the time, clinic faculty were not on the tenure track, were treated as second-class faculty with unusual titles or as non-academic staff attorneys, were paid much less than classroom faculty and had little contact with them, had high turnover, and sometimes were inexperienced recent graduates. Washburn rejected all of these models. Clinical training was viewed as an important and integral part of a legal education. Thus, Washburn was in a tiny vanguard of schools that hired experienced lawyers as clinical teachers, assigned them regular academic rank, paid them accordingly, and put them on the same tenure track as other new faculty. It seemed desirable, however, that the Clinic Director be familiar with Kansas law and procedure and have experience with the types of cases most likely to qualify under the student practice rule. These factors trumped any concern about in-breeding. Dean Spring's classmate, Don Rowland '59, thus became the first Clinic Director. He had practiced in Hays and most recently had been Judge of the Probate, County and Juvenile Courts of Ellis County. Rowland quickly became an impassioned advocate for the clinical method. "Perhaps the key to learning law in the academic sense is motivation," he said. "What better motivation could there be than the total professional responsibility for a client's very real legal problems?"

Rowland started working in the summer. The Governor's Committee on Criminal Administration had funded a new statewide summer prosecution program for law students. The program, which continued and expanded in numbers throughout the 1970s, assigned students to prosecute cases in county attorney offices throughout Kansas.[636] Nine Washburn students participated during the first summer and Rowland visited each office to which they were

---

636. Students that first summer received a $1,000 grant to cover expenses during the eight-week program. *The Legal Clinic: Practice Perfects*, THE CIRCUIT RIDER 2 (June 1971).

53. Donald F. Rowland '59, Professor 1970–1988 and
first Director of the Washburn Law Clinic

assigned. Kathy King '71 prosecuted a felony, a robbery charge, to conviction
in the Montgomery County District Court.

Of necessity, the in-house program built slowly through the first year.
An office was designated for the Law Clinic, with a secretary and phone.
Seven students enrolled in the fall, handling thirty-five cases. In the spring,
there were seventeen interns who had eighty-seven cases. Keeping up with
that many students and that many cases taxed the ability of a single faculty
member. "Professor Rowland is usually found running from courtroom to
courtroom and courthouse to courthouse in beautiful downtown Topeka,
to appear with and supervise interns who are trying cases."[637] To provide
some help, 3L Phil Knighton '71 was appointed as student coordinator to
help manage office affairs.

---

637. *Id.* at 3.

The program was popular. In its second year, students could receive up to four hours of credit per semester and thirty students enrolled. The number of cases mushroomed to 345. The office space initially assigned became inadequate. The southwest corner of the lower level was remodeled as a clinic office, with work space for secretaries and student coordinators and a private office for client interviews. The location meant clients could park in the south lot and would not have to wander through the building to find the clinic office. The new quarters did nothing, however, to ease the burden on Professor Rowland. In addition to in-house interns, he supervised fifty-seven students receiving credit for externship placements that year, including eighteen in the summer prosecution program.

Limiting academic credit to four or fewer hours made clinical teaching challenging. Students had to learn basic skills in interviewing, counseling, negotiation, and office practice, not to mention the substantive law, before they could handle their first cases. Yet the time spent learning those skills limited their time to practice them. Also, court appearances often conflicted with classroom courses students were taking. The faculty's answer was to create the Clinical Semester, beginning in the fall of 1972. Clinic students were required to enroll in a thirteen-hour package of classroom, simulation, and live client courses "scheduled and interwoven in a way that hopefully will result in maximum benefit for the students."[638] The package included seminars, some already part of the curriculum, in Trial Techniques, Office Practice and Management, Negotiation and Settlement, Interviewing Technique, and Ethics and Professional Responsibility, plus a general Clinical Seminar. The clinical semester constituted nearly half of the elective hours and nearly all of the fifteen ungraded hours a student could count toward graduation.

Such a dramatic expansion of the clinical program would not have been possible without additional teaching resources. Happily, expansion of the program appealed to CLEPR, which approved an additional grant of $38,500 over two years to add a second full-time faculty member and additional adjunct professors from the local bar to teach components such as Office Practice and Management. Mary M. (Billie) Parr '47, was recruited from the Topeka Legal Aid Society to be Assistant Director of the Law Clinic.

---

638. Raymond L. Spring, *The Dean's Report to the Bar*, 11 WASHBURN L.J. 331, 335 (1972).

Most law school clinics limited their scope to a single topic of substantive law, but Washburn's clinic was open for the general practice of law. Each intern's caseload could include civil, criminal, probate, and mental competency cases, as well as administrative proceedings. Thus, "each case offers the intern an essentially new experience," rather than being repetitious.[639] Interns also traveled to the state penitentiary to assist lawyers in a new Legal Services for Prisoners program, the third of its kind in the country, representing inmates in civil matters. This association continued for two decades.

Cases were selected with the goal that they could be opened and concluded in a single semester by the same intern. However, interns learned their obligations of professional responsibility ordinarily meant they should continue to represent their clients until cases were concluded, even if that was beyond the end of the semester.

The Clinic used a high-volume model of case selection that was compatible with the Ford Foundation's goal of expanding the availability of legal services to the poor. Increasing academic credit itself required increased numbers of cases. During 1972–73, the Clinic accepted 627 cases, an average of thirteen per intern, and each intern logged approximately 130 billable hours per semester. The following year, interns averaged seventeen cases each. Approximately thirty interns enrolled each regular semester and a smaller number of summer interns kept the Clinic operating year-round. Students seeking to enroll exceeded available spaces by 50% and they competed for selection. Second-year students could volunteer as law clerks for the interns, conducting interviews and doing investigation and research. Even though they received no academic credit, many 2Ls did so because it improved their chances for selection as interns the following year.

The Clinic now was supported by three secretaries and three student assistants. One student assistant coordinated a voluntary program for 1Ls that included court observations, police ride-alongs, and visits to correctional institutions. The volume of students and cases was too large for two professors to supervise alone, so classroom teachers helped supervise students. Dean Spring reported in March 1974, "During the past year, twelve non-clinical faculty supervised one or more cases, and all of the remainder rendered some advice or assistance on particular problems. Indeed, some have even ventured

---

639. Spring and Rowland, *supra* note 635.

so far as to suggest that they 'wouldn't mind spending a year or so in full time clinical work.'"[640]

The Clinic quickly outgrew the remodeled area it occupied on the lower level. The solution was to put back into service two of the portable units that had housed the Law School following the tornado. They were installed southeast of the law building, west of Carruth Hall, and gave the Clinic five times more space. One unit housed the secretaries and student directors, a conference room and a small library. The other unit had ten small offices interns shared and used for client interviews. Professors Rowland and Parr continued to maintain their offices on faculty row in the main building, reinforcing the student perception that clinic professors were full partners in the academic program.

Inspections related to the CLEPR grants gave Washburn confidence its program was "highly successful in comparison with others around the country."[641] Washburn's leadership in the field led CLEPR President William Pincus to accept Washburn's invitation to be the 1973 commencement speaker. Added national recognition followed. Professor Rowland was invited to be on a panel of clinic directors at CLEPR's annual meeting. Dean Spring was asked for three consecutive years to speak at national conferences sponsored by CLEPR. At these meetings, Spring heard descriptions of less well-conceived programs at some other schools. He gained confidence that "ours is moving in the right direction and that at no law school may a better clinical experience be gained by law students than that which we now offer."[642] Spring and Rowland co-authored a lead article for CLEPR's monthly newsletter, attributing the success of Washburn's clinic to its being integrated as a visible and substantial part of the student's academic experience and located at the law building itself, rather than being a separate, essentially extracurricular activity conducted "on the side" at a location away from the law school where other students did not see it.[643] Spring expanded on this theme in a law journal article in which he described the various models of clinical education, from those offered "on the side" and "on the cheap" to fully integrated programs like Washburn's:

---

640. *Id.* at 5.

641. Raymond L. Spring, *The Dean's Report to the Bar*, 11 WASHBURN L.J. 331, 339 (1972).

642. Raymond L. Spring, *The Dean's Report to the Bar*, 13 WASHBURN L.J. 393, 396 (1974).

643. Spring and Rowland, *supra* note 635.

If this diversity of program and view point is allowed to continue much longer, those who predict the future of clinical education is limited by the extent to which outside grant support continues may well be proven correct. The time for experimentation, it would seem, must soon come to an end, and time and thought and even money now must be invested in an evaluation of the experiments that have been occurring. Doubtless such study will show more than one form of clinical education has value, just as torts need not be taught by all teachers in precisely the same way. Each school may be able to accomplish ultimate goals in the "making of a lawyer" in somewhat different ways. Hopefully, it also will be possible to establish some criteria to use in determining whether a clinical program in a law school has viability as a part of the overall academic program, or whether an academic program has viability without the existence of such a program. Then it will be time for the agencies of accreditation to take a stand.[644]

Washburn received a third CLEPR grant in 1974, for $38,000 over two years, to double the number of clinical faculty. Joel Meinecke '69 was Public Defender in Shawnee County before joining the faculty. He increased opportunities for students to defend criminal cases. Randall Jones, a 1971 KU graduate, supervised civil cases, which he had handled as a staff attorney for the Topeka Legal Aid Society. Interns were assigned cases so that they worked with each clinic faculty member. More faculty supervisors meant more cases could be accepted. In one six-month period, interns conducted 1,112 initial interviews and 602 cases were opened. Billie Parr professed to "know of no other program in the country where the experience is as broad."[645]

Grant funders rarely support mere maintenance of programs and CLEPR was no exception. The major innovation supporting the 1974 grant was creation of the Second Year Clinic Block. Students electing this three-hour course now received academic credit for working as law clerks for interns and for classes focusing on professional responsibility issues and office management procedures, designed to prepare these students to be effective interns as 3Ls.

---

644. Raymond L. Spring, *Realism Revisited: Clinical Education and Conflict of Goals in Legal Education*, 13 WASHBURN L.J. 421, 430 (1974).

645. *Legal Clinic Program Provides Training, Public Service*, WASHBURN REV., Apr 21, 1976, at 2.

An additional component of the grant was to make the previously voluntary first-year program a structured course and to award one graded hour of credit for it. Wisely, the course was changed to credit/no credit after one year. The course was an elective but was a prerequisite for enrollment in later clinical courses. It was called the F.L.I.P. (Freshman Law in Practice) program and Professor Meinecke coordinated it. It included the observation component as before but now included a classroom component Meinecke team-taught with Dr. Roy Lacoursiere of the Menninger Foundation which focused on the intersection of behavioral sciences and the law.

Dean Spring expressed pride that Washburn "pioneered" in clinical education. "For this effort we have earned a deserved reputation as one of the premier law schools of the nation in this *avant garde* approach to legal education (if *avant garde* can appropriately be applied to a concept that pervaded legal education until the past century)."[646] As early as 1972, however, when the Clinical Semester was inaugurated, Dean Spring acknowledged "some risk that such an intense program provides too much thrust in a single direction" but concluded that "can only be determined by trying."[647]

The intensity of clinical supervision necessitates lower student-faculty ratios than for classroom courses, making clinics expensive. While CLEPR grants offered the lure of "free" money, once they expired, continuing costs had to be covered from the school's operating budget. Each new grant required a new initiative. In 1975, Spring and Rowland proposed an additional CLEPR grant application, to make the first-year course required and to permit the hiring of a fifth clinical faculty member. Some faculty resisted, and four untenured junior faculty joined Roy Bartlett in voting against it, not because of opposition to clinical education generally but because of concern that an excessive percentage of limited financial and faculty resources were being committed to the Clinic at the expense of other priorities.

A sizable majority of the faculty endorsed the grant proposal and CLEPR's approval led Benjamin Farney to join the faculty for one year in the new position. Farney had been Probate Judge in Johnson County for twelve years and worked with Washburn during the previous six years when it offered an

---

646. Raymond L. Spring, *Summation: The Dean's Report to the Bar*, 17 WASHBURN L.J. 515, 521 (1978).

647. Raymond L. Spring, *The Dean's Report to the Bar*, 11 WASHBURN L.J. 331, 335 (1972).

annual summer program for Special Court Judges. When Farney left to enter private practice, Bill Rich was hired for the second year of the grant. Rich was the first clinician who graduated from an out-of-state law school, Boalt Hall at Berkeley in 1975, but he was a native Kansan and had returned to practice with the Legal Aid Society in Wichita before entering law teaching.

The required first-year clinical program made sense in theory, providing all students an initial exposure to the Clinic as part of a three-year progression of clinical experiences. In practice, it proved unpopular with students who had difficulty deciphering its purpose. The first-year program was discontinued when the two-year grant expired. Student interest in the Clinical Semester diminished, as some students came to believe the commitment of thirteen hours in the third year too severely curtailed their ability to take classroom electives and others found it difficult to juggle the time demands of the Clinic with extracurricular activities such as law journal or moot court or part-time employment. Before the 1976–77 academic year, Professor Rowland and the clinic faculty reluctantly agreed to award variable credit for the Clinical Semester, giving flexibility in the amount of work interns had to undertake.

When his deanship ended, Spring made no apologies for pushing the envelope of innovation. "Pioneering is not without its risks," he wrote. "The leader often tears his britches on the brambles....We have, quite consciously, taken clinical education as far and quite probably further than it can be taken and still fit within a law school curriculum....I think we have been right. There is no way you can know what you can do until you have tried and found the limit. Few schools have had the courage to do this, and I am proud Washburn did."[648]

AN ADDITION, SO SOON?

The euphoria of being in a modern building soon gave way to the cramped feeling of overcrowding. Just months after the tornado, when the University scaled back the faculty's original plan for a 60,000 square foot building,[649] mostly by cutting library space, Dean Howe warned President Henderson not to formulate future plans based on current requirements:

---

648. Raymond L. Spring, *Summation: The Dean's Report to the Bar*, 17 WASHBURN L.J. 515, 521 (1978).

649. Minutes, Washburn L. Sch. Ass'n Board of Governors (Oct. 2, 1971).

[I]n planning a building care must be taken that we do not erect a structure that will be obsolete shortly after completion. Present plans for a 40,000 square foot structure may not be adequate. This is a matter that should be considered by all concerned. I, personally, am undecided on the point, but other new law buildings for student bodies that will be of our approximate size have approximately 50,000 to 85,000 square feet.[650]

Howe's warning was not heeded. The rationale in part was that the start of construction should not be delayed by the time required to raise money needed to construct space that would not be needed until years later. What happened, of course, was that the school outgrew the building in less than three years. The library was designed to hold 65,000 volumes, roughly twice the post-tornado collection. The year before construction was completed, however, the AALS adopted a requirement that every member school have at least 60,000 volumes by January 1, 1975. Meeting the requirement would leave few empty shelves.

Washburn had the smallest library of any AALS member school. Almost all schools already had libraries exceeding 60,000 volumes, or close to that number.[651] Work began in the fall of 1970 to develop a priority acquisition list for orderly expansion of the collection to meet the AALS requirement. Financing collection growth was a separate issue. An AALS standard effective in 1968 required member schools to have a minimum book budget of $40,000. Washburn's book budget for 1970–71 was only $20,000 from university funds, plus $6,082 from Title II federal funds and a Cities Service Foundation grant. Expenses for continuations and binding consumed almost all of the university appropriation, leaving little for new books.[652] Dean Spring was confident that the school's failure to comply with the standard while it occupied the trailers was "completely defensible," but saw nothing that would excuse failure to comply once the new building was occupied.[653] He even urged that $15,000 of the funds raised in excess of the cost of the new building be held in reserve, rather than placed in endowment, to augment

---

650. John E. Howe, "Annual Report, School of Law July 1, 1965–June 30, 1966, To: President John Henderson."

651. Letter from Acting Dean Raymond L. Spring to Eugene W. Hiatt, Chair, Finance Committee, Washburn Board of Regents (Dec. 11, 1970).

652. *Id.*

653. *Id.*

the book budget in the likely event university funding could not increase rapidly enough to meet the AALS minimum.[654]

The alumni board's Library Committee proposed, as a partial fix, a strategy reminiscent of the one used to meet the volume count crisis in 1913. It recommended that the school urge retiring attorneys to donate their libraries. Duplicate volumes not needed for the collection could be used for exchanges. The committee concluded that out-of-state alums could be especially helpful, even if they weren't retiring, by filling gaps in the library's collection of state-specific materials.[655] Initial concerns about the cost of acquiring the required volumes were allayed in part in 1971 when, soon after his election to Congress, Representative Bill Roy '70 arranged for the Law Library to be designated as one of two federal depository libraries in his district.[656] This meant the library received free all materials published by the Government Printing Office that it wished to select. Not only were the library's holdings of federal materials greatly enhanced, the funds it previously used to purchase them could be used for other priorities in expanding the collection. The acquisitions budget was increased by 75% in 1971, to more than $40,000 annually. In 1972, the collection grew by nearly 25% and there were nearly 55,000 volumes on the shelves. Many volumes were in dead storage in what had been designed as a processing room on the first floor. Even with that stopgap measure, shelf capacity was expected to be reached in as little as two years.

The faculty Library Committee reported in May 1972 that "the present capacity of the library for students, books, and staff is inadequate, and will in the near future be almost hopeless."[657] Accreditation standards required library seating for 325 students for a student body of 450, but there were only 140 student seats in the library. Three librarians, a secretary, and student assistants occupied an office designed for the Director, who had moved her office to a study carrel. The Library Committee projected a need, with a target date of 1985, for library space housing a collection of 150,000 volumes, plus space for micro-materials and audio-visual materials, for 400 library seats, half in carrels or study rooms, and for six library staff. Beginning in 1973, new faculty had

---

654. *Id.*

655. Report of the Library Committee, Washburn L. Sch. Ass'n, Dec. 4, 1968.

656. *WU's law library U.S. depository*, TOPEKA ST. J., Aug. 25, 1971.

657. Minutes, Washburn U. Sch. of Law faculty meeting (May 8, 1972).

to be assigned offices in converted student study carrels on the second floor of the library. Ultimately, five faculty members had such offices. In addition, there was no space in the main building for the Law Clinic and the tornado-era trailers it occupied already had exceeded their expected useful life.

Dean Spring alerted the alumni Board of Governors in October 1971 that an addition would be needed much sooner than originally anticipated, and the following year board President Warren Shaw '31 alerted the alumni generally.[658] Some members of the alumni board doubted another fundraising effort could succeed so soon after the last one but ultimately concluded it had to be done. The University insisted fundraising for the addition be delayed until fundraising was completed for the University's new main library, and then insisted that commitments to fund construction costs be in place before architectural planning would be authorized.

A campaign to raise the estimated $850,000 cost was announced in the fall of 1974. The Board of Governors reconstructed the system of regional solicitation that had been successful after the tornado. Gerald L. Goodell '58 agreed to chair the campaign. Dean Spring later acknowledged that Goodell's "unflagging optimism and willingness to pursue new avenues in the face of early marginal reports proved a bouyant stimulus to the rest of us on the firing line."[659] By the end of the year, gifts and pledges totaled $200,000 and 60% of the gifts were for $500 or more. In early January 1975, the Mabee Foundation, again influenced by Don Moyers '34, issued a challenge grant, committing to contribute the final $200,000 if the school raised the remainder of the expected construction costs. The Mabee challenge grant provided needed stimulus and by June 1 the goal was met. Ultimately, the cost exceeded $1 million and the University used part of its general capital improvement fund to make up the difference.

The same architects, Coolidge and Coolidge, who designed the building also designed the addition, and would design the 1992 addition as well, thus providing continuity of design. While the building originally was constructed to permit the addition of two floors, totaling 19,000 square feet, it was not desirable to locate the Clinic on an upper floor. Thus, a separate L-shaped

---

658. Minutes, Washburn L. Sch. Ass'n Board of Governors (Oct. 2, 1971); Raymond L. Spring, *The Dean's Report to the Bar*, 11 WASHBURN L.J. 331, 338 (1972); *Growth Discussed At Annual Luncheon*, 3 THE CIRCUIT RIDER 1 (June 1972).

659. Raymond L. Spring, *Turning the Corner: The Dean's Report to the Bar*, 14 WASHBURN L.J. 429 (1975).

building with two levels was built on the northwest corner of the main building and connected to it by a covered walkway. Clients enter the top floor from
the north at ground level. That floor was laid out as a model law office, with
a reception area, four client interview rooms, rooms for student directors,
a secretarial area, and a work area for interns with a small, working library.
Faculty offices were on the lower level, including some that would be assigned
to non-clinical faculty, as well as a conference room, an interview room with a
one-way mirror permitting observation of mock interviews from the conference room, and a sixty-five seat classroom that could be configured easily as
a courtroom for sections of Practice Court and Trial Techniques which could
not be accommodated in Robinson Courtroom. Few law school clinics at the
time had facilities specifically designed for them. When Washburn's new clinic
opened, CLEPR featured it in a new book about law clinics.[660]

The cost of the separate building for the Clinic left funding to add only one
floor to the main building. It increased shelf capacity by more than 50%, to
more than 100,000 volumes. The building project also included remodeling
of other areas. Library space on the south wall of the library's second floor
was converted to faculty offices. The law journal office on the lower level in
Room 106 was converted to a seminar room when offices on the third floor
were remodeled to house the journal staff.

Groundbreaking occurred in September 1976. Students experienced no
disruption of classes and only modest inconvenience when library materials
were moved from the library's second floor to permit remodeling. However, six
faculty members were displaced from their study carrel-offices in the library
or from offices to be remodeled on the third floor and experienced major disruption. They were herded into Room 104, a small and oddly shaped seminar
room. The arrangement made the study carrels seem spacious. The faculty
members missed even the inches lost because of Professor Elrod's pregnancy.
Conferences with students were awkward and rarely was it quiet enough to
permit concentration.

Concrete work on the Law Clinic was completed before unusually prolonged cold temperatures arrived in January. Heavy tarpaulins were placed
over the structure, permitting work to continue through the winter. However,

---

660. COUNCIL ON LEGAL EDUCATION FOR PROFESSIONAL RESPONSIBILITY,
INC., LAW SCHOOL TEACHING CLINICS: PLANS AND PICTURES 21 (1977).

54. Washburn Law Clinic has its own building

the cold weather, plus delay in delivery of structural steel, postponed work on the new top floor of the library until late January. The original construction schedule called for completion before the start of the 1977–78 academic year but the building was not ready. The dedication went ahead as scheduled on September 30, 1977, during homecoming. Judge Delmas C. Hill '29 gave the principal address, urging those assembled to take pride in the school's history and accomplishments in its 75th, or Diamond Jubilee, year. The move into the Law Clinic took place in October and the new top floor of the library was occupied in November.

CREATING A MORE VIBRANT ENVIRONMENT

With more students and more faculty, there was more activity and greater vitality in the academic environment. The Law School started a Distinguished Lecturer program in academic year 1970–71. Evidence scholar and former Dean at Iowa Mason Ladd spent three days at Washburn, teaching classes and meeting informally with students and faculty. His principal address was entitled "Are There Wonders in the Law?" He was followed the next year by Dean Robert

McKay of NYU, whose formal presentation discussed "The Selection of Supreme Court Justices." In 1972–73, the Distinguished Visitor was Dean Page Keeton of the University of Texas, who lectured on "Compensation Systems in Product Liability." The Student Bar Association started its own speaker program that year and brought Professor Arthur Miller of Harvard to campus to speak about invasion of privacy. Local treasures were tapped also. In the spring of 1972, Dr. Karl Menninger returned to the Law School for the first time in many years, presenting a series of three lectures, on the insanity defense, reform of prison conditions, the death penalty, and other topics.

Four United States Supreme Court Justices, two sitting and two retired, visited the Law School during Spring's deanship. Retired Justice Charles Whittaker was a judge for the 1970 regional finals of the National Moot Court Competition. Justice William O. Douglas, after speaking at a University-wide assembly on February 12, 1973, dropped in for Professor Dale's class in Environmental Law and spent the hour discussing recent decisions. He stayed for another hour to visit with law students generally. He signed several of his opinions that appeared in students' casebooks. The following fall, retired Justice Tom C. Clark addressed a convocation at the Law School on one of the two days he sat in Robinson Courtroom on a panel of the United States Court of Appeals for the Tenth Circuit.

In January 1977, then-Associate Justice William Rehnquist visited the school as part of the WSBA's lecture series. His address, "Sunshine in the Third Branch," was published in the *Washburn Law Journal*.[661] He spent more than an hour after his lecture in a question and answer session with students and more time visiting with them informally. The Justice traveled to Topeka alone, without the security personnel who today frequently accompany a Justice. Law Journal Editor Michael C. Manning '77 had written the letter inviting Rehnquist to Topeka and appointed himself chauffeur for the Justice. He borrowed a new Cadillac from the lawyer for whom he previously had clerked and met the Justice's commuter flight at Topeka's Forbes Field airport:

> I put on the only suit I owned and waited nervously for the three-piece, Brooks Brothers-suited dignitary to hand me his baggage and to lead him to the back seat of his chauffeured sedan.

---

661. Justice William H. Rehnquist, *Sunshine in the Third Branch*, 16 WASHBURN L.J. 559 (1977).

Nearly all of the flight's few passengers were past me now as I stood by the gate. But, there was no impressive personage headed my way....As I considered approaching the man serving as the flight's pilot, baggage handler, flight attendant and ticket agent to report my missing dignitary, I noticed in my peripheral vision a man who appeared to be waiting for someone as well. He wore a wrinkled and tattered trench coat like TV's favorite detective, Lt. Columbo.

He also wore Hush Puppy desert boots and an old fishing hat with its brim pulled down all around. "God, I hope Justice Rehnquist does not think this man is one of our professors," I thought to myself.

The man kept nudging nearer to me and making inane small talk I ignored. As the last passenger passed me by, the rumpled man said, "You are dressed like you are waiting for someone important." I was dismissive and abrupt to the rumpled old stranger as I stared straight ahead and said, "Please leave me alone; I am here to pick up a member of the United States Supreme Court." He said, "What a coincidence! I am a member of the Supreme Court as well. How about giving me a ride into town too?" He laughed and introduced himself as "Bill Rehnquist."... He jumped into the front seat with me and promised he had a suit for the speech and that he would not wear his desert boots.[662]

Rehnquist attended a reception with the faculty the evening before his lecture and Manning drove him back to his hotel. On the way, Justice Rehnquist asked Manning for the names of places within walking distance where he could get a beer. He didn't want a nice place, just a nearby beer joint frequented by locals. Manning offered to drive him to one but the Justice said his back needed the stretch of a walk. The following morning, he told Manning about his evening. He had struck up a lively conversation with several locals about sports, politics, and other typical bar fare. The person on the stool next to the Justice, a person named Gary, said he was a truck driver for Pacific Intermountain Express.

The rest of the stoolers announced what they did as well. All were blue collars and the Associate Justice really had enjoyed the evening. Near

---

662. Michael C. Manning, *Rehnquist: Big day for law student*, ARIZONA REPUB-LIC, Sept. 18, 2005, at V1, V3.

the end of the night, Gary said: "Bill, we have all told you about our jobs, where do you work?" He said: "I work in Washington." After a few misplaced comments from the boys about friends and relatives all had in Seattle and Spokane, the Associate Justice corrected the misapprehension and said: "no, I work in Washington, D.C."

"Wow, what do you do there, are you a fed?" "Well, I kind of am. I am a Justice on the Supreme Court." At that point the stoolers all erupted in laughter and slapped him on the back saying: "Right, ole man! Admit it, you're just a darn clerk in the Ag Department out here to check out our farmers." The Associate Justice just smiled and laughed with them.[663]

In 1971, the Law School's commencement became another opportunity to hear from distinguished guests. Through 1970, law graduates participated in University-wide commencement exercises at Memorial Auditorium. When graduating law classes of record size threatened to over-extend the already lengthy University exercises and exceed seating capacity at the Auditorium, the argument supporting the Law School's natural desire for a separate ceremony became compelling. The Law School commencement on May 15, 1971, was held in White Concert Hall, where 800 guests heard AALS President Alfred Conard, a professor at the University of Michigan, speak on the topic "Macrojustice." The following year, ABA President and future Watergate prosecutor Leon Jaworski was the featured speaker.

Robinson Courtroom was used for every imaginable legal proceeding, giving students the opportunity to observe proceedings first-hand. Shortly after it was dedicated, State Senator Harold S. Herd '42 convened a hearing of a Senate Judiciary Subcommittee there. In March 1972, the Municipal Court conducted a day-long docket there. In 1973, Dale E. Saffels '49, then chair of the Kansas Corporation Commission, conducted a three-day hearing in the courtroom on Gas Service Company's application for a rate increase. The Kansas Commission on Civil Rights regularly held hearings there and the National Labor Relations Board met there in May 1974.

There was curricular experimentation besides the Law Clinic. A summer foreign study program was offered in 1974, for the first time in six years. Classes

---

663. E-mail from Michael C. Manning to James M. Concannon (June 24, 2003) (on file in Washburn Law School). Manning expanded his account of the story following Justice Rehnquist's death in 2005. Manning, *supra* note 662.

were held at Brunel University in Uxbridge, England, on the outskirts of London, and students lived in flats on the Brunel campus. Professor Ahrens taught Legal History and Professor Kratochvil taught Trusts. Members of the law faculty at Brunel team-taught with them and arranged visits to local courts and other legal institutions.

While some experiments succeeded, others did not. A two-week orientation for entering students became possible in 1972 when students were permitted to start law studies only in the fall. It seemed to work well but was shortened when a semester-long Law and Legal Methods course was added. A required course in Jurisprudence was added to the first-year curriculum in 1972, in response to a report of the Kansas Bar Association's Committee of Liaison with Law Schools that expressed "surprise, and some concern" that law schools were not offering the traditional Jurisprudence course but instead were attempting to introduce its basic principles by the pervasive approach.[664] Dean Spring described the

> debate within the faculty, and substantial difference of opinion, on whether the first year was the appropriate time for such a course. Some pragmatists, like myself, even offered the suggestion that the best time to study Jurisprudence in depth is perhaps after five or ten years of exposure to the hard realities of practice. Of course the practical answer to that is that by then, few, if any, have either the time or inclination to do so. In the end the question was resolved by considering the character of the entering students. Their fresh and eager attitude, their willingness to challenge and indeed what appears their almost insatiable desire to *be* challenged—all of these attributes led us to conclude the appropriate time is at the beginning. We shall see.[665]

The experiment was a disaster and was discontinued after a single year. Nearly half the grades Professor Levine awarded were Ds and Fs, and Dean Spring ultimately had to persuade him to raise some of them. Students who failed the course were not required to retake it. The required course in Jurisprudence was replaced by a required first-year course in Law and Legal Methods and, more than a decade later, by Law and Legal Systems, a sort of Jurisprudence Lite, that Ray Spring, among others, would teach.

---

664. Raymond L. Spring, *The Dean's Report to the Bar*, 11 WASHBURN L.J. 331, 336 (1972).

665. *Id.*

55. Bruce Levine, Professor 1971–2000

Many students in the required class on Jurisprudence have difficulty imagining that two decades later the same Professor Levine would be so beloved that graduating seniors four times would elect him Professor of the Year. Levine remained methodical throughout his teaching career, emphasizing a textbook's table of contents as an organizational tool, but in his early years at Washburn he was perceived as rigid. Clad in a dark suit, invariably with a white shirt and dark tie, he still followed the formerly common practice of requiring students to stand to recite. "Recitation is an electric experience, and for the poorly prepared, a high voltage shock," a feature story in the student newspaper reported during Levine's second semester at Washburn. "'In mustering a high level of classroom tension day after day,' Levine explains, 'the student is sharpened'....The exchange is between advocates and the business is serious."[666]

---

666. New Washburn Law Prof "*Lives The Law,*" CASE AND CANE (Feb. 1972).

THE EVOLVING MISSION OF THE *JOURNAL*

Washburn Law Journal was an integral part of the school's writing program. More students were encouraged to write for the *Journal* and its pages came to be dominated by student work. For example, volume 9 in 1969–70 included eight notes and seventeen comments, constituting 46% of the volume's 484 pages. Volume 10 had fourteen notes, sixteen comments, and one student essay, filling 57% of the volume's 531 pages. By volume 14, the percentage of published student material, sixteen notes and forty-five comments, exceeded 80% of the *Journal's* total pages. Although funding from the Washburn Law School Association permitted the *Journal* to grow to 714 pages that year, it contained just 125 pages of articles other than student work, by far the smallest number since the *Journal* expanded to three issues annually. There were only two authors from outside Kansas. One was a Washburn graduate and the other was an Arkansas practitioner who discussed the new Kansas comparative negligence statute. Editor-in-Chief Harker Russell '75 noted in issue one that sixty-five second-year students were writing articles. "Our efforts to encourage participation by any student willing to contribute the time and effort necessary to prepare an article of publishable quality have been rewarded by record growth this year."[667] In issue two, he described a decidedly local mission: "Hopefully this growth will enable the Journal to perform more effectively its twofold purpose—improving the student's legal research, writing and analysis skills and providing the Kansas bar with a useful, high quality legal publication."[668] The next year, Editor-in-Chief William Sidlinger '76 reported that 110 students were writing in the hope of being published.[669] Dean Raymond Spring '59 lamented that budget constraints limiting the size of the *Journal* made it "impossible to publish so much as half of those notes and comments that merit publication."[670] The pages devoted to non-student work dwindled to just ninety of 568 pages.

Case comments consistently averaged between five and six pages from volume 9 through volume 15. Notes grew from, on average, fifteen to seventeen pages to twenty to twenty-three pages. However, the burden of editing the work of

---

667. *Obiter Dictum*, 14 WASHBURN L.J. v (1964) (issue one).

668. *Obiter Dictum*, 14 WASHBURN L.J. v (1975) (issue two).

669. *Obiter Dictum*, 15 WASHBURN L.J. iv (1975) (issue one).

670. Raymond L. Spring, *Of Books, Fische and Terminals: The Dean's Report to the Bar*, 15 WASHBURN L.J. 415, 421 (1976).

so many different students taxed the capacity of the senior staff. As volume 16 Editor-in Chief Michael C. Manning '77 saw it, "Deadlines were routinely slighted and editorial control lacked the thoroughness that is the hallmark of a reliable legal periodical; there were too many articles and too few editors with 48-hour days."[671] Beginning with volume 16, the number of students invited to write for the *Journal* was reduced significantly. Manning's staff concluded that page constraints on comments had hampered in-depth analysis. In volume 16, the average comment grew to almost eight pages with the additional space "provided for authors to engage in more detailed development and analysis of the case."[672] The senior note was expanded too, so it provided more thorough documentation. There was renewed emphasis on lead articles of interest nationally, recognizing that the *Journal* needed to become once again more than a local publication. Volume 16 featured articles, all based on addresses at Washburn, by Professor Raoul Berger of Harvard Law School,[673] retired Supreme Court Justice Tom C. Clark,[674] and Justice William H. Rehnquist.[675] With external funding again from the Washburn Law School Association, volume 16 grew to 800 pages but the percentage of pages devoted to student work declined to 76%.

Volume 17 published a somewhat more manageable fourteen notes and twenty-five comments. Editor-in-Chief Vivian Wiberg '78 expressed the pleasure of the Board of Editors "with the favorable response of our subscribers to changes in the *Journal* format last year."[676] The volume 17 board instituted a writing competition in which students could earn a position on the *Journal* staff even though they were not among the more selective group of students invited on the basis of grades. Competition among students seeking to be published became more intense each year thereafter.

Also during academic year 1977–78, the Wichita law firm today known as Foulston Siefkin LLP increased its involvement with both Kansas law schools. At Washburn, it chose to underwrite an annual lecture, but with a twist. The

---

671. *Obiter Dictum*, 16 WASHBURN L.J. v, vi (1976) (issue one).

672. *Id.* at v.

673. Raoul Berger, *The Tug-of-War Between Congress and the Presidency—Foreign Policy and the Power to Make War*, 16 WASHBURN L.J. 1 (1976).

674. Justice Tom C. Clark (Ret.), *The Continuing Challenge of Advocacy*, 16 WASHBURN L.J. 243 (1977).

675. Rehnquist, *supra* note 661.

676. *Obiter Dictum*, 17 WASHBURN L.J. v (1977) (issue one).

firm provided an honorarium that was significant enough to attract leading thinkers and to entice them to expand the lecture into a scholarly article for publication in the *Washburn Law Journal*. The lecture was scheduled for the day following the annual law journal banquet, at which the Foulston Siefkin lecturer could give less formal remarks and mingle with students and faculty. The first Foulston Siefkin lecturer was Vern Countryman from Harvard and the series continues today.

ENTERING THE COMPUTER AGE

As library shelves neared capacity and plans for off-site storage were made, the school embraced the use of microfiche as a way to expand library holdings and acquire materials for which there never had been space. A fact sheet about the proposed building addition, presented to the Board of Governors in 1974, suggested that many materials then on shelves would, in time, be replaced by microfiche and that "it might well be that there will never be a need for further expansion."

In the fall of 1975, Spring noted the addition would include substantial space for audio-visual and micro equipment "and, hopefully, a computer terminal."[677] The computer age arrived sooner than that, when a Lexis terminal, just one for the entire school, was installed that academic year. At that point, it provided access to decisions only for a limited number of years and only for nine states. However, because of leadership and funding by the Kansas Bar Association, Kansas was one of those states. Professors Kuether and Concannon were sent for training in Kansas City and they trained other faculty. Instruction in computerized research was integrated into the Legal Research and Writing class. However, those wishing to use the one Lexis terminal had to schedule an appointment on a sign-up sheet.

The following year, Washburn participated in a pilot project of the Consortium on Computer Assisted Legal Instruction (CALI) and sent Professor Concannon to a CALI training conference at Harvard. CALI exercises were used in several courses at Washburn that year and Dean Spring was excited about the opportunity these exercises provided for student feedback resembling one-on-one instruction, with the computer offering "speed, accuracy

---

677. *Annex funds donated to Law School*, WASHBURN REV., Sept. 3, 1975, at 12.

and consistency of response far beyond that which could be expected of even the best professors."[678]

ACTIVE STUDENTS

During the 1971–72 academic year, the Student Bar Association waged a successful, five-month long battle to gain control of the full amount of the $10 per semester student activity fee that law students, like all University students, paid. Previously, WSBA received approximately $6 of that fee but the remainder funded activities of the undergraduate Student Association in which law students rarely participated. WSBA President Rick Tucker '73 persuasively argued that WSBA supported its own student newspaper, *Case and Cane*, and had its own yearbook in the form of the annual placement booklet. He also argued that the funds provided were insufficient to meet other WSBA obligations, such as operating the placement service, funding travel to moot court competitions and ABA Law Student Division conferences, as well as other activities. Law students' arguments, endorsed by Dean Spring, ultimately persuaded the undergraduate Student Council and, by a slim majority, the University General Council, after a presentation by Linda Elrod '72. However, University administrators refused to concur, viewing the proposal as furthering unwanted "tendencies for the Law school to be separate from Washburn University anyway"[679] and promoting "a feeling of divisiveness."[680] President Henderson ultimately came around to support the proposal when it was coupled with an $8 per semester increase in other student fees retained by the University, apart from the activity fee. The speakers program WSBA started the following year was one of the new initiatives its increased resources made possible.

Washburn students in the 1970s added to the school's tradition of success in moot court competitions. The school in 1971 became a charter member of the Order of Barristers, which recognizes outstanding participants in a school's advocacy program each year. Phil Harley '74 was named top oralist and John Ambrosio '72 was second best oralist in the 1971 Jessup International

---

678. Raymond L. Spring, *Of Books, Fische and Terminals: The Dean's Report to the Bar*, 15 WASHBURN L.J. 415, 420 (1976).

679. *Gen. Council grants Student Bar Assoc. full monies from activity fees allotment*, WASHBURN REV., Nov. 22, 1971.

680. *Regents discuss activity fees*, WASHBURN REV., Jan. 19, 1972.

Law Competition but they lost in the regional finals to the University of Texas, which had higher scores on the memorials. Harley represented Washburn a record six times in interschool competitions. He repeated as top oralist in the 1973 Jessup regional, winning the votes of all twelve judges. This time, he and his teammates, his then-spouse Marcia Harley '74, and Bob Keeshan '75, together with memorial writers Ray Connell '76 and Rex Linder '74, won the regional competition and competed as one of eight teams in the national finals in Washington, D.C. There, they won one round before being eliminated.

Keeshan teamed with Robert Prentice '75 and Alan Rupe '75 in 1974 to place second in the regionals of the National Moot Court Competition and competed in the national final rounds in New York City. During academic year 1977–78, Washburn students were top oralists in two different regional competitions, Dennis Dow '78 in the National Moot Court Competition and Lloyd Swartz '79 in the Jessup Competition.

As enrollment grew, the school elected to compete in additional competitions. The ABA Law Student Division began sponsoring a moot court competition each spring and in 1976, Randy Fisher '76 and David Gray '76 won the combined Eighth and Tenth Circuit competition. Its unique format judged only oral arguments and did not require students to prepare a brief. In 1973, Washburn competed in the inaugural ABA Client Counseling Competition and finished second in the regional rounds, losing to the eventual national champion, New Mexico.

In 1972 and again in 1976 Washburn was elected to the governing Board of Editors of the National Conference of Law Reviews. The 1976–77 staff was the first in a number of years to publish all of its issues before graduation. It also completed work on the final issues of the prior volume, as had become a common practice. This surge of productivity created a problem for the alumni Board of Governors because all dues-paying members were entitled to receive the *Journal* and a dispute had to be resolved whether they should receive all issues actually published during the dues year or only the single volume allocable to that academic year.

Actually, preparation of an additional issue was started that year and completed by the next Board of Editors. The extra issue, funded by $1,500 contributions each by the Student Bar Association and the alumni Board of Governors, published the papers of the first Washburn Environmental Law Conference, organized by David Pierce '77 and held March 24–25, 1977. The conference focused on water, air, energy, and land use issues confronting Midwestern states. Technical experts introduced the topics and explained environmental effects and scientific alternatives. Law professors and lawyers from government agencies, including G. William Frick, General Counsel of the Environmental Protection Agency, then discussed the effectiveness of legal controls and suggestions for change. Sadly, the extra issue was published as volume one of an anticipated annual series of Midwest Environmental Law Conference Papers, rather than as an additional issue of the *Washburn Law Journal*. Thus, the innovative conference papers are not found in many libraries and have not been cited as widely as they deserved to be. A second Midwest Environmental Law Conference was held the following year, but its papers were not published.

Students also succeeded in writing competitions. In the spring of 1976, David Pierce '77 and Bill Sidlinger '76 won first and second place, and $700 and $300, respectively, in a competition for Kansas law students sponsored by the Kansas Association of Defense Counsel. Pierce financed a significant portion of his legal education from writing competitions, twice winning the American Trial Lawyers Association regional Environmental Law Writing Competition.

The Student Bar Association was active nationally too. During academic year 1970–71, it for the first time submitted a request for funding to the ABA Law Student Division and received the largest grant in the nation, $480, to support WSBA's long-standing Legal Assistance Program.[681] In 1973, Paul Perez '74 was elected Secretary-Treasurer of the ABA-LSD and Washburn was the only school west of Chicago represented on the six-member executive committee. In 1972, WSBA created the Kansas Legal Research Board, staffed initially by a student director and three researchers who prepared memoranda for attorneys throughout Kansas at a modest hourly rate but one that was higher than the going rate for law clerking in Topeka. WSBA even coordinated distribution and tabulation of student evaluations in the spring of 1972.

A fictitious student achieved more front page notoriety than any real student. He was Ned Oliver Primmer, the invention of Larry Mundy '77. By the time Mundy enrolled, Primmer already had earned a significant number of academic credits at several Kansas colleges and was a statewide Notary Public. Having Primmer take the LSAT was neither feasible nor prudent but his name did appear on the seating charts of Mundy's first-year classes and those for the fall semester of his second year. Mundy simply scanned the classroom and

---

681. CASE AND CANE (Feb. 2, 1971).

signed Primmer's name on the seating chart in a seat that was vacant. Unfortunately, in the fall of 1975, a student who enrolled several days late came to his first Evidence class and chose to sit in the vacant seat Mundy had picked for Primmer. In the due course of several weeks, Professor Concannon determined it was the late-arriving student's turn to recite and called on him. "How would defendant argue that objection, Mr. Primmer?" he asked. After a few moments of silence, he repeated, "Mr. Primmer?" The student in the chair knew the professor's eyes were locked on him but his facial expression showed he had no clue why. "My name is Jones," he finally mumbled. The professor observed a group of students, including Mundy, in the wing area of seats to his right exhibiting much mirth, and resolved to check the matter out after class. Primmer's name was not on Professor Concannon's official class roster. He consulted Professor Kuether, who found Primmer's name on his seating chart for Decedents' Estates. Handwriting similarities pointed to Mundy but were inconclusive because of block lettering used in signing the seating charts. Concannon and Kuether set out, Columbo-like, to find conclusive evidence. They gathered seating charts from first-year classes the prior year. On one of them, Primmer's name was signed using both capital and small letters and one of the small letters had distinctive characteristics. Writing samples were gathered from Mundy's papers from prior semesters. The following morning, Kuether presented the evidence in his Decedents' Estates class and Mundy offered no defense. Nancy Scherer '77, a student in the class, recalled that "The professors delighted in exposing Ned as a fraud, and while the class admired their sleuthing abilities…there was a sense of sadness at having lost Ned to reality."[682]

The following fall, when Mundy was a 3L, he applied for a position after graduation as Law Clerk for United States District Judge Richard Rogers. Upon hearing the Ned Primmer story from Professor Concannon, Judge Rogers had his law clerk, Robert Prentice '75, send Mundy a rejection letter that urged him "to be consoled by the fact…you were one of the final two candidates…[H]owever, Judge Rogers concluded that your high qualifications and winning personality were overshadowed by the similarly fine attributes of another applicant, Mr. Ned Primmer." The letter did suggest that "If, for some reason, Mr. Primmer is unable to accept this position, we intend to offer it to you, should

---

682. *Reflections on Dean Monk's Years At Washburn*, 27 CIRCUIT RIDER 8 (Summer 1988).

you still be available." A separate letter from Prentice offering Ned the position was sent to Mundy's address the same day, just three days before Christmas. It indicated that "At the start of your employment, you will be working with a visiting judge from the State of New York, Judge Joseph Force Crater. You and Judge Crater will have a lot in common and I am sure you will get along swimmingly." Crater was a New York Supreme Court Justice of legend, who stepped into a taxi in New York City in 1930 and vanished. Mundy's call to Concannon at home, begging for confirmation that he actually had been chosen for the job, gave Concannon an unanticipated opportunity to administer a coup-de-gras. He suggested the only way Mundy could be sure was to call the Judge himself at home. Mundy quickly regained his wits, sending Judge Rogers a letter, signed by Primmer, declining the position. "My activities to vocalize the plight of the Nonentities have caught the ear of the federal executives, and I have been appointed to the post of Deputy Underassistant to the Assistant Secretary of the new Bureau of Missing Persons." Ned recommended Mundy as an acceptable second choice. The legend of Ned Primmer spread in succeeding years and the *Topeka Capital-Journal* printed a front page feature story about Primmer before Mundy left employment with Judge Rogers.[683]

A Washburn chapter of Phi Delta Phi Law Fraternity was formed and its signature activity, started in 1975 and continued each spring for more than twenty-five years, was the annual Faculty Roast. There were skits and impersonations of faculty and time always was allocated for the faculty's rebuttal. In the mid-1980s, musical numbers composed by Nola Wright '84 rivaled in quality those at the Kansas Bar Association's annual meeting Bar Shows. Patrik Neustrom's '77 impersonation of Professor Levine caused many in the audience to believe the Professor was playing himself. On the other hand, some Roasts were too long and did not earn even one thumbs up. The 1976 Roast extended significantly past midnight, due to ad-lib skits that made the faculty happy it attended a pre-Roast marinade. The final two Roasts of Spring's deanship used an Academy Awards theme, with professors receiving "Silver Spring" Awards. The proclivities of faculty, both real and imagined, were exaggerated. The premise of a skit one year was a lawsuit by Professor Elrod's tongue, that appeared on-stage in a wheelchair, claiming Elrod had bitten it off while talking too fast. Another year, the student portraying her

---

683. *Missing: Ned O. Primmer*, TOPEKA CAP.-J, Feb. 2, 1980.

talked at warp speed while writing on a blackboard with her right hand and immediately erasing it with her left.[684]

TRANSITION

Faculty were active within the profession and in public affairs. Dean Spring and Professors Ryan, Treadway, and Kratochvil added volumes on criminal law, criminal procedure, the probate code, and the corporation code to the *Vernon's Kansas Statutes Annotated* series, joining those authored by Professors Fowks and Howe. Faculty scholarship focused almost exclusively on Kansas law and appeared principally in the *Washburn Law Journal* and the *Journal of the Kansas Bar Association*. Professor Ryan, aided by four students, completed the Kansas Law in Education project, providing elementary and secondary teachers a massive notebook of materials they could use to teach about the legal system. Two faculty members served on AALS committees in 1972, Dean Spring on the Committee on Law School Administration and Professor Kratochvil on the Committee on Special Opportunities and Needs of Smaller Law Schools.

During academic year 1970–71, faculty participated in a monthly television series, "Trial Brief," shown on the University's public television station, KTWU. The following year, the school collaborated with the Kansas Bar Association's Real Property, Probate and Trust Section to offer a twenty-week "Short Course on Estate Planning" on KTWU, the first extended televised CLE course in the nation. In June 1972, the school hosted the first Practicing Law Institute CLE program offered in Kansas, on real estate finance, again co-sponsored with the Real Property, Probate and Trust Section. Beginning in 1970, the school cooperated with the Kansas Supreme Court to offer annual programs for judges, frequently for special court judges and also for new judges following each election. In 1972, the school entered a formal agreement with the Kansas Bar Association and the University of Kansas School of Law that created a Kansas Joint Committee on CLE to co-sponsor all continuing legal education programs in the state, with the KBA taking the lead. KU was considering an aggressive plan to offer CLE. However, Kansas was still years away from mandatory CLE, and KBA leaders worried that competition among the three entities would not serve Kansas lawyers well.

---

684. Elrod, *supra* note 628, at 888.

Students did not close Washburn University to protest the Nixon administration's invasion of Cambodia, as students did at KU, but that invasion
ultimately led Professor Ahrens to file suit against President Nixon in the
United States District Court in Kansas City, seeking to enjoin the bombing
for lack of constitutional authority. "I have felt for a long time that Presidents
have been overstepping their bounds in regard to executive privilege," Ahrens
was quoted as saying. "Nixon is not alone in this. President Truman went
into Korea on much the same basis. He should have consulted with Congress
first."[685] Ahrens did not question the President's right to respond to an attack
without notifying Congress but felt Vietnam and Cambodia were examples of
waging war without the required involvement of Congress. He acknowledged
it was an uphill battle. "The courts tend to regard executive power as a political
question rather than a legal one. However, the courts have reversed themselves,
as in the case of voting rights, and we are hopeful they will reverse themselves
in this case as well." The District Court did not and dismissed the case.

Professor Elrod succeeded John Howe as Executive Secretary of the Washburn
Law School Association in January 1978 and reinstituted quarterly publication of *The Circuit Rider*. Only two issues had been published in the previous
three years and they had focused principally on fundraising for the building addition and for annual gifts to the new Foundation Fund the Board of
Governors established within the Association. Elrod immediately expanded
the publication to eight pages and concentrated on Law School and alumni
features. She also added short articles by faculty and alumni on timely legal
issues. One *Circuit Rider* article, by David Pierce '77, even was cited as authority
in a judicial opinion.[686]

El Slover stepped down as Assistant Dean in 1976 and Dean Spring selected
Carl Monk to replace him. Spring's own rapid entry into administration a
decade earlier, in his second year of law teaching, made his choice of an untenured faculty member who was starting only his third year of teaching less
of a surprise. That Spring would select Monk even though Monk had been
one of the faculty members who just one year earlier unsuccessfully opposed
Spring's plan to submit the fifth CLEPR grant for the Law Clinic would surprise

685. *Dr. Ahrens sues President Nixon*, WASHBURN REV., Sept. 12, 1973.
686. *Scully v. Overall*, 17 Kan. App. 2d 582, 840 P.2d 1211 (1992), citing David
Pierce, *July 1 Is Deadline for Filing Claims to Preserve "Unused Mineral Interests,"* 25
THE CIRCUIT RIDER 6 (Summer 1986).

only those who expect deans to hold grudges, something Spring never did. Spring later expressed "constant amazement" that Monk "regularly performs in only 70 to 80 hours a week duties that should reasonably require 120. His fresh approach, enthusiasm, and complete commitment to a high standard of quality have been the perfect catalyst to the administration of our school."[687]

The student-faculty ratio continued to improve because two of the three faculty members hired for 1976–77 filled new positions. One was the grant-funded position in the Clinic that Ben Farney filled. As Spring had predicted, Washburn was able to hire professors with prior law teaching experience for the other positions. Gregory Pease had taught for four years at Ohio Northern University and was Assistant Dean when he left. After graduation from law school at New Mexico, Pease had been law clerk for Judge Oliver Seth of the Tenth Circuit. Colin Kaufman came to Washburn after two years as a Teaching Fellow at Harvard while he earned an LL.M. He received his J.D. from the University of Texas, then practiced in Corpus Christi and served as Trustee in Bankruptcy in the Southern District of Texas. Kaufman immediately showed promise as a scholar, publishing two articles in the *Washburn Law Journal*. He stayed just one and one-half years before his wife's serious illness forced him to return to Texas in mid-year so she could receive medical treatment and be near her family. Kaufman later taught at St. Mary's Law School and prepared supplements for *Corbin on Contracts*.[688]

Late during the 1976–77 academic year, David Dale was invited to spend the following year teaching at the National Energy Law and Policy Institute at Tulsa's law school. Myrl L. Duncan was hired as Visiting Professor for the year of Dale's leave of absence. Duncan was completing a two-year clerkship, following his graduation from Georgetown Law Center, with Kansas Supreme Court Commissioner and later Court of Appeals Judge J. Richard Foth. Dale decided not to return after his year at NELPI and Duncan was hired for the permanent position.

---

687. Raymond L. Spring, *Summation: The Dean's Report to the Bar*, 17 WASH-BURN L.J. 515, 518 (1978).

688. Kaufman later entered private practice. Surprisingly, he was disbarred in Texas in 2004, based on allegations he failed to safeguard and promptly disperse client funds, charged unconscionable fees, and engaged in conduct involving dishonesty, deceit, or misrepresentation in connection with a bankruptcy client. *In re Kaufman*, 282 Kan. 36, 141 P.3d 500 (2006).

56. Gregory Pease,
Professor 1976–present

57. Myrl L. Duncan,
Professor 1977–present

When John Howe and Otto Kratochvil announced they would retire at the end of academic year 1977–78, there was more hiring to do. Ronald C. Griffin and Paul B. Rasor replaced them. Griffin taught the previous four years at the University of Oregon, after completing an LL.M. at Virginia. His law school years at Howard Law School overlapped for one year with Carl Monk's and the two of them renewed their acquaintance when both attended a two-week long AALS conference on law school teaching techniques. Griffin became Washburn's first black full-time faculty member, teaching Contracts among other courses. Rasor, a graduate of Michigan, practiced in Alamagordo, New Mexico, for six years and took over Howe's courses in commercial law.

Soon, there was an even more significant vacancy to fill. In September 1977, just before dedication of the new addition, Spring announced he would leave the deanship and return to full-time teaching at the end of that academic year. Assistant Dean Monk did not consider applying for the position, believing the school needed a leader more experienced in legal education. In fact, Monk was one of three faculty members elected to the search committee. However, the search was doomed from the outset, not by a lack of acceptable candidates[689]

---

689. One candidate who rejected Washburn's offer, Elwin Griffith, accepted the

58. Ronald C. Griffin,
Professor 1978–2011

but by a University policy refusing to grant tenure immediately to the person selected. None of the acceptable candidates would assume the position without the security tenure would provide to press a reluctant University administration to address the Law School's priorities and resource needs. When President Henderson prepared to offer the position to a candidate who might have accepted it without tenure, the faculty felt obliged to invoke the accreditation standard that no dean should be hired over the stated objection of a majority of the faculty. Ultimately, in mid-summer, Carl Monk was asked to be Acting Dean for one year while the search continued.

Spring reflected in his final Dean's report on his decision to step down. "I took this step neither in bitterness and frustration (as some have done) nor in protest or under pressure (as some have done). Rather I made the decision with some sense of satisfaction at goals achieved." In addition to a real desire to return to the classroom, which "I thoroughly enjoy,...there are other contributions to be made to our profession in my special fields of interest, and I hope to participate in making some of them."[690]

---

deanship at DePaul that year.

690. Raymond L. Spring, *Summation: The Dean's Report to the Bar*, 17 WASH-

He did just that, becoming one of the nation's leading authorities on law and mental disability. He helped organize the second National Conference on the Legal Rights of the Mentally Disabled, held in Topeka just four months after he left the Dean's office. That fall, he offered a new course on this subject, team teaching with psychiatrist Dr. Roy Lacoursiere. Two major articles led to his 1983 book, *The End of Insanity*, in which he argued for the abolition of the insanity defense. That in turn led to his 1984 appearance on the PBS program Firing Line, along with Dr. Walter Menninger, to discuss what host William F. Buckley described as "the revolutionary implications of his proposed reform." Rarely did Buckley seem as respectful of a guest or more willing to admit his guest knew more about a topic than he did.

Spring and LeCoursiere, together with a member of the University of Cincinnati faculty, published three editions of the textbook *Psychiatrists, Patients & Lawyers: Law and the Mental Health System*, which began as materials collected for their class at Washburn. The book quickly became the most popular text for courses on the topic at law schools nationwide. Other articles and international presentations followed.

Late in 1981, Spring pursued a "pet project" that he had kept on hold while the Law School addressed more urgent concerns. He proposed in a letter to Dr. Walter Menninger development of "a significant program" in mental health law. "In fact," he wrote, "I think a case could be made that some of us have been derelict in not developing such program long ago. Our position is probably unique, or nearly so, among law schools in terms of the range and depth of resources in the mental health community."[691] Not only would potential lawyers benefit from understanding mental health law issues, Spring thought psychiatrists would benefit from understanding the legal system in which they often play an important role.[692] Dr. Menninger, along with Dr. Herb Modlin, pursued the joint venture on behalf of the Menninger Foundation,[693] and it ultimately would lead to creation of a Certificate in Mental Health Law at Washburn. Spring received a joint appointment to the faculty of the Karl Menninger School of Psychiatry and Mental Health Sciences, annually giving lectures to Menninger residents and using law students to present mock trials.

BURN L.J. 515, 524 (1978).

691. Letter from Raymond L. Spring to Dr. Walter Menninger (Oct. 29, 1981).
692. *Id.*
693. Letter from W. Walter Menninger to Raymond L. Spring (Nov. 4, 1981).

7

THE MONK YEARS (1978–1988)

During his initial months as Acting Dean, Carl Monk was not a candidate for the permanent position. He did ask to be replaced on the search committee, but that was because of his workload. In fact, he fought to overturn the prohibition on awarding tenure that thwarted the search for an external Dean the previous year. Monk assumed he would return to being Assistant Dean, possibly as early as January, and undertook to do the work of both jobs. However, when enrollment in the Clinic plummeted that fall, he readily accepted Billie Parr's offer to help with administration and preparation for the accreditation inspection scheduled for the spring. Faculty Secretary Paul Rasor captured Parr's assignment by inventing for her the title "Assistant Dean for Institutional Studies Pro Tempore." Monk persuaded Ray Spring to chair the Self-Study Committee, a responsibility not usually assigned to just-retired deans, and not solely because they usually elect a sabbatical on the conclusion of their deanships. However, Spring was not on sabbatical and Monk and Spring were more on the same page than are many deans and their successors.

Monk gave literal meaning to the word "acting" in his title. He informed students that class section changes no longer would be approved based on professor preference or work schedules. He believed requirements for faculty scholarship and for tenure should be strengthened. At a July faculty meeting just eleven days after he assumed the position, Monk appointed a committee to recommend new promotion and tenure standards for new faculty members hired to begin teaching in August. He won University approval to hire three

59. Carl C. Monk, Dean 1978–1988,
Professor 1976–2010

new faculty members for academic year 1979–80, to address anticipated ABA/ AALS concerns that the student-faculty ratio of 32:1 was too high.

Monk quickly tackled the school's two most critical problems, the clinical program and the law library, making what alumni association President Gerald Goodell '58 later described as "constructive, although difficult, personnel changes."[694] The dedication of the Clinic addition in 1977 ironically had coincided with a dramatic decline in clinic enrollment. At a meeting of the alumni Board of Governors the morning after the dedication, then President-elect Goodell reported "serious criticism currently exists" among members of the Topeka Bar, students and alumni about the operation of the Clinic. Worse than that, "Law firms in Topeka have expressed serious concern as to whether or not graduates who have taken the legal clinic semester should be given the same consideration as graduates who have not received the legal clinic credit."

694. *President's Corner*, 18 THE CIRCUIT RIDER 2 (Spring 1979).

Questions were raised "about the educational value of the Legal Clinic and its future impact upon the entire Washburn Law School."[695] Rumors that firms had these concerns led increasing numbers of students to fear enrollment in the Clinic would harm their employment prospects. Concern became crisis after Monk became Acting Dean when only nine students enrolled in any Clinic course in the fall of 1978, just five in the Clinical Semester. In late August, the University administration directed Monk to prepare a report evaluating the program and making recommendations for its future.

The root causes of the bar's concerns and of the enrollment decline were many, some fact and some fiction. One fiction affecting both employers and students was that clinic students disproportionately failed the bar examination. Dean Monk refuted that fiction, reporting in posted notices and in the alumni magazine that 94% of the graduates who completed the Clinical Semester since its creation had passed the bar examination, compared to 91% of all graduates.[696] Ray Spring had tried in his final Dean's Report to refute other fictions, such as that one-third of the school's budget was allocated to the Clinic. However, it was fact that Washburn's expenditure of $159,250 of its own dollars in 1977–78 on clinical education, excluding grant funding, placed it twelfth among 130 reporting schools in CLEPR's *Survey & Directory of Clinical Legal Education* and the eleven schools spending more all were in major metropolitan areas. Because those schools "undoubtedly have substantially larger total budgets," Monk concluded "Washburn thus committed a larger percentage of its own resources to clinical education than any other law school in the country."[697]

To determine what else was fact, questionnaires were sent to all graduates of the clinical program since 1973, all current students, faculty, local judges, adjuncts who had taught in the program, members of the Board of Governors, and all 1977 and 1978 graduates. More than 560 responses were returned. While there was high praise for the supervision students received from clinical faculty, concerns about the administration of the clinical program and about its structure, particularly the way it limited enrollment in elective courses, were statistically significant responses. Unfavorable experience with the first-year

---

695. Minutes, Washburn L. Sch. Ass'n Board of Governors (Oct. 1, 1977).

696. *Acting Dean Comments on Clinic and Library Reports*, 18 THE CIRCUIT RIDER 1, 7 (Winter 1979).

697. Memorandum from Carl Monk to Vice President for Academic Affairs Robert Haywood (Nov. 2, 1978).

and second-year clinical programs was another factor cited for not enrolling in the clinical semester.

The frequency of proposals in the mid-1970s to expand the Clinic, while other needs were not met, was another contributing factor, because faculty debates about those proposals affected student perceptions. There had been resistance to submitting the fourth CLEPR grant, for the required first-year program, and Professor Rowland's proposal to make the second-year clinical course a prerequisite to enrollment in the elective two-hour externship course had been defeated. When retired Justice Tom C. Clark argued in the *Washburn Law Journal* that one year of clinical training should be a prerequisite for graduation, following twenty-four months of classroom instruction,[698] then-Assistant Dean Monk felt compelled to oppose Clark's proposal in the following issue of the *Journal*.[699] Students could not help but perceive the division within the faculty and many mistook opposition to further expansion for opposition to the concept. Professor Rowland did not hide from students his disagreement with Monk and others who opposed his proposals.

Early in the fall of 1978, Acting Dean Monk placed responsibility for policy decisions for the Clinic with a reconstituted five-member Clinic Committee, with the majority being classroom faculty, including the chair, Professor Concannon. One purpose was to make certain the Clinic was not merely a means "to ease the transition into law practice" but rather insisted on the same rigorous analytical process and mastery of substantive law that classroom courses did, while using a different and challenging teaching method.[700] While Professor Rowland had favored the "legal aid" model of clinical education in which students handled large numbers of cases, emphasis now was placed on smaller caseloads. Evaluation of "the case's potential for presenting novel or complex issues which have substantial educational value" became a major factor in selecting cases.[701] A further mandate to the Clinic Committee was to consider possible curriculum changes, such as abolition of the second-year program

---

698. Hon. Tom C. Clark, *The Continuing Challenge of Advocacy*, 16 WASHBURN L.J. 243 (1976).

699. Carl C. Monk, *Mandatory Advocacy Training: Caveat Emptor*, 16 WASHBURN L.J. 584 (1977).

700. Carl C. Monk, *The Dean's Report to the Bar*, 19 WASHBURN L.J. 440, 444 (1980).

701. *Id.* at 445.

and offering one-hour clinic experiences tied to classroom electives, such as Domestic Relations. The Committee's composition was intended to make clear to students that the classroom faculty supported clinical education. Monk placed Professor Meinecke in charge of day-to-day administrative details, without the title of Director, and gave the Clinic Committee responsibility to designate the professor who would be the day-to-day manager in future semesters.

Not solely because of low enrollment but also to emphasize to students that Clinic faculty were an integral and equal part of the entire faculty, Professors Meinecke and Jones taught a substantive law class in Criminal Law. Even Professor Rowland was assigned a classroom course until enrollment permitted his reassignment to supervise interns full-time. Professor Rich already had substituted the classroom course in Debtor-Creditor Rights for clinical supervision in the spring of 1978, when Professor Kaufman had to leave and Clinic enrollment had declined. When the first-year course was abandoned that fall, Rich became a classroom professor full-time. There were now four professors teaching in the Clinic and three devoted part of their time to other duties.

In early November, Dean Monk submitted his report to the Vice President for Academic Affairs. He described the changes he had implemented and plans to increase publicity, both to better inform the bar about the clinic program and to assure students would make informed choices of electives. Monk's report ended somberly. "There is of course no guarantee that these changes will increase enrollment.... The program should, under this new setup, be given at least one, and probably two years to see if enrollment will justify its continuation."[702] Happily, the changes led to a turnaround in enrollment more quickly than that. As soon as spring semester 1979, it returned nearly to traditional levels. A year later, students seeking to enroll exceeded the Clinic's capacity, triggering the school's policy of giving graduating seniors preference in enrollment.

The self-study preparing for the accreditation inspection identified the Law Library as an area requiring attention. While Spring's deanship saw significant growth in staff (from only Professor Warren and Ruth Gough to a staff of six, including four professional librarians), size of the collection (from 30,000 to 80,000 volumes), and book budget (from $18,000 to $86,500), the library still was understaffed, the collection still was among the smallest at long-established schools, and the materials budget barely covered the cost of

---

702. Memorandum, *supra* note 697.

continuations. Professor Bartlett, as a former Law Librarian, used funding from his Kline Summer Sabbatical in 1978 to tour law school libraries in the region and recommended changes needed at Washburn. Monk concluded additional external validation would be needed to persuade University administrators and the Board of Regents to provide necessary resources. The alumni Board of Governors authorized funding to hire a consultant, Roger Jacobs, who had been Law Librarian at Southern Illinois University and currently was Librarian of the United States Supreme Court.

The Jacobs Report contained many useful suggestions. It helped gain University approval to create a new Reference Librarian position that Professor Warren agreed to fill, serving until her retirement in December 1984. A search commenced for a new Director of the Law Library. Because of the increasing complexity of the position, a Masters in Library Science became a minimum qualification, along with a law degree. The University administration also accepted Jacobs' recommendation that the base library acquisitions budget be increased to $130,000. Shortly before the inspection, the University even agreed to a one-time additional appropriation of $20,000 to address weaknesses in the collection. The inspection team confirmed Jacobs' evaluation of the library's needs. The positive steps the University already had taken in response to Jacobs' recommendations led the team to conclude there were "signs of a good beginning on a program of improvement for the Law Library" and that progress of the library "appears bright."

The dean search proceeded simultaneously with all of Monk's initiatives. Four additional candidates came for interviews in September. An offer was extended to Steven Smith, who then was Associate Dean at Louisville. During extended negotiations, Smith insisted on commitments for additional resources for the library, new faculty positions, faculty salaries, and faculty research. When the University declined to make those commitments, Smith declined the offer. Monk then announced at a faculty meeting on December 8, 1978, that he had become a candidate. Though he was only 36 years old, his accomplishments, including the additional budget commitments he had obtained for personnel, led him "to believe I would enjoy the work in the next years," he told the local newspaper. "There are some additional commitments I'm interested in for the law school."[703] A motion at that faculty meeting by

---

703. *Monk is recommended for WU law dean post*, TOPEKA CAP.-J., Feb. 13, 1979.

Professor Bartlett to make offers to two additional external candidates before re-opening the search to internal candidates died for lack of a second. As the new semester started in January, the search process focused on Monk.

Monk had more leverage to negotiate on behalf of the Law School than he appeared at first blush to have as a legal educator for less than five years. First, the University did not want to have a second failed search. Second, Monk had interviewed at another law school and had received an offer to be its dean. Further, he effectively argued that the ABA and AALS accreditation committees would look on the school more favorably, not only regarding the library but also on other issues as well, if the University began to address the resource issues identified in the school's self-study before, rather than after, the inspection visit. The University developed a detailed set of "Assumptions for the Law School," covering matters from budgets to teaching loads.[704] Finally, by February, the University made sufficient commitments for Monk to agree to accept the deanship. When the Personnel Committee of the Regents formally recommended him, University Provost Robert Haywood "expressed relief that the drawn-out selection process has apparently come to an end.... They (law school deans) are just hard to find."[705]

The ABA/AALS inspection team arrived less than three weeks after Dean Monk's appointment. It described him as being "as energetic and articulate as he is well-informed" and as combining "a willingness to step forth in new directions with a sensitivity and respect for the long course of the development of the Law School." Monk had a reputation for teaching his classes "like a preacher on the stump"[706] and he pressed the University with the same evangelical fervor to meet the Law School's needs. He negotiated to double the budget for faculty travel to professional conferences and to create a permanent line item of $40,000 for research assistants to help faculty increase scholarly productivity. This also had the effect of increasing student scholarship funds by $15,000, the amount of scholarships previously awarded to research assistants. The University committed to hire two additional clerical staff for the library, as recommended in the Jacobs report. For the first time, a professional staff person, Susie Peters, could be hired as Director of Placement and Alumni Relations. Previously a

---

704. Memorandum from Provost Robert Haywood to President John Henderson (Jan. 17, 1979) (on file in Mabee Library).

705. *Id.*

706. *Dean Reviews Past Year*, 19 THE CIRCUIT RIDER 12, 14 (Summer 1980).

student served as Placement Director, paid in part by the WSBA and supervised by Professor Fowks as Faculty Advisor. Future Kansas Supreme Court Justice Lee Johnson '80 was the last Student Director as a 2L. Patti Schlosser replaced Peters in 1981 and was succeeded by Sandy Zagar in 1985, when coordination of CLE programming was added to the job description.

THE LARGEST FACULTY RECRUITMENT EVER

The recruitment of new faculty for the 1979–80 academic year produced the greatest change in the faculty of any recruitment in the school's history. When the dust settled, there were eight new professors, nearly one-third of the resulting faculty, and six of the eight remained through the school's centennial year, twenty-five years later. The AALS Faculty Recruitment Conference was held separate from the AALS annual meeting for the first time in 1978. Even in advance of the December conference, it was clear it would be a significant year for recruitment. In addition to the three new positions the University had committed to fund, Washburn was seeking a new Library Director and a new administrator for the Clinic. Professor Meinecke, influenced by the turmoil that declining Clinic enrollment caused, had decided to enter private practice. The possibility that additional positions would open following the Recruitment Conference was apparent. The Faculty Recruitment Committee was so concerned about the number of faculty to be hired that it scheduled interviews each twenty minutes during the two-day conference, even though the unwritten norm was thirty-minute interviews. In none of my twenty-plus years as a member of that committee did the feeling of exhilaration at the conclusion of the conference match what the committee felt that year. The number of quality candidates the committee interviewed was high and the committee felt there was a better than usual likelihood Washburn could successfully recruit them. The committee felt it succeeded in conveying the exceptional collegial relationship that existed at Washburn and that Washburn did not suffer from what Dean Monk called the "squabbles and in-fighting that characterize some law faculties." Several new faculty members "identified this as the primary consideration in selecting Washburn despite more lucrative offers from other schools."[707]

---

707. Carl C. Monk, *The Dean's Report to the Bar*, 19 WASHBURN L.J. 440, 442

One astonishing obstacle to recruitment had to be overcome. The University's policy was to pay in full the travel expenses of faculty candidates who accepted offers or did not receive offers after interviewing on campus. However, it would only reimburse half the travel expenses of candidates who declined offers. Not only was there the risk the best candidates would not interview because of this policy, it was embarrassing even to have to explain it to them. The Law School Foundation readily agreed to Monk's request to reimburse the other half of the travel expenses, if necessary.

The faculty's highest priority was recruitment of a specialist in taxation and it found one in Randall Roth. A 1974 graduate of Denver who completed an LL.M. in tax the following year at Miami, he had started law teaching just that fall at Hamline where he would be selected Professor of the Year. However, he was a native Kansan and family ties made the offer from Washburn attractive. Two brothers, James Roth '66 and Kent Roth '79, both graduated from Washburn. Roth quickly developed a national reputation as a lecturer. It is unlikely anyone in America presented more continuing education programs for lawyers and accountants than he did during his three years at Washburn. One year, he spent more than forty weekends away from Topeka delivering lectures. Yet, he made time to publish several articles in tax journals and was popular with students who, like those at Hamline, elected him Professor of the Year. Roth's desire to reduce the frequency of travel by having CLE attenders come to him was among the factors that led him to join the law faculty at the University of Hawaii in January 1983. Roth became one of the leading public figures in the state and at one point took a leave from the Hawaii faculty to serve as Chief of Staff for the Governor.

James B. Wadley and Nancy G. Maxwell were the first two candidates interviewed in Chicago who received offers, and both accepted. After earning his law degree from Tulane, Wadley had spent seven years at the University of Florida, first as Director of its Eastern Water Law Center and then of its Land Use Law Center. He held a joint appointment with the Schools of Agriculture and Law. He was writing a treatise on Agricultural Law with Florida Professor Julian Juergensmeyer and wanted to develop a teaching specialty in the area. Kansas was a natural place to do so and Washburn was eager to develop a unique program meeting local and regional needs. Maxwell was completing an LL.M.

(1980).

60. Nancy G. Maxwell,
Professor 1979–present

61. Allen Easley, Professor 1979–2004,
Associate Dean 1991–2004

at Harvard after a year as Assistant Professor of Law at her alma mater, North Dakota. Because she had practiced law for two years before that in Grand Forks, persuading her of the quality of life in a town the size of Topeka was not the hard sell it sometimes was for other faculty candidates. Maxwell was the first of many faculty candidates for whom placing a two-career family was a recruitment issue. It helped that Dean Monk was able to sweeten the pot by arranging a one-year joint faculty appointment between the Law School and Washburn's Journalism Department for her spouse, Ted Frederickson, and that Fredrickson had been for one year a classmate of Professor Duncan at Georgetown.

Additional faculty positions opened after the Recruitment Conference. Monk persuaded the University, as part of negotiations after he was offered the deanship, to permit the line item that had been reserved for an outside dean to be filled with a new faculty member instead. Another of the candidates interviewed in Chicago, Allen K. Easley, became the school's first Asian-American faculty member. He too was completing an LL.M., as part of a two-year Teaching Fellow program at Temple. He had practiced with a firm in Philadelphia and clerked there for United States District Judge Herbert Fogel. Like several other new faculty members that year, Easley assumed he would get his start in legal education at Washburn and move on within a few years. Like most of them, he changed his mind. Just a year after his arrival, on July 26, 1980, he married Guen Villarreal, who had become Assistant Law Librarian in 1976. She later completed her J.D. in 1984.

During spring break in March 1979, Professor Treadway suffered a mild stroke while he was in his office grading mid-term papers. We were able to dissuade him from driving himself home. Sadly, he was unable to teach again. Jean Reeves, his successor as General Attorney at the Santa Fe Railroad, and Kay Adam '76 agreed on just several days' notice to complete his classes. Treadway had carried the equivalent of a full-time teaching load for part-time pay and Monk successfully argued a full-time replacement was needed. This position was filled in the spring semester of the following academic year by John Lungren, who previously taught at Lewis University's law school in Chicago for two years.

The final vacancy was created late in the spring semester when Professor Jones decided to leave law teaching and move to Seattle. Like Meinecke, he had been affected by the controversy that low clinic enrollment spawned. Monk determined that the number of full-time equivalent (FTE) faculty teaching in the Clinic should be reduced to three, from the peak of five. The school still needed Jones' replacement to teach a .5 FTE load in the Clinic to reach the desired 3.0 FTE because Professor Parr agreed to continue as Assistant Dean. That left her only .5 FTE in the Clinic. A new model of a clinic faculty member who could teach both in the classroom and in the Clinic was appealing, because it gave flexibility in making teaching assignments as enrollment rose and fell in the Clinic. It became the school's model for hiring clinic professors for many years. Sheila Reynolds was well-suited for this new model. She had been Staff Attorney for Legal Aid Societies in Kansas City and Topeka and most recently was Legal Services Developer for the Kansas Department of Aging. She was a law school classmate of Professors Jones and Concannon at KU.

The new Library Director was John E. Christensen, whose law degree from Brigham Young and Masters of Library Science from the University of California-Berkeley met the enhanced requirements for the position. He was a protégé of legendary law librarian Roy Mersky at Texas, where Christensen served as Assistant Librarian for three years and became active in the American Association of Law Librarians. Dean Monk happened to share a cab at an AALS meeting with Mersky and his co-author Myron Jacobstein and asked for their help in filling the vacancy. Mersky suggested Washburn had an opportunity with Christensen to catch a rising star in the field before he had risen too far.

62. Sheila M. Reynolds, Professor 1979–2009

For Christensen, it was an opportunity to modernize and enlarge a library with potential for growth and to take it into the computer age.

The position as administrator of the Clinic was the last to be filled, by Michael Kaye. At one level, Kaye, who after graduation from Cleveland-Marshall College of Law earned an LL.M. in International Law from NYU and then became a graduate fellow at the University of Grenoble Institute of Comparative Law, would seem an unlikely director of a clinic representing indigents. However, Kaye had been an Assistant Public Defender and a criminal defense lawyer in private practice in California for many years. He taught for two years at Lincoln University Law School in San Francisco. The year before coming to Washburn he was Assistant Dean there.

Among the new faculty members, Kaye had the most difficult assignment. He was the first Clinic faculty member who was not a member of the Kansas bar when he was hired. While the title of Clinic Director was rarely used in his early days on campus, Kaye had the challenge of "directing" a colleague, Professor Rowland, who as the founding and former director was not happy with many of the changes that had been made. Maintaining student inter-

63. Michael Kaye, Professor 1979–present

est in the Clinic and a relatively stable enrollment were critical and required continued effort to rebuild the Clinic's credibility among students.

The arrival of the eight-member faculty class of 1979 completed a dramatic change in the character of the institution in the decade since the new building was dedicated. The faculty now numbered twenty-seven, including the two deans and two librarians. They held degrees from eighteen different law schools and eight of them had earned LL.M.s. Few law schools, particularly within the region, could boast such a high percentage of faculty with advanced law degrees or such diverse educational backgrounds. Two-thirds of the faculty had been hired in the past six years and seventeen faculty members had seven or fewer years of law teaching experience.

The sheer number of "young turks" meant they could set law school policy if they all agreed on an issue, even a non-academic one. For example, although the faculty banned smoking from classrooms in 1974, several faculty members still smoked during faculty meetings. Not long after he arrived, Professor Roth, a health-conscious marathon runner, was prepared to move to ban smoking there too. The votes likely were there to pass the motion, but it was a sensitive issue on which to confront senior faculty. There was discussion at a faculty meeting[708] but Dean Monk was able to negotiate a voluntary cessation of smoking that avoided a formal motion.

There were other growing pains. As more faculty with varying expectations rotated through the Legal Methods and Legal Research and Writing courses, some students complained that workloads for their section exceeded those of other sections. Sometimes, first-year students in the A section complained that their professors graded harder than B section professors, or vice versa, putting them at a disadvantage when invitations to join the Law Journal staff were issued and firms offered 1L clerkships. Increasingly, some students selected upper level electives based on the professor's reputation for grading, either high or low. Thus, during academic year 1982–83, the faculty adopted voluntary grade distribution guidelines and uniform requirements for the Legal Methods and Research and Writing classes that specified what assignments would be required, their due dates, and their weights in the final grade. The grade distribution guidelines were far more sophisticated than the ones the faculty had adopted in 1921. They were not meant to raise or lower grades but sought instead to mirror the core range of grades currently being given. Separate guidelines were set for first-year required large section courses, for methods and research classes, for upper-level required courses, and for large electives, but all the guidelines retained substantial flexibility. Small section seminars were exempt from the guidelines. Most faculty voluntarily complied with the guidelines, although there was some resistance, and first-year grade averages rarely varied more than .01–.03 between the A and B sections thereafter. An attempt failed in May 1980 to eliminate the requirement that dated back to 1950 that one faculty member act as a proctor in each examination room, but the attempt was an early step that led in January 1985 to the school's first Honor Code to govern student conduct, not just during examinations but in all law school activities.

WASHBURN'S IN-HOUSE TEACHING CLINIC

Because of the youth of the faculty and the positive experiences Dean Monk and Professors Griffin and Slover had when they attended two-week long

---

708. Minutes, Washburn U. Sch. of Law faculty meeting (Dec. 11, 1979).

AALS summer workshops on law teaching, Monk urged the faculty to try to replicate the experience in-house, through a weekend teaching clinic. Only Bob Fowks among twenty-three faculty who taught in the classroom declined to participate and he already planned to retire at the end of the following fall semester. As the appointed weekend neared, March 7–9, 1980, it was "viewed with varying degrees of anxiety"[709] by many faculty. The anxiety arose because the principal activity of the weekend, showing to one's faculty colleagues 15–20 minute videotaped segments of one's classes, risked diminished self-esteem. However, group discussions of techniques that succeeded and those that failed, including suggestions for being better classroom teachers, were conducted in supportive ways, highlighting effective techniques as often as criticizing poor ones. The tapes prompted discussions of problems all professors face, from issues affecting the atmosphere in a classroom, such as how to respond to flawed answers students give, without appearing intimidating to other students, to technical issues such as using a blackboard more effectively.

The weekend "united us even further"[710] and ended with professors feeling exhilarated, though exhausted. The faculty viewed the experience as being "without exception…an unqualified success."[711] A substantial part of the weekend's success was attributable to two outside facilitators who acted as group leaders, Dean Richard Huber of Boston College School of Law, who had been a leader in starting the AALS summer workshops, and Professor Barry Zaretsky of Brooklyn Law School, a participant with Washburn professors in prior national teaching clinics. They led plenary sessions about the goals and major problems of legal education, then put their groups at ease by using videotapes of their own classes to illustrate a model of self-evaluation and supportive critique. Time was set aside for two faculty members to teach live classes, to remind us what it was like to be a student. A major effect of the weekend was to cement a bond of mutual trust and respect among Washburn faculty members and a commitment to being better teachers. Comments by Huber and Zaretsky that the quality of teaching at Washburn exceeded that at a number of schools with national reputations helped too. Faculty members arrived on the Monday morning after the teaching clinic to find in their mailboxes

709. Washburn University Law School Self-Study Committee Report, at 4 (Feb. 1986).

710. *Id.*

711. *Dean Reviews Past Year*, 19 THE CIRCUIT RIDER 12, 13 (Summer 1980).

a challenge to the "Jets," Huber's group, from the "Sharks," Zaretsky's group, for a teach-off, under the Kansas Avenue Bridge on Saturday night, "no holds barred" and "your choice" of weapons. Nancy Maxwell quickly answered on behalf of the Jets, who as luck would have it included all the women professors: "Yah!, But—The Sharks don't got no Chicks!"

Students that Monday morning must have thought they had been transferred involuntarily to a new law school. Everyone did something differently. For example, for my entire teaching career prior to that weekend, I had taught class sitting at the desk at the front of the class, close to the multiple textbooks, statute books and other materials characteristic of a statutory course. My colleagues saw a caged animal on my videotape and suggested that student attention and interaction would improve if I allowed myself to move around. I haven't taught seated since. Nancy Maxwell experienced the same transformation.

Washburn's in-house teaching clinic was the first of such magnitude to be conducted at any law school. Huber and Zaretsky encouraged the school to share the model with other schools. Because I chaired the planning committee, I joined Dean Huber in describing the clinic during the Teaching Methods Section program at the next AALS annual meeting, in San Antonio, and Dean Monk and various faculty members made presentations about it at subsequent AALS meetings, as long afterwards as 1991,[712] and in other venues, such as summer meetings of the Mid-Continent Association of Law Schools and the Central States Law School Association. Professors Rich and Zaretsky prepared a paper describing and analyzing the weekend. Over the next three years, more than fifty law schools requested information about the teaching clinic so they could consider conducting their own programs.

The success of the teaching clinic led Monk to appoint a standing Committee on Professional Development. Building on the teaching clinic, the committee encouraged informal exchanges of classroom visits. When leading legal educators from around the country visited the campus to present lectures or participate in other programs, the committee organized up to half-day professional development sessions with them. For example, after Professor Curtis Berger delivered the Logan Lecture in Property Law in April 1982, he spent the afternoon discussing with the faculty the desirability of imparting humanistic values in the classroom. An afternoon session two weeks later, when Professor James J. White

---

712. From the Dean's Desk, 29 THE CIRCUIT RIDER 3 (Winter 1990).

of Michigan presented the annual Foulston Siefkin Lecture, expanded on the prior discussion by focusing on the extent to which law schools can influence students' values effectively. When former Iowa Dean and AALS President-Elect David Vernon taught in the Council on Legal Education Opportunity program for minority applicants that Washburn hosted that summer, the faculty had an afternoon session with him too. Sometimes non-lawyers shared their insights. In February 1983, Dr. Janice Redlish of the American Institute for Research in the Behavioral Sciences discussed techniques for teaching legal writing and in April that year Dr. Ron Burris of the Center for Computer Assisted Legal Instruction led a discussion of new ways to use computers in legal education. The Professional Development Committee's mission went beyond classroom teaching. It sponsored discussions of ways faculty could be more productive scholars and formalized a program to provide feedback for drafts of articles.

INCREASING FACULTY SCHOLARSHIP
AND NATIONAL VISIBILITY

Like no one in the school's history, Dean Monk pushed faculty to higher levels of scholarly writing, particularly in out-of-state journals, and of participation in the affairs of legal education nationally. He did it both by providing needed resources and by example. In addition to increasing funding for students to serve as research assistants and for travel to professional conferences, Monk persuaded the University to approve a slight reduction in the faculty teaching load, freeing more time for research, although the teaching load still was the third highest nationally in 1980–81. He negotiated with the administration to return faculty to nine-month contracts in 1979–80 so those inclined to write significant articles would have the uninterrupted time required to do so, free of the obligation of summer teaching. In April 1979, after being confirmed as Dean, Monk announced a new system of merit salary increases, initially with three categories, which would reward those who met publication expectations in addition to being good teachers.

The new incentives and resources soon produced results. Many professors published nationally between 1980 and 1983. Ray Spring's article on the insanity defense was published in the *Detroit College of Law Review*.[713] Myrl Duncan had

---

713. Raymond L. Spring, *The Insanity Issue in a Public Interest Perspective*, 1979

a lead article in the *Harvard Civil Rights—Civil Liberties Law Review.*[714] Linda Elrod[715] and Sheila Reynolds[716] both published in the University of Louisville's *Journal of Family Law.* There were articles by Bill Rich in the *Brigham Young Law Review,*[717] Allen Easley in the *Georgia Law Review,*[718] John Lungren in Utah's *Journal of Energy Law and Policy,*[719] Banks McDowell in the *McGill Law Review* in Canada,[720] Ron Griffin in Notre Dame's *Journal of Legislation,*[721] and Randy Roth in several tax journals.[722] John Christensen authored the first LEXIS training manual for law students, published by its creator, Mead Data Central. Jim Wadley, who was completing a four-volume treatise *Zoning: The Law in Florida* with Julian Jurgensmeyer when he arrived at Washburn, continued to collaborate with Jurgensmeyer and in 1982 they published a two-volume treatise on *Agricultural Law,* the first of its kind nationally. Wadley also had articles in the *South Dakota Law Review*[723] and the *Northern Illinois Law Review.*[724]

Monk led by example. He was appointed to the AALS Professional Development Committee in 1981, largely because of his innovation in professional

---

DETROIT CO. L. REV. 603 (1980).

714. Myrl L. Duncan, *The Future of Affirmative Action: A Jurisprudential/Legal Critique,* 17 HARV. CIV. R.-CIV. LIB L. REV. 503 (1982).

715. Linda D. Elrod, *Housing Alternatives for the Elderly,* 18 J. FAM. L. 723 (1980).

716. Sheila Reynolds and Roy B. Lacousiere, *Interminable Child Neglect/Custody Cases: Are There Better Alternatives,* 21 J. FAM. L. 239 (1982).

717. William Rich, *The Role of Lawyers: Beyond Advocacy,* 1980 B.Y.U.L. REV. 767 (1980).

718. Allen K. Easley, *Buying Back the First Amendment: Regulation of Disproportionate Corporate Spending in Ballot Issue Campaigns,* 17 GEORGIA L. REV. 675 (1983).

719. John Lungren, *Solar Entitlement: A Proposed Legislative Model,* 4 J. ENERGY L. & POL'Y 171 (1983).

720. Joel Levin and Banks McDowell, *The Balance Theory of Contracts: Seeking Justice in Voluntary Obligations,* 29 MCGILL L. REV. 24 (1983).

721. Ronald C. Griffin, *The Problem of Black Consumers and Commercials: A Proposed Legislative Solution,* 10 J. LEGIS. 135 (1983).

722. E.g., Randall Roth, *Can lender be charged with recurring taxable income as a result of an interest free loan?,* 52 J. TAX. 136 (Mar. 1980).

723. James B. Wadley, *Federal Seed Act: Regulation of Seed Sales and Remedies Available to the Seed Purchaser,* 27 S. DAKOTA L. REV. 453 (1982).

724. James B. Wadley, *The Future of Government Regulation of Agriculture: Biting the Hand that Feeds Us,* 3 NO. ILL. L. REV. 299 (1983).

development at Washburn. President David Vernon named Monk Chair of that Committee in 1983. Vernon had participated in Washburn's program and wanted the Committee to facilitate similar in-house efforts by other schools. Monk was re-appointed Chair for 1984. In 1982, Monk was elected Secretary of the AALS Section of Administration of Law Schools and spoke about "Faculty Governance" at the ABA's New Dean's Workshop. Monk accepted appointment as a member of accreditation site inspection teams at law schools at Campbell University in North Carolina and Mississippi College during academic year 1980–81, at Whittier and Texas Tech during academic year 1982–83, and at Brigham Young in the fall of 1983. He served on five more inspection teams during the remainder of his deanship. Despite the burden of administration, he published an article in 1981 in the *Journal of the Kansas Bar Association* on media access to court proceedings. He used a sabbatical in 1985, something unusual for a dean, to write another article on media and the law that the *Missouri Law Review* published.

Faculty became more visible nationally and many were invited to teach at other schools. Jim Concannon was Visiting Professor at Washington University in St. Louis during the summer of 1979. During academic year 1980–81, Bruce Levine and John Kuether visited at the University of Baltimore and Temple University, respectively. Myrl Duncan spent that year earning an LL.M. at Columbia and taking the classes required for the S.J.D. he completed in 1988. The following year, Ron Griffin was Visiting Professor at Notre Dame and Randy Roth visited at Hawaii during the spring semester. Ray Spring visited at St. Louis University during the summer of 1982. Paul Rasor visited in 1983–84 at the University of Detroit Law School and then from 1986 until 1988 at the University of Texas, where he was the first Visiting Professor ever selected to receive the Texas Excellence in Teaching award. Bill Rich was Visiting Scholar at Syracuse during a fall 1983 sabbatical and Carl Monk was Visiting Scholar at Brooklyn Law School in the fall of 1985 during his sabbatical, while Rich served as Acting Dean. Washburn faculty members who taught elsewhere gained an appreciation of the unique collegiality they had at their home school. Only one of them, Randy Roth, ultimately left to teach at another school—and that school had the unfair advantage of being in Hawaii.

In announcing new merit salary standards, Monk acknowledged that the nature of the student body and the roles Washburn graduates were likely to play meant classroom instruction and student needs would remain the primary

obligations of faculty, so that faculty as a whole might be "less involved in beneficial non-classroom activities than our colleagues at some other schools."[725]
Likewise, he acknowledged that some faculty "have strengths and interests in
other areas equally important to professional development and the law school.
Abandoning those activities in favor of a stringent publication requirement
would be the height of folly." He pledged to implement increased rewards
for scholarship in a manner that would "preserve the positive, constructive
atmosphere that exists within our faculty." In addition, the new standards for
promotion and tenure adopted a broader definition of scholarship than at
some other schools, for example by recognizing the scholarly value of interdisciplinary research and writing clinicians were especially likely to do and of
pro bono work preparing briefs on important issues of first impression.

While there was broad support for enhancing the school's visibility, some
faculty still worried the increased rewards for national scholarship would
detract from the school's tradition of faculty accessibility to students and its
emphasis on quality teaching and service to the local legal community. Other
faculty, even those committed to publication, reacted against what seemed like
increased bureaucracy. Paul Rasor, known for his irreverence, distributed a
"Faculty Credit Card" to each of his colleagues listing eleven different activities
a faculty member might complete and assigning a point value to each of them.
Four activities received one point, four more received five points, two received
ten points and the last one received twenty points. The card indicated it could
be punched only by a one-of-a-kind Great Punch kept in the sole possession of
the Dean. Faculty who completed a listed activity were to take the card to the
Dean "to receive your well-deserved punch." Minimal annual achievement was
met by one punch for each one-point activity. However, extra credit was to be
given for credit cards showing no punches for one-point activities. Publishing
a law review article was worth one point but publishing an "important, well-
written law review article with fewer than 20 footnotes" was worth five points.
Publishing a law book was worth one point but publishing an "important law
book with no cases in it" was worth five points. Making a speech to experts
in the faculty member's field was worth one point, while making "your area
intelligible to someone without expertise" was worth five points. At the end,

725. Memorandum from Carl C. Monk to All Faculty, "*Merit Salary Increases.*"
(Apr. 27, 1979).

Rasor sought to pad his own score by awarding ten points to faculty members who "anonymously publish scurrilous, disrespectful commentary on merit raises" and twenty points to those who "confess to [the] above."

Students caught the spirit of national involvement too. Art Bredemeyer '83 was elected Chair of the ABA's Law Student Division in 1982. Kirk Nystrom '79 twice was named Liaison for the Law Student Division to the ABA Committee on Law and National Security. Students revived *Case and Cane* in March 1982, publishing an interview with Tim O'Brien of ABC News when he was at Washburn as the keynote speaker for a Media and the Law Seminar. *Case and Cane* promptly won the ABA-LSD Award of Excellence as the best student newspaper in the Tenth Circuit.

Washburn was selected to host the 27th Annual Meeting of the National Conference of Law Reviews, held on March 26–28, 1981. The training program attracted 138 newly-elected editors from seventy-seven schools. Because University funds to support the conference were limited, alumni responded to solicitations for funds by *Law Journal* faculty adviser David Ryan and made the conference possible. Featured presenters included ABA President William Reece Smith, Jr. and Professor Henry Weihofen from New Mexico, whose text *Legal Writing Style* was widely used in law school classes. Local experts led seminars too, including Professor Spring, who discussed lead article solicitation, and a representative from Menninger, who discussed stress management.

Washburn's Catholic Law Student Association and Christian Legal Society, in cooperation with WSBA and the ABA Law Student Division, organized three annual Midwest Regional Conferences on Theology and the Law, beginning in 1978. Topics included "The Lawyer as Counselor," "The Lawyer and the Code of Professional Responsibility," and "Capital Punishment." Women's Legal Forum sponsored Women in the Law Conferences in 1984 and 1985. Washburn collaborated with the William Allen White School of Journalism at KU to present four Media and the Law seminars between 1979 and 1985, targeting both journalists and media lawyers and drawing as many as 144 participants. The thirtieth anniversary of the decision in *Brown v. Board of Education* was celebrated May 17–18, 1984, with the dedication of a commemorative sculpture entitled "Common Justice" near the east entrance to the Law School, a half-day

64. David L. Ryan '65,
Professor 1968–2005

65. James B. Wadley,
Professor 1979–2009

panel discussion in Robinson Courtroom, and a lecture at White Concert Hall. Coretta Scott King had agreed to present the lecture but when illness prevented her from attending, her daughter Bernice King delivered her remarks.

Dr. Karl Menninger once again returned to the Law School, six decades after he first taught Criminology. He delivered two lectures in March and April of 1982 in Michael Barbara's seminar on Sentencing and Correction. Distinguished speakers who presented William O. Douglas Lectures included: former U.S. Attorney General Ramsey Clark; Robert Kutak, Chair of the ABA Committee that produced the Model Rules of Professional Conduct; noted constitutional law scholar Professor John Nowak from Illinois; and tax scholar Boris Bitker from Yale. Foulston Siefkin Law Journal lecturers included Arthur Miller from Harvard, renowned evidence teacher Irving Younger from Minnesota, and commercial law expert James J. White from Michigan.

THE RURAL LAW CENTER

There were many incentives for Washburn to develop distinctive programs that other schools did not, or could not, offer. Unique programs could help student recruitment, enhance national reputation, and answer in part the recurring question, "Why does Kansas need two law schools?" Hiring Jim Wadley in 1979 gave Washburn the intellectual resource to exploit Kansas-centered opportunities in the field of agricultural law. Washburn created the Rural Law Center in 1980. It had three principal goals. One was to develop a curriculum of courses in agricultural law and related topics which would prepare students for a rural practice. A second goal was to be a significant source of research on issues important to practitioners in rural areas. The third goal was to disseminate information that would enhance the delivery of legal services in rural areas. Creation of the Rural Law Center had a side benefit beyond these goals. There were few specialists in this field and other schools already were expressing interest in hiring Wadley away from Washburn. The twelve-month contract that came with being Director of the Rural Law Center helped Washburn fend off what would have been more lucrative offers of nine-month contracts.

The first of the Center's goals was the easiest to achieve, as courses such as Agribusiness Law, Government Regulation of Agriculture, Rural Law Seminar, and Regulation of Agricultural and Public Lands all were added to the curriculum. Because it was a Rural Law Center, not an Agricultural Law Center, the eclectic Professor Wadley could bring within the Center's umbrella a wide range of subjects that interested him, from Legal Problems and Issues of Rural Development to Patents, Copyrights and Trademarks. Washburn soon was recognized by the ABA Forum Committee on Rural Law and Agribusiness as the only law school offering, as part of studies for the J.D., a formal program exposing students to the problems and perspectives of a rural law practice.[726] Only the LL.M. program at Arkansas offered more courses related to agricultural law.

Wadley sought almost single-handedly to fulfill the Center's other two goals as well. He wrote books and scholarly articles that were published nationally as well as columns for magazines and other publications to which Kansas farmers subscribed. He spoke at symposia sponsored by other law schools and at programs throughout Kansas, such as those sponsored by the Extension Service of Kansas State University's Department of Agriculture. Aided by student research assistants, he produced pamphlets dealing with practical legal problems in rural areas, such as a step-by-step guide to obtaining ap-

---

726. James B. Wadley, *Rural Law Center Progress Report and Memorandum in Support of Curriculum Proposals* (1982).

proval for ground water wells used for domestic purposes. An index of student seminar papers was prepared and distributed. Later, students researched issues identified by the Kansas Department of Agriculture. Wadley worked closely with Secretary of Agriculture (and future United States Senator and Kansas Governor) Sam Brownback. The two co-authored a textbook, *Kansas Agriculture Law*, in 1987.

From the outset, Dean Monk and Professor Wadley understood that grant funding would be needed to achieve the Center's second and third goals fully. There were too many other priorities for the school's operating budget. Initial optimism about prospects for funding was dampened when a joint proposal the Center and the Kansas Water Resources Research Institute at Kansas State University submitted to the Department of Interior was put on indefinite hold. A proposal to renew the school's federal Clinic Legal Education Experience grant for a fourth year in 1983–84 which included a clinical experience in rural law was not funded. Periodically throughout the next decade, the Center pursued major grants from private foundations and Congressional earmarks without success. The Center occasionally negotiated modest service agreements, such as one in 1985 with Kansas Legal Services, Inc. to support expansion of its services to poor farmers through rural offices. This $10,000 annual contract covered the costs of research by students and recent graduates supervised by Professor Wadley, who also conducted training programs for lawyers in field offices. However, external funding was never found for the additional faculty member who could share the Center's core teaching load, thereby freeing time for Wadley to focus more on research and outreach, or for a recent graduate assistant who could assume part of the research/outreach function. A few faculty members taught occasionally in the area, notably Professor Duncan, who once team-taught Water Law with Wadley and thereafter periodically taught the course himself and whose published research for his S.J.D. included work on farmland preservation and rural water conservation. However, the Center was too much a one-man show to fully achieve its goals, despite Wadley's valiant effort.

FINANCES AND THE FOUNDATION

The 1978 dean search and the accreditation inspection were times of revelation for alumni, particularly Gerald Goodell '58, the President of the Washburn Law School Association and its representative on the dean search committee. With these processes proceeding simultaneously, the need to reduce the student-faculty ratio, to make salaries competitive, to increase the library acquisitions budget and support staff, and to enhance staffing for the placement office and other student services became readily apparent. The University's reliance on the Law School as a "cash cow" had to be reduced. Goodell and other alums joined Acting Dean Monk in pressing the University for action on these issues both before the accreditation site visit and after the inspection team's report was received, and to its credit, the University responded. It increased the Law School's operating budget by 30% for 1979–80, when the eight new faculty members arrived. Direct expenses exceeded tuition revenue and state aid by about $100,000 that year, requiring the University to allocate some of its local property tax revenue to support the Law School. The operating budget increased by 20% more the following year as the budget for new books in the library neared the national median. Monk gave credit where credit was due, telling those attending the Washburn luncheon at the Kansas Bar Association meeting in 1980:

> I do not now nor will I ever stand here as an apologist for the University; my commitment is to the law school and my only job is to effectively represent the law school in the university community. But by the same token I will not unfairly and without basis in fact criticize University support. The simple fact is that regardless of what may have been true in the past, today Washburn Law School enjoys much greater support than do most law schools in the country.[727]

Of course, given the University's limited sources of additional funds, Dean Monk and alumni leaders like Goodell could expect the University to provide adequately only for the basic needs of legal education. They recognized that the margin of excellence to compete with better-financed state and private schools had to come from private giving. Particularly was this true regarding scholarships. The self-study identified scholarships as a priority because Washburn's tuition was more than twice that of state schools with which it competed for students, particularly KU. Too many students who might have chosen to attend Washburn were deterred from doing so by the high relative cost. Alumni leaders had been discussing the need for an organized fundraising

---

727. *Dean Reviews Past Year*, 19 THE CIRCUIT RIDER 12, 14 (Summer 1980).

effort since the 1950s, but, except for the significant scholarship fund created by donations not needed for the new building in 1969, little progress was made. In the mid-1970s, the alumni board established a separate sub-account called the "Foundation Fund" and a line was added to alumni dues statements on which alumni could make voluntary extra contributions. This step produced modest contributions but also some resentment.

Dean Monk attended an AALS-sponsored law school development conference and learned that Washburn was behind other schools in its lack of a well-structured annual giving campaign. He advised alumni that KU had received over $80,000 in contributions the previous year. The alumni board in 1980 authorized formation of a separate 501(c)(3) tax-exempt entity, the Washburn Law School Foundation. The board concluded an entity separate from the University was needed to assure alums that donations earmarked for the Law School would actually be used to improve the Law School and not as a substitute for University funding of basic needs. The control issue that led the Board of Governors to want a separate Foundation led President Henderson to oppose it. "'Can you entrust to another body a phase of operation of the university?' he asked the Regents. He reminded the Regents they had agreed on a general policy that all money-raising campaigns should be run out of the office of the vice-president for institutional advancement."[728] Monk was never a slave to a chain of command, and he took this issue, like many during his deanship, directly to the Regents, meeting with them individually in advance of the meeting of the full board. It did not hurt the Law School's case that Henderson's influence with the board was waning and his sixteen-year reign as president would end within a year. Alumni Board President Rae Batt reported the outcome in plain words reflecting its importance: "These funds will be outside the university and will not be subject to their control."[729]

The structure of the Foundation was exquisitely simple, providing a system of checks and balances. Its board had three members, the Dean of the Law School, an appointee of the Board of Governors, and an appointee of the University's President. The Dean and law alumni member could outvote a University appointee who sought to use Foundation funds to pay for basic needs the University should provide or for purposes that were not Law School

---

728. *WU regents tentatively OK budget*, TOPEKA DAILY CAP., Mar. 13, 1980, at 2.
729. *President's Corner*, 19 THE CIRCUIT RIDER 2 (Spring 1980).

priorities. The alumni and University representatives could outvote a runaway Dean, and the Dean and University representative could prevent use of funds for an alumni priority that was not in the long-term interest of the school. None of these scenarios ever transpired, perhaps because of the structure, and the Foundation Board always acted with consensus. J. Robert Wilson '39 agreed to be the first president of the Foundation and pledged $10,000 to get it started. He served until his death in 1982, when Gerald Goodell succeeded him and continued as president through 2001. President Henderson named University Provost Robert Haywood as the University representative. University Treasurer Louis (Gene) Mosiman succeeded him in 1982 and held the position until his retirement in 1998. Mosiman received the Law School Association's Honorary Life Membership that year in recognition of his loyal service to the Foundation Board.

Concurrent with creation of the Foundation, Monk began to explain to alumni the school's need for private giving, primarily for scholarships. Monk's 1980 Dean's Report to the Bar announced that an organized effort to create an annual giving program would begin later that year. Class agents were recruited for every class since 1930 to solicit classmates by mail for annual gifts. Soon, donors of $1,500 or more were named Delmas C. Hill Fellows and received a numbered print of Professor Wadley's painting of the Law School. Dean Monk presented print #1 to Judge Hill at the 1982 Law Institute.

Alumni activities increased too, even when the dean was not asking for money. At the urging of Charles L. Davis, Jr. '43, Washburn sponsored an alumni luncheon during the 1982 ABA convention in San Francisco. Forty-one alumni and guests attended. The luncheon became an annual event and years later Davis created an endowment to defray part of the cost.

Dues-paying members of the Washburn Law School Association reached nearly 800 and remained high despite Washburn Law School Association President Jim Barnett's report in the fall of 1982 that an audit had revealed misappropriation of Association funds by the Association's treasurer, an alum. The Association filed suit to recover its losses of more than $100,000.[730] The treasurer was bonded and by the summer of 1983 Barnett was able to report not only that all losses and interest had been recovered, as well as expenses,

---

730. *Lawsuit filed against Topeka attorney,* TOPEKA CAP.-J., Oct. 23, 1982; *Law School Alumni's Treasurer Charged with Theft of Funds,* WICHITA EAGLE-BEACON, Jan. 19, 1983.

but also that "due to the generous additional contributions made by some of our members during the time when the status of funds was questionable, we actually are now financially ahead of what we would have been had the unfortunate situation not occurred."[731]

RE-EXPANSION OF THE CLINIC

Dean Monk had described as permanent the reduction in the number of full-time equivalent faculty teaching in the Clinic to three, from the high of five. However, several factors made a cautious re-expansion of the Clinic desirable. The two most important ones were the rapid turnaround in student demand following the restructuring of Clinic administration and the availability of new grant programs. The new grant programs were, in turn, a response to criticism by Chief Justice Warren Burger that many trial lawyers were not competent for their work, often because of deficiencies in their legal education, and to a task force report commissioned by the ABA Section on Legal Education and Admission to the Bar. While the so-called Cramton Report, named for task force Chair Dean Roger Cramton of Cornell, praised law schools for teaching analytical ability and knowledge of the law, it urged them to expand training in performing basic legal skills and in diligence and ethical responsibility.[732] While Monk accepted "the general thrust of this report," he observed that individualized instruction in skills would require substantial increases in resources for legal education, at a time when budgets were being strained to maintain existing programs and university administrators were accustomed to providing legal education on the cheap. Further, he attributed much of the criticism of lawyers to lack of preparation, something that "is seldom the result of an inadequate education."[733] Because law school lasts only three years of a forty-year professional life, Monk's view was that law schools should do what they do best:

---

731. *The President's Corner*, 22 THE CIRCUIT RIDER 2 (Spring 1983). Strangely, in 1990, a later treasurer of the Association resigned when irregularities were discovered in other accounts at the bank by which he was employed, although the Association's account there was not involved.

732. Carl C. Monk, *The Dean's Report to the Bar*, 19 WASHBURN L.J. 440, 446 (1980).

733. *Id.*

To concentrate on skills training to the detriment of sound analytical reasoning would sacrifice the best opportunity for inculcating good analytical skills in future practitioners. We should however take advantage of opportunities to improve skills training when we can do so without sacrificing the traditional emphasis on analytical skills.[734]

Such an opportunity arose almost immediately when the United States Department of Education, shortly before the start of academic year 1980–81, created a new Law School Clinical Experience Program to fund expansions of clinics. The grant program was particularly attractive because it allowed requests for funding for equipment in addition to personnel. Washburn sought to identify innovative and fundable proposals that it did not have to commit to fund from its own resources after the expiration of the grant. The faculty approved a one-hour internship that students would complete in connection with a substantive class. Few, if any, law schools had tried such a program and the grant application sought funding for a full-time faculty member to coordinate it. The application also sought $12,000 to purchase a word processing computer for the Clinic. No doubt most law schools wanted to include computers in their grant applications but Washburn was able to make a strong case for it since the Clinic building had been constructed to facilitate operation of a model law office. The objective was to permit students to experience not only "how the computer fits into a law office and how briefs, letters and other memoranda of law...could be speed-copied, printed, filed and called up for research"[735] but also how it could be used for calendaring, checking conflicts of interest, and other functions. An initial project would adapt routine domestic relations pleadings and enter them in the word processor.

Because successful grants would not be announced until after the fall semester started, the grant period for the initial year ran January 1–September 30. The grant request totaled $62,000, with some funding also earmarked to upgrade the Clinic library. Grant recipients could apply for additional grants in succeeding years, and Monk expressed optimism about the likelihood of renewal. However, Monk realized that it might be impossible to hire an experienced clinical teacher for the position if it would end in the middle of the

---

734. *Id.*, at 447.
735. *Law school purchasing new electronic word processor*, WASHBURN REV., Mar. 25, 1981.

fall semester if the grant were not renewed. Thus, in seeking the University's approval to submit the grant application, he sought contingent funding of $10,000 to assure the position could continue from October 1 though December 31. President Henderson balked at even that contingent commitment. Monk once again was forced to lobby the Board of Regents to gain approval to submit the application.

The Department of Education approved the grant request and renewed it for two additional years. David Boeck, a law school classmate of Nancy Maxwell at North Dakota and former director of the clinical program there, filled the new position during the spring and summer of 1981. The grant was renewed for 1981–82 so that the list of substantive courses offering the one hour internship could be more than doubled: Public Benefits Legislation, Domestic Relations, Juvenile Law, Law and Mental Disability, Administration of Criminal Justice, and Advanced Civil Procedure. Enrollment in the one-hour internship almost tripled that year and during the spring semester sixty students were enrolled in some Clinic course. Dixie Moss (now Madden) held the position that year and the next, when the renewal of the grant permitted the position to be converted to a twelve-month contract. Moss was a native Kansan who graduated from law school at Ohio State University and had taught in the clinic there for one year.

A FRESH START WITH A NEW PRESIDENT

John Howe expressed "a great deal of confidence" in President Henderson early in his presidency, believing "[h]e will not bend over backward to favor the law school, but I am certain that he will not cut our throat."[736] Ray Spring and Henderson actually were friends who had cabins near one another at Lake Wabaunsee. On the other hand, Monk and Henderson almost immediately and often thereafter were at loggerheads. Monk was an advocate for the Law School and its pressing needs and frequently met resistance from Henderson. When the Law School sought approval from the Board of Regents in 1978 to apply to host a Council on Legal Education Opportunity summer workshop in 1979 targeting prospective minority law students, Henderson surprised everyone at the Regents' meeting by opposing the proposal. Monk was able to persuade the Regents to approve the application anyway. Monk knew that

---

736. Letter from John E. Howe to Melvin C. Poland (Nov. 28, 1966).

first-time applicants rarely were selected to host CLEO programs but the fight with Henderson was worth it because the Law School would be in a better position when it applied again in later years. Remarkably, Henderson rejected the next year's application too, only to have the Regents once again override his objection. CLEO chose KU to host the program instead. Monk later attributed the decision to CLEO's "perception…that the administration of Washburn University was not committed to the program. Unfortunately, that perception was correct."[737] Not long after Monk also won his battles to create the separate Law School Foundation and for approval of the Clinic grant, there were reports that renewal of Henderson's contract was an issue with the Regents,[738] although ultimately it was extended. By December 1980, however, Henderson announced his resignation, as of the end of the academic year, and the local paper reported rumors he had fallen from favor with the Regents.[739]

Rocky relationships with the rest of the campus extended beyond the president's office. At the time, a University-wide Committee on Promotion and Tenure (UCPT) made recommendations to the Provost on all applications for promotion or tenure. In early February 1981, the committee voted not to recommend promotion from Assistant to Associate Professor for one of the new faculty members hired in 1979, despite the unanimous recommendation of the tenured faculty at the Law School. Monk went ballistic, in part because of comments of committee members exhibiting bias against the Law School. One member's comment, "When I saw your faculty contracts it sure got the hair up on my back," was improper, Monk wrote to Provost Robert Haywood, "even when made in jest."[740] Worse, the comment of another member, "My vote will be based on your teaching load being half of what mine is," was not made in jest. Another member questioned the award of credit for prior teaching to this professor, even though that question was beyond the committee's jurisdiction. The faculty member in question already had proven to be one of the Law School's best teachers and comments of UCPT members convinced Monk "that it is probably

---

737. Memorandum from Carl C. Monk to Dr. John Green (Oct. 26, 1981) (on file in Mabee Library).

738. *Henderson's contract, future at WU debated*, WASHBURN REV., Apr. 30, 1980, at 1.

739. *Henderson quits Washburn job*, TOPEKA CAP.-J., DEC. 11, 1980, at 1.

740. Memorandum from Carl C. Monk to Robert Haywood, Provost (Feb. 10, 1981) (on file in Mabee Library).

impossible for a person not trained in law to understand, much less judge the quality of legal scholarship."[741] He proposed changes so that recommendations for promotion or tenure for law professors would be made by the Law School directly to the Provost or the President. He pledged to fight for the changes if the Provost and President didn't agree to them. "Whatever the outcome of such a fight, it could only result in widening the gap between the law school and the 'main university.'"[742] Provost Haywood reversed the UCPT recommendation against promotion. The incident ultimately led to new procedures restricting review by the campus-wide committee of promotion and tenure recommendations to a determination whether the recommending School or the College had followed its prescribed standards in making its recommendation.

The law faculty did little to attract allies across campus. Law professors hardly ever attended University general faculty meetings. When they did, it often was en masse, to vote as a block against a proposal many elsewhere on campus supported. Once, for example, Monk rallied the troops to oppose scheduling the University's spring holiday around Easter weekend every year, on the ground that the University's calendar should not be tied so closely to a single religion.

There were high hopes that relations, at least at the presidential level, would improve when President John Green arrived during the summer of 1981. WLSA President Jim Barnett '59 expressed the belief that "we're entering into a new relationship with the University through his efforts that will be of tremendous benefit to both the University and the Law School."[743] Green's previous experience in academia included positions at three universities that had law schools, including Miami in Florida and most recently the University of Houston. Thus, it was thought, he would be more familiar with the needs of a law school and the ways they differed from undergraduate programs.[744] In fact, he decentralized the administrative structure, with the result that the Dean of the Law School, unlike other deans, reported directly to the President.

Green spoke to law alums at their 1982 luncheon during the Kansas Bar Association annual meeting. There was much to like. He had implemented full-cost academic accounting for programs and admitted,

741. *Id.*

742. *Id.*; Memorandum from Carl C. Monk to Dr. John Green (Oct. 6, 1981) (on file in Mabee Library).

743. *The President's Corner*, 21 THE CIRCUIT RIDER 2 (Winter 1982).

744. *From the Dean's Desk*, 20 THE CIRCUIT RIDER 2 (Summer 1981).

In the past, it was obvious that the law school, to a certain extent, was subsidizing other operations of the university. This has stopped, and we are now in a posture of the law school utilizing all of its direct revenues. I believe you can surmise from my comments so far that as long as I am president of Washburn University, the Law School will receive my utmost support and attention.[745]

Remarkably, the University had never had a full-time fundraiser and Green announced plans to hire one. He expressed the hope that the Law School could be named for an endowed gift of between $3 and $5 million and that funds could be raised for scholarships, chairs, and "the much-needed law school addition to house more library books" that was part of the newly-developed five-year plan.

BOBBY'S BOYS

Bob Fowks retired from full-time teaching in mid-academic year, 1980–81. He continued to teach part-time for several years while acting as Assistant Vice President and Trust Consultant for Southwest State Bank and later as consultant for the Kansas Bar Association. He had taught full-time for twenty-nine years.

Fowks was a teacher of legend, described by his students as "vivid" and "zestful," and as having an "animated classroom style" and a "quiet sense of humor."[746] He understood that learning occurs when students are caught off guard. He taught Agency during Ray Spring's first semester as a law student:

> Bob wasn't there one day, and Mrs. J., the law school secretary, came in after awhile to say that class had been cancelled and we could leave. The first person to open the door to leave the room was faced by Fowks who said, 'Who told you that Mrs. J had the authority to dismiss my class?' That was just one example of how Bob made the classroom so much fun.[747]

---

745. *Dr. Green Cites Progress For Law School*, 21 THE CIRCUIT RIDER 13, 14 (Spring 1982).

746. *Remembering Professor Robert J. Fowks*, 20 the CIRCUIT RIDER 12–13 (Fall 1991).

747. *Id.* at 12.

Fowks was a member of the Selden Society and continued to spend the majority of the first semester of Civil Procedure teaching the common law forms of action and common law procedure long after the Federal Rules were in force in most states, including Kansas. Not every student appreciated his approach. When the first semester exam covered only the common law writs and did not contain a single question about Kansas or Federal procedure, Kay McFarland '64 wrote at the bottom of her exam that "the test questions were about as relevant as testing a medical student on how a broken leg should be set in 1720."[748] Others like George Erickson '66 appreciated Fowks' method because it

> stressed the historical aspects of the law and taught that you can understand today's legal procedure if you also understand the history of how the laws were developed....The course was very alive. We were required to prepare original writs...and by doing so we learned to establish a recognizable legal right.

> Bob had a way of teaching that just captured your imagination....He used to have a model of a knight—'Charlie'—that he used as a prop in equity class...and he used Charlie to describe how one went before the king to get equity.[749]

It became a tradition each year Fowks taught Labor Law for students in the class to strike at some point during the semester, establish a picket line outside the classroom, and carry picket signs demanding shorter class hours and making other demands. Some picket signs addressed conditions of education: "Black Letter Law, Not War Stories." Others were more personal. The signs "do not describe me in glowing terms at all," Fowks told a reporter. However, "the theory behind this is these people are going to be lawyers....It gives them some understanding of what goes on in a picket line. There are some leaders, some followers, some hot heads, some cool heads. It's sort of like a psychiatrist who gets analyzed so he'll know what the problems of the client are."[750]

When Fowks retired, Linda Elrod '72 wrote that she was

---

748. Teresa Sittenauer, *Women and Minorities Enrich Early Topeka*, TBA BRIEF-INGS 26, 27 (April 2005).

749. *Id.*

750. Professor 'pickets,' TOPEKA ST. J., Nov. 20, 1973.

66. John Braun, '80, pickets during annual strike in Professor Fowks'
Labor Law class; Fowks was Professor 1950–1951 and 1953–1980

fortunate to have had the opportunity to see Bob not only from a student's perspective but also as a colleague on the law faculty. Any teacher is judged not only by what is imparted in black letter law, but also what is instilled through values, feelings and by the example that is given. Bob's enthusiasm for the law, his love of the common law, his devotion to students and the educational process are inspirations to those who knew him. Bob's keen sense of humor—his ability to laugh at himself and his theatrical classroom manner have left their mark on those who studied under him. Bob encouraged students to participate in the educational process. Whether he was playing a Shire Reeve serving a Breve Originale from the 14th century or whether he was portraying a tough labor boss—cigar and all—arguing with a recalcitrant labor law class, Bob made learning fun.[751]

---

751. Linda Elrod, *Bob Fowks Resigns After 30 Years*, 20 THE CIRCUIT RIDER 1, 7

Fowks was, as Elrod described him, a "helpful tutor for young professors" and "constantly aware of his obligations to the school and to the profession and went far above the call of duty to perform."

The faculty subpoenaed Fowks to a retirement reception and, in typical Fowks-fashion, he recited a Latin answer. Faculty members who could carry a tune, and some who couldn't, joined in singing "Bobby's Boys," to the tune of the 1964 Chad Mitchell Trio song "Barry's Boys" about Republican nominee for President, Barry Goldwater:

> We're the bright young men who want to go back to 1310;
> We're Bobby's boys;
> We're the kids with a cause, yes it's pleadings like Grandpa-pa's
> We're Bobby's boys;
>
> At the old law school we fight the new young turks;
> We'll never be caught dead voting with those jerks;
>
> We fancy the time when forms were forms and writs were writs
> And you felt so damned secure just knowing which were which;
>
> When his students start to picket, he tells them all to stick it,
> Cuz they're Bobby's boys'
>
> When they said he was scurrilous, he became well, quite furillous
> They're Bobby's boys;
>
> So if you don't recognize de bonis asportatis
> With Bob you'll simply be persona non gratis;
>
> Now you may think some of his ideas are queer,
> Such as equity will never aid a volunteer;
>
> And we're always right, although some may think we're slightly trite;
> We're Bobby's boys;
>
> And we'll prove that it's true—common law pleading is best for you;
>
> Thoughts too deep for tears pervade the court
> When we assumpsit bring and godlike waive the tort;

(Winter 1981).

You can join the crew; he knows what's best for you;

So come join up with Bobby's, not the Haywood-Hill-Monk lobbies;
Come join up with Bobby's boys.[752]

NEW FACES

Four retirements brought new faces to the faculty, as did the frequent visits
Washburn professors made at other schools. The same year Fowks retired,
1980–81, Billie Parr concluded her third year as Assistant Dean and returned
to full-time supervision in the Clinic, where extra help was needed to meet
revived student demand. She retired after the spring semester of 1982, although
she was coaxed out of retirement in the fall of 1983 to fill in as Associate Dean
when her successor in the position, Bill Rich, was granted a sabbatical. Roy
Bartlett retired after the fall semester in 1982,[753] at the same time Randy Roth
left to join the Hawaii faculty. Then, El Slover retired at the end of the spring
semester in 1983.

Several of the new professors who arrived in these years had long tenures.
Michael Barbara '53 came first, in 1980–81, initially as a visitor when three faculty
members were on leave, then replacing Fowks in a permanent position. Barbara
was a widely respected District Judge in Topeka, who one year was selected by
the Kansas Trial Lawyers Association as Trial Judge of the Year. He was a popular
adjunct professor in Trial Advocacy during his years on the bench. Barbara was
well-connected statewide and upon joining the faculty was in constant demand
as a continuing legal education speaker and expert on numerous public issues
such as sentencing and corrections. He was granted a leave of absence in 1983
to serve as Governor John Carlin's Secretary of Corrections and ultimately
served for two and one-half years. Barbara was more physically fit than most
of his students. For nearly two years, even after turning 60 years old, he never
lost to a law student in racquetball. Finally, in the spring of 1982, he lost the
championship match of the first annual student-faculty racquetball tournament. The following year, the tournament's title, "Quash the Judge," reflected

---

752. *Id.* at 9.

753. He died January 4, 1995. Ray Spring '59 described him in a memorial published in 34 THE CIRCUIT RIDER 15 (Spring 1995) as a "trusted teacher and loyal
alumnus," a lover of all history and "an incessant reader on all subjects."

67. Professor Charlene Smith and Barb White, the Dean's Administrative
Assistant, compete in the student-faculty racquetball tournament

student determination to assert the physical supremacy of youth, but Barbara
remained a force in the tournament until his retirement in 1993.

Billie Parr's retirement afforded Michael Kaye an opportunity to become a
full-time supervisor in the Law Clinic, happily "forsaking the joys of administration" as Clinic Director.[754] After several offers were rejected, the search for
a new Director initially seemed to have a positive outcome with the hiring of
Warren Hill for 1982–83. He had been an Assistant United States Attorney and
most recently served as Regional Director in Chicago for the Legal Services
Corporation. Previously, he taught for five years at the law school at Ohio State
University and for one year at the University of Pennsylvania. Unfortunately,
a misstatement on his application led to denial of his application for admission to the Kansas bar on motion and he left the faculty before the end of the
academic year. A second search for Clinic Director led to the hiring in 1983–84
of the school's first full-time Hispanic faculty member, Robert W. Piatt, Jr. He

---

754. Carl C. Monk, *From the Dean's Desk*, 21 THE CIRCUIT RIDER 2, 5 (Summer
1982).

had taught in the clinic at the University of Oklahoma and was practicing in New Mexico when he was hired. The Department of Education grant ended that year when the proposal to renew it to extend the Clinic's services to rural clients through the Rural Law Center was not funded. The loss of the grant position held by Dixie Moss left 3.5 full-time faculty teaching in the Clinic.

In anticipation of Roy Bartlett's mid-year retirement, Charlene Smith joined the faculty in 1982–83 to replace him in what then was a year-long Torts class. Like Allen Easley before her, she had completed the LL.M. Teaching Fellows program at Temple University. She had taught at several undergraduate universities before earning her law degree at Hamline. Monk persuaded President Green that the University for the first time should pay half of a new faculty member's moving expenses.[755] That, plus Dean Monk's final offer during negotiations of the first harvest of asparagus each year from Professor Pease's garden, sealed the deal. Smith taught at Washburn for more than twenty years.

Bartlett's retirement also created a need for a faculty member for 1983–84 to teach international and comparative law, preferably a specialist. Roth's departure created a critical need to hire a tax professor that year. Primarily because of the difficulty often encountered in recruiting a tax professor, the Faculty Recruitment Committee planned an aggressive recruitment and for the first time interviewed candidates prior to the national Faculty Recruitment Conference, targeting tax LL.M. programs. Dean Monk interviewed candidates at Harvard and Boston University while attending a conference in Boston, and Monk and the Committee's Chair, Professor Concannon, interviewed candidates at NYU and Columbia while attending a conference in New York. Such an aggressive recruitment would not have been undertaken solely for the International Law position. Ironically, the aggressive recruitment did not produce the school's new tax professor but it did produce its new professor of International Law. At NYU, Monk and Concannon interviewed Liaquat Ali Khan and they were so impressed with him they urged him to interview with the full committee at the recruitment conference in Chicago. A native of Pakistan, Khan was an engineer who earned his LL.B. at the University of Punjab. He was completing his S.J.D., writing his thesis in the area of comparative constitutional law. The smallest city in which he had ever lived was Houston. Khan later acknowledged

---

755. Memorandum from Carl C. Monk to Dr. John Green (Feb. 23, 1982) (on file in Mabee Library), reporting that the new policy was influential in Smith's decision to accept Washburn's offer.

that he signed up to interview with Monk and Concannon "on a whim"[756] and that had he not done so in New York, it was unlikely he ever would have considered coming to Washburn or even interviewing with Washburn's team in Chicago. Yet he came, and he has stayed to this day.

The new tax professor came not from the standard recruitment process but from faculty contacts. John Christensen recommended that the recruitment committee consider J. Wendell (Jim) Bayles, who had been Christensen's tax professor at the University of Utah. Bayles graduated at the top of his class at Utah in 1965 and earned an LL.M. at NYU in 1966 before entering private practice. He then was on the full-time faculty at Utah from 1972 through 1978, including a year as Associate Dean and visits at Brigham Young and Texas, before returning to private practice. He missed teaching and the Mormon connection at Washburn though Christensen and Jim Wadley made Washburn and Topeka attractive. He came to Washburn without interviewing at any other school. For many years, he returned "home" to recruit students at Utah and Brigham Young and his efforts made Washburn a leading alternative to the Utah schools for Mormon students.

In 1983, at the mid-point of his decade as Dean, Monk reflected on how far the school had come in its past twenty years.[757] Between 1963 and 1973, enrollment had more than tripled, from 175 to 592, while the faculty had not quite doubled, from eight to fifteen. The fifteen faculty members held J.D.s from just nine law schools, although they did hold seven advanced degrees. Between 1973 and 1983, enrollment had remained relatively constant, growing only by twelve to 604, but the full-time faculty had nearly doubled, from fifteen to twenty-eight, including the deans and librarians, and the number of courses offered had grown from sixty-two to 100. Faculty members now had degrees from twenty different law schools and twelve had earned LL.M.s, two had earned S.J.D.s, and a third was working toward an S.J.D. Equally important, the number of other law schools at which faculty had taught had grown from three in 1973 to twenty-two in 1983.

Looking ahead, Monk correctly anticipated that the frequency with which new faculty would arrive would decline sharply in the next decade. No more than three professors would reach the normal retirement age by 1993 and the

---

756. *Faculty Profiles*, 27 THE CIRCUIT RIDER 21 (Fall 1988).

757. Carl C. Monk, *Dean Seeks Alumni Ideas and Support*, 22 THE CIRCUIT RIDER 1 (Summer 1983).

68. Professor Ali Khan becomes U.S. citizen

69. James W. Bayles,
Professor 1983–2000

school could not expect a significant increase in budgeted positions. Indeed, it would be 1988 before the next new tenure-track faculty member would arrive. Monk warned that as the faculty increasingly became tenured and was not reinvigorated annually by the arrival of energetic new faculty members, special efforts would be required to assure it maintained productivity and continued to develop professionally.

A PROVEN SCHOLAR

The hiring of Banks McDowell as a visitor in 1982–83 and as a tenured professor beginning in 1983–84 was a boost for the school's self-esteem and a validation of its efforts to increase its national visibility. He held the Austin B. Fletcher Professorship at Boston University and was a nationally respected scholar. McDowell had been Chair of the Faculty Senate at Boston and the distraction of constant, time consuming battles he was forced to wage with Boston's controversial President John Silber made the collegial atmosphere at Washburn look attractive. Indeed, when he retired, he described his years at Washburn as the most productive of his career.[758]

758. Banks McDowell, *Reflections on Thirteen Years at the Washburn Univer-*

McDowell came for a "look-see" visit, so that both he and the school could evaluate whether he should stay. McDowell brought the perspective of one who had taught at an elite eastern school for twenty-three years. His nature was to be provocative and to challenge all assumptions. "I thought my role ought to be to shake up the community by raising matters rarely discussed in public in Kansas. This coincides," he wrote, "with my personal view of a teacher's job—to force people to think and be curious, rather than just give information. In my role as a sometimes gadfly, I was always met with toler-ance, and at least polite attention."[759] His description of insights, his own and those of others, as "intriguing" became a trademark.[760]

McDowell's article in *The Circuit Rider* describing the differences between his former and new schools[761] demonstrates both his affection for his new school and the restless spirit that could lead him to stay at arm's length. Students and faculty at both schools, he thought, reflected the values of their regions. At Boston, they "are aggressive, sophisticated, ambitious, cynical, impatient, and talented." At Washburn, they are "cooperative, hard-working, polite, trusting as well as trustworthy, and talented." He found he could "teach the students essentially the same way, using the same materials, at the same levels of complex-ity and sophistication, and get about the same results." However, he perceived that each school clearly had its own model or ideal "of the kind of lawyer it is trying to train," and the different models had different consequences. Boston University's model was an elite one of training "highly specialized partners" in major metropolitan firms, which led to highly specialized courses and emphasis on federal and public law.

> The faculty were disdainful of students in the bottom half of the class and deliberately aimed their teaching at the top ten percent. This at-titude was picked up by students, who were embarrassed or guilty if they were not in the upper half of the class. This, of course, increased the tension and competitiveness among students enormously. Another

---

sity School of Law, 34 WASHBURN L.J. 215, 216 (1995). This article was part of a seventeen-page tribute to Professor McDowell.

759. *Id.* at 215.

760. James M. Concannon, *A Fond Farewell*, 34 WASHBURN L. J. 218 (1995).

761. Banks McDowell, *A Visitor's View of Washburn Law School*, 22 THE CIRCUIT RIDER 5 (Spring 1983).

70. Banks McDowell, Professor 1982–2004

consequence of such an elite model was great pressure on the faculty to try to build national reputations as scholars, so that they had little time to spend with students outside of class and particularly resented demands on them made by weaker students.

By contrast, McDowell saw Washburn's model in the early 1980s as training general practitioners in smaller Kansas communities, with the consequence that the curriculum had a high percentage of required courses that emphasized "breadth of coverage, rather than depth of any particular problem, and a rather strong emphasis on teaching Kansas law." The strong populist or egalitarian attitude required of those who will represent all segments of a community

is reflected in the school itself where students are cooperative rather than competitive and the faculty place as much or more emphasis on helping the weakest student in the class as the strongest. The faculty here regard their primary obligation to be good teachers. Other obligations, such as scholarly writing, community service, or professional consultations, while recognized as important, are given a lesser priority than teaching.

While he acknowledged that models are a necessary way "of organizing what a school is doing," in McDowell's view the models didn't fit very well because diverse student bodies in fact will engage in many different kinds of practice and scatter geographically. "Less than ten percent of B.U.'s graduates went into the kinds of elite practice they were being trained for. And not more than twenty percent of Washburn's graduates have the kind of practice the model here seems to contemplate." A problem with Washburn's model, in McDowell's view, was that it required breadth of coverage to expose students to the variety of substantive areas of law a generalist encounters, at the sacrifice of "an in-depth, thorough, sophisticated study of a fairly narrow area, the sort of complete examination a first rate specialist must make." Still, he concluded, "The egalitarian and people-service orientation of the Washburn model seems to me much preferable as values for professional people over the elitist notions inculcated at Boston University." Further, he saw Washburn as

> a school in transition and the model is gradually being altered. The good features of a cooperative, egalitarian, populist professional will unquestionably be retained. But there is being added an element of more sophisticated and specialized training.…If I had to choose between the two models of legal education, the one I taught under for a number of years at Boston University and the one being refined at Washburn, the one used here strikes me as a substantially better starting point. Washburn is a good law school and on the move towards getting better.

That, he explained, is why he accepted the faculty's offer to make his stay at Washburn permanent.

CHANGING DEMOGRAPHICS

Washburn no longer was a school overwhelmingly populated by Kansans. Nearly 22% of entering students in 1978 (47 of 218) claimed out-of-state residence and one-third received their undergraduate degrees from schools outside Kansas, including universities in China and Ghana. The percentage of women reached

22% and minority enrollment was up to 5%. In 1981, 30% of the fall entering class were women and women were 29% of the entire student body. The next year, women were 35% of the entering class. The percentage of women in the entering class remained relatively constant at approximately 33% for the next few years. The 1986 Self-Study determined that the acceptance rate for women applicants was higher than for men, 74% compared to 63%, and that the yield of acceptances of offers of admission, 42%, was the same for both groups. However, women comprised only 29% of the applicant pool.

The diversity of the faculty grew dramatically too. By 1985–86, there were four minority and four women full-time teachers, together 31% of the total, one of the highest percentages in the nation.

AGGRESSIVELY SEEKING STUDENTS

During the years of essentially open enrollment through the early 1960s, surprisingly few resources were devoted to student recruitment. A "field of dreams" philosophy was in place—open the doors and they will come. Perhaps not surprisingly, that philosophy largely continued as applications began to far exceed the seats available. The Assistant Dean, as Chair of the Admissions Committee, oversaw activities of the admissions office but the office was staffed only by a clerical employee.

Dean Monk knew immediately, as the former Assistant Dean, that the traditional recruitment philosophy had to change. Substantial declines in applications to law schools were forecast to begin nationally within the next five years and would be a threat to the quality of the applicant pool.[762] Improved student recruitment might avoid the undesirable choice between lowering admission standards and reducing enrollment solely to maintain, rather than improve, quality. The growing tuition gap between Washburn and the schools with which it competed meant "many applicants whose first choice is Washburn are going to other schools because they cannot afford Washburn."[763] Increasing scholarship dollars was an essential solution but would take time. An active student recruitment program might help more immediately. Monk appointed

---

762. Carl C. Monk, *The Dean's Report to the Bar*, 19 WASHBURN L.J. 474, 480 (1979).

763. Carl C. Monk, *The Dean's Report to the Bar*, 20 WASHBURN L.J. 440, 448 (1980).

Professor Rich to chair a Student Recruitment Committee and obtained approval for a $5,000 recruitment budget for 1980–81.

One committee recommendation was to reinstate the option to start law school in the spring semester. The rationale was that increasing numbers of college students were graduating in December and no more than a dozen law schools nationally, and very few in the Midwest, permitted them to start in January. Thus, Washburn could recruit well-qualified students from throughout the country who wanted to start law school immediately and who, if forced to wait until the following fall, would have more options closer to their homes and might not consider Washburn. The initial January class in 1981 targeted fifteen students. The target for the fall class, starting in 1980, was reduced by thirty students, from 220 to 190, to make fall classes more selective too. However, the yield on admission offers increased in the fall of 1980, producing 199 new students, so the goal of reducing enrollment to 205 students annually was not reached until the following year.

The entering credentials of the initial January classes were somewhat higher than for fall classes, as predicted, but there were some surprises. There were fewer December graduates than expected but more older students who decided to switch careers at times during the year that did not match the fall admission cycle. For example, five of the sixteen students entering in January 1982 had graduate degrees, including one Ph.D. Also, while there were applicants from throughout the country, as expected, the January classes frequently had higher percentages of Kansas residents than expected, because the yield on offers of admission to well-credentialed Kansans was much higher than the yield for similar students for the fall class. However, seven of the sixteen January students in 1983 were graduates of out-of-state schools. The target of fifteen students was raised to twenty-five in 1985 to maximize the positive impact of the class on student credentials.

In 1981, Monk finally persuaded the University to budget resources to hire a full-time professional, Dottie Harder, as Director of Admissions. College pre-law advisors were invited to attend conferences at the Law School every other year and the Law School paid for travel expenses. There was outreach too, as Harder visited campuses throughout the region and gained a reputation for the personal attention she gave applicants. Ed Kainen's '88 experience was typical. He and his best friend, Nick Cox '88, were scheduled to graduate in December from a Florida college. They planned to attend the same law school, but because they wanted to start immediately, their choices were limited. They both applied to Washburn but decided to attend a law school in Texas. They planned a trip to Texas to make arrangements and to rent an apartment. They called to make appointments with the appropriate people at the school.

> When we arrived at the law school, we were told the person with whom we had the appointment was "not there and wouldn't be back for at least a week," "there was no one else who could show us around," and "could we please come back next week."…
>
> As we sat in the car and mulled over our situation, we decided that since we had already driven over 1,000 miles, driving another 800 or so to Topeka wouldn't be a big deal. However, unlike our trip to Texas, no one in Topeka knew we were coming, we had no appointment, nor had we made any advance arrangements.
>
> We arrived around noon on a cold November day.…[W]e were at the back of the car putting on our jackets…when a friendly woman walked by us and smiled. In an attempt to be friendly, I made the offhand remark, "this sure is a lot colder than we're used to in Florida." The nice woman looked at us without missing a beat and matter-of-factly said "you must be Ed Kainen and you must be Nick Cox." We were both dumbfounded as neither of us had ever been to Kansas before and no one knew we were coming. She introduced herself as Dottie Harder, the Admissions Dean, and continued by telling us that there had only been two applicants from Florida that year and we must be those applicants. Before we had a chance to relate our unfriendly reception in Texas or how we ended up in Topeka, she suggested that we meet her in an hour so she could spend the remainder of the afternoon showing us the school and answering our questions. That's exactly what happened.
>
> That afternoon we had Dottie's undivided attention. To us, it appeared that her only goal was making sure we walked away with a positive impression of Washburn. We did. Needless to say, we decided to forfeit our deposits and reservations in Texas and attend law school at Washburn.[764]

---

764. Email from Ed Kainen to James Concannon (Oct. 25, 2007).

A special priority for Dean Monk and faculty members who came of age during the civil rights movement was increasing minority enrollment. It was important to the WSBA as well and it sent a representative in the fall of 1978 to a minority recruitment seminar in Texas.[765] Also that fall, Hispanic students organized a Washburn chapter of La Raza Legal Alliance and minority recruitment became one of its priorities. The group sent students to recruit at Kansas schools and the next fall sponsored a two-day "Minorities and the Law Seminar" for prospective students.[766] The school's commitment to affirmative action was touted in a news release distributed to Hispanic publications, and then in a videotape.

There were many obstacles to minority recruitment. Historically, the legal profession and many law schools nationally had not welcomed minority students. Many qualified minorities who would have been excellent attorneys did not consider a career in law. Effectively changing that perception would require contact with minority students early in their college years, or even in high school, and this was not something a single law school could do effectively. While high tuition rates were an obstacle for many applicants, they more frequently burdened minority applicants. As late as 1984, Washburn's scholarship budget for all entering students was only $64,100. However, there were steps an individual school could take. Washburn was more willing to consider factors beyond numeric credentials in evaluating applicants and to accept greater risk in admissions, when there were reasons to believe numeric credentials did not fully reflect potential to succeed, to achieve the critical mass of minority students that would encourage more minority applicants. In addition, a school could provide as much support as possible to students who did enroll. In the spring of 1984, a tutoring program was started for all law students who had GPAs below 2.0 and new Associate Dean Sheila Reynolds expanded the program in the fall of 1985 to all entering students whose LSAT and GPA placed them at higher risk of not succeeding.

The Council on Legal Education Opportunity (CLEO), funded by an annual congressional appropriation, helped both with screening and finances. Each year it conducted regional six-week summer workshops for minority applicants in which they took mini-courses in two first-year substantive classes, including

---

765. *W.S.B.A. Completes Busy Fall*, 18 THE CIRCUIT RIDER 10 (Winter 1979).
766. *Seminar designed for future law students*, WASHBURN REV., Dec. 5, 1979.

mini-exams, and a condensed course in legal writing. The courses were taught by faculty members from various schools who prepared individual evaluations of the students which were sent to all law schools to which they had applied, for use in making the admission decision. CLEO students who were admitted received financial assistance from CLEO to defray part of their expenses for all three years. Washburn became a participant in CLEO, providing funding either for a Washburn student to be a teaching assistant in the program or for a faculty member to be one of the instructors. The school's first black faculty member, Ron Griffin, became active in CLEO. When a Washburn faculty member did not teach in the program, one ordinarily went for at least a day to recruit students. Of course, the school hosting the program, if it did well, had an advantage in student recruitment. Ordinarily, host schools that did well also were approved as host for a second year. KU hosted three consecutive programs from 1979 through 1981 and saw its minority enrollment increase significantly. Washburn finally was selected, over three other applicants, to host the Midwest regional program in 1982. Professors Rich and Griffin administered the program and Professor Easley taught one of the classes. In addition to attending classes, the thirty-two student participants met with Governor John Carlin, Kansas Supreme Court Justice Harold Herd '42, and Charles Scott Sr. '48, local counsel in *Brown v. Board of Education*. Washburn was the host site again in 1983, selected over two other applicants.

Progress was slow but the school's affirmative action efforts paid off. Minority enrollment in the first-year class was still just 5.6% in 1983 but grew to 12.9% in 1985 and 15.9% in 1986 before reaching 18.4% in 1988. Among fifteen schools in the six states surrounding and including Kansas, Washburn had the fifth highest minority enrollment by 1984–85, the third highest in 1985–86, the second highest in 1986–87, and the highest in 1987–88 and 1988–89.

THE TWO LAW SCHOOL ISSUE REINCARNATED

Once Washburn had a new building in 1969 after the tornado, the two law school issue receded from the public spotlight. However, it did not go away. It surfaced twice during Ray Spring's deanship. When KU announced plans to ask the 1974 legislature for planning money for a new law building, the *Topeka State Journal* opined that a merger of the two law schools on the Washburn campus should be considered "before locking in the two-school system even more firmly with construction of another building at Lawrence."[767] No one was interested in the suggestion. The issue resurfaced in a different form in 1976 when the Legislature's Educational Planning Commission, the so-called 1202 Commission, conducted an interim study of whether Washburn University should be made part of the Kansas Regents system. Max Bickford, Executive Director of the Kansas Board of Regents, thought the timing was poor, since college enrollments were projected to decline by one-third in the 1980s. More-over, he thought Washburn Law School "was likely to be the biggest obstacle" to state affiliation. "Those who are already against Washburn's becoming a state school will ask 'Why should the state have two law schools thirty miles apart?'"[768] KU's new law building also complicated the matter. President Hen-derson and the Washburn Regents initially were undecided whether to support or oppose state affiliation, balancing potential long-range improvements in funding against an undesirable loss of autonomy. Ultimately, they opposed the plan and the 1202 Commission recommended against state affiliation.

The two law school "problem" resurfaced whenever the issue of state affiliation resurfaced, and the University exhibited schizophrenia regarding state affilia-tion. Consecutive years of deficit budgets led Washburn's Board of Regents in the spring of 1981, during the search for a successor to President Henderson, to endorse state affiliation as a way to solve the University's financial difficulties and ease what some perceived to be the excessive property tax burden borne by Topekans. The 1981 Interim Legislative Budget Committee thus was charged with studying a bill bringing Washburn into the state system. The Shawnee County legislative delegation endorsed the idea, but Governor John Carlin expressed opposition.[769] When the bill was introduced, Monk immediately began to compile data demonstrating the Law School's contributions to legal education and to the State, such as that more judges in Kansas graduated from Washburn than from any other law school and that fifty-seven of 105 County Attorneys were from Washburn. Other data showed that clinic students devoted over 4,000 hours annually to representing clients entitled to court-appointed counsel, saving the county and state over $100,000 annually. Monk documented the faculty's contribution to state government, particularly volunteer hours for continuing

767. *Editorial, Do we need two law schools?* TOPEKA ST. J., Oct. 15, 1973.

768. *Bickford says WU state question a political one*, WASHBURN REV., Sept. 22, 1976, at 2.

769. *State takeover of WU endorsed*, TOPEKA CAP.-J., Aug. 13, 1981, at 1.

judicial education that many other states had to pay for.[770] He acknowledged in his annual report that alumni were not unanimous on the issue but pointed out that only one state with a population larger than Kansas had only one law school and that state, South Carolina, had its law school in the state capital. He expressed confidence Washburn would continue to make significant contributions "whether as part of the state system or as a strong independent law school."[771]

By the fall of 1981, concerns arose that the University might be turned into a two-year community college or merged into the University of Kansas. Washburn had a new president and there were five new members of the Board of Regents, including three lawyers, Louis Eisenbarth '54, Carol Duffy McDowell '75 and Jim Slattery '75. McDowell said she no longer saw the question as being who would finance the University. "'The feedback I get is that if Washburn goes state it would not continue to be a four year college, have a law school or remain a separate entity,' McDowell said. 'The legislature is not so much concerned with the continuation of a four year quality liberal arts college.'"[772] Slattery wanted to find some way to stop tuition increases but acknowledged "the political reality of maintaining two law schools within 30 miles of each other raises a real question about the induction of Washburn into the state system while maintaining the law school."[773] To the surprise of local legislators,[774] President John Green concluded that matters were moving too fast. "My review convinced me that Washburn was being treated unfairly. There was bad press all over the state, with statements such as 'we don't want Washburn.' Misinformation about Washburn in the press and in the legislative committee hearings was gross."[775] He rejected the committee's comparison of Washburn with Emporia State, Pittsburg State, and Fort Hays State because Washburn's mission and

770. *From the Dean's Desk*, 21 THE CIRCUIT RIDER 2 (Spring 1982).

771. Carl C. Monk, *The Dean's Report to the Bar*, 20 WASHBURN L.J. 697, 700 (1981).

772. *New board members enthused about Washburn*, WASHBURN REV., Sept. 2, 1981, at 8, 9.

773. *Id.*

774. *WU change surprises Bunten*, WASHBURN REV., Sept. 30, 1981 (quoting Representative Bill Bunten's comment, "I am confused on how things can change so much in six months." He declared the state affiliation issue surely would not be subject to legislative consideration for at least two years.).

775. *Dr. Green Cites Progress For Law School*, 21 THE CIRCUIT RIDER 13 (Spring 1982).

programs were different. He concluded the economic benefit of Washburn to Topeka more than justified its local tax levy and that tuition, though high, was still the best investment a student could make.[776] Green developed "a strong anti-state affiliation position."[777] He asked the Interim Committee to delay its study until he and his staff could complete a five-year plan for the University and consider alternate funding options. "'There are not enough facts on the table.' Green said, 'Is it in the best interest of this institution to go state?...We're looking at the needs of Washburn University and how to finance them.'"[778]

Remarkably in this environment, Washburn proposed that the 1982 Legislature grant state aid at a higher rate than for undergraduates for each credit hour taught to Kansas residents in the Law School, recognizing the significantly higher cost of graduate, professional education. However, a newspaper story in the middle of the session erroneously reported that the University supported elimination altogether of credit hour aid for law hours, undercutting the more than seventy letters of support for the differential alums had sent to legislators.[779] The University clarified its position but the $3 per credit hour differential that ultimately passed was far less than the University sought initially. By 1984, the differential was only $1.

Following the close of the 1983 legislative session, Speaker of the House Mike Hayden suggested the state might decide to eliminate duplicate programs at various state colleges to achieve cuts in funding for higher education. He told a group of law students at KU that "the legislature might decide that it didn't want to spend money on two law schools that are so close together."[780] Early in 1984, the Kansas Board of Regents, after several months of study by a subcommittee, recommended reductions in the target sizes of entering classes in the state's medical school from 200 to 175 and in the state's veterinary medical school from 105 to 100, but recommended the target size of the KU law school class remain at 200. The Regents' report prompted a study by the Legislature's 1984 Interim Budget Committee of the adequacy of the state's supply of physi-

---

776. *Id.*

777. *Id.* at 14.

778. *Green gains support for statehood delay*, WASHBURN REV., Sept. 30, 1981.

779. Memorandum from Carl C. Monk to Dr. John Green, Mar. 31, 1982 (on file in Mabee Library), referring to an article in that morning's local paper.

780. David C. Topliker, *The Grass Roots Report*, INDEPENDENCE NEWS, June 25, 1983.

cians, veterinarians, and lawyers, and whether admissions policies of the state's professional schools should be adjusted. The study was expanded to include consideration of policies at Washburn and whether "there is a continued need for two schools of law in Kansas."

The Interim Committee scheduled a public hearing for August 24. Monk and KU's Dean Mike Davis consulted about the most effective way to present the law schools' case. They drew on the experience of the two Arkansas law schools in responding to a similar legislative study several years earlier, in which a strong position taken by the state bar association was thought to have been decisive. Kansas Bar Association President Darrell Kellogg asked the KBA's Legal Education and Admissions Committee, chaired by Elwin Cabbage '56, to recommend to the KBA Council what the bar's position should be. The Committee held a special meeting on July 27. Both schools were represented on the Committee, with Associate Dean Bill Rich substituting for Dean Monk. There was consensus that Kansas was well served by two law schools operating concurrently, that diversities in curriculum and in the expertise of faculty not only allowed students to select the school that best met their needs but also enhanced continuing legal education, and that the schools cooperated closely while maintaining their separate identities.[781] There also was consensus there was no need to adjust enrollment at the two schools legislatively, despite the often-voiced complaint that there were too many lawyers. The Committee noted the burgeoning volume and complexity of new laws and regulations. It unanimously concluded the number of lawyers in Kansas "is not such as to negatively affect the quality or cost of legal services." It further recommended that the two schools "should be allowed the freedom to exercise their academic integrity in determining enrollments" in light of market forces.[782]

In fact, Washburn already had reduced the target size of its entering class from 220 to 200, responding to the decline nationally in applications which was expected to continue, and KU was planning a fall class of 175, twenty-five below its former target, for the same reason. The two schools submitted data to the Legislature's Interim Committee showing their placement rates were higher than the national average and that attrition rates were only 15% between enrollment and graduation. At the public hearing on August 24, the Deans

---

781. Minutes, Kansas Bar Association, Legal Education and Admissions Committee, July 27, 1984.

782. *Id.*

testified that nationally as many as 40% of graduates do not enter private practice and that reductions in the number of law students would not necessarily
reduce the number of practicing lawyers. Dean Davis attributed the increase
in the number of lawyers to a public demand for more legal expertise. Regent
John Montgomery noted that because law schools have large section classes,
small reductions in class size result in limited monetary savings. He also noted
that because average LSAT scores at KU were higher than at Washburn, reducing class sizes at KU would not result in fewer law school graduates unless
Washburn maintained or reduced the size of its entering class. Dean Monk
noted that Washburn considered various non-quantifiable factors in making admission decisions and that if LSAT scores were the primary criterion,
Washburn's average would be higher. He shared the data first compiled three
years earlier showing the variety of services Washburn Law School provided
to the community and state. He highlighted the school's unique programs,
including the Rural Law Center and the Law Clinic with its new mediation
component.[783] Monk noted that the State spent only $780 per Kansas resident
law student at Washburn, less than 20% of the direct cost of educating the
student. Under the University's full-cost accounting formula, the State paid
only 13.1% of the Law School's operating expenses. After the Deans spoke,
Elwin Cabbage presented the views of the KBA.

The presentations were effective. The Interim Committee's conclusions
and recommendations, issued November 29, contained only two paragraphs
about the law schools. The Committee concluded "that the two law schools are
cooperatively monitoring the quality of their applicant pools as they establish
enrollment levels" and proposed no changes in their enrollment policies. The
Report even "commends the schools as to their cooperation in such matters."
Further, in light of the testimony that not all graduates enter the practice of law,
"the Committee concludes that two law schools may not necessarily constitute
an unnecessary duplication; and, therefore, it does not propose elimination
of one of the two schools."[784]

There were other flirtations with state affiliation during Dean Monk's tenure.
Each time, someone publicly warned that the Law School's fate was uncertain.

783. Extensive excerpts from Dean Monk's testimony are reprinted in Carl C.
Monk, *From the Dean's Desk*, 23 THE CIRCUIT RIDER 2 (Summer 1984).

784. *Proposal No. 32—Supply of Physicians, Veterinarians, and Lawyers,* INTERIM
STUDIES OF THE KANSAS LEGISLATURE 467, 475 (1984).

For example, in response to a request by Washburn's Board of Regents that the legislature study long-range funding of the University, another interim study was authorized following the 1985 session, not only to review options for state aid but also to study the feasibility of state affiliation. Speaker Hayden endorsed a plan for Washburn's entry into the state system as of July 1987. Over time the plan would equalize tuition with other Regent schools and replace the local property tax with a county-wide sales tax, but it would also cap Washburn's enrollment at present levels. On September 11, 1985, Washburn's Regents endorsed state affiliation but with the proviso that Washburn must enter the state system with all of its programs, including the Law School, intact.[785] Senator Joseph Harder, chair of the 1985 Interim Study Committee, objected to that proviso, saying "I couldn't guarantee the law school would remain."[786]

The 1989 session, the year after Monk's departure as Dean, was thought to be the optimal year for a state affiliation proposal. The proposal was serious enough that Wayne Stratton '58, John Hayes '46, Dick Hite '53 and I drafted a letter explaining the issues which the Law School Association Board of Governors sent to all alums. The letter urged them to contact their legislators, regardless of their views about state affiliation generally, to express support for adequate funding for the University and of the Law School as a statewide resource. In posturing prior to the session, the Kansas Board of Regents refused to endorse state affiliation, citing four conditions that would need to be met, among them "removal of any conditions attached to Washburn's affiliation that would impinge upon the authority of the state regents to organize, manage and control the school."[787] However, when Mike Hayden, now Governor, included state affiliation in his Margin of Excellence plan to increase funding for Regents schools, the Kansas Board of Regents endorsed it because it was part of the package.[788] Stan Koplick, Executive Director of the state board, emphasized that the bill satisfied the Board's criteria because "there were no strings attached to bringing Washburn under its jurisdiction, such as a requirement that the

---

785. The Regents reaffirmed that Washburn must be "a free-standing university, with the schools and programs now established intact, including the school of law" in a resolution dated March 12, 1986.

786. *House Speaker makes proposal*, WASHBURN REV., Oct. 25, 1985.

787. *Regents fail to back WU admission*, TOPEKA CAP.-J., Dec. 16, 1988.

788. *Regents back Hayden plan for Washburn*, TOPEKA CAP.-J., Feb. 18, 1989.

Washburn University School of Law remain in existence."[789] However, ten days before the bill was introduced, when asked by Sen. Richard Rock '50 during a hearing before the Senate Ways and Means Committee whether the state board had considered whether Washburn's law school "would be redundant," Koplick responded like a politician: "Even if you wanted to do something about the Washburn law school you probably couldn't do it. I really don't know anyone who has a serious proposal to abolish the Washburn law school, least of which is the Kansas Board of Regents."[790]

Various factors combined to doom each state affiliation proposal and most had nothing directly to do with the Law School: opposition from State Regents schools that feared dilution of state funding for higher education when the pie of state dollars was sliced an extra time; opposition from community colleges, whose increases in state funding often were used to determine increases for Washburn, which feared loss of an ally and the votes of the Shawnee County delegation for future budget increases for them; opposition from city officials who opposed retention of any local tax to support the University because most other cities with Regents schools were not burdened with local taxes; tight budget times for the state that made the cost projection for state affiliation of $6 to $8 million in the first year financially unfeasible; and ambivalence at Washburn when particular proposals would extract too great a loss of the University's identity. Through it all, the two law schools in the 1980s were on the same page on the issue.

Indeed, interaction between the two schools increased. In 1982, the schools began jointly offering a bar review course for Kansas, with roughly the same number of lecturers from each school, at a price substantially below the price of other courses nationally. When the course finally was discontinued in 2004, Kansas was the last state with a free-standing comprehensive bar review, not affiliated with national provider Bar-Bri. In early 1985, Flip Kissam from KU was invited to give a professional development program on his paper "The Decline of Law School Professionalism." In September that year, the Washburn faculty hosted the KU faculty for a lamb roast at Clinton Lake. It was with some trepidation that Bill Rich was designated chief cook, since his previous service in that capacity for a faculty pig roast resulted in

---

789. *Id.*

790. *Legislator questions status of law school*, LAWRENCE J.-WORLD, Jan. 31, 1989.

very rare pork. He had attempted to cook the pig in a pit dug in the ground but agreed to roast the KU lamb above ground.

REDUCING ENROLLMENT ANYWAY

While Washburn Law School opposed legislation forcing it to reduce enrollment, Dean Monk and the faculty actually wanted to do so voluntarily. Applications to law school nationally declined significantly for the entering classes of 1983 and 1984 and were projected to continue to decline for three or four more years.[791] While applications had held steady at Washburn in 1983 and 1984, it became clear early in the 1985 admissions cycle that Washburn would catch up with the national three-year decline in 1985, with a decline in applications of as much as 25%. More broadly, a smaller student body would benefit the academic environment in many ways: a better student-faculty ratio, smaller sections for large classes, and more opportunities for seminars. More selective admissions would help to maintain credentials in the short term and would produce in the long term a student body with higher credentials. The improvements in quality of the academic program also would make the school more competitive for top applicants. Dean Monk presented, in concept form, the idea of reducing enrollment at the Washburn Board of Regents retreat on December 1, 1984.[792] As Monk later put it, if "we view the current decline in applicants as an opportunity rather than a catastrophe, and engage in effective long-range planning we can significantly improve what is already a growing positive reputation."[793] In a memo to Dean Monk later that month, Associate Dean Rich projected the financial implications of reducing the size of the entering class from the current 200 students annually to 125 annually over three years. The plan would reduce the school's total enrollment to 340

---

791. Memorandum from Carl C. Monk to President John L. Green, Jr., Academic Affairs Committee, Washburn University Board of Regents (Apr. 5, 1985) (on file in Washburn Law Library).

792. Remarks of Dean Carl C. Monk Prepared for Board of Regents Retreat, Dec. 1, 1984. Monk bluntly reminded Regents that despite dramatic progress in recent years, there was a "simple truth: Washburn University seriously neglected its law school for a period of years; that serious neglect resulted in Washburn reaching near bottom levels of funding...by the early 1970's. We are still paying for that neglect..."

793. Memorandum, *supra* note 791.

by 1989–90. The total credit hours taught would fall from the current 16,100 annually to approximately 10,200. The obstacle, of course, was that there was no apparent way to replace the tuition revenue and state aid that would be lost because of the reduction in credit hours. The lost revenue could not be offset by budget cuts because the budget only barely met basic needs, if that, and tuition would have to nearly double in just five years, from $93 per credit hour to $177 per credit hour for Kansas residents, just to maintain the current operating budget without any increases. Such an increase in tuition would make Washburn's already higher tuition even less competitive with KU and other public schools.

As recently as 1982–83, the Law School was the only unit on campus to generate a profit under the University's full-cost accounting formula.[794] While the Law School's budget by 1984–85 marginally exceeded the tuition and state aid it generated, its budget allocation was substantially below the proportion of the University's credit hours taught at the Law School. Monk persuaded the central administration that a smaller entering class was desirable and that it should support a more modest reduction than Rich outlined, to 150 new students annually. "For the last ten to fifteen years the law school has generated significant profits for the University. It is clearly justifiable for the University to demonstrate its commitment to maintaining a quality law school by a significant…increase in its subsidy to the law school."[795] To improve the proposal's chances for approval, Monk suggested that improved demographics in the applicant pool by the mid-1990s might permit the increased subsidy to be temporary, for ten or twelve years.

Still, there was the problem of state aid that would be lost if credit hours declined. Before the 1985 session, Monk and David Monical, Washburn's Vice President for Planning and its representative before the Legislature, devised an ingenious approach to increase the differential, by tying it to reductions in enrollment, thus quelling fears the State would be "creating an 'open-ended' new fiscal note for Washburn."[796] Washburn proposed to reduce the entering class to 150 to 160 students, in phases over three years, in exchange for the Legislature granting state aid for resident hours in law at one and one-half

794. *Id.*

795. *Id.*

796. Carl C. Monk, *From the Dean's Desk*, 23 THE CIRCUIT RIDER 2, 16 (Fall 1984).

times the rate for undergraduate credit hours. The beauty of the proposal was that, while it would cost the state more money during the phase-in period, when the reduction was fully implemented the State would be spending no more dollars for hours taught at Washburn Law School than the State was spending in 1984–85. Plus, the timing was right politically. No one could have hoped for a more favorable report than the one issued by the 1984 Interim Budget Committee, and it undercut any argument that the State presently was spending too much for Washburn Law School. In addition, House Speaker Hayden already was preparing his candidacy for Governor in 1986. While he had been openly critical of judges and was viewed as hostile to the bar, Washburn's plan appealed to him. Through it, he could help reduce the number of lawyers, without extra cost, and curry some favor with voters in Topeka. Dean Monk met with Hayden and ultimately won his support. The bill passed and Governor Carlin signed it. When Washburn announced it was reducing law enrollment, it attributed the decision to the school's desire to enhance the quality of instruction and also to the publicly palatable goal to "deal with any oversupply of lawyers that may exist."[797]

When the bill enlarging the law school differential passed late in the 1985 session, the January class already had enrolled and many offers of admission to the fall 1985 class already had been extended. Nevertheless, the fall class in 1985 fell to 140, from 181 in the fall of 1984. Still, the Senate passed a bill during the 1986 session that would have terminated the law school differential as of 1988. It was described as "a less-than-subtle message…that the school had better cut down the size of its law school."[798] Its real purpose may have been, like sunset legislation today, to force the Legislature to monitor law school enrollment and re-authorize the differential only if the school adhered to the agreed enrollment reduction. Still, Dean Monk and President Green sent a joint letter, dated March 17, asking law alums to write to their Representatives in the House and urge that the bill be killed. It was. The target of 150 entering students was reached in 1986–87, with 125 students starting in the fall.

The enrollment reduction was a bold move. No other American law school made a voluntarily reduction of this magnitude. Total enrollment of 432 in 1987

---

797. *Washburn School of Law plans to reduce enrollment*, TOPEKA CAP.-J., Apr. 30, 1985.

798. *Bill threatens law school aid*, TOPEKA CAP.-J., Apr. 8, 1986; *Bill approved reducing aid to law school*, TOPEKA CAP.-J., Apr. 10, 1986.

was the school's smallest since 1971. When reductions were fully phased in after four years, total enrollment declined by more than 25%, from 571 to 421. The student-faculty ratio improved dramatically and quickly, since the University administration only required the Law School to commit to reduce the faculty by two positions, one through anticipated attrition, to help finance the reductions. Despite the reductions, the credentials of the 1985 and 1986 classes actually declined slightly, since applications declined at Washburn and most other schools nationwide. However, the reductions in enrollment meant Washburn's credentials improved vis-a-vis other schools that did not reduce enrollment.

ACTIVISTS

Washburn faculty members for years had been active in public affairs and had assisted pro bono litigation. That activism increased during the Monk years. Remarkably, new members of the Washburn faculty had the opportunity to participate in *Brown v. Board of Education*. In 1979, local lawyers claimed that, due to racial imbalance in the schools, the school district still was not in compliance with the Supreme Court's mandate in the case. The District Court had never entered an order terminating the original case. Professors Bill Rich, Ron Griffin, Myrl Duncan, and Allen Easley volunteered to be part of the litigation team[799] and helped to develop the strategy that Linda Brown Montgomery, whose father Oliver Brown had been the lead plaintiff in the original litigation on her behalf, would seek to intervene in the action to assert the claim as a parent on behalf of her own child, who was affected because of the district's failure to desegregate the schools fully. No reported case had ever permitted intervention in a case so long after judgment, but Professor Easley, who was in his first semester at Washburn and was the Civil Procedure teacher in the group, helped prepare the brief that led the court to permit intervention to reopen the case.

Bill Rich may hold the Washburn record for pro bono service. In 1978, eight prisoners at the Lansing Correctional Facility filed an action *pro se* claiming that overcrowding at the prison violated their civil rights. United States District Judge Richard Rogers asked Rich personally to represent the plaintiffs. Rich declined to do that but agreed to accept the appointment as a Washburn Law Clinic case,

---

799. *Local racial balance issue to be re-judged*, WASHBURN REV., Dec. 12, 1979.

71. Bill Rich, Professor 1977–present, Acting
Dean 2006–2007, Associate Dean 1981–1985

with assistance from Kansas Legal Services for Prisoners, which kept an office in
the Clinic at that time. Rich was in the midst of transition from clinic supervision to classroom teaching but agreed to be the lead lawyer from the Clinic for
the case. Students participated actively. In 1980, the parties entered a consent
decree, agreeing to plans for corrective actions, renovations at the prison, and
improved safety and health measures. Rich, through the Law Clinic, monitored
compliance with the consent decree. Happily, it was after Professor Mike Barbara
concluded his term on leave as Secretary of Corrections that Rich concluded
compliance was lacking. In 1985, Rich persuaded the United States Department
of Justice to investigate. It issued a report finding unconstitutional overcrowding,
life-threatening safety risks, medical care that was indifferent to serious needs
of prisoners, and grossly inadequate medical care.[800] On the basis of that report,
Rich sought to modify the consent decree and to have it enforced.

---

800. *WU clinic to file plea for prisoners*, TOPEKA CAP.-J., Jan. 1, 1986.

The Department of Corrections was not in a position this time to settle. Helping Rich litigate such a major case was a rare opportunity for various Clinic students for several years. They participated in interviews, preparation of both lay and expert witnesses for depositions, research, and drafting. They were involved at each stage. However, litigating such a case was expensive and there was no line item in the school's budget to cover the expenses. Fortunately, Rich obtained funding from the Edna McConnell Clark Foundation in New York which gave the Clinic the resources to litigate the case vigorously and, ultimately, successfully. The Clinic's position would require substantial state appropriations for the Department of Corrections. Not surprisingly, some legislators and influential public figures criticized what they viewed as extravagant demands by the Clinic and questioned why it, as a publicly-funded program, should be permitted to sue to force expenditure of other public funds. The criticism became particularly ticklish when it was voiced in the context of the University's requests for increased state aid or its periodic proposals for state affiliation. Clinics at other schools have faced similar challenges when they have handled controversial cases and there always is the risk that a school's governing board will buckle under the pressure. While individual Washburn Regents and University administrators occasionally were squeamish, lawyer members of the board understood that once the Clinic accepted appointment by the District Court as counsel, it had the professional responsibility to pursue the action vigorously. They persuaded the board to be resolute in support of the Clinic's continued involvement in the case.

Ultimately, the case expanded to include conditions at other state prisons. Practitioners Dwight Corrin '80 and Roger Theis joined the Clinic as co-counsel in the expanded case. The District Court in 1991 made findings in favor of the prisoners and ordered appropriate remedies. While the Clinic had not sought attorney fees following the 1980 consent decree, Rich concluded that he would not be representing his clients appropriately if he did not seek a portion of allowable attorney fees this time, to make clear that there were financial consequences for the State when it failed to comply with court orders regarding prison conditions. The resulting award of fees and expenses was used to repay the funds advanced by the Clark Foundation and to create two funds, one to monitor compliance with the decree until the case was closed in 1998 and the other to underwrite litigation expenses in other Clinic cases that the Clinic's indigent clients were unable to reimburse.[801]

HIJINKS INSIDE AND OUTSIDE THE CLASSROOM

As he rushed to complete assigned material in the last class in Civil Procedure II of the spring 1981 semester, Dean Monk's lecture was interrupted by the sound of music and a young woman dancing down the aisle toward his podium. Students had chipped in a quarter or fifty cents each to have a "Belly Gram" delivered to him. As the dancer reached the podium, Monk told the class, "I don't know whether to laugh, cry or prepare a resume."[802] The latter option no doubt seemed optimal the next morning when Monk awoke to find his picture with the dancer filling four columns of the front page of the local paper, which speculated that students were trying to "jolly up the good dean" before their Saturday exam. "That was a sneaky trick to avoid 10 minutes of class," Monk observed when the dancer finally left the room. Later students achieved gender neutrality, presenting Linda Elrod with a birthday "male-o-gram," which included a carrot as the only prop.

Hijinks were not restricted to birthdays. Leap year became an excuse for students to celebrate All Cynic's Day on February 29, 1984. There was little doubt who they would choose as Washburn's Most Cynical Professor. They presented an aluminum foil halo to the winner, Greg Pease, in his 11:00 a.m. Property I class.

Sometimes faculty were responsible for the startling events in class. Clothing was a common prop. To emphasize in his class on Secured Transactions the extraordinary powers of the Trustee in Bankruptcy, Paul Rasor would rip off his shirt, like Clark Kent, to reveal "Super Trustee," who proceeded to void preferences and exercise the Trustee's other strong arm powers. David Ryan breezed into class wearing a biker's jacket embroidered with the phrase "Fuck the Draft" when he taught the landmark case determining the First Amendment protection afforded to such speech. Professor Elrod lacked a similar pedagogical purpose for the clown costume she wore to class each Halloween. There simply

---

801. The history of this litigation is described in detail in William R. Rich, Prison Conditions and Criminal Sentencing in Kansas: A Public Policy Dialogue, 11 KAN. J. L. & PUB. POL'Y 693 (2002).

802. *Washburn law lecture halted by belly dancer*, TOPEKA CAP.-J., Apr. 29, 1981.

72. Professor Paul Rasor becomes Super Trustee

was not enough time for her to change clothes before racing to be room mother for afternoon parties at the elementary schools her children attended.[803]

Over time, I became known for using hypotheticals involving sheep. The more mirth and raised eyebrows they provoked, the more inclined I became to use them. It may have started when I explained that while the Sixth Amendment gives criminal defendants a broad right to confront their accusers, it was not as broad as an Oklahoma prosecutor thought it was when he felt compelled in a trial for bestiality to bring the enraged ewe into the courtroom. Some student responses were predictable. Sheep routines became a standard part of the faculty roast and I did nothing to discourage them, usually drinking beer from a Woolite container. A fall 1983 Civil Procedure class was interrupted when I was arrested by former United States Marshal Bert Cantwell '83 for abandonment and non-support of a lamb offspring and was subjected to a

---

803. Linda Diane Henry Elrod, *Washburn Law School Celebrates a Century of Welcoming Women*, 42 WASHBURN L.J. 853, 887 (2004).

shotgun wedding with the lamb's mother, played by Candace McFadden '85. A full-blown reception with a wedding cake followed in the Robing Room.

Some student responses were wholly unpredictable. My practice is to arrive at my classroom five or more minutes before class starts. Upon arriving for my 8:00 a.m. Civil Procedure class one morning, I found a live lamb chained to the podium. It clearly was a stealth project since very few students were present yet and no one was hanging around to claim credit. As the clock reached the top of the hour I expected someone to come and take the lamb away, but no one did. Finally, I concluded I had to go ahead and start the class. The lamb, which had tolerated the noise and hubbub calmly up to that point, became unnerved by the silence and began bleating rhythmically. I looked at the lamb and said, "You didn't complain like that last night," and went on with the class. After fifteen minutes that seemed like thirty, workers from the University's physical plant came with bolt cutters for the chain and took the lamb away. Surprisingly, the perpetrators never came forward to claim the credit they deserved, although years later Jonathan Dalton admitted some involvement, an easy thing to do for someone who had transferred to a St. Louis law school.

Because I taught Evidence and Civil Procedure in the fall semester, I routinely had 220–230 papers to grade after the fall semester throughout the 1970s and early 1980s. Not infrequently, the spring semester was well underway before grades for the second class were posted. I was unusually late the year of the Iranian hostage crisis. Students kidnapped from my office one of the stuffed sheep that was part of a growing collection of gifts from students. Notices quickly were posted on the student bulletin board indicating the hostage would be released only upon timely posting of the grades. Soon, a Polaroid picture of my "frozen assets" was posted. The sheep was blindfolded and posed sitting in a plastic container filled with ice. Ultimately, I posted the grades on a yellow posting sheet, reminiscent of the yellow ribbons being used to support the real hostages, and the stuffed animal was released overnight at my office door.

Phi Delta Phi's annual roast of the faculty often drew on themes from popular culture. Skits patterned after "Saturday Night Live" were common and an LSN segment (Law School News) became a regular feature. Titles of the productions usually were provocative, even if the skits weren't always. In 1987, the title was "No Stone Unturned, No Nerve Too Raw." Students produced the "Roast Post" to promote the show and launch their initial salvos. There were some standard jokes, such as Professor Kuether's annual promotion from

"Captain Confusion" to "Major Confusion," or even to "General Confusion." Speculation that Dean Monk had imposed a limitation that no new faculty hires could be taller than he was led the 1980 Roast, which used a television show theme, to feature "Sixty Midgets," in which reporters visited a law school taught by pygmies. Professors were not above submitting good lines for the script through back channels. In the years before grading guidelines were adopted, Jim Wadley was notorious for giving high grades, mostly A's and B's. In one skit, Bruce Beye '82, playing Saturday Night Live character-law student Chico Escuela, used a line offered by Professor Concannon. Chico was asked who he was taking for Property. "Jim Walley," he replied. "Jim Walley been velly, velly good to me!" "Don't you mean Jim Wadley?" he was asked. "No. Jim Walley," Chico replied. "Ain't no D in Walley." The faculty also presented rebuttal at the end of each Roast, sometimes responding in song, as when Paul Rasor sang "You've Got To Flunk A Student Or Two," a parody on the song "Oliver," and when Ron Griffin responded to complaints about late grading of papers by singing, "Tomorrow. Tomorrow. We'll grade them tomorrow...." Sometimes a song produced a feel-good moment, as when Rasor played The Beatles' tune "Imagine" on his guitar and sang lyrics on the theme "Imagine there's no law school.... "

Faculty members often exploited their colleagues' quirks for amusement directly, rather than through back channels. Professor Duncan never has been shy about sharing his views and the hallway near his office often reverberates with his pointed comments on current events. After the first two weeks of the fall semester in 1980, when Duncan was in New York starting his S.J.D. program, his six colleagues on the third floor claimed in a letter to him that they were "suffering delirium tremens due to the near total silence on the floor." They even claimed to have "heard someone say 'due process' in a normal tone of voice." Fearing they would be "forced into unnatural productivity," they urged him, "as our Pied Piper to craziness to send us an audio cassette of the Best of Myrl Duncan—be sure to include the classic 'Bullshit' and the bellowing 'Goddammit.' Whenever it gets too quiet, one of us will sneak into the hallway, turn on a tape recorder and give us the fix we need."

The spirit of comradery between students and faculty that has long character- ized Washburn was particularly high when many faculty were not much older than their students. Faculty members competed in the student racquetball and golf tournaments and fielded a team to meet the challenge of a student all-star

73. Faculty dressed as characters from the Wizard of Oz

74. Faculty prepare for their rebuttal

75. Paul Rasor singing

team in slow-pitch softball. They even entered a team in the student basketball tournament, with the condition that they be allowed to use an alumni ringer or two, such as former NAIA All-American Doug Baker '75. In one game, Linda Elrod's nose got in the way of a ball dribbled by Mark Hutton '79 and by Monday morning her face was black and blue. Students who had not attended the game asked her what happened and her off-hand response, "Oh, Mark did it," set off a firestorm of rumors that she was the victim of spousal abuse by her then-husband Mark Elrod '72. The faculty soon realized its level of talent did not justify entering a team in the tournament but it continued to play an exhibition game against a student team. The faculty lobbied hard to make sure the student team did not have too many stars. In 1980, the faculty actually won the game 47–46, although students protested calls by the referee, Carl Monk, and that the faculty had twelve players on the court at the end of the game.[804]

Students entered teams in the summer slow-pitch softball leagues in Topeka for four summers beginning in 1980 and recruited Professor Concannon to be

804. *WSBA Sponsors Basketball Tournament*, 19 THE CIRCUIT RIDER 10 (Summer 1980).

76. Dean Monk pitches during a faculty-student softball game

manager. The first year, an adult theater at 21st and Gage, the Cedar Cinema, sponsored the team and offered the bonus of free admission for team members wearing their jerseys. The manager came up with the team's nickname, the Blues. The next year, the team switched both sponsors and vices when the College Hill bar Quincy Magoo's agreed to be sponsor and offered a free pitcher of beer for team members wearing jerseys. The team was more creative in finding sponsors than it was on the field, at least when the team tried to compete in Division 1 leagues. Each year the team was assigned to a lower division and in 1983 won the league in Division 5 A. The manager promptly retired, taking his cue from New York Yankees manager Billy Martin, who resigned after winning the World Series.

MOOT COURT AND TRIAL ADVOCACY

The Law Journal for many years held a spring banquet to celebrate student achievements and, after 1977, to enjoy after-dinner remarks by the Foulston Siefkin Lecturer. In 1978, the Moot Court Council decided it should have a spring celebration too. The first one was little more than a party at a student's apartment. By the second year, there was a banquet at the Student Union with a speaker, Hon. James K. Logan of the United States Court of Appeals for the Tenth Circuit. The next year's banquet was at the Ramada Inn and Professor James McElhaney from Case Western Reserve Law School, a nationally acclaimed lecturer on trial advocacy, was featured speaker.

In 1978, Robert Keeshan '75 and Randall Fisher '76 organized what they believed to be the second alumni Order of Barristers Club in the nation. They sent a membership list to the forty-six Washburn graduates in eight classes who had been selected as Barristers, suggesting the list might be useful for referrals. They also sought dues and contributions to support the moot court program, which "became one dependent on meager funds" after the death of Professor Robinson, who had frequently funded special needs off-budget. The Club's first project addressed a recurring problem. Washburn competitors too often had won oral arguments but lost competition rounds when oral argument scores were combined with brief scores. The Club thus funded an award for the best intramural brief.

Washburn teams earned trips to the final rounds of the National Moot Court Competition twice during Monk's deanship. Karen Wedel '84 and Michael O'Hara '84 finished second in the 1982 regional competition, defeating host Creighton and the University of Nebraska in preliminary rounds and KU in the semi-finals before losing to another University of Nebraska team in the finals. Wedel was named Top Oralist in the competition. The 1985 team of Larry Pitts '86, Debra Vermillion '86, and David Mitchell '86 also finished second in the regional and Pitts received the American College of Trial Lawyers Award for best oral argument in the final round.

Students competed in new competitions. In 1987, Martha Mullen '87, Kent Hall '88, and John Smith '88 argued in the championship round in the second annual Jerome Prince Memorial Evidence Law Competition, held at Brooklyn Law School, placing second among nineteen teams. They received the Best Brief Award. Rob Beal '83 and John Jurcyk, Jr. '84 received the second place brief award in the Wagner Labor Law Competition in New York in 1983. Teams entered mock trial competitions in addition to moot court competitions. In both 1987 and 1988, Washburn teams competed in the championship round of the American Trial Lawyers Association's regional Trial Advocacy Competition. The 1987 team included Roger Warren '88 and Jim Jarrow '88 as attorneys and

Sarah Foster '89 as a witness. Team members in 1988 were Nicholas Cox '88 and Tracey Samantha Fitzpatrick '88 as attorneys and Thomas Black '89 and Kristine Stockwell '90 as witnesses.

A SERIES OF FIRSTS IN THE LIBRARY

John Christensen did everything the faculty that hired him hoped he would do to modernize the library, and more. Today's law students will be amused that the installation of technologies now taken for granted, or even known only as obsolete relics, were hailed as major accomplishments. They ranged from simple things, such as his immediate acquisition of a second photocopier and negotiation of a price reduction from ten to five cents per copy, to the more innovative. At the time, access to LEXIS was through a direct telephone line to St. Louis and, in exchange for reduced charges, law schools were denied access between 1:00 p.m. and 4:00 p.m., the period of peak access by practitioners. Christensen devised a plan by which the law libraries in seven mid-western states that had St. Louis phone lines used their phones during the three down hours to process interlibrary loan requests.[805] The first WESTLAW terminal was installed in 1982 and Dean Monk could not resist commenting that "Washburn is now the only law school in the state with both LEXIS and WESTLAW."[806]

Washburn re-catalogued its collection so that it could subscribe to OCLC (Online Computer Library Center), a support service then serving 2,000 North American libraries, including sixty law libraries. As a result of subscribing to OCLC, the Law Library's holdings were included in the Kansas Union Catalog, allowing attorneys throughout the state to determine at their local libraries whether Washburn held a book they needed.

Among Christensen's major initiatives were formalizing an interlibrary loan service and networking with other libraries to coordinate acquisitions. He initially developed a combined list of looseleaf holdings at the Washburn and Supreme Court libraries, then early in 1981 concluded an agreement by which the two libraries would exchange card catalog entries. The library purchased LAWNET COM I, the first computer-output-microfiche product. It contained

---

805. John E. Christensen, *Networking Aids Washburn Law Library Users*, 20 THE CIRCUIT RIDER 5 (Winter 1981).

806. Carl C. Monk, *From the Dean's Desk*, 22 THE CIRCUIT RIDER 2, 11 (Spring 1983).

77. John Christensen, Library Director
and Professor 1979–present

card catalog entries from approximately fifty major research law libraries, facilitating interlibrary loan requests. The Library coordinated acquisitions with the Supreme Court and KU Law Libraries, avoiding unnecessary and expensive duplications without sacrificing ready access to materials. The success of that partnership led Christensen to help form a consortium of eighteen law schools in seven mid-western states that reduced overall acquisition costs for members by having different schools develop larger collections in particular substantive areas and share those materials through interlibrary loan.

　　Washburn was among the first twenty law schools to join the Center for Computer Assisted Legal Instruction, which develops and distributes programmed exercises students use to learn or reinforce legal principles and skills in a variety of courses. Initially, CALI exercises required use of an Apple computer and this was one of the few times the library maintained a small number of these computers. In 1986, the Library added videodisk technology that was particularly useful in Evidence and Trial Advocacy classes. Students watched a trial in real time and lodged objections by keystrokes on a computer. The software generated an appropriate response to the objection and provided feedback about objections students missed.

In 1983, Christensen arranged for a one-year trial of OnTyme II electronic mail by mid-west law schools. Later, the library joined the ABANET electronic mail system and could receive mail from any ABANET user. The school assured alums in 1986 that "The mail is checked twice daily, Monday through Friday, at 9 a.m. and 4 p.m."[807] The University ultimately installed more sophisticated e-mail capability on its main frame computer and in April 1988 Christensen conducted a faculty development session to explain how to use it and other emerging technologies. Some faculty were mossbacks and resisted the rush toward e-mail, notably Professor Duncan. While one might have thought an environmentalist like Duncan would welcome a technology that would reduce the use of paper, he worried it also would reduce faculty interaction and ultimately diminish collegiality.

As early as 1980, Christensen expected schools ultimately would transmit documents by telefax. However, it was 1983 before the mid-west schools planned a demonstration project.[808] In 1984, Washburn became one of only seven law school libraries to acquire a telefacsimile machine, after a national survey Christensen conducted determined that "many of the major academic libraries will be acquiring telefax equipment within the next year or two."[809] No one foresaw the full potential of fax machines. Monk noted documents could be sent "at relatively high speed" and that, "over twenty county recorder offices in Kansas plan to install similar equipment—thus opening up a potential channel for distributing legal information to remote areas of the state."[810] Washburn's machine transmitted at the state-of-the-art speed of about forty-five seconds per page, but could also be used with the slower machines in most Register of Deeds offices that required about three minutes per page.[811] By 1986, a *Circuit*

---

807. *Library Adds Materials, Rearranges To Cope with Space Shortage*, 25 THE CIRCUIT RIDER 12 (Fall 1986).

808. *Faculty News and Notes*, 23 THE CIRCUIT RIDER 11 (Summer 1983).

809. Carl C. Monk, *Dean's Annual Report to the Bar*, 23 THE CIRCUIT RIDER 5, 6 (Spring 1984).

810. *Id.*

811. John E. Christensen, *Telefacsimile Service Initiated*, 23 THE CIRCUIT RIDER

Rider article noted that the school could fax "to anyone with access to a unit," not just to Register of Deeds offices, but assumed the public office would be the primary source of access in remote counties.[812]

Christensen offered an elective course on Law and Computers as early as the spring of 1983. By 1985–86, there was a Computer Literacy Center with six Zenith microcomputers available for student use, including one funded by the Student Bar Association to assist students in applying for jobs, and a growing library of software. In the spring of 1987, both LEXIS and WESTLAW brought in five dedicated terminals for two weeks to train students in on-line research. Modems were added to permit simultaneous searches by three additional terminals in the Computer Literacy Center, although the vendors still limited those searches to evenings and weekends.

Librarians began to innovate, not merely providing portals through which users could try to find what was "out there" but also by helping them find it through user-friendly menus and by adding original content. The Washburn Law Library Information Service (WALLIS) was unveiled in 1987, using the University's Prime minicomputer. It was accessible through computers in the library and then externally by dial-up using a modem for users registered with the University's Academic Computer Center.

The library also expanded the breadth of the physical collection. The acquisitions budget grew over time to near the national median, and the number of new titles added each year put Washburn in the top quarter in that category. In March 1981, the library became the first selective depository of publications of Kansas state agencies. In 1985, it became a depository for the Nuclear Regulatory Commission for documents relating to the Wolf Creek nuclear power plant and received annual funding to maintain the depository. The library made a greater commitment to microfiche than most other schools, to add important but irregularly used materials such as records, briefs, and transcripts of oral arguments before the United States Supreme Court, the *Congressional Record,* and other government documents that would consume many feet of shelf capacity if maintained in hard copy. By 1987, nearly 40% of the library's 197,476 volumes, 75,796 in all, were microforms. Even so, the stacks filled rapidly and little-used materials were stored in Morgan Hall in the area

---

10 (Fall 1984).

812. *Telefacsimile Aids Kansas Attorneys*, 25 THE CIRCUIT RIDER 3 (Winter 1986).

formerly occupied by the University Library. The portion of the collection in off-site storage rose to almost one-third by 1988.[813]

Growth of the collection required the library to be more user-friendly. Immediately after he arrived, Christensen placed "Quick Reference" sections on each floor, containing the same basic materials, and created a single tax research center. A weekly *Washburn Law Library Bulletin* alerted users to additions to the collection. A current awareness service made the contents pages of legal periodicals conveniently available the day they arrived. Trained professionals soon provided reference service seven days each week.

Library staffing necessarily expanded from the Library Director, three professional librarians and three staff members in 1978 to the Director, 5.5 professional librarians and seven support staff by 1988. A strategy to help both student recruitment and library staffing led to a Library Internship program in which librarians already holding MLS degrees could pursue law degrees part-time at Washburn while working part-time in the library, being paid at professional rates rather than at the modest rate for student workers. In 1984, there were five such interns, bringing the number of staff members with MLS degrees to eleven.[814] This internship program is part of the reason so many Washburn graduates today are Law Librarians at other law schools.

Travel funds were provided for library staff to attend conferences and to interact with professional colleagues. John Christensen served as the librarian member of an ABA/AALS inspection team at Campbell Law School in North Carolina. Washburn hosted the annual meeting of the Mid-America Association of Law Libraries in the fall of 1981.

One of the debates in legal education nationally in the mid-1980s was whether law libraries should be put in charge of all computer and technology functions of a law school or whether faculty and administrative functions should be supported separately. Some deans and faculties worried that librarians might place library priorities above those of faculty and staff. Monk initially opted to maintain some independence between library and other functions. During 1986–87, Anne Spencer was hired as a Microcomputer Specialist while she was on leave from the faculty at Baker University. Spencer adapted soft-

---

813. John E. Christensen, *Washburn Law Library: What a Difference a Decade Makes*, 27 THE CIRCUIT RIDER 4, 5 (Fall 1988).

814. Carl C. Monk, *Dean's Annual Report to the Bar*, 23 THE CIRCUIT RIDER 5, 7 (Spring 1984).

ware programs for use in the admissions, alumni, development, and other administrative offices and offered training for faculty and staff.

In June 1985, Monk and the faculty Technology Committee, chaired by Professor Bayles, announced a plan to provide professors with computers for their offices. Faculty members had to put up 20% of the cost and the school would pay 80%, up to a maximum of $1,200. Wearing his tax professor hat, Bayles assured faculty their 20% share would be tax deductible as an employee business expense, which at the time did not have to exceed a percentage of gross income. The same 80%–20% split was used for faculty travel expenses. At the time, the recommended Zenith computer with dual disk drives and 320K of memory cost $1,349. About half the faculty took advantage of the plan the first year.

ALTERNATIVE DISPUTE RESOLUTION

Washburn was among the first law schools to offer a course in what today is called alternative dispute resolution. Bob Fowks developed a course in Arbitration Techniques in the early 1970s, which included both classroom instruction and simulations, and he taught it regularly until his retirement. Later that decade, a course in Negotiation and Settlement was added. It was taught for many years by Jan Leuenberger '61 as an Adjunct Professor. A new grant in 1984 from the United States Department of Education's Clinical Legal Education Experience program facilitated expansion of the school's offerings in ADR. A mediation component was added to the third-year Clinic internship. It included classroom instruction about mediation, role playing, and mediation of actual cases, primarily disputes involving domestic relations and neighborhood conflicts. The program was interdisciplinary in its approach, blending behavioral science and law.[815] Instead of hiring a new full-time faculty member, the school hired a non-lawyer mediation specialist, Susana Valdovinos-Hall, to implement the program. The federal grant was renewed for three more years and Valdovinos was able to attend law school part-time while teaching the mediation component in the Clinic. She earned her J.D. in 1988 and continued to teach the mediation component, as well as classroom courses, as Visiting Professor the year after the grant expired.

---

815. Bill Piatt and Susana Valdovinos-Hall, *The Birth of a Mediation Program*, 23 THE CIRCUIT RIDER 11 (Fall 1984).

THE SUMMER ABROAD PROGRAM BECOMES PERMANENT

Washburn had conducted summer study abroad programs in 1968 and 1974, the latter at Brunel University in Uxbridge, England. In 1985, the program once again was offered at Brunel and a foreign summer program has been offered regularly ever since. While many law schools merely send U.S. professors overseas to teach courses, Washburn has always been committed to offering courses that emphasize comparative or international approaches and to team-teaching with members of foreign faculties. Linda Elrod and Charlene Smith organized the 1985 program. Students took three two-hour courses during the five-week session, Comparative Property and Land Use Planning that Elrod taught with Brunel Professor Patrick Polden, Comparative Constitutional Law that Smith taught with Brunel's Martin Coleman, and Comparative Legal Systems for which Elrod and Smith collaborated with Brunel's Hillary Astor. Polden would become a mainstay of the program, teaching nearly every summer for more than a decade.

Classes were taught each morning for four days each week, giving students long weekends to travel. An afternoon field trip was scheduled, on average once each week. Some field trips were repeated almost every year, such as to the Uxbridge Magistrate's Court, to the Old Bailey, to an Inn of Court, and to Parliament. Others were selected to complement the particular courses taught that year, such as trips to a land title office, to solicitors' offices, or to Lloyd's of London. While faculty accessibility to students long has been a hallmark of Washburn's open door policy in Topeka, faculty and students had far more interaction abroad. Elrod and Smith participated in each other's classes and partied with students in addition to teaching them.[816]

Twenty-eight students enrolled in 1985, including three from KU. Perhaps because 1985 was the first opportunity for students completing both their first and second years to attend, enrollment in future years usually was smaller and first-year students predominated. World events had the potential to impact the program. Students went to London in 1986 despite Irish Republican Army bombings there that spring, but Jane Bennington '87 wrote that they "were first hand observers of the British sadness at so many Americans' decision not to

---

816. Linda Elrod, *Reflections on an English Law Program*, 24 THE CIRCUIT RIDER 3, 4 (Summer 1985).

travel in Europe because of international terrorism."[817] The school sent brochures and posters about the program to other schools and students from other
schools enrolled nearly every summer, although the all-time high was just nine
students from five other schools among twenty-four students in 1988. Thus, the
summer program was not a profit center for the school. Student-faculty ratios
were far lower than for regular summer classes stateside. Washburn students
had to complete ninety hours to graduate whether they went to London or not,
so their tuition represented "new revenue" only if they would have enrolled in
another school's summer abroad program if Washburn's were not available.
Still, the program has always been viewed as being well worth the investment.
On one hand, students broadened their perspectives in ways not possible at
home. After the first program, Pat Horner '87 described its effect this way:

> We were forced to look at ourselves in the context of a different culture.…
> [W]e were almost continually re-evaluating our American style of liv-
> ing, our legal system and ourselves. Through this re-evaluation process
> most, if not all of us, finished the program with a new appreciation of
> our country and its legal system as well as some valuable insights into
> our English heritage. In addition, we developed a new appreciation for
> ourselves and each other.
>
> In time our law careers will benefit from this intense foreign learning
> experience. We have gained an added dimension to problem-solving by
> observing how another country settles its legal disputes. We have gained
> insights from our experiences gained abroad that will help us weigh
> problems and solutions not just from the American legal perspective.
> This gives us a broader base from which to draw upon when looking
> for answers or solutions to a problem.[818]

On the other hand, professors invariably thought they learned far more
than the students and that the perspective they gained led to better teaching
and better scholarship back home. Faculty members welcomed the luxury
Linda Elrod described after the first summer of "opportunities to meet and

---

817. Jane Bennington, *Hail, Britannia—1986*, 25 THE CIRCUIT RIDER 3 (Fall
1986).

818. Pat Horner, *Summer School in England 1985*, 24 THE CIRCUIT RIDER 9, 10
(Summer 1985).

share ideas with other law faculty, to observe a variety of teaching techniques and to do some creative and reflective thinking."[819] Numerous opportunities to converse with British faculty while preparing for classes, on field trips, and during dinners and lunches broadened faculty horizons. For this reason, faculty members who had never taught in the program always were given preference, as long as a British faculty member was available to team-teach with them, over faculty members who had taught in it previously.

Relations with Brunel went beyond the summer program. Professor Geoffrey Woodroffe came to Topeka in April 1986 to present a William O. Douglas Lecture about the European Economic Community, then team-taught with Paul Rasor in the London program that summer. Woodroffe also taught in the summer of 1988 and several years thereafter, and returned to Topeka many years later to participate in an Ahrens Chair in Torts seminar. Professor Coleman brought ten Brunel students to study at Washburn during the summer of 1987. The early part of the program concentrated on classroom instruction. During the latter part, local firms, judges, and government agencies provided field placements for the students. Coleman hoped to repeat the program regularly. However, law students in Great Britain are undergraduates and costs limited the number who could participate. Brunel students came to Washburn only one other time, accompanied by Professor Polden.

MANDATORY CONTINUING LEGAL EDUCATION

Beginning in 1972, Washburn was party to a joint agreement with KU and the Kansas Bar Association to provide continuing legal education, with the KBA coordinating all programs, providing support staff, and pocketing all profits. The agreement exempted the Washburn-Topeka Bar Association Annual Law Institute from joint sponsorship because it started in 1957. The Institute celebrated its silver anniversary in 1982. On behalf of the Topeka Bar Association, Phil Lewis '35 presented a silver tray to Professor Ahrens to recognize his twenty-five years of work coordinating the Institute with little or no staff support.

Lawyers were not required to attend continuing education programs and, compared with today, there were relatively few programs offered, even by the KBA. Many lawyers attended the Washburn Institute as much to have social

---

819. Elrod, *supra* note 816, at 4.

time with other lawyers as to attend the presentations. There always was a "symposium" hour and dinner following the Institute, usually with a speaker. Costs were kept at a break-even minimum.

The Joint CLE agreement worked imperfectly, like most compromises. For the schools, CLE often was an issue of visibility, both within the state and nationally. KU understandably was unhappy that Washburn was permitted to continue with a program in its own name because of its prior link to a local bar association. When Professor Lonnie Rose at KU arranged for a National Institute of Trial Advocacy regional institute to be held at KU and indicated it would be offered there annually, Washburn objected that this violated the spirit of the Joint Agreement, particularly since a NITA-style program already was being offered under the agreement, rotating its location between the two schools. Feathers at the KBA could be ruffled too, especially when the bar's financial bottom line was affected. Kansas lawyers usually volunteered their time as speakers and as authors of chapters in handbooks. Some lawyer members of the Joint CLE Committee were unhappy because law professors usually were paid honoraria to present programs and received royalties when they were sole authors of handbooks.

The KBA emphasized programs that would attract large audiences and it was not economically feasible for the KBA to sponsor in-depth, extended programs for specialists, because of overhead costs. The law schools, with less overhead, could do that and in-depth programs often appealed to faculty more than basic programs. The Joint CLE Committee authorized the law schools to experiment with two- and three-day programs and they both offered two of them in the summer of 1984. Linda Elrod and Paul Rasor teamed with Bankruptcy Judge Robert Morton and then-practitioners Jerry Elliott and John Pearson to present a three-day program on "Current and Continuing Bankruptcy Problems." It attracted forty-seven registrants. Randy Roth returned from Hawaii to join Jim Bayles in a three-day program for thirty-three lawyers entitled "Sophisticated (But Sensible) Tax Planning Strategies." The next year Professor Bayles coordinated a two-day seminar on "Tax Planning with Real Property," with Professor Ed Hood from UMKC and Tim O'Sullivan '75. The second program that summer was entitled "Cutting the Ties that Bind—Handling Property Issues and Child Custody in the 80's." Professors Elrod, Maxwell, and Reynolds, and Mediation Specialist Susana Valdovinos-Hall served as faculty along with judges, practitioners, and professors from

Washburn's School of Business. Nearly fifty attorneys attended a two-day Family Law Institute in 1986 focusing on negotiation strategies and drafting skills. The Family Law Institute became an annual event. The same summer, Professors Barbara, Concannon, and Kaye organized a three-day Advanced Trial Advocacy Institute.

The continuing education landscape changed with the Kansas Supreme Court's adoption in 1985 of a rule requiring each lawyer to earn at least ten hours of continuing legal education credit each fiscal year. Lawyers worried unduly how they would meet the requirement. Washburn's twenty-eighth annual Law Institute was held less than four months into the fiscal year but attracted 320 registrants, more than double the previous high. It was the first Institute to be held over two days, beginning on Thursday afternoon. Twenty-one hours of instruction were offered, in overlapping sessions, and registrants could earn nine total hours of CLE credit. It is not clear in hindsight why the program was not organized to enable registrants to earn the entire ten hours of credit needed for the year but it was fortunate it was not, since the building and the staff were taxed to handle the capacity crowd as it was.

Of course, it took no genius to anticipate that there would be many lawyers who would not be as diligent as those attending the Institute in fulfilling their CLE requirements early in the fiscal year. One also could anticipate that many lawyers would be unhappy about the billable hours lost to complete the requirement, particularly if they had to attend two or more programs to do so. A faculty CLE committee chaired by Professor Concannon thus planned a "year-end" program entitled "Recent Developments in the Law" through which lawyers could earn all ten hours needed on the last possible day, June 30, and by staying to attend the program on July 1 could earn all hours needed for the next fiscal year as well. Each topic was assigned two hours so lawyers who had completed some of their hours could register for only the number of hours needed. The June 30 program drew a huge crowd and a large number of registrants completed all ten hours. Predictably, attendance declined on July 1, as many June 30 registrants assumed they would have occasion during the next year to attend another program, but many of them returned the next June 30. This "Procrastinator's Special" program has been offered at year-end ever since and some professors have used it to introduce a "captive" audience to emerging topics such as Bioethics and the Law and computerized legal research that many lawyers in the early days would never have chosen in a stand-alone

program. Many lawyers came to rely on the program to fulfill CLE requirements and commented they would be in trouble if Washburn ever canceled
it. When the Supreme Court raised the annual requirement to twelve hours,
the July 1 program was dropped and a June 29–30 program was substituted,
offering eight hours each day.

Numerous new CLE providers entered the Kansas market, seeing potential
profits. The KBA dramatically increased the number of its offerings and the
size of its CLE staff. While some KBA officers were concerned about restraint
of trade issues, the view prevailed that the CLE agreement should be kept
intact. The Bar feared the loss of faculty as speakers if the state's law schools
offered comprehensive CLE schedules, particularly if the schools paid honoraria
to speakers but the Bar eliminated such payments. The two law schools felt
the need to show their flags among CLE providers. However, a survey of law
schools in states that already had transitioned to mandatory CLE led Washburn
to conclude it "should not look to CLE as a substantial source of revenue."[820]
Modest profits were thought to be possible which would, at minimum, cover
the cost of adding administrative staff to coordinate programs and help with
understaffed functions besides CLE, provide additional compensation for faculty speakers which bar programs would not, and support other needs such as
faculty research stipends. On the other hand, limiting the extent of Washburn's
involvement in CLE seemed desirable so faculty would not be distracted from
the school's primary goal of increasing scholarly writing. By September 1985,
Gerald Goodell '58, wearing the hat of KBA President, brokered a new agreement to continue joint sponsorship of all CLE programs, in which the schools
agreed to limit the programs they would offer to eighty hours per year. The three
entities agreed to hold semi-annual meetings to coordinate schedules, to avoid
undesirable overlap and duplication, and also to share a total of 25% of their
net profits with each of the other two entities, up to a maximum of $10,000
per year per entity. The expectation was that this revenue sharing would be a
sufficient inducement for faculty to continue to present KBA programs, even
without honoraria, because their efforts for the KBA would help generate some
funds for their school.[821] The two schools quickly entered a side agreement that

---

820. Bill Rich, *Acting Dean's Desk*, 24 THE CIRCUIT RIDER 2 (Fall 1985).

821. Letter from James M. Concannon to Dennis P. Harwick, et al., "Re: Board
of Governors' Special Committee to Review the Relationship Between the KBA and
the Kansas Law Schools" (Apr. 2, 1999).

they would not make payments to each other but would keep all profits from their respective activities except for the Bar's share.

The new CLE agreement worked more imperfectly than the original one. Over the years, KBA members of the Joint CLE Committee complained that the schools violated the agreement when they offered the identical program on different days in different locations, for example to serve small audiences in rural counties, and only counted the presentation once toward the limit on the number of hours of instruction the schools could offer. The schools too complained about creative accounting in the Bar's calculation of its net profit or loss from CLE. The Bar Association had two main sources of revenue, dues and CLE fees, and one of the inducements to pay dues was a lower charge to members for CLE. Yet, no portion of dues was allocated as CLE revenue. The Bar Association of course performed numerous important functions that were not revenue-generating, such as its legislative program, and these functions were supported by dues. However, the Association had a strong incentive to allocate as much overhead as possible to CLE rather than to activities that produced no revenue. The incentive was enhanced by the public relations value of being able to represent to members that fees for CLE programs were being kept as low as possible, and only covered costs. The indirect costs charged to CLE, including salaries, nearly equaled direct CLE expenses and constituted approximately 40% of all of the Bar's indirect costs, with the result that the net profits the Bar had to share with the schools were negligible. Annual squabbles over accounting made it clear the new agreement was flawed. The schools thought it was unfair that the Bar Association was the only party to the Joint Agreement that was recovering its indirect costs related to Bar-administered CLE. Expenditures from the schools' operating budgets for secretarial support, student research assistants, and other costs faculty incurred in preparing lecture outlines and handbooks for the KBA were not being reimbursed. The schools argued that law students should not be forced to pay for these costs through tuition so that the KBA's budget could be balanced.[822] By December 1988, a revised agreement provided for payment annually of a flat amount of $5,000 to the schools to offset their expenses supporting KBA programs, regardless whether the Bar's internal allocation of overhead produced a net profit or loss from CLE.

---

822. *Id.*

366 Washburn Law School History

VISITORS FOR THE SHORT AND LONG TERM

Leaves of absence for faculty to visit other schools or, in the case of Mike Barbara to serve in state government, as well as departures from the faculty too late in an academic year to conduct national searches for permanent re-placements, led Washburn to hire more Visiting Professors during Monk's deanship than during any previous period. Recruiting visitors for one-year positions that have little or no likelihood of becoming permanent positions presents challenges. Topeka does not rank high on many urban professors' lists of getaway destinations. Not surprisingly then, some visitors had local ties, such as Bill Ward, a 1971 KU law graduate who visited in the spring of 1979, and Diane Acker, a Harvard graduate who returned to Kansas where her father was President of Kansas State University. Others were Washburn graduates. Emily Kofran '80 taught in the Law Clinic as Visiting Professor in 1987–88. David Pierce '77 got his start in law teaching in the spring of 1981, teaching Administration of Criminal Justice and Legal Research and Writing, before enrolling at the University of Utah and earning its first LL.M. in Energy Law. He returned as Visiting Professor for academic year 1986–87, after two years as Assistant Professor at the University of Indiana-Indianapolis. In 1987, he organized the first class reunion, an idea that should have been implemented many years earlier. Pierce's class of 1977 turned out in huge numbers.

In many instances, Washburn professors used their contacts to recruit visitors from elsewhere. Michael Kaye knew Eric Schneider well when they both practiced in San Francisco and the opportunity to visit at Washburn in 1980–81 allowed Schneider to enter law teaching a year earlier than he expected, since an extended stay in Greece prevented him from attending the faculty recruitment conference. The next year, he joined the University of Baltimore law faculty and later served three years there as Associate Dean and one year as Interim Dean. While Mike Barbara served as Secretary of Corrections during academic years 1983–85, Mark Dobson and Larry Benner were Visiting Professors for one year each, teaching Evidence and criminal law courses. Dobson was a VISTA attorney, then staff attorney, in Wichita's Legal Aid Office from 1973 until 1975, overlapping briefly with Bill Rich, and had taught with Nancy Maxwell at the University of North Dakota in 1977–78. He had joined the faculty at Nova in Florida in 1980 and remains there today. Benner was well acquainted with Sheila Reynolds and her husband Lowell Paul and, like Schneider, was attracted to visit while he was abroad, serving as Legal Counsel for the Ombudsman Commission of Papua, New Guinea. Benner has been a member of the California Western faculty in San Diego since leaving Washburn.

Two visitors stayed far longer. Due to the reduction in enrollment in 1985, the departure of John Lungren that year meant his position was lost through attrition. It was Washburn's good fortune not only that Jean Reeves retired from the position of General Attorney for the Santa Fe Railroad at the same time and was too vigorous to retire completely but also that the railroad retirement board ruled that he could not be paid for any legal employment, even teaching. Reeves had taught Business Associations for the last half of the spring semester in 1979 when Professor Treadway was ill and now volunteered to teach, without pay, both sections of the classes on Agency and Partnerships and on Corporations. He expressed "gratitude for the opportunity of sharing the joy and enthusiasm of young people."[823] A graduate of the University of Nebraska School of Law, Reeves was honored as an Honorary Life Member of the Washburn Law School Association in 1987. He continued to teach full loads, even summer classes, until macular degeneration forced him to retire in August 1991. While Washburn President Norman Plass in 1902 pointed to the presence of "the headquarters of the great railroads, with their special attorneys" as a reason Topeka was the ideal place to start a law school,[824] he could not have imagined that two of those special attorneys, Treadway and Reeves, would serve for fifteen years combined as full-time faculty members.

Ellen Byers was another rarity, a person with full-time law teaching experience who was forced to relocate to Topeka when her husband, an F.B.I. agent, was transferred to the Bureau's Topeka office. A 1981 law graduate from Georgetown who had been an Assistant United States Attorney, Byers had taught criminal law courses at St. Mary's in San Antonio as Visiting Professor in 1985–86. Washburn had openings only for visitors in 1986–87. Byers' background in criminal law made her a good fit as Washburn implemented small section classes combining substantive courses with Legal Methods. Almost every year there was a need for a visitor, sometimes just three-quarters or one-half time, and the faculty felt fortunate she was locked in by her location. She did not teach from 1990 through 1994 when she had small children and was writing a

---

823. *Faculty Profiles*, 27 THE CIRCUIT RIDER 28 (Fall 1988).
824. WASHBURN COLL. BULLETIN 9–10 (Nov. 1902).

novel, but otherwise was Visiting Professor until 1999 when she ceased being
a visitor and began teaching full-time in a new year-long writing program.

RETREAT AND CURRICULUM REVISION

Monk saw expanded professional development activities as critical once the
school's core faculty stabilized in academic year 1983–84. That spring, the faculty
held a full weekend retreat at the restored Elms Hotel in Excelsior Springs,
Missouri, seeking to identify priorities and plan for the future. The retreat
also served as the first step in preparing for the ABA/AALS inspection in 1986.
There were outside facilitators, Dean Richard Huber from Boston College,
who had been a facilitator of the 1980 in-house teaching clinic, and Dean Jack
Mudd from Montana. Another resource was Professor Willard Pedrick from
Arizona, who was sent by the AALS Professional Development Committee as
an observer to prepare a report for inclusion in the Committee's *Manual on
Law Faculty Development*. As in 1980, the faculty divided into two groups for
discussions. Extended sessions were devoted to assessing strengths and weaknesses in three areas: (1) academic program, with one group focusing on the
first-year curriculum and the other on the upper-level curriculum, including
such issues as whether there was overemphasis on appellate decisions and the
adversary model, particularly in the first year, and what the balance should
be between teaching of theory and skills; (2) student recruitment, including
minority recruitment; and (3) how professors should allocate their time, balancing Washburn's traditional open door policy and availability for student
counseling with increased demands for scholarship, while still leaving time
for personal lives. Ad hoc committees were appointed for each of these three
topics to follow up on retreat discussions and to recommend needed changes.
   Pedrick, the outside observer, concluded:

> It was plain at the end of the first full day of the retreat that the sentiment
> of virtually all of the faculty members was that this was a useful exercise.
> They found themselves in dialogue with their colleagues on matters of
> importance to the school and its program but matters which they rarely
> had time to address in the setting of the day-to-day routine of the law
> school and their duties there. Further, it was apparent that this faculty
> has a very real sense of collegiality.... [W]hile there are undoubtedly

some differences in viewpoint on legal education, the impression given the outside observer was that this was a faculty characterized by mutual respect and ambition for the law school tinged, a bit, by some individual anxieties about the new dimensions of expectations for younger and newer members of the faculty.[825]

Predictably, the ad hoc committee on curriculum developed the most concrete proposals and had the most lasting impact. For many years, Washburn had more required courses than most law schools. The required courses produced a "liberal arts" education of sorts, but inhibited specialization and smacked of paternalism. Revolutionary change was proposed, and adopted for academic year 1986–87, which gave students far more autonomy than ever before. However, a liberal arts exposure was retained. After completing the first year, students were required only to complete two courses in each of six broad categories of courses: The State and the Individual; Social Legislation; Economic Relationships; Use, Distribution and Transfer of Property; Resolution of Disputes; and Perspectives. Only Evidence in the category of Resolution of Disputes and Professional Responsibility in the Perspectives category, now a graded class with two hours credit, were specifically required, although new upper level writing and oral presentation requirements also were mandated. In the first-year curriculum, the separate Legal Methods course was abolished but each entering student in the fall semester would take one substantive class in a small section with an additional hour of credit so that legal methods could be taught in the context of the substantive class. Some 1Ls had their small section in Criminal Law and others had it in Property. A perspectives course, Legal Systems, was added to the spring semester and initially Professor Khan taught both sections. An additional hour was added to Legal Research and Writing, making it a three-hour course, and it was taught as a seminar, with all assignments drawn from a single substantive area of law that was announced in advance so that students could select a seminar that interested them. We remained confident that using members of the permanent faculty member to teach legal writing was preferable to using recent graduates to teach the course, as many other schools did. The ad hoc committee believed the opportunity to teach legal research in a substantive area of interest would make

825. Willard H. Pedrick, *Comments on the Washburn Faculty Retreat of March 30–April 1, 1984* (Apr. 17, 1984).

the faculty member's turn in the rotation to teach the course less burdensome. Constitutional Law I was moved into the first year and Civil Procedure II and Property II were made upper level electives.

BIG GIFTS

Fundraising was a priority for John Green when he became Washburn's new president. In 1982, he created the position of Vice President for Development and Dean Monk was instrumental in Green's selection of Robert Hartsook '79 for the position. Monk understood the need for a University fundraiser who would solicit as vigorously on behalf of the Law School as for other units of the University, particularly from dual degree alums. That fall, the University commenced a $23 million capital campaign and it included $7 million for the law school. That total included scholarships, faculty chairs, and $2.5 million for an addition to the building, primarily to accommodate the rapidly expanding library.

The school received the three largest gifts in its history during the next five years, gifts that would significantly enrich the Law School's program. The first was in 1983, a gift to the Washburn Law School Foundation by John Shamberg '37 of nearly thirty acres of land at 119th Street and Blackbob Road in Olathe, appraised at $404,000. Shamberg explained his gift:

> If it had not been for Washburn Law School, I doubt that I would ever have had the opportunity to enter into the legal profession or even go to law school. Through this gift, I hope I am able to repay, in some small way, the debt I owe to the school and, at the same time, perhaps encourage other graduates who have done well in their careers financially to assist in the current fund-raising effort . . .[826]

Shamberg had been frustrated when he was President of the Washburn Law School Association with the University's effort to rebuild the Law School after the tornado. Thus, having a separate Law School Foundation to receive his gift added to his confidence in making it. At the time, the tract was farm land. Today, it is in the middle of a thriving shopping and residential area. The Foundation held the land, as the city grew around it, until 2004 when it contracted to sell the tract for $2.6 million.

---

826. *Shamberg Makes Largest Law Gift*, THE CIRCUIT RIDER 1 (Winter 1984).

78. John E. Shamberg '37

In 1986, Gerald Michaud '51 and the members of his law firm, all Washburn graduates, Richard Cordry '75, Patrick Michaud '76, Andrew Hutton '79 and Mark Hutton '79, committed $1 million to create a Chair in Tort Law. Instead of naming it for themselves, they named it in honor of the professor who taught Torts to all of them, James R. Ahrens. "We want to show our appreciation for the excellent education we received from the Washburn faculty," Gerald Michaud said.[827] "Jim Ahrens…has made substantial contributions to the quality of legal education at Washburn. The Chair will permanently recognize his role in making the law school what it is today."[828] The Chair was fully funded by 1988 and a celebration was held in Robinson Courtroom in July, just days before Monk's term as Dean ended.

---

827. *Michaud Firm Endows Ahrens Chair in Tort Law*, 25 THE CIRCUIT RIDER 1 (Fall 1986).

828. *Wichita law firm to give $1 Million to Washburn*, TOPEKA CAP.-J. 1, 2 (June 18, 1986).

The Estate of Duffie Hindman '24 provided the largest gift in the University's history, more than $4 million. He made much of that fortune accepting assignments of mineral rights in oil and gas leases he procured for clients who couldn't pay for his services. His first philanthropic priority was giving back to the community that made him successful, so $3 million was designated for scholarships for graduates of high schools in Rooks County who attend Washburn University, including both undergraduate and law programs. Dean Monk persuaded Hindman to designate the fourth million as an unrestricted fund for the Law School, which has been used ever since for the priority purpose of scholarships.

In addition to these gifts, there were pledges of more than $3.5 million of deferred gifts for the law campaign.

A single Vice President for Development serving the entire University could not devote the time to conduct fundraising for the Law School at the level it needed. One of the Law School Association Board of Governors' initiatives in 1985 was to fund for the first year a one-half time Law School Development Director to institutionalize an alumni annual giving campaign. Previously, the Placement Director administered a system using class agents to solicit annual gifts. Gifts to the annual fund had grown from $18,512 in 1978–79 to more than $40,000 annually by 1981–82 and Monk expressed appreciation to alums for that accomplishment, but also reminded them that annual giving at KU was twice that at Washburn, even though tuition there was only half that at Washburn. "We must close the gap if we are to continue to make the progress we all seek."[829] In early 1986, the school's new Development Director oversaw the first student phonathon to seek annual gifts, as part of the University's phonathon. The chair of the student committee, Barbara Head '86, would later become a Development Director herself. In the two nights allocated exclusively to the Law School, students raised $6,505 in pledges, more than 10% of total annual gifts the prior year.

Increasing scholarship awards was essential if the school's student recruitment goals were to be met. However, increasing annual giving and endowments takes time and dollars were needed quickly. As of early 1986, endowments held by the University restricted to the Law School totaled just $870,000 and the Foundation's

---

829. Carl C. Monk, *Dean's Annual Report to the Bar*, 25 THE CIRCUIT RIDER 11, 14 (Summer 1986).

79. Students call alums during the annual Phonathon in 1997

assets were just $600,000, including the Johnson County land that was not liquid. Monk persuaded the University for the first time to designate a portion of the University's general fund scholarship budget to the Law School, to be used for minority scholarships. He also succeeded in having a portion of the University's unrestricted endowment, including the Finnup scholarship endowment that was not restricted to any academic unit, designated for law scholarships. By cobbling together funds from these various sources, plus external grants for CLEO graduates, total scholarship awards rose from $31,150 in 1978–79 to $122,024 in 1984–85 and $181,403 in 1985–86. One-third of the available funds was targeted to recruit minority students and the actual percentage was 40% in 1985–86.

The alumni Board of Governors endorsed an Alumni Scholars Program as part of the University's capital campaign, targeting applicants with the highest credentials. The Board's Vice President, Richard Hite '53, took the lead in soliciting gifts from firms and individuals in Wichita. By late 1986, there were eleven gifts to start the program, seven endowments and four pledges of annual gifts. At the end of the capital campaign in April 1988, there were thirty-one gifts or pledges to the program, totaling $750,000. Monk asked the Alumni Board also to solicit funds to underwrite summer research stipends for faculty engaged in significant research, a key strategy identified in the self-study for increasing faculty scholarship. Four stipends were awarded for the summer of 1986.

A SPECIAL COMMENCEMENT

The Law School was privileged to have Justice Harry A. Blackmun of the United States Supreme Court as speaker at the 1986 commencement ceremonies. In his remarks, the Justice urged students "to work hard to find solutions to the numerous problems confronting society today, to hold fast to their ideals and to uphold the ethics of the profession."[830] He and his wife Dottie spent the entire weekend on campus, arriving in time for a gala reception at the Top of the Tower for members of the graduating class, faculty, alumni, and members of the judiciary. On Saturday morning, he conducted a question and answer session at the Law School and that evening attended a dinner honoring him and other honorary degree recipients at President Green's home.

Blackmun warned the school that, because he was the author of *Roe v. Wade,* right-to-life groups often picketed his speeches, and they did. Melissa Ness '87 had a conversation with Blackmun:

> She was eight months pregnant and had attended a small group discussion with the Justice and mentioned her involvement with the Kansas Chapter of National Abortion Rights Action League. Justice Blackmun walked up to her and her husband at graduation and asked when the baby was due. He then turned to her husband Larry and said, "Take care of her and this baby…they've got important work to do."[831]

A wonderful picture of Ness talking with the Justice was printed in *The Circuit Rider.*

THE NEXT INSPECTION

It is remarkable in hindsight that Dean Monk was away on sabbatical the semester before the ABA/AALS inspection in the spring of 1986. That he was is a

---

830. *Blackmun Delivers Address,* 25 THE CIRCUIT RIDER 1 (Summer 1986).
831. Elrod, *supra* note 803, at 853.

80. 1986 Commencement speaker U.S. Supreme
Court Justice Harry Blackmun with Melissa Ness '87

reflection of the confidence with which the school approached the inspection.
The Self-Study expressed justifiable satisfaction with the school's progress in
the past seven years. There was a genuine team spirit Professor Smith later
described this way: "Being at Washburn Law School is an absolute delight. The
collegiality can't be surpassed; there is a great support from other faculty. The
school is of the type that encourages faculty-student contact which is very
conducive to learning and sharing ideas—more than at other places."[832] The
school had been able to recruit experienced teachers like Bayles and McDowell
because, as Bayles put it, "Washburn was an excellent law school that was in
the process of building an even better quality institution."[833]

The Self-Study acknowledged the urgent need for additional space for the
library, seminars, and administrative functions, and that much work remained

---

832. *Faculty Profiles*, 27 THE CIRCUIT RIDER 33 (Fall 1988).
833. *Id.* at 11

to be done on student recruitment, diversifying the student body, increasing student scholarships, refining the academic program, and increasing library holdings and access to technology. However, the thrust of the Self-Study was that the school was on the right track and needed primarily to continue the many initiatives that were in progress. It reported that within the last two years twenty-three of twenty-six faculty members had published, though an especially broad definition of "publication" was used in compiling the data.

The faculty encountered enough adversity in pursuing its goals to keep it from becoming cocky. Although the capital campaign announced in 1982 included $2.5 million in private funding for a library addition, no significant contributions had been received by 1986. Even before he received the ABA and the AALS inspection reports, Dean Monk anticipated they would insist that the school report progress on the addition. Thus, Monk asked the Library Committee, chaired by Professor Duncan, to start in the fall of 1986 to develop a plan identifying precise space needs in square feet for each academic and administrative function. In early 1987, President Green created a University committee to plan the addition and Monk appointed Law School representatives. However, the school still was no closer to the fundraising goal. The reduction in enrollment enabled the school to buy a little time. Enough study tables were removed from the top floor of the library in the summers of 1986 and 1988 so that 924 linear feet of shelving could be erected.

One of the Self-Study's goals, membership in the Order of the Coif, would not be achieved. Years earlier, J. Robert Wilson '39, made a contribution to the newly-created Law School Foundation to cover the costs of applying for membership. In late 1983, Samuel D. Thurman, Past President of the Order of the Coif, agreed to be a consultant to assist in preparing the application and he ultimately encouraged the school to submit it in the fall of 1987, after the conclusion of the accreditation process. Monk thought the time was right in light of the faculty's increased scholarly activities and the improvement in the credentials of the entering class the reduction in enrollment was expected to bring. He surely was motivated also by the opportunity Coif membership would have given to end his deanship on a high note. However, the review committee concluded the application was premature. It expressed concern about inadequate space in the library, about whether the school over the long term could attract sufficient numbers of high credentialed students, and about the extent to which the faculty still published in local journals rather than in national journals. The faculty concluded the first two concerns could be satisfied in the future, by completing the addition and by more vigorous student recruitment and fundraising for scholarships. However, the faculty debated whether it wanted to satisfy the third concern, fearing it would require abandonment of the school's traditional role in the local legal community and change the character of the institution. There was agreement, at least, that where the topic of faculty scholarship permitted it to be published either locally or nationally, national publication was preferable.

LITIGATION

During the last half of Monk's deanship, the Law School administration and in varying degrees the entire faculty were distracted by the need to defend five lawsuits that were brought against the school. By 1983, Fred Phelps and four of his children had graduated from the Law School and a fifth child was in school and would graduate in 1985. Three more Phelps children applied for admission to the fall 1983 class. Two of these applicants were denied admission and the third was placed on a waiting list. The three applicants filed suit against the University and four individual defendants, President Green, Dean Monk, Associate Dean Rich, and the University's Affirmative Action Director Carol Vogel. United States District Judge Frank Theis later summarized plaintiffs' contention as being "that they were discriminatorily denied admission to the Washburn University School of Law in retaliation for their association with civil rights work, their association with the law firm of Phelps Chartered, and their association with Fred W. Phelps, Sr."[834] When the one plaintiff who had been placed on the waiting list was not admitted from that list, a second lawsuit was brought by that plaintiff, claiming "that he was retaliated against for having filed the previous lawsuit."[835] Discovery in the cases predictably was extensive and time consuming. All three plaintiffs applied again for admission to the fall 1984 class. The one applicant who had been wait listed the previous year was admitted. Applications of the other two plaintiffs again were denied and they filed a new lawsuit. Theories in this case included claims of reverse discrimination and that rejection of their applications was in retaliation for their having brought the prior suit.[836] This case was assigned to Judge Wesley

---

834. *Phelps v. Washburn Univ. of Topeka*, 634 F. Supp. 556 (D. Kan. 1986).
835. *Id.*
836. 2 *lawsuits against WU dismissed*, TOPEKA CAP.-J., Feb. 12, 1986, at 8.

Brown. Those plaintiffs subsequently brought yet another action, this one assigned to Judge Dale Saffels, claiming their rights were violated when, after the third suit was filed, they were denied an opportunity to pursue their claims through the University's grievance procedure. These suits continued even after the two plaintiffs were admitted at Oklahoma City University Law School.[837]

In February 1986, Judge Theis granted summary judgment to the University and the individual defendants in the first two cases. He wrote:

> Plaintiffs have failed to controvert the objective evidence...[W]hen the objective evidence is viewed from the perspective that the Washburn admissions committee used for all applicants, it overwhelmingly demonstrates that the plaintiffs simply were not qualified for admission to the law school.[838]

With respect to claims of bias on the part of admission committee members Rich, Easley, Smith, Griffin, and Ahrens, and two student members, the court "carefully examined the circumstances of the transactions to see if the plaintiffs can draw any reasonable inferences that panel members have negative sentiments because of the Phelps participation in civil rights activities."[839] The court reviewed the record and concluded:

> In sum, the evidence is not susceptible to the attributions plaintiffs place upon it . . . . Indeed, the Court finds it remarkable that many of the quoted passages attest to the strong civil rights interests of the individual committee members. Furthermore, there is simply no evidence that any anti-Phelps sentiment affected the evaluated procedure. No inferences can be drawn from the evidence that individual members of the committee denied the plaintiffs admission to law school because of their civil rights activities.[840]

Furthermore, the court concluded that plaintiffs' vicarious minority theory failed to state a cause of action "because the Phelps are not a protected group under section 1981."

---

837. *Id.*
838. *Phelps v. Washburn Univ. of Topeka*, 634 F. Supp. 556 (D. Kan. 1986).
839. *Id.*
840. *Id.*

While the Phelps claim that the admissions committee denied them admission in retaliation for their civil rights activities, the Court must examine the structure of this argument in somewhat more depth. The plaintiffs assert the following tautology: the plaintiffs' father and the family's law firm, Phelps-Chartered, are associated with blacks and the cause of civil rights; the plaintiffs in turn associate with their father and the law firm; therefore, plaintiffs are so associated with blacks and civil rights as to have standing to sue under section 1981. In short, the plaintiffs explain that "Phelps equals Black," dk. no. 41, p. 20, and claim that they "should be accorded the benefit of minority status protection."

Parenthetically, the Court would note that these same plaintiffs have filed a separate suit, Phelps v. Washburn University of Topeka, Civil Action No. 84-4199, in which they accuse the same defendants of reverse discrimination. In Case No. 84-4199 the Phelps argue that they have been denied admission to the law school because of the affirmative action treatment given to black applicants. The Court finds it passing strange that in the present case that plaintiffs claim to be the victims of discrimination because they are considered black, while in Case No. 84-4199 the same plaintiffs claim to be the victims of discrimination from the same set of circumstances because they are white.

... [T]he Court has discovered no cases in which a party has attempted to claim protected status under section 1981 because the party has associated with another party who has associated with a protected class.[841]

Judge Theis also granted summary judgment in the second suit, regarding the waiting list. Because the yield of acceptances of offers of admission for the fall of 1983 exceeded the target size of the class, no students were admitted from the waiting list.

Judge Theis later granted the University's motion for an award of attorney fees and costs. The local newspaper reported on the award and the plaintiffs' plans to appeal it:

In his order dismissing the suits and awarding the fees, Theis said the Phelpses should pay for defense of the suits because of the "frivolous"

---

841. *Id.*

and "groundless" nature of the claims. Evidence presented to support the Phelpses' claims, Theis said, was "rife with speculation, innuendo and hearsay."

"The very filing of these suits was utterly unreasonable," Theis wrote.

An award of attorneys' fees against a plaintiff in a civil action is reserved by judges as a sanction against the unnecessary filing of lawsuits, Theis said.[842]

The same article reported:

Marge Phelps said she also thought it was noteworthy that Washburn rejected the advice of the insurance carrier responsible for the university's defense in the remaining two lawsuits and rejected a settlement offer pitched by the Phelpses once the three younger Phelpses had been admitted to law schools.

The settlement would not have required Washburn to pay the Phelpses money, she said, but would have involved a 'mutual walk' agreement by which the Phelpses would not pursue their claims and the university would not ask for attorneys' fees. According to an affidavit supplied by a Washburn faculty member and filed in the cases, when Washburn rejected the settlement agreement, the insurance carrier withdrew its defense.

"Now tax money is paying for these (cases) because they (Washburn) wanted to rub our faces in it," Marge Phelps said.[843]

The next day's newspaper printed Monk's response:

Monk…disputed statements by Marge Phelps that the university's insurance carrier had withdrawn from defending the law school in the suits because Washburn had rejected a cost-free settlement. Phelps said the law school, and hence the taxpayers, were now paying for the law school's defense.

Monk said the law school was represented in the lawsuits by legal counsel, provided by two insurance carriers.

---

842. *Phelps firm to appeal award of fees to WU,* TOPEKA CAP.-J., Aug. 21, 1986.
843. *Id.*

"One insurance carrier has specifically said to us that we should pursue attorney fees," Monk said. "That is the best way to deter frivolous lawsuits of this type."[844]

On the same day the first of these stories appeared in August 1986, Judge Brown granted summary judgment to the University in the third case.[845] By that time, Judge Saffels had already granted motions to dismiss most of the claims in the fourth case.[846] In December, the Phelps' appeal of the award of attorney fees was dismissed for lack of appellate jurisdiction since there was no final, appealable order until the amount of fees awarded was determined.[847] Ultimately, the matter was settled by agreement and by the delivery to the University of twelve cashier's checks in the amount of $1,000 each which did not bear the name "Phelps" as remitter.

Judge Theis' orders led to high hopes that the distraction and disruption of litigation soon would be over. Those hopes were quickly dashed. On September 2, Clinic Director Bill Piatt, an Hispanic-American, filed suit against the University. The local newspaper described the suit as

> charging that he had been discriminated against on the basis of his race and in retaliation for his defense of racial minorities and the Phelps family of attorneys....

> In the lawsuit, which was filed on his behalf by the Phelps attorneys, Piatt claims that the law school retaliated against him after he provided affidavits to the Phelpses supporting their positions in other lawsuits against the law school.[848]

The article included Dean Monk's response to the suit and his defense of the school's affirmative action program:

> "We have a higher percentage of minority faculty and students than most law schools in this region," Monk said....

---

844. *WU law dean says lawsuit unfounded*, TOPEKA CAP.-J., Aug. 22, 1986.

845. *Judge dismisses Phelps lawsuit*, TOPEKA CAP.-J., Aug. 26, 1986.

846. *Phelps v. Washburn Univ. of Topeka*, 632 F. Supp. 455 (D. Kan. 1986).

847. *Phelps v. Washburn Univ. of Topeka*, 807 F.2d 153 (10th Cir. 1986).

848. *Faculty member files suit against Washburn law school*, TOPEKA CAP.-J., Sept. 3, 1986, at 28.

"I'm very saddened that Bill feels the way he does," Monk said. "The absurdity of the claim is revealed when he admits in the complaint that he has always received the highest salary increase awarded to any faculty member."[849]

Piatt left the faculty at the end of academic year 1986–87 and became a visiting professor at Southern Illinois University. Washburn would not be the only law school at which Piatt would become embroiled in controversy or against which he would assert a claim of discrimination.[850]

FREE SPEECH

The four years of litigation were a distraction not just for faculty and administrators but also for students, particularly the last year when all students read the accusations and responses in the newspaper and some had daily contact with participants on both sides of the Piatt litigation. Society's struggles with race and gender issues, and soon with sexual orientation, would have sparked debates and divided students anyway, but the litigation made issues of race and discrimination particularly sensitive by putting a spotlight on the Law School's extensive affirmative action program and support for minority students. The data used to refute claims in litigation that the Law School's affirmative action efforts did not go far enough could be used by those who opposed affirmative action to argue those efforts went too far. The title of the 1987 Roast, "No Nerve Too Raw," unwittingly may have captured it: nerves were raw.

In January 1987, a new student paper, the *Washburn Law Digest*, replaced *Case and Cane*, and with Sean Scally '88 as editor it made investigative reporting

849. *Id.*

850. Carlos Guerra, *Departure of controversial law dean is welcomed in some quarters*, SAN ANTONIO EXPRESS-NEWS, Oct. 30, 2006; Melissa Ludwig, *The case against Bill Piatt*, SAN ANTONIO EXPRESS-NEWS, Nov. 12, 2006. After Piatt's contract as Dean of St. Mary's Law School in San Antonio was not renewed, he filed a complaint with the EEOC alleging discrimination, resulting in a 2007 settlement. Piatt's spouse Rosanne also filed a complaint against the school with EEOC after her non-tenure-track contract was not renewed at the end of the 2008–09 academic year. Mary Alice Robbins, *The Final Exam*, TEXAS LAWYER, Apr. 27, 2009, found at http://www.law.com/jsp/tx/PubArticleTX.jsp?id=1202430263848.

its mission. A school whose dean has a specialty in First Amendment media law might be expected to have an active student press and the new publication stirred the pot. Its lead story about the lawsuit filed by Professor Piatt gave the attorneys for the parties equal time to air their positions, providing additional fodder for discussion among students. According to the paper, Piatt's lawyer "suggested 'a scenario which is not far from the truth. Let's say in the last five years, there have been 100 white students admitted (to WU) per year, and twenty minority students. But two minority students graduated while ninety-five of the whites have graduated which gives you 95% graduation rate for whites and 10% for the minorities.'"[851] It also quoted Associate Dean Reynolds' response "that she was 'deeply disturbed that anyone would make a false allegation of this sort. Reactions to such false statements could be extremely damaging to minority students at WU.'"[852]

That same month, rumors circulated in the student body that the Black Law Students Association had amended its constitution to limit voting rights and eligibility to hold office to members who were black. An "underground" second newspaper, *Justin Case*, written and published privately by two students, printed an article entitled "How Do You Spell Discrimination?," purportedly written by a member of an unnamed student organization who wanted to be more involved. "If only I could be an officer . . . any officer. . . but. . . unfortunately members of my race can't be officers in this club," the story said, "Oh, I forgot to tell you what club I belong to. . . YOU GUESS!" Several BLSA members, already feeling under siege in the affirmative action debate, complained. Twenty-three faculty members signed "An Open Letter to the Washburn Law School Community" seeking to dispel any perception by minority students that there was a hostile environment at Washburn:

> We believe the vast majority of students in this school are in agreement with the value of a diverse student body, and abhor bigotry in any form. Most recently, however, statements have been published in <u>Justin Case</u> which might variously be read as open bigotry, subconscious racism, or simply misguided attempts at humor. Whatever the intent, such statements have the invariable effect of causing undeserved pain.

---

851. *WU Lawsuit Over Discrimination of Minorities, Freedom of Speech*, washburn law digest 1, 4 (Jan. 26, 1987).

852. *Id.*

We recognize and defend the right of every individual to his or her opinion on any subject, and to public expression of that opinion. We also recognize that it is not appropriate for faculty members to impose their views on students. We believe, however, that bigotry and intolerance should have died long ago.

We hope students who believe as we do will make that view clear to fellow students who may have been 'targets' of the statements in Justin Case. They should know that they are not only welcome here, but wanted—as respected members of this law school community.

If faculty members thought their open letter would quiet the controversy, they were wrong. The editors of *Justin Case* promptly issued a response, purporting not to disagree that a concerted effort to promote diversity "is the appropriate course for the school to take," but defending the factual accuracy of their claim about the amendment to BLSA's constitution and contending that the amendment violated the University's policy that registered organizations could not engage in discrimination. The March issue of the mainstream newspaper, *Washburn Law Digest*, devoted five pages to the controversy, reporting divergent views about the validity of the amendment and the propriety of allocating student activity fees to a student organization with such a policy. It provided a forum for a student's claim that the faculty's letter was "an effort to 'chill' the freedom of speech of those individuals whose political and philosophical persuasions are different from those of the administration." The student decried "strife, contention and intimidation" as producing "an atmosphere incompatible with academic pursuits. I hope that the open letter to the Washburn law school community was signed by most of the faculty members as a result of a misguided attempt to support admirable principles as opposed to a 'subconscious totalitarianism' which is becoming increasingly prevalent among the law school administration."[853] BLSA's president was quoted as saying he "just wished this thing would die."

All of a sudden, it seemed that every hot button issue of the day aroused students. The same issue of the *Digest* reported that "the emergence of" a bulletin board on the lower level for a new student group, the Washburn

---

853. *See* WASHBURN LAW DIGEST (Mar. 1987), which also reprinted in full the JUSTIN CASE article, the Open Letter, and the editors' response.

Law School Lesbian and Gay Information Network, had "stimulated several responses" because, although it had not sought funding from WSBA, it had been allowed to use a spare bulletin board without charge and to keep confidential the membership list it filed when it registered with the Law School administration. The next issue of *Washburn Law Digest* reported there was a division of opinion about whether WSBA's allocation of $30 from the activity fee to Christian Legal Society was improper because of the establishment clause of the First Amendment. It also reported claims that 200–300 copies of the prior issue were found in a trash can in a women's bathroom.

With new editors the next academic year, an abbreviated *Washburn Law Digest*, like the Law School itself, was calmer and focused more on good news.

MONK

Carl Monk was a master strategist who routinely brainstormed issues with a kitchen cabinet of faculty and Foundation President Gerald Goodell before selecting the best way to proceed. When I succeeded him as Dean, I described his "good judgment in handling difficult situations and his tenacity as an advocate for the law school, within the university and beyond."[854] He had a gift for building consensus. He frequently did so before faculty meetings at which issues important to him were on the agenda by going from faculty door to faculty door. By the time the meeting was held, irreverent faculty expected him to appear wearing an engineer's hat and addressed him as "Casey Jones."

Monk never met Professor Swede Larson but they were from the same stock, sharing a propensity to use earthy language. A faculty member once asked Monk's Administrative Assistant Diane Milligan if Monk cursed as much around the office as he did outside it. She responded that she hadn't heard cursing like that since the last time she helped wallpaper a ceiling. Monk was an avid baseball fan and often organized faculty outings to Kansas City Royals games. He delighted in berating umpires for perceived bad calls and Monk's piercing voice could be heard throughout Royals Stadium. Monk took special pride at one game when an especially "creative" yell caused a normally stoic umpire at first base to turn around and look at him. Monk and other faculty

---

854. James M. Concannon, *From the Dean's Desk*, 27 THE CIRCUIT RIDER 3 (Fall 1988).

members occasionally joined students when the WSBA chartered a bus to go to a Royals game. They joined a large group of students one year for a road trip immediately after the last final exam in the spring. Beer flowed freely and the post-finals celebration became rowdier and rowdier. Another law student attended the game with his father, a minister, and sat about fifteen rows behind the WSBA group. After a particularly loud outburst by a member of the group, the father asked his son, "What would the Dean of the Law School think of such conduct?" The son replied, "Dad, that IS the Dean of the Law School."

Monk was intense but also could take a joke. A rash of thefts from the library led him to advise the faculty by memorandum in February 1981 that locks might be changed, with the result that faculty would be unable to access the library when the building was closed. Professors Rasor and Concannon promptly distributed a twelve-step proposal from a self-appointed Committee to Reassess Access Procedure (C.R.A.P.). Proposed steps included institution of a "buddy system...under which no faculty member is allowed to enter the building alone after hours," keeping blackboard chalk in the vault, that "the doorway to the audio-visual room should be cemented shut," and even that "answer keys should be prohibited." A later memorandum from the Dean, prompted by the same security concerns, suggested faculty members would need to place their waste baskets outside their offices each evening. This prompted distribution of a report from the Committee to Reduce Unwanted Debris (C.R.U.D.).

Monk always was a popular teacher. Mike Manning's '77 first day as a law student was Monk's first day as a teacher. Having watched the movie "Paper Chase" the night before, Manning worried as he saw "this diminutive 'rookie' professor strut to the platform of Civil Procedure...a Wall Street refugee with a Napolean complex and a rural Oklahoma twang."[855] It was not long, however, before he realized he had a "remarkable teacher." Nancy Scherer '77 was in the same class. She later recalled:

> [T]here was a lot of humor in his classroom, initiated by very witty and somewhat irreverent class members who recognized that Dean Monk was willing to engage us at a personal level, even when he was the object of the humor. The class celebrated the birth of his first child by presenting him with a petition alleging long-arm jurisdiction in Kansas, arising

---

855. *Reflections on Dean Monks' Years at Washburn*, 27 THE CIRCUIT RIDER 8, 9 (Summer 1988).

from the tortious out-of-state conception of his child. He accepted the petition with grace, retorting that he had underestimated our comprehension of his lectures on in personam jurisdiction.[856]

Monk considered leaving the deanship after seven years. It was at the suggestion of Vice President and Provost Robert Haywood that he instead took a one-semester sabbatical in hopes of "avoiding administrative burnout."[857] Associate Dean Bill Rich served as Acting Dean in Monk's absence during the fall semester of 1985. The sabbatical succeeded in extending Monk's term an additional two and one-half years. However, in December 1986, Monk announced he would resign as Dean on June 30, 1998, and return to full-time teaching. He timed the announcement to give the school the chance to plan during the spring for an effective search for his successor that could be conducted as soon as classes started in the fall. At the time, Monk said, "The accomplishment of which I am proudest is the quality and diversity of the faculty. They graduated from many different schools. Over half were hired during my time as dean."[858] Former students and other alumni understood what he had accomplished. As Brad Haddock '80 wrote, "Under his leadership, Washburn School of Law has effectively overcome its image as a state-oriented law school and has gained a continually improving reputation as an outstanding regional, and perhaps national institution."[859] Over the next seventeen months, alumni donated $11,000 to create the Dean Carl C. Monk Law Scholarship Fund. Dick Hite '53 announced its creation at the 1988 KBA meeting during the final Washburn alumni luncheon of Monk's deanship.

The Board of Regents granted Monk the title Distinguished Professor of Law and awarded him a sabbatical for the fall of 1988. During the 1987–88 academic year, he was offered the deanship at another law school but ultimately turned it down. However, he did accept the invitation of Betsy Levin, Executive Director of the AALS, and long-time Washburn friend Richard Huber, now President of the AALS, to serve a two-year term as Deputy Director in the Association's Washington D.C. office. "'Carl has a wonderful ability to delegate and has experience on AALS committees,' Huber said. 'With his high energy and persistence,

---

856. *Id.* at 8.

857. CASE AND CANE, Mar. 1986.

858. *Wagnon, Monk resign positions*, 27 WASHBURN REV. 5, Feb. 6, 1987.

859. *Reflections on Dean Monk's Years at Washburn, supra* note 856.

he is exactly the right person at the right time for this position.'"[860] The follow-ing year, he elected to spend his deferred sabbatical at the University of Hawaii William S. Richardson School of Law and stayed there the second semester as a Visiting Professor. He returned to full-time teaching at Washburn in 1991–92, but only for one year. He was selected to succeed Betsy Levin as Executive Di-rector of the AALS the following year. Monk became only the fifth person to hold the position, the others coming from the faculties at Texas, Duke, UCLA and Colorado. When he announced he would resign at the conclusion of his sixteenth year in that position, his term far exceeded that of any other Execu-tive Director. Late in his term, he spearheaded an AALS initiative to create the International Association of Law Schools and served as its first President. He earned praise for his "visionary leadership," and for "his inclusive approach, his thoroughness and careful consideration of the issues facing legal education, his integrity, his kindness to and his light touch with his colleagues in legal education, and his wise counsel."[861] Monk remained a member of the Washburn faculty, on leave of absence, throughout his years as Executive Director, probably setting the record for the longest "leave" in the history of legal education. University policy ordinarily limits leaves of absence to two years but the Regents made an exception in Monk's case because he was serving a national organization of which a University department was a member. Making an exception was wise since Monk's leadership role in legal education has enhanced Washburn's vis-ibility nationally. Monk returned to teach at Washburn for one last year during academic year 2009–10. "I love teaching and being around students," he wrote in his resignation letter to the AALS Executive Committee, "and I want to have that opportunity again before I retire."[862] After retiring at Washburn, he was ap-pointed as Visiting Professor at American University, near his home in Virginia.

THE LONGEST SERVING FACULTY MEMBER

Coinciding with Monk's departure as Dean, Professor Ahrens retired, forty years after joining the Washburn faculty. He taught more years at Washburn than

---

860. *Dean Monk Appointed As New AALS Deputy Director*, 27 THE CIRCUIT RIDER 17 (Summer 1988).

861. Email from Nancy Rogers, AALS President, to the AALS listserv (May 24, 2007).

862. *Id.*

81. James R. Ahrens, Professor 1948–1988

anyone else. The faculty organized a dinner to express its appreciation to both Ahrens and Monk. Ahrens' children did more, arranging for the Topeka High School band to lead a parade through the campus for the Professor and his wife Marge. One daughter held a sign, "40 Years In Ahrens' Wilderness." Mayor Doug Wright '73 proclaimed the day "Professor James R. Ahrens Day" in Topeka.

Ahrens' first trip in retirement was a visit to Pakistan, where he spent his first eighteen years while his father worked as a missionary. By remarkable coincidence, Ahrens lived in a home in Lahore during that period which was only blocks away from the home where, years later, Professor Ali Khan grew up.

The stories about Ahrens are legendary. Jan Leuenberger '61 concluded that when he graduated, "to explain a tort, I would need to wave my arms in the air, that this was some type of ritual of reverence for the *Palsgraf* case."[863] Though

863. Jan W. Leuenberger, Class Notes, Washburn School of Law Alumni Weekend, Aug. 25–26, 1995.

he taught large, required classes in Torts and Constitutional Law, one year he gave no A's in Constitutional Law, rejecting the protest of one person who tied for top paper, Linda Elrod '72, that she should have received an A. Another year, Ahrens failed to note correctly the date he was to give an exam. He received a call at home from the Dean's office, telling him that his students were in the classroom waiting to take the test. He had not prepared the exam yet but began to think of questions as he drove to the Law School. He walked into the room, wrote out the first question on the blackboard, told students to start writing answers to that question, and went to his office to draft the remaining questions for the test. In the late 1970s, students in the Torts classes taught at the same time by Ahrens and Professor Bartlett conspired to switch classrooms. When Ahrens arrived at his classroom and started to teach, he looked at the strange assemblage quizzically. To his credit, he figured out what the students had done more quickly than Bartlett, who proceeded with his lecture and tried to call on students using his regular seating chart. Ahrens had to break the news to Bartlett when he arrived and offered to trade classrooms for the day.

Few people demonstrated greater commitment to the school than Professor Ahrens. Until the size of the graduating classes became too large, Ahrens and his first wife Geri annually hosted a brunch at their home for graduating seniors. They regularly attended student social functions and dances. Throughout his lengthy retirement, he regularly has attended class reunions of his former students and other Law School events and was an active participant in discussions at Ahrens Chair in Tort Law Seminars.

8

THE CONCANNON YEARS
(1988–2001)

The search for Carl Monk's successor had unexpected twists. Before it even began, Washburn President John Green announced his resignation, effective June 30, 1988, the same day Monk planned to step down. Soon, long-time University Provost Robert Haywood announced he would retire then too. Concurrent searches to fill these positions complicated the dean search.

During the final exam period in May 1987, the faculty held a half-day retreat to discuss the search. There was substantial consensus that having the fresh perspective of an outside dean was desirable. In the fall, three external candidates interviewed on campus. The faculty found only one of them acceptable and in mid-December voted to recommend that an offer be extended to him. That candidate was the same Steve Smith who had been offered the position in 1978 but declined it. Smith had remained on the faculty at Louisville. When he applied for the Washburn position for the second time, he was on leave serving as the first Deputy Director of the Association of American Law Schools.

Rarely does one have greater leverage to obtain commitments essential for a school to make significant progress than when an offer to be the dean has been extended but not yet accepted. Smith's assessment was that, "No one could be more effective than Carl Monk has been in pressing the needs of the law school within the Washburn structure. And yet, the law school now finds itself at a dangerously low level of financial support."[864] During negotiations that extended for

---

864. Letter from Steven R. Smith to Thomas E. Wright, Chair (Apr. 4, 1988).

several months, Smith developed a list of "benchmark" schools with which he wanted Washburn to be compared. He sought commitments from the Board of Regents that the Law School initially would reach national averages, then reach benchmark school averages, in faculty salaries, library resources, and research support. The board balked, in part because it was unwilling to tie the hands of a new president who had not yet been named. Soon after Dr. John M. Duggan was selected in March to be President, Smith met with him. Duggan expressed strong support for the Law School as the "jewel in the crown" of the University, a phrase Monk used repeatedly as a member of the presidential search committee, but was unwilling to make specific commitments until he arrived on campus and assessed the situation University-wide. The Board of Regents, of course, backed Duggan's decision. On April 4, Smith sent a letter declining the Board's offer. He expressed disappointment but still attempted to help the school:

> Throughout the search I have been very impressed by the potential the law school has....However, potential does not last forever: it is either realized or lost....This is an instance in which a substantial delay to study the situation could "plan to death" the existing potential.[865]

Later that spring, Smith accepted the deanship at Cleveland-Marshall College of Law at Cleveland State University, a position he held for eight years before becoming Dean at California Western School of Law in San Diego in 1996.

There was no other acceptable external candidate and it was too late in the academic year to reopen the search nationally. Faculty members were unsettled by the uncertainty about where we would turn next. Monk already had accepted an offer to succeed Steve Smith as Deputy Director of the AALS, so he could not extend his term another year even if he had been willing to do so. Naming a caretaker Interim Dean for a year while another search was conducted was undesirable. There was a critical need to commence fundraising for the library addition, and the school needed a credible advocate who could establish an effective working relationship with the incoming president, who had no previous experience at a university with a law school. At the end of the week Smith's rejection letter arrived, Associate Dean Sheila Reynolds, a member of the search committee, came to my office and asked if I would be willing to apply for the position.

---

865. *Id.*

82. James M. Concannon, Dean 1988–2001,
Professor 1973–present

I had never wanted to be Dean. I enjoyed the classroom and the opportunities I had to participate in bar activities and public affairs. I had managed political campaigns and had experience raising money for them, but I did not think I would enjoy the parts of administration involving personnel and hassles with university bureaucracy. When the search started, I had been as adamant as any faculty member that it was time to hire from the outside.[866] By

866. Undated 1987 memorandum from Jim Concannon to Allen Easley, in response to the Faculty Development Committee's request for input on the impending Dean search, "Ten Tips on Choosing a New Dean Who Will Be Good for the School (or at Least Save Us from Litigation)." I argued that a "dean able to provide national perspective on legal education would help us" and that hiring a person of national stature would benefit us both nationally, from the endorsement our ability to do so would provide, and locally "when final compromises are made on the bill to admit Washburn to the state system."

April, however, our options were limited. After talking with Carl and thinking about it over the weekend, I told Sheila I was willing to do it, provided she agreed to remain as Associate Dean. I went to faculty members' offices to see what they thought of the idea.

My application was put on a fast track. The search committee hastily arranged for a formal interview and, by April 19, I had lunch with alumni representatives on the committee. A presentation to the faculty followed. Incoming President Duggan and I met on one of his visits to Topeka. Soon, there was a recommendation to the Board of Regents that I be named Dean. The Board's regular procedures would have placed the issue on the Board's June agenda. However, I was leaving May 20 to teach in our summer program in London and would not return until June 30. Thus, the issue needed to be resolved before I left. The Board scheduled a two-hour executive session for an interview at the conclusion of its regular agenda on May 11.

The Board understandably was nervous about the forced choice it was presented and about having only an internal candidate after the virtue of hiring an external candidate had been extolled throughout the search. I was nervous too, knowing that a Board that was unwilling to make commitments for additional resources to its preferred external candidate was not going to make those commitments to a default internal candidate a month later. Yet, I could not permit the Board to believe that, by hiring internally, it could avoid having to address the Law School's resource needs. Thus, five days before the interview, I sent the Regents a letter expressing my full agreement with the goals Steve Smith had set. I acknowledged that hiring a new president had made Smith's deadline for committing to meet those goals unrealistic but added, "Nevertheless, any candidate for Dean would share Steve Smith's reluctance to accept the position without commitments being made to the law school. I want to be Dean only if the entire University is committed to continuing the progress the law school has made."[867] I expressly asked that the Board endorse the preliminary plan for the law library addition that was on its May 11 agenda, which Dean Monk was not certain would be approved.

The University's on-again, off-again approach to state affiliation was on again, and my letter firmly expressed the belief that "we must not enter the fight for state affiliation without having faculty salaries and other basic support for the

---

867. Letter from James M. Concannon to Thomas E. Wright, Chair (May 6, 1988).

law school at least at parity with the KU Law School. To do so would place at risk the role of the law school, not only in Kansas but also nationally." I pledged that if selected as Dean I "would develop a plan for the next three to five years that recognizes the distinctive character of professional education."

Two days after the Board meeting, I attended my first alumni event as Dean-designate, the Class of 1938 reunion luncheon. Because I did not want to exhibit jet lag on my first day as Dean and because I previously had committed to be co-coordinator with Mike Barbara in July for the Kansas Bar Association's annual eight-day trial advocacy institute, I persuaded Monk to continue in the job through the normally slow month of July, so I could start fresh August 1.

In hindsight, there were more reasons to choose an internal candidate than I realized when the search for Monk's successor commenced. The Law School needed to raise $1.25 million for the library addition in approximately eighteen months. An external dean would have required that long or longer to become sufficiently acquainted with alums to ask for their help comfortably and effectively. By contrast, after teaching large, required classes for more than fifteen years, I had taught at least 2,700 of what we determined to be 4,300 living alums. In addition, I already was well acquainted with many graduates from earlier years. Moreover, Steve Smith did not view the new dean's primary responsibility as being a fundraiser. He expected the University Development Office to do most of the work, but that office lacked the infrastructure to accomplish the task. My view, to the contrary, was that the dean had to be the principal fundraiser and that fundraising should be controlled by the law school, not the central university. Further, as I joked with the Regents during my interview, after asking for money for various political candidates, it would be easy to ask for money for a good cause.

THE LIBRARY ADDITION

At the same May 11 meeting at which I was selected as Dean, the Board of Regents authorized preparation of preliminary concept drawings for the building addition and committed itself to issue $2.5 million of bonds to cover two-thirds of the estimated $3.75 million cost of construction. The University then was authorized to levy property taxes in Topeka for three distinct purposes: operations, fringe benefits, and capital improvements. Proceeds of the latter levy backed issuance of the bonds.

Architect Phil Coolidge warned that construction costs could be as high as $100 per square foot, compared to $21 per square foot when his firm designed the building twenty years earlier, after the tornado. The proposal to the Board recommended an addition occupying 32,000 square feet. The building committee's charge had been to meet the Law School's space requirements for the next twenty years. The space recommended was less than the committee determined was needed, but it was thought to be as much as the Regents would approve at a point when fundraising had not begun. The camel's nose was under the tent, however. Professor Duncan, as chair of the building committee, visited nine law libraries during the summer of 1988 to make comparisons. The committee worked with Coolidge to assure the plan included essential space, so the preliminary concept drawings presented for Board approval in November called for a larger addition of 37,227 square feet. The University's Vice President for Planning, David Monical, and Treasurer Gene Mosiman met with the building committee throughout the process and supported the expanded project. A statutory cap on the mill levy for capital improvements limited public funding to the $2.5 million approved in May. The increase in space raised the estimated cost to $4 million. Because the actual cost could not be known until the project was put out for bids, it could not be known with certainty how much private fundraising would be required, and there was some anxiety that even if we met our fundraising target it might turn out not to be enough. Whatever the difference, the cash basis law meant it would have to be raised through contributions and pledges before groundbreaking could occur.

The number of alums making annual gifts to the Law School still was small. However, alums who did not give regularly had responded to the post-tornado and 1977 building campaigns, with many contributing their fair shares but with few making large gifts. We sought to use fundraising for the library addition to create a culture of larger gifts and regular gifts. For the year-end solicitation in 1988, we drafted a special letter for non-donors, asking them to designate their "first gift to the annual fund" for the library addition. Knowing that people respond better to personal solicitations than form ones, I began a practice that I continued throughout my deanship of personally signing every fundraising letter and of adding personal notes to former students and alums I knew. Ultimately, more than 750 alums, one of every six, contributed to the building campaign.

Face-to-face solicitations started in earnest as well. President Duggan and I made several visits together during his first months on campus. John Corkhill '48 agreed to chair an alumni steering committee and was a tireless volunteer solicitor. During my first year as Dean, I traveled to fourteen states and more than forty Kansas cities, many of them more than once, asking for contributions. Our Development Director Sandy Vogel organized those trips so tightly that I often met with alums in seven or eight different offices in a single day. Those visits proved to be important not merely to meet the immediate goal of the library campaign but also to rekindle long-term interest in supporting the school by alums who had been visited rarely before, if at all.

Nevertheless, the urgent need to meet the fundraising goal could be met only by major gifts. Ultimately, just twenty-six gifts of $10,000 or more accounted for $950,000, approximately two-thirds of the total raised. Two of the largest gifts were unrestricted estate gifts from non-alums that we allocated to the addition. Alums had vital roles in both gifts. Dorothy Palmquist's bequest of $384,397 still ranks among the largest gifts the school has received. She attended Washburn as an undergraduate for two years before completing her degree at Kansas State in 1926. She and her husband owned a thriving metal-working business in Topeka which had sales offices in several states. She lived just south of the Law School at 1875 MacVicar. Mrs. Palmquist "had left money to Kansas State and she wanted to be fair to Washburn by leaving money to it as well."[868] Her attorney and Law School Foundation President Gerald Goodell '58 suggested the Law School was a worthy recipient of her Washburn gift. The main floor of the Law Library is named in honor of Mrs. Palmquist.

The second estate gift, of more than $69,000, was made by Alma H. Gavitt. She told her lawyer, former Acting Dean Howard Jones '28, that she wanted both to honor the memory of her late husband, C.S. Gavitt, and to leave behind something that would be lasting and worthwhile to the community. Jones encouraged the gift to the Law School and today the federal taxation area of the Law Library is named in honor of the Gavitts.

Other alums who were in-house counsel worked from the inside to obtain major gifts from their corporations. For example, many Washburn graduates had held significant positions with Southwestern Bell Telephone Company

---

868. Conversation with Mrs. Palmquist's friend, Eugene VanVranken, as reported by Gerald Goodell.

and its predecessor, AT&T. At the time, Jack Lorenz '59 was general counsel of Bell Publications, Inc., and Duke Dupre '73 was about to become general counsel of Southwestern Bell in Texas. They worked with Larry Dimmitt '68 and other Washburn graduates in the Kansas corporate office. The result was an $80,000 contribution to underwrite the thirty-station Southwestern Bell Computer Lab that helped to launch the Law School's leadership in legal information technology over the next decade.

Brad Haddock '80 similarly mobilized Washburn graduates who comprised half of the thirty attorneys in the corporate legal department at Koch Industries, Inc. The $10,000 gift that resulted set the stage for a later major gift for an endowed scholarship. Corporations in Topeka contributed too, both because their Washburn lawyers urged them to do so and also because they wanted to support their local University, which made the library addition its top fundraising priority. Merchants National Bank, KPL Gas Service Company, and Hallmark Cards each gave $25,000, Bank IV of Topeka gave $20,000, Stauffer Communications gave $15,000, and Security Benefit Group, Capital City Bank and Trust, and AmVestors Financial Corporation each gave $10,000.

Three alumni personally made gifts of $50,000. T.M. (Tim) Murrell '49, Chairman of AmVestors Financial Corporation, was the first to do so, in the fall of 1988, giving critical momentum to the campaign. Edwin Linquist '50, Chairman of Linquist and Craig Resorts and Hotels, already had written his check before he arrived for lunch in the Dean's office early in the spring of 1989. His son Ed, Jr. '89 and daughter-in-law Becky '89 were then 3Ls completing their final semesters and knew first-hand how crowded conditions were. Arthur G. Johnson, Jr. '49, retired Clerk of the United States District Court of Kansas, made his contribution shortly thereafter, appropriately to name the Government Documents Area in the addition. The Reference Area in the Library is named in recognition of the Linquist gift and the Murrell gift is recognized in the entry foyer with a bronze sculpture by Glenna Goodacre, sculptor of the Vietnam Women's Memorial.

Plans for the addition included a room to house special collections and memorabilia reflecting Kansas legal history. Kent P. Smith '66, a former Law Clerk to Judge Delmas C. Hill '29, committed $25,000 to name it the Delmas C. Hill Kansas Room. I was able to tell Judge Hill about the gift and our plans for the Kansas Room before his death in December 1989.

83. The 1992 addition completed the current law building

By mid-July 1989, contributions and pledges totaled $1,058,000. The University persuaded the 1989 Kansas Legislature to increase the cap on the mill levy that could be used for capital improvements. The principal purpose of the increase was to meet other capital needs of the University but it gave flexibility to go forward with the library addition even if bids came in higher than expected. It meant we could set a firm target of $1.25 million for private fundraising.

As fundraising continued through the end of the year, the building committee and the architect continued to tinker with building plans and ultimately settled on an addition of 33,000 square feet which doubled the size of the library and increased the size of the building by 50%. Kietzman Construction Company of Topeka submitted the low bid of $4.225 million. The bid was approximately $250,000 less than the next lowest bid and it was approved by the Board of Regents at its January 1990 meeting. Site preparation began in March at the southwest corner of the building. A formal groundbreaking ceremony, with 150 donors and friends in attendance, was held on the north lawn on the sunny, but blustery, morning of April 24.

The architect estimated that construction could be completed in time for the fall 1991 semester. The four stories of new space abutting the west wall and two stories abutting the south wall would be completed first. The walls between the addition and the existing building then would be removed and the library would be moved in its entirety into the addition. Then, the original library area and other areas of the building would be renovated. The building project involved much more than the library. The addition included a new 75-person classroom and a 24-person seminar room, both on the lowest floor, replacing the classroom and seminar room on the second floor. That space was used to consolidate in a single area near the Dean's office administrative functions that had been spread throughout the building. It included the Career Services Offices, which had been on the southwest corner of the first floor, the Admissions Office, which was in an uninviting and windowless area in the middle of the second floor, as well as the Development Office. The addition also included new faculty offices, a Faculty Reading Room, new space for the Law Journal, Moot Court, and the Student Bar Association, and, for the first time, a separate room shared by other student organizations. There even was a confined room for smokers that subsequently was converted to a seminar room when the building finally was declared smoke-free.

Of course, classes continued throughout construction and the fact that the addition affected all four floors presented logistics challenges. There was too much jackhammering to do to confine it to times classes were not in session. The noises, one student observed, "are a little unusual, kind of like listening to an orchestra's percussion section without the rest of the orchestra."[869] Arrangements were made to use quiet classrooms elsewhere on campus for final exams. One contingency plan even called for bringing back into service as office space for faculty and student organizations one of the portable buildings that had been part of Law Village after the 1966 tornado. Noise and inconvenience did prompt a number of faculty members to do much of their work at home when they were not teaching classes. Each day seemed to present a new challenge. Diane Milligan, the Dean's Administrative Assistant, described some of the problems: "All day long there's something. In their digging, the construction workers have hit some important pipes and wires out there. We've had the phones go out, water and air conditioner lines have been hit, and of course there's the parking problem."[870] The contractor took over the two rows of

869. *Library Addition Progressing Quickly*, 29 THE CIRCUIT RIDER 4, 5 (Winter 1990).

870. *Id.*

parking closest to the building's south side. Our argument that students still were able to park closer to the building than was possible at most American law schools did not diminish the fervor or frequency of their complaints. Still, students and staff coped with the disruption overwhelmingly with perspective and good humor. "They had to expand, and I'm glad for the implications for the law school," one student commented. "After all, your J.D. is only as good as the reputation of your school."[871]

Even the best laid plans often fail, and the initial timetable failed for two principal reasons. First, renovation of areas located in the original building could not proceed without removal of asbestos from the ceilings. That process proved to be more time-consuming and disruptive than anticipated. Second, the general contractor became insolvent. On a cold Monday morning in January 1991, we arrived at the Law School to find that the contractor's trailers were gone, the tools were gone, and the workers were gone. The contractor could not be found for more than a week. The resulting delay certainly was disruptive. However, matters could have been much worse. The outer walls of the addition had been completed and the new space was fully enclosed. More importantly, pursuant to standard University policy, the project was bonded. The bond was issued by Trinity Insurance Company in Texas. We later learned that Trinity already had decided, due to loss experience in the industry, that the Washburn bond would be the last construction bond it issued. While Trinity could have re-bid some sub-contracts, which would have produced major delay, happily it reaffirmed the sub-contracts, hired a supervisor, and put people back to work. In completing the project, Trinity spent nearly $500,000 more than the remaining payments from the University on the Kietzman bid. I later joked that we should name a floor in the addition for Kietzman Construction Company, since the bond meant that the amount by which Kietzman underbid the project to get the work was the equivalent of a major gift to the campaign.

Following Kietzman's departure, Professor Duncan, Chair of the building committee, and Martin Wisneski, the Library's Director of Technical Services and its liaison to the project, became even more like mother hens than they had been previously, injecting themselves into construction issues on a daily basis and acting as advocates for the Law School with the architect, the Build-

---

871. *Id.*

84. Ed Linquist '50 cuts a ribbon at the 1992 dedication of the
library addition, along with Becky '89 and Ed Linquist, Jr. '89

ing and Grounds Department, and the construction supervisor to assure the
Law School's quality goals would be met and that corners would not be cut
to reduce the bond company's losses.

The new space was sufficiently complete that "The Big Move" of the entire
library collection from its existing shelves to the addition could be done over
the Memorial Day weekend in 1991. Wisneski's elaborate planning made it
possible for volunteers quickly to move books to the desired locations. The
process would be repeated in reverse when renovation of the existing building
was completed. Renovation required that the main library entrance be closed.
Students and faculty had to take a circuitous route using a back stairwell to
reach a temporary entrance on the second floor. When the fall semester started
in 1991, many professors occupied temporary offices, and it often was expedi-
ent to go outdoors to get from one floor to another.

The finished product was worth the wait and the Law School was back to
normal operations by the spring semester of 1992. The dedication was held
Saturday, June 13, immediately following the Kansas Bar Association's annual
meeting in Topeka. The date was selected to make it convenient for alums from

throughout Kansas to attend, to assure we would be comfortably settled into the addition despite any last minute delays, and to increase the likelihood of favorable weather. More than 300 people attended the ceremony and Alumni Association President Terry Kilroy '77 reported that "you could feel the excitement in the air."[872] A gala dinner followed the ceremony.

The Judge Delmas C. Hill Kansas Room was elegant, with a parquet floor, oak wainscoting and ceiling beams, paneling, and fabric wall coverings. There were bookshelves for faculty and alumni writings and rare books. We wanted to display Kansas legal memorabilia and recreate the appearance of a turn-of-the-century law office. June Windscheffel, wife of Arno Windscheffel '34, chaired a committee of spouses of Washburn alums which solicited graduates to donate appropriate items. Members included Martha Davis (Mrs. Clayton '29), Helen St. John (Mrs. Harry '34), Ruth Marie Fromme (Mrs. Alex '39) and Marjorie Steerman (Mrs. Everett '27).[873] United States District Judge Dale Saffels '49 arranged for the donation of the desk, conference table, and chairs used by United States District Judge George Templar '27, as well as two lamps that had been on the ends of the judge's bench in the main courtroom the court formerly used in Topeka's main post office. United States District Judge Pat Kelly '53 donated eyeglasses he found in his desk that belonged to Judge Hill. The many other donated items included a 1760 indenture under seal on lambskin conveying property in Great Britain and Justice Richard Hopkins' bowler hat that was hung on an antique coat rack. The Phi Alpha Delta cane rack that had been used in Boswell and Carnegie Halls was restored and alums were invited to donate for permanent display canes they had carried as senior law students. The cane rack has two freestanding places, one on each side, with inscriptions reserving them for Deans Harry K. Allen and Antrim Hambleton '14. Initially, we planned to use the Kansas Room primarily for special occasions and receptions, but we quickly concluded it was the ideal place for placement interviews. There was no better place to showcase our students and make visiting firms feel special. The fall after the dedication, on October 16, 1992, a panel of Tenth Circuit Judges which heard arguments in Robinson Courtroom participated in a ceremony hanging Judge Hill's portrait in the room, as did lead donor Kent

872. *President's Message*, 31 THE CIRCUIT RIDER 3 (Summer 1992).

873. *Kansas Room Committee Seeking Antique Furnishings*, 30 THE CIRCUIT RIDER 31 (Fall 1991).

85. The Kansas Room features Kansas legal memorabilia

Smith '66, who was in Topeka as the Law School's honoree in the University's Alumni Fellows program.

The addition included a Faculty Reading Room, adjoining but separate from the Robing Room at the rear of the courtroom which since 1969 had doubled as the faculty and staff lounge. Mark '77 and Lisa Heitz made sure it was inviting, supplying not only plush leather chairs, attractive furniture, and wall coverings but also the services of an interior designer. Their gift was in memory of grandparents Oscar Waggoner '12 and Eva M. Garner Waggoner.

CAMELOT LOST

Jack Duggan was everything the campus hoped a new president would be, and much more. He charmed community leaders and alums, inspired the confidence of the faculty, promised higher standards, and increased the energy level of the campus. The change of tone provoked comparisons to the Camelot days when John Kennedy went to the White House. There was optimism for the University's future and the Law School shared it. Dean Monk had established a positive personal relationship with Duggan while serving on the presidential search committee and during Duggan's early visits to campus. So high was confidence in Duggan that the Law School did not vigorously oppose Duggan's decision no longer to have the Dean of the Law School report directly to the President, even though this restructuring meant the new Vice President could be a greater threat to the Law School than his predecessors. In part to make clear to Duggan the Law School's special status, Monk arranged for the Law School Foundation to pay part of the premium on an insurance policy that was part of the compensation package that persuaded Duggan to accept Washburn's offer.

Duggan emphasized fitness and played tennis with Monk and me. Then, suddenly, in mid-November 1988, Duggan was in the hospital, and within days he was dead from pancreatic cancer. His tenure as President lasted just five months.

Predictably, the Board of Regents named new Vice President for Academic Affairs Robert L. Burns as Interim President. It subsequently determined that it was too late in the academic year to launch an effective search for a new president and set the search for 1989–90. Burns welcomed the additional time as Interim President, since it was an opportunity to show by his performance that he should be retained as President. There were reasons for the Law School to be apprehensive of that scenario. Before becoming Vice President, Burns had been Dean of the College of Arts and Sciences. In that capacity, he had clashed frequently with Dean Monk, opposing several Law School initiatives. Monk had recommended that Duggan hire an external candidate, instead of Burns, as Vice President. As Dean-designate, I made the same recommendation, though my comments were more measured than Monk's. We were not persuasive enough.

One of Burns' first acts as Interim President was to ask former Dean Ray Spring '59 to serve as Interim Vice President for Academic Affairs. Spring was widely respected throughout the campus and had consensus support from the undergraduate deans. He had been active in University governance since leaving the deanship, particularly on the Athletics Committee, and was a visible fan of Ichabod teams. The undergraduate deans, who sometimes found themselves competing with one another, had greater confidence in the neutral good judgment of a former law dean than of someone selected from a particular undergraduate unit. An added motivation for Burns may have

86. Professor Allen Easley succeeded
Sheila Reynolds as Associate Dean

been a desire to enhance the Law School's confidence in his administration and forestall open opposition to his candidacy to be the next president.

Spring's unexpected move to Morgan Hall just before the spring semester of 1989 presented scheduling problems. Jalen O'Neil '87 agreed to teach one of his spring classes as Visiting Assistant Professor and became a full-time visitor while Spring continued as Interim Vice President during the presidential search. Even after Spring returned to full-time teaching, O'Neil continued as Visiting Professor while Monk was on his year-long sabbatical and thereafter when Monk was granted an extended leave of absence to serve as Executive Director of the AALS. She continued to teach Criminal Law, Legal Research and Writing, Civil Procedure II, and Bioethics and the Law through 2001.

In the midst of the upheaval in the University administration, Associate Dean Sheila Reynolds expressed her desire to return to full-time teaching. I persuaded her to stay an additional year, through academic year 1990–91, so that we could rely on her experience to handle unexpected events in-house while I still traveled frequently, furthering our fundraising agenda. The extra year also helped us maintain continuity as a new president took the reins of the University. Reynolds invariably organized her time each day with precision and used that skill to balance deftly and calmly the demands of administration and clinic supervision. I tried to persuade her to stay yet another year, but to no avail. I asked Allen Easley to replace her and he would serve in the position, remarkably, for thirteen years.

THE LAW SCHOOL FINANCING PLAN

The phased reduction in the size of entering classes from 220 students to 150 students annually gave Washburn the fourteenth best student-faculty ratio among all ABA schools in 1989–90. It also meant that the Law School was no longer a cash cow for the University. Direct revenues generated by the Law School from tuition, state aid, and miscellaneous sources declined in 1986–87 and again in 1987–88 because of the planned decline in enrollment. Despite higher tuition rates, direct revenues barely returned in 1988–89 to the amount generated in 1985–86. On the other hand, operating expenditures continued to rise modestly, an average of 4% annually, during that period. Direct revenues, which had exceeded the school's operating budget in 1982–83 by more than $171,000, soon fell short of operating expenses. As a result, revenue from the local property tax authorized for general university operations was used to fund part of the Law School budget. Of course, it was appropriate that the Law School, as a major unit, share fairly in property tax revenues. As enrollment declined, the amount of property tax revenue allocated to the Law School increased from $316,000 or 13.5% of operating expenditures in 1985–86 to $692,000 in 1988–89, and to more than $800,000, nearly 27% of law operating expenditures, in the 1989–90 budget. While tuition and expenditures at the Law School usually rose at the same percentage rates as in other units, the law salaries to which the percentage rates applied were generally higher than those elsewhere on campus. Thus, the raw dollars required to fund increases for Law School operations grew rapidly.

Even though the Law School finally was receiving its fair share of University resources, it was not enough to fund the school's needs. The property tax allocated by the University had not been used for program improvements but to replace lost tuition and state aid that supported existing programs. The Law School was hard-pressed to claim entitlement to further significant increases in property tax support. Yet, by academic year 1988–89, the median salary for full professors at Washburn was the eighth lowest among 174 ABA accredited schools, and three of those lower than Washburn were in Puerto Rico. The ranking in 1989–90 was still 14th lowest. Perhaps more significantly, Washburn was 18.7% below the ABA median, despite increases made possible by an increased state operating grant to the University. There was an immediate risk that Washburn could not recruit or retain talented faculty. Needs for technology, library materials, new academic programs, and student activities were not being met by budget increases. The Law School could not improve if increases in its operating budget were limited to the same rate as for other campus units.

New thinking was needed. We were fortunate that the University's Vice President for Planning, David Monical, understood that the Law School differed from other campus units in its need to compete nationally for students and faculty. He was a rare University administrator who was willing to think outside the box. He was tired of receiving annual statistical reports showing that Washburn compared poorly with other schools in available resources and agreed we should do something about it. In any other year, the Vice President for Academic Affairs might not have been receptive to a new approach to funding the Law School, but, not surprisingly, Ray Spring was. Throughout the fall of 1989, Monical, Spring, and I brainstormed to develop a win-win plan that would benefit both the Law School and the rest of the University. University Treasurer Gene Mosiman, who had the remarkable ability to insist on rigid adherence to governing financial principles while still finding a way to facilitate good ideas, also participated and was supportive. By February 1, 1990, we had a final draft plan. The Law School agreed to finance all increases in its operating budget from increases in tuition or its proportionate share of increases in state aid and to forego any increase in property tax revenue. In return for assuming responsibility to finance budget increases in this way, the Law School would be granted greater autonomy to increase its tuition and its operating budget by percentage rates higher than in other campus units. A target after four years was for faculty salaries to be not too far below the national median and, in light of the goal to achieve state affiliation, at least to match KU, where the median salary for full professors then ranked 113th among 174 schools and was only 5.8% below the national median.

The plan reflected several premises. It contemplated significant increases in tuition, not only immediately as we increased expenditures to competitive levels but also in the long term to fund quality improvements. The risk was that higher tuition rates would cause applicants to choose less expensive schools, diminishing the credentials of the class. We discounted the risk for several reasons. First, our tuition already was almost 2.25 times the tuition at KU, which then had the twelfth lowest tuition of all ABA schools. Thus, we already were losing applicants who were forced to choose between the two schools on the ground of cost alone. Second, while our resident tuition already was higher than that at most public law schools, there were only four states where Kansans could pay a lower non-resident tuition than our resident tuition, even if we increased it dramatically. Our non-resident tuition, the 14th lowest nationally, would remain attractive to non-residents who were not admitted to public law schools in their home states. Our tuition was far lower than at any of the private schools, which far outnumber public schools. We concluded, more importantly, that students would pay for quality and that we should not artificially restrict tuition increases at the expense of quality. This conclusion was borne out as applications reached a record high in 1992 of 1009, despite a 30% increase in resident tuition over three years. We further concluded that the only effective way to recruit applicants deterred by Washburn's cost was to persuade alumni to increase private giving for scholarships.

Another important premise of the plan was that the Law School's obligation to fund budget increases applied only to the operating budget. Several significant items traditionally had been excluded from that budget. For example, it did not include fringe benefits. A separate and unlimited mill levy paid for all benefits university-wide. Allowing the Law School to use the dedicated mill levy for increases in fringe benefits did not deprive the remainder of the University of funds that could be used for any other purpose. Also excluded from the operating budget were physical plant expenses, including utilities, which were certain to increase once the building addition was completed, and general institutional support, such as centralized purchasing services, for which private universities usually charge overhead to departments.

File cabinets throughout academia bulge with good plans that never were implemented. There were high hurdles to be crossed before we could implement the plan for the 1990–91 budget. Interim President Burns had to approve its submission to the Board of Regents and the Board had to agree.

The greatest risk to the plan was opposition by other units on campus, where many faculty members already resented that law faculty salaries were higher than theirs and might feel that the Law School should not have an advantage simply because tuition elasticity gave it the ability to afford enhancements not thought to be affordable elsewhere. Interim President Burns' roots in the College of Arts and Sciences made us particularly wary. However, Burns' initial reaction was positive. He sent a copy of the plan to the Chair of the Board of Regents with the comment, "It is a significant change for us, but I believe it is a positive move for the University."[874] Burns asked Ray Spring to meet with the other deans and asked University Treasurer Gene Mosiman to meet with the faculty representatives to the Board of Regents. As expected, some reactions were lukewarm. There were comments that more time was needed for review. Mosiman reported that the faculty representatives expressed concern that the plan would cause considerable problems if non-law revenues declined so that non-law budgets declined while the law budget increased.[875] Still, he reported that "they seemed to have an open mind" that the plan might work if non-law revenue were increasing. I had followup meetings with the other deans, emphasizing that, by freezing the Law School's property tax support, the plan would make more dollars available to other units than if the plan were not adopted, and arguing that even though law salaries were higher than in other units they were much further below peer medians than those of other units. Ultimately, the other deans did not oppose the plan.

We sought to neutralize other potential sources of opposition and rally support. Law students might have protested the tuition increases. I attended a meeting of the Student Bar Association to explain the proposal. I shared in detail the comparative resource data on which the plan was based and emphasized that every dollar of increased tuition would be added to the Law School budget. The WSBA agreed to support the plan. I outlined the plan to the alumni Board of Governors at its February meeting. It expressed its support and endorsed a major endowment raising campaign for scholarships and other needs which we would call Law School 2000.

The reservations some on campus expressed gave Burns pause. As the deadline for submitting agenda proposals to the Regents loomed, he "continue[d]

874. Memorandum from Robert L. Burns, President, to Ann Garvin, Chair (Feb. 2, 1990).
875. Memorandum from Louis E. Mosiman to Dr. Robert Burns (Feb. 6, 1990).

to ponder" the matter and wondered if it would be "possible (and helpful)" to implement the plan for the upcoming year but to allow time for additional review whether its use should be continued.[876] However, he realized "the method should be ongoing if it is to be helpful," and after one final meeting sent the plan as proposed to the Regents. The role the presidential search played in Burns' decision-making process cannot be known. Fear of alienating strong supporters could explain his hesitance to sign off on the plan. On the other hand, I was the Law School's representative on the search committee and the committee was in the midst of interviewing Burns as well as external candidates. The committee's report to the Board, and the Board's selection of the new president, would not take place until the issue of the law finance proposal was resolved, one way or the other. Burns thus might have perceived a significant downside from opposing the plan.

The Board approved the Financing Plan at its March 1990 meeting. Regents who were law graduates, particularly Mayor Butch Felker '72, expressed concern that increased tuition would prevent deserving students from being able to afford to attend law school, but the commitment by the Board of Governors to aggressively seek scholarships diminished their concerns sufficiently.

BATTLES WITH THE NEW PRESIDENT

The presidential search soon wound to an end. I concluded the strongest candidate was the president of a private college in Idaho. However, because achieving state affiliation was the Board's highest priority, it preferred a candidate with experience working with a state system. That narrowed the field of finalists to two, Burns and Hugh L. Thompson, who was President of the Kokomo branch of the Indiana University system. The Board was bitterly divided and selected Thompson on a 5–4 vote.

Even before Thompson's arrival on campus, we eagerly shared details of the Financing Plan with alums, seeking to boost their morale about the school's prospects and to enlist their support. The Board of Governors sought to lay groundwork for the forthcoming fundraising campaign in a presentation during the Kansas Bar Association's 1990 annual meeting in Overland Park

---

876. Memorandum from Dr. Robert L. Burns to Ray Spring, Vice President for Academic Affairs (Mar. 1, 1990).

at the Washburn luncheon that nearly 300 alums attended. The presentation forthrightly described the stark budget concerns that led to the plan. It was a time before Powerpoint, so we used a slide show and laser pointer. We told alums that the plan over time would assure "an adequate base level of funding," but I stressed that "it will not be possible to provide through student tuition all of the quality improvements" that would "set this law school apart." Additional resources were needed "to take advantage of unique program opportunities." Examples included a Trial Skills Center, an energy law program unrivaled in the Midwest, and a partnership with Menninger to develop a signature program in mental health law. I described the importance of creating full-tuition scholarships so we could compete for academic leaders despite the significant tuition increases the plan made certain for the foreseeable future. The President of the Board of Governors, Dick Hite '53, then used slides to show the large disparity between alumni annual giving to KU and to Washburn. In the four years before the library campaign commenced, our annual giving had averaged less than $53,000 while annual giving at KU grew 45% to almost $250,000. Hite also described disparities in the endowments of the two schools, particularly for endowed professorships. He encouraged those in attendance to begin annual gifts and pledged that the Board of Governors would develop a plan to address the Law School's financial needs for the remainder of the decade.

To acquaint alums who did not attend the luncheon with these plans, we printed portions of the presentations in the summer issue of *The Circuit Rider*.[877] Dick Hite described the Board's long-range planning in the winter issue. He argued that "[t]he merit scholarship program must be substantially expanded to maintain the current academic standards," and solicited ideas.[878] Bill Kurtis '66 narrated a videotape describing the plan and the need for additional resources. We played it for various audiences, including at "Inner Circle" dinners in a number of cities that sought input from alumni leaders.

Graduates responded positively. Annual giving grew to more than $208,200 by 1991–92 and to more than $244,000 the next year. As a result, we were able to increase the non-grant funded scholarship budget by 66% in just four years, from $247,000 in 1988–89 to a record $409,000 for 1992–93.

---

877. James M. Concannon, *New Law School Improvement Plan Offers Opportunity for Quality Change*, 29 THE CIRCUIT RIDER 3 (Summer 1990).

878. Richard C. Hite, *President's Page*, 29 THE CIRCUIT RIDER 2 (Winter 1990).

Not surprisingly, Hugh Thompson's priorities during his initial year on campus kept him from focusing on the Financing Plan. We thus were able not only in the budget he inherited but also in the next one to make significant improvements in faculty salaries, expand the scope of our academic support program, increase the number of inter-school competitions in which Washburn students participated, add library materials, and increase other parts of the operating budget.

The Financing Plan worked during its initial two years exactly as we expected. By 1991–92, the median salary for full professors ranked 132nd among 174 schools, just one position away from the third quartile and the highest ranking Washburn had enjoyed for a decade. The gap below the national median closed to 9.7%. We were able to fill a position in the Law Clinic that we had been unable to fill in two searches since Don Rowland retired. Faculty recruitment for other positions benefitted. While our salary offers still were below national averages, the Financing Plan meant we could assure candidates that we could make appropriate increases in future years. In addition, despite significant tuition increases, applications increased 41% over two years and 58% over three years. Credentials of matriculating students rose sharply.

President Thompson had never been associated with a law school or similar professional school. Further, the mathematics of the plan were complicated and it was never clear he fully understood how the plan benefitted the University as well as the Law School. In any event, he was not sympathetic to the premise that it was appropriate to treat different campus units differently or to grant one unit greater autonomy. As a result, Thompson and I battled each other throughout his presidency.

The first battle erupted when the Financing Plan appeared to be working too well, in a way that was wholly unanticipated. The University's various attempts to achieve state affiliation had led the Law School to argue that it was imperative that its resources increase to at least match those at KU. In the two years after our plan was adopted, the median salary for full professors at KU actually declined by $1,100, primarily because of retirements of senior faculty and the promotion of junior faculty to full professor. KU's median fell below Washburn's in 1990–91, probably for the first time in history, and by 1991–92 its median was substantially below Washburn's. It fell to the lowest 9% of all schools and 21% below the national median.

There were reasons Washburn's median should have been somewhat higher even if both schools were funded at proper levels. Washburn's full professors had significantly more experience than their counterparts at KU. For example, the twenty-four Washburn faculty members holding the rank of full professor had in the aggregate fifty more years of experience since receiving their law degrees than the twenty-four most senior full professors at KU, and began their law teaching careers twenty-nine years earlier. The most recent date of graduation of a Washburn full professor was 1978, while KU had full professors who graduated in 1983 and 1984. In addition, twelve full professors at Washburn held advanced law degrees, compared with just two at KU. Notwithstanding all these facts, it violated the traditional order of things for Washburn's resources to exceed those at KU. Making matters worse, 1991–92 was the year of the ABA/AALS accreditation inspection at KU, and it was readily apparent that concerns would be expressed about the school's compliance with standards regarding law school resources.

President Thompson was prone to accept as gospel truth any criticisms or concerns expressed by those outside the University. Stan Koplick, Executive Director of the Kansas Board of Regents, persuaded Thompson that the State Board was concerned that law salaries at Washburn were higher than at KU and that Washburn's effort to achieve state affiliation might be harmed as a result. Thompson relayed those concerns to the Chair and Vice-Chair of Washburn's Board, Lanny Kimbrough and Dean Ferrell. Thompson expressed concern about increases I might propose for 1992–93.

What Thompson did not realize was that the state Board's interest was not prompted directly by Washburn's salaries but instead by a proposal by KU's law dean, Bob Jerry, to increase his school's resources dramatically by charging a fee earmarked for the law school.[879] Because tuition increases in the Regents system went into the State general fund and could not be earmarked for the unit that generated them, Jerry had to describe his proposed three-year increase of $40 per credit hour as a dedicated "fee." Jerry wisely sought to blunt the criticism expected in KU's accreditation report by having in place added funding for the library and for increases in faculty salaries for 1992–93 significantly higher than the 2.5% increases that were forecast elsewhere in

---

879. Memorandum from Robert H. Jerry II to Kansas Board of Regents Tuition and Fees Committee (May 8, 1992), entitled "Proposal Concerning KU School of Law Funding, Tuition, and Fees," found as Attachment VII of Recommendations of the Tuition and Fees Committee to the Kansas Board of Regents, Fiscal Affairs Agenda Item 2, Kansas Board of Regents meeting (June 25, 1992).

the state system and in the undergraduate school at Washburn as well. Jerry understood that student fees at KU could rise dramatically without harmful effects, and he and I had talked in detail about how our plan was working.

I alerted Thompson, Kimbrough, and Ferrell about KU's fee proposal in a memorandum in February 1992. I realized that it would not be prudent politically to propose another double-digit percentage salary increase but felt that the plan was at risk in its entirety if we permitted its premises and goals to be undermined by events at KU so soon after its adoption. Thus, I proposed an average salary increase of 7–7.5% and argued that would keep us on track toward the Plan's target by reducing slightly the gap between Washburn's median and the national median. I mentioned our own accreditation inspection, scheduled for 1992–93:

> The salaries of Washburn law faculty never were tied to salaries at K.U. when the K.U. law school was on the ascendency; in light of the credentials and experience of our faculty and in light of the funding mechanism we have devised that does not require the use of other University resources, Washburn's salaries should not be tied to those at K.U. when it is on the decline.
>
> …
>
> If we continue to make modest progress next year and with the Law School Financing Plan in place to assure a competitive level of funding in the future, I do not believe we will face substantial criticism from the inspection team about the financial support of the law school. If, on the other hand, the modest gains of the past two years appear only to be a blip on a generally downward spiral, I believe we can anticipate such criticism.

I was invited to make a detailed presentation about the Financing Plan's performance at the March Board of Regents meeting. It was uneventful. The University's internal budget committee approved my budget proposal unanimously. Less than two weeks before the April board meeting, however, Thompson expressed to the Vice President an unwillingness to recommend increases beyond 5%. The Vice President relayed Thompson's position to me. His rationale was that increases in law were too much greater than increases in other units. Well before 8:00 a.m. the following morning, I slipped under his office door a lengthy memo explaining yet again that law faculty salaries still were further below those of their peers than were salaries in any other campus unit.

Thompson did not want to be in a position that would permit us to hold him responsible to our alums for a reduction in our budget proposal. Thus, he had the Secretary to the Regents conduct a telephone poll of Board members asking whether they supported my 7.3% proposal, the 2.5% increase that was available elsewhere on campus, or "a compromise" of 5%. Given the way the issue was presented, without supporting rationales, and given that there were two new members who had not attended my March briefing of the Board, it is not surprising that the majority expressed support for the compromise.

Reacting against such uninformed decision making by poll and fearing the long-term implications, we determined we had to go directly to the Board. I distributed to each Regent a detailed memorandum explaining the rationale and background of the budget proposal. I requested individual meetings with them and six Regents agreed to meet. Nine days before the April meeting, I sent an "Urgent Request for HELP" to members of the Law School Association Board of Governors, asking that they contact President Thompson and Regents they knew to emphasize that "alumni support continued progress at the law school under the Law School Financing Plan and that the support of law alumni for various other initiatives of the University hinges upon the continued progress of the law school."

Dick Hite wrote to Thompson, noting the many years of antagonism between the University and the Law School "which caused many law school alumni to believe that the law school was not receiving fair treatment." He cited the Financing Plan as an integral component of the alumni Board's plan to increase private giving and argued that failure to approve the budget would "impair the success of alumni fundraising efforts and renew the old antagonism."[880]

Only six Regents attended the April meeting. Two favored the 7.3% proposal, two felt the Law School should receive the same 2.5% increase as other units, and two favored the 5% compromise. Based on what he knew about the views of the three absent members, the Chairman concluded there was majority support for at least 5% and directed that figure be used when the budget was submitted for final approval in May.

Alumni continued to pressure Thompson to recommend approval of the Law School's original proposal. Foundation President Gerald Goodell urged reconsideration because of the "very negative impact upon the Law School 2000

---

880. Letter from Richard C. Hite to Dr. Hugh Thompson (Apr. 15, 1992).

campaign" and forecast that the action at the April meeting "will be considered by many alumni to be a reversal" of the plan "to make Washburn Law School competitive with the law schools against which Washburn recruits highly qualified students and faculty."[881] Bill Bunten '56 made the issue the dominant topic at a meeting of the Washburn Alumni Legislative Network in Wichita.

Internally, we sought to make the best of the outcome. We used the disapproved salary funds to increase other budget line items, such as for technology, and received permission to keep promises to newly-hired faculty by granting them somewhat larger increases. At a faculty meeting, I described the outcome as "not disastrous" but said that it was "disheartening to see the Board vote for mediocrity, not excellence, and to take steps that rekindle the old wars between the Law School and the rest of the University." I said I did not blame the Board members.

> They are volunteers and when the issue is presented to them in the way it was, with no rationale for our proposal and only the concerns of the President, I can understand their response. The problem is the lack of presidential leadership. Our increases last year were much greater than undergraduate increases as compared to this year, and they went through without one word from any Board member—and they would have this year if the President had exercised the leadership to say, 'This is the right thing to do.'"

I shared with faculty what alumni had done to support the Law School's proposal and vowed "to put unrelenting pressure on the President over the next year to make sure this doesn't happen again."

However, there was an even bigger surprise at the May Board of Regents meeting. As in April, only six Regents attended, but it was a different six. The two law graduates who in March supported the 7.3% budget, Mayor Butch Felker '72 and Mark Heitz '77, were absent, as was Francine Hines, who ultimately supported the 5% budget. Those present voted 4–2 to approve the University budget except for the Law School salary budget, which was to be re-submitted as a 2.5% budget for approval in June. The Board's rules required action to be approved only by a majority of a quorum. Near the end of the Board's discussion, Thompson, clearly influenced by alumni contacts, for

---

881. Letter from Gerald L. Goodell to Dr. Hugh Thompson (Apr. 28, 1992).

the first time publicly stated a position, urging the Board to approve the 5% proposal. He first told the Board, "a Plan that is adopted sometimes has to be changed," but added failure to adopt the 5% plan would "send the wrong message" to the alumni and the alumni endowment building effort. Kimbrough, one of the two dissenters, said, "Maybe I shouldn't say this, maybe I should. There are law alums all over the state who have bought into the plan who are very influential in their communities." Ferrell added, "they have done a really good job over there in the law school and we ought to do this." The reasoning of two Regents, who simply opposed increases in any unit beyond those of other units, though inconsistent with the Financing Plan, was intellectually defensible. However, Regent John Montgomery from Junction City, the appointee of the State Board of Regents, supported their position with the astonishing argument that Washburn professors were paid more for working three-fourths time than KU professors were being paid for working full-time. In fact, Washburn's highest paid faculty members were paid less than the highest paid faculty members at KU. It was not until the next morning that we determined the reason for Montgomery's error. He did not understand the elementary point that Washburn's budget listed academic year contracts as .75 FTE while KU listed them as 1.0 FTE.

The implications of the unexpected action of the plurality of the Board were not easy to determine. The Board seemed to have approved the recommended tuition rates for the Law School but not its budget. That would mean the University would capture the excess tuition, effectively repealing the Financing Plan. It felt like we were at war. I sent letters to the four plurality Regents explaining the factual error in the information Montgomery provided. Alumni expressed outrage. Bill Bunten '56 resigned from the Alumni Legislative Network. I spoke with the three Regents who missed the April meeting and they stated they did not support the plurality's action. Mark Heitz '77 committed to take the lead at the June meeting to see that the majority view prevailed.

I sought internally to keep pressure on President Thompson and to make it clear we would not allow the issue to go away. My 1991–92 Dean's Annual Report, submitted later in May, was one sentence long: "Although Academic Year 1991–92 saw extraordinary achievement at Washburn Law School, it will be viewed in hindsight as a disastrous year because of the University's retreat from its commitment to allow the Law School through its own resources to become competitive with peer law schools." Twenty paragraphs of accomplishments were relegated to a footnote.

The Kansas Bar Association meeting that year was in Topeka and the Washburn luncheon was the day after the June Regents meeting. We had expected the luncheon to be a festive occasion, celebrating completion of the library addition that we would dedicate two days later. Early in the year, we invited Thompson to attend the luncheon and he had accepted. We now determined we would introduce him at the head table but would not invite him to speak. I prepared two versions of remarks for the luncheon, so that I could choose the appropriate one depending on the outcome of the Regents meeting. Both described the many accomplishments of the year, but Thompson would not have enjoyed the version I planned if the Board adhered to the decision of its May plurality. I'm sure he knew that. However, the Board restored the 5% budget plan and the version I gave acknowledged that the President had urged it to do so. However, I knew this would not be our last fight with Thompson. We had an opportunity to impress on him that our alumni would be there for the next fight too. I observed that the Kansas Board of Regents and staff, instead of providing needed resources at KU's law school through the increased fees Bob Jerry proposed,

> have sought to convince Washburn's leadership that Washburn's chances of state affiliation will be harmed if our law school is too much stronger than its counterpart at Lawrence. And, amazingly, they have had some success with that argument.
>
> ...
>
> Every law alum in this room has always known that the best way to assure the future of the law school in the event of state affiliation is for us to be in the strongest possible position we can attain. I hope there will be two strong law schools in this state, viewed as important parts of the Kansas education system. If, however, there is to be only one strong law school, it was our commitment, when we asked you to support the Law School Financing Plan two years ago, that law school would be ours.
>
> It is not enough to be linked with the state's other law school in hard times for the state. We aspire to be among the best law schools in the Midwest and in the nation. You have a right to insist upon nothing less.
>
> ...

It is clear that within the next year we must reeducate our Board of Regents about the wisdom of the improvement plan you have supported. We may be forced to call upon you to make it clear to the Board that your support for the legislative and other initiatives of the general University is dependent upon the continuation of the commitment the University made in the Law School Financing Plan to excellence, not just adequacy. Your continued support has never been more vital to us.

The enthusiasm of the audience's response added exclamation points that President Thompson could not miss. We printed these remarks in the next issue of *The Circuit Rider*, seeking to rally alums who had not attended the luncheon.

VANISHED

Because we expected Carl Monk to return to Washburn after his two years as AALS Deputy Director and then his deferred sabbatical, we hired visiting professors during his absence. Arthur Chaykin was Visiting Professor for two years. For 1990–91, Lawrence E. Williams, Jr., a faculty member at District of Columbia School of Law, was recruited as a visitor to teach part-time in the classroom, including Civil Procedure in the fall semester, and part-time in the Law Clinic while Professor Kaye was on leave teaching at Whittier Law School. Williams arrived in Topeka with his wife, and he began working with other clinic faculty members on August 6. When the semester started, he taught the only Civil Procedure class scheduled during the first week. Students arrived for his class the next week but Williams did not. His wife initially explained that an emergency required him to return to the east coast but that he would return soon. By the end of the week, it was apparent to her and to us that he was not coming back, but we heard nothing from him. A resignation letter finally arrived on August 30. Williams wrote that he was compelled to make "an irrational, unreasonable and inexplicable move...." Later, a faculty member at District of Columbia School of Law told us that Williams left Topeka to join one of his former students, whom he married after obtaining a divorce. Even later, we were told he that had been convicted for stabbing the former student to death.

Former professor Joel Meinecke, then in private practice, agreed to devote nearly half of his time during the fall semester to supervising Clinic students. I took over Williams' Civil Procedure class, but because of my travel schedule and administrative responsibilities, the only option was to combine his class with mine and to teach all 150 students in the large classroom in the Henderson building across campus, just as Ray Spring had done with the Criminal Law classes in 1974 when Kurt Morgan departed during orientation week. We had to replace the textbook Williams was using with the one I was using. I conducted several initial sessions with his section to cover material my section already had covered. At the first of those sessions, I tried to turn the situation into a 1L learning opportunity about legal methods. I asked students how they would decide what to do when a faculty member vanishes. Eventually, someone suggested one might ask if there was precedent for the situation. At that point, I explained how Dean Spring had handled Professor Morgan's departure. I then asked what the holding of the precedent was. I suggested a possible holding might be that, whenever a faculty member vanishes, the Dean takes over the class and moves it to Room 100 in the Henderson building. I suggested that such a broad holding would have presented difficulties if the vanishing faculty member had taught a course like Estate and Gift Tax and suggested that the holding of our precedent likely was narrower than that. Needless to say, by that point, the class was hoping Professor Williams miraculously would reappear.

SPECIALIZATION: CERTIFICATE PROGRAMS

In 1983, Jim Wadley proposed to establish a Certificate in Rural Law as part of the Rural Law Center. The certificate would be awarded to students who completed fifteen of the ninety hours required for the J.D. degree in specified courses, with an average GPA of 3.0, and also completed an advanced research paper in one of several courses, as a Directed Research project, or as a Law Journal comment or note. The proposal was controversial and was not approved. Some faculty members, led by Banks McDowell, opposed it because they opposed specialization in the J.D. program, believing that students needed a liberal arts exposure to law and that the certificate courses would consume too many of the limited number of elective hours available to students. Wadley sought to blunt that concern by arguing that "the prototypical example of the rural lawyer is that of a general practitioner and this proposal should not be considered as an attempt to encourage specialization."[882] He thus brought under the rural

---

882. *Proposal and Requirements for a Certificate in Rural Law at Washburn Uni-*

law umbrella such courses as Administrative Law, Estate Planning, Municipal Corporations, Public International Trade, Private International Trade, State and Local Taxation, and Taxation of Gifts and Estates. As many as eight of the fifteen hours needed for the certificate could be in these courses. Defining a certificate with such broad reach prompted opposition by other faculty members, who were concerned that it did not require sufficient specialization to assure that recipients would develop expertise in core rural law principles. Adding incentives for students to enroll in courses in which higher than average grades typically were awarded was a concern for a few faculty members.

Thus, it was not until 1991 that Professor Spring developed Washburn's first certificate program. Its premise was different and it had a different focus. The Certificate in Law and Mental Health was awarded jointly by the Law School and Menninger, which had cooperated in various ways for seven decades. Now, to prevent dilution of the law school's "liberal arts" requirements, the certificate could be earned only with additional commitment by students, beyond the core J.D. degree. Students had to complete 96 hours, rather than the normal 90, including at least fifteen hours in specified courses. Participation in a Colloquium with psychiatric resident physicians at Menninger was required. In 1992, Professor Bayles developed a 96-hour Certificate in Taxation that allowed graduates to demonstrate specialization in tax courses without completing an LL.M. Next, in 1994, Professor Wadley developed a Certificate in Agricultural Law. It included a directed research component that would become a standard requirement of certificate programs in future years. A fourth certificate program, in Family Law, was added that same year, and a certificate in Environmental Law was created soon thereafter.

FAMILY LAW QUARTERLY

Increasingly, law schools created additional opportunities for their students to benefit from the law journal experience apart from the school's main journal. Linda Elrod's initiative and her extensive involvement in the American Bar Association's Family Law Section led to the location of a second journal at Washburn. In 1982, she became the Kansas reporter for the annual "Law in the Fifty States" issue of *Family Law Quarterly,* the Section's scholarly journal that

---

versity School of Law to be Administered by the Rural Law Center (1983).

is distributed to nearly 20,000 Section members nationwide. The next year she chaired the Section's committee on the Schwab Essay Contest. By 1988, Elrod had been Chair of the Section's Amicus Curiae Brief Committee and a member of its Publications Board and the Board of Editors of the *Quarterly*. She then was elected to a three-year term on the Council of the Section and was named Associate Editor of the *Quarterly*. The Section's practice was to rotate the location of the *Quarterly* among law schools every three to five years and to use a Student Editorial Board at the host school to edit and cite-check articles. At the time, the *Quarterly* was located at the University of Denver, where Professor Tim Walker was Editor-in-Chief. As Associate Editor, Elrod undertook responsibility for the "Law in the Fifty States" issue and enlisted student research assistants from Washburn to help.

In 1992, the Council of the Section voted to relocate the *Quarterly* to Washburn. The Council has elected to keep it at Washburn ever since. Because of Elrod's success in upgrading the content and scope of the articles published, the *Quarterly*'s stature grew steadily. One measure of the influence of a published article is the number of times the article is cited in other legal publications. Research published in 2000 in *The Journal of Legal Studies* ranked the *Quarterly* 15th among all specialized legal periodicals in the average number of times each article had been cited in the previous ten years.[883] An earlier article, purporting to assess the prominence of the authors who chose to publish articles in each journal, concluded the *Quarterly* was the 76th most prestigious journal among the 284 specialized journals published by American law schools.[884]

Rose Mulvany '83 was the first student editor-in-chief of the *Quarterly* after it was moved to Washburn. An office was assigned for the *Quarterly* staff, initially on the lower floor of the Law Clinic and thereafter on the third floor of the main building just three doors away from Professor Elrod's office.

STUDENT SUCCESSES

Success in national competitions grew in frequency in the 1990s. For the second time in four years, Washburn placed second among thirty law schools in the

---

883. Fred Shapiro, *The Most Cited Law Reviews*, 29 J. LEGAL STUD. 389, 395 (2000).

884. *An Empirical Evaluation of Specialized Law Reviews*, 26 FLA ST. U. L. REV. 813 (1999).

Jerome Prince Evidence Moot Court Competition, hosted by Brooklyn Law School in April 1990. Mike Kuckelman '90 and Trey Pettlon '91 received the Best Brief Award and argued in the final round before a panel that included Justice Antonin Scalia. That same spring, Ronald Small '90, Doug Witteman '91, and Suzanne Zimmerman '91 received the Top Respondent Brief Award at the August Rendigs Products Liability Moot Court Competition, held in Cincinnati. In 1994, Chris McCurdy '95 and Patrick Reavey '95 received the award for Top Respondent's Brief among twenty-two teams in the National Environmental Moot Court Competition hosted by the Salmon P. Chase School of Law at Northern Kentucky University. Their brief on the issue of state jurisdiction over federal military installations for environmental clean-up was reprinted in the *Northern Kentucky Law Review*. They defeated teams from Yale and Wayne State. At the 1995 J. Braxton Craven Memorial Constitutional Law Moot Court Competition at the University of North Carolina School of Law, Rhonda Crowley '96, and John Carpinelli '96 received the award for overall Best Brief among twenty-six competing schools. In March 1997, Washburn's team of Steve Heck '97, Stacy Friend '98, and James Crawford '98 received the second place award for Best Brief in the Judge Conrad B. Duberstein National Bankruptcy Law Moot Court Competition at St. John's University. The same weekend, David Hansen '97 was named Top Oralist at the Evan A. Evans Constitutional Law Moot Court Competition at the University of Wisconsin. Another Top Oralist Award went to Eric Kraft '99 at the Giles S. Rich Intellectual Property Moot Court Competition at Suffolk Law School in Boston in March 1998. His teammate Scott Liljegren '99 received the second place award for Top Oralist.

In 1993, eligibility for membership in the Order of Barristers was expanded to include students who had competed in trial advocacy competitions and no longer was limited to students participating in moot court competitions.

Washburn students also excelled in competitions involving lawyering skills besides trial and appellate advocacy. In February 1995, Jerry Parrish '96 and David Perry '96 finished third in the national final rounds in Miami of the ABA National Negotiation Competition. Competitors negotiated international business transactions. Washburn had earned one of sixteen places in the national finals when its team tied for first place in its regional competition. Washburn returned to the national finals two years later after finishing second in the regional competition. Team members that year were Ken Fenley '97 and Shannon Wead '97.

Students excelled individually as well. Marilyn Horsch '90 received the 1990 Edward L. Dubroff Memorial Award for Best Writing on Immigration and Nationality Law. The award included a $1,000 prize. Kate Lynch '92 also won a cash award for first place in the 1992 Schwab Memorial Essay Contest sponsored by the ABA Family Law Section. Her paper on abrogation of adoption was published in the *Family Law Quarterly*, ironically in the first issue published by the Washburn student editorial board.[885] In 1991, the *CCH Labor Law Journal* published Tracy Lough's '91 article on the Worker Adjustment and Retraining Notification Act. She prepared it as a class project for Professor Jean Reeves, who encouraged her to submit it for publication. William S. Hein & Co. in 1994 published another class project, "Limited Liability Companies," by Mary Virginia "Ginny" Moore '96, prepared for Professor John Christensen's Advanced Legal Research class, as volume 17 of its series *Legal Research Guides*. The following year, Moore published articles on third-party liability in malpractice cases in *National Public Accountancy* and on "Comparable Worth" in *Public Personnel Management*. That same year, "Legal Malpractice" by Patrick Reavey '95 was added to the Hein *Legal Research Guide* series.

Phi Delta Phi legal fraternity chose Karl Hesse '92 as the 1992 recipient of the J. Will Pless International Graduate of the Year Award. Hesse was chosen from more than 150 nominees based on scholarship and service to the fraternity. Jae Lee '95 received the 1994 ABA Student Service Award, recognizing her work to establish Washburn's Asian Pacific American Law Student Association, to create awareness of issues of concern to Asian Pacific American communities, and to recruit students.

Students were active in professional organizations too. Washburn students formed a chapter of the National Association of Public Interest Law in 1989. Ainka Kweli '94 was elected national Vice President for 1993–94. Stan Wolfe '98 was elected national President of the Native American Law Students Association for 1997–98, in just the second year that Washburn had a NALSA chapter. During 1998–99, 2L Angela Boeck '00 served as Student Director of the ABA's national Volunteer Income Tax Assistance (VITA) Program and was the ABA-LSD's representative to the Public Contract Law Section. Washburn received the Governor's Trophy as the best ABA Law Student Division chapter

---

885. Kathleen M. Lynch, *Can Adoptive Parents Change Their Minds?* 26 FAM. L.Q. 257 (1992).

in the Tenth Circuit in 1989, and again in 1994 and 1995. Mike Montero '96 in 1995 and Paula Hickman '98 in 1997 were elected Circuit Governor. Rick Penalta '92 was ABA-LSD Liaison to the Real Property Division of the ABA Section of Real Property, Probate and Trust Law for 1990–91. Carolyn Powell '01 served as the Law Student Division Liaison for 2000–01 to the Unmet Needs of Children: America's Children at Risk Task Force. In 2001, Adam Espinosa '02 was elected Vice President of Committees for the Hispanic National Bar Association Law Student Division and Andrew Kynaston '02 was ABA-LSD Liaison to the Family Law Section.

Students made the annual Barrister's Ball a charity event. Faculty members donated items for silent and live auctions, including dinners at their homes or restaurants, pool parties, rounds of golf, and the like. The most popular auction item was David Pierce's Spam-a-Lot, a dinner for ten students at which each dish was made from a gourmet recipe for Spam. The winning bid one year was $3,000. Students usually selected a law-related charity to receive the net proceeds. The fall 2000 ball produced record contributions of $5,000 each to CASA and to Kansas Legal Services, Inc.[886] Another popular charity event was Kiss-the-Pig. Students put money into mason jars designated for willing faculty members and the professor whose jar had the most money had to kiss a pig during a noon-hour ceremony on the patio. Professors who were in the lead were not above making last-minute contributions, hoping to win the honor for a colleague. Professor Wadley provided the pig, although sometimes it was a donkey or other farm animal.

THE MEMO

The principal meeting each year of America's law school deans is held during the mid-year meeting of the American Bar Association. I arrived in Boston for the 1993 meeting in the early afternoon of Tuesday, February 2. When I checked in at my hotel, the clerk recognized my name immediately. "Oh, Mr. Concannon," she said. "We have three messages for you." Two were from my Administrative Assistant Diane Milligan and one was from Associate Dean Allen Easley. Each read, "Call your office ASAP!"

---

886. *WSBA Donates Barristers Ball Proceeds*, 39 THE CIRCUIT RIDER 18 (Spring 2001).

Around noon that day, alums in Wichita had begun calling the Dean's office asking about a memorandum that was circulating rapidly among Wichita lawyers. One of them faxed a copy. It was a memorandum from KU law school Dean Bob Jerry to KU's Vice Chancellor Del Brinkman entitled "ABA Accreditation; Washburn; Funding the KU Law School." It was dated two months earlier, November 30, 1992. In it, Jerry argued that all state funding for Washburn Law School should be eliminated and used instead to address deficiencies in the budget of the KU Law School. One portion of Jerry's rationale was incendiary enough to incite every Washburn student and alum and was certain to produce headlines:

> The state has assisted in the advance of a low-quality law school, with a faculty whose credentials cannot even compare to ours, with a student body (I believe to be) composed of more non-residents percentage-wise than our own, and with a student body of significantly lower quality; at the same time, the state has failed to provide adequate resources to fund the state's one public law school. In a sentence, the state law school is in the process of being leveled while a low-quality law school gets improved.

Jerry acknowledged in the memo that "[t]here is room in Kansas for a second law school" and that it should be at Washburn, but he argued it should be a private school charging "whatever tuition it needs to sustain its operations" and with no limitation on the number of non-resident students it enrolls.

> This would mean that high-quality Kansas residents would receive a state-subsidized education at KU; lower-quality Kansas residents would still have an option to get an education in Kansas (i.e., at Washburn), but they would have to pay more—which is reasonable, because at a certain point the state should not be in the business of subsidizing the graduate education of lower-quality students....If the state is concerned that some high-quality Kansas residents may not get admitted to the KU Law School and thereby receive the state's support, part of this reform could include a slight expansion (e.g., 15 resident students per class) of the KU School of Law....

The coincidence that there were reports that a bill might be introduced that very week to "privatize" Washburn's law school and merge the remainder of Washburn with KU was striking. The day before the memo surfaced, Washburn

428 *Washburn Law School History*

University's alumni network had been advised that "the details of how such a proposal could be accomplished are unclear. Nevertheless, this proposed legislation has been discussed in both the House and Senate among rank and file legislators as well as the leadership."[887]

No one from the press had called yet about the memo, but the call was inevitable. Easley and I immediately began discussing strategy for our response. I asked David Monical, then Executive Assistant to the President and Washburn's lobbyist at the Legislature, to join the discussions. We all were concerned what might happen if the press contacted President Thompson about the memo, since he was not sufficiently informed to respond effectively and, we feared, not adept enough to do so. Monical agreed to urge Thompson to say as little as possible and to direct inquiries to me or Monical, if possible. By then, it was late enough in the day that we were reasonably confident the morning papers would not report the memo, so we decided it was prudent to wait until the next morning to advise Thompson, giving us more time to develop a strategy and reducing the risk he would develop his own. We wanted to be able to give him, and others who might be contacted, a page of talking points about the achievements of the Law School and the prominent roles of its graduates in state government and the legal profession in Kansas. We also wanted to have ready data about the diverse backgrounds of Washburn's professors, such as the number who had earned advanced degrees beyond the J.D., 14 of 26, compared to just two on the entire faculty at KU who had done so. Happily, we recently had accumulated most of the needed data for other purposes, in anticipation of state affiliation proposals, in response to requests from the Kansas Board of Regents, and to support the Law School Financing Plan. We merely needed to update the data. I dictated on the phone early Wednesday morning a memo to send to Monical—we did not yet travel with laptops or use email while on the road.

Being in Boston had several advantages. I had the luxury to spend several late night hours that Tuesday brainstorming with former Dean Carl Monk, refining our theme for responding to the media, and drafting precise language to make certain points. In addition, on Wednesday it was Allen Easley who had to handle all the walk-in inquiries as faculty, staff, and students learned in waves about

887. Washburn University Alumni Legislative Network, Update 93-1 (Feb. 1, 1993).

the memo, and in some instances urged harsh responses. He had to field many calls from alums too. He did an extraordinary job of sharing what we knew, and what we didn't, and offering assurance we would respond appropriately.

I never doubted Jerry's later statement that he did not intend for his memo to become public. It clearly was prompted by the site evaluation report following KU's accreditation inspection which led the ABA Accreditation Committee not only to express concerns about KU's overall resource base and how far KU's faculty salaries and other funding had fallen below national medians but also to require a report about remedial action. By February, when the memo was leaked, Jerry was again proposing as the solution the separate law school fee of $40 per credit hour that he sought unsuccessfully the year before. When he wrote the memo in November, however, Jerry's response was not to complain about the denial of the fee increase but instead to complain about Washburn's funding.

> [S]tate support, when combined with the tuition dollars that Washburn Law School gets to retain, has created a situation I never thought I would witness: Washburn Law School's resource base exceeding that of the KU Law School.... Washburn Law School has accomplished its growing prosperity by appealing to the Washburn regents 'to catch up with KU.' But the best interests of Kansans are served if Washburn tries to be the best school possible with its own resources (on a private model), and the state provides one state law school of sufficient quality and at a sufficiently competitive price that Kansas residents will not need to go outside Kansas for their education.

Finance was not the only issue at KU and the other issues influenced our strategy. KU had endured sixteen months of bad publicity stemming from allegations by women students of sexual harassment involving law professor Emil Tonkavich and further allegations that various claims of sexual harassment by both present and former students had not been handled appropriately.[888] Since the beginning of the 1992 fall semester, a special university committee had been conducting hearings in a proceeding to dismiss Tonkavich from the University. For inexplicable reasons, committee members were not given release time to conduct the hearing promptly, so hearings were held weekly

---

888. *KU law school on nightmarish ride*, TOPEKA CAP.-J., Feb. 5, 1993; Letter to KU Law School Alumni from Robert H. Jerry II (Nov. 22, 1991).

and, like a water torture, produced weekly news stories reporting new, lurid details and recounting the full history of the proceeding.

An anonymous source finally faxed the memo to three Topeka news media the next day, late Wednesday afternoon. KSNT-TV broke the story in a brief report on its 10:00 p.m. news. The *Topeka Capital-Journal* treated it as a bigger story and assigned reporter Lisa Sodders to cover it. She immediately called to interview any official at either university who would talk with her. David Monical gave her the data we had readied for distribution: five of seven Kansas Supreme Court Justices were Washburn graduates, and only one was from KU; 65 of the 105 county attorneys in Kansas graduated from Washburn; and 75 of the 146 District Judges held Washburn degrees, including 50 of the 79 judges sitting outside the four largest counties. Sodders obtained a KU alumni newsletter that listed only 54 graduates who were District Judges and verified with the Kansas Board of Regents that 66% of Washburn graduates in 1991 were employed in Kansas compared to 44% at KU. Monical told Sodders with some amusement, "Dean Jerry seems to be implying that the bulk of the legal infrastructure in the state of Kansas has graduated from a second-rate law school."[889] Although the banner headline on the front page of the Thursday paper read "KU dean belittles WU law school," the story reported all the data Monical provided, the comparison of the number of advanced degrees earned by faculty members at each school, plus the results of the summer 1992 Kansas bar examination at which Washburn's pass rate for first-time takers was 95% compared to 92% at KU. Positive information about Washburn that never would have been printed had we issued a press release now was a newsworthy product of investigative reporting. A graphic compared numeric credentials of entering classes at both schools and the article reported that Washburn had more than 1000 applicants for 150 openings, despite the fact that Washburn's tuition was almost 2.5 times the tuition at KU. Sodders reported Allen Easley's observation that it was clear many qualified applicants were not being admitted at either school:

> "This is not an issue where we're drawing distinctions between qualified applicants at KU and unqualified applicants at Washburn," Easley said. "Every admitted student at both law schools is highly qualified.

---

889. *KU dean belittles WU law school*, TOPEKA CAP.-J., Feb. 4, 1993.

"The more important question is—more than entrance credentials—is what they do when they leave. I think our graduates are doing more to serve Kansas."[890]

Monical told Sodders, "In terms of support for the state's legal infrastructure, the return which the state of Kansas gets is much higher for the $700,000 invested in Washburn than for the 2 plus million dollars invested in KU."[891] In a similar vein, I tried to diminish the role of state funding and emphasize the role of tuition: "We have clearly worked very hard to improve the quality of our program in a responsible way. Student tuition covers 64% of our total operating budget."[892]

As chance would have it, Bob Jerry had been away from Lawrence for several days and did not arrive in Boston until late Wednesday. He thus was unavailable to talk to Sodders before the Thursday article was printed. The only KU official who would comment was the executive vice chancellor who had "no comment on the contents of the memo because it was a private communication" but did say it did not represent the view of KU.[893] I talked with Sodders several times that Wednesday. My goal was to say up front something that would redirect the focus, and she printed it first: "'I'm both shocked and disappointed to think that Dean Jerry would take this approach to the problems he's facing,' Concannon said."[894]

Jerry sought me out as soon as I arrived at the continental breakfast at the deans' meeting on Thursday morning. Our working relationship always had been positive, and he clearly was embarrassed. He speculated that the memo would be more harmful to KU's interest than ours. Both of us were certain the story would grow throughout the day, rather than subside, but neither of us anticipated how large it would grow. I spent nearly the entire day in my hotel room, where the phone rang continuously. Lisa Sodders continued to interview me, and the *Capital-Journal* assigned another reporter, Sherry Pigg, to interview Jerry. Four other reporters submitted pieces. State Senator Richard Rock '50 described the incident as "a reporter's dream and a legislator's or

---

890. *Id.*
891. *Id.*
892. *Id.*
893. *Id.*
894. *Id.*

administrator's nightmare."[895] The Friday *Capital-Journal* devoted two and one-half pages and eight separate stories to the "flap," including a four-column front page point-counterpoint piece reporting Jerry's reaction on one side and my response on the other. Our pictures were set off against one another in the closest approximation of the 60 Minutes format of Shana Alexander versus James J. Kilpatrick that the paper could accomplish with file photos.

When Sodders asked me Thursday morning what I thought had motivated the memo, I gave the response we had planned: "If you look at the first sentence of it, it appears to be the concerns of the ABA accreditation committee" about the law school's resource base. "I certainly support his efforts to increase funding for his law school through increased student fees. Adequate funding is vital to a quality program. I understand the budget frustration that prompted it; I can understand when you're trying to convince your internal administration to help you, you might go a little overboard." Our redirection strategy worked. The banner headline on page one of Friday's *Topeka Capital-Journal* proclaimed "KU law school on nightmarish ride," and the lead paragraph reported that internal problems during the past sixteen months, including the sexual harassment investigation, had produced a "public relations nightmare" for KU.[896] A second front page article, "Resource base a concern at KU law school" noted that the accreditation document expressing concern about KU's resources "that prompted" Jerry to write the "controversial memo" was not public information. Jerry found it necessary to assure the reporter "there is absolutely no reason to think there is any problem with our school's accreditation."[897]

The formal statement Jerry issued made it clear why he had been so eager to talk with me early Thursday: "I met with Jim this morning to express my regret that someone would attempt to damage the positive relationship between us and our schools, and to apologize for the misunderstandings that have developed because of my poor choice of words in a private communication."[898] He expressed regret at his use of "some extremely casual language in that memo, because I believe that Washburn School of Law has made tremendous strides under the excellent leadership of Jim Concannon, has many outstanding alumni

895. *Anecdotes and notes on the KU-WU flap*, TOPEKA CAP.-J., Feb. 5, 1993.
896. *KU law school on nightmarish ride*, *supra* note 888.
897. *Resource base a concern at KU law school*, TOPEKA CAP.-J., Feb. 5, 1993.
898. *KU: Bob Jerry's REACTION*, TOPEKA CAP.-J., Feb. 5, 1993.

in the state and nation and is a quality institution."[899] He stood by his concerns about funding for his institution but maintained, "I have always thought that Kansas needs two quality law schools, as it has today."[900] When asked about my reaction to his apology, Jerry said, "He's a very gracious person. He's a class act. I respect him a lot. Jim reacted the way that I hope I would in a similar circumstance. I hope that we can restore and build up the positive relationship that did exist…so all of us can make progress in the programs we offer."[901]

I sought to take the high road, but also to stay on message. When asked how the memo would affect relations between the schools, I responded,

> I'm convinced from talking to Bob this morning that he regrets his statement, and in the future he will address the ABA accreditation committee and concerns about the KU law school by taking positive steps to improve his school. I'm convinced he regrets not only the release of the statement, but the statement itself. There are so many areas where we need to cooperate for the betterment of the Bar, and I'm sure we'll continue to do so.[902]

I rejected the suggestion that the memo reflected the general mindset of faculty members at KU. "They know what our faculty do, and we know what their faculty do. When you've got that information, you have a respect for one another."[903] Other questions gave opportunities to emphasize that while Washburn had more non-resident students, many ultimately stayed in Kansas, "becoming an important part of the Kansas legal community" and that "[w]e've had many calls from alumni here who have been unbelievably supportive of the law school. They're willing to do absolutely anything for us."[904]

Sodders decided to test that assertion by calling lawyers in Topeka. She reported that Washburn graduates were "steaming."[905] "'It's a lot of baloney, is what it is,' fumed Mark L. Bennett, Jr. ['61]"[906] Shawnee County Commis-

---

899. *Id.*
900. *Id.*
901. *Id.*
902. *WU: James Concannon's RESPONSE*, TOPEKA CAP.-J., Feb. 5, 1993.
903. *Id.*
904. *Id.*
905. *KU comments steam WU law school grads*, TOPEKA CAP.-J., Feb. 5, 1993.
906. *Id.*

sioner Don Cooper '90 expressed "disbelief 'because I've always felt the state of Kansas was fortunate to have two quality law schools, and I still feel that way.'"[907]

Other graduates responded with wonderful sarcasm. Joel Meinecke '69, who had become first Assistant Shawnee County Attorney, professed, "I've always considered myself in the presence of greater minds when I'm with KU graduates."[908] Shawnee County District Judge Frank Yeoman '73 revealed that in his first probate matter that morning he had been asked to approve a substantial bequest to the KU Endowment Association. "I wonder if they think I'm competent to sign this?"[909] Chief Justice Richard Holmes '53 may have had the greatest line. When a reporter reached him in his chambers, he commented, "I'm just sitting here wearing my dunce cap." Washburn lawyers, he added, "hold their own in court. No, we don't have any special instructions when a party is represented by a WU Law graduate."[910]

Student reaction was newsworthy too. Sherry Pigg was unable to persuade any student at KU to comment for publication and was able to report only that students there gathered in small groups to read Jerry's statement about the memo and to discuss it.[911] Predictably, Washburn students were more vocal, voicing what a reporter described as "anger and near disbelief."[912] Robert Beattie, Jr. '93 called for Jerry's resignation, adding that he had turned down a scholarship offer to attend KU after visiting both schools. "I thought this was the better school."[913] Other students found more humor in the situation, "using the 'second-rate' student remark as a mocking excuse for not having an answer" to a question in class.[914] Barbara Peterson '93 "envisioned Jerry having a 'pomposity tantrum. I have the impression he was lying on the floor, pounding his fists, kicking his feet, having a red face. I'm still unemployed, but I'll be applying for (Jerry's) position next week.'"[915] Allen Easley scheduled an open meeting with students Thursday afternoon to update them about what

---

907. *Id.*

908. *Anecdotes and notes on the KU-WU flap, supra* note 895.

909. *Id.*

910. *Id.*

911. *Id.*

912. *WU students take remarks with disgust,* TOPEKA CAP.-J., Feb. 5, 1993.

913. *Id.*

914. *Id.*

915. *Anecdotes and notes on the KU-WU flap, supra* note 895.

we knew and to make it clear "the law school was proud of the students and they should be proud of themselves."[916]

The buzz was not confined to the legal community. The 240-member Downtown Topeka Rotary Club met at noon on Thursday. Its custom is for members to put pocket change into cups at each table to donate to charity. No charity had yet been designated for February. "A voice from the audience suggested the money should go to the Washburn Law School."[917] Before introducing guests, Webb Garlinghouse asked Washburn law graduates to stand. "About 25 stood. Garlinghouse said, according to the latest news reports, those were the inferior lawyers. He then asked the 'superior KU lawyers' to stand. Five stood."[918]

The plan to minimize President Thompson's involvement largely succeeded. When a reporter predictably called him, he suggested that the two law schools "have better things to do than compare themselves to each other. 'No one's going to benefit from this; it's just going to hurt legal education. It's just an unfortunate incident.'"[919] However, Thompson in letters to the Kansas Board of Regents and KU's Chancellor diverted from the message we wanted to emphasize by seeking to relate the incident to his larger view of higher education. "This reinforces what I've been saying: We need a master plan for higher education because we've been approaching it in a fragmented way. We're not getting at the root cause. Our institutions of higher education probably are underfunded."[920]

Perhaps the most important audience, viewed in the long term, was the Legislature. Washburn again was proposing an increase in the state operating grant to the University, part of which went to the Law School, and its broader goal continued to be full state affiliation. Rep. Denise Everhart '89 worried that the memo "gives credence to proposals we've heard to make Washburn a satellite campus of KU and then kill the law school. There is a law school out there that doesn't want to compete with Washburn and may try to harm Washburn."[921] The "satellite campus" proposal she mentioned had been championed by a member of the Kansas Board of Regents from Wichita, Don Slawson, and early speculation identified Slawson as a likely source of the leak of the memo.

---

916. *WU students take remarks with disgust, supra* note 912.

917. *Anecdotes and notes on the KU-WU flap, supra* note 895.

918. *Id.*

919. *The memo trail,* TOPEKA CAP.-J., Feb. 5, 1993.

920. *Id.*

921. *Memo's meaning for Washburn pondered,* TOPEKA CAP.-J., Feb. 5, 1993.

The memo, according to The Associated Press, "ignited a firestorm" at the Legislature.[922] Rep. Don Smith '50, whose family included five Washburn lawyers over three generations, including a former Chief Justice, declared on the House floor that the memo was "highly inappropriate" and that Jerry "should spend his time, really, taking care of the administrative problems" at KU.[923] Sen. Marge Petty '90 thought the memo "might have an effect, in at least pointing out the competition among educational institutions in Kansas.... Washburn is apparently doing a very, very good job of educating lawyers. It wouldn't hurt if the memo is not forgotten."[924] Legislators from Lawrence felt obliged to declare that their delegation "certainly doesn't feel that way about Washburn law school graduates" and described the situation as "tragic," but Sen. Sandy Praeger did suggest the memo's effect might turn around: "If Washburn quickly capitalizes on the attack to raise alumni money, 'that might show that the law school really doesn't need a piece of the Washburn operating grant.'"[925] The verdict of the *Capital-Journal*'s legislative reporter was that the memo was a "public relations bonanza" for Washburn.[926] Legislators were "extremely impressed" by the statistical data the memo caused to be published and the "controversy served as a vehicle for Washburn to better inform legislators regarding the nature of its law school and its contributions to the state."[927] Ultimately, the memo's effect was to "derail any immediate attempts to 'privatize' the law school and merge"[928] Washburn into KU. No one later in the session wanted to risk reopening the debate about state funding for the Law School.

By Saturday, a *Capital-Journal* editorial entitled "Washburn's class action" declared that "the regrettably incendiary relationship of Kansas' two schools of law has been effectively defused."[929] It referred to Jerry's apology and included generous remarks about me, adding that "[i]nstead of hunting for Jerry's head,

---

922. *KU Law School dean's remarks ignite firestorm at Statehouse*, HUTCHINSON NEWS, Feb. 5, 1993. The AP stories were printed in many newspapers throughout Kansas.

923. *Id.*

924. *Anecdotes and notes on the KU-WU flap, supra* note 895.

925. *Id.*

926. *Memo's meaning for Washburn pondered, supra* note 921.

927. *Washburn University Alumni Legislative Newsletter*, Update 93-2, Feb. 12, 1993.

928. *Id.*

929. *Washburn's class action*, TOPEKA CAP.-J., Feb. 5, 1993.

as Concannon had every right to do, the Washburn law school dean graciously attempted to mend fences."[930] It repeated much of the positive data we had provided and suggested "the incident might inadvertently boost Washburn's image in the state."[931]

Bob Jerry tried to do the right thing too. On Monday, after returning from the ABA meeting, he came to Washburn unannounced to apologize to students he found in the commons area of the first floor.

> I introduced myself and told each student that I wasn't there to ask them to change their views about me, but I wanted them to know I was a big enough person to walk into their school and shake their hands and look them in the eye and tell them I was sorry for things I put in that memo that I really don't believe are true....And I wished them each good luck in their studies.[932]

Students initially were bewildered when they were approached by a stranger introducing himself as Bob Jerry. Most "were gracious, even if they weren't all ready to forgive him." Some thought he was "courageous." Others doubted the sincerity of the gesture, expressing uncertainty whether the apology was "for what he wrote or for the fuss that arose after his memo became public."[933]

News items, both serious and humorous, continued to appear for several weeks in the *Capital-Journal*. One serious one, confirming that Washburn Law School actually did spend more per student in its operating budget than did KU, included a quote I hoped prospective students would read: that our budget "allows us to spend money on students that all law deans would like to spend" to "make our students successful."[934] Another, analyzing State Regent Slawson's proposal that the Law School become free-standing, stressed how low tuition was at KU compared to ours. In the same story, I was able to address the "free-standing" issue by pointing out how intertwined our Law School and the University were and how they cooperated on expenditures in ways that benefitted both, such as coordinating acquisitions at the Mabee and

930. *Id.*

931. *Id.*

932. *KU dean ventures into the lion's den bearing apologies,* WICHITA EAGLE, Feb. 10, 1993.

933. *Id.*

934. *WU outspends KU $2,500 a student,* TOPEKA CAP.-J., Feb. 13, 1993.

Law Libraries to avoid duplication. "It's almost like you'd have to dig a moat to separate us from the rest of the university," I commented.[935]

Other items were tongue-in-cheek. Legislative writer Martin Hawver speculated that even if Dean Jerry was correct that Washburn spent more per student, it might be appropriate "given that much of the WU class time is apparently remedial education." He asked if the same formula should be used "as in the school finance formula, where vocational education students are counted as 1.5 pupils for budget purposes? Sounds reasonable, because from what we read in the faxes, a lot of WU law students are on the rebound from barber college anyway, just casting around for a vocation where they can work indoors in the winter, possibly as a judge."[936] An editorial cartoon depicted a KU fighter jet that had launched a "Washburn memo" missile in which pilot "Capt. Bob Jerry" was reporting "Washburn target destroyed…am returning to base" as the missile was turning around to aim at the rear of his jet.[937]

There was news coverage in most daily papers statewide and in the *Kansas City Star*. The *Chronicle of Higher Education* even reported the incident nationally under the headline "Robert Jerry may be in line for this year's Bryant Gumbel Tact-in-Memo-Writing Award." The headline in *The Wichita Eagle* was "The case of the insulted law school,"[938] and the following day the *Eagle* reported details of the ABA Accreditation Committee's report in which KU's "ability to afford a top-quality law school is being questioned."[939] The incident was fodder for editorial writers: "Snob Hill Law School" proclaimed the *Chanute Tribune*. The *Hutchinson News* suggested the data showed the state "may be getting its money's worth on its Washburn spending" and "might cause the Legislature to take a harder look, not at the money spent on Washburn, but at the money spent on the KU Law School."[940] The *University Daily Kansan* called for Jerry's resignation,[941] and that prompted a letter in response signed by almost all members of the KU law faculty supporting Jerry. Other editors, including those in Regents communities Lawrence and Emporia, thought the

935. *Law school viewed as appendage of Washburn*, TOPEKA CAP.-J., Feb. 9, 1993.
936. *Remedial funds for WU school?*, TOPEKA CAP.-J., Feb. 7, 1993.
937. *Opinion*, TOPEKA CAP.-J., Feb. 9, 1993.
938. *The case of the insulted law school*, WICHITA EAGLE, Feb. 5, 1993.
939. *Low salaries at KU law school concern ABA*, WICHITA EAGLE, Feb. 6, 1993.
940. *Chewing words*, HUTCHINSON NEWS, Feb. 7, 1993.
941. *Jerry should resign*, UNIVERSITY DAILY KANSAN, Feb. 18, 1993.

effort to admit Washburn to the state system was behind the flap and warned in headlines "Washburn no bargain."[942] The *Wichita Eagle* opined that the flap should not obscure the fact that law schools were producing too many lawyers and that eventually consolidation of the schools would have to be addressed.[943]

I was astonished that, despite massive media coverage, no story ever reported that Washburn's Dean was a graduate of the University of Kansas law school. I worried that would become another target for media frenzy, especially when we responded to a reporter's request for a list of all faculty members showing their degrees and the schools from which they received them.

The public finally lost interest in the controversy but lawyers, being lawyers, kept it alive in the legal community. Mike Merriam '76 distributed two poems at a Topeka Bar Association luncheon. David Bruns '93 drew a full-page cartoon for the March TBA newsletter depicting a Jayhawk sporting a "K.U. Law" tattoo with its foot in its beak.[944] The cartoon accompanied a satiric short story entitled "Landfillers v. Snobhillers." The Crawford County Bar Association invited Bob Jerry and me to be the after-dinner speakers at its annual bench-bar day in April. I used the occasion to present Jerry with a one-year Honorary Membership in the Washburn Law School Association, based on his having done more to advance the interests of Washburn Law School during the past year than any other non-alum. The Leavenworth County Bar Association presented me with its coveted Smiling Bull Award and I am certain the memo was what prompted the award. The Wichita Bar Association devoted an entire skit to the incident in its bar show during the Kansas Bar Association annual meeting in June. The chorus sang the tune "Dean Jerry" to the music of "Officer Krupke" from West Side Story:

Verse 1

Group: Dear Kindly Dean Bob Jerry
         You gotta understand

942. *Washburn no bargain*, LAWRENCE J.-WORLD, Feb. 11, 1993, reprinted as a guest editorial in many other papers. A similar view was expressed in *The Law-School War*, EMPORIA GAZETTE, Feb. 8, 1993.

943. *"C" word? The need for two laws schools is the real issue for Legislature*, WICHITA EAGLE, Feb. 23, 1993.

944. TBA BRIEFINGS, Mar. 1993, at 3.

Someone leaked your memo
You've gotten out of hand.

You said we're pretty lousy
We're really not that bad

All: Golly, Moses, natcherly we're mad.

All: Gee Professor Jerry
We're very upset
We think you need a lecture on knee jerk etiquette.

Group: We're not all that preppy
We're misunderstood
All Ichabods are really good.

All: We are good. We are good.
Ichabods are good.

Group: Gee Bob, we're so misunderstood.

Verse 2

Solo 1:   Dear Kindly Dean Bob Jerry
I looked at old KU
But people down at Washburn
Taught me how to sue
You said I couldn't Rock Chalk
You said low quality

All: Dean, you've got no personality.

Solo 2:   Hey, professor Jerry, you're livin' a dream.
You'll never get a lot of bucks by being so mean.
Your ivory tower is missing some bricks.
Just ask your colleague, Tonkavitch.

All: Eeek!

All: Tonkavitch, Tonkavitch
Tonkavitch, vitch, vitch.

Solo 2:   Oops, Bob, there goes another glitch.

Verse 3

Solo 3:   I came to KU Law School.
            I heard it had some class.
            Nobody ever told me,
            The Dean's a horse's ass.

            I met some friends from Washburn
            We took the bar review

All: Jerry, we have got some news for you!

Solo 3:   Gee, Professor Jerry, you've got it all wrong.
            A pompous little memo
            And you're history, so long.
            The media made you a snub and a geek
            Your (spit) apology is weak.

All: It is weak. It is weak.
            It is weak, weak, weak.
            Too late (spit) you couldn't stop the leak.

            The trouble is you're jealous.
            The trouble is you're rude.
            You didn't want to tell us.
            We read it in the news.
            Your problem is we're growing.
            Your problem is we're grown.
            Jerry, you've got problems of your own.

All: Look, Professor Jerry it's time to concede
            That half the Supreme Court has got a Washburn degree.
            You have to admit that your memo was rude.
            Gee, Professor Jerry, K Who?

ANOTHER BATTLE WITH PRESIDENT THOMPSON

Despite the lessons that should have been learned from the incident with Dean Jerry's memo, President Thompson could not resist revisiting the issue of the Law School Financing Plan. In April 1994, he lamented to his senior administrative staff that the plan was "killing us." He described law faculty salaries as "hurting us externally," referring to published reports about an American Association of University Professors study showing that university-wide Washburn had the highest salaries in the state, a fact that was true only because inclusion of the disproportionately large proportion of law faculty distorted the data. He complained that law salaries also were "killing us internally,"[945] exaggerating wildly, by more than 100%, the number of law faculty members who would be receiving in excess of $100,000 in the next year and ignoring the fact that a larger number of faculty members at KU were receiving more than that amount in the current year.

As soon as I saw the minutes of the senior staff meeting, I asked for a meeting with Thompson and had a notepad full of bullet points. I told him how appalled I was by his "affirmative misstatements of fact," his "ignorance or indifference to critical facts I would have thought a competent administrator would want to know before drawing conclusions," and his "lack of understanding of how the Law School Financing Plan provides more money, not less," for the remainder of the campus. I provided updated data showing that KU's new law school fee had led to progress in solving its resource issues. Despite Washburn's modest improvements, three candidates had declined our offers that year to fill a faculty vacancy and we previously lost a candidate who joined the KU faculty instead. "Perhaps your comments to the senior staff reflect a belief that we should not compete for the best possible faculty in the national market but instead should be satisfied with whomever we might hire locally," I told Thompson. "No one else has such an inferiority complex about this institution and all of our constituents would reject such a commitment to mediocrity." Because KU's budget issues likely were short-term only, I asked if Thompson could agree that our budget should at least be comparable with the budget at KU. When to my surprise he said he could, I sent a confirming memorandum immediately after returning to my office.[946]

945. Minutes, Washburn U. senior staff meeting (Apr. 29, 1994).
946. Memorandum to Dr. Hugh Thompson from James M. Concannon, Dean

The issue piqued the interest of several Washburn Regents, including not surprisingly the Regent Washburn still had in common with the state board, John Montgomery. Thompson promised the Regents a comprehensive reevaluation of the Financing Plan prior to the spring 1995 budget cycle. A committee including Vice Presidents Wayne Sheley and Gene Mosiman plus David Monical and me concluded that the plan was working as intended and that student credentials had increased despite tuition increases. However, there was a greater likelihood the issue would go away if the Law School conceded something. I agreed to reduce the Law School's share of future increases above the current state operating grant to 8.7% from 13%. The 13% figure had been selected initially so that the amount of state aid allocated to the Law School would be the same as when state funding for Washburn was based on the number of resident credit hours taught. At that time, the legislature allocated one and one-half times the amount for law hours that it allocated for undergraduate hours. Thus, although the Law School taught less than 13% of the resident credit hours, the hours it taught generated 13% of the state aid. My rationale for eliminating the 50% add-on for future operating grant increases was that the legislature would not forever have adhered to the law differential had it retained the credit hour model for Washburn aid. This recommendation as well as the full report were accepted without fanfare by the Board of Regents at its January 18, 1995 meeting. The Financing Plan would not again be an issue during my deanship. It would earn high praise during ABA/AALS accreditation inspections both in 1992–93 and 1999–2000.

THE PROFESSION FOCUSES ON FAIRNESS AND EQUALITY

In 1990, the Kansas Bar Association appointed three task forces, to study the Status of Women, the Status of Minorities, and the Quality of Life in the profession and to make recommendations for improvement. Both Kansas law schools were represented on the task forces on minorities and women; Ron Griffin served on both task forces and Charlene Smith served on the task force for women.

Legal education was only one of many topics the task forces considered. Students at both Washburn and KU completed separate questionnaires in

(May 13, 1994).

1991 about issues of gender and race. The questionnaire on gender issues, for example, asked whether students had either witnessed or experienced various types of gender discrimination by students, faculty, adjunct professors, staff and administration, or student groups. There were 600 responses in all to that questionnaire, 265 at Washburn, including 111 by women. Predictably, the percentage of students, both women and men, who answered that they had witnessed discriminatory conduct by other students was higher than the percentage who answered that they had experienced it, but both numbers were unacceptably high at both schools. As an illustration, 71% of women and 51% of men respondents at Washburn reported they had witnessed "unwanted sexual teasing, jokes, remarks, verbal abuse or questions" by other students, while 40% and 11%, respectively, responded that they had experienced such conduct. On a few questions, Washburn's women reported a significantly higher level of unacceptable behavior by fellow students than did their counterparts at KU. For example, 32% of women at Washburn reported they had experienced unwanted pressure from other students for dates, compared to 10% at KU. However, KU Dean Bob Jerry was insistent that the Task Force's final report include only aggregate data combining responses from both schools.[947] The hearings at KU on sexual harassment charges against Professor Emil Tonkavich were in full swing at the time, and release of school specific responses about faculty would only have fueled the public relations nightmare by showing that higher percentages of women at KU reported witnessing and experiencing acts of gender discrimination by professors than their Washburn counterparts.

The task forces' recommendations for legal education were not revolutionary, e.g., that faculty and administrators should eliminate unintentionally stereotyping women. We distributed the survey results and the recommendations to the faculty to raise awareness of the issues and of student perceptions. Happily,

947. Letter to The Hon. Mary Beck Briscoe, Chair, from Dean Robert H. Jerry (Feb. 19, 1992). I acknowledged that had been the schools' understanding when they agreed to distribute the questionnaires but argued that the report needed to make it clear that there were differences in the responses at the two schools on some questions. Not surprisingly, the student newspaper at KU eventually acquired the unabridged report and published KU's school-specific data. *Survey reveals perception of bias at KU School of Law,* UNIVERSITY DAILY KANSAN, Sept. 15, 1992. Jerry's response expressed concern about the survey's methodology, the vague phrasing of questions, and the failure to define some terms, including "gender bias." *Dean questions survey method,* UNIVERSITY DAILY KANSAN , Sept. 16, 1992, at 2.

when the KBA Board of Governors asked for a report on the steps each school was taking in response to the recommendations, we were able to respond that we had implemented many of them prior to the report's release. For example, even before the Task Force on the Status of Minorities recommended adoption of plans to increase the number of minorities who applied for and were appointed to summer and judicial clerkships, Washburn joined KU, UMKC, and UM-Columbia as participants in a First-Year Minority Clerkship Program sponsored by the Kansas City Metropolitan Bar Association. Twenty firms and corporations participated in 1990, although unfortunately the number of participants declined the next three years. The Task Force further recommended adoption of plans to increase recruitment and retention of minority students. Washburn already had done so and was able to report that its 15.3% minority enrollment in 1990–91, that placed it third among forty-four schools in our twelve-state region, had risen to 15.8% for 1992–93. We attributed that success, in part, to Washburn having one of the highest percentages in the nation of full-time professors who were minorities, 18.5% or five of twenty-seven, including the deans and law librarian,[948] a figure that would grow to seven of twenty-seven in 1995–96. We were able to make a comparable report in response to the recommendation of the Task Force on the Status of Women that the schools "should declare that women have a place in the law school community." One-third of our twenty-seven professors were women and ten women were adjunct professors. We also reported that during the spring of 1990, Washburn had been among the first schools to adopt the November 1989 AALS Statement of Good Practices by Law Professors in the Discharge of their Professional Responsibility, prescribing standards of appropriate faculty conduct. The first two Law Colloquium courses, on Feminist Jurisprudence in the fall of 1990 and Critical Race Theory in the spring of 1993, examined many of the issues raised by the task forces, and in the fall of 1992, Professor Judy Trent Scales from the University of Buffalo led a faculty development discussion of "Sameness and Difference in the Law School Classroom."

Despite these initiatives, there was more work to do. One Washburn student was moved in a letter to the editor of a national women's magazine to complain of "flippant remarks in class regarding women's legal issues," that "guys

---

948. Washburn Law School Report to the Kansas Bar Association Board of Governors, Report of Recommendations of the Task Force on Minorities (Oct. 22, 2002).

ridiculed our Women's Legal Forum by forming a Men's Legal Forum that goes to strip bars one night a week," and most unfortunately about "blonde" jokes a new professor told in class.[949]

The KBA created the Committee on Professionalism, Equality and Quality (COPEQ) to follow up on progress in meeting the task forces' recommendations, not only for legal education but also for the courts, law firms, and state and local bar associations. In my 1994 report to COPEQ, I noted the disconnect between our success in recruiting minority students and the low number of minority graduates who remained in Kansas to practice. "Of 22 minority graduates at Washburn in 1993, only 8 are employed in Kansas or Kansas City, Missouri—only two in private practice. Of 27 minority graduates in 1992, 13 are employed in Kansas or Kansas City, Missouri—five in private practice."[950]

The same report described our plans to create a mentorship program pairing enrolled students with members of the Topeka Bar Association, to enhance students' exposure to professional values. However, the report cautioned that initiatives by the KBA focused only on the two Kansas schools would impact a smaller segment of the KBA's future membership than bar leaders might assume, given that of the 454 new lawyers admitted to practice in Kansas in 1993, exactly 50% graduated from law schools other than Washburn or KU; programs reaching all new lawyers would be needed.

Studies at several other law schools showed that women students had less academic success compared to male students than their entering credentials predicted they would have.[951] Our 1995 report to COPEQ, to the contrary, confirmed that when several classes at Washburn were examined, women were found to be disproportionately represented in the top half of the classes and among the very top ranked graduates as well. In the fall of 1994, the average GPA for women was 2.77 and for men was 2.75. In the 1994 graduating class of 129 students, thirty-one women ranked in the top half in class rank while only twenty-four women were in the lower half. Women in that class had sixteen of the highest twenty-seven grade point averages. The 1995 class had 154 graduates. Thirty-eight women were in the top half in class rank and

949. Kelli Eads '93, *Letters from readers*, GLAMOUR 32 (May 1992).

950. Report to the Kansas Bar Association Committee on Professionalism, Equality and Quality: Update of 1992 Report (Apr. 14, 1994).

951. Lani Guinier, et al., *Becoming Gentlemen: Women's Experiences At One Ivy League Law School*, 143 U. PA. L. REV. 1 (1994).

thirty-three were in the lower half. Nineteen of the twenty-nine graduates with the highest GPAs were women. Four of the five senior editor positions on the *Washburn Law Journal* that year were held by women.[952]

As the KBA Task Force surveys showed, however, race and gender issues are fraught with tension, and the school's "attempts to encourage tolerance and respect have not always been smooth."[953] Washburn was not immune from anonymous postings of offensive messages on billboards or the anonymous placing of hateful or harassing messages in the mail folders of some students. On one occasion, a student organization removed material it had displayed on its bulletin board and placed notes of apology in student mail folders.[954] After incidents in November 1997, the two Deans felt compelled to issue a statement to the student body emphasizing Washburn's commitment to tolerance.

GLOBALIZATION

Washburn was among the first schools to recognize that graduates needed a global perspective of law, even when they attended a Midwestern law school and had no plans to practice in a large firm. The summer study abroad program continued at Brunel University in West London through 1992, but problems with facilities and institutional issues there that made Brunel faculty unwilling to co-teach prevented us from offering the program in 1993. After a one-year hiatus, the Law School in 1994 arranged to use facilities on the Hampstead campus of Kings College, closer to downtown London, and recruited British faculty from a number of different schools, occasionally including Brunel, as co-teachers. The summer program remained there until it was moved to Utrecht University in the Netherlands in 2004.

Expanding appreciation of international issues on Washburn's own campus also became a priority. Washburn eagerly participated in Sister Law School Programs that were part of ABA initiatives to assist in legal reform in newly-liberated and developing countries. The first of those was the Central and East European Law Initiative (CEELI), targeting countries that formerly were part of the Soviet bloc. Its Sister Law School program matched each participating

---

952. Letter to Marcia Poell Holston, Executive Director, Kansas Bar Association, from James M. Concannon (Sept. 21, 1995).

953. Washburn University School of Law Self-Study Report 1999, at 5.

954. Minutes, Washburn Student B. Ass'n (Sept. 8, 1998).

foreign law school with three American schools and funded travel by faculty members from those countries to observe first-hand the American system of legal education, to consult with U.S. professors on curricular reform, and to develop cooperative relationships that would benefit the foreign schools. Washburn volunteered to host a one-week visit in April 1992 by one of twelve East European law deans. Vice Dean Laszlo Bodnar of the Faculty of Law of Josef Attila University in Szeged, Hungary, arrived at Washburn after stops at California Western in San Diego and Emory Law School in Atlanta. His busy schedule included observations of classes, visits with groups of students and faculty, visits to state and federal courts and a Topeka law firm, and the monthly luncheon of the Topeka Bar Association. He even got a taste of law school humor by attending the annual Faculty Roast. He presented a lecture for students about legal reform in Hungary.

In the fall of 1993, the ABA Section of International Law and Practice organized a similar Central and Latin America Law Initiative, funded in part by the United States Information Agency. It brought to Washburn Dean Jackson Parada from the University Dr. Jose Matias Delgado in San Salvador, El Salvador, one of nineteen law schools in the country. Parada was presiding officer of the Council of Law School Deans there.

When the ABA extended its Law Initiative to Africa in the spring of 1995, Washburn hosted Professor Fidelis Kanyongolo, senior head of the Department of Law of the University of Malawi. As a student, he had been ushered out of a law school class and held in jail for nine months for political reasons. Washburn offered assistance to his school in developing Internet capabilities and sent boxes of duplicate and outdated books his school was eager to acquire.

Washburn's priority to expose students to international perspectives was not limited to the Sister Law School programs. The Law School underwrote week-long visits, one during the spring semester of 1996 by Professor Tatiana Zrazhevskaya, Director of the Department of Constitutional and Administrative Law at Voronezh State University and an advisor on constitutional law issues to the Duma in Russia, and another in March 1997 by Michael Coper, who held a chair in constitutional law at Australian National University in Canberra and later became Dean there. Astrid A. M. Mattijssen spent portions of three academic years at Washburn, twice while on sabbatical from Utrecht University in the Netherlands. During her first visit in 1993, she joined faculty members teaching a Colloquium on Human Rights. When she returned for the

1996 spring semester, she collaborated with four Washburn faculty members to teach the three-week course on Comparative Human Rights: Women, Gays, and Lesbians, a collaboration she repeated in the spring semester of 2001 with six Washburn professors.

The Harry R. and Leila J. Logan Endowment for Lectures in Property Law underwrote a ten-day visit in March and April of 2000 by Professors John Michael Milo and Frederik Willem Grosheide from the Mollengraaff Institute for Private Law at Utrecht University. Their principal lectures, respectively, discussed European perspectives on property law and expansions of copyright law.[955] Their interest in visiting Washburn arose when they met Professor Nancy Maxwell while she was at Utrecht during a research sabbatical. Another of Maxwell's collaborators, Caroline Forder from the University of Maastricht in the Netherlands, visited Washburn for a month in September 2001 while researching a book on marriage and marriage-like institutions.

Large numbers of international visitors lectured at Washburn during several periods.[956] In a span of just six weeks during March and April of 1998, Washburn hosted lecturers from five countries on four continents.[957] Eugene Clark '78, then Dean of the Law Faculty at the University of Canberra in Australia, returned to Washburn to compare trends in legal education and the legal profession in Australia and the United States, focusing on recent mergers of Australian law and accounting firms. Other visitors included: Professor Neal MacCormack, a jurisprudence scholar from the University of Edinburgh in Scotland; Professor Dermot Walsh of the University of Limerick in Ireland, who commented on peace accords reached there just days before he arrived in Topeka; Tatsuo

---

955. *Visitors from the Netherlands*, 38 THE CIRCUIT RIDER 7 (Spring 2000).

956. For example, international visitors during eighteen months from 1993–95 included not only Dean Parada and Professor Kanyongolo but also: Professor Richard Grimes of Sheffield Hallam University in England, in October 1993; Professor Jan-Harm d'Kluwen of the University of Limburg in the Netherlands, in April 1994; Professors Eugene Clark '78, then at the Law Department at the University of Tasmania, and Martin Tsamenyi, co-director of the Environmental Law Center at the University of Wollongong in Australia, also in April 1994; Raul Granillo Ocampo, Ambassador to the United States from Argentina, where he previously had been a law professor at two schools and a provincial Supreme Court Justice, in October 1994; and in March 1995, Rose Migiro of the University of Dar Es Salaam in Tanzania, who was spending the week at KU as part of the ABA's African Law Initiative.

957. *International Visitors Share Perspectives*, 37 THE CIRCUIT RIDER 5 (Fall 1998).

Tanaka, General Counsel of Japan's Consulate in Kansas City, who spoke on international trade issues; and Raquel Alvarado Beltran and Dr. Zoraida Avalos Rivera, a prosecutor and prison administrator, respectively, in Peru. Highlights the following spring included a lecture by Oscar Arias Sanchez, former President of Costa Rica and 1987 recipient of the Nobel Peace Prize,[958] and a presentation by Dean Ray Friel from the University of Limerick during a visit to recruit Washburn students for Limerick's LL.M. program. The relationship with Limerick evolved into more formal exchanges of faculty and students, with Professors Ron Griffin, Rogelio Lasso, and Loretta Moore traveling to Limerick during 1999–2000 and two students studying there for a semester.

In later years, the Ahrens Chair in Tort Law brought numerous international visitors to campus. In addition, co-teachers from Washburn's summer abroad program lectured at Washburn on occasion; for example, Julian Killingly from the University of Central England in Birmingham visited in September 1995.

One last initiative involved the Supreme Court of Justice of the Republic of Paraguay. The Partners of the Americas Program had paired Paraguay with the State of Kansas in 1968. Dr. Russell Smith at the School of Business maintained ongoing contacts with officials from Paraguay and learned that, after years of political instability in the country, Paraguay's Supreme Court sought assistance from an American law school in developing judicial training programs, improving legal education, arranging for exchanges of scholars and practitioners, and enhancing the role of the judiciary. We negotiated a Cooperation Agreement, and Minister Elixeno Ayala, a member of the Court, and Dr. Mario Ramos Reyes, Consul General of Paraguay in Kansas, joined Washburn President Jerry Farley and me in signing it in Robinson Courtroom on December 9, 1999.[959] We began implementation in March 2000, hosting a two-month library internship by Arnaldo Levera Gomez, a computer technician in the Research, Legislation, and Publications Division of the Court, who was in the fifth of the six years of law school studies required in Paraguay. Washburn librarians trained him to make available on the Internet court opinions and other legal materials. Unfortunately, further political instability

958. *Nobel Peace Prize Winner, Guest Speaker at Law School*, 37 THE CIRCUIT RIDER 10 (Spring 1999).

959. *Washburn University Signs Cooperation Agreement with the Supreme Court of Paraguay*, 38 THE CIRCUIT RIDER 6 (Spring 2000).

in Paraguay and in its courts precluded the extensive exchanges the agreement contemplated. However, by September 25, 2003, the Law School was able to host the co-directors of Paraguay's Center for Documentation and Archive for the Defense of Human Rights, Judge Luis Maria Benitez and Rose Palau Aguilar, who described the Center's "archive of terror," documenting human rights abuses by a number of South American countries.

AHRENS CHAIR IN TORTS

Funding of the $1 million Ahrens Chair in Tort Law was completed during the summer of 1988, shortly after Professor Ahrens retired and became Professor Emeritus. A reception and press conference on July 26 celebrated creation of the Law School's first Chair. I appointed a special faculty search committee to select a Visiting Professor to be the first Ahrens Chair Professor for fall semester 1989. It would be no ordinary torts scholar but the leading living authority on torts, John W. Wade, a former Dean and then Professor of Law Emeritus at Vanderbilt University School of Law. Wade had collaborated with the late Dean William Prosser to compile the leading casebook on torts. Wade also was the author of casebooks on Restitution and Legal Methods. Wade had been a Visiting Professor at Texas, Columbia, Cornell, Michigan, and Pepperdine before coming to Washburn. At Washburn, he taught both Torts I and an upper level class in Advanced Torts. While advancing age limited his stamina, Wade, along with his wife Mary, was an active participant in the life of the school, and he even made a CLE presentation.

The next Ahrens Chair Professors were Taunya Lovell Banks from the University of Maryland in the spring of 1992 and Carl S. Hawkins from the J. Rueben Clark Law School at Brigham Young University during the spring of 1994. Banks was well known to many faculty members and was a law school classmate of Professor Griffin at Howard. She had come to Topeka in May 1990 to lead a one-day faculty mini-retreat discussing the special needs of minority students and the characteristics of successful academic support programs. Hawkins formerly had been Dean at BYU and currently was Professor of Law Emeritus. He taught Advanced Torts and Remedies and was a co-facilitator for the faculty retreat that spring in Council Grove. Hawkins had been a member both in 1979 and 1986 of the ABA/AALS accreditation teams that visited Washburn. His multiple visits gave him a unique perspective:

I observed [in 1979] that Washburn had a good law school....One thing that was clear was the law school's diverse faculty. They were younger and more productive, and the character of the institution was being influenced by some new young appointments to the faculty who were very talented people. The one big problem I saw here in 1986 was the lack of adequate space in the law library, and that certainly has been well corrected since then.

Washburn has always been distinguished for good teaching, and one thing that became evident after being here for awhile was that Washburn enjoys tremendous respect in the region and in the Kansas bar....The law school has been adding to its reputation in recent years without diminishing any of its established strengths because more of the faculty have done productive research and writing that has reached a national audience.[960]

Persuading nationally renowned scholars to spend an entire semester as a Visiting Professor in Topeka proved to be challenging. Topeka was not at the top of many leading scholars' lists of "must see" destinations. Professors emeritus like Wade and Hawkins were willing to make such commitments but the pool of emeriti was small. Although we persuaded Taunya Banks to accept our offer, her active involvement in activities nationally meant she often had to be absent from Topeka after she finished teaching classes for the week during the semester-long visit. Thus, the faculty tried a new model during the 1996 spring semester, the Ahrens Chair Symposium. The new model was to bring together for a single weekend many of the leading scholars and practitioners in the nation to discuss hot topics in Torts. The *Washburn Law Journal* was an immediate beneficiary since it was able to publish the papers of the symposium. The hope long-term was that faculty visitors would find the experience sufficiently stimulating that they would want to return in the future for a full semester as the Ahrens Chair Professor. However, the symposium format was so successful that it became the longer-term model, with multiple visitors coming to Topeka each year.

The first symposium, entitled "The Impact on Tort Law of 'Loser Pays' and 'Honesty in Evidence,'" featured an all-star team of professors, including: Thomas

---

960. Sandy Vogel, *A View From the Ahrens Chair in Tort Law*, 33 THE CIRCUIT RIDER, 13 (Summer 1994).

87. Professor Charlene Smith moderating an Ahrens Torts Seminar

D. Rowe, Jr. of Duke University; Francis E. McGovern, the Francis H. Hare Professor of Torts at the University of Alabama; Joan Vogel of the University of Vermont;
David Faigman of Hastings College of Law; and Twila Perry of Rutgers-Newark
University. Professor Geoffrey Woodroffe, a frequent co-instructor in Washburn's
summer abroad program, came from Brunel University in West London to
share his insights about the "loser pays" rule in Great Britain. Nationally known
litigators Kenneth Chesbro from Cambridge, Massachusetts, Bert Black from
Baltimore, and Thomas W. Henderson from Pittsburgh also participated on
panels, along with Dr. Joe Cecil from the Federal Judicial Center. Respected local
litigators acted as responders, including Richard C. Hite '53, Wayne Stratton '58,
Lynn Johnson '70, Cynthia Sheppeard '84, and Jerry Palmer. Besides students,
attendance was by invitation only and limited to leading litigators and judges.
Gerald Michaud '51 was featured speaker at the symposium dinner, and Third
District Congresswoman Jan Meyers spoke at a luncheon the following day.[961]

Professor Charlene Smith coordinated the symposium, effectively using
her contacts nationally to recruit prominent speakers, and planned local arrangements. She coordinated seven more Ahrens Chair programs before her
retirement in 2003. The format was refined and sessions were expanded so that
the symposium was offered as a class in Advanced Torts for which students
received academic credit and in which seminar papers were required. For

---

961. *Tort Reform Symposium Featured Nationally Renowned Panels*, 35 THE CIR-
CUIT RIDER 11–12 (Spring 1996).

example, the fall 1997 course was conducted over five weekends, with each weekend devoted to a different topic: mass toxic torts; business torts; privacy; liability of a background defendant when a crime has been committed; and tort law in the twenty-first century. Fifteen professors visited, three each weekend, including: Marshall Shapo of Northwestern; Robert Rabin from Stanford; Edmond Kitch from Virginia; Regina Austin from the University of Pennsylvania; Gary Schwartz from U.C.L.A.; and, for the second consecutive year, Francis McGovern, who had moved to Duke. Thereafter, the course usually was taught as a mini-course, condensed to fill four to six weeks of the semester, often with breaks between segments. The same large number of visitors usually participated, but they were encouraged to come in smaller groups and to stay longer, often up to two weeks. The course often focused in depth on a single topic. Topics areas varied each year, permitting Professor Smith to recruit scholars with different expertise. The class increasingly included a comparative law perspective, since the generous funding for the Ahrens Chair made it possible to bring torts scholars to Topeka from every corner of the globe. Gerald Michaud '51 and Professor Ahrens were frequent and active participants in class sessions. Dinners at faculty members' homes permitted students to interact informally with our visitors.

Both semesters in 1999–2000, the Ahrens Chair class featured an experiment in distance education using interactive video technology. Students at Nova Southeastern University in Florida enrolled in the same course with Washburn students. Twice each semester, visiting professors spent one week teaching in Topeka while Nova students participated in real time through a video connection and then spent the next week teaching in Fort Lauderdale while Washburn students joined in electronically from Topeka.[962] The seminars brought to Topeka torts scholars and practitioners from seven countries on four continents.[963] The first session in September examined "Tort Law in the 21st Century" from a comparative perspective. Visitors included: Professor Ulrich Magnus from Hamburg University in Germany, who was Executive Vice-Director of the European Centre of Tort Law; Professor Stephen M.D. Todd of the University of Canterbury in Christchurch, New Zealand; and Professor Michael Green from

---

962. *Ahrens Chair Hosting International Tort Scholars*, 38 THE CIRCUIT RIDER 6 (Fall 1999).

963. *Advanced Torts Seminar Uses Distance Learning Technology*, 38 THE CIRCUIT RIDER 13 (Spring 2000).

the University of Iowa, a Co-Reporter for the *Restatement of Torts*. Later sessions attracted international scholars of similar caliber, including: Professors Derek Morgan and Celia Wells from the University of Carduff in Wales; Geraint Howells of Sheffield University in England; Tsuneo Matsumoto from Hitosubashi University in Japan; and Jane Stapleton from Australian National University. Professor (and later Dean and President) William Powers from the University of Texas participated in Topeka, and James A. Henderson from Cornell was a Fort Lauderdale participant. The *Albany Law Journal on Science and Technology* published Professor Smith's article analyzing this new teaching model.[964]

Ahrens Chair visitors relished the opportunity to visit informally with each other and with Washburn students and faculty. Following the fall 2000 class, Professor Caroline Keenan of the University of Bristol in England wrote, "Washburn has a unique program, one for which it is justly world famous.... It was such a pleasure to be involved in discussions with such bright and interested students. I feel that my thinking about the whole area of tort liability of public institutions in cases of child abuse has developed considerably as a result of their contributions."[965] Keenan at the time was Visiting Scholar at the University of Waikato in New Zealand. The Ahrens Chair seminar permitted her to spend time with her co-author of a forthcoming book on legal responses to allegations of child abuse, Laura Hoyano, who came to Topeka from Wadham College at Oxford in England. Hoyano agreed that Washburn students were "generally of a very high caliber indeed, with maturity and insight into the public policy facets of imposing tort liability" in that area. She praised the vision of the faculty in emphasizing international perspectives. "It is important that tort scholars and students adopt a comparative approach to common problems adopted by other legal systems."[966]

MORE THAN TORTS

Major conferences that Washburn hosted were not limited to torts issues. Professor David Pierce organized a two-day symposium in March 1994, entitled

---

964. Charlene L. Smith, *Distance Education: A Value-Added Model*, 12 ALB. L.J. SCI. & TECH 177 (2001).

965. *FALL 2000 International Torts Scholars*, 39 THE CIRCUIT RIDER 14 (Fall 2000).

966. *Id.*

"The Future Course of Oil & Gas Jurisprudence." To fund the conference, Pierce used the Harry and Leila Logan Lecture Fund and a grant he secured from the Rocky Mountain Mineral Law Foundation. Pierce had arranged for Washburn to become the Foundation's twenty-ninth law school member just three years earlier. Pierce brought seven of the preeminent scholars in the field to Topeka to join him in critically evaluating core issues: Professors Bruce Kramer from Texas Tech; Richard Maxwell from Duke; John Lowe from Southern Methodist; Owen Anderson from Oklahoma; Patrick Martin from Louisiana State; Gary Conine from Houston; and Robert Beck from Southern Illinois. It was not a CLE program. Attendance was by invitation only. Panels of practitioners and industry leaders from throughout the region were assigned to be responders to each professor's presentation. Participants, both academic and practitioner, described the symposium as "the best intellectual discussion of oil and gas law they had ever attended."[967] Conference papers were published in a special symposium issue of the *Washburn Law Journal*, along with articles by Professors Ernest Smith of Texas and Jacqueline Lang Weaver of Houston, who were unable to attend the conference but wanted their articles to be included in the same issue because it would be such a valuable resource in the field.

In March 1995, Washburn hosted the Sixth Annual Midwestern People of Color Legal Scholarship Conference. Professor Ron Griffin coordinated the conference, which brought together twenty-two minority faculty members from throughout the Midwest who presented works in progress for discussion and critique and shared ideas for enhancing production of scholarship.

LAW COLLOQUIUM

There were other curricular innovations. When a decade had passed since the in-house teaching clinic, faculty members who had been energized by it recognized a need to collaborate on teaching issues again. They developed a team-taught Law Colloquium, an eight-week mini-course that was offered five times in six academic years starting in 1990. It was so unique it was featured in an issue of the weekly *National Law Journal*:

---

967. *National Oil and Gas Symposium at Washburn Featured in Special Issue of the Washburn Law Journal*, 33 THE CIRCUIT RIDER 16, 17 (Summer 1994).

When academics think of team teaching, they usually mean a course taught by two faculty members.

But at Washburn University School of Law in Topeka, Kan., when they talk about team teaching a course, they mean a whole team—as in football team.

...[U]nofficially these one-credit courses are called "potluck" teaching because as many as 13 professors combine to teach a one-hour course, with each professor bringing his or her own dish to a semester-long picnic of ideas on a specialized topic....

[I]s this the most efficient use of faculty time, having as many as 13 professors sitting in one room for two hours per week to teach a one-credit course? "All faculty participants do it as volunteers and as such are increasing their work load," says Professor [William] Rich. "So it's very efficient from a law school financial standpoint. It draws [a faculty member's time], but in professional development terms, it has been worth it for those who participate. The faculty learns a lot, it provides an opportunity for collaboration and gives us a common subject area...."

Nina W. Tarr, another of the potluck professors at Washburn, says she knows of no other school where so many professors gather to teach one course.

"It won't work at every school, because at some schools you can't get three teachers to have lunch together, much less teach together and sit while others teach."[968]

What was required to maximize participation was a topic that overlapped a wide range of traditional subjects. Eight professors agreed to teach an initial Colloquium on Feminist Jurisprudence on Thursday evenings in September and October of 1990. Professors Rich and Smith coordinated the course. Each participating professor developed materials illustrating the application of feminist theory to the professor's area of substantive expertise, including criminal law, family law, constitutional law, and law practice. Several practicing lawyers

968. *Megateam to Teach Single Course on NAFTA at Kansas' Washburn*, NATIONAL L.J., Dec. 20, 1993.

enrolled in the one-credit course, for sixteen hours of CLE credit, along with forty students. Each class had a one-hour plenary session, followed by a second hour of small group discussions led by faculty members. Students submitted journals weekly, responding to the assigned materials and class discussions, and professors gave feedback.

Students and professors found the course stimulating and professors quickly realized they were incorporating insights they learned not only in the classes they taught but also in their scholarly writing. Faculty members resolved to replicate the format in the spring of 1993, but with a new topic about which they wanted to learn more. This time, the topic was Critical Race Theory. Ten faculty members[969] and more than 100 students participated. Two of the eight sessions were led by guest lecturers, Professors Kellis Parker from Columbia University and Rennard Strickland, then at the University of Oklahoma.

The following fall, the Colloquium focused on Comparative Human Rights, and this time a visitor collaborated with Washburn professors for the entire course. Astrid Mattijssen from Utrecht University and the Clara Wichmann Institute for Women and the Law in the Netherlands compared the ways Dutch and American courts dealt with discrimination, including issues of sexual orientation. The class examined the European Convention on Human Rights, the International Covenant on Civil and Political Rights, and the Convention on the Elimination of All Forms of Discrimination against Women.[970]

The spring 1994 Colloquium had a different focus and drew on the expertise of faculty specializing in business issues. It analyzed ramifications of the recently ratified North American Free Trade Agreement (NAFTA) in such diverse areas as labor law, insurance, immigration, environmental law, and energy law. Professor Ron Griffin began organizing the course even before the final vote in Congress to approve the agreement. Faculty from other Washburn departments, including the Dean of the School of Business, and business and labor leaders participated with law professors and adjuncts. The NAFTA Colloquium was featured, along with a picture of Professor Griffin teaching

969. Participating faculty members were: Ron Griffin, Cathy Lesser Mansfield, Loretta Moore, Allen Easley, Charlene Smith, Nancy Maxwell, Nina Tarr, Rogelio Lasso, Bill Rich, and David Ryan. *Students and Faculty Participate in Critical Race Theory Class*, 32 THE CIRCUIT RIDER 12 (Summer 1993).

970. *International Law Colloquia Featured in National Law Journal and U.S. News and World Report*, 33 THE CIRCUIT RIDER 11, 12 (Summer 1994).

the class, in *U.S. News & World Report*'s annual article focusing on significant developments in legal education.[971]

The spring 1996 Colloquium may have been the most ambitious of all. The topic was Professionalism, and a record twenty faculty members participated. In addition, twenty-three practicing lawyers and judges and three faculty members from UMKC and KU either made plenary presentations or led discussions with small groups of the seventy-three students enrolled. Weekly sessions focused on the history of the profession and civility, lawyer criticism of the judiciary, diversity, pro bono obligations, attorney-client relations, business aspects of the profession, public agency lawyers, and the role of law schools in promoting professionalism. The active participation as small group leaders each week by leaders of the profession like retired Supreme Court Justices Richard Holmes '53 and Harold Herd '42 emphasized to students the importance of the topic to their careers. For 2L James Martin, the course "put the basic courses into perspective. It gave me an idea of what it's like in the private practice. I really enjoyed it—I had access to and advice from judges, justices, practicing lawyers, and professors. The professionalism exhibited in the course exemplified why the students like it here so much."[972] 1L JoLynn Brown '98 described professionalism issues the course explored as "sensitive" and believed the course gave "students a context for the dialog that they are already having....As important, it puts law in a human context."[973]

The focus on professionalism extended beyond the Colloquium. For three academic years, the Law School co-sponsored a program with Phi Delta Phi law fraternity, "Making Ethics Interesting," which awarded CLE credit to attract practitioners to join student participants. In the spring of 1998, the Law School joined with the KU Law School, the Kansas Supreme Court, and the Kansas Bar Foundation to sponsor a two-day conference on Professionalism and the Law. Washburn hosted the program the first day and KU hosted the second day. Professor Sheila Reynolds was among nationally recognized scholars on ethics who made presentations. There also were panel presentations on judicial ethics and the future of the legal profession, a keynote address by Judge Deanell Reece Tacha of the United States Court of Appeals for the Tenth

---

971. *Going International*, U.S. NEWS AND WORLD REPORT 66, 70 (Mar. 21,1994).
972. *Professionalism emphasized in special class...*, 35 THE CIRCUIT RIDER 10 (Spring 1996).
973. *Id.*

88. Hon. Sam A. Crow '52

Circuit, presentation of awards to winners of a state-wide writing competition for high school students, and the first public exhibition of a photographic history entitled "The Face of the Law in Kansas" which now is on permanent display in the lobby of the Kansas Judicial Center.[974]

An ongoing initiative in professionalism was the Law School's participation in Topeka's Sam A. Crow American Inn of Court, organized in 1992. The American Inns are built on the British model and emphasize civility, professionalism, and enhancing litigation skills. The Inn holds monthly dinner meetings at which pupillage teams of members present programs on these topics. Senior lawyers and judges serve as permanent Masters of the Inn, lawyers with 5–15 years of experience participate as Barristers, and lawyers with 0–5 years of experience are Associates. From the outset, the Inn's founder, Judge Crow '52, was commit-

---

974. *Washburn Co-Hosts Major Conference on Professionalism*, 37 THE CIRCUIT RIDER 8 (Fall 1998).

ted that law students should participate each year as Pupils. That commitment extended to his making a financial contribution each year to cover meals and other incidental costs for students. As many as fourteen students do so each year, and from the Inn's inception through 2006, more than 175 students eagerly participated as Pupils. From the outset, I have served as the Inn's Administrator and the Law School has provided staff support. One student, Eric Kraft '99, was a member of the pupillage team that won the national Best Program Award in 1999 for "Lawyers in Love, Or The Ethics of Lawyering When Related to or Involved with a Lawyer, Client or Adverse Party." There is an annual joint meeting of all Kansas Inns. Student members had a special opportunity on January 13, 2001, to attend the joint meeting at which United States Supreme Court Justice Stephen Breyer spoke. The meeting was held in conjunction with Judge Tacha's elevation to the position of Chief Judge of the Tenth Circuit.

RETHINKING THE CURRICULUM

There were curricular innovations besides the Colloquium and Ahrens Chair seminars. For example, United States Bankruptcy Judges John Flannagan '64 and James Pusateri volunteered to be field supervisors for one or two students each semester in Bankruptcy Court Externship, a program Professor Griffin administered. Then, beginning in 1992, they co-taught Advanced Bankruptcy, focusing on Chapter 11 proceedings, for students who had completed the basic course on bankruptcy.[975] In the spring semester of 1997, four lawyers in the Kansas Death Penalty Defense Unit, including Ron Wurtz '73 and Jeff Moots '91, taught a seminar on capital punishment. That same spring, Legislative Workshop was restructured so that students no longer had widely varying experiences working with individual legislators. Instead, Revisor of Statutes Norman Furse '67 taught classes about the legislative process and gave students the opportunity to do in-depth research on a bill. Professor Wadley developed a new course entitled "Creative Thinking," in which rappelling was an optional, but popular, exercise.

In addition to new courses, there were significant changes in core courses. For many years, Legal Ethics was a one-hour course, credit/no credit. We

---

975. *Federal Judges Teach Advanced Bankruptcy Course*, 32 THE CIRCUIT RIDER 18 (Summer 1993).

could only hope the fact that distinguished judges such as Jerome Harmon '35, J. Richard Foth, Bob Abbott '60, and Terry Bullock taught it would impress students with the seriousness of their professional obligations. A consistent theme of my early visits with alums, however, was a lament about the decline in professionalism among members of the bar.[976] We gave Legal Ethics a new name, "Professional Responsibility," to suggest that students should learn more than merely how close they could come to the line without being subjected to discipline.[977] We increased the number of credit hours from one to two and converted the course to a graded course to encourage students to devote as much time to the course as to any other. After all, who would want a grade of D or F in Professional Responsibility permanently inscribed on a transcript? Judge Bullock liked the greater emphasis on ethics, and agreed to teach the course in the new format each semester, even during the summer, until Professor Sheila Reynolds began teaching one section when she returned to full-time teaching after being Associate Dean. We wanted to make a statement to students that Professional Responsibility was so important that full-time faculty members would teach it. Professor Reynolds focused her scholarship on professional responsibility issues as well. Judge Bullock has been remarkable in his commitment to training students in professional responsibility issues. Not only did he teach Washburn students from 1969 until 2008, he taught similar classes at KU for almost as long. He was a deserving recipient of the Washburn Law School Association's 1988 Honorary Life Membership.

The Academic Success Program was restructured in 1996 and Professor Lynette Petty '87 agreed to coordinate it. Previously, supplemental instruction (SI) groups were open only to students identified as "at risk" academically. Expanding the SI program to all first-year students eliminated any unintended stigmatizing effect. Upper-level students were trained in techniques to promote active learning, and then facilitated small discussion groups linked to the Civil Procedure and Contracts classes. Data showed that students in SI groups, on average, had higher grades than those who declined to participate, although the participation rate soon became so high (88% in the fall of 1998) that the lack of an adequate control group called into question the statistical significance of the difference. Still, the faculty concluded the SI groups were

---

976. *From the Dean's Desk*, 28 THE CIRCUIT RIDER 3 (Fall 1989).
977. *Id.*

"diverse, stronger and much more educationally effective than those from before the program was restructured."[978] The smoker's lounge included in the 1992 addition was a dispensable luxury and we converted it to a seminar room that the large number of SI groups could use.

Changes recommended by a special Trial Advocacy Skills Curriculum Committee in 1997 enhanced the consistency of the experience of students taking the courses in Pretrial Advocacy and Trial Advocacy. A full-time faculty member assumed responsibility for course design, selecting teaching materials, teaching a classroom component, and coordinating the adjunct faculty members who critiqued student simulations in small sections. An Advanced Trial Advocacy course was added.

Other major changes in the core curriculum were made at the end of the decade, resulting from the self-study for the 1999 accreditation site visit. At one time, Washburn was quite progressive by having full-time tenured or tenure-track faculty, or long-term visitors like Jalen O'Neil '87 and Ellen Byers, teach Legal Research and Writing, rather than hiring adjunct faculty or recent graduates to teach the course. While a few faculty members enjoyed teaching the class and chose to do so each year, assignments were rotated among most other faculty members so that each would take a turn every four to six years. I even taught a section while I was Dean in the spring of 1995 on the theory that it might make other faculty members less resistant to taking their assigned turns. The advantage, of course, was that tenured faculty members were more experienced legal writers. However, multiple disadvantages came to outweigh that advantage. It was difficult to keep current on advances in research technology when one only taught the course every few years. Scheduling was disrupted when faculty members had to drop a course they regularly taught to rotate into the writing course. Worst of all, we effectively were restricted to requiring only one semester of legal writing in the first year.

During the self-study, the faculty reached consensus to make Legal Analysis, Research, and Writing a year-long, six-hour course, taught by faculty members who would devote most of their teaching load to the course. The course would include materials on legal methods, which previously was taught as a one-hour add-on to a substantive law class, and legal systems, which had been the subject of a separate course until it was abolished in 1998. Four faculty members

---

978. Washburn University School of Law Self-Study Report at 5 (1999).

would be needed to implement the change, three to teach forty-two students each in the fall, and one to teach the twenty-five students entering in January. The flexibility of the Financing Plan let us make the change immediately in the fall of 1999. Our budget to support the new faculty lines was approved in mid-spring. Professors O'Neil and Byers committed to teach the new course and we jettisoned the qualifier "Visiting" from their titles.

We had not interviewed research and writing teachers at the fall faculty recruitment conference in Washington, but quality candidates for the other two vacancies were still available. At many other schools legal writing was then, and remains, a teaching ghetto in which writing teachers are treated as second-class faculty. Commonly, they were assigned different titles, paid far less than faculty members teaching doctrinal courses, assigned crushing teaching loads, denied a vote or even the right to attend faculty meetings, given no support for professional development, and expected to remain only a year or two. We designed our new positions to be attractive by comparison. Washburn Law School had rejected creation of classes of faculty for nearly thirty years. Our research and writing teachers would have the same titles, e.g. Associate Professor, were paid the same as other faculty members with comparable experience, were full members of the faculty with the right to vote, and had the same perquisites, such as eligibility for summer research stipends. To make the positions even more attractive, and hopefully to reduce the burnout that many writing teachers experience, each writing professor would be able to teach one doctrinal course each year in addition to the research and writing class. We did not place the positions on tenure track, in part because we did not want to force gifted writing instructors like O'Neil, who did not want to devote time to traditional scholarship, to do so on pain of losing their jobs. However, we assured applicants of our intent that these be permanent positions and that if they did produce quality scholarship, they later could request that their positions be converted to tenure track.

Our program was unique in another way. Unlike most schools, we did not designate a Director of the Legal Writing Program. Having a Director made sense at schools that hired recent graduates to teach on short-term contracts and used an experienced writing director to supervise them and coordinate the various sections. Neither Byers nor O'Neil wanted to be Director, and the limited teaching experience of the two new faculty members we hired made them seem unlikely candidates to become Director immediately. However, they all were experienced lawyers and coordinated the new program effectively by consensus.

For the first time, we used interactive video technology to interview candidates before inviting them to campus. Both of the new professors we hired received law degrees from Duke University. Alex Glashausser was a 1995 graduate who had clerked for Judge Albert J. Engel of the United States Court of Appeals for the Sixth Circuit. He taught legal writing and legal process as Adjunct Professor at Ohio State University's College of Law during his last year of practice with a large firm in Columbus. His first doctrinal class was Remedies, which Bruce Levine had taught before his retirement. Peter Cotorceanu had earned an LL.B. in New Zealand at Victoria University in 1980, before completing his American law degree in 1982. He had been Adjunct Professor for nine years, teaching Legal Skills at William and Mary's Marshall-Wythe School of Law, while practicing with his own firm, Knicely and Cotorceanu, in Williamsburg, Virginia. His doctrinal course was Decedents' Estates.

The other major curricular change in advance of the 1999 site visit was to eliminate the "distribution requirement" that had been in effect since 1985 and forced students to take ten electives from six categories of courses. While the faculty remained committed to a diverse selection of upper-level courses, the distribution requirement unnecessarily complicated enrollment decisions and resulted in exaggerated student fears of being unable to enroll in a course needed to meet the requirement. The faculty concluded that most students would take a diverse course load voluntarily, because of a desire to be well-prepared for the bar exam if for no other reason, so retained only the requirement that students take one course from a list of "Perspective" electives.

EVOLUTION IN THE LAW CLINIC

Most of the tumult in the Law Clinic subsided with Professor Piatt's departure in 1987. The search the following year was not merely for a new faculty member but a new director. The faculty chose Nina W. Tarr, a 1979 graduate of the University of Iowa College of Law, who had been Clinical Supervisor in the Civil Litigation Clinic at William Mitchell College of Law in Minnesota from 1984 to 1986 and then taught at Northern Illinois College of Law. She developed consensus to restructure the format of the Law Clinic so that students usually worked with a single faculty member on particular types of cases, rather than working on cases in varied areas with multiple faculty members. The rationale was that the same skills could be taught in any area but that students would learn more in depth by focusing on a single topic in which they had a special interest. Emphasis was placed on smaller caseloads that were carefully screened for their educational value and on more intensive supervision. That emphasis continues today. Compared to the 602 cases opened in six months in 1975, just 185 cases comprised the Clinic's caseload during the entire calendar year 2004. The purchase of case management software in 1996 permitted clinic students to learn modern law office management techniques.

Tarr was energetic and anxious to reestablish the national visibility of Washburn's Clinic. She quickly became a frequent speaker at regional and AALS conferences for clinical law teachers. She arranged for Washburn to host the Midwest Conference in October 1989. The conference attracted 50 clinical teachers for sessions discussing whether clinics should limit their scope to representing the poor or expand to include public interest law activities and representation of fee-paying clients.[979] By 1992, Tarr was a member of the Executive Committee of the AALS Clinical Law Section and a member of the initial Board of Directors of the Clinical Legal Education Association. She chaired a committee that started the Association's *Clinical Law Review*, then served on its Board of Editors. For those efforts, she received CLEA's 1995 Annual Award. In 1994, she was one of two American professors who acted as consultants for a week-long conference at Sheffield Hallam University in England, which sought to form a clinical education association there. Sheila Reynolds was active nationally too, making presentations about Washburn's unique collaboration with Menninger, "Using Psychiatric Residents in Law Clinics" and "Designing a Mediation Program," at the 1990 AALS Clinical Legal Education Conference at the University of Michigan.

There was an unexpected change in the Clinic faculty shortly after Tarr arrived. Professor Don Rowland's spouse, Dr. Mary Rowland, a senior administrator at the University, died suddenly in May 1988. Professor Rowland elected to leave law teaching in December, retiring as Professor Emeritus. He served as Acting City Attorney in Topeka for four months.

Visiting Professors filled Rowland's position for two years while we searched unsuccessfully for his successor. Finally, Loretta Moore filled the Rowland va-

---

979. *AALS Midwest Clinic Conference*, 28 THE CIRCUIT RIDER 11 (Fall 1989).

cancy in the fall of 1991, adding an alternative dispute resolution component to the Clinic in addition to supervising students handling civil cases.

Moore was a 1978 graduate of Washington University Law School in St. Louis and had taught there while she was a partner in a firm specializing in civil litigation. She sought opportunities in the community for students to practice mediation. Starting in the fall of 1994, clinic interns provided on-site mediation in the Small Claims Division of the Shawnee County District Court. Also, interns accepted referrals from the Better Business Bureau of Northeast Kansas and the Topeka Housing Authority. The following fall, Moore negotiated an agreement with Kansas Attorney General Carla Stovall for clinic students to mediate cases in which consumer complaints filed with her office alleged matters beyond the scope of the Consumer Protection Act. Initially, five interns worked on forty cases ranging from breach of contract to breach of warranty, shoddy workmanship, and unsatisfactory service. The premise of the program, according to Moore, was that "the mediation process tends to preserve the consumer and business relationship.... [Eighty] percent or more of these cases are resolved through mediation and the compliance rate is substantially higher than with those cases that go through the legal system. This way both parties come out feeling like it's a win-win situation."[980] By 1996, students had the option of a separate 1–4 credit hour ADR Internship in the Clinic. By completing it, they could become certified as mediators under the Kansas Supreme Court Rule 902. Three new courses were added in 1998, Negotiation & Mediation Skills, Advanced Mediation, and Advanced Arbitration, bringing to thirteen the credit hours offered in alternative dispute resolution.

A three-year grant in early 1992 from the United States Department of Education permitted Washburn to add an additional faculty member in the Clinic and expand opportunities for students in the areas of ADR and mental health law. The grant permitted Moore to devote more of her time to ADR, and Lynette Petty '87 became the Visiting Professor supported by the grant, supervising students in mental health and disability matters. As a grant position, it was not tenure track but it was a twelve-month position, which meant Petty was available to teach along with the Clinic Director during summer sessions. A five-year $200,000 grant from Torchmark Corporation, which its

---

980. *Washburn law student mediators ease AG's consumer caseload*, 34 THE CIR-CUIT RIDER 12 (Spring 1995).

Chairman Ron Richey '51 arranged following expiration of the DOE grant, maintained the ADR program and facilitated a transition to hard dollar funding of Petty's position. Because the Financing Plan generated the hard dollars and the position remained non-tenure track, the University did not object and barely even noticed when we made the position a permanent one. Petty assumed one-fourth time administrative responsibility as Assistant Dean for disability issues. In 1999, we quietly dropped "Visiting" from her title when two other visiting positions became permanent ones in the expanded legal research and writing course.

Nina Tarr left Washburn in 1995 to start the first in-house clinic at the University of Illinois. A significant attraction was that both of her parents had been faculty members at the University and still lived nearby. Tarr's replacement as Clinic Director was Julie Kunce Field, a 1985 graduate of the University of Chicago School of Law who had clerked for United States District Judge John Oliver in Kansas City, Missouri, and practiced with a firm in Boston. Field thereafter was a member of the clinic faculty at the University of Michigan for six years, the last four as Director of its Women and the Law Clinic. She handled a high-profile case for a Michigan undergraduate student who had lost custody of her daughter because she put the child in daycare while she attended classes. Field appeared on CNN, Good Morning America, and similar programs, and she continued her involvement in the case after arriving at Washburn at the start of the 1996 spring semester until its successful conclusion.

Two-career family issues limited Field's stay at Washburn to two and one-half years. Her spouse was a particle physicist, and permanent positions for them are not abundant in Kansas. When he was offered a position at Colorado State University in 1998, Field resigned, determining there were more opportunities for her to work as a lawyer in Colorado than there were for him in Kansas. Washburn granted her a formal leave of absence, in part on the remote chance she would change her mind, but mostly for any help that status might give her in seeking a position there. Sadly, she was forced to leave law teaching to practice in Fort Collins, although she later was recruited to be Coordinator of Clinical Programs at the University of Denver College of Law for two years. In 2010, she was appointed as District Judge in Larimer County.

Professor Reynolds served as Acting Director of the Clinic for 1998–99 during a national search for Field's replacement. The new Director, John J. Francis, had been Clinical Supervising Attorney at Hofstra for five years. Before that,

89. David E. Pierce '77, Professor 1986–1987 and 1989–present

he had been a trial attorney for the Criminal Defense Division of the New York City Legal Aid Society. He received his J.D. in 1989 from American University. In 2007–08, he became the school's longest serving Clinic Director.

A STABLE AND MORE PROLIFIC FACULTY

Except in the Law Clinic, there was remarkably little turnover in the permanent faculty. I argued successfully that my becoming Dean meant that we had a faculty vacancy to fill. The University had recognized at the start of the dean search that a new line would be created for an externally hired dean and ultimately agreed that hiring an internal dean should not change its commitment. The new position allowed us in 1989 at last to hire David Pierce '77 as a permanent member of the faculty.

For nearly four years after graduation, Pierce had a solo practice in Neodesha, Kansas, and wrote a newsletter for prosecutors and law enforcement officers, before deciding to change careers. He was accepted as the first LL.M. candidate at the University of Utah Energy Law Center, for 1981–82. He spent the spring 1981 semester as Visiting Professor at Washburn, teaching Criminal Procedure and Legal Research and Writing. For two years after earning the LL.M., he was an attorney for Shell Oil Company in Houston, where he taught as an adjunct faculty member at the University of Houston Law Center. In 1984, he became an Assistant Professor at Indiana University—Indianapolis School of Law. Pierce was a native of Pittsburg, Kansas, and he maintained his Kansas ties while he was in Indiana, completing the first volume of his two-volume *Kansas Oil and Gas Handbook* under a contract with the Kansas Bar Association.[981]

By 1986, Pierce wanted to be closer to home and was prepared to leave law teaching for private practice to do so. However, Dean Monk hoped Pierce would remain in academia and arranged for him to be Visiting Professor at Washburn for 1986–87, filling in for a faculty member who was on leave. Pierce spent 1987 through 1989 as Visiting Associate Professor and Associate Director of the National Energy Law and Policy Institute at the University of Tulsa College of Law, working with Director Kent Frizzell '55. Still, Pierce's heart was at Washburn and he was willing to do just about anything to return. The only vacancy for 1988–89 was for Clinic Director and Pierce applied, knowing it was a long shot. He had never been a clinician and knew he would be teased if he proposed the only oil and gas law clinic in the nation, so he developed a characteristically well-thought-out proposal to introduce bankruptcy and debtor-creditor work into the Law Clinic. Undaunted by the faculty's decision to hire an experienced clinician, he expressed his willingness to become Dean when it became clear Steve Smith would reject Washburn's offer. The position he accepted in 1989 fit him better, and he has become one of the premier authorities nationally in the field of oil and gas and energy law. Within days of his arrival, he presented the first Washburn-sponsored CLE programs outside Kansas, "Basic Federal Natural Gas Regulation," in Dallas, Houston, Oklahoma City, and Tulsa.

Professor Michael Barbara '53 retired from full-time teaching in December 1991. He continued teaching Criminal Law and Evidence for two years in the fall semester, then taught only Evidence for five more years, even commuting

---

981. I was chair of the Handbook Task Force of the KBA CLE Committee at the time and recall having to allay fears of committee members about entrusting the project to a "foreigner."

to do so after he moved to Wichita. It was in effect a "phased retirement" that we effected several years before the University adopted a formal phased retirement policy. The Law School Financing Plan gave us the flexibility without fanfare to pay him a pro rata share of his faculty salary, rather than the modest compensation emeritus and adjunct faculty receive, while also adding an entry-level full-time position.

There were only two other vacancies. Paul Rasor left law teaching in 1992 to pursue a Ph.D. in religious studies at Harvard. He was far younger than the typical Professor Emeritus, but we awarded the title anyway, confident it would benefit both Washburn and Rasor in the scholarship on law and religion he planned to produce. Since 2005, he has been Professor of Interdisciplinary Studies and Director of the Center for the Study of Religious Freedom at Virginia Wesleyan College. Banks McDowell retired in January 1995, two years after being the seventh faculty member since 1970 to be named Distinguished Professor of Law. The retirement of Jean Reeves in 1991 created a void in the area of Business Associations. However, because he had been an unpaid volunteer, there was no budget line item to use to fill it. David Pierce agreed to teach those classes temporarily, and we resolved to shift resources when there were later vacancies.

The extraordinary stability of the faculty meant only five members of the permanent faculty in 1990 had departed by 1998. The faculty was committed to using the limited vacancies to diversify the faculty. All newly hired tenure-track faculty members during those years were women or minorities.

Rogelio Lasso filled Mike Barbara's line in 1991, arriving the same year as Loretta Moore. A 1985 graduate of the University of Minnesota School of Law, he had spent six years as a litigator with the Chicago law firms of Peterson & Ross and Holleb & Coff. Initially, he taught Payment Systems and upper-level civil procedure courses Allen Easley had to abandon to become Associate Dean.[982] Soon, Lasso abandoned the Uniform Commercial Code to teach Torts. Charlene Smith had been our only full-time Torts teacher since Jim Ahrens retired in 1988, except when Ahrens Chair visitors were available to teach the second section. Lasso became one of the faculty leaders in using technology in the classroom. He delighted in being outrageous in the classroom. He was

---

982. *Associate Professor of Law Rogelio Lasso*, 30 THE CIRCUIT RIDER 18 (Fall 1991).

strong-willed and independent, occasionally storming out of faculty meetings after a flash of temper. I often kidded him that we had gotten two faculty members for the price of one, Rogelio and his evil twin "Skippy."

Cathy Lesser Mansfield filled Paul Rasor's line in 1992, inheriting the Payment Systems class from Lasso, a section of Business Associations from Jean Reeves, and Rasor's class in Consumer Credit Transactions. A 1987 graduate of the University of Virginia School of Law, she had practiced in Phoenix for five years with Brown & Bain and in the Urban Indian Law Office of Community Legal Services. Mansfield, who had been "composer, lyricist and musical director for the musical version of the Story of Job,"[983] exhibited potential to be an outgoing and creative teacher, but her career at Washburn, like Julie Kunce Field's, was cut short because of two-career family issues. Her spouse was a partner in the Phoenix firm of Lewis & Roca. While we used our contacts to seek opportunities for him near Topeka, none matched his criteria for a lateral move. One year, he in effect had a one-person branch office of Lewis & Roca in Topeka, and another year they commuted. The birth of twins made that arrangement untenable and, in 1994, Mansfield left law teaching to return to Phoenix. Three years later, she was able to reenter law teaching at Drake University when her spouse agreed to accept a position with a Des Moines firm.

Michelle Rabouin replaced Mansfield, joining the faculty in 1995 after a year as Visiting Professor at Texas Southern Law School. She taught at Washburn for four years and published three articles during that time. Then, after a year as Visiting Professor at Texas Wesleyan in Fort Worth, she left law teaching to return to her home base in Denver.

Steven A. Ramirez joined Rabouin and Field in the new faculty class of 1995. He was a fitting replacement for Banks McDowell, quickly becoming a prolific scholar writing on corporate, banking, and securities law issues and the need for diversity in the boardroom. There were two-career family issues to be resolved before Ramirez accepted our offer, too. His spouse and classmate, Mary, was an assistant United States Attorney in the antitrust division in Chicago. After the faculty voted in early December to extend an offer to Steve, we immediately contacted United States Attorney for Kansas Randy

---

983. *Associate Professor Cathy Lesser Mansfield*, 32 THE CIRCUIT RIDER 14 (Summer 1993).

Rathbun '78 to determine the likelihood of a rare opening in that office. In fact, he already had conducted interviews for a pending part-time opening and was nearing a decision. Mary's experience impressed Rathbun and she flew to Kansas from a holiday vacation in Florida to interview on New Year's Eve. She received an offer to which she had to respond promptly, and that sealed Steve's decision to come to Washburn. Mary began work in her new position in February, months before she and Steve moved to Topeka from Chicago.

A 1986 graduate of St. Louis University School of Law, Steve Ramirez had no naiveté as an entry level faculty member, since his sister had been a member of the faculty at Northeastern Law School in Massachusetts since 1988. Ramirez was well prepared. He had been a Senior Attorney for the Resolution Trust Corporation, an Enforcement Attorney for the Securities and Exchange Commission, and then a partner at Robinson, Curley & Clayton in Chicago. In an interview for *The Circuit Rider,* he exhibited the intensity and ambition that made him successful. "We live in a competitive environment....I was determined to outwork my opponents and distinguish myself by my client service....Litigating complex cases...takes the maximum level of focus."[984]

Until an amendment in 2009 increased the age, K.S.A. 20-2608 precluded Kansas Supreme Court Justices from standing for retention after they became seventy years old. We had that statute to thank for another addition to the faculty. It forced Hon. Harold Herd '42 to leave the court in 1993 after fourteen years of service. However, he was far too vigorous and intellectual to retire. We both on occasion would visit after work a popular local bar called The Vintage, along with David Monical, Executive Assistant to Washburn's president. We talked about what Justice Herd might do next. I knew he would be an exceptional teacher and role model for students. The idea appealed to him, as did having an office in Topeka and secretarial support. He didn't want to teach full-time, and that was a good thing, because we did not have a vacant full-time line item or funding for a new position. I made my best offer: he would have the title Distinguished Jurist-in-Residence, teaching Constitutional History during the spring semester of 1994. Few people are so well-read on the topic, and Herd traced the roots of the American Constitution to Roman times. He enjoyed teaching and students enjoyed him. Soon, he agreed to teach one course each semester, adding a course in Kansas Constitutional Law. He made

---

984. *Three new faculty join Law School,* 34 THE CIRCUIT RIDER 21 (Fall 1995).

valuable contributions to faculty meetings and participated actively in the life of the Law School. He continued to teach, for very little more than expenses, until he retired in 2001 to practice law with his son Skip '89 in Caldwell and complete construction of his library there. He received the Washburn Law School Association's Distinguished Service Award in 1995.

Increasing Washburn's visibility was a priority. The University of Calgary chose David Pierce for its Natural Resources Law Chair for the spring of 1995. Myrl Duncan was awarded the Natural Resources Law Institute Fellowship the following year at Lewis and Clark University in Oregon. Linda Elrod was invited frequently to be a Visiting Professor and spent semesters at Washington University in St. Louis and Florida State University. In 1996, Bill Rich was selected to serve on the innovative AALS Resource Corps, whose eleven members were trained to be facilitators of faculty retreats nationwide on such topics as long-range planning, curriculum reform, teaching innovation, developing a scholarly culture, and expanding diversity. Rich is one of the few original members who continues to serve on the Resource Corps.

Faculty members published more widely. Some co-authored law school textbooks. West Group published: Paul Rasor's book, Rohner, Spanogle, Pridgen & Rasor, *Consumer Law*, 2d ed. in 1991; David Pierce's book, Kuntz, Smith, Anderson, Lowe & Pierce, *Cases and Materials on Oil and Gas Law*, 3d ed. in 1998; and Linda Elrod's book, Krause, Elrod, Oldham & Garrison, *Cases, Comments and Questions on Family Law*, 4th ed., also in 1998. The second edition of Ray Spring's book, *Patients, Psychiatrists, and Lawyers, Law and the Mental Health System,* was reviewed favorably in the *Journal of Legal Medicine*.[985]

Other professors wrote treatises or texts on topics in their fields. Banks McDowell's 1989 book *Deregulation and Competition in the Insurance Industry* received the American Risk and Insurance Association's Clarence Arthur Kulp Memorial Award in 1991 for the outstanding original contribution to the literature of risk and insurance.[986] McDowell's later books focused on legal ethics: *Ethical Conduct and the Professional's Dilemma: Choosing Between Service and Success* in 1991 and *Ethics and Excuses: The Crisis in Professional Responsibility* in 2000, after he became Professor Emeritus. In 1989, David Ryan co-authored, with Professor Emeritus Bob Fowks and Dr. Max Halley '66, *Medical Malpractice*

---

985. Martin Firestone, *Book Review*, 19 J. LEGAL MEDICINE 151 (1998).

986. *Professor Banks McDowell Receives National Insurance Award*, 30 THE CIRCUIT RIDER 15 (Fall 1991).

Solutions: Systems and Proposals for Injury Compensation. Callahan & Company published Linda Elrod's *Child Custody Law and Practice*, which Elrod updated with annual supplements. A reviewer called this treatise a "virtual must" for family lawyers, concluding that Elrod "demonstrates the rare gift of being able to provide historical data within the context of the practical reality of where the law is today....[F]ew authors possess the range of talents needed to create a quality law book....Elrod's book is a rare gem indeed."[987] Professor Bill Rich joined Chester James Antieau, who had taught at Washburn from 1951 until 1953, as co-author of the three-volume Antieau & Rich, *Modern Constitutional Law*, 2d ed., published by West Group. Antieau invited Rich to be his co-author after they met during the summer of 1994 when Antieau used an office at the Law School during an extended visit to Kansas to see his daughter. Rich wrote two volumes and assumed responsibility for producing supplements for all three volumes. Professor Ali Khan published two books. *The Extinction of Nation States—A World Without Borders* was selected in 1996 by Kluwer Law International to be volume 21 in its twenty-year series *Contemporary Issues in International Law*. Kluwer also published his next book, *A Theory of Universal Democracy: Beyond the End of History*, in 2003. Jim Wadley had responsibility for three chapters in *Thompson on Real Property*.[988] David Pierce joined other co-authors in the seven-volume treatise, Kuntz, *The Law of Oil and Gas*, in 1997. In addition to writing books, faculty members published articles in many journals nationally, too many to list here.

Yet, while faculty self-studies in 1992 and 1999 committed, respectively, to "emphasize faculty responsibility for scholarship" and to "increase scholarly productivity," they also acknowledged misgivings about making scholarship in national journals the school's overriding priority. For example, the 1992 self-study, discussing the 1987 denial of the school's application for membership in the Order of the Coif, mentioned the faculty consensus that "when our writing does not have a unique appeal to our region," submission to journals with "a more national audience" was encouraged. However, it added that "we remain committed to being a significant resource to our region and we believe that scholarship devoted to state and local concerns is a worthwhile faculty

987. H. Joseph Gitlin, *Custody Book Combines Big Picture and Sharp Focus*, 18 ABA FAMILY ADVOCATE, No. 3 v (1996).

988. Chapters 47 on *Water Rights*, 50 on *Agricultural and Farm Land*, and 79 on *Foreign Ownership*.

endeavor." The 1999 self-study produced a revised definition of "scholarship" that moved into the definition of service less rigorous products such as briefs and CLE materials. However, the definition the faculty adopted was not as restricted as one initially proposed, which would have counted only law review articles and books and would have discounted publications with a local focus. The revised definition thus continued to include "rigorous publications approaching, for example, Kansas legal issues, in a scholarly fashion, as well as the drafting or analysis of legislation which includes a sophisticated analysis of legal issues." Further, while the 1999 self-study set as a high priority the hiring of new faculty "who demonstrate strong interest in scholarship," in the next breath it emphasized, "More needs to be done, however, to make sure that new faculty will understand and participate in some of the unique aspects of the law school faculty community." It urged that mechanisms be developed for "more faculty interchange, with emphasis on activities to foster the spirit of collegiality that has long existed at this institution."

Additional incentives for scholarship included larger summer research stipends. I clarified the often determinative role of scholarship in setting merit salary increases. The 1999 self-study endorsed reduced teaching loads to give time for major projects. The same self-study led to creation of a standing faculty committee on scholarship, charged with assisting faculty authors in placing finished products and obtaining both internal and external reviews of drafts. In April 2001, the committee held the first Faculty Scholarship Seminar for students and practicing lawyers, showcasing recent articles by five faculty members.

WASHLAW

Even before ground was broken for the Library addition, John Christensen had become a leader and innovator in expanding access to legal information and the use of technology. The previous chapter described Washburn's role in the early 1980s in developing union lists of holdings in multiple libraries, making the Mid-America Law School Library Consortium a cost-effective means of coordinating expensive acquisitions and sharing materials, providing resources to practicing lawyers by fax, and in 1987 developing one of the first in-house electronic information systems (WALLIS) in a law school. By 1989, Washburn was one of the seventeen Consortium schools selected to combine their catalog records using then-emerging CD-ROM technology, funded by

a U.S. Department of Education College Library Technology and Cooperation Grant. Christensen's heroics in meeting the deadline for submission of
the grant application were lauded in the *Law Library Journal.*[989] The project
was like most that Christensen submitted—it brought his Law Library free
equipment or software, this time an extra CD-ROM workstation.[990] In 1992,
Christensen won a $185,000 grant for the Consortium from the same DOE
grant program for its then nineteen members to expand access to materials
online, facilitate transforming information from one format to another, and
beta test the use of scanning technology.[991] Naturally, the scanning device
purchased with grant funds was housed at Washburn.

Christensen foresaw clearly that technology would become dominant in
legal research and law practice but had to persuade some faculty holdouts and
other users who could not believe technology would be more than a novel
supplement to book-based research. Christensen often took a moment during faculty meetings to extol the virtues of advances in technology and nudge
faculty to try them. The University had to be nudged too. Computing support
from the main campus often was inadequate to meet the Law School's needs.
"The campus choice of technologies did not include systems in use in the
mainstream legal community,"[992] so the library staff had to develop support and
design capability. Plus, the Law School's computer gurus were more prescient
than those across campus. For example, the director of the campus computer
center decided to implement a campus-wide computing model relying on a
mainframe computer accessed by "dumb terminals," rather than relying on
PCs. The plan had the advantages of lower cost and ease of maintenance.
However, we knew it would not prepare our graduates for the computing
environment they would find in practice and would hinder innovation in
the use of computers and access to new programs. Our persistence won the
Law School an exemption from the plan, once we responded to the argument
that the computer center lacked staffing to maintain PCs by saying we would

989. Richard C. Amelung, *The Mid-America Law School Library Consortium
Catalog on CD-Rom*, 85 LAW LIBR. J. 801 (1993).

990. John E. Christensen, *New Technologies In The Law Library*, 28 THE CIRCUIT
RIDER 12, 13 (Summer 1989).

991. John E. Christensen, *Launching the Law School into Cyberspace Leadership*,
34 THE CIRCUIT RIDER 8, 10 (Fall 1995).

992. Washburn University School of Law Self-Study Report (1999).

maintain them ourselves. At the same time, the Law School cooperated with the main campus when positive technology outcomes resulted. The Law Library and Mabee Library jointly chose the Innovative Interfaces catalog system and worked with other Topeka research libraries to create the Associated Topeka Libraries Automated System (ATLAS), a public access joint catalog with links to full text resources through the Internet. In 1996, the Law Library initiated a project with the Kansas appellate courts to distribute online the full text of decisions within thirty minutes of their release.

By academic year 1994–95, Washburn had the fifth largest collection of CD-ROM materials of any American law school library and the fourth largest number of titles in microfilm or microfiche format. Combining these materials with hard copy volumes, Washburn was 20th among all law schools in the number of titles held. I wrote to alumni that we had become "one of no more than a half dozen law schools that are the most technologically sophisticated" and were "committed to using new technologies to maximize the resources available to our students...."[993]

Plans for the Library addition sought not only to make Washburn state-of-the-art but also to facilitate incorporation of technology yet to be developed. For example, fiber optic cable was placed throughout the addition and in administrative offices, even though it could not yet be connected externally. By the fall of 1992, the library had installed a local area network and it was expanded to administrative and faculty offices the next year.[994] In early 1993, fiber optic and coaxial cable was laid to link the Law School directly to the University's Academic Computer Center and Media Center. It opened Internet access to all workstations on the Law School's local area network and permitted greater utilization of graphics, imaging, and multi-media applications, as well as classroom access to cable television shows such as Court-TV and satellite programs.[995] Overhead monitors and VCRs were added to each classroom as part of the project.

The Library staff assumed responsibility for supporting all uses of technology throughout the Law School. Between 1993 and 1999, the number of staff

993. James M. Concannon, *From The Dean's Desk*, 34 THE CIRCUIT RIDER 3, 5 (Fall 1995).

994. John E. Christensen, *Network Infrastructure—Washburn's vital link*, 34 THE CIRCUIT RIDER 13 (Fall 1995).

995. John E. Christensen, *Library Update*, 32 THE CIRCUIT RIDER 15, 16 (Summer 1993).

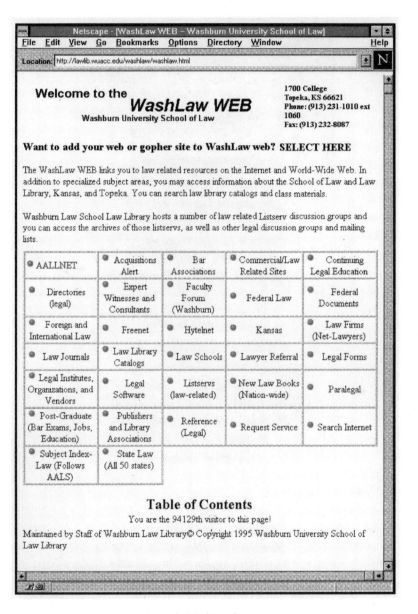

90. An early WashLaw homepage

91. WashLaw homepage in 2011

members devoting most of their time to computer functions rose from two FTE to six. It was fortunate that the computer expert among classroom faculty, Allen Easley, was Associate Dean. He was able both to provide useful input in planning for technology and to evaluate proposals independently to help set resource priorities. A faculty standing committee on technology, first appointed in 1997, provided feedback and direction to the library computing staff.

Christensen's early goal was that, on the completion of the library addition, attorneys and other users would be able to access WALLIS,[996] which originally served only Washburn-based users. It had screens listing select bibliography for each law school class, research guides and library service guides that could be downloaded, and bar admission information for each state. There was a database of court and administrative decisions which could be searched by a limited number of key words. However, technological advances allowed Washburn to move rapidly beyond the relatively narrow initial focus of WALLIS.

---

996. Christensen, *supra* note 990, at 15.

The librarians developed a vision of a widely-accessible electronic resource for legal information. The Dean's office had the good sense not to impede their pursuit of that vision. They made Washburn a leader among law schools known for its innovation on Wall Street and in every corner of the globe.

In May 1993, the American Association of Law Libraries accepted Washburn's proposal to host its electronic information service LAWNET.[997] AALL members include more than 5,000 librarians at law firms, corporations, courts, and law schools. That same spring, Washburn launched WashLaw as the successor to WALLIS. WashLaw's driving force was Mark Folmsbee, who became Associate Director of the Law Library in 1990. Folmsbee was a computer guru. He received his J.D. from Valparaiso School of Law in 1982 and an M.L.S. from the University of Illinois in 1986. He came to Washburn from Gonzaga Law School, where he had been Reader Services Librarian since 1987.

WashLaw's menu provided "direct links to the most useful law, government, and library-related resources across the Internet."[998] Initially, users had to have accounts on Washburn's mainframe computer, but Folmsbee and the Library staff set about making it accessible by alumni and then literally the world. Various Internet websites developed specialties in particular topics but Washburn's librarians set a goal, one many of their peers thought was too ambitious for a non-commercial site to attempt, of sorting and providing comprehensive access to all legal information that was available anywhere on the Internet.

Researchers were drawn to WashLaw almost immediately. The February 1994 issue of *The Internet Letter* reported that WashLaw was "becoming accepted nationwide as a reliable source for legal and government information on the Internet." Then, WashLaw was reviewed favorably in the March/April issue of *Law Library Lights*, the newsletter of the Law Librarian's Society of Washington, D.C., in a report, "Best of the Internet: A Review of Selected Internet Resources."

Folmsbee was selected to design and oversee a special computer laboratory at the January 1995 AALS annual meeting in New Orleans to introduce law professors nationwide to the legal and educational resources available on the Internet. WashLaw, of course, was the gateway used in the lab to access materials, and Washburn librarians were featured presenters. The lab was so popular that Folmsbee was asked to repeat it at the 1996 annual meeting. He

---

997. Christensen, *supra* note 995.
998. *Id.*

chaired the American Association of Law Libraries Automation Special Interest Section, then was elected to the AALL Executive Board for 1998–2001.

Accolades kept coming. *The Internet Guide for the Legal Researcher*, published by Don MacLeod, librarian at New York's Cravath, Swaine & Moore, described the AALLNET site Washburn maintained as "perhaps the best law gopher on the Internet…This should be the first stop for the serious legal researcher." The July 1995 Update declared WashLaw "perhaps the most comprehensive law-related site on the Internet." In November that year, the monthly newsletter *Legal Resources via the Internet* rated WashLaw the best of all law school legal research sites and the only law school site among five sites receiving "five star" ratings. It praised WashLaw, located in what it described as "the technology mecca of Topeka, KS," for "its currency and breadth of legal information."[999]

WashLaw was not a one-shot wonder. In July 1996, it was named one of the top three sites in the first "Best of the Web for Lawyers Award" by *legal.online* which concluded, "The original indexer of legal sites on-line remains among the most exhaustive and continues to innovate."[1000] *The New York Times* listed the Washburn and Harvard sites as the two "Places to Go" for online legal research.[1001] Don MacLeod purported to end the debate in the second edition of his *Internet Guide* in 1997:

> If only one law-related index page were allowed on the Internet, this one would be the one to choose. For the sheer breadth and inventiveness of preparation, WashLaw Web from Washburn University School of Law in Topeka, KS is the best all-around law resource on the Internet, period.[1002]

Several decisions were key to WashLaw's success. None was more critical than that a team approach would be used to maintain it. Each librarian and many members of the non-professional staff were assigned topics for which they were responsible for "identifying significant resources, building menu struc-

---

999. *WashLaw Web Rated Top Law School Research Site*, 35 THE CIRCUIT RIDER 9 (Spring 1996).

1000. *WashLaw Web Named Best of the Web*, 35 THE CIRCUIT RIDER 8 (Fall 1996).

1001. *Your Own Law Library (No Shelves Required): Taking in the Sites*, N.Y. TIMES (May 12, 1997).

1002. DON MACLEOD, THE INTERNET GUIDE FOR THE LEGAL RESEARCHER 2D 4:7 (1997) ("Its all-inclusive pull-down menu of links offers a mind-boggling array of law resources that link to every imaginable resource.").

tures, and programming the technical links required to make using WashLaw Web a simple process for the researcher."[1003] Not only did this division of labor prevent the departure of a single key person from disrupting the reliability of WashLaw, it meant each member of the team had an ownership interest to see that WashLaw succeeded and could take pride in the many accolades that person's work helped to generate.

The comprehensiveness of WashLaw occasionally led to controversy. There was a link to a site that compiled lawyer jokes. Some visitors thought some of the jokes were too crude for a law school site; others found the whole notion of a law school linking to lawyer jokes offensive. The issue even became a topic of discussion at an alumni Board of Governors meeting.[1004] Given the role of law libraries to share, rather than to suppress, information users may find useful, the link stayed on WashLaw but the label was changed from "Lawyer Jokes" to "Legal Humor" and it was made clearer that the presence of a link to any site was not an endorsement of its content.

Folmsbee was ingenious in finding partners to help fund WashLaw's constant expansion, or to host parts of it. When the Topeka Area Bankruptcy Council sought to make previously unpublished opinions of the United States Bankruptcy Court of Kansas available online, the Council contributed a server and the library staff created the site. When the City of Topeka wanted to provide electronic access to ordinances and other materials, Folmsbee negotiated the same trade. While WashLaw's size could cause technical difficulties and Folmsbee acknowledged that "if our partners are having problems with their server, then [their sections] might go down,"[1005] Folmsbee's tenacity and 24/7 attention kept the site both going and growing.

During academic year 1997–98, Scott Campbell, the Computer Librarian at Louisville's law school, conducted a survey to determine the number of network servers each law school had. He reported that twelve schools had none, 76 schools had 1–3, 62 schools had 4–8, 25 schools had 9–15, and one school had 23:

> "I'm not sure how much individual schools want this information disseminated, so I decided not to mention any names. I will make one

---

1003. Christensen, *supra* note 991, at 8.

1004. Minutes, Washburn L. Sch. Ass'n Board of Governors (Nov. 19, 1999).

1005. Wendy R. Leibowitz, *Growing Pains of Big Legal Sites Part II: Where Do We Go Now?*, NATIONAL L. J., B18 (Mar. 9, 1998).

exception to answer the question that is probably on everyone's lips: the school with 23 servers is Washburn, although God only knows what they're doing with all of them."[1006]

The Director of Information at Hofstra University School of Law offered an explanation the next day: "As for what Washburn is doing with 23 servers, Mark Folmsbee is planning to put in a bid for Netscape now that they are looking for buyers."[1007]

Recognition would come to WashLaw constantly for its preeminence in the field: #1 ranking in July 1998 by *LegalWorks Interactive* in "Top Legal Links—The Best of the Legal Web;" "best law library site" by the spring 1998 newsletter *legal.online*, chosen by a panel of legal professionals and Internet experts; listing with Yale and Cornell in the "Top Law Library" list in 1998 on *The Law Engine*; listing with Cornell as "Legal Research Starting Points" in the Spring/Summer issue of *Contact*. In addition, local and specialty bar publications highlighted it, bringing attention to Washburn in theretofore unlikely places: *Michigan Bar Journal*, *California Lawyer*, *Chicago Lawyer*, as well as *Trust and Estates*, *Searcher*, and *Law Practice Management*.[1008] The latter publication ultimately named WashLaw as one of seventeen initial inductees in its ABA TechShow "60 Sites in 60 Minutes" Hall of Fame that it no longer would feel compelled to feature each year.[1009] Textbooks used in legal research courses praised it.[1010] Other law schools even directed their students and graduates to WashLaw in their library resource guides and in articles in their alumni publications about Internet research.

WashLaw's dominance of the field was confirmed by scholarly research. Robert Vreeland applied principles of citation analysis to measure and evalu-

---

1006. Email posted by Scott Campbell to teknoids@listserv.law.cornell.edu, Feb. 11, 1998.

1007. Email posted by Gary P. Moore to teknoids@listserv.law.cornell.edu, Feb. 12, 1998.

1008. *WashLaw Again Named Best Legal Web Site*, 37 THE CIRCUIT RIDER 7 (Fall 1998).

1009. *WashLaw Web Named to ABA TechShow Hall O' Fame*, 40 THE CIRCUIT RIDER 12 (Fall/Winter 2002).

1010. *See, e.g.*, JACOBSON, ROY MERSKY AND DONALD DUNN, FUNDAMEN-TALS OF LEGAL RESEARCH 782 (7th ed. 1998) ("just about the most all-inclusive site available").

ate law library websites objectively, using the two criteria of "luminosity" and "visibility." "Luminosity is a measure of how many other URLs a site points to. The premise is that better sites have more links. Visibility measures the number of other sites that have pointers to the site being evaluated, since this reflects a collective endorsement of the targeted site."[1011] Vreeland found WashLaw to be by far both the most luminous and the most visible site. Washburn

> appears to be following a "two-power standard" like that of the Royal Navy during the 19th Century—its collection of links is larger than the second and third largest collections [at Emory and Georgetown] combined. In part this is accomplished by creating "deep links" to remote sites in order to provide direct access to specific resources.[1012]

The number of external links to WashLaw also exceeded the combined total of the second and third place schools.

Christensen was an early advocate of use of e-mail and he and Folmsbee recognized before most others in legal education its potential to transform the way scholars interacted with one another in an "invisible college,"[1013] and to permit students to interact with faculty anytime day or night. Space on a Washburn server was set aside for electronic discussion groups, and a number of Washburn faculty members became list owners in their areas of expertise, including family law, oil and gas, agricultural law, health law, and clinical law.

In 1994, Washburn hosted twenty listservs, including those for Deans of AALS member schools, AALL Law Library Directors, CLE directors, and members of law journal boards. By 1995, Washburn hosted 60 listservs, more than any other site in the world. Understanding that every use of a listserv helped expand Washburn's reputation as a leader in technology, we then created a separate listserv for use by lawyers in each of the 50 states. A software program was modified so that listservs could be created automatically from enrollment data for each law school course.[1014] By 1998, the number of external lists had grown to 250 and there were experiments with live chat sessions.

1011. *WASHLAW Website Premiere [sic] Internet Source*, 38 THE CIRCUIT RIDER 14 (Spring 2000).

1012. Robert C. Vreeland, *Law Libraries in Hyperspace: A Citation Analysis of Worldwide Web Sites*, 92 LAW LIBRARY J. 9 (2000).

1013. Christensen, *supra* note 991, at 8.

1014. *Id.* at 11.

Professor Pierce offered Washburn's first CLE program using interactive video in November 1994. In addition to a live audience in Topeka, lawyers in Liberal also participated in "Environmental Management of Routine Oil & Gas Transactions." The program originated in the interactive video classroom of the Kansas Department of Education since there was not yet adequate interactive video capability on campus. Law Library staff later supported a University Media Center project that equipped a campus classroom with a codec and T1 phone line for interactive video. Christensen accurately predicted in 1995 that "[t]eaching innovations might include a course from a specialist at another law school or classroom presentations led by a prominent alum in St. Louis, Denver, Washington, D.C., or other city."[1015] By 1999, we used interactive video for the Ahrens Chair seminar and to conduct some initial interviews with faculty candidates. Christensen secured a competitive grant from unrestricted University funds for a "Teaching Teachers Technology" project to train interested faculty members in the use of eight enhancements of teaching. By the spring of 2001, there was wireless access to the Internet throughout the Law Library, and the Technology Committee's proposal to expand access to the entire building was approved the following fall, despite misgivings by some faculty about the risk that students would be too easily distracted from class discussions. At the start of the new millennium, *The National Jurist* magazine listed Washburn among the thirty "Most Wired Law Schools" and placed Washburn Law Library among the top twenty law school libraries, based on comparisons of collections, facilities, and staff resources.[1016]

RATINGS AND RANKINGS

Rankings have been an obsession for many stakeholders in legal education, including alumni, applicants, and academic administrators since *U.S. News & World Report* published its first ranking of the "top 25" law schools in 1990. However, various sources purported to rank schools many years before *U.S. News* got into the business. For example, in 1980, *The Gourman Report* purported to rate all graduate and professional programs not only in the United States but also at international universities. By 1987, it was in its fourth edition. The author,

---

1015. *Id.*

1016. *Washburn Law Library Among Top 20*, 39 THE CIRCUIT RIDER 11 (Spring 2001); *Washburn Law School Among the 30 "Most Wired," Id.*

Dr. Jack Gourman, claimed he used an unexplained methodology to evaluate fourteen criteria and produce an overall grade for each law school between 2.00 and 5.00 with precision of .01. No two law schools received the same grade. In 1987, Washburn ranked 102 of 175 schools with a grade of 3.18, just ahead of West Virginia at 3.17 and just behind Texas Tech at 3.19. Legal educators found *The Gourman Report* laughable, but alumni and university administrators, upon learning only of the overall ranking, occasionally took it seriously. In 1984, Dean Monk had to respond to an inquiry from a member of the Board of Regents who was concerned that Washburn did not have a higher rating.

As early as 1976, the Council of the American Bar Association's Section of Legal Education and Admissions to the Bar issued a statement rejecting any law school rating system, observing that "[q]ualities that make one kind of school good for one student may not be as important to another." The Council reaffirmed its statement in 1985 and 1987 and was pro-active in seeking to avoid the proliferation of rankings. In August 1987, *U.S. News & World Report* editor David Gergen asked each law school dean to identify the ten institutions that "offer the best graduate programs in law." The ABA Consultant on Legal Education, James P. White, expressed to Gergen the Council's view that "law school ratings are of little value and, indeed, may mislead the public. In an era of greater consumer protection, we must assist in preventing law school constituencies from being misled."[1017] No doubt hoping to persuade Gergen that the project was not well thought out, White observed that "graduate programs in law" were understood to include only programs leading to an advanced degree, such as an LL.M. or S.J.D.

The project was delayed but *U.S. News* was not deterred. In the fall of 1989, it asked deans and selected lawyers, judges, and legal educators to rate each law school by quartile for quality and asked deans to supply extensive statistical data about their schools. Respondents could not anticipate how the results would be reported but *U.S. News* promised to publish them in March 1990. Leaders of the four principal organizations serving legal education, the ABA Section of Legal Education, the AALS, the Law School Admission Council, and the National Association of Law Placement, issued a joint statement in February seeking even before the rankings were published to undermine their credibility:

1017. ABA Memorandum D8788-17 to Deans of ABA Approved Law Schools, from James P. White, Consultant (Aug. 31, 1987).

> We believe that any ranking or rating of law school, based upon data the magazine has asked deans to provide, must be meaningless or grossly misleading. The survey does not, and could not, measure many important factors involved in evaluating the quality of law schools. Statistics cannot reflect such factors as the quality of the faculty, curricular offerings, adequacy of library resources, and quality of life. Most importantly, the U.S. News and World Report ranking or rating is, in significant part, based on responses of legal educators, judges, practicing lawyers, and others who could not possibly know enough about each of the 175 accredited law schools to rank or rate the law schools by quality quartiles. This survey is designed more to sell magazines than to inform the public about the relative merit of law schools.[1018]

Sighs of relief in many quarters greeted publication of the rankings, since *U.S. News* chose to list only the top 25 schools, although there surely was consternation at schools that expected to be listed among the top 25 but were not. Soon the listing was expanded to the top 50 schools and by 1992 initial fears were realized when the magazine began to list all schools by quartile. Washburn was placed in the third quartile. Considering the rankings' emphases on LSAT scores and a school's reputation nationally among judges and hiring partners at large law firms, to which few Washburn graduates applied to be clerks or associates, the ranking was not a surprise. Lacking a name indicating state affiliation or athletic teams regularly appearing on television, Washburn simply was not known to many respondents.

U.S. News rankings became more misleading in 1994 when schools were spread among five "tiers." The "tiers" did not equate to "quintiles" in which 20% of schools would be found in each tier. Instead, the magazine spread the top half of rated schools in the top three tiers (1–25, 26–50, 51–88) and placed the remaining half of schools in the fourth and fifth tiers (89–132, 133–176). In effect, the fourth "tier" was the third quartile and the fifth "tier" was the fourth quartile. Washburn remained in the same group in which it had been previously, but being in the fourth of five tiers sounded worse.

In 1995, Washburn was in the fifth tier. We were unable to identify a reason, since reputation ratings actually increased three places among academics, to the

---

1018. AALS Memorandum 90-15 to Deans of Member Schools from Betsy Levin, Executive Director (Feb. 26, 1990).

second highest level we have ever recorded, tied for 119th among 177 schools, and increased two places among lawyers and judges to a tie for 122nd. Our median LSAT was the same, 154, that it had been the prior two years. Because the fifth "tier" (i.e., fourth quartile) included eight schools in the fourth quintile, we concluded that the factors *U.S. News* considered placed Washburn near the line between the third and fourth quartiles, so that minor statistical variations could lead to a shift of tiers. That conclusion was reinforced the following year when Washburn was back in the fourth of five "tiers" even though its median LSAT slipped two points and the rest of its statistical profile was essentially unchanged. By 1997, *U.S. News* reverted to just four "tiers" and Washburn was in the third tier that year and the next.

The flaws in the *U.S. News* methodology have been described in numerous articles and will not be repeated here in detail.[1019] Despite the flaws, the preoccupation of alumni and applicants with the rankings meant they could not be ignored. A magazine should not be able to set goals for legal education, but some schools allowed *U.S. News* to do so, with insidious results. There were reports of schools altering their admissions processes, seeking to select half the entering class based on the highest LSAT scores, regardless of GPA, and half the class based on GPA, regardless of LSAT scores, seeking to boost both medians. Some schools became less willing to rely on factors other than LSAT and GPA to achieve greater diversity. Some schools that, unlike Washburn, operate part-time programs, admitted applicants with lower credentials only to the part-time program, since *U.S. News* considered LSAT and GPA scores only of students in the full-time program. Other schools encouraged applications by those with credentials that meant they were unlikely to be admitted, to produce a low percentage of applicants who were admitted which would make the school appear to be more selective. Schools sought to influence likely "voters" in the reputation surveys by identifying them and sending them a flurry of slick mailings. Some established public relations departments, diverting

---

1019. See, e.g., Nancy B. Rapoport, *Why U.S. News & World Report Shouldn't Want to Be Compared to Time and Newsweek*, 60 OHIO ST. L.J. 1097 (1999); Stephen P. Klein, Ph.D. and Laura Hamilton, Ph.D., *The Validity of the U.S. News and World Report Ranking of ABA Law Schools*, (Feb. 18, 1998), available at http://www.aals.org/reports/validity.html; Theodore P. Seto, *Understanding the U.S. News Law School Rankings*, Loyola Law School—Los Angeles Legal Studies Paper No. 2007-25, available at http://ssrn.com/abstract=937017.

resources from education to advertising. Sadly, a few submitted erroneous data in response to *U.S. News* requests, for example by reporting means rather than medians, by using scores of admitted students rather than enrolled students, or by excluding lower LSAT scores of students admitted conditionally.[1020] In addition, there was the phenomenon of strategic voting in the survey of academic reputation. Deans and faculty members had incentives to advance their own school's interest by rating their school in the first tier, and by rating in the lowest tier all schools with which their school competed for students. More broadly, the desire to keep one's own school from declining in the ratings gave an incentive to rate low all schools that in the prior year, or even in any prior year, had been ranked in a tier below one's own school's tier. One might find strategic voting distasteful, but one could do harm to one's own school if one did not vote that way while competitors did.

Leaders of legal education responded in imaginative ways, but they failed to diminish the pernicious effects of the rankings. Dean John Sexton of NYU, as President of the AALS, and others met with the publishers in 1997 and sought to persuade them to abandon the rankings altogether, or at least to limit them to the 25 or 50 schools that might be thought to have actual national reputations. When *U.S. News* refused, Sexton, Carl Monk, and others held a news conference urging the magazine to cease publication of rankings and releasing a critique of the validity of the magazine's system the AALS had commissioned by a senior research scientist with the Rand Corporation.[1021] One year, the AALS even paid to have an advertisement in the ratings issue, although it was forced to tone down its criticism as a condition of publication. The ABA Section of Legal Education ultimately changed its annual law school questionnaire so that schools only reported LSAT and GPA for entering classes at the 75th and 25th percentiles and no longer reported medians. The hope was to deprive *U.S. News* of a statistic it needed for its rankings and to reduce incentives for schools to distort the admissions process in search of higher medians. *U.S. News* was undeterred, continuing to ask schools to report medians even though

1020. *LSAT Scores, Disturbing Discrepancies*, U.S. NEWS & WORLD REPORT 82 (Mar. 20, 1995).

1021. Stephen P. Klein, Ph.D. and Laura Hamilton, Ph.D., *The Validity of the U.S. News and World Report Ranking of ABA Law Schools* (AALS 1998); Laura Johannes and Jonathan Walsh, *Most Law Schools Assail Ratings by U.S. News and World Report*, WALL STREET J., Feb. 19, 1998.

it lacked any way to verify that schools reported them accurately. Eventually, the magazine itself computed what it labeled a median but what in fact was an average of the 75th and 25th percentile scores.

Deans in 1998 developed a six-page joint statement, "Law School Rankings May Be Hazardous to Your Health!," which the Law School Admissions Council mailed to 97,000 takers of the LSAT that year, and again in later years. It was signed by 164 deans. It identified twenty-one variables that applicants find important, to greater or lesser degrees individually, in choosing a law school, none of which is a factor in the *U.S. News* ranking system, including: breadth and support of alumni network; breadth of curriculum; clinical programs; collaborative research opportunities with faculty; commitment to innovative technology; cost; externship options; faculty accessibility; intensity of writing instruction; interdisciplinary programs; international programming; location; public interest programs; quality of teaching; racial and gender diversity within the faculty and student body; size of first-year classes; skills instruction; and specialized areas of faculty expertise. "If the list above includes variables that you consider important," the deans wrote to applicants, "it does not make sense to defer to a system of ranking that ignores them." In addition, they wrote:

> *U.S. News* focuses predominantly on those aspects of law schools that can easily be counted, despite the far greater importance of those aspects that cannot easily be counted. Moreover, like all such systems, *U.S. News* attaches arbitrary weights to those few factors it does include.

> For example, according to *U.S. News*, the median undergraduate GPA of a law school's most recent entering class is five times more important in assessing a school's quality than a school's bar exam success. But why five times, instead of six times, or four times, more important, or more important at all? *U.S. News* similarly assumes, by implication, that the quality of your experience as a law student depends four times more on the LSAT scores of your classmates than on a school's student-faculty ratio. Does that reflect *your* concerns? *U.S. News* weighs a school's overhead budget twice as heavily as its library size. What do *you* think? In fact, the weights attached to all the variables are just *U.S. News & World Report* inventions. Even minor adjustments in this weighting would change some rankings significantly, and the assigned weights are dubious.

...You are simply being misled if you treat some rankings, of which *U.S. News* is a prominent example, as even a competent and conscientious presentation of the limited information they purport to convey.

THE HAPPIEST LAW STUDENTS ON EARTH

Of course, most deans who signed the joint statement to applicants were not above touting to their own applicants and alumni favorable rankings their schools received. Nor was I. *The National Jurist* magazine, distributed nationally to law students and pre-law students, devised a "Best Law Schools" ranking that sought to capture a number of the important measures omitted by *U.S. News.* Cooperating with *Princeton Review,* which publishes an annual guide for applicants about law schools, *The National Jurist* in 1994 surveyed 18,000 law students at 165 of the 176 accredited schools, measuring their relative satisfaction with the quality of their education. To increase responses, representatives went to each law school, set up a table in the commons areas, and encouraged students to complete a questionnaire on the spot. Washburn ranked first in the nation in the category of student satisfaction with Quality of Faculty, based on responses to four questions. Washburn was fifth in Overall Student Satisfaction, based on responses to all eleven questions in the survey, behind only Washington & Lee, Seton Hall, Notre Dame and Texas. "The best law professors are hiding out in Kansas," the April 1994 issue reported, adding that Washburn "students gave their school high marks in faculty-student relations, quality of teaching and faculty diversity. Students said accessibility and friendliness are the primary reasons they think their professors are the best."[1022] The magazine featured students testimonials:

> "They really care about training us for life and not just for our professions," Washburn second-year student Michael Card said. "They care about our lives and not just our academics."

> Jae Lee, a third-year student from Argentina, said her professors have helped her assimilate to law school and American culture. "Even though they didn't have the tools to help me (with my English), they helped me emotionally," Lee said.

1022. *The Best Law Schools,* NAT'L JURIST 12, 14 (Apr. 1994).

Second-year student Clayton Skaggs said Washburn professors use the Socratic method, but they put students at ease rather than intimidating them. "They kind of make you proud to be in law school, to learn something and to challenge yourself." Skaggs said....

"I think the law school at Washburn has a high degree of diversity considering that there aren't that many professors to begin with," Card said.

There was reason to celebrate the positive publicity and we did, with a pizza and beer party for the entire student body, faculty, and staff on a Friday afternoon in late April.

The National Jurist repeated the survey for its April 1996 issue, reaching 28,000 student respondents at 170 schools. This time, Washburn ranked second in Overall Student Satisfaction, behind only Washington and Lee, and actually received the highest ranking in two of the three sub-categories, Faculty and Facilities. Washburn had the eighth highest score in the third category, Quality of Life, which included questions about competitiveness among students, sense of community, and equal treatment of women and minorities. The still almost new building addition contributed to the facilities ranking, as did students' rating of Washburn's research resources, including both the library and computer databases. In the faculty category, Washburn students expressed by far the highest agreement that "Faculty comprises a broadly diverse group of individuals." The article reporting the rankings, with the headline "The Happiest Law Students on Earth," again gave Washburn extensive coverage, including a picture of students presenting me the regional Bronze Key Award our ABA Law Student Division won. After noting that students were pleased with Washburn's new surroundings, the author reported:

> But it takes more than just a building to keep a student body among the five most satisfied in the country for two years running. Schools like No. 2 Washburn and No. 1 Washington and Lee also have outstanding faculties, administrators and deans, students say.
>
> "I think that the faculty here is quite diverse, so you're exposed to a lot of different viewpoints, a lot of different perspectives, which is nice," said Tris Felix, a third year at Washburn.... "They are very responsive to the students," he said. "As a result, the students have a lot of confidence in them..." Good professors can do more than impart valuable

92. Students celebrate the Law School's high
national ranking in overall student satisfaction

knowledge in the classroom—they can teach lessons by example as well. "There's a camaraderie with the faculty members amongst themselves, and there's a camaraderie between the faculty and the students," said Washburn's Felix.

Washburn's dean, James Concannon, agrees that having faculty members who work together displays a good model for students at his school. About once a year, more than a dozen Washburn professors team teach eight-week colloquia…, Concannon said. "The faculty really works as a team (and) students see the positive benefit of everyone working in the common interest," he said.[1023]

1023. Shanie Latham, *The Happiest Law Students on Earth*, NAT'L JURIST 20–22 (April/May 1996).

My penchant to celebrate such positive publicity, as well as orientations and graduations, with beer as an option, among other treats, probably contributed to the overall level of student satisfaction. However, the response was not uniform. When Washburn President Hugh Thompson appeared on a local radio talk show, an anonymous caller asserted that the dean of Thompson's law school had mandated that beer be served at all law school events and asked what the president planned to do about it.

BOOMS AND BUSTS IN THE APPLICANT POOL

Applications to Washburn increased throughout the first half of the 1990s at a pace far exceeding national trends. While the number of applicants nationally increased just 1% for the fall 1992 class, applications to Washburn increased 12%, to 1009, from 901 the prior year. The difference reflected more than the documented national phenomenon of applicants applying to a greater number of schools. Applications were 56% higher in just three years and 92% higher than the 524 applications received in 1986. I reported enthusiastically to alums that "The heightened selectivity from nearly 7 applicants for every place means that this year's class once again will have the highest credentials in the history of the law school."[1024] The increases cannot be attributed to what in hindsight seem to be bland recruiting materials. Rather, they likely reflected the attractiveness of the building addition, increases in alumni giving that, beginning in 1991, supported awards of three-year full tuition scholarships to the most outstanding applicants, and the personal attention of Admissions Director Dottie Harder and her staff. In addition, the Alumni Association Board of Governors in 1990 approved a mentorship program that increased alumni involvement in student recruitment. We matched a graduate with an admitted applicant who either was then attending college in the graduate's hometown or resided there before leaving for college. I sent letters encouraging alums to share their insights about legal education and the legal profession while, of course, touting Washburn's unique advantages. It was nice to be able to ask alums throughout the country to do something specific to help the school besides writing a check.

1024. *From the Dean's Desk*, 31 THE CIRCUIT RIDER 2 (Summer 1992).

When Dottie Harder retired in 1992, her successor, Janet Kerr '87,[1025] increased Washburn's visibility by attending additional LSAC regional recruitment fairs and joining more caravans of admissions officers visiting targeted undergraduate schools. There were obvious advantages in having a Director of Admissions who was a lawyer with a major corporation, Southwestern Bell, and who had been a successful student. In 1994, third-year student Terence O'Malley '95 produced an effective sixteen-minute videotape, entitled "A Commitment to Students," that we sent to pre-law advisors and admitted applicants. He was an experienced photographer and video editor and used equipment and facilities at KTWU and the University Media Center. The cost was a small fraction of what an advertising agency would have charged to produce a tape of similar quality.

Not only was it important to encourage applications, it was important to find new ways to encourage enrollment by applicants Washburn admitted. We mailed them "Washburn Law School Updates," highlighting activities and accomplishments at the school. We also mailed them *The Circuit Rider* when it seemed helpful for recruitment. In 1996, we created a listserv to facilitate communication with admitted applicants. These initiatives seemed to work at first. While the number of applications plummeted nationally, Washburn held steady, at 974 in 1993 and 991 in both 1994 and 1995, and the classes in those three years had the highest numeric credentials ever, a median LSAT of 154 and median GPA of 3.27.

Washburn made recruitment of minority students a priority when Carl Monk was Dean, long before many other schools did so. As other schools became more aggressive in recruiting minorities, Washburn worked harder to stay ahead of them. There were targeted mailings and visits to historically black colleges. Significant scholarship dollars were committed to this priority, with up to one-third of the school's scholarship budget awarded to minority students in some years. Funds were allocated to student organizations, such as the Black Law Students Association, Hispanic American Law Students Association, Asian American Law Students Association, and Native American Law Students Association, to support their student recruitment efforts. The results were dramatic. By 1989–90, Washburn's percentage of minority enroll-

---

1025. Kerr was unaware that the position was vacant until she attended the dedication of the library addition in June 1992. We already had interviewed several candidates, but I assured her a prompt application would be considered.

ment was the highest among forty-four schools in the twelve-state Midwest and Great Lakes region. The following year, Washburn was third in the region, behind only Michigan and Iowa. Washburn's commitment to diversity deserved to be rewarded, and it was. Associate Dean Sheila Reynolds prepared a successful grant application in 1989 to the Patricia Roberts Harris Fellowship program of the United States Department of Education. It underwrote three-year $16,000 per year scholarships that Washburn used to recruit two outstanding minority students who had financial need. The following year, Washburn was awarded two new Patricia Roberts Harris Fellowships, and in 1992, when funding for the law school component of the Harris Fellowships was reduced, Washburn was one of just twelve schools to receive awards. Only one school was granted a larger number of awards than Washburn's three. That a school of Washburn's size and location could receive Patricia Roberts Harris Fellowships in three of four years was remarkable. Terence O'Malley revised his 1994 student recruitment videotape to target minority students, adding new footage. Delano Lewis '63, then President of National Public Radio, taped the narration of "A Commitment to Diversity" during a campus visit. Washburn enrolled twenty or more minority students for twelve consecutive years, beginning in 1985, with a peak of thirty-four students, 22.5% of the entering class, in 1994.

After bucking the national trend of declining applications for four years, Washburn joined the trend in 1996. Application volume fell that one year from 991 to 719. Because of declines in applications elsewhere, we predicted that our percentage yield, i.e. the percentage of enrollment by admitted applicants, would be no better than the previous year. Thus, we extended the same number of offers of admission as we had in 1995, even though doing so required admission of a higher percentage of the applicant pool. When the overall yield unexpectedly rose 8%, the result was an entering class of 182 students, thirty-two over the target and the largest class by far since 1984. An unfortunate companion result was that the median LSAT fell two points to 152, the lowest median since 1991. In 1997, applications declined again to 649. Initially, it was possible to explain the decline as reflecting Washburn "catching up" with the national trend of declines. As the 1999 self-study later observed, "The national application volume dropped by 27% from 1991 to 1997; during the same time period applications to Washburn dropped by 28%." That explanation became untenable in 1998 when applications fell precipitously again, to just 500, the lowest number since 1986. There were one-third fewer applications that year from Kansas residents than in 1995, and applications from non-residents fell a whopping 58% over the same period. Applications from minority students were down by nearly one-half from 1994, and the percentage of minorities in the entering class predictably fell to 13%. Although the 75th percentile LSAT fell only one point, reflecting the positive impact of merit scholarships, the median fell three points. The result could have been worse but Washburn's yield was exceeded by only 28 law schools and was the highest for resident students (70%) since 1987 and for non-residents (39%) since 1991. Even though the number of non-resident applicants declined more than for residents, the differences in yield meant that the entering class in 1998 had 47% non-residents, tying Washburn with Colorado for third place among public schools in the percentage of non-residents in the entering class, behind only Virginia and Michigan.

The data suggested that we were effective in recruiting students who chose to apply but that our effectiveness in enticing applications had declined. We concluded that increases in our tuition were not the reason for the decline in applications. Throughout the decade, increases in public funding of higher education were so small in many states that many public schools were forced to raise tuition significantly. By the end of the decade, fewer law schools had resident tuition rates that were lower than Washburn's than in 1990, before the Law School Financing Plan was implemented. Further, while our resident tuition was still higher than at KU, in percentage terms our tuition was much closer to KU's, only 30% higher, than it had been in 1990 when it was 2.25 times higher. KU was experiencing declines in applications too. However, we feared the decline in our applications might accelerate, particularly from non-residents, and that yields might erode, when, as we expected, the 1998 decline in median LSAT caused us to fall in the 1999 *U.S. News* rankings.

Thus, we undertook in the fall of 1998 to reexamine recruitment strategies. Current students completed a questionnaire asking them to compare Washburn's recruitment efforts to those of other schools. We asked Professor Peter Winograd, a former President of the Law School Admissions Council and long-time Associate Dean at the University of New Mexico, to review Washburn's recruitment strategies, publications, and admissions process, and to make recommendations for improvement. Dean Winograd's report, following a February 1999 campus visit, recommended numerous changes to increase not only the size of the applicant pool but also the yield. Many recommendations confirmed tentative conclusions an ad hoc recruitment committee had reached. Cost-benefit analysis suggested that directing more recruitment resources at Kansas and nearby states, and less at distant states, was a strategy likely to augment the applicant pool. Our drab, black-and-white catalogue that was designed to be a comprehensive information source was transformed, with the assistance of an advertising agency, into a full-color promotional piece. It included a new logo, vetted by a surprising number of faculty members who claimed to have taste in such matters. The new catalogue was first used to recruit the class of 2000. The upgrade included complementary brochures highlighting special programs and targeting particular groups, as well as rewriting all correspondence to prospective students. We also revamped webpage content. Applicants for the first time had the opportunity to submit applications online, and seventy of them did so during the first three months.[1026] It was too late to impact significantly the 1999 entering class. However, minority enrollment did rebound to 19% that fall. The faculty's self-study that year speculated that a *National Jurist* magazine article reporting that Washburn's percentage of minority faculty, 19%, exceeded that of all but five other schools may have been a factor in the improved yield among minority applicants.

We sought new ways to reach prospects. Admissions Director Janet Kerr '87 for several years taught Washburn's undergraduate mock trial course and used it to recruit outstanding students to the Law School. In February 2000, the Law School co-hosted with the Political Science Department the American Mock Trial Association regional competition, showcasing the school to 150 potential law students representing eleven Midwest colleges. The competition was well organized and returned to Washburn in later years.

We sought to make greater use of our alums too. We identified the undergraduate schools in our region from which law alums had graduated and sent information about them to prelaw advisors and applicants at those schools. Alumni Board of Governors President Allan Caldwell '73 believed that having alums make presentations at their alma maters would be effective, and he tried out the idea at his, Evangel College in Missouri. During a joint discussion among faculty members and alumni board members in March 2001, support

---

1026. *Applying to Washburn Law Via the Web*, 38 THE CIRCUIT RIDER 12 (Spring 2000).

was expressed for Professor Bill Rich's idea to provide funds that feeder undergraduate schools could use to target scholarships for their students who had been admitted to Washburn. The idea made sense, both as a recruitment tool and as an inducement for alums to give, or give more, because their gifts would benefit both of the institutions they attended. Unfortunately, the next Dean declined to implement the idea.

GIVING BACK

The need to solicit alums for contributions for three building projects completed in just twenty-three years between 1969 and 1992 precluded consistent solicitation of alums for contributions for scholarships and academic programs. Alums loyally contributed to the 1969 and 1978 building campaigns, but there was no systematic follow-up to translate that loyalty into annual gifts and gifts of endowment for other purposes. We vowed to seize that opportunity after the 1992 campaign.

We tried to create a culture of annual giving. It was not rocket science to conclude that if an alum made several consecutive annual gifts, there was a high likelihood that alum would make a gift every year thereafter. We wrote different solicitation letters for donors at different levels of giving, for sometime-donors, and for non-donors. We asked those in the latter group to donate what for them would be the equivalent of one billable hour, a request meant to acknowledge the difference between the circumstances of those in public service positions compared to those practicing in large firms. We listed how much donors had contributed previously and asked prior-year donors to increase their gift to a specific amount. Often the increase corresponded to the percentage tuition had increased that year. The practice produced unusual numbers. If tuition increased 11.4%, an alum who had contributed $250 the prior year was asked to give $278.50. The number of alums each year who sent the precise amount requested was high; happily, many others rounded up.

Development Director Sandy Vogel reorganized the student phonathon so that prior donors who had not responded to the letters sent in the late fall would be called early in the spring. One goal was to recruit as many students as possible to make calls. We developed incentives for them, or student organizations they wanted to help, to do so. Besides assuring that we reached as many alums as possible, we knew that any student who made calls would be more inclined later as an alum to respond positively when called. We celebrated Phonathon successes each year with a party at my home.

Numbers of donors were important. In 1990–91, Mark Heitz '77 chaired a Development Council the Board of Governors created to contact alums in Topeka, Wichita, Kansas City, and selected other Kansas cities. In 1994, the Development Council expanded statewide. Mert Buckley '77 was chair and sixteen regional councils in Kansas had regional chairs. In all, 149 alums served on the regional councils, personally soliciting non-donors and sometime-donors. Sandy Vogel tirelessly supported the efforts of the regional councils and I traveled to meet with most of them. The result was 155 first-time donors and forty-seven former donors who renewed their support, with gifts totaling $17,820.[1027] The impact of gifts those donors made in later years was much larger.

As important as the number of donors was, increasing the size of gifts was critical too. Alumni Board of Governors President Dick Hite '53 had the inspiration to begin an annual black-tie dinner honoring all donors of $1,000 or more. He believed that having a first-class, exclusive event would encourage those attending to renew their gifts at the same or higher levels the following year and lead other alums to increase their gifts so they could be part of the group. The first Dean's Circle Dinner was held at the Carriage Club in Kansas City, Missouri, on September 7, 1991. Lynn '70 and Jacque Johnson hosted an elegant cocktail party before the dinner at their nearby home in Mission Hills. Hite was right. The dinner became a popular event and the number of Dean's Circle members grew steadily each year.

These efforts paid off. After averaging approximately $50,000 annually before fundraising for the building addition started in 1988, annual giving soared to more than $126,000 in 1990–91, excluding endowments, with 23% of alums contributing. It rose to more than $208,000 the next year and to more than $244,000 the next. The 1996 Phonathon achieved $100,000 in pledges for the first time, exceeding its goal by 20%. Contributions that year from faculty, faculty emeriti, and staff totaled $39,700, including eleven gifts at the Dean's Circle level, an impressive expression of commitment to the institution. The percentage of alums contributing in 1996–97 grew to 31%, and Washburn had the twenty-third highest rate of giving of all law schools. The peak was reached

---

1027. *149 Alums Participate in Development Council*, 34 THE CIRCUIT RIDER 28 (Fall 1995).

93. Reception hosted by Lynn Johnson '70 before first Dean's Circle Dinner

in 1999–2000, when 36% of alums contributed, the second highest rate of giving among all public law schools, behind only the University of Virginia, and the eighth highest rate among all schools, behind private schools only at Yale, Washington & Lee, Marquette, Vanderbilt, Pennsylvania and Harvard.[1028] Astonishingly, all thirty-two graduating classes from 1967 through as recently as 1998 had participation rates of 30% or higher and the rate was at least 25% for fifty-two consecutive graduating classes.[1029] Annual giving that year, excluding endowment and capital gifts, was $437,168, an increase by a factor of almost nine since the start of the building campaign. I regularly touted these levels of alumni support to prospective students as the strongest testimonial we could provide of the high quality experience, both educationally and personally, they would have if they chose Washburn. We highlighted the data in our revised catalogue and on our website.

1028. *Alumni Contributors Rank Washburn Law School Eighth Among Law Schools*, 39 THE CIRCUIT RIDER 29 (Spring 2001).

1029. *Solid Foundations at the Law School*, 39 THE CIRCUIT RIDER 3, 38–39 (Fall 2000).

LAW SCHOOL 2000

To increase annual giving by $5,000, many non-donors have to be persuaded to begin making gifts. A gift of endowment of $100,000 accomplishes the same result instantly, and forever. The total value of endowments that benefitted Washburn Law School as of 1990 was barely more than $4 million, and one in six of those dollars represented the value of land that was not producing income. Prodded by President Dick Hite '53, the Board of Governors committed to initiate a campaign to increase the Law School's endowment, as soon as fundraising for the building addition was completed. Planning for the campaign actually began in December 1989, prior to the April groundbreaking.[1030]

We understood that people are motivated to give to a program of accomplishment rather than one that faces difficulties. Thus, we emphasized accomplishments, like the new Financing Plan. However, we also sought to explain the extent of the need and make alums realize their gifts to the building fund should not be their last. Dick Hite and I presented sobering data at the 1990 Washburn luncheon during the KBA annual meeting showing that alumni giving at KU's law school exceeded giving at Washburn dramatically, both for annual gifts and for endowments. For example, there were six named professorships there compared with only the recently funded Ahrens Chair at Washburn. Because Washburn's tuition then was 2.25 times higher than tuition at KU, Washburn would need an endowment of $13.3 million, even assuming an unlikely 8% rate of return, to equalize tuition for our students with tuition at KU, yet even that amount would not enable us to match full tuition scholarships KU was able to award from its substantially larger endowment. Dick Hite's message was that for Washburn to compete and succeed, our alums would have to respond. That fall, we invited alums we hoped might make significant gifts to attend "Inner Circle" dinners in a number of Kansas cities. Bill Kurtis '66 narrated a video highlighting the issues and the school's priorities. The University's new president, Hugh Thompson, attended the Topeka dinner. Foundation President Gerald Goodell '58 agreed to chair the campaign steering committee and Senator Bob Dole '52, Gerald Michaud '51, and John Shamberg '37 signed on as Honorary Chairs. By early 1993, we had a brochure for use in solicitations, "The Case for Law School 2000." Bob Hartsook '79, now nationally known as

1030. Letter from Richard C. Hite to Dean James Concannon, Terry Kilroy and Lynn Johnson (Dec. 20, 1989).

a fundraising consultant, conducted workshops for the steering committee and the Board of Governors and advised Development Director Sandy Vogel and me quarterly.

Anyone who agrees to join a steering committee for an endowment campaign knows that he or she is expected to make a gift during the "quiet phase" of the campaign, before it "goes public." Steering committee members responded wonderfully with early pledges, as did many members of the Board of Governors. Gerald Goodell '58, Lynn Johnson '70, Mark Heitz '77, Joseph W. Morris '46, Richard Hite '53, and Bradley Post '54 all made early gifts or short-term commitments of six figures or more. In addition, Norman Pozez '80 made a seven figure commitment over a longer term.

Estate gifts in excess of $250,000 came from the estates of Wallace Fisher '33 and Reginald '27 and Mae Labunker. We displayed in the reception area of the Dean's office one of several pieces of sculpture Fisher sent me, made from manzanita root from his property in Lakeside, California. One of my fondest memories is of joining him, in my dress shoes but with my tie loosened, in climbing the small mountain on his property that he loved.

The Law School received more than $375,000 from the estate of Susan Stussy '94 barely six years after she graduated as a non-traditional student. The estate of George Ramskill '33 provided in excess of $100,000 for the Law School and Keith Quail '37, Bill Bunten '56, and Glenn L. Archer '46 created significant charitable remainder trusts benefitting the school. We learned of one deferred gift that we did not solicit directly, from the estate of John Schovee '56, that eventually will net the Law School nearly $1.4 million.

Koch Industries, Inc., made the largest corporate gift in the school's history in June 1994. There were more Washburn law alums at Koch than from any other school. Koch lawyers had taught our International Business Transactions class as Adjunct Professors and lectured in other courses, thus expanding the school's relationship with the company. Koch's general counsel Allan Caldwell '73 joined the Board of Governors in 1992 and collaborated with other Washburn graduates internally to encourage the gift. Dick Hite '53 worked externally with Don Cordes, former General Counsel and then a Koch Vice President. We proposed a Koch Scholars program that would provide a full scholarship for all three years to an outstanding applicant, selected after interviews with our Financial Aid Committee in which a Koch lawyer would participate. It would pay for tuition, books, a living expense stipend, and, after the student completed the first year, a research assistant stipend to work with a faculty member. There also would be an opportunity for the Koch Scholar to have a summer internship at the company to learn its market-based management principles. The concept was that we would recruit and, hopefully, keep in Kansas, an academic leader who otherwise would attend law school elsewhere. Initially, the company suggested it might fund two such scholarships at $250,000 each. We countered that it was important to be able to offer one such scholarship each year and Koch ultimately increased its commitment to $750,000. Having the Washburn Law School Foundation as recipient of the gift, separate from the University, was essential. Charles Koch, the Chairman of Koch Industries, and his brother Bill Koch were on opposite sides of high profile litigation that was nearing trial in federal court in Topeka. Mindful of the advantages of creating a positive impression among potential jurors, Bill Koch had made many philanthropic gifts in the Topeka area, including a major gift of art history materials to Washburn University. Koch Industries' gift to the Foundation both matched the plaintiffs' publicity initiative and helped to attract top quality students the company one day might want to hire. The Koch Scholars program was phased in the following year by naming 3L Lisa Agrimonti '96 and 2L Steve Torline '97 as recipients in addition to entering 1L Heather Randall '98.

The Law School 2000 campaign did not raise the full amount that we optimistically set as our initial target. Sandy Vogel's departure from the Development Office in 1994 to pursue seminary studies slowed momentum, as did her successor's decision to do the same thing four years later. Still, at the end of my thirteen years as Dean, cash payments received by the Law School during those years, for both annual giving and endowments, totaled nearly $11 million. Perhaps as important, nearly forty alums had included the Law School in their estate plans or made other deferred gifts and pledges that would provide significant resources in future years.[1031]

One last major gift arrived just days before the end of fiscal year 2001, a $520,000 remainder gift to create the Richard S. Righter Distinguished Professorship. Righter started law studies at Washburn in 1916 after he graduated from Washburn College. His studies were interrupted after one year by World War I and Righter completed his LL.B. at Harvard after the war. He became

---

1031. *From the Dean's Desk*, 39 THE CIRCUIT RIDER 3 (Spring 2001).

a partner in the Kansas City law firm of Lathrop, Crane, Sawyer, Woodson & Righter. Washburn did not solicit his gift and we did not even know about it until after the death of those for whom he had designated life estates. His trust specified that the remainder was to be used to create a named professorship at Washburn Law School which would pay the full salary of a full-time professor. By the late 1990s, even a gift as large as his was insufficient to do that, and his trust provided that if Washburn declined to accept the gift on the stated terms within a ten-year period, the trustee was to make the gift instead to one of four other colleges in the region. It was clear, however, that Righter's overriding purpose was to have a named professorship at the Law School and to have his entire gift used for the salary of that professor. We were fully prepared to do those things. One of the trust officers administering the Righter Trust was, happily, Clark Bradshaw '69. He obtained releases from the four schools of their claims to the funds, and on that basis the trustee was willing to designate the Foundation to receive them. Ultimately, Linda Elrod would be named the first Richard S. Righter Distinguished Professor of Law.

Not surprisingly, our disagreements with President Thompson extended to fundraising. When Thompson arrived, the University's Development Office reported to the President. It was understaffed. Many campus entities besides the Law School conducted their own fundraising, including the Mulvane Art Museum, KTWU-TV, and athletics through the Ichabod Club. By 1992, Thompson concluded that all University fundraising should be centralized. One option was to transfer the University's development function to the separate Washburn Endowment Association, which previously had responsibility only for investment of endowment funds. It seemed odd that a president would consider an arrangement in which the president had less control over fundraising. However, with state affiliation still the University's top priority, the proposed structure was the same one Regents schools like KU used. Converting to that structure was thought to be a way to remove an obstacle to incorporation in the state system.

The Law School had no stake in whether central University fundraisers were on the University's payroll or that of WEA. However, I felt strongly that preserving the Law School's fundraising autonomy was critical. There were many reasons, not the least of which was that forcing us to rely on a central database would have reduced the amount we raised. Our alumni database was more current and more accurate than the one maintained by the University, in part because of the frequent professional contacts law graduates have with the Law School. Indeed, the University Development Office once directed that we not send for inclusion in the University's database records of contributions to the Law School Foundation or changes of address we discovered, because staff shortages there meant those items could not be processed. In addition, our software permitted us to do more with the information we had.

The Law School Foundation assured donors that their donations to the Law School could not be siphoned off for other uses. Further, we carefully had built an expectation by our alums that they would be solicited separately by the Law School, so that they would not mistakenly respond to a solicitation from the University in the erroneous belief their gift would be credited to the Law School. While in earlier years many law graduates had undergraduate degrees from Washburn, only 9% of the entering class in 1991 had bachelor's degrees from Washburn, and the percentage was only 13% for the nine years from 1983–91. Graduates lacking other Washburn degrees might give to their undergraduate institutions, or even to KTWU if they lived in its viewing area, but they were unlikely to make unrestricted gifts to the University.

One risk of a centralized structure was that it might undermine the existing agreement that unless there was a reason to believe law-only graduates might give elsewhere, they would be solicited only by the Law School and not by the central University. There were enough breaches of that agreement under the existing fundraising structure. Dual degree alums expected to be solicited both by the undergraduate school and by the Law School, but solicitation solely by a central development office likely would create the confusion we had worked hard to avoid. Adequate mechanisms already were in place to coordinate activities so that dual degree alums were not solicited by both entities at the same time. The bottom line, however, was that when annual giving to the rest of the University was just $170,000 and annual giving to the Law School exceeded $235,000, it was unlikely that centralization would benefit us.

It was difficult to shake Thompson of his belief that unrestricted gifts to the University would grow if the separate campus fundraising entities could be reined in. Indeed, following the bitter disagreement in 1992 about the Financing Plan, Thompson's desire to rein in the Law School's autonomy in fundraising grew.

By early 1994, the University completed negotiations to shift its fundraising staff to WEA, which changed its bylaws so that its president could become the University's chief development officer. However, structural issues were still to be resolved and, in May, Thompson sought to bolster his position by bringing three consultants to campus to examine "fundraising policies and procedures, organizational structure, staffing, etc."[1032] and to advise on the feasibility of a capital campaign. Predictably, they all endorsed greater centralization, including making all fundraisers WEA employees. One did propose what he described as "a centralized de-centralized model of development" with a prospect clearance system for all campus entities, "not to restrict anyone's efforts, but to provide a firm communications basis as to who is soliciting which donors for which projects."[1033] They warned that it would take several years to prepare for a capital campaign but suggested that the campaign should embrace all campus fundraising priorities rather than having separate campaigns by individual units. Our Law School 2000 Campaign already was underway, and we could not wait for the University to be ready to launch its own campaign. In fact, we had delayed some parts of our campaign to permit the University to complete fundraising for the Bradbury Thompson Alumni Center. We moved forward with the campaign, although not without challenges from Thompson, who at one point claimed he was unaware of our campaign, despite having attended one of the early dinners to promote it. At another point, he questioned whether the Board of Regents had ever approved it, although we won that argument too, since a pledge from the Alumni Association to support the campaign was an explicit premise of the Financing Plan on which the Regents relied in approving it.

In 1995, Jerry Clevenger became President of WEA. He pursued centralization aggressively. We spent substantial time over the next six years fending off what we perceived to be bad ideas. We coordinated contacts but preserved the Foundation's autonomy. A call Clevenger and I made jointly on a law-only alum, who had made it clear that the Law School was his only philanthropic interest at Washburn, was the final straw for me. Clevenger consumed most of our time talking about other units on campus and what the University's other fundraising priorities were. When I suggested at the airport that the alum might have been offended by the presentation, Clevenger responded by explaining his philosophy of fundraising: "Ready, Shoot, Aim." I never made another call with him. He left the University abruptly, just days before the end of my deanship.

1032. Memorandum from Hugh L. Thompson, President to Washburn Board of Regents and others (Mar. 22, 1994).

1033. Jack H. Miller, *Report to Washburn University on Future Directions for Development* (July 14, 1994), at 14, 15.

REMODELING

The renovation in 1992 did not include the Law Clinic building. The medium-sized classroom/courtroom on its lower level, Room 150, had never worked well and professors avoided having classes there whenever possible. It had theater seats with fold-down arm tables that were ill-suited for notetaking or having multiple textbooks open simultaneously. The platform for the professor's podium was small and more than one faculty member tripped off of it. The built-in blackboard was so small that a portable blackboard was permanently stationed in the room. Between fall and spring semesters in 1996–97, we gutted the room, replaced its sloping floor with a stair-stepped floor, and removed the platform to put the professor's podium on the floor. We installed a larger blackboard and regular classroom tables and chairs. There were ports at each seat with electric outlets.

Standardized multi-media teaching stations were installed for the first time in the fall of 1998, in Room 150 and in two of the larger classrooms in the main building. All of the classrooms had them by 2000.

Robinson Courtroom remained unchanged for more than thirty years after its dedication. Even the original blue carpet was still there. The courtroom had been quite functional. United States District Judges Sam A. Crow '52 and J. Thomas Marten '76 even conducted civil jury trials there, in September 1994 and April 1999, respectively, so that students could observe trials conveniently.[1034] Nevertheless, the courtroom showed its age. As an evidence teacher, I regularly clipped articles about advances in courtroom technology. I asked our technology gurus in the library to work with interested faculty to determine what we would want to include in a state-of-the-art courtroom and what it

---

1034. In the 1994 case, *Tighe v. B.C. Christopher Securities Co.*, plaintiff asserted theories of negligent misrepresentation and promissory estoppel in connection with a short-term loan to the developer of a subdivision. After a four-day trial, the jury awarded $86,700 on the promissory estoppel claim. Counsel were Washburn graduates Steve Cavanaugh '80 and Dan Biles '78. *U.S. District Court Conducts Jury Trial in Robinson Courtroom*, 33 THE CIRCUIT RIDER 15 (Summer 1994). Post-trial proceedings were resolved in an opinion at 1994 U.S. Dist. Lexis 6470. The 1999 case, *Rodriguez v. IBP, Inc.*, resulted in a plaintiff's verdict for $411,000 on a claim of wrongful termination from employment. David Alegria '87 was plaintiff's counsel. *Marten Hears Jury Trial at Law School*, 37 THE CIRCUIT RIDER 10 (Spring 1999). The last reported opinion in the case is at 243 F.3d 1221 (10th Cir. 2001).

likely would cost. During initial planning, we determined that asbestos abatement would be needed before wiring could be installed in the ceiling, just as it had been needed prior to the 1992 addition. Happily, the University had funds earmarked for asbestos removal, so a two-month abatement project was completed during the summer of 2000, not only in Robinson Courtroom but also in the three main classrooms on the first floor, in part because some wiring for the courtroom project would go through the floor into the ceilings below and in part because abatement would be needed before any major renovation of the classrooms could proceed.

The Americans with Disabilities Act presented another complication. The extent of remodeling planned for the courtroom meant it had to be brought into compliance with the ADA. The only access to the judges' bench was by three narrow steps and there were big steps up to the two witness boxes and the top row of the jury box. Installing a lift to the judges' bench was rejected for aesthetic reasons and because it would consume too much space. Ultimately, the solution was to build a ramp that went around the west witness box and remove the wooden panel on the west end of the bench. To have a grade on the ramp that complied with the applicable code, however, the bench itself had to be lowered by eighteen inches. Restoring the appearance of the bench required more skilled work than ordinary woodworking. ADA compliance added nearly $60,000 to the project cost.

The planning committee sought to incorporate all the gadgetry needed to prepare students for careers as twenty-first century litigators:

> separate cameras focusing on the attorney at the podium, the judge, and the witness, with the ability to display them on split screens; microphones and speakers throughout the courtroom;

> a presentation podium with recording equipment, a document camera, and a control panel permitting files to be projected from computers plugged in there, at counsel tables, the judge's bench, or on the witness stand to monitors in each of those locations, to a flat screen mounted on a wall behind the witness box and to a pull-down screen in front of the gallery;

> video teleconferencing capability not only for trial or deposition testimony but also for guest lecturers from remote locations, without incurring travel expenses;

Internet access;

and capability for remote broadcast that would facilitate offering CLE programs.[1035]

After much debate, the committee rejected the added cost of installing individual monitors in the jury box, opting instead to wheel in portable monitors in the rare instances in which we hosted actual jury trials. We acquired a "smart board" that could be used for that purpose and many others.

Private funding was required for the entire cost, projected at well in excess of $300,000. Our annual giving letter asked donors to add a technology surcharge to their annual gifts. Ralph Foster's '50 gift was triple matched by Kansas Power and Light Company. However, we could not start the project until the full cost was in the bank. We anticipated we would have to solicit a number of other alums to reach the goal.[1036] In fact, we only had to ask one. Bernie Bianchino '74 was President-elect of the Law School Association Board of Governors and understood the impact of technology better than most of us, having been a vice-president for Sprint Corporation and U.S. Sprint, general counsel for the then start-up Qwest Corporation, and later CEO of Pegasos PCS in Mexico. Bianchino immediately sensed the competitive advantage the project would give Washburn. He committed $300,000 to name the Bianchino Technology Center in the courtroom, allowing construction to begin on April 26, 2001, after the last spring semester class was held there. The new technology was already in constant use when the formal dedication ceremony was held in October 2002, honoring Bernie and his spouse Marilyn. Michael C. Manning '77 demonstrated how he had used technology in various cases, including the Lincoln Savings/Charles Keating cases which brought him national attention.[1037]

The Courtroom was not the only area of the building impacted by the ADA. The recessed area known as "The Pit" in the commons areas outside the main classrooms on the first floor was inaccessible to students who used wheelchairs, and one of them complained. The area wasn't used for instruction but students

---

1035. *Training Tomorrow's Lawyers: Integrating Technology*, 38 THE CIRCUIT RIDER 15 (Spring 2000).

1036. *From the Dean's Desk: Summer 2000—Transition and Change*, 38 THE CIRCUIT RIDER 5 (Spring 2000).

1037. *Michael Manning Keynote Speaker*, 41 WASHBURN LAWYER 37 (Fall/Winter 2002–03); *Bianchino Technology Center Dedication, id.*, at 38.

socialized there and it filled with people during receptions and other events. Ramps weren't feasible because of the extent of the drop-off, and installing a lift would have required significant structural changes in the walls and floor on one side of the pit. We elected the path of least resistance. During the break following the fall semester in 1998, we filled the pit with sand and put a new floor over it. We installed a kiosk for computer access in the middle of it. The WSBA committed $6,500 from its capital improvements fund for furniture, and we matched that amount from Law School funds.

CELEBRITY

The campaign of Senator Robert Dole '52 as the Republican Party's 1996 nominee for President brought Washburn Law School significant national exposure. Dole scheduled the announcement of his candidacy in Topeka for Monday morning, June 10, 1995. Mark Heitz '77 not only was active in the Dole campaign but also was President-elect of the Law School Association Board of Governors. Seeing an opportunity to feature the Law School in national media, Heitz suggested that the Law School host a reception to honor its distinguished graduate on Sunday evening, June 9, before his announcement. The Dole campaign thought that was a wonderful idea, as long as it could charge invitees to raise funds for the campaign, which it planned to do somewhere in Topeka anyway.

The lower level of the building was transformed on Sunday morning: student bulletin boards were removed, memorabilia from Dole's years as a law student were hung, and the entire floor assumed the appearance of a national convention hall. Kansas political leaders who never before had been to the Law School considered the event a command performance. National media broadcast footage of Dole arriving for the event and there was extensive print media coverage. The work of the Law School staff was extraordinary. By Monday morning, all student bulletin boards were back in place and there was no evidence that anything unusual had happened on the first floor. Dole returned frequently to the Law School, giving the commencement address in 1998 and keynoting an April 1999 presentation on Disabilities and The Law, discussing the impact of the Americans With Disabilities Act he helped pass.[1038]

1038. *Dole Lectures on Disabilities and the Law*, 37 THE CIRCUIT RIDER 4 (Spring 1999).

94. Senator Bob Dole '52 with Mark Heitz '77 at a Law School reception the evening before Dole announced his candidacy for President

The Law School received a different kind of publicity in the spring of 1994 when it was featured in two episodes of the short-lived CBS television situation comedy "Tom." The title character Tom, played by Tom Arnold, and his wife, appropriately named Dorothy and played by Alison LaPlaca, returned to Kansas to live on a farm and raise their family.[1039] In the premiere episode, Dorothy applied for admission to Washburn Law School. She ultimately was admitted to the fall 1994 class after Tom visited the Admissions Office to insist that she be admitted even though her application was submitted late. The episode included a film clip of the actual Washburn University cornerstone on the campus but the fictional Hollywood set of the Admissions Office was far from modern. Worse, the admissions director was stern and intransigent, unlike the real-life director Janet Kerr '87. The episode concluded with Dorothy wearing a Washburn Law School sweatshirt Tom had purchased to celebrate her admission. In a later episode, Dorothy was urged by her lawyer father to attend a nearby law school from which he graduated and to which she could have been admitted, but Dorothy expressed a strong preference to attend Washburn. The decision to have Dorothy apply to Washburn Law School was

---

1039. *Law School Featured in CBS Television Series*, 33 THE CIRCUIT RIDER 13 (Summer 1994). The description that follows is based on the text I wrote for this article.

made by the show's executive producer, Steve Pepoon, a native of Paola. His brother Mike is a Wichita lawyer who graduated from that nearby law school. We gladly sent Steve Pepoon the sweatshirt, a catalogue, and other props for use in the show. On the theory that any national publicity was positive so long as Washburn's name was spelled correctly, I was prepared to recommend an honorary degree in 1997 for Dorothy if the show lasted three years.

Sometimes, opportunities to host celebrities arose in unexpected ways. Ellyn Atherton's '89 father had worked in Colorado for many years for *Forbes* magazine publisher Malcolm Forbes. That connection led Forbes to agree to be the 1989 graduation speaker. A not insignificant factor also was his hobby of collecting honorary degrees. Forbes was frequently in the news at the time as companion to actress Elizabeth Taylor. He flew into Topeka on his own Boeing 727, the green and gold plane he named "The Capitalist Tool." My straight face did not persuade him when I suggested that we had renamed the local airport Forbes Field especially in honor of his visit. He took the welcoming party on a tour of the plane—there was a bedroom suite with a waterbed and above it one of the then-popular helium filled balloons with bouncing feet. He gave each of us a plastic model of the airplane as a souvenir. Christel Marquardt '74 arranged with Governor Mike Hayden for the Law School to host a reception for Forbes prior to commencement at the Governor's mansion, Cedar Crest. Nearly 150 lawyers and Kansas business and community leaders attended. It was a beautiful day and the presence of a hot air balloon, another of Forbes' hobbies, added a distinctive touch.

Forbes shared the secret of his success at a press conference: "I had a father who owned a business who wasn't mad at me when he died." For those not fortunate enough to have such lineage, Forbes later advised graduates, "if you're able to do what turns you on, you're going to be a success. You may not be the richest, and you may not climb the highest mountain, but you're a success because you're doing what you want to do." This "psychic income," he said, needs to be considered when evaluating job satisfaction.[1040]

There was consensus among alumni leaders and some on campus that we should not pass up the opportunity to ask Forbes for a contribution. It was a long shot and I had difficulty devising a comfortable way to do that, within

---

1040. *Malcolm Forbes Speaks at 1989 Law School Commencement*, 28 THE CIR-CUIT RIDER 7 (Summer 1989).

just hours of meeting him. As we walked back alone from the commencement ceremony to a reception at the Law School, I told him the most creative suggestion had been to ask him to be the first person ever to turn a public university into a private one. Before I could mention a specific project, Forbes deftly cut the discussion short. "You wouldn't be doing your job if you didn't ask," he said.

REUNIONS

The success of the class of 1977's tenth anniversary reunion that David Pierce organized prompted interest in making reunions an annual event. In 1989, fifty-eight alums attended a tenth-year reunion of the class of 1989 and sixteen of the forty-four members of the class of 1964 attended a twenty-fifth year reunion. Starting in 1990, we encouraged classes regularly to return for reunions on the zero and five anniversaries of their graduation. Five classes gathered in Topeka that year. The classes of 1950, with twenty-three members in attendance, and 1985, with forty-five members, had the highest percentage turnouts. The number of classes grew to nine at the August 1994 reunion weekend. A faculty member, or sometimes a reunion class member, offered a free CLE program each year, with the happy byproduct that trip expenses might be deductible for CLE attendees. Ordinarily, there was a separate class event one evening, often at the home of a Topeka class member, and an all-class dinner the other evening. Often, there was golf too. Retired members of the faculty, particularly Jim Ahrens, regularly attended to visit with former students. In 2000, the class of 1965 underwrote expenses to have Professor Bill Harvey join its reunion, thirty-two years after Harvey left Washburn.[1041] A special reunion was held on June 8, 1996, the thirtieth anniversary of the tornado, bringing together graduates from the 1966–69 classes. Bill Kurtis '66 came from Chicago to retell the story of the "big blow" and Dean John Howe, Professors Ahrens and Spring, and John Shamberg '37 shared their recollections. There also was the debut showing of a high quality video history produced by Terence O'Malley '95 which blended news film, photographs, and interviews with professors and students who described the tornado and its aftermath.[1042]

1041. Harvey discussed Hillary Rodham Clinton's suit against him when he was chair of the Legal Services Corporation. *Washburn School of Law Reunions*, 39 THE CIRCUIT RIDER 18 (Summer 2000).

1042. Slider, *supra* note 521, at 31.

Reunions attracted many graduates from throughout the nation who had not returned to the school for many years, if at all. We were surprised that sometimes the turnout was poorest among those who lived closest to the school and regularly had other opportunities to attend Law School events. The demands reunions placed on the staff meant we usually scheduled all classes the same weekend, but the chosen weekend might be ideal for one class but less so for another. Large numbers meant successful reunions, but small turnouts for a class discouraged those who did attend, particularly from afar, from returning five years later.

Reunions fit into a larger strategy of rekindling alumni interest in the school and encouraging alumni involvement, particularly by alums outside Topeka. Asking alums to contact prospective students fit that strategy too. Martin Wisneski, the Library's head of technical services, wrote a software program to generate an alumni directory from our database. A national publisher, the Harris Company, had produced a directory in 1986, but it omitted many alums who did not respond to the company's questionnaire, was sold to alums at a high cost that discouraged purchases, and was out of date when it was printed. Wisneski's program meant we included every alum about whom we had information and the information was current within days of mailing the directories. The cost was so low, $6.41 including postage, that we sent it free in 1993 to dues paid members of the alumni association. Alums had the option to receive it on a computer diskette. Updated directories followed in 1996 and 1999.

The directory and a subscription to the *Washburn Law Journal* were tangible benefits of paying dues annually to the Association. Dues supported distribution of *The Circuit Rider*, now called *The Washburn Lawyer*, to members and non-members alike. Some law schools elect not to charge dues to members of their alumni organizations, instead absorbing the costs of alumni outreach in their tuition-supported budgets or using contributions to cover them. Even at Washburn, alumni activities are far from fully self-supporting. Thus, it was important to encourage membership by making the Association a visible sponsor of alumni reunions and receptions, as well as events for future members, such as a welcoming reception for new students and a luncheon honoring graduating seniors each year.

Shortly after I became dean, a committee of the Board of Governors recommended a substantial increase in the $25 annual dues, to generate more resources to support law school programs. I persuaded the Board not to do that. I feared that our effort to increase annual giving significantly would be undermined if alums perceived their alumni dues to be their contribution to the school. The Board did, quite appropriately, raise the cost of a life membership from the bargain price of $250 to $500.

TELEJURIST

Students jumped on the technology bandwagon. Four students in 1993 organized the Communications Law Society and it soon had thirty-five members. Its most ambitious project was an electronic journal dedicated to novel legal issues spawned by emerging communications technologies. *Telejurist* was one of the first law student publications available electronically. It was launched on the Internet on January 21, 1994, with the push of a button during a media event in the Computer Lab. It included twenty short articles, one by Professor Griffin and the rest by sixteen student authors, on topics "ranging from electronic monitoring of employees in the workplace to the liability issues raised by the practice of telemedicine; the latest in cable TV must carry litigation to new multimedia techniques being used in the courtroom."[1043] The Kansas Bar Association donated printing services for a hard copy version and it was sent to other law schools, scholars in the field, and communications groups and organizations. A second issue was produced in both formats the following year, with nine articles. However, when the Society's founders all graduated in 1995, no student stepped forward to become the editor.

CONSTRUCTING CHANGE

As early as 1951, an AALS bylaw forbid discrimination by member law schools against racial minorities and women. The AALS continued its leadership when in 1990 the bylaw was expanded to cover other forms of discrimination as well, such as discrimination based on sexual orientation. Washburn was a flash point in the implementation of this principle of human dignity and equal opportunity.

Following her arrival at Washburn in 1982, Charlene Smith became the first openly lesbian or gay member of the law faculty. Nancy Maxwell later revealed

1043. *Communications Law Society Publication Telejurist Transmitted Worldwide Via Internet*, 33 THE CIRCUIT RIDER 13 (Summer 1994).

publicly that she was a lesbian. Some lesbian and gay students elected to be visible, while others elected not to be for a variety of reasons, sometimes because
of uncertainty about how prospective employers would react. Students in the
mid-1980s formed the Washburn Law School Lesbian and Gay Information
Network, with Professor Smith as advisor, adopting a form of organization
that permitted its membership list to remain confidential.

In 1989, the law faculty unanimously adopted the "Good Practices of Law
Professors in the Discharge of Their Ethical and Professional Responsibilities"
that the AALS had distributed earlier that year. By doing so, the faculty affirmed
that "Discriminatory conduct based upon such factors as…sexual orientation…
is unacceptable in the law school community." Consistent with that affirma-
tion, the Law School's Equal Opportunity Statement in the next catalogue, for
1991–93, was revised to include discrimination based on sexual orientation.

For years, the Law School permitted student groups to install bulletin boards
on the walls surrounding the large classrooms on the lower level of the building. In 1989, the WLS/LGIN decided it should have a bulletin board too and
received permission to use a bulletin board that previously had been used by
a then-defunct student organization. The display caught the attention of the
infamous Fred Phelps who, on the stationery of his campaign for Governor,
challenged the use of tax money to "promote homosexual" activities.[1044] I responded that student groups paid for the bulletin boards, that neither public
nor private funds were used, and that protecting the rights of free speech and
the free flow of information were important principles for the Law School.[1045]

Throughout the next decade and beyond, members of the Phelps family
referred pejoratively to Washburn's "fag law school" on signs they carried and
in the relentless barrage of faxes they distributed. They picketed the school and
special events with regularity. Professor Smith was depicted crudely on signs
and in faxes, as were other faculty members and administrators. It became a
badge of honor to be called a "fag" by the Phelpses and some were embarrassed
they had yet to achieve the designation.

Various developments kept the issue in the headlines, including a ban on
gays and lesbians serving in the military. At its January 6, 1990 meeting, the
AALS House of Representatives amended Bylaw 6-4 to add sexual orienta-

---

1044. *Phelps blasts bulletin board*, TOPEKA CAP.-J. 10-F (Dec. 10, 1989).
1045. *Id.*

tion, as well as age, handicap, and disability, to the list of grounds upon which law schools are not permitted to discriminate. The amendment passed on a voice vote without audible dissent. While resistance developed from some schools, such as religious schools and schools in states where only "unlawful" discrimination was prohibited, the AALS ultimately was able to persuade all schools to come into compliance with this non-discrimination policy.[1046] The amendment to Bylaw 6-4 also provided that "[a] member school shall communicate to each employer to whom it furnishes assistance and facilities for interviewing and other placement functions the school's firm expectation that the employer will observe the principle of equal opportunity" without discrimination on any of the prohibited grounds.

On January 15, 1990, I wrote a memorandum formally directing Assistant Dean and Director of Placement Sandy Zagar to advise employers of the requirements of Bylaw 6-4 and to take all necessary steps to assure we were in compliance with it. In August, the AALS Executive Committee promulgated a regulation, ECR 6-19, that made explicit what most legal educators assumed Bylaw 6-4 meant, that schools were prohibited from making the services of their placement offices available to employers that did discriminate. New regulations are not effective for sixty days, to provide an opportunity for schools to object. However, it seemed appropriate for Washburn to lead rather than follow, given the composition of its faculty and student body and the fact that Carl Monk was AALS Deputy Director at the time.

The strategy of the Department of Defense was to request permission to interview at each school, as it had done previously, and to see what happened. When the assurances of compliance we requested from the military branches were not returned, we advised them they could not use law school facilities for interviews in the fall of 1990. One branch signed and returned the form but responded to a further inquiry by confirming it would not enlist gay or lesbian students. It was then barred from using the law school too. Of course, we were aware that military lawyer positions had been a source of employment for many Washburn graduates through the years. The goal of the bylaw amendment was to push the military to change its recruitment policy, not to deny graduates jobs. When representatives of the military asked if they could post notices in

---

1046. Barbara J. Cox, *AALS as Creative Problem Solver: Implementing Bylaw 6-4(a) to Prohibit Discrimination on the Basis of Sexual Orientation in Legal Education*, 56 J. LEGAL ED. 22 (2006).

the building advising students how to contact them to arrange for interviews elsewhere, we acknowledged they were free to do so to the same extent that anyone else could post notices, since the bylaw merely prohibited schools from furnishing "assistance or facilities for interviews and other placement functions." We even advised them that interviews in the University's placement office in Morgan Hall would not be a violation of Regulation 6-19, and the military branches arranged to conduct them there. When contacted by a newspaper reporter, I said "we would love to have them recruiting here" but was more willing than I should have been to use the cover the AALS bylaw provided for schools to do what was right.[1047] Nevertheless, a few alums wrote in protest, including an unhappy J.A.G. officer. On the other hand, when KU continued to allow military recruiters to interview while it "made up its mind what to do," an editorial at KU urged its law school to "look to Washburn's example."[1048] Washburn University subsequently amended its non-discrimination policy to include sexual orientation, and military recruiters then were not allowed to use even the undergraduate placement office. They had to use off-campus sites until action by Washburn's Board of Regents reopened the main University's placement facilities to them. From the Law School's perspective, after the predictable initial hubbub, the system worked smoothly and with little controversy for several years.

Congress changed that by adopting the so-called Solomon Amendment II in 1996. An earlier version of the Solomon amendment had been interpreted only to preclude law schools that barred military recruiters from receiving grants from the Department of Defense, a hollow sanction. Solomon II made legal education blink because it denied students eligibility for three federal loan programs if the military services were denied the opportunity to interview in the same places as other prospective employers. The AALS Executive Committee relented in August 1997, announcing it would excuse non-compliance with ECR 6-19 and permit a law school to provide placement services to military recruiters, "as long as a school provides 'amelioration' in a form that both expresses publicly the law school's disapproval of the discrimination against gays and lesbians by the military and provides a safe and protective atmosphere for gay

1047. *Law school bars military: WU cites policy on homosexuals*, TOPEKA CAP.-J. 11-A (Sept. 25, 1990).

1048. *Discrimination: The KU Law School should do the right thing and ban military recruiters, as Washburn does*, UNIVERSITY DAILY KANSAN 4 (Dec. 4, 1990).

and lesbian students."[1049] We continued to exclude military recruiters in the fall of 1997 because Solomon II sanctions were triggered only by a letter of inquiry by the Department of Defense and we did not receive one until March 18, 1998. We responded in April that we would permit military recruiters to interview at the Law School. A committee, chaired by Nancy Maxwell, met during the summer and recommended ameliorative steps that should be implemented. The faculty unanimously adopted its report on September 24.

Schools varied in the ameliorative steps they implemented. Some elected to be rude, merely providing military recruiters a room without the amenities, such as water and coffee, they provided to other employers. At Washburn, we chose to be hospitable but clear spoken. On September 30, 1998, Allen Easley and I co-signed a letter we placed in each student's mail folder, explaining that military recruiters would again be interviewing at the Law School despite the inconsistency between the military's hiring policy and the Law School's non-discrimination policy. While "[a]n individual's sexual orientation has no legitimate relevance to practicing law—in the military or elsewhere," we wrote, "we find it unacceptable that the burden of the Law School's compliance with its policy of nondiscrimination be borne by the neediest of our students." We later also distributed a resolution the faculty adopted unanimously to publicly reaffirm its conviction that discrimination by employers based on sexual orientation could not be justified. Copies of the resolution were posted on walls near the interview rooms on the days when military recruiters were in the building, and a notice was included in future student placement handbooks. The ad hoc committee created a lapel button that students and faculty could choose to wear on days military recruiters conducted interviews to express solidarity with gay and lesbian students who could not ask to be J.A.G. officers if they told of their sexual orientation.

The visibility of the return of military recruiters and the implementation of ameliorative steps created far more controversy than did the former system for interviews. Students on both sides of the issue were upset, and some alums were too. In our joint letter, Dean Easley and I emphasized that "[o]ur quarrel is with the military's irrational policy of discrimination. It is not with the individuals who will be on campus as recruiters or with our students who will

---

1049. Memorandum from Executive Director Carl Monk to Deans of AALS Member and Fee-Paid Schools, August 13, 1998, *reprinted in* AALS NEWSLETTER 8 (Nov. 1997).

interview with them. Washburn Law School has never been 'anti-military.'"
Nevertheless, a recent Washburn graduate who was excited to return to her
alma mater to recruit for the J.A.G. had the misfortune to be the first recruiter
to visit the school following adoption of the new procedures. She left dismayed
by the tension-filled reception she experienced. Ultimately, we held a town
hall meeting to discuss the history of the non-discrimination policy. Happily,
tensions subsided as the new procedures became the only institutional memory
of future student bodies.

Through the years, WLS/LGIN was visible in other ways. In April 1996, it
sponsored a regional conference, "Constructing Change: Seeking Our Human
Rights." Program topics included the impact of the criminal justice system on
gays and lesbians, forms of legal relations for gays and lesbians, and a Hawaii
Supreme Court decision on gay marriage. Two nationally known speakers
participated, Professor Ruthann Robson from City University of New York
and Evan Wolfson, senior staff attorney at the Lambda Legal Defense and
Education Fund. That conference was followed by "Constructing Change II"
in January 1997 and "Representing the Invisible" in March 2001.

WINGS OF FREEDOM

Gerald Michaud '51 agreed to serve on President Thompson's campus beau-
tification committee. He wanted the Law School to be part of the beautifica-
tion. A major collector of large bronze sculptures, he learned that renowned
Colorado sculptor Sandy Scott had created the mold for a limited edition of
bronze eagles, called "Wings of Freedom." The first had been perched on the
rim of the Grand Canyon and a second had been purchased for the Resthaven
Gardens of Memory in Wichita.[1050] Michaud commissioned the third eagle,
to be placed on the west lawn of the Law School, one block south of 17th and
MacVicar. The eagle has a wingspan of twenty-two feet and measures ten feet,
two inches from the tip of its beak to the end of its tail. It weighs 3,000 pounds
and a Wyoming foundry required twelve weeks to cast and weld together its 110
pieces. It is mounted on a six-foot foundation built from sixty tons of Kansas
limestone rock. Native wildflowers surround it. Floodlights that illuminate it in
the evening cast a giant shadow of the eagle on the west wall of the Law Clinic.

1050. *Giant eagle descends upon WU*, TOPEKA CAP.-J. 1-A (May 7, 1997).

95. Gerald Michaud '51 (left) with
Dean James Concannon at dedication
of "Wings of Freedom"

As construction was nearly complete, I joked that we planned to lobby the University to change its mascot from the Ichabod to the Ichabird. At the dedication ceremony on May 16, 1997, during commencement weekend, I suggested more seriously that "Wings of Freedom" would be our silent, but powerful response to the hate picketers who so often darkened that street corner, and did so that day.

Michaud and his spouse Shannon later donated two other bronze sculptures from their personal collection, the first, of Benjamin Franklin holding a copy of the Constitution, in the fall of 2000, and the second, of Thomas Jefferson writing the Declaration of Independence, in 2002 to celebrate the graduation of Cameron Michaud '02 and her spouse Greg Drumright '02. They are on permanent display at entrances to the law building.

Other tangible gifts added class in other ways. In December 1999, Dr. John Davis, a retired Topeka optometrist whose hobby of sixty years was collecting autographs, donated his collection of signatures of 87 of the 112 United States Supreme Court Justices. It was the first time he had donated part of his collection. At commencement the following May, Ramona Eidenmiller, whose only direct connection to the Law School was that her niece was married to Linden Appel '77, donated to the Law Library the three-DVD-ROM set of "The Law Practice of Abraham Lincoln: Complete Documentary Edition." The gift was in honor of Ambassador Delano Lewis '63, that year's Honorary Doctor of Laws recipient, who had spoken at commencement ceremonies Mrs. Eidenmiller attended the previous year. The compilation, which required fifteen years to complete, has 14 GB of data, including 100,000 documents and 250,000 pages.

GONE TOO SOON

Our decade of minimal faculty turnover ended swiftly and tragically at the end of the fall semester of 1998. John Kuether was to be on sabbatical the following spring semester to do research. He didn't feel well when he taught his last fall class the week after Thanksgiving or when he attended the annual faculty/staff holiday potluck lunch the next day, but none of us thought anything about it. He had played golf the week before and always appeared healthy despite smoking too much. He often commented that his practice was to "fill up on the vegetables before eating any of the good stuff."[1051] He soon felt so bad that he consulted his doctor and was unable to write exams for his classes. A trip to the Mayo Clinic was required to determine he had small cell cancer in the lungs which had spread with lightening speed. Two weeks later he died.

It was John's twenty-fifth year of law teaching and, almost exclusively, he had taught large, required classes. Knowing John's incredible attention to detail, I felt compelled to calculate that he had taught 6,823 students and to observe at his memorial service that, on average, each graduate since 1974 had taken 1.5 classes from him. We received emails, notes, and calls from many of them. At the time, his tenure as a faculty member was the eighth longest in the school's history.

Linda Elrod described Kuether as a person "who could talk about anything and he seemed to know something about everything. He would sit for hours with a scotch (or beer) in one hand, his pipe dangling in the other, discussing

---

1051. Recollection of Jalen O'Neil '87.

96. John F. Kuether, Professor 1973–1998

terrorism in the Middle East, black holes in space, the advantages of wood burning stoves, or the details of living trusts."[1052] Patrick Polden of the Brunel University faculty, with whom Kuether had taught in England, wrote that his "intellectual curiosity, which was unabating, and his passionate anxiety both to learn and inform were impressive and endearing."[1053] At his memorial service, I commented that he:

> modeled for his students better than any of us so many of the traits and skills that are essential to high quality lawyering: that meticulous attention to detail…, a tenacious approach that never let go of a problem until

---

1052. Linda Henry Elrod, *Remembering Washburn's JFK*, 38 WASHBURN L.J. 3 (1998). Other profiles of Kuether are found in *Special Faculty Features*, 27 THE CIRCUIT RIDER 9, 22 (Fall 1988), and Patti Slider, *They're Famous for Their Dedication to Teaching*, 35 THE CIRCUIT RIDER 13, 18 (Fall 1996).

1053. Letter from Patrick Polden to Linda Elrod (May 29, 1999).

it was solved, an ability to see and the will to look for every imaginable side of an issue even when others only saw one side at the start. How often you would ask him what you thought was a good question and, instead of a direct answer, his response would begin, "Now if you want to make it harder…" I'm not sure he ever met a precedent case he couldn't distinguish. He modeled a special work ethic—I'm not sure the word "no" was in his vocabulary when a student or colleague or alum asked for help or there was something to do to make students' experience at the school better. He formed opinions as strong as anyone I know and could argue long and forcefully for them. Yet as a colleague observed this week, he may have been the least judgmental person any of us has ever met.[1054]

I mentioned that John and his wife Annie, who was elected to the Kansas House of Representatives in 1996, had been

catalysts for the social interaction that helped build collegiality and bond the faculty. We will always remember the TGIO parties—thank God it's over—they hosted on the last day of each semester after we had finished classes and before we had papers to grade—and how they always wanted you to stay—to linger longer at the end—because that's when the really serious conversations—the fun part—could start. And you could always count on them, for the same reason, to linger among the last to leave the other events we had. That's a good part of why it's so hard to accept that John has left us so early—he's never been early before. But I'm sure, having brought us together again, John would have us linger longer now—and would have us share maybe more than one more for the road.[1055]

We were jolted again just two years later by the sudden passing of Ray Spring in March 2001. He had begun a three-year phased retirement in 1999–2000 but stayed fully engaged in the life of the school, reminding us at a faculty meeting less than three weeks before he died, held to discuss the selection of the next dean, how much different the Law School was from the institution he attended and presided over as Dean. He had experienced health problems, including

1054. *Remarks by Dean James M. Concannon at Memorial Services for Professor John F. Kuether, January 16, 1999*, 37 THE CIRCUIT RIDER 12 (Spring 1999).
1055. *Id.* at 13.

surgery in 1996, most stemming from emphysema. At his funeral, I expressed

> regret that our five newest faculty members and recent students never
> had the chance to know the vigorous Ray Spring…who had the choice
> when to be soft-spoken. Ray remained one of our very best and most
> popular teachers even after complications from bypass surgery robbed
> his voice of the ability to reach the back of our large classrooms. In an
> odd way, students may have appreciated each word more, concentrating,
> and therefore learning, even more. His perseverance and grace, never
> complaining even when he had to take an oxygen tank with him, taught
> much about professionalism—and about tenacity when he insisted on
> playing nine holes of golf in the student tournament when he wasn't
> strong enough to play eighteen.

> One of Ray's former students emailed me this morning from Wisconsin.
> She had participated in a number of mental health community activities
> in which he was involved. She wrote, "Professor Spring not only gave
> me a good grasp of the subject matter: more importantly, he showed
> me the way that I want to practice law. He showed me that in a hectic
> and competitive profession, people can still come first."[1056]

NEW BLOOD

We knew the pace of change in the faculty would increase, even before the
untimely deaths of Professors Kuether and Spring. Charlene Smith started
a three-year phased retirement in 2000–01, in connection with her move to
Florida. Each year, she taught full-time one semester, then spent two or three
weeks in Topeka the other semester as coordinator of the Ahrens Chair seminar.

Bruce Levine retired after the first summer session in 2000, concluding
twenty-nine years at Washburn. At the time, his was the fifth longest tenure
in the school's history. He left with four Outstanding Professor of the Year
Awards and the 1999 Honorary Life Membership awarded by the Washburn
Law School Association. The 1988–89 class "coined the phrase "Levine-ology'

1056. James M. Concannon, *In Memoriam*, 40 WASHBURN L.J. 377 (2001); *In Memoriam—Ray Spring*, 39 THE CIRCUIT RIDER 21 (Spring 2001). Other profiles of Spring are in *Special Faculty Features*, *supra* note 1052, at 34, and Slider, *supra* note 1052, at 14.

for his method and philosophy in teaching."[1057] He explained that philosophy in five essays published over more than a decade.[1058] At the end, he wrote:

> Students have come to my office periodically for, what some have expressed as, "a shot of confidence." It takes just a few moments to reconnect with them. It gives real meaning to my life at the law school to touch their lives, primarily in academic and career conversations but when needed, in personal conversations as well. The sense of a joint endeavor, a feeling that we are engaged together in the work of the profession, sets the stage for the conversation. What I seek to develop is a community of interest in the work of the law school and for a life in the law.[1059]

The effect of the various departures was that two new full-time professors plus one visiting professor were hired for the 2000–01 academic year, in addition to the three new professors who started in 1999. Richard Lavoie replaced Levine in the area of taxation, after having been Visiting Professor the prior two years, first at Capital University in Ohio and then at Syracuse University. He also taught the section of Secured Transactions John Kuether previously taught. Megan Ballard took over Kuether's courses in Trusts and Property and also taught Civil Procedure II. She had both her J.D., in 1994, and LL.M., in 1999, from the University of Wisconsin and had practiced with Perkins, Coie, L.L.P. in Seattle and Foley and Lardner in Madison.

Another addition in 2000–01 was Lavoie's classmate in the 1988 graduating class at Cornell Law School, Carol Vizzier. The 1999 self-study recognized that growth in administrative functions had outpaced growth in the administration. The Dean's external responsibilities steadily consumed a greater proportion of his time. The Associate Dean's role spanned both academic affairs and student affairs, and even though Lynette Petty had assumed a one-fourth administrative

---

1057. *Bruce Levine Retires from Teaching*, 39 THE CIRCUIT RIDER 7 (Fall 2000). Other profiles of Levine are in *Special Faculty Features*, *supra* note 1052, at 23, and Slider, *supra* note 1052, at 16.

1058. Bruce Levine, *Legal Education—A Personal Reflection After Twenty Years*, 27 WASHBURN L.J. 330 (1988); Bruce Levine, *Thoughts in Preparation for the Last Lecture*, 29 WASHBURN L.J. 18 (1989); Bruce Levine, *An Issue of Professional Identity*, 32 WASHBURN L.J. 35 (1992); Bruce Levine, *An Education In Law—For What Purpose? "The Trust We Impose On the Law Student,"* 34 WASHBURN L.J. 516 (1995); Bruce Levine, *Conversations*, 39 WASHBURN L.J. 207 (2000).

1059. Levine, *Conversations*, *supra* note 1058.

load to handle ADA issues and academic support, the Associate Dean's position was overburdened. The solution was a new position, Associate Dean for Student Affairs, to which the functions of advising students and chairing the Admissions and Financial Aid Committees would be transferred, freeing Allen Easley to focus on academic affairs and increasing faculty scholarship. The new administrator would oversee new initiatives to rejuvenate student recruitment and visit additional college campuses and recruitment fairs. Vizzier had been a litigator in New York City and most recently had administered the pro bono program at Milbank, Tweed, Hadley & McCloy, L.L.P. Although the new position was not tenure track, there was the possibility to teach one class and Vizzier filled the void Professor Spring left in Law and Mental Disability for one year.

Jalen O'Neil '87 took a leave of absence in the fall semester of 2000 for the birth of her child. She returned to teach in the spring semester but then requested a full-year leave of absence for 2001–02. Because she taught the smaller January class, she also taught a one-half load of substantive law classes. Using her line item and one-year savings from other leaves, we were able to hire a Visiting Professor to teach the research classes and another class, and also to hire a three-fourths time visitor to cover O'Neil's class in criminal law and other needs as well. Our decision to hire Mary K. Ramirez for the latter position likely was the deciding factor that led her spouse, Professor Steve Ramirez, to remain at Washburn and reject an offer from Loyola University School of Law in Chicago. Steve had an expanding reputation as a provocative and prolific scholar, and Loyola was not the first school that sought to woo him away from Washburn. Loyola offered Mary a short-term position in its writing program, but its writing positions were not tenure-track and her preference was to teach substantive law classes. We agreed to consider her seriously for a permanent position if a vacancy occurred in her areas, but also made clear that it would be an open and aggressive national search. There was understandable concern by some faculty members about the impact of having spouses on the same faculty and that, once she was teaching at Washburn, she would have too much advantage in a later national search. However, her credentials in academia as Editor-in-Chief of the *St. Louis University Public Law Forum* and in practice as Assistant United States Attorney matched those of candidates we regularly interviewed in national searches. Her credentials, plus our common desire to keep a rising star like Steve, overcame the faculty's concerns. While O'Neil planned to return to teaching eventually, she received an additional leave for

2002–03 and again for 2003–04 before resigning to focus on family responsibilities. What those leaves meant, of course, was that there was a full-time Visiting Professor position for Mary Ramirez in those years, teaching writing courses in addition to Criminal Law and Criminal Procedure.

GRADE INFLATION

The Law School's voluntary grading guidelines had been revised only modestly, in 1991 and 1992, since they were adopted in 1982. Students frequently complained that average grades at many other schools were higher and that they, as a result, were at a competitive disadvantage in the job market. Of particular concern to those seeking jobs in Kansas was that the average GPA at KU was higher. I routinely responded that employers were logical and would realize that the significant number was a student's rank in class, not the student's grade point average. Indeed, for alums who conducted interviews regularly at Washburn, the consistency of grades over time gave them confidence that they knew what a student's grades meant. I concluded it was appropriate, however, to prepare a memorandum explaining our grading guidelines and what different grade point averages meant in light of them. We distributed it to employers who used our Career Services Offices and students could choose to send it to employers they contacted directly.

Still, students had one irrefutable point. Regardless of logic, some employers set a GPA threshold for applicants, e.g., at least a 3.0. In those instances, our guidelines meant that a smaller percentage of our graduates were eligible to be in the applicant pool than comparable students at some other schools. Leveling the playing field for our graduates seemed uncontroversial but there was devil in the detail. Changing the grade guidelines to raise the median GPA in a graduating class from 2.86 to 3.0, for example, would raise the grades of not just the top half of the class but of the entire class. The concern was that higher GPAs might give a false sense of security to those who, statistically, were at the greatest risk of not passing the bar examination on the first attempt. Within a decade, the scaled score required to pass the Kansas exam increased from 125 to 130, and then to 133. No matter whether our bar results exceeded or fell below the state average for first time takers, the correlation between bar performance and quartile of the graduating class was exceptionally high. The correlation concerned us even though an "Annual Program Achievement

Ratio" published in the Fall of 2000, using data from the ABA's *Official Guide to Law Schools*, placed Washburn in the top quarter of schools, 41st, in "value added," based on comparison of bar results with the numeric profile of the class when it entered.

The correlation between bar results and rank in class led me, on the last day of fall examinations in 2000, to send a letter to the members of the class of 2001 who statistically were at the greatest risk. It discussed the correlation explicitly, suggested students should think of the increases in the scaled score required to pass as the equivalent of increasing the performance requirement from a C level to a C+ level, and urged them to review with faculty members their just-completed exams, or even answers to sample bar questions, with the goal to correct in advance exam taking technique errors that the bar exam's short question format magnify.

There was a dissonance between sending that letter and raising the grading curve. Nevertheless, I appointed a faculty-student committee, chaired by Professor Reynolds, to study the issue. It used research on grading practices nationally and enlisted the assistance of a statistician from Washburn's Mathematics Department. Data the Committee gathered showed there was disparity between our average grade and the average of ten regional schools and that the disparity was larger at graduation (.16 GPA) than in the first year (.08 GPA). The disparity at graduation was highest vis-a-vis KU, .39 GPA. In May 2001, the faculty approved new guidelines. The permissible range of median GPA for each class was narrowed, for example, from the former median of 2.60—2.80 in a large first-year class to a median of 2.70—2.80. The median was increased for upper level classes to 2.90—3.0. To make the guidelines more a norm and less voluntary, the Associate Dean for Academic Affairs now could require consultation by a faculty member before posting grades that deviated from the guidelines. Also, (-) grades were added to the existing system of (+) grades. Rationales included reducing the instances in which students who performed differently received the same grade, giving faculty members who insisted they had an absolute standard for an "A" a way to adhere to that standard but still use grades of "A-" to meet the guidelines, and also giving faculty members reluctant to give a harsh "D+" a more aesthetically palatable option of a "C-" for substandard performance. Implementation of (-) grades had to be delayed, pending installation of new administrative software campus-wide.

The new grading guidelines would have increased the number of graduates awarded academic honors. That was not their intent. Thus, the following fall, the faculty changed the requirements for academic honors. For example, *magna cum laude* now is awarded to the top 5% of the class, rather than to all students with a 3.6 GPA or higher, *cum laude* is awarded to the next 5% and Dean's Honors are awarded to the next 25%. A GPA of 3.9 still is used in define *summa cum laude*.

COMMENCEMENT

I chose not to attend my own law school commencement ceremony. Through 2001, I attended twenty-eight commencement ceremonies in penance for that rash act. Not surprisingly, though, in my early years as Dean I streamlined the ceremony, eliminating first in 1989 the invocation, then in 1992 the alma mater, which few law students had even heard before, and finally in 1993 the color guard. We continued the practice of having members of each graduating class select the graduation speaker. The budget we set for an honorarium eliminated many high-dollar nominees and the distinguished alums students frequently chose usually gave better speeches anyway. When Ed '89 and Becky '89 Linquist attended the commencement ceremony for a cousin in 1999, they volunteered that they could not remember who their speaker had been. It had been Malcolm Forbes and the Linquists were close friends of Ellyn '89 and Rod '89 Atherton, who had arranged for Forbes to speak. If I ever needed proof that extravagant expenditures for commencement speakers were not worth it, that was it.

We traditionally accommodated reasonable student requests to tinker with the ceremony, particularly when there was no fiscal note. At the suggestion of the graduates, a formal hooding was incorporated into the ceremony in 1988. Three faculty members now place the hood over the head of each graduate after the graduate's name is announced and before the graduate proceeds across the stage to receive a faux diploma. Even when there was added cost, we supported student initiatives. While I preferred having the post-commencement reception in the law building, so that students and their families would spend their last minutes on campus at the Law School, the size of the crowd taxed the building's capacity. In 1996, we moved the reception to the new Bradbury Thompson Center and upgraded the reception to include champagne. In 1999, we added a reception for December graduates, recognizing their desire

97. Grand Marshal David Ryan '65 and the St. Andrews Pipes
and Drums lead the procession march to commencement

for closure on their academic careers and the likelihood that many of them
would not return for the May commencement ceremony.

Students in the class of 2000 complained that having their commencement
ceremony in a gymnasium, Lee Arena in the Petro Center, was not sufficiently
dignified. They proposed moving the ceremony downtown, to the Topeka
Performing Arts Center. I doubted that it was a good idea to have the ceremony
away from the campus, but I didn't have to press my view. The proposal came
too late to be implemented, because of the tight schedule of the University's
various commencement ceremonies. We did accede to the class's request to
add pizzazz to the ceremony by having the Kansas City St. Andrews Pipes and
Drums lead the processional. For thirty years, the Law School had used music
for the processional composed by Professor Edward Robinson in 1969 for the

ceremony dedicating the new building. Traditionalists like Professor Ryan opposed the change, but we concluded it was the students' ceremony, not ours, and the bagpipers became a new tradition. Kevin E.J. Regan '81 frequently is one of the pipers. The 2001 class raised the location issue earlier in the year. Given my *laissez faire* attitude about commencement and my confidence that the central administration would never approve moving the ceremony downtown, I told WSBA President Anthony Springfield '01 that I would not push for the change but that I would not oppose it if WSBA persuaded the University administration to make it. My plan was to let the University be "the bad guy," rather than the Law School. To my astonishment, University administrators altered the usual graduation timetable to make it happen. Putting the best face on it I could, I commented during the ceremony that we had returned to the site where law graduates received their degrees in the 1960s and through 1970, when they were included in University-wide exercises at Memorial Auditorium, TPAC's predecessor. The ceremony returned to White Concert Hall on campus in 2002, and, because limited seating capacity there required a complicated ticket system, it was back in "the gymnasium," Lee Arena, by 2003.

TWO INSPECTIONS

Improved facilities because of the 1992 addition and program improvements implemented because of the Law School Financing Plan led to an achievement that Washburn had not experienced for decades: the ABA Accreditation Committee did not identify any issues of compliance with accreditation standards after the March 1993 site inspection that required further action by the school or a report back that the committee frequently requires. This achievement was repeated the next site visit, in October 1999.

The goals established in a self-study for one inspection begin the preparation for the next inspection. The 1993 self-study identified twelve new goals under three broad headings: preparing students to serve the profession better; continued strength of the faculty; and ongoing assessment and improvement of academic programs. Many of the 1993 goals involved what were called "second generation" issues. For example, while we had achieved the 1986 goal to increase the diversity of the faculty and student body, now we wanted to strengthen tolerance and respect for that diversity and to "foster a climate of inclusiveness and full participation."[1060] That included finding new ways to instill in students a greater appreciation of the values of professionalism and civility. Another 1993 goal was to build on the stability and lack of turnover of the faculty by increasing faculty responsibility for scholarship and providing added support for it, including improved faculty technology skills and international study. Some academic program issues overlapped faculty scholarship issues, such as whether the legal research and writing course was structured appropriately, since the rotation of different full-time faculty members into the course each year put significant demands on their time to write.

The faculty described the 1993 self-study as a transitional document, and the site inspection team agreed. While the team found the goals and self-evaluation to be "realistic" and "worthy,...focused, clear and authentic expressions of this faculty's effort," it agreed with the faculty's assessment that the "process of further defining our long-range vision" was at hand. To that end, the faculty scheduled its first weekend-long retreat off-campus in ten years, at the Cottage House in Council Grove in March 1994. Dean Judith Wegner of the University of North Carolina and Professor Charles Calleros from Arizona State University facilitated the retreat, along with Visiting Ahrens Chair Professor Carl Hawkins from Brigham Young University. One session was devoted to the "vision" issue and three other sessions were devoted to the three broad categories of goals from the self-study. The academic program session examined our skills training and writing programs in light of the so-called McCrate Commission Report that identified skills and values lawyers should have before assuming sole responsibility for representing clients. The faculty scholarship discussion led to biweekly faculty gatherings the following fall to discuss works in progress and ideas for scholarly articles. It also led to the distribution weekly of reports of faculty scholarly and service activities, and more broadly law school news, so that faculty members had a clearer sense of what their colleagues were doing. Ideas mentioned during the "vision" discussion were creating Centers of expertise, taking advantage of technology to develop interactive classrooms, and adopting new methods of teaching and problem solving that recognize that students have different learning styles.

While some goals discussed at the 1994 retreat led to significant action, the 1999 self-study recognized that we did not effectively establish priorities dur-

---

1060. *From the Dean's Desk*, 32 THE CIRCUIT RIDER 3, 11 (Summer 1993).

ing the retreat. For some, diversity was the overriding issue. For others, it was scholarship. For still others, it was some other priority. "Post-retreat activity did not generate the sense of direction or satisfaction that we had experienced in years following prior retreats."[1061] That may in part have been an inevitable byproduct of the maturation of the faculty. Young teachers attending the 1980 in-house teaching clinic had not yet fully developed unique teaching styles. The 1983 retreat was not about tinkering with what had worked successfully but instead was about major restructuring of the curriculum, first generation issues of recruiting a diverse student body and faculty, and time allocation issues with which all faculty members then were struggling. By contrast, by 1994, most professors were established authorities in their fields and felt they understood which goals they best could advance. In fact, they did that, and the 1999 self-study reported significant progress toward meeting each of the goals from the 1993 self-study.

Alumni became more actively involved in setting and achieving the school's goals. As President of the Board of Governors, Hon. Christel Marquardt '74 used her contacts as a member of the ABA House of Delegates and her impending election to the ABA Board of Governors to arrange for a consultant from the ABA national office, Delores Gedge, to lead a strategic planning session at the November 1998 board meeting. Members considered "our strengths, weaknesses, current image, desired future image, dreams, threats and goals."[1062] Asked to identify the greatest advances in the school since they graduated, members listed the library, the diversity of the student body, the quality of the faculty, improvements to the physical plant, the quality of the students, and increased use of technology. However, they cited as weaknesses "Washburn's lack of a national reputation, ability to recruit students, lack of sufficient scholarship funds, placement opportunities and ability to communicate its centers of excellence and identity."[1063] Marquardt appointed four separate committees, including both board members and other alums, to develop initiatives to achieve the goals the Board identified: Communications; Education; Funding; and Technology.

1061. Washburn University School of Law Self-Study 1999, at 2.

1062. Christel E. Marquardt, *President's Message*, 37 THE CIRCUIT RIDER 2 (Spring 1999).

1063. Washburn University School of Law Self-Study Report 1999, at 19.

THE RIGHT TIME TO LEAVE

The 2000 fall semester marked the start of my thirteenth year as Dean. Only nine current deans at accredited schools had served longer in their positions. It had not been possible to consider returning to full-time teaching before then. The University's new president, Dr. Jerry Farley, started in 1997 and I resolved to stay as Dean until it was clear he would be a supporter of the Law School, rather than an antagonist as his immediate predecessor and earlier presidents often had been. We could not have hoped for a more positive change. Farley became the chief cheerleader for the University. His enthusiasm in articulating the University's strengths, including those of the Law School, inspired both internal and external constituents. For the first time in several years, we invited the president to attend the Law School's Dean's Circle Dinner, and we actually hoped he would come. He steered the University away from its former emphasis on part-time, non-traditional students and focused on recruiting high school seniors to be full-time traditional students. That required modern campus housing, more vibrant campus life, and innovations such as a new leadership program. This shift in focus had indirect benefits for the Law School since the greater numbers of students majoring in liberal arts and business it attracted to the campus meant there were more students who were likely to consider graduate studies in law and, once they were here, we had advantages in recruiting them.

Though confidence in Dr. Farley developed rapidly, by 1998 we were beginning preparations for our accreditation inspection. It would not have been prudent to have been a lame duck dean either the year before the site visit or during it. Plus, it would have placed a significant burden on my successor to inherit the site visit during his or her first year. Once the inspection was successfully behind us, however, I concluded it was the right time to leave the deanship. The Law School would complete its 100th year in September 2003. The celebration of the centennial would be an opportunity for new initiatives and a significant fundraising campaign that would extend well past the school's 100th birthday. I either had to leave when I did, to give the new dean time to plan for the centennial, or I had to remain as Dean for as many as five more years to see the centennial campaign through. I felt we would benefit from new ideas. I called a meeting on August 30 to tell the faculty of my decision to return to full-time teaching.

9

CENTENNIAL (2001–2003)

Washburn had just four deans in forty-two years from 1959–2001. Only Fordham University School of Law in New York had fewer deans during the same period. Not since John Howe became Dean in 1959 had a new Dean been hired from outside the Washburn faculty. Thus, the desirability of hiring an external candidate versus an internal one was much debated in the hallways outside faculty offices and in the student commons area. Nearly 40% of the faculty had never been through a dean search.

The impact the *U.S. News & World Report* rankings had on the search cannot be overstated. In responses to questionnaires distributed during the 1999 accreditation self-study, students (18%) and recent graduates (27%) identified as the school's greatest weakness, not a shortcoming in the education it provided, but "its low national ranking." The first of seven goals the alumni Board of Governors set in its self-evaluation process was to "improve the national image of the Law School."[1064]

The obvious internal candidate, if there was to be one, was Allen Easley. He was the third-longest serving Associate Dean in the country, beginning his tenth year. When Easley later received the alumni association's Honorary Life Member Award, I commented that there had been "no important decision, policy choice or memorandum on which I did not seek his input or that he did not improve significantly."[1065]

1064. H. Allan Caldwell, *President's Message*, 39 THE CIRCUIT RIDER 2 (Fall 2000).

1065. Remarks at the Washburn Law School Association luncheon at the Kansas

Easley debated whether to apply. He wanted to be dean. However, he knew that our last three deans had not applied at the outset of the search and had been selected only after the search failed, either for lack of acceptable candidates or because preferred candidates declined the position. He also knew that, despite having respect for Easley, some faculty in addition to students and alumni were convinced that hiring from the outside was needed to boost Washburn's reputation scores and reverse its fall to the lower tier in the *U.S. News* rankings. Easley considered not applying and simply being available if the pool of candidates was not as strong as we hoped. On the other hand, none of the three recent "inside" deans were pursuing such a strategy when they refrained from applying initially. I urged him, if he wanted the job, to apply for it. It remains difficult to assess whether his initial strategy would have worked better.

Because Easley was widely known and highly regarded nationally, his presence in the applicant pool no doubt deterred a number of well-qualified candidates from applying, on the assumption that the search was a formality that was predestined to lead to Easley's selection. He had served on ten accreditation inspection teams in just seven years, three times as chair and four times as summarian for the AALS. That led to his appointment in 2000 to a three-year term on the AALS Membership Review Committee, which would include one year as chair. The same year, Easley was named to the Annual Questionnaire Committee of the ABA's Section on Legal Education and Admissions to the Bar, and he ultimately would chair that committee too. He also served on the Section's Law School Administration Committee, which among other tasks plans the biannual conference of Associate Deans. His expertise in technology would lead to his appointment as Chair of the AALS Special Committee on Faculty Recruitment Services and as a member of the planning committee for the AALS workshop on the Impact of Information Technology on Law. Ultimately, in 2003, he would be elected to a three-year term on the AALS Executive Committee.

However, there were external applicants. The search committee conducted initial interviews with the most promising of them during the AALS annual meeting in San Francisco in early January, then narrowed the pool to five finalists for campus interviews. One of them withdrew after the campus interview to accept a position outside legal education, leaving Easley and three external candidates. The only one of them who previously had been a dean was Dennis

---

Bar Association annual meeting, June 2004.

98: Dennis R. Honabach, Dean 2001–2006

R. Honabach, who was Dean for three years, starting in 1996, at Western State University, a freestanding, state-accredited school in Fullerton, California. He oversaw the combination of the school's two campuses and prepared the school to apply for provisional accreditation by the ABA. When that was achieved in 1999, he left the deanship and became Director of the school's new Entrepreneurial Law Center. A 1973 graduate of Yale Law School, Honabach had practiced for two years with Kirkpatrick, Lockhart, Johnson & Hutchinson in Pittsburgh, and then spent thirteen years on the faculty at Vermont Law School. Thereafter, he taught for three years at Rutgers-Camden in New Jersey and for six years at the District of Columbia School of Law. Washburn graduate Glen-Peter Ahlers '87 was the D.C. school's Library Director and Honabach's colleague during the first two of those years, and Ahlers recommended him favorably. Honabach was Associate Dean during his final four years in D.C. He had taught primarily in the areas of Business Organizations, Commercial Law, and Contracts, although he also had taught Torts.

While neither of the other external candidates was found unacceptable by a majority vote of the faculty, one of them had been a legal educator for only six years, and neither of them generated significant enthusiasm among faculty members. Honabach was the most experienced of the external candidates and essentially was the only viable candidate for those who wanted new blood from the outside. There was spirited debate in each constituent group, and many individuals expressed their views in memoranda to President Farley. Leaders of the Student Bar Association requested, and were granted, a meeting with him. A majority of them urged an external appointment.

By the early March deadline for submitting comments, we worried that raw nerves left by spirited debates put in jeopardy the broad support the new dean would need. I sent an email to the faculty, staff, and student body. It praised "our students for the active role they have played in the search process and for the passion with which they have expressed their views." It suggested that no one should be surprised that there were strongly held, and often divergent, views of the strengths and weaknesses of the candidates and about what the outcome should be. The intensity of views merely showed that all stakeholders "care very deeply" about the school's future:

> None of us knows today who our next Dean will be. However, we can commit today that, regardless of which candidate is chosen, we will do everything we can to help the new Dean be successful and move this Law School to a higher level of achievement. Those of us in the Law School family who have cared about this school, whether for one year or more than forty, must demand nothing less of ourselves.

On April 4, Dr. Farley advised the faculty he had selected Honabach.

Given that the *U.S. News* rankings had been such a major theme of the dean search, Honabach used them in his negotiations. We already had implemented a number of new student recruitment strategies, many suggested by our consultant, seeking to improve the credentials of the entering class. Farley agreed, in addition, to seek to raise the yield among high LSAT/ high GPA students who already had been offered admission to the fall 2001 class by providing extra scholarship dollars from University resources.

Another factor in the rankings that could be impacted immediately was the student/faculty ratio. When we revamped the legal writing program in 1999, the four faculty members hired to teach in it received non-tenure-track renewable contracts, in part because we wanted time to make sure we had selected the right model and in part because we did not want to burden them with the obligation a tenure-track position includes to produce scholarship, given the time commitments the writing program would impose on those teaching in it. However, to give us an edge in recruiting quality teachers, we had advertised that writing professors might have an opportunity to convert to a tenure track later on. By the spring of 2001, three of them, Glashausser, Cotorceanu and Byers, had begun scholarly writing projects and expressed interest in the conversion. Because instructors who do not occupy tenure-track line items count only as a fraction of a faculty member in computing the ratio, even though they are full-time, converting them to tenure track immediately improved the ratio, without any fiscal implications. With Honabach's endorsement, my June 19 memo requesting the change was swiftly approved for the 2001–02 academic year.

To facilitate a smooth transition, we wanted Honabach to meet as many alums as possible. He returned to Topeka for commencement weekend in May. Many alums accepted invitations to attend the Alumni Association's annual barbeque lunch for graduating seniors and their families, held under a large tent west of the law building. We also invited members of the Board of Governors and other alumni leaders to a dinner at my home after commencement to honor the commencement speaker, ABA President-elect Robert Hirshon, and to introduce Honabach. While Honabach was unable to attend the Washburn luncheon at the Kansas bar meeting in June in Vail, he prepared an open letter for *The Circuit Rider* that was published just after he took office.[1066] I wrote in my final column that "[a]ll of us are delighted that we were able to attract as our new Dean a person with such breadth of experience in legal education." I expressed optimism that he would "bring a welcome, fresh perspective that will permit him to see many opportunities to improve the education we offer students."[1067]

Wisely, Honabach asked Allen Easley to continue as Associate Dean, reducing the extent of transition required. Easley soon was invited to apply for deanships elsewhere. After declining an offer to be Dean at John Marshall Law School in Chicago in the spring of 2003, he announced he would leave the

1066. *An Open Letter from Dennis Honabach to Washburn University School of Law Alumni*, 39 THE CIRCUIT RIDER 5 (Spring 2001).
1067. *From the Dean's Desk*, 39 THE CIRCUIT RIDER 3 (Spring 2001).

position of Associate Dean at the end of the 2003–04 academic year to return to full-time teaching. Instead, he left to become President and Dean at William Mitchell College of Law in Minnesota. Four years later, he became Dean at the University of La Verne College of Law in California.

Honabach's deanship lasted five years, until he left to become Dean at the Salmon P. Chase Law School at Northern Kentucky University. His was the shortest deanship since the single year Glenn Archer '46 served in 1947–48 before leaving to lead Americans United for Separation of Church and State.

THE CENTERS

At its weekend retreat in Council Grove in the spring of 1994, the faculty included as part of its ten-year vision the development of centers in areas in which faculty members had special expertise.[1068] The 1999 self-study committed the school, as a way to establish regional or national leadership, "to develop proposals of, and establish if feasible, one or more 'centers of expertise.'" Recognizing that the Rural Law Center had not achieved its full potential because it had become, in effect, the Jim Wadley Center, the self-study identified six attributes a center should have: (1) multiple faculty members in the same general area; (2) regular scholarly publications; (3) advanced curricular offerings; (4) a visiting scholar or lecture series; (5) regular CLE offerings; and (6) commitment of law school resources to promote the center's visibility.

Family Law was an obvious candidate for a center, since we had four professors, Elrod, Maxwell, Reynolds, and Petty, teaching in the area, plus an extensive curriculum, substantial scholarly publications, including the *Family Law Quarterly*, and an annual CLE program. The self-study identified other areas in which we had sufficient faculty expertise, including environmental/natural resources/rural law, clinical law, and mental health and disability law. Indeed, in July 1998, Senator Robert Dole '52 authorized the University to seek funding for a Center on Disabilities and the Law that would bear his name and recognize his leading role in the adoption of the Americans With Disabilities Act. This center was particularly attractive since potential donors who had no connection with the Law School might give to it, because they wanted to honor Senator Dole or had a special interest in mental health and disabilities. For that reason,

---

1068. *From the Dean's Desk*, 33 THE CIRCUIT RIDER 3, 10 (Summer 1994).

we agreed that the larger staff of fundraisers for the Washburn Endowment Association would undertake the project. Dole attended a reception to which we invited potential donors, following his lecture in Robinson Courtroom on Disabilities and the Law in April 1999.[1069] Unfortunately, in September 2000, Menninger confirmed reports that it would leave Topeka to merge with the Baylor College of Medicine in Houston. All of Menninger's psychiatric residents, who interacted with law students completing the Certificate in Mental Health Law, transferred to Texas in July 2001 before the merger was even complete. The loss of Menninger, plus the sudden death of Ray Spring in March 2001 undercut major premises of the proposed center's program. The faculty even was forced to discontinue the certificate program in December 2001.

The 1999 self-study identified as additional areas for possible centers technology and the law, which could build on WashLaw's success, and state and local government law, which could exploit the opportunities Washburn's location in the capital city provide. We believed students would have particular interest in the latter specialty, since Washburn's 1997 graduates accepted employment in government and public service positions, other than judicial clerkships, at the highest percentage rate of any law school in America, 35.4%. Yet, a credible center could not rely solely on an adjunct faculty, and no full-time faculty member ever had the primary interest in this area needed to be the anchor of a center.

Shortly after the 1999 accreditation team's visit, Professor Reynolds led a further discussion of ideas for a center.[1070] The self-study acknowledged that all ideas for centers could not be implemented at once, since that would mean we would fail to develop genuine leadership in any one area. Its goal thus was to focus on one area and devote adequate resources so national recognition could be achieved. The underlying assumption was that, for a center to have all six attributes, a substantial endowment would be needed.

Honabach had a different idea, one he had used when he recommended that Western State create "two signature programs" designed to "establish an

---

1069. *Dole Lectures on Disabilities and the Law*, 37 THE CIRCUIT RIDER 4 (Spring 1999). At a reception with potential donors following his presentation, Senator Dole announced his commitment to endow the Robert J. Dole Scholarship Fund for Law Students with Disabilities that he had funded through annual gifts for thirteen years.

1070. Minutes, Washburn U. Sch. of Law faculty meeting (Nov. 3, 1999).

identity in our market."[1071] One could describe it as a "field of dreams" approach: build it and the endowment will come. With that approach, the Children and Family Law Center was a no-brainer and the faculty voted in November 2001 to proceed to develop it. It merely required the packaging for marketing purposes of components that already were in place. Only one other school offered students the opportunity to staff a specialty journal in the field. After fifteen years, Washburn's annual Family Law Institute was an established CLE program. Most importantly, the center's Director, Linda Elrod '72, already was a nationally recognized star in the field. In addition to serving as Editor of the *Quarterly*, she achieved an unusual honor for an academic when she was elected Chair of the ABA Family Law Section for 2000–01. Elrod had published articles in respected journals nationwide and was a sought-after speaker at programs not only throughout the nation but in other countries as well. She was co-author of a widely-used law school textbook and sole author of a leading treatise. Elrod used her many national contacts to create opportunities for students by linking the Center with entities such as the ABA Child Custody Pro Bono Project, the ABA Center for Children and the Law, and the National Association of Counsel for Children.

Soon, the faculty approved two more centers: the Center for Excellence in Advocacy and the Business and Transactional Law Center, which debuted in the fall of 2002. Compared with family law, preexisting programs in these areas did not meet as many of the self-study's criteria. However, in the case of the Advocacy Center, Washburn long had been known for training trial lawyers and already had in place a vibrant Law Clinic, which would come to be described separately from the centers as a "signature program." Additional credibility came from the Bianchino Technology Center in Robinson Courtroom, which allowed advocacy classes to teach state-of-the-art trial techniques and showcased demonstrations by leading litigators. Professor Michael Kaye was appointed Director of this center and he was energized by the opportunity. He regularly invited practitioners and judges to share their insights in lectures and classes, then to meet for in-depth discussions with small groups of students. Starting in the spring of 2004, the Center each semester selected an Advocacy Scholar in Residence to spend several days, up to a full week, at

---

1071. Letter from Dennis R. Honabach to Professor John J. Francis, Chair, Dean Search Committee (Nov. 23, 2000).

Washburn. Professor Doug Colbert of the University of Maryland School of Law was the first Advocacy Scholar.

Professor Steve Ramirez was named Director of the Business and Transactional Law Center. Ramirez had become a prolific author of law journal articles in these areas, often with emphasis on diversity issues. Not surprisingly, he set a scholarly agenda for this Center, beginning with a seminar in October 2002 on the landmark Sarbanes-Oxley Act, followed by a Corporate Counsel Institute in March 2003.

All three centers created student societies. Each also formed advisory councils of alumni and other leaders in their respective fields. For example, the Business and Transactional Law Center's Advisory Council included Washburn graduates who were leading business law practitioners at major law firms in Kansas, Dallas, and Washington, D.C., and presidents and C.E.O.s of companies not only in Kansas but also from throughout the United States, such as Norman Pozez '80, chairman of Uniwest Construction, Inc. in Washington D.C., and Robert Bigelow '67, managing director of Blue Ridge Asset Management, LLC in Denver. The Council included graduates who were or had been senior attorneys with some of America's largest corporations, such as Paul Hoferer '75, vice president and general counsel for Burlington Northern Santa Fe Railway Corporation, Bernie Bianchino '71, vice president for Sprint Corporation and U.S. Sprint and general counsel for Qwest Corporation, Duke Dupre '73, general counsel for various Southwestern Bell Corporation entities including Southwestern Bell Texas and SBC Communications, Terry Anderson '64, senior corporate counsel for Northrup Grumman Corporation in Los Angeles, Gerald Aaron '66, senior vice president and secretary of Lone Star Steakhouse and Saloon, Sue Jean White '80, general counsel for Shell Chemical Corporation, Teri Wilford Wood '78, associate general counsel for IBM Corporation and formerly for American Express Corporation, and Delano Lewis '63, C.E.O. of C&P Telephone Company and later NPR Corporation in Washington, D.C.

Sophisticated upper-level courses were added in each center's area. In family law, for example, new courses were approved in Domestic Violence, Adoption, and Financial Issues in Divorce, and the former course in Juvenile Law was split into two courses, Juvenile Offender Law as well as Children and the Law. The Business and Transactional Law Center added Federal Corporate Law and Law and Finance. Advanced Evidence was approved for the Advocacy Center, which later offered condensed one-hour courses on topics such as

Voir Dire and Depositions. Starting in May 2004, it offered as an alternative to the traditional semester-long Trial Advocacy course a week-long Intensive Trial Advocacy Program (ITAP), immediately after commencement in the spring. It also could be offered between the fall and spring semesters. Like the full semester course, ITAP used the successful model of the National Institute for Trial Advocacy. Alums volunteered to critique student performances in exercises throughout the week and in trials that were staged the final weekend at the Shawnee County Courthouse. Remarkably, some alums devoted their entire week to ITAP, including Bill Ossmann '77, who served as co-director with Professor Kaye. In the fall of 2003, Hon. Sanford Brook, Chief Judge of the Indiana Court of Appeals and a member of NITA's Board of Directors, conducted a one-day training program for the center's trial advocacy teachers, both full-time and adjunct.

The Law School's free hour, which formerly was a single hour on Friday morning, was moved to noon and expanded to all five days of the week. Initially, Mondays and Wednesdays were reserved for student organizations, and Tuesdays and Thursdays were reserved for events sponsored by the administration, the career services office, and the like. The Centers frequently hosted guest speakers during the free hour and sometimes there even were competing programs. Student attendance was high, spurred perhaps by what came to be an indispensable inducement, a free lunch, but interest was high as well. Students were encouraged to attend the increasing number of CLE programs the centers sponsored. The goal of CLE programs evolved from drawing large crowds to examining issues in more depth. For example, in November 2003, at the start of the centennial celebration, the Advocacy Center sponsored a three-day National Death Penalty Defense and Mitigation Conference. A featured topic was the newly-adopted ABA Guidelines for the Appointment and Performance of Defense Counsel in Death Penalty Cases. With partial funding from the ABA, the National Association of Criminal Defense Lawyers, Amnesty International, and five local organizations, the conference attracted speakers and participants from throughout the region, and even from as far away as Arizona and Florida. Two months earlier, the Family Law Center presented "The Role of Judges and Lawyers in High-Conflict Custody Cases," and it later repeated the program in Wichita. The following spring, the Business and Transactional Law Center held a two-day conference on "Diversity in Corporate America."

Washburn already offered a Certificate in Family Law, and it was logical that the other Centers offer certificates as well. For a time, the Business and Transactional Law Center offered two certificates, one in Corporate Law and one in Transactional Law, although there was substantial overlap of courses. Honabach sought generally to increase the number of students who earned certificates, and particularly to do so in the subject areas of the Centers. That would add to the Centers' credibility and visibility, helping to create a "buzz" about them. While the original requirement that students complete 96 credit hours to earn a certificate, rather than the normal 90, assured that earning a certificate was a significant achievement and did not detract from the "liberal arts" education we wanted a law graduate to have, it also meant that few students would undertake the additional expense and work required. The 1999 self-study reported that only eleven students had earned certificates during the three previous years. At Honabach's urging, the faculty approved elimination of the requirement that students complete additional credit hours to earn a certificate, standardized core requirements of all certificates, and required that a certificate advisor approve each student's proposed course of study. The number of certificates awarded predictably grew.

The Law Clinic enhanced its "signature program" status too. Starting in the fall of 2003, one Master's degree student each semester from Washburn's Department of Social Work completed a required clinical field placement by offering social work services to Clinic clients in cases ranging from child in need of care to family law and even to criminal law. The program filled the void that had been left by the departure of Menninger's psychiatric residents, helping interns learn the value of working with professionals in other fields.[1072]

CHANGE

An observer easily could conclude that Honabach viewed his role as being an agent of change. There were many changes, and many attempts to make others, besides the Centers and certificates. Early in his first year, at a meeting with the writing faculty which Jalen O'Neil '87 attended even though she was on leave, Honabach suggested a radical restructuring of the program, switching to the

---

1072. *Washburn Law Clinic*, 42 WASHBURN LAWYER 42, 43 (Fall/Winter 2003–04).

model of hiring recent law school graduates to teach on short-term contracts for low pay, thus freeing budget resources for other uses. He even suggested that grading of student memos could be contracted out to lawyers around the country. O'Neil recalls that when she expressed difficulty imagining how she would explain to her students that she would teach them, but a stranger would grade them, Honabach leaned across the table, shook his finger at her, and said "Don't resist me, Jalen."[1073]

Both ideas for the writing program seemed odd to many because the faculty had so recently and with such unanimity rejected ideas like these in the 1999 self-study, when it opted despite a clear understanding of the budget implications for the model using experienced writing professors. They seemed odder still because three of the professors teaching legal writing had just received tenure-track appointments with Honabach's blessing. The overwhelming majority of the faculty continued to resist Honabach's idea of short-term, capped contracts, but in February 2003, the Curriculum Committee recommended a "middle ground" approach.[1074] It was to hire a tenure-track director for the writing program and thereafter to hire new writing faculty either on long-term, renewable contracts or on a separate legal writing tenure track, with no expectation of scholarly writing and with salaries that were one-fourth or one-fifth less than those of tenure-track faculty. The faculty voted to go forward with hiring a director but deferred decision on the committee's second proposal until the new director was selected. Substantial sentiment remained to continue with regular tenure-track positions and, on the other side, even Honabach supported delay since delay meant that his minority position on the status issue might be bolstered if the new director recommended hiring recent graduates.

There was optimism that we could successfully conclude a search for a Director for 2003–04, despite starting the search in the middle of the spring semester. That optimism was unfounded. Thus, we decided to hire Visiting Professors to fill not only that position but also other writing positions that opened for 2003–04 due to shifts in teaching responsibilities. These developments gave Honabach the opportunity to implement temporarily his concept for the writing program, without faculty approval, by paying three Visiting Assistant

1073. Memorandum from Jalen O'Neil to James Concannon (Oct. 2007).
1074. Memorandum to the Faculty from the Curriculum/Skills Committee, entitled "Writing Program Proposal" (Feb. 3, 2003).

or Visiting Associate Professors hired to teach legal writing in 2003–04 and one in 2004–05 salaries far lower than salaries of the writing professors they replaced, even though they all had comparable experience since law school and one even had prior law teaching experience. The issue of the status of writing faculty was at last put to rest during academic year 2004–05 when the faculty approved the recommendation of new Director Lyn Goering '87, supported by her extensive study of best practices nationally, to retain the model of having experienced, tenure-track writing professors.

A change Honabach found easier to implement was a reduction of the number of moot court competitions students entered. During 2000–01, twelve teams competed in nine competitions. By 2002–03, just seven teams competed in five competitions, and a low of five teams participated in three competitions in 2004–05. The former approach sought to maximize the number of students who benefitted from the experience of competition, but too much authority was delegated to the Moot Court Council, which sometimes selected competitions to enter based more on the appeal of their location than the depth in the subject matter our students likely had acquired from their courses. The new approach sought to increase the school's success in competitions by having teams composed only of our top competitors. Responsibility for directing the program was shifted in 2003–04 from the Council to the Faculty Advisors, who became more hands-on in directing team preparation. Visiting Professor Stephanie Mathews organized a special advanced course on brief writing and oral argument to train moot court competitors. Sometimes, competitions were selected that complemented the centers, as in the spring of 2003, when two Washburn teams competed in the Domenick L. Gabrielli National Family Law Moot Court Competition for the first time since 2000, at the University of Albany in New York. However, the practice was not systematic, as 2003 was the final year in which Washburn competed in the Dean Jerome Prince Evidence Law Competition.

For years, the Law School permitted its students to apply up to thirty credit hours taken at another law school toward a Washburn degree. This policy accommodated a student who had decided to practice in, for example, Oregon, by allowing the student to take the third year of classes at one of Oregon's law schools. The policy was student-friendly, allowing the student to become more familiar with local law there, to assist not only with the bar exam and with practice but also with the student's search for employment through networking with local lawyers. However, student-friendliness had financial implications, since the student paid tuition to the Oregon school, not to Washburn. The number of students taking advantage of the policy originally was small and usually was counterbalanced by the number of students from out-of-state schools who visited at Washburn as 3Ls under a similar policy. By 2000, however, Washburn was experiencing a negative annual flow of visitors, principally because UMKC implemented a program by which students could earn an LL.M. in taxation by taking only fifteen credit hours after they received their J.D., rather than the normal thirty hours, if they took fifteen hours in tax courses at UMKC as a 3L. In effect, the student was able to use those fifteen hours both as hours toward the Washburn J.D. and as the first fifteen hours toward the LL.M., but UMKC received the tuition. UMKC tax professors even came to the Washburn campus to recruit students for the program. That was too much for Honabach. The faculty voted to reduce the number of hours as a visiting student at another school which counted toward the J.D. to six, except under a small number of unusual circumstances.

Change went beyond academic matters. Honabach imposed a dress code for administrative and classified employees, banning blue jeans, which did not heighten morale. The WSBA even took up the issue, after an officer reported that "one of the ladies in the law clinic had talked about how the dean doesn't let them have a casual day. This is important to the staff. She suggested as a fundraiser that faculty and staff could pay to wear blue jeans."[1075]

Marketing and branding were center stage for change. The alumni magazine was upgraded to a full color publication, with a new, professionally produced format and a theme for feature stories in each issue. Even the name was changed, from *The Circuit Rider* to *The Washburn Lawyer*. While alums who received it knew which school produced *The Circuit Rider*, the concern was that others, including deans of other schools who received it and voted in *U.S. News* surveys, might not. So committed was Honabach to change that the phrase "Washburn Law School" disappeared from official use. When we did not use the official name, "Washburn University School of Law," we were to use "Washburn Law." The rationale may have been to distinguish Washburn from law schools that were not affiliated with a university, which often used the name "_____ Law School," or it may simply have been to sound more Ivy League. Expenditures

---

1075. Washburn Student B. Ass'n Minutes, Nov. 12, 2003, at 7.

for postage soared, as Washburn joined the many law schools that targeted mailings to potential *U.S. News* voters. The school's web pages were upgraded and made jazzier, and researchers logging on to WashLaw were greeted by a more prominent display of the school's logo and name. By the conclusion of the centennial celebration in 2006, the school had its second new logo in just seven years.

New brochures were produced for the centers. CLE brochures were redesigned. Old brochures were redone. The Admissions Office produced new viewbooks each year and more resources were allocated to achieving a better yield among admitted applicants. Previously, scholarship awards were limited to the amounts available from alumni contributions or grants. In academic year 2002–03, Washburn for the first time awarded scholarships funded by the school's operating budget. It of course meant that all students were paying higher tuition so that additional scholarships, or larger ones, could be awarded to some students, but the Law School Financing Plan gave us the flexibility to do so. Both our admissions consultant Peter Winograd and members of the 1999 accreditation inspection team had suggested the idea. The line item was relatively small at the outset, $100,000 in the first year, but the amount grew to $300,000 and then to $400,000 in the next two academic years. The awards appeared to have significant impact. The 2003 entering class of 187 was the largest in nearly two decades, thirty-seven over the target of 150, yet, the class had a significantly higher median LSAT than the prior year's entering class. The extra students necessitated the hiring of a visiting professor to teach an additional section of Legal Analysis, Research, and Writing.

In the fall of 2002, Honabach added a public service component that became an annual feature of the new student orientation. The laudable goal was to emphasize that professionalism includes commitment to community service. Local news coverage on a slow news day and an article in the October issue of *The National Jurist* were bonuses.[1076] The workday at the Abbott Community Center drew 150 of the 165 entering students, as well as some 2Ls, 3Ls, and professors, who painted and cleaned, and organized the Center's library and card catalog. While voluntary student participation was exceptional, faculty heard reports that Honabach later considered making participation in the workday mandatory by administrative fiat. It was a prelude to many future

---

1076. *Washburn: Public service head start*, NAT'L JURIST, Oct. 2002, at 17.

disputes about faculty governance issues. Only the faculty could establish prerequisites for graduation.

"Orientation" soon evolved into "First Week," in which new students began one of their substantive classes and the professors in those classes were expected to front-load materials on legal methods, legal systems, case briefing, and study skills so that students would have less of a learning curve when they started their other courses. Like so many "new" ideas in legal education that bear many similarities to ideas that have been tried before, this one closely resembled the one- or two-week-long orientations Washburn conducted in the early 1970s.

The 1999–2000 accreditation report confirmed the faculty's assessment that the administrative staff was lean. Honabach expanded it dramatically. The functions of alumni relations, including production of the alumni magazine and event planning, were spun off from the duties of the Director of Career Services, and soon the new person responsible for alumni relations had an assistant. Later, a position was added to focus on public relations and marketing. A new staff person was added in the Dean's office so that Assistant to the Dean for Administration Betty Fischer could devote more time to being fiscal officer and chief of staff.

Not only did the new positions give Honabach an opportunity to bring in his own people, rapid turnover gave him the same opportunity in other administrative positions. Within eighteen months, there were new Directors of Development, Admissions, and Career Services. Director of Development Joyce Martin had announced even before Honabach's arrival that she would join the Washburn Endowment Association staff. Shortly after Honabach arrived, Director of Admissions Janet Kerr '87 departed to accept a position in state government. Not only was she replaced but an Associate Director was hired too. Then, following the 2002 election, Director of Career Services Judyanne Somers left to become manager of Cedar Crest for Governor Kathleen Sebelius. The theme of change extended even to the titles of offices. The Career Services Office became the Professional Development Office and the Development Office became the Advancement Office.

Associate Dean for Student Affairs Carol Vizzier's role seemed to change each year until she accepted a position as Assistant Dean at the University of Maine at the end of the fall semester, 2004. When the Admissions Office staff was enlarged, her role in student recruitment diminished, and in 2002 we returned to the practice of having a tenured faculty member, Professor Pease, chair the Admissions Committee. In the fall of 2003, Vizzier assumed responsibility from Professor Petty for the supplemental instruction program for 1Ls and the tutoring program for all eligible students. The following spring, Honabach gave her responsibility for proposing a public service program.

FACULTY INITIATIVES

The faculty had its own initiatives, such as improving performance on the bar examination. During the spring of 2002, a committee assisted by a statistician from the Department of Mathematics identified a correlation between bar performance and whether students had taken Constitutional Law II and Secured Transactions. The faculty promptly restored them to the list of required courses. During academic year 2003–04, Professors Lynette Petty '87 and Myrl Duncan, a former member of the Kansas Board of Law Examiners, offered sessions each semester for graduating seniors in which they discussed strategies for analyzing essay questions and for preparing for the bar examination, including starting early. Those sessions evolved into a more elaborate early-start bar preparation program that Petty administered, in which 3Ls viewed lectures on bar exam topics and exam writing techniques, then wrote several practice essay answers that were evaluated and returned to them. The program encouraged students to follow a disciplined approach to prepare for the multiple choice portion of the exam by providing thirty new practice questions for them to complete each week. There is consensus that the program contributed significantly to improved bar passage rates.

The faculty continued its focus on quality teaching. During academic year 2001–02, the Faculty Development Committee continued a "Let's Talk" program that had started the prior spring. Faculty members met for one-hour sessions on the last Monday each month. One month, the topic might be "Tips for Teaching a Large Class," while the next month the focus might be on seminars or how to direct students enrolled in Directed Research. Other sessions took a fresh look at writing and grading both essay and objective exams. In the spring of 2003, the Committee organized a one and one-half day on-campus retreat, "Reflecting on Teaching and Learning." Outside facilitators were Professors Gerald Hess, Director of Gonzaga Law School's Institute for Law School Teaching, and Alison Anderson from UCLA School of Law. Sessions focused on innovative teaching techniques suggested by modern learning theory and included discussion of Hess' article, "Heads and Hearts: The Teaching and Learning Environment in Law School."[1077]

The faculty increasingly became concerned about logistics issues in the summer study abroad program in London. The faculty at King's College, where classes were held, had no interest in team-teaching the courses, so professors from other institutions had to be recruited to co-teach with Washburn professors. In addition, it increasingly became difficult to obtain needed on-site support. Students found the facilities less than optimal. In 2003, Professor Nancy Maxwell explored options at several European schools. She had developed a number of contacts at Utrecht University in the Netherlands, and several of its faculty members had visited Washburn. They were interested in collaborating with us. There was concern whether our students would attend a summer program in a country where they did not speak the native language, but the Netherlands had the advantage that English was commonly used. The faculty approved moving the program to Utrecht effective with the summer 2004 program.

RENOVATION

The enlarged administrative staff meant additional offices were needed. The Professional Development Office moved from the second floor into space formerly occupied by the Student Bar Association and the Moot Court Council on the first floor. The project was completed by the fall of 2003. The office thus returned to the site of the first Placement Office in the 1970s, although it now had many more square feet than did the cubbyhole it had then. The Admissions Office acquired more space when it moved to the former Career Services Office and the space Admissions vacated was assigned to the new Alumni Director.

The three large classrooms on the first floor had remained essentially un-changed since the building opened in 1969. They still had the same blond wood tables and the same blue, orange or green plastic covered chairs. The only difference was the rooms resembled rainbows as chairs of one color originally assigned to one room came to be commingled with chairs of other colors in

---

1077. Gerald Hess, *Heads and Hearts: The Teaching and Learning Environment in Law Schools*, 52 J. LEG. EDUC. 75 (2002).

other rooms. The walls were still cinder block and the concrete floors were covered with linoleum. Large television monitors still hung from the ceilings. The blue tile walls outside the classrooms in the commons area surrounding what had been the pit shouted "'60s!" No one could be certain whether we were losing applicants because they preferred to have classes in more modern looking facilities, but there was a sense of urgency to remove any potential impediment to improving the applicant pool. Honabach persuaded President Farley that the need was immediate and that renovation should not be delayed for fundraising. Moreover, Honabach had begun to talk about constructing a new building, and it would be difficult to solicit alums to donate for a new building on the heels of soliciting them to donate so that the existing building could be renovated. Thus, on Farley's recommendation, the Board of Regents in the spring of 2003 approved $1.25 million from University funds for the project. The timetable called for construction to be completed during the summer of 2004, when the rooms would not be needed for classes.

The renovated classrooms were carpeted and had new furnishings, including power outlets on new tables. The renovation resulted in a reduction in the seating capacity of each room. That was not problematic, however, because class sizes now rarely approached 100, let alone the 135 students the original large classrooms could hold. White boards replaced ancient blackboards. The professor's stage area was redesigned to accommodate both a traditional table with a podium on top and a freestanding "sympodium" containing modern computer and electronic projection equipment. One large classroom, Room 102, finally became fully accessible to students with disabilities, not just on the back rows. The cinder block walls were covered with wood and cloth panels, with goals both to make them more attractive and to improve the acoustics. There were new wall coverings as well in the commons area outside the classrooms. That area was enlarged by removing the wooden rails that surrounded the former pit and by demolishing Room 104, an odd-shaped seminar room that never worked well as a site for classes or other activities.

The project addressed other facilities needs as well. Because additions to the faculty following the 1992 addition exceeded our expectations, we needed faculty office space. Faculty meetings no longer could be accommodated comfortably in Room 119, so the project included a new, large meeting room that could be used for them, and also for seminars and a variety of other functions. Space for the meeting room and offices was taken from the Law Library, in the

99. Room 102 before, during, and after renovation in 2004

area on the north and east ends of the third floor that formerly housed the state units of the National Reporter System. The loss of space in the library was offset, in part, by installing compact shelving in the library storage area on the lowest floor and moving second copies of National Reporter System volumes from the third floor to the storage area.

REVOLVING DOOR

After my thirteen years as Dean, there were only twelve full-time faculty members who had not been there when I became Dean. In the fall following Dean Honabach's departure just five years later, there were fourteen new faces at faculty meetings. Some departures were anticipated, through retirements; others were not.

Charlene Smith's three-year phased retirement ended in 2003.[1078] She wanted to remain at Washburn, even in a year-to-year non-tenure-track position, but Dean Honabach did not arrange it. She joined the faculty at Nova Southeastern University, Shepard Broad Law Center in Florida, although she would return to Washburn as Ahrens Chair Professor in Tort Law for 2007–08. The other Torts professor, Rogelio Lasso, also departed in 2003. Lasso often clashed with Honabach and took particular offense at what Lasso perceived to be attempts to prevent him in the spring of 2002 from teaching a Torts class as an overload at the University of Missouri–Kansas City while a UMKC faculty member was on leave. Thus, Lasso was receptive when an offer came to move to UMKC full-time. Lasso taught there for two years before returning to Chicago, where he had practiced prior to coming to Washburn, to join the faculty of John Marshall Law School.

There was a void in the tax curriculum for 2003–04 too. Jim Bayles retired, to return to Utah,[1079] a year after Richard Lavoie left to be Visiting Assistant Professor in the graduate tax program at Northwestern University, joining his bride who worked in Chicago and resisted moving to Topeka. There was

---

1078. Profiles of Professor Smith appear in *Faculty Profiles*, 27 THE CIRCUIT RIDER 9, 33 (Fall 1988), and *Washburn Law School's Vision Expanded by Faculty Arriving in 1980's*, 36 THE CIRCUIT RIDER 27, 28 (Spring 1997).

1079. Profiles of Professor Bayles appear in *Faculty Profiles*, 27 THE CIRCUIT RIDER 9, 11 (Fall 1988), and *Washburn Law School's Vision Expanded by Faculty Arriving in 1980's*, 36 THE CIRCUIT RIDER 27, 30 (Spring 1997).

yet another change when Loretta Moore elected to begin a phased retirement in academic year 2003–04. She jettisoned supervision of students in the Law Clinic but continued to teach mediation and assumed responsibility for co-ordinating an expanded Externship program.

The tax area was covered by a Visiting Professor for 2003–04, as was Loretta Moore's former role in the Law Clinic. The void in Torts coincided with Alex Glashausser's desire to substitute a full load of substantive law classes for teaching Legal Analysis, Research, and Writing, a desire that had grown since the Dean proposed restructuring the writing program. The faculty understood that the legal writing program could achieve its potential only if its faculty gained the experience that commitment to legal writing for a career would produce. Let-ting new faculty members we hired because we were confident they would excel as writing teachers use the course as a stepping stone to fill later substantive law openings seemed to many to benefit neither the writing program nor the development of substantive law specialties. Moreover, there was ongoing faculty concern that the Dean might use shifts in course loads to implement his prefer-ence to hire legal writing instructors on short-term contracts, a proposal that many believed would downgrade the status of writing teachers. On the other hand, that was a distinct issue and Glashausser had proven to be an exceptional teacher in the substantive class in Remedies he taught as well as in his writing classes. He already had written more than we had expected writing professors would be able to do. Thus, the decision to have him fill Charlene Smith's vacancy had wide support. Another legal writing professor, Peter Cotorceanu, wanted to make the same switch to substantive courses, but no vacancy fit his substantive interests well. When, beyond that, Cotorceanu perceived administrative reluctance to accommodate his request, he began to explore other options. While Lasso's subsequent departure ultimately meant that in 2003–04 Cotorceanu taught three substantive classes, including Torts, and only one semester of legal writing, he nevertheless accepted a position with Baker & McKenzie in Switzerland at the end of that academic year. When Ellen Byers left law teaching in 2005 to manage her family's ranch, following her own disagreement with the Dean, none of the four original teachers from the 1999 expansion of the writing program still were teaching in it. However, both Byers, in 2010, and O'Neil, in 2008, would return to teach in the program after Honabach left Washburn.

The school's tradition of success in retaining new faculty members who came to Washburn from outside Kansas suffered further erosion. Megan Ballard's departure in 2004 meant that only Glashausser and John Francis remained among five faculty members hired in 1999 and 2000. Two-career family issues and geographic preferences prompted Ballard to join the faculty at Gonzaga University, even though students had just voted her Professor of the Year.[1080]

NOT THE HAPPIEST LAW STUDENTS ON EARTH

Student reactions to Honabach varied. Some students thought his approach in class was merely demanding; others thought it belittled them. Steve Ramirez taught the other section of Business Associations, and it filled quickly to capacity at pre-enrollment. The WSBA discussed perceptions of antagonism between Honabach and his class.[1081] Indeed, minutes of a WSBA meeting quoted an officer as observing, "I think we spend a lot of time debating what the dean says or does."[1082]

Whether intended to do so or not, Honabach's actions aroused suspicions outside the classroom too. As one example, during the centennial year, he raised the legitimate issue of the extent to which students were accessing the Internet during classes. The way he did so, however, led to reports at three successive WSBA meetings about students "complaining that the Dean has been look-ing into classrooms and questioning students' activity on the internet...."[1083] There were "rumors that...he said something to the effect that once he kicks a few students out for an honor code violations [sic] for misuse of internet, the problem will go away," and a WSBA officer protested, "This is wrong that he said this in class and it has leaked out."[1084] Another WSBA officer reported that "a lot of people are worried" that they "could get kicked out of school."[1085] Opportunities to diminish student distrust went unused. Under the heading "Barristers ~ Great Event ~ No Dean again!" WSBA minutes reported the Vice

---

1080. Formally, both Ballard and Cotorceanu were on leave for academic year 2004–05. Ballard had a "look-see" visit, in which both sides determine whether the relationship should be made permanent.

1081. Washburn Student B. Ass'n Minutes, Mar. 31, 2004, at 1.

1082. *Id.* at 2.

1083. Washburn Student B. Ass'n Minutes, Feb. 18, 2004, at 1; *see also* Washburn Student B. Ass'n Minutes, Feb. 25, 2004, at 1, and Mar. 3, 2004, at 1 ("It's an ongoing concern that Dean Honabach is looking into classrooms.").

1084. Washburn Student B. Ass'n Minutes, Mar. 3, 2004, at 1 and 2.

1085. *Id.* at 1.

President's comment, "It bothers me that our dean has not showed up to this event again."[1086]

Of course, awareness of student perceptions could not be confined within the walls of the law building and spread to the larger legal community. It should not have been a surprise that students who had concerns about the Dean shared them with their parents or other relatives who were alums and also with lawyers and judges, alums and non-alums alike, for whom they were employed as clerks and later as associates.

RETURNING TO THE HIGHER TIER

Washburn returned to third tier in the 2003 *U.S. News & World Report* rankings, based on statistical data and surveys from the fall of 2002. There was no certainty about the reasons. The median LSAT rose one point but was the same as in three years when Washburn was placed in the fourth tier. Reputation among academics actually fell from a tie for 123rd to a tie for 132nd. Reputation among lawyers and judges likely was a significant factor, since it rose twenty-three positions, from tied for 143rd to tied for 120th, back to the pre-1999 level. The rise in the rankings seemed only to reaffirm the conclusion that the factors *U.S. News* used simply caused Washburn to be within a range of schools near the line between the tiers.

It was hard to attribute the rise in the lawyer/judge category to the new marketing effort, which was not in full force when votes were cast. That category simply is more volatile than the one for academicians, as would be borne out in the four subsequent years when Washburn's reputation among lawyers and judges improved to tied for 109th in 2004, fell to tied for 129th in 2005, improved again to tied for 105th in 2006, the highest ranking ever, but then fell again to tied for 128th in 2007. Of course, there is no correlation between such fluctuations and actual changes in program quality at a school.

The three-point jump in the median LSAT in the fall of 2003, despite a larger entering class, along with excellent placement data, solidified Washburn's position in the third tier, as did an increase of an additional point in the LSAT the following year. Even for these years, the effects of the money spent on marketing, as well as the increased emphasis on national scholarship,

---

1086. Washburn Student B. Ass'n Minutes, Nov. 12, 2003, at 4.

are difficult to gauge. No doubt because of the strategic voting described in the preceding chapter, Washburn's reputation ranking among academicians remained within a narrow range in the eight years from 1999 through 2006, seemingly impervious to the marketing effort. The fluctuation was statistically insignificant, from a high of tied for 123rd (2001 and 2002) to a low of tied for 133rd (2006). The highest ranking ever in the category was the tie for 113th in 1997, before the marketing effort started.

CELEBRATING THE CENTENNIAL

In the year prior to the Law School's 100th anniversary in 2003, the lower level of the building at 118 West Eighth Street which had been the school's first home was reopened as an Irish tavern, The Celtic Fox. On the evening of September 17, one hundred years to the day from the school's first day of classes, I stopped at The Celtic Fox after a meeting downtown. I brought along a copy of a picture of the building with signs on the west exterior wall advertising that Washburn Law School occupied the third floor. I persuaded the manager to let me go up to the third floor to look around. I climbed the same stairs students had climbed in 1903. Work had begun on the second floor to create loft apartments but the third floor seemed little changed from 1911, when the Law School moved elsewhere. Some walls had large displays of shorthand symbols, added when Dougherty's Shorthand School expanded to the third floor, but other walls bore remnants of the wallpaper pattern that can be seen in early photographs of the Law School. There was furniture, including what could have been library tables, which might have been there for a century. It occurred to me that I was standing in the very spot Dean Ernest Conant stood the day he taught the school's first class.

There had been talk about commencing the centennial celebration with a walking tour of the Law School's three downtown locations, ending at The Celtic Fox for a party. That never materialized. The following September 17, however, students and faculty who responded to an email announcing an impromptu 101st birthday celebration at The Celtic Fox took the same tour I had taken a year earlier.

The celebration of the centennial was scheduled to last three years, through the graduation of the class that entered in the fall of 2003, which would coincide with the 100th anniversary of the first commencement in 1906. A formal

Kickoff Reception was held on campus at the Bradbury Thompson Center on September 18, 2003. Ten history boards, one for each decade, were displayed on easels around the room. They contained numerous photographs as well as text. Speakers in addition to Dean Honabach and President Farley were alums Bill Bunten '56 and Carolyn Adams '81, who shared their recollections of beginning their law studies fifty and twenty-five years earlier, respectively, and 1L Sunee Mickle '06. We soon discovered the happy coincidence that a member of the fall 2003 entering class, Kelly McDonald '06, was the great-granddaughter of a member of the first entering class, Hugh McFarland '06.[1087]

Other law school events throughout the academic year, including center programs, a reunion weekend, and a special symposium on November 1, 2003, celebrating the 50th anniversary of *Brown v. Board of Education*, were packaged as part of the centennial celebration. Papers from the symposium were published in the winter issue of the *Washburn Law Journal*.[1088] Alumni receptions were held in many cities. The Law School hired an out-of-state firm to produce a hard-bound alumni directory. It was more attractive than the ones previously produced in-house, but it omitted many alums and was not as accurate.

The formal celebration of the Centennial was a festive black tie gala, held March 27, 2004, at the Westin Crown Center in Kansas City. More than 400 alums and special guests attended, including Governor Kathleen Sebelius. Keynote speaker Senator Robert J. Dole '52 spoke before dinner, because of additional personal commitments. Lighting at the podium made it difficult for Dole to read from his prepared remarks, but he spoke with great fondness, seemingly off-the-cuff, about his days as a law student at Washburn. Professor Elrod was mistress of ceremonies for the program following the dinner. A highlight was the first showing of a fifteen-minute video tracing the law school's history. President Farley made remarks. Alumni Association President Bernie Bianchino '74 recognized donors to the Centennial Campaign, including five alums who had made commitments of $100,000 or more, Senator Dole, David '79 and Hannah Fenley, David Ash Johnson '49, Eugene Ralston '66, and James Sloan '52. Dean Honabach presented concluding remarks, and their length became a standing joke to which even he would refer in later speeches. A thirty-five minute talk that begins well past 9:00 p.m. while a band is waiting in the wings

---

1087. *Washburn Law Legacies*, 42 WASHBURN LAWYER 20, 26 (Fall/Winter 2003–04).

1088. 42 WASHBURN L.J. 428 (2004).

100. Hon. Robert J. Dole '52 speaking
at the Centennial Gala in 2004

would make any group of natives restless, and Honabach magnified that effect in this one by imagining how legal education might change during the next 100 years. His "visioning" went beyond suggesting that "virtual law schools" might replace "brick and mortar law schools."

> Long before the end of this next century, we likely will employ brain scanning technology to determine just how an individual student learns. We will observe how her brain activity changes as we use different teaching methodology and then—equipped with that knowledge—we will design teaching technology to help her acquire doctrinal knowledge and master theory. To be even more outlandish, consider the possibility that those old stand-by legal nutshells and course outlines might one day be replaced by data-encoded brain implants or even by a dose of "smart chemicals?"[1089]

1089. Podium Book, Centennial Gala, Mar. 27, 2004.

Such speculation was provocative when it was read in the law review article into which Honabach adapted his speech.[1090] When heard at the gala, though, it sounded only like someone was reading interminably from a law review article. At the end, however, Honabach declared that Washburn had the physical and people resources needed to be ready for the challenges that change would bring. "Washburn Law has enjoyed a glorious past. It has established a record of success of which we are justifiably proud. At the same time, it has earned a national reputation for innovation. Be assured that we at Washburn Law will build on our successes."[1091]

1090. Dennis R. Honabach, *And Now What?: An Essay Contemplating a Course for the Second Century of the Washburn University School of Law*, 42 WASHBURN L.J. 947, 950 (2004).

1091. *Id.* at 954.

10

WOMEN AT WASHBURN LAW SCHOOL[1092]

It would be nine years after Washburn Law School opened its doors in 1903 before women in Kansas received the right to vote and seventeen years before the Nineteenth Amendment accorded women nationwide that right. It had been only twenty-two years since the first woman was admitted to practice law in Kansas, and it would be another nineteen years before the number of women ever admitted to the Kansas bar would reach fifty.[1093] It would be twenty-four years before women were admitted to Columbia Law School and forty-seven years before they were admitted to Harvard Law School.

By contrast, women were welcomed at Washburn Law School from the first day, although the number who initially chose to attend was small. Three women, Maude Bates, Anna Marie Nellis, and Ruth Welles, completed the first year with the entering class of 1903, classified among the twenty-three special students. Two other women, Zeva Bradshaw Edworthy and Louise Mary Morrison, also were listed among the special students and took at least one class. None of the women returned the following year. A classmate observed that some

---

1092. Material from an early draft of this chapter was used in Charlene Smith, *History of Women at Washburn University School of Law*, 41 WASHBURN LAWYER 4 (Fall/Winter 2002-03), and Linda Diane Henry Elrod, *Washburn Law School Celebrates a Century of Welcoming Women*, 42 WASHBURN L.J. 853 (2004).

1093. Martha J. Hodgesmith, *"Some of them [are] actually representing clients in court…" Women Lawyers in Kansas*, in REQUISITE LEARNING AND GOOD MORAL CHARACTER: A HISTORY OF THE KANSAS BENCH AND BAR 96, 98 (Robert W. Richmond, ed. 1982).

quit, of course, when they first realized the status of women at common law. They did not tarry long enough to ascertain that all the rights a woman has, even now, depend upon the statutes, and are liable to be repealed at any session of the legislature, or forever wrested from her by a constitutional convention in which she has no voice.[1094]

Only a few women took law classes during the next five years and their absence was often lamented in the student newspaper. The poorly kept quarters on West Eighth Street were thought to make the school less than appealing to women.[1095]

Jessie Junette Nye enrolled in 1909 and became the first woman graduate in 1912. She graduated from Garnett High School and taught in the public school there from 1907 to 1909. She took some college work while pursuing her law degree. Nye quickly became an active participant in the life of the Law School. Her classmates elected her Secretary of the first-year class. She became the Law School's reporter for the College's student newspaper, writing a weekly column. During the spring term of 1911, she worked as the Law Librarian, a position held by students at the time. During her last semester, she was elected County Attorney for the Practice Court and teamed with Olive White of the College to represent Washburn in an intermural co-ed debate.[1096]

Immediately after graduation, Nye became a candidate for Harvey County Attorney in Newton, but she lost by a vote of 2,308 to 1,487.[1097] She returned to Topeka and was docket clerk for the Public Utilities Commission. She soon wrote to encourage other women to study law:

> The bar of entrenched prejudice against the study of law by women is gradually breaking; it is responding to the spirit of the times, which is unquestionably a spirit of greater freedom for women.
>
> As a profession, it is as yet a new venture for women, but the few who have braved the stern and almost forbidding glances of the lawyers, the about to be lawyers, and the public at large, have found it an unusually interesting department of university training.

1094. THE KAW 46 (1906).

1095. *Law Notes*, WASHBURN REV., Dec. 9, 1908, at 2.

1096. *Debating Begins*, WASHBURN REV., Feb. 28, 1912, at 1.

1097. Patti Slider, *Jessie Nye Warren*, in JOURNEYS ON THE ROAD LESS TRAVELLED: KANSAS WOMEN ATTORNEYS 60, 62 (1998).

101. Jesse Junette Nye, 1912

The old popular query of the years gone by of, "why study or enter into the mannish profession of law?" is becoming less insistent....There is a field open and increasing demand for women lawyers. Women now acquire, hold and transfer property and the study of laws of state and nation will be a great aid to her in assisting her to meet and cope equally with others in the business world....

Since the election last November, woman is not only a citizen but a voter and for that reason, I say that we, as women of Kansas, have a new duty to train our minds and create an interest among ourselves in the governmental questions of our great state and nations....

It will soon cease to be a marvel to see young women take up the study of law. Already, Washburn people are accustomed to it....We, who are pioneers so to speak, in this branch of academic study, have found the law anything but dry and uninteresting, but since it is a study of justice, we have found it rather, rich in historical interpretation and in human interest.[1098]

Nye returned to Newton in 1931 to open a law office that she maintained for twenty-five years.

Mignon Florence Eckhart '13 graduated one year after Jessie Nye. A native of Birmingham, Alabama, she was a graduate of the University of Alabama. She was attracted to law by her interest in juvenile law and in reforming the law to serve the needs of young people. She was sophisticated:

> She was educated in Paris at one of the world's leading finishing schools for girls. She made her debut in Paris, only people of title being present. Has been entertained by a baroness at her castle in Holland; and is one of the few American girls to have been presented at the Japanese court.[1099]

Before her second year, she built a Japanese bungalow at Ninth and Buchanan Streets, "the only structure of its kind in the city."[1100] It was said that she was "different from most women who attend law school, in that she throws her entire energy into the work. She has shown more than usual ability in the trial work."[1101] Following her graduation, Eckhart for a brief time had a small practice in Topeka and enrolled in additional classes in pleading and practice and later in conveyancing. In the fall of 1913, she gave the school a large roll top desk. Before long, she left the state.

Anna Parrett enrolled in night classes in 1911. She was from Fayetteville, Arkansas, and had been a court reporter and stenographer there. No woman had ever been admitted to practice law in Arkansas and Parrett had filed suit when she was denied permission to take the bar exam there. She already had completed one year of law classes at KU and took classes at Washburn while waiting for her right to take the bar exam to be resolved.[1102]

Edna Sperry graduated in 1914. She had been Register of Deeds for two terms in Graham County and had conducted a farm loan, abstracting, and

---

1098. Jessie J. Nye, *Tells of Law as Work for Co-eds*, WASHBURN REV., Apr. 12, 1913, at 2.

1099. *Law Girl Honored*, WASHBURN REV., June 5, 1912.

1100. TOPEKA DAILY CAP., Oct. 9, 1911.

1101. *Law Notes*, WASHBURN REV., Mar. 26, 1913.

1102. TOPEKA DAILY CAP., Oct. 9, 1911.

insurance business in Horton for a year. She had studied in the office of a local attorney long enough to be eligible to take the bar examination. She enrolled in law school in the spring of 1912 as a special student, intending only to review a few subjects before taking the bar exam that summer. She soon concluded she needed a better preparation for practice and decided to stay to complete the degree program.[1103] She was one of two graduates selected to speak on behalf of her class at the Law School's annual spring banquet. After graduation, she moved to Portland, Oregon, reporting that she had entered a partnership there,[1104] but she returned in 1917 to practice law in Kansas City, Missouri.[1105] She was listed in the *Martindale Hubbell* legal directory through 1939.

Edna Hopkins and Mabel Jones were two of just six members of the graduating class of 1918. Before their class was depleted after their first year due to World War I, a classmate penned this verse:

> Mabel and Edna, we are proud of you—
> Just stay with us the whole course thru.
> With your bright faces, from day to day
> You cheer us and help us along the way.
> At law we have considerable wit,
> But you are wiser we must admit.
> You cook, and iron, and knit and sew,
> All those we cannot do—much to our woe.
> In examinations you are to a tee
> While we make sixty and seventy-three,
> You smile and work, we frown and play.
> But to be like you, we ever say
> Mabel and Edna, receive our thanks
> We're glad to have you among our ranks.[1106]

During her senior year, Jones was selected as secretary for Kansas Supreme Court Justice Henry Mason, who taught Constitutional Law at the school. Following graduation, Jones married Don Shaffer '20, who started law school as a member of her class but graduated two years later due to the war. They

1103. *Yes, There's Work for Women in Law*, WASHBURN REV., May 1, 1912, at 10.
1104. *Law School Notes*, WASHBURN REV., Feb. 3, 1915, at 4.
1105. *Law School*, WASHBURN REV., Nov. 21, 1917, at 4.
1106. *Law Notes*, WASHBURN REV., Mar. 8, 1916.

practiced together in Hutchinson in the firm of Tincher, Shaffer & Shaffer. Their son, John Shaffer '54, graduated from Washburn and returned to practice in Hutchinson.

Hopkins was the daughter of a lawyer and had taught English at Topeka High School before starting law school. She had attended Bryn Mawr and Simmons Colleges after receiving her A.B. degree from the University of Kansas. Shortly before her graduation, *cum laude*, she loaned the school her late father's entire law library to help it reach the number of volumes required by the Association of American Law Schools. Hopkins was admitted to practice in Kansas in May 1918 at the age of twenty-nine. However, she moved to New York City in October 1918, joining a nine-attorney firm, Curtis, Mallet-Prevost, Colt & Mosle, that traces its history to 1830 and today is a major international firm. She initially was employed as a law clerk before applying to take the New York bar examination,[1107] and then continued as the firm's first woman associate. She was Washburn's first "Wall Street lawyer," practicing with the firm at 63 Wall Street until 1962. A 1948 history of the firm acknowledged that as its first woman lawyer, Hopkins

> was under a psychological handicap which it was not easy to overcome. How is it that she has won out so completely? The answer is not difficult to find. Ability, thoroughness in her work, the faculty of cooperating with her associates, the confidence which she inspires in her judgment, and her success in winning the confidence of clients; these are the things that have overcome the handicap of sex and that have won for her the respect and admiration of her fellow workers. So highly have we regarded her that we have urgently invited her to become one of our partners. We deeply regret that she has declined that invitation as we believe that joining with us would add an important element to the partnership.[1108]

According to a lawyer who joined the firm in 1949, when the offer of partnership was made to Hopkins in 1938, she declined it because she did not believe it was fitting for a woman to be a partner.[1109] However, the lawyer reported

---

1107. *Law School*, WASHBURN REV., Jan. 8, 1919, at 2; *Law School*, WASHBURN REV., Mar. 19, 1919, at 3.

1108. These comments appear on page 43 of a history of the firm written by Severo Mallet-Prevost in October 1948 (copy on file in Washburn Law Library).

1109. Conversation on Sept. 17, 2007, with John Campbell, who practiced with

that she thereafter acted like a senior partner, bawling out young lawyers for not using proper English. He recalled Hopkins with fondness, noting that she had "no shyness about her," "was a tiger," and could be "caustic" and "crusty."

Women were not invited to join the Kansas Bar Association until 1935. In 1919, however, Jones and Hopkins joined Jessie Nye as charter members of the Kansas Women Lawyers' Association.[1110] Jones was elected Vice President.[1111] *The Kaw* later reported that women law students formed a Portia Club.[1112] There was speculation during the fall semester of 1920 that the national women's legal fraternity Kappa Beta Phi would create a Washburn chapter.[1113] That did not materialize. However, the rival women's legal fraternity Phi Delta Delta installed Kappa Chapter at Washburn on May 21, 1922.[1114]

Not surprisingly, given the number of practitioners and judges who taught part-time, not all the instructors treated women students as inclusively or as hospitably as they should have. At one extreme was Justice Alfred Benson. When he felt that a topic to be discussed in class would embarrass Mabel Jones, he told her, "Miss Jones, you may be excused from class attendance tomorrow."[1115] At the other extreme was attorney Ed Rooney, who reportedly remarked to the only woman in his class on Criminal Law, "It is very good for the man you marry that you are developing your mind logically. When you are cooking and your biscuits fall, instead of becoming emotional and hysterical, you will pause and think (logically) 'Now what did I do that was wrong...oh yes, I left the baking powder out.'"[1116]

More women enrolled once the Law School moved to Washburn's main campus. The catalogue issued by new Dean Harry K. Allen, in advance of the 1923–24 academic year, for the first time had a special section encouraging enrollment by women. "Recent news that a woman had been elected to the Supreme Court of Ohio," it said, "was not altogether surprising to the members of Washburn Law School, which has several women graduates among members

Hopkins at Curtis, Mallet-Prevost after 1949. He was of-counsel when we talked.
1110. *Women Lawyers Organize*, WASHBURN REV., Apr. 9, 1919.
1111. *Law School*, WASHBURN REV., Feb. 5, 1919, at 3.
1112. THE KAW 60 (1935).
1113. *Girls Legal Frat?*, WASHBURN REV., Dec. 15, 1920, at 1.
1114. Elrod, *supra* note 1092, at 875.
1115. McLane, *supra* note 3, at 9.
1116. *Id.* at 11.

of the bar." It noted that nine women currently were taking classes, that college dormitories were open to them, and that they "enjoyed the protection and care afforded by the general supervision of the dean of women over student life, …a woman of experience in this work, endowed with common sense, sympathy and tact." Still, one woman graduate from this period explained, "we tried hard to be as little trouble as possible and always stay on the front row nearest the door."[1117]

Twelve women graduated during the 1920s, including Ruth Kaster '21, who during the wartime spring semester of 1919 was the first woman to be elected President of the Student Bar Association. Women frequently were selected as officers of their classes. Lucille Horn '26 was Vice President during her last semester, and Horn, Nellie Crotts '27, and Margaret McGurnaghan '27 were elected Secretary in various semesters. Crotts and Minnie Banks '24 both served as clerk of the Practice Court. Crotts practiced law with Colmery & Smith before opening her own office in 1953. She was the first woman to be Honorary President of the Topeka Bar Association, in 1967–68.[1118]

Many of the 1920s graduates were exceptional students. Kaster was one of three women among a total of only seven students that decade who both graduated *cum laude* and completed the additional requirements to earn the J.D. degree. One of the others was Marie Russell '25, who also received the Walker Prize of $5 for the highest grades in her class and the Vernon Law Book Company Prize of five volumes of *Randall's Instructions to Juries*. Upon graduation, she was appointed Assistant to the Dean of the Law School and was Law Librarian for one year. That year, she won first prize in the national essay contest sponsored by Phi Delta Delta women's legal fraternity. She later was chosen as State Law Librarian. In 1928, Russell became the first woman Lecturer at the Law School, teaching Common Law Pleading and later Conflict of Laws as well. She continued to teach annually for 31 years. Mildred Wilson '28 was the third woman who earned the J.D., but for her, law study was a hobby while she taught at Washburn as an Assistant Professor of Bacteriology.[1119]

In addition to the three women who earned J.D.s, both Isabel Obee '24 and Margaret McGurnaghan '27 received the LL.B. *cum laude*. Obee, who graduated with her sister Phyllis Obee '24 and received the Walker Prize for highest

---

1117. *Id.* at 9.

1118. Her married name was Nellie Huffman. Elrod, *supra* note 1092, at 877.

1119. *Law Is Hobby for Wilson: Is Ichabod Prof*, WASHBURN REV., Feb. 7, 1929.

grades, practiced in a Great Bend firm for many years. McGurnaghan was fifty-one years old when she graduated, having previously spent twenty-five years with a Topeka law firm, working as a stenographer and being trained in title standards. She joined that firm after graduation and later became a partner. The firm became Wheeler, Brewster, Hunt & Goodell. She practiced for thirty-three years before retiring at age eighty-four in 1960. She was Chair of the Title Standards Committee of the Kansas Bar Association and published a number of articles in the *Judicial Council Bulletin* on title, real estate and probate issues. She was national treasurer of Phi Delta Delta women's legal fraternity for sixteen years and served as President of the Kansas Women Lawyers' Association. She began teaching at Washburn as Lecturer on Abstracts of Title and Conveyancing in 1936, continuing to teach most years through 1958–59. "Never having married, McGurnaghan considered her students to be like her children, and spent considerable time with them."[1120]

Several early women graduates besides Mildred Wilson did not practice law. Ruth Kaster '21 and Ivah Raines '23 married lawyers, Robert Webb '19 and Ralph Glenn '26, who did not want them to practice.[1121] Ruth Kaster Webb was an active community volunteer, especially at the public library. Ivah Raines Glenn did help in her husband's law office. Phyllis Obee '24 was Reno County Superintendent of Schools.

Thirteen more women graduated in the 1930s and the number grew to 17 during the 1940s. Thelma Helsper '30 was one of the first two women in Kansas to be elected County Attorney, in 1932 in Norton, where she maintained a private practice for many years. Georgia Wells '40 was elected Rice County Attorney in 1942 and 1944 and served as City Attorney in Lyons from 1962 until 1964. Lyons was also the home town of Bessie Mae Wills '40, who considered returning there to practice law with Wells. "Dean Hambleton cautioned her against it, saying he didn't know if Kansas was ready yet for women lawyers."[1122] Kansas Supreme Court Justice Walter Thiele taught her class in Wills. She recalled, "He would greet me in every class session with 'Good morning Miss Wills, what do you know about wills this morning?' It was funny at first."

1120. Laura Howard, *Margaret McGurnaghan*, in JOURNEYS ON THE ROAD LESS TRAVELLED: KANSAS WOMEN ATTORNEYS 66, 68 (1998).

1121. Elrod, *supra* note 1092, at 876 n. 162.

1122. Patti Slider, *Progressive Trio Set Pace for 1940 Class*, 36 THE CIRCUIT RIDER 14 (Spring 1997).

Wills married Elton McIntosh and while he served in the Army, she worked for the F.B.I. in Washington, D.C. "J. Edgar Hoover was not fond of women, but he had a shortage of men due to the times," she said. She was assigned to the Legislative Desk and spent substantial time at the Capitol, monitoring legislation that might affect the F.B.I. She also wrote briefs for Hoover.[1123]

Virginia Miller '41 also had a unique experience. In 1942, she was appointed Sedgwick County Law Librarian and executive secretary of the Wichita Bar Association. In 1943, she became a Deputy Sedgwick County Attorney but resigned when a former deputy returned from service in the armed forces. She then was a lawyer for the National Labor Relations Board in Washington. After the war, she became a prosecutor of Nazi war criminals for the International Military Tribunal in Nuremberg, Germany. She then settled in Nevada, where in 1958 she was the first woman to seek election as Clark County District Judge, losing by less than 200 votes.[1124] M. Maurine Hallock '43 succeeded in becoming Probate Judge for the City and County of Denver and was the first woman president of the Colorado County Judges Association.

When Washburn formed a Student Editorial Board for the *Journal of the Bar Association of Kansas*, Lorraine McMullen '36 was a member of the initial Board. Later, Martha L. Stewart '40, Dorothea Grubbs Warren '42, and Constance Lord '46 all were named to the Board, and both Warren and Lord had pieces accepted for publication. Gladys Hoskinson '41 came to law school with the encouragement of Margaret McGurnaghan, for whom she worked as a stenographer. Hoskinson joined the legal department of Southwestern Bell Corporation, initially as a secretary, but was promoted during the war to became the only woman lawyer in the Bell system.

A number of graduates in the 1930s and 1940s spent parts of their careers as the Law School's librarian and as legal educators. Immediately following her graduation, Dorothy Davidson Tyner '41 became Law Librarian and during the spring semester also filled a vacancy as Secretary and taught Domestic Relations. She was from McCracken, Kansas, and also received her A.B. degree from Washburn. In 1942, she was appointed to a full-time faculty position, holding the title Instructor of Law, the first woman to hold a full-time position at a Kansas law school and one of few to do so nationally.[1125] The Law School

---

1123. *Id.*

1124. *Pioneer attorney dies at 83*, LAS VEGAS REV.-J., Jan. 21, 2001.

1125. Herma Hill Kay identified only three women who held tenured or tenure

announced her full-time faculty appointment after Ralph Rice received a leave of absence due to World War II.[1126] She taught Property II, Federal Taxation, Domestic Relations and Legal Bibliography. She revised the tax course because she didn't like the way it had been taught.[1127] In addition to teaching, she moonlighted, doing corporate tax returns for an accounting firm.[1128] She left teaching in October 1943 to join the legal staff of the War Production Board in Kansas City, leaving Dean Hambleton as the sole full-time faculty member as enrollment declined because of the war.[1129] In August 1944, she moved to Juneau, Alaska, working as an assistant enforcement attorney for the Office of Price Administration for two years. Tyner visited Anchorage in the summer of 1945, "with thoughts of" moving there to practice law. She met with the Anchorage bar.

> They wined her and dined her, and offered to send cases her way. Afterwards, the eight men—about three quarters of the dozen or so lawyers in Anchorage—stood outside and memorialized their meeting with the attractive woman attorney by having a picture taken. Their easy camaraderie convinced Tyner to move and she became the first woman to open a private practice in the city.[1130]

---

track appointments at ABA or AALS approved law schools before Tyner taught full-time at Washburn. Herma Hill Kay, *The Future of Women Law Professors*, 77 IOWA L. REV. 5, 8 (1991). Because Tyner was hired to replace a professor who was granted a leave, she may not have been on tenure track that year.

1126. *Notes and Personals*, 10 AM. L. SCH. REV. 60 (1942). The WASHBURN COLL. SCH. OF LAW BULLETIN issued in late spring 1943 listed her, immediately below Assistant Professor Kenneth Wagner, as "Instructor of Law," a title Wagner held when he was appointed to the faculty and for many years thereafter. Both Tyner and, before her, Joyce Rodgers Tyler, who also was a lawyer, held the title "Secretary and Instructor of Law" when they held the Secretary position vacated by Emily Sanford Platt in 1941, but their teaching duties in that position were limited to part-time. Helen Loomis '43 held the position as Secretary and Instructor of Law the year Tyner served as full-time Instructor of Law.

1127. Transcript of oral history interview with Tyner, completed in 1968 by the Alaska Bar Association, at 2 (on file in Washburn Law Library).

1128. *Id.*

1129. See the discussion of the circumstances of Tyner's departure in Chapter 3, notes 339 and 340.

1130. Pamela Chavez, *The history of the Anchorage Bar Association: From the Lido*

She opened her office in October 1946 and was one of only eighteen lawyers, including the federal judge, listed in *Martindale Hubbell* for Anchorage in 1947. She interrupted private practice from 1951 to 1953 to return to federal government service and practiced law for a time in Seward. In 1961, she became Senior Law Clerk for United States District Judge Walter Hodge, and then in 1966 accepted a similar position with United States District Judge Raymond E. Plummer. In 1968, when magistrate courts were replaced by district courts, Governor Walter Hickel appointed her as District Judge for the Third Judicial District in Anchorage, the second woman district judge in Alaska. Tyner later applied unsuccessfully for appointment as a judge of the Superior Court. She served as District Judge until 1977, when she retired. She once ran for State Treasurer in Alaska as a Democrat, pledging to work to abolish the office as an elective office.[1131]

Dorothea Grubbs Warren '42 worked in the law library during her senior year. She was the first woman to be granted tenure at Washburn Law School and also the first to hold the title of Professor of Law. She was Director of the Law Library from 1967 to 1979. She continued to be Reference Librarian until she retired in 1984. Upon graduation from law school, she went to Louisville, Kentucky, as a lawyer in the Government Regulations Department of Seagram's Distillery. In 1956, she became Assistant State Law Librarian under Marie Russell '25. Dean John Howe recruited her from that position to manage the library after the tornado.

After a long career as a litigator, Mary M. (Billie) Parr '47 became the Law School's second woman tenured professor. She was the second faculty member hired to teach in the Law Clinic, in 1971. She was the first woman to serve as Associate Dean. She had been popular with her classmates, who elected her as the Law School's representative to the student council, and as a professor was both popular with and respected by her students.

Martha L. Stewart '40 also became a law professor, teaching at Loyola University School of Law in Los Angeles[1132] full-time for nineteen years beginning

---

Bar to good deeds, ALASKA BAR RAG (Jan./Feb. 2002). The story was based on the oral history taken from Tyner in 1968.

1131. Conversation with Tyner's son Franz Stangl, who attended Washburn Law School in 1976. He described his mother as "strong willed" and observed that "no one messed with her." When she started law school studies, she was married to Topeka lawyer Lyle Tyner.

1132. When hired at Loyola, she was Martha S. Yerkes, having married Marburg

102. Professor Billie Parr '47, meets with Law Clinic intern Pantaleon Florez '81

in 1965 and part-time for many years thereafter as Professor Emeritus. When she was hired at Loyola, no more than thirty women held tenured or tenure-track classroom teaching positions in ABA and AALS approved schools.[1133] She had been a part-time Instructor for eight years at Southwestern Law School, beginning in 1947, while she was in private practice with her husband in Los Angeles. She was Judge Pro Tem for the Los Angeles Superior Court in 1963 and was a member of the American Law Institute.

Clessie Gilmore '36 earned her law degree by attending classes part-time after she became the Law Librarian in 1931. Helen Loomis '42 succeeded Dorothy Tyner as Law Librarian and Secretary, and then became a Law Clerk at the Kansas Supreme Court before moving to Winfield to practice law. Elizabeth S. (Beth) Bowers '48 was Law Librarian for two years after her graduation, then was Law Librarian at Creighton Law School the following two years. Thereafter, she was a construction contract lawyer for the Corps of Engineers in Omaha,

Yerkes '41. In later years there, she was Martha S. Robinson.

1133. Kay, *supra* note 1125, at 10. Kay did not include either Dorothy Davidson Tyner or Virginia Creitz Martin in her list of women teachers. Because both were full-time teachers for only one year, Kay was unaware of them when she wrote this article and it is unclear if Tyner was on tenure track.

a hearing officer for the Federal Aviation Administration and then for the Social Security Administration, and Administrative Law Judge for the Nuclear Regulatory Commission. In 1976, she received a presidential Appointment to a panel on Women in High Level Government Positions. She was Chair of the Atomic Safety and Licensing Commission when she retired. Sen. Bob Dole '52 gave her credit for suggesting, when she was Law Librarian, that he should run for public office for the first time, as a State Representative from Russell.

Enrollment by women actually declined in the next two decades, with eleven graduates in the 1950s and only six in the 1960s. Kay Arvin '51 was an inspiration. She had been blinded in an accident before she accompanied her husband Ray Arvin '50 to Topeka when he started law studies. "Because she was bored at home, her husband encouraged her to go to class with him. Dean Schuyler Jackson suggested she enroll in classes. She came with her seeing-eye boxer, named Larkin, and did very well."[1134] She was selected to the Law Review Board. She felt she received "totally fair treatment and open acceptance" and her fondest memory was being honored at the year-end bash as "woman of the year," even though she was the only woman in her class.[1135] The Arvins practiced law together in Wichita for fifty years. She specialized in divorce, mediation, and counseling. Governor Robert Bennett appointed her to be Interim District Judge in 1978, completing the term of an elected judge who died.

Virginia Creitz '54 graduated with honors and practiced law in Wichita for six years, specializing in property law. The next six years, now known as Virginia Martin, she was Washburn's Law Librarian and taught Legal Bibliography as an Instructor. Following the tornado, at age 36, she became a full-time teacher for the 1966–67 academic year, with the rank of Assistant Professor of Law, teaching Titles, Office Practice, and Trusts and Estates. She died suddenly, after a short illness, after that academic year.[1136]

1134. Elrod, *supra* note 1092, at 881, citing minutes of Kappa Chapter of Phi Delta Delta that refer to an article about Arvin and Larkin being written for the organization's national magazine.

1135. Kay Arvin, Class Notes, Washburn School of Law Alumni Weekend, 1996 and 2001.

1136. Robert J. Fowks, *In Memoriam*, 7 WASHBURN L.J. 285 (1968). Fowks described her as "the first full-time woman law teacher in the sixty-three year history of Washburn Law School." However, no member of the faculty at the time would

103. Hon. Kay McFarland '64

No women graduated after 1958 until 1964, when Kay McFarland '64 was the only woman in her graduating class. She recalls one professor who believed women did not belong in law school and gave her a lower grade for that reason. "He had a hostile attitude."[1137] She would be a woman of many firsts: the first woman elected in Shawnee County as Juvenile Judge and Probate Judge, in 1970, and then as District Judge in 1972; the first woman to serve on the Kansas Supreme Court, in 1977; and the first woman to become Chief Justice, on September 1, 1995.

McFarland's place on the District Court was taken by Mary Schowengerdt '57, who received a J.D. rather than an LL.B. by completing the thesis required in addition to regular course work. Her thesis was published in the KBA's

have been familiar with Dorothy Tyner.

1137. *Chief justice reflects on 30 years with state's high court*, TOPEKA CAP.-J., Sept. 17, 2007, 1A, 6A.

Journal.[1138] Schowengerdt later was the first woman President of the alumni Law School Association.

Only five more women graduated between 1965 and 1969. Their lack of a critical mass may explain several examples of male chauvinism. When the Student Bar Association decided in 1965 to participate for the first time in the national Law Day celebration, one of the feature activities it planned was a beauty contest, with ten contestants in swimsuits on the law school steps.[1139] WSBA ultimately canceled the contest "because of criticism" by the campus Panhellenic Council, which also rejected a proposed compromise that the girls be "judged in shorts, slacks or stretch pants."[1140] Campaigns for student bar offices had been raucous for many years. In 1970, the appearance of two Bunnies from the Kansas City Playboy Club was credited with helping the Equitable Party sweep student elections.[1141]

The women's legal fraternity, Phi Delta Delta, remained active, despite the small number of women students, with the help of regular attendance at meetings by alumnae members. Kappa Chapter celebrated its fiftieth anniversary with a celebration at the Topeka Country Club on November 10, 1970. Professor Bob Fowks "gave a humorous talk."[1142] In the spring of 1970, Washburn's Benson Chapter of Phi Alpha Delta voted to admit to its membership three Phi Delta Delta members, Martha Steincamp '71, Linda Elrod '72, and a recent initiate, Peggy Gatewood '73.[1143] The Benson Chapter, aided by P.A.D.'s International Justice Hon. Alex Hotchkiss '27, recently had succeeded at the P.A.D. national convention in amending P.A.D. membership eligibility requirements so that P.A.D. chapters could admit women.[1144] At its October 11, 1971 meeting, Kappa Chapter voted unanimously to merge with Phi Alpha Delta, and the national

1138. Mary Schowengerdt, *The United Nations as Juridical Personalty*, 25 J. KAN. B. ASS'N 275 (1957).

1139. First Washburn Law Day Slates Beauty Contest, WASHBURN REV., Apr. 9, 1965.

1140. *Swim Suit Beauty Contest Canceled by Law School*, WASHBURN REV., Apr. 23, 1965.

1141. *Law School Elections—Playboy Bunnie Will Help*, WASHBURN REV., Sept. 30, 1970; *Equitable Party Sweeps All Student Bar Offices*, WASHBURN REV., Oct. 7, 1970.

1142. Elrod, *supra* note 1092, at 876.

1143. *Id.* at 884.

1144. *Id.*

paperwork was completed in 1972.[1145] The presence of women members did not alter P.A.D.'s traditions. The three new women members were invited to attend one of the regular "special" meetings in the basement of the P.A.D. house at 1612 College "only to discover," as Linda Elrod described it, "that it was an opportunity to view the latest confiscated adult films. Martha and I left quickly. Peggy Gatewood, however, sat in the front row, saying, 'After having three children, nothing bothers me.'"[1146] In later years, P.A.D. made half-hearted attempts to legitimize the event as a Seminar on Contemporary Community Standards, even justifying "testimony" by an expert witness. In 1983, a woman for the first time lived in the P.A.D. house, Marsha Pankewich '86.[1147]

The graduating class of 1971 had the largest number of women, five, of any class in the school's history, surpassing by one the class of 1941. One of its members, Kathleen E. King '71, won the 1968 national essay contest sponsored by the *Women's Law Journal*,[1148] earning an all-expenses-paid trip to England. In 1970, she became the first woman to represent Washburn in an intermural moot court competition, arguing in the regional rounds of the Jessup International Law Competition.

In 1972, there again was only one woman graduate, but Linda Henry Elrod '72 ranked first in her class. She became an attorney for the Kansas Judicial Council. Her path to becoming a full-time member of the faculty, which began when she taught Creditors Rights as an Adjunct Professor during the summer of 1973, is traced in Chapter Six. Today, she is one of the leading authorities in the nation on Family Law, having served as Chair of the ABA Section on Family Law during 2000–01, Editor of the Section's *Family Law Quarterly* since 1992, author of a treatise on child custody and visitation, and co-author of a casebook used at law schools throughout the country.

The number of women graduates reached six in the class of 1974. They included Christel Marquardt '74, who in 1995 would be the third woman appointed to the Kansas Court of Appeals. Marquardt initially practiced with two law firms in Topeka and one in Kansas City, before forming a small firm with her son Andrew Marquardt '92. She was the first woman elected President of the Kansas Bar Association, in 1987, was selected in 1988 to represent Kansas in

---

1145. *Id.*

1146. *Id.*, n. 209.

1147. 22 THE CIRCUIT RIDER 18 (Winter 1983).

1148. Kathleen E. King, *Civil Rights?*, 8 WASHBURN L.J. 143 (1969).

the ABA House of Delegates, and then was elected as one of eighteen district representatives on the thirty-seven member ABA Board of Governors in 1998. She chaired the ABA's Committee on Specialization and served on its Committees on Professionalism, Mediation, and Lawyer Referral. She also has been an active supporter of the Law School, serving fourteen years as a member of the Board of Governors of the Washburn Law School Association and as its President from 1998 to 2000.

Women began enrolling in law schools nationwide in much greater numbers in the early 1970s. The number of women graduates at Washburn more than doubled from six in 1974 to sixteen in 1975. The 1975 graduates used their law degrees in every way imaginable at the time. Polly Wilhardt '75 would become Chief Judge of the United States Bankruptcy Court in the District of Oregon. Darci Rock '75 was Law Clerk for United States District Judge Frank Theis, then became a leading litigator, specializing in asbestos cases, in the Washington, D.C. offices of the Houston-based firm of Bracewell & Patterson. Kathy D'Agostino (Wachsman) '75 would practice with her husband in the well-known medical malpractice firm of Pegalis, Wachsman & Erickson near New York City. Victoria Kumorowski '75 would be elected District Judge in Hutchinson and Karen Langston '75 became a District Judge in Wichita, after years as an Assistant District Attorney. JoAn Hamilton '75 would be elected State Representative and District Attorney in Shawnee County. Imelda Koett '75 would become a deputy counsel for the Bureau of Tobacco, Alcohol and Firearms, joining two classmates also working in Washington for federal agencies, Jenifer Lucas '75 at the Federal Energy Regulatory Commission and Sally Stratmoen '75 at the Department of Agriculture. Sara Miller '75 went the corporate route, with Northwestern Mutual Life Insurance Company in Milwaukee. Carol Duffy McDowell '75 would be a lobbyist and for a time Executive Director of the Kansas Trial Lawyers Association. Other class members practiced in small- and medium-sized law firms throughout Kansas.

Women no longer were novelties at the Law School. Nevertheless, being on the forefront of rapid change is never easy. When Joyce Simmons Rubenstein '76 applied for a law clerk position advertised in the placement office, she was told at the interview that the lawyer who placed the ad had "forgotten that the fairer sex might be in law school" and would not accept an application from a woman. The part-time student director of the placement office took no action because the interviewer "was an alumnus and it was a job opportunity—for a male."[1149] Members of the classes of both 1974 and 1977 recalled "Ladies Day" in Professor Fowks' class when only women were asked to recite.[1150] Professor Ahrens did not have a "Ladies Day" routinely but declared one in 1973 the day after Billie Jean King defeated Bobby Riggs in the tennis "battle of the sexes."[1151] There was appropriate push-back. Women in Professor Howe's Domestic Relations class in 1976 presented him with a live pig wearing a sign proclaiming "Male Chauvinist Pig." Howe relinquished the course to Professor Elrod the next year.[1152] When Professor Elrod in 2003 distributed a questionnaire to women graduates while writing an article for the centennial edition of the *Washburn Law Journal*, 89% responded that they "had a positive legal education experience and were accepted as an equal by faculty and students"; however, 41% of those who felt differently attended law school between 1971 and 1977.[1153]

The percentage of women students continued to grow, topping 20% for the first time in the entering class of 1978 (22%; 46 of 209) and reaching 28% the next year. Women first comprised more than one-third of the entering class in 1982 (34%) and that percentage remained relatively constant until an upward spike to 39.9% in 1988. Finally, in 1991, the percentage of women in the entering class for the first time exceeded 40% (44.6%), and women comprised 39.9% of the entire student body.

There were a number of "firsts." Mary A. Senner '70 was the first woman to be Editor-in-Chief of the *Washburn Law Journal*, in 1969–70 for volume 9,[1154] followed in 1977–78 by Vivian Wiberg '78. Of the twenty-two Editors-in-Chief from the class of 1985 through the class of 2006, sixteen were women. Marcia Harley (now Johnston) '74 was the first woman elected to the Order of Barristers. She was a member of the Washburn team that won the regional Jessup International Law Moot Court Competition in 1973 and won one round in the national finals in Washington, D.C. before being defeated. She also represented the school in the National Moot Court Competition in 1973 and in a second

---

1149. Elrod, *supra* note 1092, at 902.

1150. *Id.* at 890 n. 260.

1151. *Id.*

1152. *Id.* at 891

1153. *Id.* at 906 n 367.

1154. Indicative of the times, a reporter for the student newspaper, a woman herself, wrote, "The striking blond was all business" as she discussed publication of the *Journal*. *Woman Edits Law Journal*, WASHBURN REV., Apr. 29, 1970.

Jessup Competition. Interestingly, she now practices internationally, in one of Canada's largest firms, in Calgary, Alberta.

The rapid increase in enrollment by women was not anticipated by those who designed the new law building that opened in 1969. No restroom facilities were provided for women on the lowest floor, where most of the classrooms and the student lounge were located. In 1971, what originally was a custodian's closet, which had a sink and thus had plumbing available, was remodeled as a women's restroom by the addition of a toilet and a small mirror. That one extra stall ultimately would be insufficient to meet demand, particularly with only ten-minute breaks scheduled between classes. The facilities in the clinic building, added in 1978, did not help much because they were small and away from the seat of most law student activities. Discontent mounted and the administration did not respond quickly enough. Students in 1984, led by Susie Schwartz '85, formed an ad hoc group called W.O.M.B.S. (Women Ordering More Bathroom Stalls). The group circulated petitions demanding more facilities and threatening takeovers of men's restrooms. The petitions noted that "[e]ach relief station frequented by males accommodates 21.7 people, whereas each relief station frequented by females accommodates 36 people." The group's theme was "Toiletbusters," based on the movie and song "Ghostbusters." A short-term fix was possible, according to the group, since existing plumbing would permit installation of three more stalls in the women's restroom on the second floor. The group vowed to take the issue to the local newspaper. The administration quickly capitulated and ordered the suggested changes, but a three-column, front-page newspaper story still reported the controversy under the headline "Dean's order averts restroom takeovers."[1155] Dean Monk put the best spin on the situation he could, apologizing for the inconvenience for women students but calling it "a great problem to have," one that was "a tribute to our outreach efforts to get more good female law students in the law school." Dean Monk's successor remembered the lesson when renovations that were part of the 1992 building plan were temporarily going to close more restrooms for women than men. He converted one bathroom from men's to women's. While only some of the plumbing was usable, the inconvenience was equalized.

As discussed in Chapter Eight, data compiled in 1994 and 1995 demonstrated that women at Washburn achieved academic success exceeding that of male

---

1155. *Dean's order averts restroom takeovers*, TOPEKA CAP. J., Oct. 24, 1984, at 1.

students, contrary to the experiences of women at many other schools. For six of eight semesters between 1995 and 1999, 1L women achieved higher average GPAs than 1L men. Linda Hirchman's book, *A Woman's Guide to Law School,* ranked Washburn Law School among the fifty schools "most supportive of women's success," based on the percentage of women faculty on tenure or tenure-track, the rate at which women were selected to membership on the law review, and the percentage of women in the classes of 1996 and 1997.

However, there were challenges. Until 1979, Professor Elrod was the only one of three full-time women faculty members who taught classroom courses. She was joined that year by Professors Maxwell and Reynolds. Women professors sometimes were tested in the classroom in ways their male counterparts were not. Alan Pretnar '82 was a student in Professor Elrod's Family Law class in 1981. Pretnar was a husky man who delighted in being outrageous. One day, he suggested that all incapacitated persons should be sterilized so they could not have children. Elrod responded, "Excuse me, class. I have to scream." She turned around to face the blackboard, let out a piercing yell, turned back around, smiled, announced that she felt better, and proceeded with the class.[1156]

Cynthia Douglass '76 organized Women's Legal Forum in 1975 and served as its first president. It sponsored speakers, organized weekend conferences, and in the 1980s raised money to endow a scholarship. Its success led in the mid-1980s to the formation in response of a Men's Legal Forum. It focused far less on speakers and conferences and far more on excursions to bars. It disbanded after several graduating classes but was resurrected for a time in the 1990s.

Women students impacted women's issues. In 1986, five women, Christine Andrade '87, Shannon Crane '86, Julia Dudley '87, Lyn Goering '87, and Patricia Horner '87 joined Robert Telthorst '87 in writing the *Kansas Women's Legal Rights Handbook.* Professor Charlene Smith served as editor, and the Kansas Department of Social and Rehabilitation Services printed and distributed the handbook statewide.

Law firms were not always as quick as the Law School to embrace the entry of women into the legal profession. A number of male students elected not to interview with a firm one year at the end of the 1970s, in protest when its hiring partner did not select any of the women applicants to be interviewed.

1156. *How Do You Spell Relief? S-C-R-E-A-M,* CASE AND CANE 10 (Spring 1981). An irony is that Pretnar became a leading domestic relations lawyer in southern Illinois.

As the number of women in each class has grown, the history of women students at Washburn Law School has become simply a part of the ongoing history of the Law School. The achievements of its women graduates throughout the profession have become far too numerous to mention individually in the same way as those of the early pioneers. Many, however, have held significant public positions. They include Lillian Apodaca '85, partner in a major law firm in Albuquerque, who became President of the Hispanic National Bar Association for 1998–99. Marla Luckert '80 was the second woman elected President of the Kansas Bar Association. As District Judge in Shawnee County, she served by designation of the Kansas Supreme Court as Chief Judge. She became the second woman appointed to the Kansas Supreme Court, in 2002. Nancy Moritz '85 joined Luckert on the Supreme Court in 2010 as its fourth woman appointee. She had been a member of the Kansas Court of Appeals since 2004, following many years as Assistant United States Attorney.

Luckert's replacement on the District Court, Jean Schmidt '82, joined Nancy Parrish '85 on that court. Parrish later would be named Chief Judge. She previously was a Kansas State Senator, Secretary of Revenue for Kansas, and a member of the Kansas Board of Tax Appeals. Other graduates who have served as District Judges in Kansas include Evelyn Zabel Wilson '85 and Rebecca Crotty '77 in Shawnee County, Muriel Yates Harris '76 and Kate Lynch '92 in Wyandotte County, Kim Parker '82 in Sedgwick County, Amy Harth '94 in Paola, Rene (Vander-Yacht) Young '86 in Salina, Kim (Wiechman) Cudney '89 in Washington, and Sally Pokorny '78 in Douglas County. Maritza Segarra '88 was the first Latina to be named District Judge in Kansas, in 2007 in the Eighth Judicial District in Junction City. She was followed by Cheryl Rios Kingfisher '93 in Shawnee County in 2008. Segarra previously served for three years as District Magistrate Judge, and Kingfisher had been a Municipal Judge. Other District Magistrate Judges in Kansas have included Crotty, in Garden City before moving to Topeka, Pam Fuller '87, Janette Haverkamp '89, and Julie Fletcher Cowell '86. Elsewhere, Donna Dixon '84 has been District Judge in Roseau County, Minnesota, Quintress Gilbert '89 has been Juvenile Judge in Macon, Georgia, since 1997, Christine Holiman Hutson '91 is Associate Circuit Judge in Laclede County in Missouri, Cynthia Hartman '77 is County Court Judge in Fort Collins, Colorado, Julie Roth '87 has been Family Court Judge in Kingman, Arizona, and Patricia Kelly '95 is a Judge on the Juvenile and Domestic Relations District Court for the Fifteenth

District in Virginia. A number of graduates have served as Municipal Court judges and Administrative Law Judges.

Outside the judiciary, Donna Whiteman '81 was the first woman to serve as Majority Leader of the Kansas House of Representatives, representing Hutchinson. Later, she was Secretary of the Kansas Department of Social and Rehabilitation Services. Other House members have included: Martha Jenkins '87 and Marti Crow '93, representing Leavenworth; Denise Everhart '89 and Jill Jenkins '92 from Shawnee County; Joan Adam '88 from Atchison; Karen Griffiths '78 from Newton; and Sabrina Standifer '99, who was completing her term representing Wichita when she started law school. Marge Petty '90 from Topeka served in the Kansas Senate. Alice Device '86 was the first woman Secretary of Agriculture for Kansas and Jane Roy '70 was a member of the Kansas Corporation Commission. Cynthia Douglass '76 was Deputy Assistant Secretary of Labor for Occupational Safety and Health under Secretary of Labor Elizabeth Dole and now is an Administrative Law Judge for the Department of Labor. Linda Richey Graves '78 was a partner specializing in real estate transactions in a Kansas City law firm before assuming the non-elected, but very public, role of First Lady of Kansas from 1995 to 2003. Linda Parks '83 served as President of the Kansas Bar Association for 2007–08.

11

A COMMITMENT TO DIVERSITY

When Washburn College was founded in 1865 as Lincoln College, one of its stated objectives was "to afford to all classes without distinction of color the advantages of a liberal education." Washburn Law School from its inception welcomed African-American students and other minorities, providing a path of entry into the legal profession that was not available at many American law schools at the time. A remarkable number of the early African-American graduates had a significant impact on the development of the law and the advancement of racial justice. Indeed, three members of the National Bar Association's Hall of Fame are Washburn graduates.

Samuel E. Cary came to Washburn Law School in 1907 from Providence, Kentucky, and was the first black graduate in 1910. He joined the practice of a renowned black trial lawyer in Hill City, W.L. Sayers. They opened an office in Russell Springs, where Cary was City Attorney from 1911 until 1912. Then, he was Assistant County Attorney of Logan County under Sayers. Cary himself was elected Logan County Attorney in 1914.[1157] He moved to Denver and opened a law practice there in 1919, specializing in criminal law. "His clients 'were made up of people whom the white lawyers shunned: Blacks, Orientals, Indians and poor whites...[who] could ill afford to pay him.'"[1158] He was disbarred in 1926

1157. Elmer C. Jackson, Jr., *A Brief History of Black Lawyers in Kansas*, in REQUISITE LEARNING AND GOOD MORAL CHARACTER: A HISTORY OF THE KANSAS BENCH AND BAR 103, at 104 (Robert W. Richmond ed. 1982)

1158. J. CLAY SMITH, JR., EMANCIPATION: THE MAKING OF THE BLACK LAWYER 491 (1933)

104. Samuel E. Cary, 1910

based on a finding he had neglected clients' business, permitting defaults to be taken and suits to be dismissed. Many, including Cary, thought that racial prejudice prompted an excessive punishment. Cary was reinstated as a member of the bar in 1935 and continued to practice for ten more years until illness forced him to retire. In 1971, a new organization formed in Denver to instill professionalism among African-American lawyers was named the Samuel Cary Bar Association. An investigation into Cary's life and practice and an address by a former Chief Justice of the Colorado Supreme Court persuaded organizers that Cary was an appropriate person to honor in this way.

The second black graduate, Frederick C. Helm, began his law studies during Cary's last year at Washburn and graduated in 1912. He was well regarded by his classmates, who elected him as an officer of the first-year class, Sargent-at-Arms, and Vice-President of the first-year Arthur Debating Club.[1159] He

1159. *School of Law,* WASHBURN REV., Oct. 20, 1909, at 6; *School of Law,* WASH-

showed a talent for trial work in Practice Court. After graduation, Helm opened a law office in Wichita. He once ran unsuccessfully for judge of the city court.

The fact that his classmates would elect Helm as a class officer at the same time they elected the only woman in the class as Secretary-Treasurer suggests the Law School early on was more accepting of diversity than the society at large. Reverend Nathan A. Mitchell, a native of Jamaica who completed college there, enrolled in the Law School in 1911 and attended for one year before a new pastoral assignment caused him to move to Missouri. He told the student newspaper that he

> came to Topeka in preference to attending law school in Louisville because here, he says, he has found no race prejudice. When he applied for entrance in a college in Illinois, he found a sentiment among the students, which he interpreted as unfriendly.[1160]

Paul Brady '56, who attended the Law School forty years later, offered a similar perspective:

> I learned that Washburn had a tradition of welcoming Negro students. Nationally syndicated columnist Carl Rowan, who had served with an officer-training unit stationed at Washburn during World War II, described the campus as an "oasis of democracy set in a community of many contradictions."...
>
> I found that both the faculty and students at Washburn were generally cooperative, polite and hard-working. However, the legal fraternities on campus that controlled the student body and other social activities did not admit Negro students. Although the discriminatory practice was totally

BURN REV., Dec. 15, 1909, at 9

1160. *Legal Atmosphere Is a Drawing Card*, WASHBURN REV., May 1, 1912, at 2. Mitchell did not complete his law studies as Washburn. He left upon being named to a pastorate at a church in Columbia, Missouri. *Personals*, WASHBURN REV., Aug. 12, 1912, at 6, reported that he planned to enroll at the law school of the University of Missouri. However, black students were excluded from that law school at that time. *See Missouri ex rel. Gaines v. Canada*, 305 U.S. 337 (1938). Mitchell ultimately became a lawyer and practiced in St. Louis, Missouri. In 1925, he became "the first Negro attorney known to represent a white client" there. SMITH, *supra* note 1158, at 333, citing ST. LOUIS STAR, June 19, 1925.

inconsistent with the mission for which we were preparing, the hard work and stiff competition caused it to be one of my lesser concerns.[1161]

Professor Paul E. Wilson '40 attributed what he perceived as the greater tolerance by white students at Washburn than by their counterparts at KU in part to the Lincoln College heritage and "vestiges of New England Puritanism" that lingered from Washburn's founding. An additional factor, he believed, was that Washburn was an urban institution where white students were more familiar and thus more comfortable with their non-white counterparts than rural youths attending the state University.[1162]

EARLY NOTABLES

Elisha Scott '16, was the Law School's third black graduate. One would have guessed he would become a trial lawyer of legend. Scott received a law diction- ary for winning the Special Prize Debate as a beginning student in 1910. He was "heralded with much applause among the students as the advocate of their cause" when they were assigned the role of the criminal defendant in cases he defended in Practice Court.[1163] He and Fred Helm '12 conducted mock trials and debates in local black churches.

Scott was a descendant of Exodusters.[1164] He was helped in his early educa- tion by the Rev. Charles M. Sheldon, famed Topeka pastor, and Scott served as a model for a character in Sheldon's *In His Steps*.[1165] In his memoir about the *Brown* case, Paul Wilson '40, who argued before the Supreme Court on behalf of the State, described Scott's career as follows:

> [H]is race, combined with his extraordinary flamboyance, gained him a special place in the Topeka bar. His clients were drawn from Topeka's minority population and whites in the lower economic strata. He was known as an attorney who would go to bat for people who could not

---

1161. PAUL E. BRADY, A CERTAIN BLINDNESS 119 and 172 (1990).

1162. PAUL E. WILSON, A TIME TO LOSE: REPRESENTING KANSAS IN *BROWN V. BOARD OF EDUCATION* 60 (1995).

1163. *Law School*, WASHBURN REV., May 17, 1916, at 3.

1164. Wilson, *supra* note 1162, at 75.

1165. Jackson, *supra* note 1157, at 105.

105. Elisha Scott '16

find representation elsewhere. Thirty years after his death he remains a legend among Topeka lawyers.

An advocate of black equality, Elisha was not a visibly angry militant. He preferred to rely on persuasion and to work within the established power structure. In his time Republicans usually controlled the governments of Kansas and Shawnee County. Elisha was a Republican.[1166]

Scott was the first African-American to run for statewide office in Kansas. In 1930, he became a candidate for the Republican nomination for Attorney General. He finished third in a four-person primary election but garnered more than 40,000 votes, half the number of the winner. However, his most important work was as a lawyer. Richard Kluger described Scott this way:

> As a lawyer, he was a quick study....He had a real knack for selecting a jury, a flair at cross-examining, and a gift for dredging up obscure

1166. Wilson, *supra* note 1162, at 78.

Kansas statutes to save his clients' hides. He could be truly inventive in the defense of his clients' civil liberties...[o]r he could be shamelessly emotional, quoting scripture lavishly and falling to his knees dramatically during two- and three-hour-long summations....

Elisha Scott worked in his sometimes mysterious ways as almost the sole legal arm of the black community in his part of the country. Things got lost on his desk that shouldn't have, and sometimes he looked less courageous than others, but he kept on fighting—against the exclusion of blacks from the swimming pool of Newton, from the kindergarten in Coffeyville, from the junior high schools and the movie houses of Topeka.[1167]

Eight African-Americans graduated between 1920 and 1929, including three in the class of 1923. Notables among them include William McKinley Bradshaw '20, who practiced in Topeka and was appointed by William Smith '14 as Assistant Attorney General of Kansas, and Earl T. Reynolds '23, who while practicing in Coffeyville in 1937 was appointed by Governor Walter Huxman to the Kansas State Highway Commission. Earl's brother Raymond J. Reynolds '29 initially practiced law with Earl in Topeka, serving seven terms as President of the Topeka chapter of the NAACP and writing a column entitled "Cheers and Encores" for the local paper. After unsuccessfully challenging incumbent Warren Shaw '31 for election as Municipal Judge in Topeka, he moved in the mid-1940s to California. In 1954, Reynolds became the first African-American appointed as Deputy City Attorney in San Francisco. Governor Ronald Reagan then appointed him in 1969 as Judge of the Superior Court in San Francisco. Judge Reynolds was a member of the inaugural class of inductees in the National Bar Association Hall of Fame in 1986.[1168]

Another graduate of the 1920s, Loren Miller '28, also achieved fame in California, and nationally too. He initially practiced with Elisha Scott '16 but moved to Los Angeles in 1930. Initially, he was a journalist, publishing the *Los Angeles Sentinel*, a weekly newspaper for the black community,[1169] and writing for the *California Eagle*, which he subsequently purchased in 1951.

1167. RICHARD KLUGER, SIMPLE JUSTICE 385, 387 (1975).

1168. *Alumni Profile: Judge R.J. Reynolds*, 28 THE CIRCUIT RIDER 10 (Summer 1989).

1169. Martha Imparato, *Washburn alumnus prominent in early California civil rights movement*, WASHBURN ALUMNUS 18 (Fall 2007).

106. Hon. Loren R. Miller '28

Miller reentered law practice in 1934. A friend and client described him as "so dynamic that other lawyers would actually postpone their own cases just to hear him."[1170] He "won the respect of his people for the valiant efforts he… waged in litigating race covenant cases,"[1171] representing more than 100 clients by 1947.[1172] In 1945, he successfully defended injunction actions seeking eviction of Hollywood actresses Hattie McDaniel, Ethel Waters, Louise Beavers, and others successful African-Americans from homes they purchased in the ritzy West Adams Heights area known as Sugar Hill, a case that caught the attention of *Time* magazine.[1173] Miller argued three cases before the United

---

1170. JOSH SIDES, L.A. CITY LIMITS: AFRICAN AMERICAN LOS ANGELES FROM THE GREAT DEPRESSION TO THE PRESENT 99 (2003).

1171. Smith, *supra* note 1158, at 489.

1172. *Loren Miller*, 7 WEST'S ENCYCLOPEDIA OF AMERICAN LAW 213 (1998).

1173. Carlton Jackson, *Hattie: The Life of Hattie McDaniel* 89 (1990); *Victory on Sugar Hill*, TIME, Dec. 17, 1945, at 22.

States Supreme Court, two of them involving racially restrictive covenants.[1174] Miller joined Thurgood Marshall in arguing *McGhee v. Sipes*, the Michigan case combined with a Missouri case that produced the landmark decision in *Shelley v. Kraemer*,[1175] in which the Supreme Court held that judicial enforcement of racially restrictive covenants was state action and was barred by the Fourteenth Amendment.[1176] That decision led to dismissal in California of the white landowners' appeal in Miller's Sugar Hill case.[1177] He argued alone the follow-up case of *Jackson v. Barrow*,[1178] in which he had been counsel in the California state courts, which applied *Shelley* to invalidate damage judgments against white sellers whose sales violated restrictive covenants.[1179] Miller reflected on the victory in *Shelley* in *The Nation* magazine:

> The successful termination of the long battle against racial covenants illustrates both the weakness and the strength of a political democracy, its weakness because the courts were so laggard in protecting a civil right that the highest court in the nation says has existed since 1868, its strength because a disadvantaged minority was finally able to vindicate that right.
> …
> [N]ow that the legal basis of residential segregation has been destroyed, the job of educating Americans to live together without strife and without reference to race rests on the very groups that filed supporting briefs in the Supreme Court. If they believe that the ghetto is the evil proclaimed in their briefs they should set about their educational task without delay. The legal victory will be a hollow triumph unless the battle against residential segregation is also won in the field of public opinion.[1180]

1174. In addition to the two cases discussed in the text, he also argued *Collins v. Hardyman*, 341 U.S. 651 (1951).

1175. *Shelley v. Kraemer*, 334 U.S. 1 (1948).

1176. Miller's role in the NAACP strategy to fight restrictive covenants and in the arguments in *Shelley* is described in Mark Tushnet, MAKING CIVIL RIGHTS LAW: THURGOOD MARSHALL AND THE SUPREME COURT 1936–1961 89–98 (1994).

1177. JILL WATTS, HATTIE MCDANIEL 239, 259 (2005).

1178. *Jackson v. Barrow*, 346 U.S. 249 (1953).

1179. Miller's account of *Shelley* and *Jackson* is Chapter 22 of Loren Miller, THE PETITIONERS: THE STORY OF THE UNITED STATES SUPREME COURT AND THE NEGRO 321–329 (1966).

1180. Loren Miller, *A right secured*, THE NATION, May 29, 1949, at 600. The title

From 1935 through 1947, the Federal Housing Administration "furnished a model race-restrictive clause for builders and subdividers" and "refused to guarantee home-construction loans unless race restrictions were inserted in subdivision deeds."[1181] Miller has been called the first lawyer "to win an un-qualified verdict outlawing residential restrictive covenants" in sales involving FHA or VA financing.[1182]

Miller joined as counsel on the briefs in *Brown v. Board of Education* and on amicus briefs in civil rights and First Amendment cases on behalf of the NAACP,[1183] the ACLU,[1184] and the National Lawyers Guild.[1185] He later authored a book analyzing the Supreme Court's role in the civil rights movement.[1186] He also served on the Executive Board of the National Bar Association. Miller "explored the possibility of running as a Democrat for Congress, a prospect that excited many in the black community."[1187] In 1964, three years before his death, Miller was appointed by Governor Edmund Brown as Judge of the Municipal Court in Los Angeles.[1188] The State Bar of California in 1977 created the Loren Miller Legal Services Award in his honor.[1189] Black lawyers in Seattle, including Philip Burton '48, who formed a local chapter of the National Bar Association named it the Loren Miller Bar Club.[1190] There is even a Loren Miller Elementary School in Los Angeles.

Ambrose Woodard '26, who was described as a "highly skilled trial lawyer,"[1191] and Fred Helm '12 became judges before either Reynolds or Miller did, if only

is drawn from the December 1946 report of the Truman Administration's special Committee on Civil Rights, *To Secure These Rights*.

1181. *Id.*

1182. *Loren Miller,* 7 WEST'S ENCYCLOPEDIA OF AMERICAN LAW 213, AT 214 (1998).

1183. *Collins v. Hardyman,* 341 U.S. 651 (1951).

1184. *Garner v. Bd. of Pub. Works,* 341 U.S. 716 (1951), and *Castaneda Gonzales v. Landon,* 350 U.S. 920 (1955).

1185. *Parker v. Cty. of Los Angeles,* 338 U.S. 327 (1949).

1186. Miller, *supra* note 1179.

1187. Smith, *supra* note 1158, at 489.

1188. *New Judge Reluctant Member of Profession,* L.A. TIMES, May 17, 1964.

1189. Email from Amina Hassan, Ph.D. to James Concannon (May 3, 2007). Dr. Hassan was writing a biography of Miller.

1190. The name was changed a decade later to the Loren Miller Bar Association. www.lmba.net/

1191. Jim Lawing, *Before Brown v. Board of Education: Desegregating the Bench,*

briefly. In May 1952, Sedgwick County had three elected District Judges and one Judge Pro Tem who was filling in for a fourth elected judge who was absent due to illness. The Kansas Bar Association convention was in Kansas City and the three District Judges, the Judge Pro Tem, and more than 100 members of the local bar attended it. Kansas law provided that a Judge Pro Tem could be selected to replace an absent District Judge by ballot of those members of the bar who were "present" before the Clerk of the District Court.[1192] At a "hurriedly-called session" on Thursday, May 22, what a reporter described as an "insurgent stay-at-home group" of nine white lawyers, including Gerald Michaud '51 and Keith Sanborn '50, gathered in the Clerk's office and elected Woodard, Helm, and two other black lawyers as Judges Pro Tem.[1193] The evening newspaper printed a front-page photograph of the four being sworn in. It reported that Woodard, who was named Presiding Judge Pro Tem, insisted that an American flag be in the photograph and said, "I think we ought to send this picture behind the Iron Curtain.[1194] Contacted in Kansas City, Presiding Judge Clair Robb '33 described the election as "all in fun," doubting there would be enough judicial business to keep all four judges busy.[1195] The terms of three of the new judges ended automatically when the District Judges they replaced returned from the convention. Because Woodard had been elected to replace another Judge Pro Tem, the court's Presiding Judge concluded that Woodard "may, if he wishes" continue as Judge Pro Tem until the absent District Judge's term expired in October.[1196] Unseating the previously selected Judge Pro Tem was an unintended consequence and the prospect prompted some controversy.[1197] However, Woodard told the morning newspaper that although "he was getting some fun out of it Thursday,...he definitely would resign" at the close of court business at noon on Saturday, permitting the former Judge Pro Tem to resume his duties.[1198] "The job does not pay enough," he added. Despite the

---

BAR-O-METER 16, 18 (July 2002).

1192. GEN. STAT. KAN. 1949 20-306.

1193. *Young Legal Lights Name Four Judges*, WICHITA BEACON, May 22, 1952, 1, at 18; *Judge Thinks Bar Action Unnecessary*, WICHITA BEACON, May 23, 1952, 1, at 6.

1194. *Young Legal Lights Name Four Judges*, supra note 1193.

1195. *Judge Thinks Bar Action Unnecessary*, supra note 1193.

1196. *Id.*

1197. *Lawyers Split Over Election of Colored Attorneys to Bench*, WICHITA EAGLE, May 23, 1952, at 8.

1198. *Id.*

brevity of the four judges' terms, in later years "decorum in Wichita's legal community required the four lawyers…to be addressed by the honorarium 'Judge,' at least on formal occasions."[1199]

Enrollment by African-Americans declined in the 1930s, with only two graduates. Wendell P. Sayers graduated in 1935. Sayers was the son of the famous Hill City lawyer, W.L. Sayers. His uncle, John Q. Sayers, spent a year taking classes at Washburn in 1912–13, although he already was an experienced lawyer who had been admitted to practice based on reading law in his brother's office. Wendell Sayers later would be an Assistant Attorney General in Colorado. A third black student that decade, Charles Bledsoe, did not complete an LL.B. but did complete forty-eight credit hours while attending part-time between 1931 and 1937, when he was employed as a Topeka fireman. He was permitted to take the bar exam in 1937, apparently based partly on law office study.

THE SCOTTS AND *BROWN V. BOARD OF EDUCATION*

Three sons of Elisha Scott graduated from Washburn Law School in the 1940s. Elisha Scott, Jr. graduated in 1942. He left practice with his father after 1948, moving to Flint, Michigan to take over the practice of his uncle. John Scott '47 and Charles Scott '48 practiced with their father. They were just young lawyers, thirty-two and thirty years old, respectively, when they, along with Charles Bledsoe, filed the "case of the century," *Brown v. Board of Education*, in the United States District Court of Kansas. During a presentation about *Brown* at the Association of American Law Schools annual meeting in January 1991, Professor J. Clay Smith, Jr. of Howard Law School referred to these Washburn graduates as "unsung heroes":

> *Brown v. Board of Education* was commenced by some lawyers in Topeka, Kansas who had graduated from Washburn University School of Law, Charles Scott and others.…[T]here were some crusty, poor lawyers who didn't get a lot of money to support this litigation.…[T]hey sacrificed an awful lot for the principle of freedom and justice.…They were able to explain in deed and in word what they were doing and the reason that they were doing it and in a language that the people could understand. As a consequence the people supported the litigation and they understood

---

1199. Lawing, *supra* note 1191.

107. John Scott '47   108. Charles Scott '48

the destiny and the words of freedom and justice in simple terms....I'd
have to tip my hat to Washburn for producing a Charles Scott.[1200]

In Smith's view, as the son of "a great civil rights warrior in the Midwest...
Charles Scott was destined to file this lawsuit."

By the time of the *Brown* trial, Elisha's prime years were behind him. His role
was limited and his input mostly was through his sons. The transcript shows
he spoke only once, making an objection that was overruled. Charles and John
carried much of the load of preparing the case for trial before a three-judge
panel of the District Court, then shared responsibilities at trial with Robert
Carter and Jack Greenberg of the NAACP national office. According to Paul
Wilson, while neither Charles nor John

> had inherited Elisha's flair for showmanship, they were regarded as sound
> and competent lawyers and were generally respected by the Topeka bench
> and bar. Neither was inclined toward militancy, but both were active in

---

1200. Transcript (on file in Washburn Law Library).

109. Hon. Raymond J. Reynolds '29 and Elsie
Faciane '92 stand beside "Common Justice"

the NAACP and shared the concerns of Topeka's blacks. When Charles
Bledsoe sought their help they were ready, willing, and able to move.[1201]

Bledsoe for a time chaired the legal committee of the Topeka branch of the
NAACP and was the first person to contact the national NAACP Legal Defense
Fund for assistance in the case. It was he who brought the Scott brothers into
the case as co-counsel.[1202]

A need was first identified in 1975, during preparation for Topeka's participation in the nation's Bicentennial, to commemorate the *Brown* decision and
the role of Washburn lawyers in it. Years of fundraising and planning followed.
On May 17, 1984, the 30th Anniversary of the Supreme Court's initial decision, a
statue entitled "Common Justice" was dedicated in the main lobby outside the
dean's office at the Law School. Bernice King, daughter of Martin Luther King,

1201. Wilson, *supra* note 1162, at 78.
1202. *Id*. at 75.

Jr., gave the principal address during ceremonies in White Concert Hall. The next day, Charles Scott Sr. and Professor Clay Smith were among the speakers at a symposium on school desegregation held in Robinson Courtroom. The statue is designed from bronze, wood, and steel. Two angular, bronze columns extending upward represent the concept of equality. The two columns separate at the base and are of different shapes, symbolizing the fallacy of "separate but equal." The design suggests Kansas textures resembling wheat and various grasses. The two columns are angled differently at the top, each having a unique slant. The upward thrust and space between the columns suggest the struggle for national unity.

Later, the Brown Foundation for Educational Equity, Excellence and Research was created to enhance the legacy of the *Brown* decision by, among other initiatives, designating the Monroe School as a National Historic Site. Washburn provided the Foundation office space in a vacant office on the lower floor of the Law Clinic building, starting in November 1993, and until the Foundation's activities grew to require larger quarters. The Law School partnered with the Foundation, the Kansas State Historical Society, and the Kansas Committee on the Humanities to obtain a grant from Hallmark, Inc. to underwrite the collection of oral histories from surviving participants in the case. Another joint project was the development of a twelve-panel display tracing the history and the litigation that led to the *Brown* decision. It is displayed on the main floor of the Law Library and additional copies have been used for traveling displays. The Law School took advantage of visits by dignitaries who came to Topeka to speak at Brown Foundation events, such as when Jack Greenberg gave brief remarks at commencement when it coincided with his appearance at the Foundation's anniversary celebration of the May 17 decision.

Although John Scott practiced in Topeka throughout the Brown litigation, he later went to Washington and was an attorney for the Department of Interior for thirty years. Charles Scott, Sr. became general counsel for the Kansas Commission on Civil Rights and later served as a hearing officer for the commission.

A POST-WAR ENROLLMENT BOOM

More African-Americans enrolled following World War II, many taking advantage of the G.I. Bill like other veterans. In all, there were eleven graduates in the 1940s. James P. Davis '48 and Bill Glenn '49 were elected as class officers in successive years. Six African-Americans were members of the class of 1948, the largest number in a single class until 1989. Besides Davis, who became Assistant Wyandotte County Attorney and later was elected as Wyandotte County Commissioner and then to the Kansas House of Representatives, and Charles Scott, Sr., the 1948 class included A. Price Woodard, Jr., the son of Wichita lawyer Ambrose Woodard '26, and Philip Burton, who became a renowned civil rights lawyer in Seattle, Washington. After serving as a Deputy Sedgwick County Attorney, Woodard, Jr. was elected to the Wichita City Council in 1967 and then as the first black Mayor of Wichita in 1970. Burton served as President of the Seattle NAACP. He was instrumental in the desegregation of Seattle's schools. He filed a suit that led in 1963 to the Seattle school district's first program for voluntary transfers to improve racial balance. His 1977 suit concluded with a consent decree under which the school board implemented mandatory desegregation city-wide, including forced school busing. He worked in 1967 for enactment of the state's Fair Housing Act. When he died in 1995, he was praised by Seattle's mayor as "first and foremost a champion of civil rights and the rights of human beings....He was one of the most articulate spokespersons for all disadvantaged individuals."[1203] He was the second Washburn graduate selected for the National Bar Association Hall of Fame. Seattle's NBA chapter annually presents a Bar Exam Preparation Scholarship in his name.[1204]

By 1949, the Law School had 1000 graduates. Bill Glenn '49 was the twenty-third black graduate. There were thirteen more black graduates during the 1950s. Many of them had substantial impact on the profession. William S. (Sandy) Price '50 became Chief Judge of the District Court for the 68th District in Michigan. Leonard Hughes '52 served as Judge in Kansas City, Missouri, and thereafter was a highly respected member of the local bar. Samuel Jackson '54 became Vice President of the American Arbitration Association and Director of its Center for Dispute Settlement. He was active in political life in Washington, D.C., receiving three presidential appointments, the first by Lyndon B. Johnson in 1965 as one of the original members to the United States Equal Employment Opportunity Commission, and the second by Richard M. Nixon in 1969 as Assistant Secretary of Housing and Urban Development.

1203. *Philip Burton, Lawyer and Civil Rights Pioneer, Dies After Long Illness*, SEATTLE POST-INTELLIGENCER, Aug. 1, 1995.

1204. www.lmba.net/scholarships.aspx

That year he contributed an article for the *Washburn Law Journal*.[1205] He left government service after Nixon's first term to practice in Washington with the firm of Stroock, Stroock & Lavan but continued to be involved in Republican Party politics. President Reagan appointed him to the Presidential Housing Commission in 1981.

Sherman A. Parks '55 became the first black appellate judge in Kansas when he was appointed by Governor Robert Bennett as an original member of the Kansas Court of Appeals in 1977. Parks was retained by Kansas voters at the general elections of 1980 and 1984 and served more than ten years before he retired. He started his career in private practice, then was Assistant Shawnee County Attorney for five and one-half years, Assistant Attorney General for three years, and Deputy Assistant Secretary and Chief Counsel for the Kansas Secretary of State for six years. He was the first black lawyer to be Adjunct Professor of Law at Washburn, teaching Criminal Law and Procedure from 1969 to 1976. He served two different four-year terms on the Law School Association's Board of Governors, beginning in 1964 and 1988. He became the first black member of the University's Board of Regents in 1968, serving eight years, and was its chair for the 1971–72 term. He received the honorary degree Doctor of Laws in 1990 and the Law School Association's Distinguished Service Award in 1987.

Paul Brady '56 was the first black federal Administrative Law Judge in United States history and later was Chief Judge of the appellate division for the southeast region. Before his appointment as ALJ, he was an adjudicator for the Social Security Administration, a supervisory trial attorney for the Federal Power Commission, and a hearing examiner with the Department of Health, Education, and Welfare. He is the most recent Washburn graduate inducted into the National Bar Association's Hall of Fame.

Among other graduates of the 1950s, Felix Neals '58 became a state Administrative Law Judge in New York City and G. Edmond Hayes '57, who practiced in Wichita, was the first black lawyer appointed to the Kansas Board of Law Examiners.

There were only three black graduates in the 1960s. One, William Harris, Jr. '63, served as general counsel for the Kansas Department of Revenue before

---

1205. Samuel C. Jackson, *Using the Law to Attack Discrimination in Employment*, 8 WASHBURN L.J. 189 (1969).

110. Delano Lewis '63 meets with Dean Concannon and Jim Wright '63

joining the Office of Legal Counsel for the EEOC in Washington. E. Bernard Hurd '68 served as Deputy City Attorney and Assistant District Attorney in Topeka after a career as a JAG lawyer. He taught courses at Washburn in alternative dispute resolution and trial advocacy as Adjunct Professor.

Delano E. Lewis '63 has had as varied and as influential a career as any graduate. He did traditional legal work for only three years, briefly in private practice in Topeka with P.A. Townsend, then as staff attorney in Washington for the Internal Security Division of the Department of Justice, and finally as a lawyer for the EEOC. He spent the next three years in the Peace Corps, first as Associate Director in Nigeria, where he helped evacuate volunteers when the Biafran war broke out, and then as Director in Uganda. There followed four years of political activity during which Lewis was Legislative Assistant to Republican Senator Edward Brooke of Massachusetts and then Administrative Assistant to Democrat Walter Fauntroy, delegate to the House of Representatives from the District of Columbia. In 1973, Lewis entered the private sector with C & P Telephone Company in Washington, becoming its President in 1988 and its C.E.O. in 1990. In 1994, he accepted a new challenge as President and C.E.O. of National Public Radio, serving four years and successfully guiding it through attempts in Congress to cut its funding. He retired briefly but soon accepted appointment by President Bill Clinton in 1999 as the United States Ambassador to South Africa. Lewis' law school classmate John Conway '63, Chief Judge of the United States District Court in New Mexico, administered the oath in ceremonies in the Grand Hall of the top floor of the Department of State, and I attended the celebration. Lewis has maintained close ties with Washburn, returning frequently to speak at the Law School. He was the 1999 commencement speaker and in 2000 received the honorary degree Doctor of Laws. In 2009, the Kansas Native Sons and Daughters selected him Kansan of the Year.

Two of the nine black graduates of the 1970s became District Judges in Kansas, Greg Waller '72 in Sedgwick County, where he is Chief Judge of the Criminal Division, and J. Dexter Burdette '77 in Wyandotte County. Enrollments in the 1980s rose dramatically, with 32 graduates. Deryl Wynn '86 was the first black graduate to become a partner in a major Kansas City firm, McAnany, Van Cleave & Phillips. Both Wynn and William Thornton '92 were gubernatorial appointees to the Kansas Board of Regents. In 2009, Thornton became Kansas Secretary of Commerce. Jerry Seales '88 was a Senator and leader of the United Labor Party in Grenada before his appointment as Magistrate in 2006 and as Chief Magistrate in 2008.

Several black women took courses at the Law School as early as the 1940s but none completed law school until the 1970s. The first black woman who attended Washburn who became a lawyer was Teresa Walters, who enrolled in 1973. She completed one and one-half years at Washburn before transferring to Creighton Law School for family reasons and graduating there in 1976. She was a lively and outgoing person whose interest in politics took her to Washington, D.C. Later, she owned a small business in Texas, became the Republican Party nominee in 1994 for State Comptroller and two years later for the U.S. House of Representatives. In September 1997, she was named by *Headway* magazine as one of the twenty most influential black conservatives in America, jointly with her then-husband John Doggett, who achieved notoriety as a witness during the confirmation hearings for Justice Clarence Thomas. In 2004, she again sought election to Congress but lost the primary election.

It was 1977 before Washburn had its first black woman graduate. There were three of them. Linda Jeffrey '77 had a distinguished career as Assistant

Attorney General, Shawnee County Counselor, and then as City Attorney of
Topeka.[1206] An editorial praised her when she left that position:

> Linda Jeffrey is a public servant in the highest sense of the word....Jeffrey
> has attacked her job as city attorney each day since being appointed in
> 1994 with incredible optimism, passion and verve....In the most difficult
> days of combat between the former mayor and city council in the past
> few years, Jeffrey was an oasis of reason and civility. And all along you
> got the sense that she utterly adored her job.[1207]

Jo Elaine Heaven '77 was the first black woman to serve as Research Attorney
for the Kansas appellate courts, for Judge Sherman Parks '55 of the Court of Appeals. She later practiced in Coffeyville. Brenda Stidham '77 practiced in Texas.

Suddenly, black women were interested in careers in law. Fifty-one of the
103 black graduates from 1977 through 1998 were women. Quintress Gilbert
'89 was the first to become a judge, serving the Bibb County Juvenile Court
in Macon, Georgia. Her classmate, Joyce McCray Pearson '89, was the first to
become a legal academic, starting as Associate Director of the law library at
the University of Louisville School of Law. She now is Professor of Law and
Director of the Law Library at the University of Kansas School of Law.

While modest activities to recruit students generally began in 1961, there
was no special focus on recruiting minority students until there were no black
students in the 1968 or 1969 entering classes. In 1970, the alumni Board of
Governors joined with the Topeka Bar Association to endow a Minorities in
Legal Education scholarship. However, there was no formal, on-going program to increase the admission of minorities[1208] until an Ad Hoc Committee
on Minority and Disadvantaged Students was appointed in the fall of 1972.

By the late 1970s, however, Washburn Law School had expanded active
recruitment of minority students, far earlier than many other law schools.

1206. Jeffrey chose Washburn over three other schools to which she was admitted, KU, Washington University in St. Louis, and Case Western Reserve in Cleveland. She later wrote that her "race was not an issue for me in law school as it relates
to the administration, the professors, or the other students." Linda P. Jeffrey, *Once
upon a Time*, 42 WASHBURN L.J. 941, 943 (2004).

1207. *City Attorney Linda Jeffrey*, TOPEKA CAP. J., June 21, 2001.

1208. *WU law school students stress need for minority recruitment*, WASHBURN
REV., Apr. 19, 1972.

Washburn sent representatives to minority recruitment fairs sponsored by the Law Schools Admissions Service. Twice, in 1982 and 1983, Washburn hosted summer institutes for the Council on Legal Education Opportunity and in other years sent faculty members or student teaching assistants to participate in CLEO programs hosted by other schools. By 1989–90, Washburn had the highest percentage enrollment of minority students among the forty-four law schools in a twelve-state Midwest region. Washburn's success in diversifying its student body led the United States Department of Education to award Washburn Patricia Roberts Harris Fellowships, providing full-tuition scholarships for entering minority students, three times in four years between 1989 and 1992.

A Washburn chapter of the Black Law Students Association was formed as enrollments grew. Among the alumni invited to speak at annual spring banquets recognizing graduating seniors were Judge R.J. Reynolds '29, Delano Lewis '63, Barbara James '80, and Sherman Parks, Jr. '75, the latter on the evening BLSA honored his father, Judge Sherman Parks '55. Lewis later narrated a minority student recruitment video and created a scholarship for students with backgrounds and interest in the fields of corporate or telecommunications law.

Washburn followed the practice of many schools during most of the first half of the twentieth century of noting a student's race on the student's unofficial transcript. This practice facilitated the identification for this chapter of the school's earliest African-American students. Identifying the school's first students among other minority groups is not done as reliably, since that information does not appear to have been recorded on transcripts as systematically. The first Hispanic graduate likely was Rosendo Alonzo '36, who also received his undergraduate degree from Washburn. After graduation, he was employed by DuPont in Mexico City and later was President of Mexico's Junior Chamber of Commerce. Apparently, more than twenty years passed before Washburn had its next Hispanic graduates, Manuel Mendoza in January 1958 and Philip Leon in June 1958. Both later had children who earned law degrees at Washburn, Lisa Mendoza '84, Marcos Mendoza '89 and David Leon '91. The first Hispanic woman to become a Washburn lawyer appears to be Susan Carmona '79, now known as Susan Salsbury after marrying her classmate Doug Salsbury '79.

The La Raza Legal Alliance was formed as a new student organization in 1978. Its members solicited funds for a new scholarship named Si Se Puede. The organization later was renamed the Hispanic-American Law Students Association.

James Marquez '73 achieved distinction as United States Attorney for Kansas and as General Counsel for the United States Department of Transportation from 1983 to 1985. Joseph Bribiesca '77 was the first Hispanic graduate to become a state court District Judge, in Wichita. In 2007, Maritza Segarra '88 was the first Latina to be named District Judge in Kansas, in the Eighth Judicial District in Junction City, after serving as District Magistrate Judge there for nearly three years. Cheryl Rios Kingfisher '93 served as Municipal Judge in Topeka, then was appointed District Judge in 2008. Lillian Apodaca '85 was President of the National Hispanic Bar Association in 1998–99. David Flores '88, who was Washburn Student Bar Association President as a 3L, served as President of the Fort Worth Hispanic Bar Association.

There was a graduate of Asian-Pacific heritage as early as 1949, Meyer Ueoka. He returned home to practice in Hawaii, as did four other members of the Ueoka family who earned law degrees at Washburn. Shoko Sevart '73 was the school's first Asian-Pacific woman graduate, and first minority woman graduate generally, just a few years after arriving in the United States from Japan.[1209] Togiola T.A. Tulafono '75 returned to his native American Samoa where he became District Judge in 1978, Senator in 1980, Lieutenant Governor in 1996, and Governor in 2003 upon the death of the incumbent Governor. He subsequently was elected in 2004 and 2008 to four-year terms as Governor.

Recruitment of students from Korea received an unexpected boost in the late 1990s when a graduate, Ji-Su Kim '96, wrote the only Korean language guidebook to American law schools.[1210] While he wrote generally about legal education in the United States, the fact that Kim had chosen to attend Washburn prompted many readers to want to do the same. Kim completed a law degree from Korea's most highly regarded school before coming to Washburn, then returned to practice in Seoul. A chapter of the Asian Pacific American Law Student Association was started in 1993. Jae Lee '95 received the 1994 ABA Student Service Award, in part for her leadership in organizing the Washburn chapter.

Harold ("Doc") Doherty '33 may have been the school's first graduate who was part Native-American. Montie Deer '72, a member of the Muscogee Creek Nation, served as District Judge in Wichita from 1983 until 1994, and became Chair of the Federal Indian Gaming Commission in November 1998.[1211] He

1209. Elrod, *supra* note 1092, at 889.

1210. Email from Inho Hwang to Alex Glashausser (July 18, 2003).

1211. He spoke about the responsibilities of the Commission in a presentation

later taught at the University of Tulsa College of Law. Susette Schwartz '85 appears to have been the first Native-American woman to graduate, although she did not know of her Osage Indian heritage until after she graduated.[1212] It was not until 1995 that there was a sufficient critical mass to prompt formation of a Native-American Law Students Association chapter. Its members immediately became active in the national organization and 1L Stan Wolfe was elected national President for 1997–98.

There is no record of accommodations made during the Law School's early years for students with disabilities. The first blind graduate likely was John Vanlandingham '44. Blind since the age of six, he used Braille, his own system of shorthand, and special devices. His wife read assignments to him and other college students assisted as readers in some of his courses.[1213] He "made excellent grades" and served as President of the Student Bar Association. His ambition was "to prove that a blind man can do anything any other person can do."[1214] Upon graduation, he was elected Kingman County Attorney. Another blind student, Reese Robrhan '45, frequently studied with Vanlandingham. He practiced in Topeka. They were followed by Kay Arvin '51, who practiced in Wichita.

in Robinson Courtroom in April 2001. *Montie Deer Talks About Indian Gaming*, 39 THE CIRCUIT RIDER 15 (Spring 2001).

1212. Elrod, *supra* note 1092, at 894.

1213. *Blind Graduate of Law at Washburn Sets Out on Career*, undated 1944 newspaper article, glued to the back of Vanlandingham's transcript.

1214. *Id.*

12

A TRADITION OF PUBLIC SERVICE

From the Law School's first days, Washburn graduates established a tradition of public service. A list compiled in 1917 by Thomas Amory Lee identified thirty-seven of the school's sixty-nine initial graduates, from the ten graduating classes from 1906 through 1915, who had held government positions, at every level from city and county to state and federal.[1215] That tradition continued throughout the years. In the summer of 1926, when the Law School had fewer than 260 living alums, twenty-one of them won primary elections in Kansas.[1216] Six years later, forty-three graduates won primary elections. When the Law School hosted a dinner for its graduates serving in the 1955 Kansas Legislature, ten of the forty members of the Senate attended, along with fifteen of the 125 members of the House of Representatives.[1217] Washburn law graduates comprised 15% of the legislature. The members of the 1997 graduating class entered government or public interest positions, other than judicial clerkships, at the highest percentage rate, 35.4%, of any law school in the nation that year.

The number of Washburn graduates who have excelled in public service as members of a legislature, trial judges, and administrative law judges, and in other important positions is too large to list them all by name. However, Washburn lawyers have achieved distinction at the highest levels of all three branches of government, and many of them clearly would have been identified during their law school days as future leaders.

1215. WASHBURN COLL. SCH. OF LAW BULLETIN 14–17 (Mar. 1917).

1216. *Laws Enter Politics*, WASHBURN REV., Sept. 15, 1926, at 1.

1217. *Faculty Entertains Former Law Grads*, WASHBURN REV., Feb. 4, 1955, at 3.

THE LEGISLATIVE BRANCH

A Washburn graduate was a member of Congress in all except two terms between 1919 and 2011. In all, eleven Washburn-trained lawyers, including nine
graduates, have served in Congress, seven Republicans and four Democrats.
The best known, of course, is Senator Robert J. Dole '52, who represented
Kansas for four terms in the House of Representatives and for twenty-eight
years in the United States Senate. He was his party's leader in the Senate for
twelve years, twice serving as Majority Leader. He was the Republican Party's
nominee for President in 1996, after having been its nominee for Vice-President
in 1976 with Gerald R. Ford. His public life is well documented but his time
at Washburn is less so.[1218] Dole completed his law degree in two and one-half
years and combined his law hours with undergraduate hours he earned at the
University of Kansas and the University of Arizona to receive an A.B. degree
from Washburn, even though he never enrolled in undergraduate hours at
Washburn. When he started classes in Boswell Hall in 1949, he still was recovering from the wounds he suffered from German gunfire in northern Italy
in 1945. His right hand was shattered and he was teaching himself to write
left-handed, with great difficulty, due to a weakened left arm. Because of his
limited ability to take notes, he focused on listening. He carried a bulky thirty-
pound device to class, supplied by the Veterans Administration and called a
Sound Scriber, that made plastic records of the lectures. He took them home
and replayed them, slowly and painfully creating class notes but in the process
learning the material well. "I'd pace back and forth in our apartment with a
book or notes in my hand, committing as much of the lecture material as
possible to memory, including the various legal cases, citations, and rulings.
I'd quote the material aloud until I could dictate it back."[1219] As the first exam
approached, in Torts, Dole knew he physically was unable to write for the four
hours typically required for a law school exam. He asked Professor Jim Ahrens
if he could dictate the exam to a secretary. It was long before the passage of
the Americans With Disabilities Act and there was no secretarial staff other
than Christine Johnson. Ahrens suggested, "Why don't you outline the high

1218. Tom Brokaw's book THE GREATEST GENERATION erroneously reported
Dole was a graduate of the law school at the University of Arizona. He only took
undergraduate classes there while being treated for his wartime injuries.
1219. BOB DOLE, ONE SOLDIER'S STORY 262 (2005).

points of your answer to each question—not too long or detailed but just give a sense of the points you would cover and the ideas you would discuss." Dole wrote only five or six pages, but received a grade of A. When another student complained the he had filled two blue books but had received a much lower grade, Ahrens let him read Dole's paper as a model of brevity and precision.[1220] Most professors allowed Dole to take oral exams or to dictate answers to his wife Phyllis who "would write them on the test papers."[1221]

Dole graduated *magna cum laude* and was one of the three Associate Editors of the Law Review Board. His comment, urging adoption of a statute to abolish common law marriage in Kansas, was published in the *Journal of the Bar Association of Kansas*.[1222] Fifty years passed before the legislature passed such a statute, and then it restricted common law marriage only by those under eighteen years of age.

Dole sought election as Treasurer of the Student Bar Association and won. The Law Librarian, recent graduate Elizabeth Bowers '48, befriended Dole during his first year, and he credits her as the most influential person in persuading him to consider politics.[1223] She suggested he run for the state legislature from his home town, Russell. He did and won the 1950 general election. Dole served in the House of Representatives during his final year of law school.

Following graduation, he served four terms as Russell County Attorney and maintained a part-time civil practice before his election to Congress in 1960. He was counsel of record in seven cases before the Kansas Supreme Court, the most famous of which was an original proceeding in quo warranto in which he persuaded the Court to declare the oil and gas severance tax law unconstitutional because the subject of the act was not clearly expressed in the title.[1224]

Dole maintained close ties with the Law School throughout his distinguished career, returning frequently to speak at commencements, most recently in 1998, and at other events or programs, such as one on the Americans With Disabilities Act. He endowed the Robert J. Dole Scholarship for Students with Disabilities and later a Professorship in the Center for Law and Government.

1220. David Maraniss, *Exploring How Dole Thinks; Clues Lie in His Kansas Roots; War Wound and Senate Service*, WASH. POST, A01 (Aug. 4, 1996).

1221. Dole, *supra* note 1219.

1222. Robert J. Dole, *Common Law Marriage*, 20 J. KAN. B. ASS'N 217 (1951).

1223. Dole, *supra* note 1219, at 263–65.

1224. *State ex rel. Dole v. Kirchner*, 182 Kan. 622, 322 P.2d 759 (1958).

He twice received honorary degrees from Washburn, an Honorary Doctor of Laws degree during the dedication of the new law building in 1969 and an Honorary Doctor of Civil Laws degree in 1985. On April 9, 1995, the night before he announced his successful campaign for the Republican Party nomination for President, Dole returned to campus as guest of honor at a reception on the lower floor of the law building.

After Dole, the next longest serving Washburn law graduate in Congress was Clifford R. Hope '17, who was elected fifteen times to the House of Representatives and served for thirty years between 1927 and 1957, initially representing the Seventh Congressional District and later the Fifth District, as reapportionment reduced the number of Kansas representatives. A Republican, he was chair of the House Committee on Agriculture for four years. Richard Nixon confirmed he would have named Hope as Secretary of Agriculture if he had won the presidency in 1960.[1225] While in law school, Hope was a champion debater, representing Washburn in several intercollegiate debates, and was president of his class. After graduation and service in World War I, he practiced law in Garden City, was elected to the Kansas House of Representatives in 1920 and served three terms there before election to Congress. He was elected Speaker of the Kansas House during his third term, at age 31.[1226]

Homer Hoch '09 was the first Washburn graduate elected to Congress, in 1918. He was a Republican, representing the Fourth Congressional District, and served seven terms. He began law school at George Washington but returned to Kansas to serve in 1907 and 1908 as private secretary to his father, Governor Edward W. Hoch, before completing his legal studies at Washburn. Hoch practiced law in Marion and edited the *Marion Record* until his election to Congress. After he was defeated for re-election in 1932, he served the following six years as a member of the Kansas Corporation Commission, many as chair, before his election to the Supreme Court in 1938. He served until his death in 1949.[1227]

A third Washburn-trained lawyer joined Hope and Hoch in Congress in 1931, Harold C. McGugin, a Republican from Coffeyville. He attended the law

1225. Bob Beatty, *From Washburn to Washington*, WASHBURN ALUMNUS 18 (Fall 2001).

1226. CLIFFORD R. HOPE, JR., QUIET COURAGE: KANSAS CONGRESSMAN CLIFFORD R. HOPE (1997).

1227. In Memoriam, 169 Kan. v (1949).

111. Hon. Homer Hoch, 1909

school for more than two years between 1912 and 1915 but also had read law for a sufficient additional period that he was permitted to take the bar exam in January 1915 without completing his law degree. He took a post-graduate course at one of the Inns of Court in London on his way home from World War I. He served one term in the Kansas House of Representatives before winning two terms in Congress. He became a vigorous opponent of the New Deal. "Various authors describe his oratory whilst in Congress as 'fiery,' 'violent,' and ' flamboyant,' while Congresswoman Kathryn O'Loughlin nicknamed McGugin the 'fire eater.'"[1228] He unsuccessfully sought re-election to Congress twice more. He contracted an incurable disease while serving in World War II and died shortly after the end of the war.

Denver D. Hargis '48, also from Coffeyville, was the first Washburn graduate to represent the Democratic Party in Congress, winning election in 1958 when Democrats were unusually successful statewide. He had been Mayor for five years while practicing law and had sought election to Congress unsuccessfully

---

1228. Beatty, *supra* note 1225.

in 1956. Hargis was defeated for re-election but remained in Washington for six years as a consultant to the Departments of Defense and Commerce during the Kennedy and Johnson administrations.

Bob Dole '52 and Garner E. Shriver '40 both arrived in Congress in 1961, the year Hargis left it. Like Dole, Shriver was selected for the Law Review Board and published an article while he was a student.[1229] He was a member of the Kansas legislature for fourteen years before serving fourteen years in Congress. He remained in Washington for six years as counsel to the Senate Veterans' Affairs Committee before returning to Wichita to practice law.

The three Washburn graduates most recently elected to Congress all have been Democrats. Dr. Bill Roy '70 practiced medicine in Topeka while attending law classes with his wife, Jane Roy '70. He defeated an incumbent to win the first of two terms in Congress in the fall elections following his graduation. While there, Roy was a principal architect of federal H.M.O. legislation. In 1974, he unsuccessfully challenged Bob Dole for election to the United States Senate in one of the most hotly contested races in Kansas history, losing by fewer than 14,000 votes. Roy later taught the course in Health Care Law at the Law School. James C. Slattery '74 was a member of the Kansas House of Representatives his last two years of law school and served a total of three terms. He then served six terms in Congress, beginning in 1983, before becoming his party's nominee for Governor of Kansas in 1994. He then entered private practice in Washington with the politically influential firm of Wiley, Rein & Fielding. Slattery has been a frequent speaker at the Law School and has endowed a law scholarship. Washburn's most recent member of Congress, Dennis Moore '70, was elected in 1998 and reelected five time to represent the Third Congressional District. The district includes heavily Republican Johnson County, where, despite being a Democrat, Moore was elected three times as District Attorney.

Two other House members started their law studies at Washburn. Albert M. Cole completed his first year at Washburn in 1922–23 before receiving his degree from the University of Chicago in 1925. He served four terms in the House as a Republican between 1945 and 1953. Joe Skubitz started law school in the summer of 1938 but joined the staff of Kansas Senator Clyde Reed and did

---

1229. Garner E. Shriver, *Recission of a Third Party Beneficiary Contract Before the Beneficiary's Acceptance of the Contract*, 8 J. KAN. B. ASS'N 253 (1939).

not complete his degree until 1944, at George Washington. Also a Republican, he served eight terms in the House between 1963 and 1978.

Three Washburn graduates in addition to Clifford Hope have served as Speaker of the Kansas House of Representatives. A member of the first graduating class, William Vernon '06 of Larned, was Speaker for the 1933 and 1934 sessions, Dale M. Bryant '26 of Wichita was Speaker for 1949–50, and Clyde Hill '40 of Yates Center was Speaker for 1965–66.

THE EXECUTIVE BRANCH

No Washburn graduate has been Governor of Kansas, although several, including Democrats Jim Slattery '70 and Dale Saffels '49 and Republicans Warren Shaw '31 and Kent Frizzell '55, have been the nominees of their parties. One graduate, Jack Campbell '40, was Governor of New Mexico, serving from 1963 to 1967. Togiola T.A. Tulafono '75 has been Governor of American Samoa since 2003, when after more than six years as Lieutenant Governor he succeeded a governor who died. He has been elected twice to four-year terms. Paul V. Dugan '64 served as Kansas Lieutenant Governor from 1979 to 1983. Republican Glenn Cogswell '47 in 1958 and Democrat Jack Glaves '50 in 1960 were their parties' nominees for that office.

Six graduates have been Attorney General of Kansas. They were John Dawson '06 from 1911 to 1915, William A. Smith '14 from 1927 to 1930, Harold Fatzer '33 from 1949 to 1956, Kent Frizzell '55 from 1969 to 1971, Robert Stephan '57 from 1979 to 1995, and Paul Morrison '80 from 2007 to 2008. Tom Van Sickle '66 was State Treasurer in Kansas from 1973 to 1975.

United States Attorneys for Kansas have included George Templar '27, Robert J. Roth '55, James Buchele '66, James J. Marquez '73, E. Edward Johnson '51, Benjamin L. Burgess '72, Randall K. Rathbun '78, Jackie Williams '71, and Eric Melgren '85. Lanny Welch '87 served for two years as Interim United States Attorney after Melgren's appointment as District Judge.

Presidential appointees in the executive branch include: Richard B. McEntire '34, who was appointed by President Truman as a Republican member of the five-member Securities and Exchange Commission from 1946 until 1953 and became its Vice Chairman in 1950 and later Acting Chairman; Samuel Jackson '54, appointed by President Johnson in 1965 as one of the original members to the United States Equal Opportunity Commission and then by President Nixon in 1969 as Assistant Secretary of Housing and Urban Development; Kent Frizzell '55, appointed Under Secretary of the Department of Interior and as Acting Secretary in 1975 by President Ford; Robert J. (Jack) Corber '50, appointed as a Commissioner of the Interstate Commerce Commission for 1975–76, also by President Ford; and Delano E. Lewis '63, appointed by President Clinton in 1999 to be U.S. Ambassador to the Republic of South Africa. Other federal department heads include: M. Cynthia Douglass '76, Deputy Assistant Secretary of Labor for the Occupational Safety and Health Administration from 1989 until 1992; Edward B. Chapman, Jr. '49, Commissioner of the Federal Housing Administration under President Eisenhower; Bradley J. Buckles '74, Director of the Bureau of Alcohol, Tobacco, and Firearms from 1999 until 2003; James J. Marquez '73, General Counsel for the Department of Transportation; and William Olmstead '74, Executive Director of the Administrative Conference of the United States from 1988 to 1994.

APPELLATE JUDGES

Twenty graduates of Washburn Law School have been Justices of the Kansas Supreme Court, a larger number than from any other law school. Remarkably, the first three graduates of a Kansas law school to serve on the Court all were graduates of Washburn, even though it opened twenty-five years later than KU's law school. The earlier Justices either read law in an office or graduated from out-of-state law schools.[1230] The first two Washburn graduates to serve on the Court, John Dawson '06 and William A. Smith '14, became Chief Justice. Dawson and Edward Sloan '06, the third Washburn graduate to sit on the Court, were two of the seventeen members of Washburn's first graduating class. Their remarkable careers are described in Chapter One. Dawson was elected to the Court in 1915 and served for thirty years. He was Chief Justice from 1937 until 1945. Sloan, appointed to fill an unexpired term, served twenty-one months between 1931 and 1933.

William A. Smith '14, the school's second Justice, served for twenty-six years, beginning in 1930, and was Chief Justice for ten months in 1956. Like Dawson, he was Attorney General for two terms before his election to the Court. He

---

1230. As noted in Chapter 1 at note 37, Justice Judson S. West, who became a Justice in 1911, attended classes at the University of Kansas law school. However, he did not graduate.

gained notoriety in 1926 when he was the only one of seven candidates for Attorney General who vowed to fight to exclude the Ku Klux Klan from Kansas, a position thought to have cost William Allen White election as Governor two years earlier. During his four years as Attorney General, Smith waged another high-profile battle, persuading the Kansas Board of Medical Examiners to revoke the license of John R. Brinkley, the infamous goat gland doctor from Milford. Smith was a legendary figure in Republican politics, even while on the Court.[1231] Like Justices Dawson and Sloan, he was a frequent participant in Law School events and was a part-time Lecturer on Public Utilities for two years shortly after joining the Court. Smith was the first of three generations of Washburn lawyers. Two sons and two grandchildren graduated from the Law School. One son, Don C. Smith '50, became an activist Democrat and was District Judge and later State Representative in Dodge City.

FIVE CHIEF JUSTICES

In all, five Washburn graduates have served as Chief Justice. Harold R. Fatzer '33, whose twin brother was his classmate, was appointed to the Court in 1956 and served for more than twenty-five years, including the last six as Chief Justice. Like Dawson and Smith, Fatzer was Attorney General before joining the Court. As Chief Justice, he led a successful effort to amend the Judicial Article of the Kansas Constitution and oversaw the resulting unification of the District Court and reinstitution of the Court of Appeals. He also pushed for construction of the Kansas Judicial Center. Fatzer was instrumental in raising the funds needed to rebuild his alma mater after the tornado destroyed Carnegie Hall. Washburn awarded Fatzer the honorary degree Doctor of Laws in 1971.

Richard Holmes '53 and Kay McFarland '64 were appointed to the Court within two days of one another in September 1977. Holmes had been in private practice in Wichita. McFarland had been elected in 1970 as Probate Judge and then in 1972 as District Judge in Shawnee County. Holmes became Chief Justice in 1990 and served five years until McFarland succeeded him whe he retired in 1995. She served as Chief Justice until 2009. Both Holmes and McFarland received the honorary degree Doctor of Laws from Washburn, in 1991 and 2009,

---

1231. Brian J. Moline, *Bill Smith, The Jurist as Politician*, 57 J. KAN. B. ASS'N 31 (Nov./Dec. 1988); *see also* Encomium, 188 Kan. v at vii (1961).

respectively. McFarland served one term on the Law School Association Board of Governors and later was the Law School's Washburn Alumni Fellow for 2005. She was a member of the initial class of recipients of the Distinguished Alumni Recognition Award in 2007.

OTHER EARLY WASHBURN JUSTICES

Homer Hoch '09 was the fourth Washburn graduate to sit on the Court, serving for ten years after his fourteen years as a member of Congress. He is the last Kansan to serve both in Congress and on the Kansas Supreme Court.

Lloyd M. Kagey '27 holds the distinction of having served the shortest term in the Kansas Supreme Court's history, just thirty-five days. His judicial "fifteen minutes of fame" came after Ed Arn resigned from the Court in March 1950 to seek the Republican nomination for Governor, and William J. Wertz was appointed to replace him. Wertz filed for election to the position for the full term that would begin January 8, 1951. However, state law at the time provided that appointments to fill vacancies in state offices were effective only until the next general election and required a separate election to fill the vacated seat from December until the start of the new term. For unexplained reasons, neither Wertz nor his opponent for the full term filed as candidates for that separate election. Kagey did, and defeated M.T. Bartlow of Topeka. It was not the first time Kagey became a judge this way. In early 1948, Wertz had been appointed to fill a vacancy as District Judge in Sedgwick County. That year, too, Wertz filed for election to a full term but not for the separate election for the short term after the general election. Kagey did, and won.[1232] Kagey contracted polio in 1940, was paralyzed from the waist down, and used a wheelchair as Assistant County Attorney in Sedgwick County from 1941 to 1947. When Kagey won election to the Supreme Court, Wertz vacated his chambers and Kagey heard the December docket of cases with the Court. A temporary ramp was installed so he could ascend the bench. He authored five opinions.

The separate election required to fill the final days of an unexpired term when a vacancy was filled by appointment had been a trap for the unwary before. When Justice Sloan decided not to seek election in 1932 to a full term after his appointment in 1931 to fill a vacancy, Walter Thiele filed as a candidate

---

1232. TOPEKA DAILY CAP., Nov. 29, 1950.

for the new term commencing in January 1933 but "through inadvertence" neither Thiele nor his opponent nor anyone else filed as a candidate for the brief term between the election and the start of the new term. The KBA president described the situation:

> This made it possible for almost anyone, by a concerted effort, to have his friends write his name in the blank space left for that purpose, a sufficient number of times to insure his election. Several persons had started a campaign to that end and the leading candidates were entirely unfit to hold such an office even for a brief period of weeks. The election of one of them would have been a disgrace to the bench and bar of the state.[1233]

Although the Bar Association had "never before taken part in a political contest," it regarded the situation "as so serious that the Association could not afford to ignore it." Through the efforts of lawyers throughout the state, "a catastrophe in Kansas politics [was] averted."[1234] Justice Sloan was elected for the unexpired term on a write-in vote "by an overwhelming majority."

The story of Clair Robb '33 also is a special one. He started his law studies at KU but was one of a number of KU students who transferred to Washburn in the early 1930s. Robb resided in Dean Allen's home in 1937 when Allen became a member of the Supreme Court. Robb "confidently remarked that someday he would take the Dean's place on the bench. Justice Allen promised that if he did fulfill his ambition, he could have his robe."[1235] A colleague observed that "Clair's destiny in the field of law was influenced to a large degree by one person," Dean Allen. "I know of no person that revered another such as Clair did Justice Allen." Robb moved to Wichita to practice law and became District Judge there. He was elected to the Supreme Court in 1954. At his swearing-in, he in fact wore the robe Dean Allen had worn, "thereby fulfilling the prophecy uttered nearly 20 years before."[1236] Robb served until his death in 1965.

When Robb died, Justice Fatzer was Washburn's only graduate on the Court. Robb's replacement, Robert H. Kaul, at least had a Washburn connection even though he was not a graduate. He completed one and one-half years of law studies at Washburn before transferring to KU.

1233. Gilbert H. Frith, *Comments of the President*, 1 J. KAN. B. ASS'N 234, 235 (1933).
1234. *Id.*
1235. *In Memoriam*, 197 Kan. xxiii at xxv–xxvi (1966).
1236. *Id.*

SIX OF SEVEN JUSTICES

Fourteen of the twenty-one Justices appointed to the Court between 1966 and 2010 were Washburn graduates. Alex M. Fromme '39, a past President of the Kansas Bar Association who had practiced law in Hoxie, served on the Court between 1966 and 1982. Perry L. Owsley '38 from Pittsburg sat with him between 1971 and 1978. Both taught the course Washburn then called Legal Ethics during their years on the Court. Fromme's first "opinion" had been a case comment published in the *Journal of the Kansas Bar Association* when he was a member of the Law Review Board.[1237] Owsley was the school's Law Librarian during his second year, a part-time position filled in those years by a student.

Justices Holmes and McFarland were appointed in 1977, and then Harold Herd '42 joined the Court in 1979. He had been a State Representative and State Senator from Coldwater. The next Washburn appointees were Tyler C. Lockett '62, who previously was District Judge in Wichita, and Donald Allegrucci '63, who was a member of the legislature while practicing law in Pittsburg. Bob L. Abbott '60, a past President of the Washburn Law School Association, was elevated from the position of Chief Judge of the Court of Appeals in August 1990. For more than two years thereafter, until Harold Herd's retirement in January 1993, six of the seven Justices were Washburn graduates. Herd was forced to retire because of a statute preventing Justices from seeking retention after age seventy. The still-vigorous Herd then spent eight years as Distinguished Jurist in Residence at the Law School, teaching Constitutional History and State Constitutional Law.

Six of the seven most recently appointed Justices are Washburn graduates. In January 2003, Marla J. Luckert '80 and Robert L. Gernon '69 joined Justices McFarland, Allegrucci, and Abbott. Luckert was the second woman elected President of the Kansas Bar Association and, when appointed, was a District Judge in Shawnee County, serving as Chief Judge. Gernon was elevated from the Kansas Court of Appeals, to which he had been appointed in 1988 after nine years as District Judge in Brown County, where he also was Administrative Judge. Following Gernon's untimely death in 2005, Eric Rosen '84 became Washburn's next appointee to the court. He was a highly-regarded District Judge in Shawnee County. In January 2007, Lee A. Johnson '80 was elevated from the Court of

---

1237. Alex M. Fromme, *Eminent Domain—Appeal from Condemnation Award— Bond-Sufficiency*, 7 J. KAN. B. ASS'N 274 (1939).

Appeals to the Supreme Court. His selection was hailed as an example of the virtue of merit selection. A Republican Governor, Bill Graves, appointed him to the Court of Appeals in 2001 and a Democrat Governor, Kathleen Sebelius, appointed him to the Supreme Court. Luckert and Johnson are the first classmates from Washburn to serve together on the court since Justices Dawson and Sloan. In 2009, Governor Sebelius named W. Daniel Biles '78 to the Court. He practiced law with Gates, Biles, Shields & Ryan in Overland Park, and was counsel to the Kansas Board of Education for many years. Finally, in 2010, Governor Parkinson appointed Nancy Moritz '85 as a Justice. Moritz is believed to be the first former Research Attorney for the appellate courts to be appointed as an appellate judge. She worked after graduation for Justice Herd and then clerked for United States District Judge Pat Kelly '53. Moritz had served since 2004 on the Court of Appeals, following years in private practice in Kansas City with Spencer, Fane, Britt & Browne and as Assistant United States Attorney.

THE COURT'S COMMISSIONERS

The non-voting position of Commissioner of the Supreme Court was created in 1963, to help the Court dispose of a rising number of appeals. The first Commissioner was Earl Hatcher '23, who served for eight years. Hatcher was the long-time Supreme Court Reporter and compiled the extraordinary digest of Kansas decisions, *Hatcher's Kansas Digest*. He taught as Lecturer at the Law School beginning the year following his graduation and chaired the committee raising funds for the Law School's new building after the tornado. He received the Law School Association's Distinguished Service Award in 1968 and the honorary degree, Doctor of Laws, at the building dedication in 1969. In 1965, Hatcher was joined by a second Commissioner, D. Jerome Harmon '35. Harmon had served almost 20 years as District Judge in Columbus and taught at the Law School for seven years after joining the Court. He was awarded the honorary degree LL.D. in 1990.

THE KANSAS COURT OF APPEALS

When the Kansas Court of Appeals was created in 1977, four of the seven initial judges were Washburn graduates. Harmon, as the senior Commissioner, became Chief Judge. He was joined by Washburn graduates Bob L. Abbott

'60, a practitioner from Junction City, Sherman A. Parks '55 of Topeka, the first black appellate judge in Kansas and Lecturer for many years at the Law School on Criminal Law, and Corwin A. Spencer '39, who practiced in Oakley with two sons who were Washburn graduates.

In addition to Harmon and Abbott, two other Washburn graduates have been Chief Judge of the Court of Appeals. J. Patrick Brazil '62 was District Judge in Eureka before being named to the Court in 1985 and became Chief Judge in 1995. Judge Brazil served on the Law School's alumni Board of Governors. Gary L. Rulon '72, practiced law in Emporia before his appointment in 1988 and served as Chief Judge from 2001 until 2011. Other Washburn members of the Court have been: Robert Gernon '69; Christel Marquardt '74, the third woman to sit on the Court; David S. Knudson '66, who formerly was a District Judge in Salina; Lee A. Johnson '80, who practiced in Caldwell; Thomas E. Malone '79, who was District Judge in Sedgwick County; Stephen D. Hill '75, who was Chief Judge of the Sixth Judicial District in Paola; Nancy Moritz Caplinger '85; and most recently David E. Bruns '84, who had been a District Judge in Topeka. The first docket of cases both Marquardt and Caplinger heard was with a panel of the Court sitting in Robinson Courtroom.

OTHER STATES

Washburn graduates have been appellate judges in other states as well. Gordon Sloan '35, son of Justice Edward R. Sloan '06, was Justice of the Oregon Supreme Court from 1958 to 1970. Zerne Haning '62 was Judge of California's Court of Appeals for the First Appellate District in San Francisco from 1983 until 2000.

FEDERAL JUDGES

Six Washburn graduates have been United States District Judges for the District of Kansas. Delmas C. Hill '29 was the first, appointed by President Truman in October 1949. He was Chief Judge from 1957 until 1961, when he became the only graduate to sit on the United States Court of Appeals, appointed by President Kennedy. Before becoming a judge, Hill practiced law in Wamego, was Pottawatomie County Attorney for two terms, was an Assistant United States Attorney, and then was general counsel of the Kansas State Tax Commission. He served as a Captain in the Army during World War II and was a member of the prosecution staff in 1945 during the trial of General Yamashita in the Philippines. In recognition of Judge Hill's loyal support of the Law School, Washburn awarded him the honorary degree Doctor of Laws in 1958. The Kansas Room in the law building is named in his honor. He was instrumental in the successful campaign to rebuild the school following the 1966 tornado and endowed one of the school's first significant scholarships.

George Templar '27 was Washburn's next appointee as District Judge. He was selected by President Kennedy in 1962, even though he was a member of the opposite political party. He had served sixteen years in the Kansas Legislature, including two terms in the Kansas Senate, while practicing law in Arkansas City. Templar worked as a motorcycle policeman for the City of Topeka while earning his LL.B. *cum laude* and served as President of the Student Bar Association. Like Judge Hill, he later was awarded an honorary Doctor of Laws degree.

Dale E. Saffels '49 was appointed District Judge in 1979 by President Carter. He received his J.D. *cum laude*, was a member of the Law Review Board, and was Vice President of the Student Bar Association. He practiced law in Garden City, was twice elected County Attorney, then served eight years in the Kansas House of Representatives, the last two as Minority Leader. Following an unsuccessful campaign as the Democrat nominee for Governor in 1962, he served eight years as a member of the Kansas Corporation Commission, the last seven as its Chair.

Patrick F. Kelly '53 was a highly respected trial lawyer before his appointment by President Carter in 1980. He served as Chief Judge from 1992 until 1995. He had practiced with three different firms in Wichita before opening his own practice. Kelly was President of the Kansas Trial Lawyers Association in 1967. He was selected to join the American College of Trial Lawyers, the International Academy of Trial Lawyers, the International Society of Barristers, and the American Board of Trial Advocates. Kelly received the Distinguished Service Award from the Law School Association in 1991.

These four judges share an unusual characteristic. Although each had been active and had success in politics, each lost campaigns for the last, and highest, elective office he sought, as member of Congress in the case of Delmas Hill and Patrick Kelly, and as Governor of Kansas in the case of Democrat nominee Dale Saffels and Republican primary election candidate George Templar.

Sam A. Crow '52 was elevated by President Reagan in 1981 from the position of United States Magistrate Judge to District Judge. Crow previously practiced in Topeka. Judge Crow has been especially active with the Law School. In 1992, he took the lead in organizing the third American Inn of Court in Kansas, now named the Sam A. Crow Inn, in Topeka. He personally has underwritten membership costs for twelve to fourteen Washburn law students to be Pupils each year, giving them the opportunity to interact with and learn from leading trial lawyers and judges in the community. The Law School Association awarded Crow its Distinguished Service Award in 2000.

The next Washburn graduate to join the federal bench was J. Thomas Marten '76 in 1996, appointed by President Bill Clinton. His great uncle, Judge Delmas Hill, was influential in Marten's selection to be Law Clerk for United States Supreme Court Justice-Retired Tom C. Clark, who maintained an active schedule hearing appeals with Circuit Courts throughout the country. Marten thereafter was a lawyer for the Kutak Rock law firm in Omaha before becoming a partner in a small firm in McPherson. Marten is the only graduate appointed District Judge in Kansas who had not previously been an activist in party politics. Judge Marten, like Judge Crow before him, conducted a civil jury trial in Robinson Courtroom so that students could observe a federal trial first hand.

Washburn's most recent addition to the District Court is Eric Melgren '85, confirmed by the Senate in the waning days of the 2008 session. He practiced with Foulston Siefkin LLP in Wichita before becoming United States Attorney for Kansas in 2002. Melgren had been active politically and his friend Senator Sam Brownback championed his nomination.

Two Washburn graduates have been Chief Judges of United States District Courts elsewhere. John Conway '63 was appointed District Judge in New Mexico by President Ronald Reagan in 1986 and served as Chief Judge before taking senior status in 2001. Joseph W. Morris '47 was Chief Judge for the Eastern District of Oklahoma from 1974 until 1978. He was appointed to the Court while serving as Dean of the University of Tulsa College of Law. His varied legal career is highlighted in chapter 13. In addition, Leland C. Nielsen served as District Judge in the Southern District of California from 1971 until his death in 1999. He did not receive his degree from Washburn but completed his first two years at the Law School before enlisting to fight in World War II. He returned to law school after the war, receiving his degree in 1946 from the University of Southern California. He was a member of the Judicial Conference Advisory Committee of the Federal Rules of Criminal Procedure for twenty years, including five as chair.

Washburn graduates who have been United States Bankruptcy Judges include: Polly Wilhardt (Higdon) '75 in Oregon from 1983 to 1999; John T. Flannagan '64 in Kansas from 1989 to 2004; Robert Berger '86, who was appointed to replace Flannagan; Dennis Dow '78 in the Western District of Missouri since 2003; and Paul L. Kilburg '74 in the Northern District of Iowa since 1993. Both Kilburg and Wilhardt served as Chief Judge. Full-time United States Magistrate Judges, in addition to Sam Crow, include John Wooley '56, John Thomas Reid '58, and Kenneth Gale '80, all in Wichita. In addition, Albert B. Fletcher '51 served from 1975 until 1985 on the United States Court of Military Appeals and was Chief Judge from 1975 until 1980. James Van Orsdol '73 was Chief Judge of the U.S. Army Court of Criminal Appeals.

13

WASHBURN GRADUATES IN ACADEMIA

Not only have many Washburn Law School graduates taught at Washburn, many have distinguished themselves as teachers at other law schools from coast to coast and also abroad. Washburn graduates have been full-time faculty members at thirty-one United States law schools, including some of the nation's most highly regarded institutions, and at six foreign schools.

Three graduates have been deans of other U.S. law schools, including one who also was a dean in Australia. Roy Lockenour '17, was the first Law School graduate to teach elsewhere. Lockenour came to Washburn from Utah and completed a bachelor's degree in 1915 at the end of his first year of law studies. He claimed in a playful memoir, "I had never heard of Washburn College until I picked a catalog out of a waste basket in a saloon."[1238] After practicing law in Wyoming, where he was a part-time United States Commissioner, he went to Chicago and earned an LL.M. from Northwestern University in 1924, followed by an S.J.D. in 1926. In 1924, he became an Assistant Professor in the Department of Political Science of Oregon State College. In 1928, he began teaching as the second full-time faculty member at the Willamette University College of Law and in 1932 was named its Dean. Willamette at the time did not qualify for membership in the AALS or even ABA accreditation. There were public debates about the law school's future. Proposals ranged from closing the school altogether due to the University's financial difficulties, to retaining it as a night school with local, part-time faculty, or continuing it with a commitment to

---

1238. Roy M. Lockenour, *A Short Story of My Long Life* 21 (1972).

112. Hon. Joseph W. Morris '47

achieve accreditation within a reasonable time.[1239] Lockenour pursued the latter course during his seven-year deanship, adding the needed additional faculty and library books to achieve provisional ABA accreditation in 1938. Willamette was among the last law schools to shift from the textbook method to the casebook method. Lockenour, "the champion of the 'new' method, had begun to intro- duce it" when he joined the faculty but was roundly criticized for pushing the change, and later called it his "downfall."[1240] At the conclusion of his deanship, Lockenour returned to the faculty and continued to teach at Willamette until 1955. Willamette annually presents the Lockenour Award in his memory to the student writing the top paper in the Professional Responsibility class.

Joseph W. Morris '47 had been a member of the adjunct faculty at the University of Tulsa College of Law for 22 years when he was named Dean there in 1972. His career as a full-time academic lasted only two years, cut short by his appointment as Chief Judge of the United States District Court for the Eastern District of Oklahoma, but few graduates were better pre- pared for an academic career. A *magna cum laude* graduate, Morris had the distinction not merely of having his student article selected for publication in the *Journal of the Bar Association of Kansas* but also of having it published as the lead article. His discussion of the ability to transfer property to the

---

1239. ERIC D. SWENSON, THE FIRST HUNDRED YEARS: AN ILLUSTRATED HISTORY 24-7 (Willamette University College of Law 1987).

1240. *Id.* at 28.

grantor and another as joint tenants was prefaced by a rare editor's note that it "covers a very timely subject in Kansas and it is believed that it will prove of considerable value to the members of the Bar" and perhaps be the subject of proposed legislation.[1241] The year after his graduation, Morris earned an LL.M. from the University of Michigan, and he completed an S.J.D. there in 1955. His career has touched as many branches of the profession as that of any graduate. Before becoming Dean, he had been general counsel of a major oil and gas company, Amerada Hess Corporation. After four years as a federal judge, he became general counsel of Shell Oil Company. Later, he was senior partner of the Tulsa law firm of Gable & Gotwals and has been active in alternative dispute resolution both nationally and internationally as a member of the American Arbitration Association.

Eugene Clark '78 held the position of Dean of the Law School at the University of Canberra in Australia from 1995 until 1997 and again during academic year 2003–04. He was the University's Pro Vice-Chancellor, the equivalent of Provost, from 1998 to 2003. His tie to Australia grew from two years teaching high school there during a leave of absence after completing his first year of law school in 1973–74. After graduation, he practiced for three years with Foulston, Siefkin, Powers & Eberhardt in Wichita before joining the faculty of the University of Tasmania Law School, a position he held until becoming a Professor at Canberra in 1994. Clark was one of two law professors selected to receive the inaugural National Teaching Excellence Awards in Australia. He has been a prolific scholar, authoring numerous books in the fields of commercial law and e-commerce. Clark made several presentations at Washburn during visits back to the United States and twice was Visiting Professor at the University of New Mexico Law School. Following his years in Canberra, he was Executive Dean of the law faculty at Charles Darwin University in the Northern Territory before returning to the United States in January 2006 to become the founding Dean of the freestanding Charlotte School of Law in North Carolina.[1242] In just two years, he led it to provisional ABA accreditation. In January 2009, he became Interim Dean at the Phoenix School of Law before returning to Australia as Professor of Business Law at Griffith University.

1241. Joseph W. Morris, *May a Grantor Convey Property Directly to Himself and Another as Joint Tenants in Kansas*, 15 J. KAN. B. ASS'N 241 (1947).

1242. *Dean of new Charlotte Law School tours the state as school prepares to open in August*, N. C. LAWYERS WEEKLY (Feb.13, 2006).

Clark is not Washburn's only graduate to teach full-time at a foreign law school. Ching Pou Shih '93 is Associate Professor in the Department of Law at Fu Jen Catholic University in Taipei, Taiwan. Shih earned his first law degree at Fu Jen and completed an LL.M. at Southern Methodist University before enrolling in the J.D. program at Washburn. At the time, his father was one of fifteen members of the Committee of Grand Justices, the equivalent of the Supreme Court in the Republic of China for constitutional questions. Attending Washburn furthered Shih's goal to return to teach at his alma mater and to be a creative scholar by bringing a comparative law perspective to legal issues in his civil law country.[1243] More recently, Scott Curry-Sumner '97 joined the Faculty of Law at the University of Maastricht in the Netherlands.

Richard C. Donnelly '38 taught at two of America's most highly regarded law schools. He was Associate Professor of Law at the University of Virginia from 1948–50, then taught at Yale Law School from 1950 until his death in June 1966. Donnelly had been a Sterling Fellow at Yale during 1947–48 while pursuing the J.S.D. degree he was awarded in 1949. Donnelly was promoted to Professor of Law in 1953 and became the Simeon E. Baldwin Professor of Law there. He taught a wide range of courses but specialized in Criminal Law, Criminal Procedure, and Evidence, and taught Law and Psychiatry. He was the lead author of a casebook on Criminal Law published in 1962 which was funded by a grant from the National Institute of Mental Health. His colleagues recognized he was "one of the earliest members of the small but respected band of innovators who brought to the study of the criminal process the range of insights to be found in the disciplines of psychiatry, psychology and sociology. Through his teachings and writings he imparted to his students his deep concern for the welfare and rehabilitation of society's offenders."[1244] Donnelly's first full-time teaching appointment was at Washburn the year after World War II ended. Donnelly early demonstrated a flair for scholarly writing, publishing two student notes before the war and then an article during his year and one-half as an Instructor, all in the Kansas Bar Association's journal.[1245]

1243. *Taipei to Topeka*, 32 THE CIRCUIT RIDER 17 (Summer 1993).

1244. FALL 1966 YALE LAW REPORT 1.

1245. Richard C. Donnelly, *The Police Power and Esthetic Zoning*, 5 J. KAN. B. ASS'N 215 (1937); Richard C. Donnelly, *Contracts in the Conflict of Laws—Kansas Decisions*, 6 J. KAN. B. ASS'N 140 (1937); Richard C. Donnelly, *Permanent Alimony in Kansas*, 14 J. KAN. B. ASS'N 205 (1946).

Arthur B. White '39 entered law teaching late in his career. After he graduated, White received the Cook Legal Research Fellowship at the University of Michigan Law School. Rousseau A. Burch, a Michigan graduate who was Dean the greater part of White's time at the Law School, recommended him for the fellowship. White then joined the Internal Revenue Service, where he was an attorney for thirty-four years, ultimately as Special Assistant in the Office of Chief Counsel. He began teaching as Adjunct Professor at Georgetown in 1965, and that led to a year as Visiting Professor and Research Fellow at Southern Methodist University Law School in 1967. When he retired from the IRS in 1974, he became a full-time academic at the Marshall-Wythe School of Law at William and Mary. He continued to teach for four years after becoming Ball Professor Emeritus in 1980.

Two members of the class of 1940 entered law teaching many years after they graduated. Martha Stewart (Robinson) '40 was among the first thirty women in the nation to hold a tenured or tenure-track position. She began as Acting Associate Professor at Loyola University in Los Angeles in 1965 and became Professor of Law two years later. She taught full-time for nineteen years, and thereafter taught part-time as Professor-Emeritus. From 1947 through 1955, she had been Instructor at Southwestern Law School part-time while practicing law in Los Angeles and earning an LL.M. from Stanford in 1953. Her principal courses were Criminal Law, Equity, Community Property, Law and Literature, and Remedies. In 1974, she was Chair of the AALS Section on Remedies. Paul E. Wilson '40 joined the faculty of the University of Kansas School of Law in 1957 after six years as Assistant Attorney General and not long after arguing twice before the United States Supreme Court on behalf of the State in *Brown v. Board of Education*. He was named Kane Professor of Law in 1968 and taught full-time until 1982. His special expertise was in Criminal Law and Criminal Procedure. He had significant roles in revisions of the Kansas codes in those areas and was editor of the *American Criminal Law Quarterly* for six years. Wilson also taught Evidence. After becoming Professor Emeritus, he continued to teach seminars on such topics as Historic Preservation and Indian Law. One of his last major presentations was an address about the *Brown* case before the Supreme Court Historical Society, delivered in the same courtroom in which he had argued it.[1246]

1246. Paul E. Wilson, *A Time to Lose*, 24 J. S. CT. HISTORY 171 (1999).

Not surprisingly, the four Washburn graduates from the classes of 1938 through 1940 who entered law teaching all were excellent students, and all four were members of the school's Law Review Board.

Three graduates from the late 1940s taught full-time elsewhere. Allen Mitchem '47 was the first to do so. A *magna cum laude* graduate, he taught Partnerships at Washburn the summer following his graduation before enrolling in the LL.M. program at Columbia Law School. That led to a position on the faculty of the University of Denver College of Law. For seven years he taught such courses as Conflict of Laws, Insurance, Military Law, Civil Procedure, Water Rights, Partnerships, and Damages. He left full-time teaching to enter private practice in Denver but continued to teach part-time.

Mitchem's classmate, Willard Van Slyke '47, took the opposite path, initially teaching part-time at Washburn while he was in private practice in Topeka. He moved to Tucson in 1961 to join the law faculty of the University of Arizona. He continued teaching such courses as Agency and Partnership, Legal Profession, and Estates after becoming Professor Emeritus in 1980.

Melvin C. Poland '49 began his teaching career at Washburn in 1951. He spent 1968 as Visiting Professor of Law at the University of North Carolina-Chapel Hill and stayed there the following year before moving to Indiana University-Indianapolis for the remainder of his career. He spent one semester as Visiting Professor at McGeorge Law School in Sacramento in 1977. He was named Cleon H. Foust Professor of Law at Indiana in 1983, and became Professor Emeritus in 1984, but continued to teach. At Indiana, Poland joined his former Washburn colleague, William Harvey, who went to Indiana in 1968. Poland and Harvey both taught with Washburn graduate David E. Pierce '77 after 1984. Poland spent some retirement years in North Carolina before returning to Kansas to live in Clay Center.

Two graduates of the early 1950s, Charles C. McCarter '53 and Kent Frizzell '55, who were partners in the Wichita firm of McCarter, Frizzell & Wettig between 1963 and 1968, became colleagues for two years on the law faculty of the University of Tulsa nearly a decade later. Their career paths were quite different, however. McCarter, who was a member of Washburn's team that tied for third in the nation in the National Moot Court Competition in 1952 and was a member of the Law Review Board, went to Yale Law School after graduation and earned an LL.M. in 1954. He spent nine years as a government lawyer, for the Kansas Attorney General, the Federal Communications Commission, and the Kansas Corporation Commission, before joining Frizzell in practice. Thereafter, McCarter practiced in St. Louis before joining the faculty at Tulsa. He then spent three years on the law faculty at Stetson College in Florida before resuming practice in St. Louis.

Frizzell's early career focused on politics. A Republican, he was elected to the Kansas State Senate and then as Attorney General of Kansas, before losing the 1970 election for Governor to incumbent Robert B. Docking. He moved to Washington to become Assistant Attorney General for Land and Natural Resources, earning national media exposure when he helped defuse a standoff with the American Indian Movement and its leader Russell Means at Wounded Knee in South Dakota. He then spent three years at the Department of Interior, initially as Solicitor and later as Under Secretary and Acting Secretary. With the change to a Democratic administration after the 1976 election, he became Professor of Law at Tulsa and Director of its Natural Energy Law and Policy Institute, a position he held until his retirement in 1992. He recruited David E. Pierce '77 to be Deputy Director of NELPI for two years.

Jerry Norton '62 has taught at two Chicago law schools, at Chicago-Kent from 1967 until 1971 and since then at Loyola University. He initially practiced with his brother Frank Norton '56 in Salina before enrolling in the LL.M. program at Northwestern in 1966. His principal teaching areas have been Criminal Law, Criminal Procedure, and Municipal Corporations. For two years, he was Editor-in-Chief of the *Chicago-Kent Police Law Reporter* and was an advisor on drafting criminal codes with the ABA's Central and Eastern European Law Initiative.

Among 1970s graduates, Helen Dupre '76 was a full-time Instructor of Law in the Legal Writing Program at the University of Arkansas-Little Rock during academic year 1981–82 and continued as a part-time teacher for several years thereafter. As noted elsewhere, David E. Pierce '77 taught at both Indiana-Indianapolis and Tulsa before returning to his alma mater in 1989 as a permanent member of the faculty. He received the first LL.M. in Energy Law awarded by the University of Utah. M. Christine Hutton '78 received her LL.M. at Harvard in 1984 and has been on the faculty of the University of South Dakota School of Law since then, specializing in Criminal Law and Procedure. She was Associate Dean there for one and one-half years. She was Visiting Professor at Thomas Cooley School of Law, at Washburn during the spring semester, 2011, and at the University of Kansas in the summer of 2011.

Shelley Ryan '87 joined Hutton on the South Dakota faculty for two years, starting in 1995, teaching Torts and Commercial Law, before joining the staff of the United States Court of Appeals for the First Circuit in Boston. Her first teaching position was as Visiting Assistant Professor at Washburn from 1990 until 1992, after being Law Clerk for United States District Judge Dale Saffels '49 and practicing with Shook, Hardy & Bacon in Kansas City. After earning an LL.M. at Harvard in 1993, Ryan taught for one year each at the University of Oklahoma and the University of Tulsa before teaching at South Dakota.

Susana Valdovinos '88 taught during academic year 1990–91 at Whittier Law School in California, after completing her LL.M. at the University of Wisconsin Law School and before returning to Topeka with her spouse, Professor Michael Kaye. Charles Masner '82 taught for five years in the George Washington University Law Clinic in Washington after receiving his LL.M. there in 1991. Jan Pierce '71 has been Clinical Professor in the Tax Law Clinic at Lewis & Clark Law School in Oregon since 2000. Gregory Lewis '74 was Assistant Professor for two years while teaching in the Law Clinic at North Dakota, Darryl Apperton '91 taught in the Legal Clinic at Northern Illinois from 2001 to 2003, and Nick Cox '88 became Elder Consumer Protection Fellow in the Law Clinic at Stetson in 2003. Montie Deer '72 was selected in 2003 as Associate Professor and Director of the Indian Law Clinic at the University of Tulsa College of Law. Mary Kay O'Malley '95 has been Associate Clinical Professor at UMKC since 2003. Don Smith, Jr. '79 is Director of the Environmental & Natural Resources Law & Policy Graduate Program at the University of Denver Sturm College of Law and is editor-in-chief of *Utilities Policy*, a peer-reviewed journal. Kim Phillips '96 was Assistant Professor of Legal Practice at Texas Tech University from 2003 until 2011, then moved to Charleston Law School to teach doctrinal courses. In 2008, Susan C. Hascall '97 joined the faculty at Duquesne University School of Law, teaching Sales and Islamic Law. Robert Coulthard '00 became Academic Excellence Professor at New England School of Law in 2008, after serving as Director of Academic Achievement at Oklahoma City University. Yolanda Ingram '95 became Assistant Dean for Student Affairs at the Cecil C. Humphreys School of Law at the University of Memphis in 2002. Marianne Deagle '95 is Dean of Career Services at Loyola University in Chicago.

Eight members of Washburn's graduating class of 1987 have spent all or part of their careers in legal education, more than any other class. Shelley Ryan '87, Jalen O'Neil '87, Lynette Petty '87, Lyn Goering '87, and Curtis Waugh '87 all have been full-time faculty members at Washburn, and Janet Kerr '87 was Assistant to the Dean for Admissions for nine years. Goering accepted offers to be Visiting Professor at the University of Arkansas-Little Rock William H. Bowen School of Law in the fall of 2009 and academic year 2010–11, then joined the permanent faculty there. Glen-Peter Ahlers '87 initially was Associate Director of the Law Library at Wake Forest Law School, then became Director for two years at the District of Columbia Law School, where he worked with future Washburn Dean Dennis Honabach. He next was Law Library Director for ten years at Arkansas-Fayetteville, then was Associate Dean for Information Services at Barry University's Dwayne O. Andreas School of Law in Florida from 2002 until 2011, when he became a classroom professor full-time. He served from 1997 until 2005 as Executive Director of the American Society of Writers on Legal Subjects, more commonly called "Scribes," that was founded in 1953. He had been editor of its quarterly newsletter, *The Scrivener*. In addition, Tim Kelly '87 has been Reference Librarian at the law schools at Nebraska and Willamette.

Washburn has produced a remarkable number of Law Librarians, in part because of a special program developed by Professor John Christensen that allowed librarians already holding a Master of Library Science degree to work part-time as professional librarians at Washburn while pursuing their law degrees. Graduates have been librarians at fifteen other schools, including eight schools at which they have been Director and two others at which they have been Interim Director.

Fritz Snyder '79 spent fourteen years at the University of Kansas Law Library, including eight as Associate Director, and has been Law Library Director at the University of Montana since 1994. He was named Associate Dean in 2000. David Ensign '82 was Associate Director of Washburn's law library before becoming Director of the Library at the University of Louisville School of Law in 1989. He was named Acting Dean there during a dean search in 2005. Joyce McCray Pearson '89 was Associate Director at Louisville under Ensign for four years after completing her M.L.S. degree at the University of Washington in 1990. She now is Professor of Law and Director of the Law Library at the University of Kansas School of Law. Nina Miley '90 was Reference Librarian for six years at the University of Oklahoma Law Library and was Interim Director for one year. She then was Associate Director of the Legal Research and Writing program for seven years before retiring. Phill Johnson '01 earned his M.L.S. and became Director of Electronic Services and Communications at UMKC

School of Law in 2005. In 2011, he succeeded Glen-Peter Ahlers '87 as Associate Dean for Information Services at Barry University. Patrick Meyer '96 became Associate Library Director at Thomas Jefferson School of Law in San Diego and most recently served as Interim Library Director. He previously was Foreign & International Law Librarian at Loyola University in Los Angeles.

Not all of the Law Librarians from Washburn are of recent vintage. Beth Bowers '48 was Law Librarian at Creighton University from 1950–52, after serving two years as Washburn's Librarian. Perhaps the most interesting story, however, is that of Herbert V. Clayton '12. He took classes as a special student during the Law School's first year while working in the Kansas State Library. It took him nine years to complete his LL.B. He continued working in the State Library and taught classes about "law books" at the Law School in 1914.[1247] As late as 1960, he was Law Librarian at McGeorge Law School in Sacramento, California.

Many graduates have used their law degrees in academic careers in University departments other than law. The Law School does not have a complete list of them all. They include academic administrators such as: Stephen Minnis '85, President of Benedictine College in Atchison; William A. Buzick, Jr. '50, who became Dean of the Business School at Fresno State University after retiring as CEO of Consolidated Foods, Inc. (Sara Lee); Richard C. Dearth '69, Dean of the Kelce College of Business at Pittsburg State University; Daniel E. Hall '88, author of several books in the field of criminal law and procedure and Dean of the Miami University-Hamilton Campus in Ohio; Vicki Brittain '77, Chair of the Political Science Department and formerly Associate Dean of the College of Arts and Sciences at Texas State University in San Marcos; John Wong '86, Interim Director of the Hugo Wall School of Urban and Public Affairs at Wichita State University and then Chair of Urban and Public Leadership at the University of North Texas at Dallas; Lowell Ewert '78, Director of Peace and Conflict Studies at the University of Waterloo in Ontario, Canada; and Delano E. Lewis '63, Interim Dean of International and Border Programs at New Mexico State University and founding Director of its International Relations Institute. At Washburn, Richard Martin '71 is Chair of the Office, Legal and Technology Department in the School of Applied Studies, and Kay Rute '80 is Director of its Legal Studies Program.

1247. *Notes of the Law School*, WASHBURN REV., Oct. 7, 1914, at 3.

Award winning professors include W. Keith Weltmer '37, first recipient of the Henry A. Bubb Award when he was Professor in the School of Business at the University of Kansas, and Robert Prentice '75, who has been selected three times as the outstanding member of the faculty at the University of Texas at Austin, where he teaches in the McCombs School of Business and was founding chair of the Department of Business, Government and Society.

Many Washburn graduates have taught full time in various departments at Kansas colleges and universities. The have taught as well at many schools nationwide. For example, Keith Maxwell '66 is a long-time member of the faculty of the School of Business at Puget Sound University in Tacoma. Robert Bock '53 taught at Western New England University in Massachusetts. James Flagg '89 teaches in the Department of Criminal Justice at the University of Central Florida. Stan Barnhill '59 was a professor of Criminal Justice at the University of Nebraska-Omaha and Central Missouri State before concluding his career at the University of Nevada-Reno from 1973–79. Robert Reeder '60 for years was on the faculty of the Northwestern Traffic Institute and published two books there. Mary Hack '68 joined the Department of Psychiatry of the Louisiana State University School of Medicine in Shreveport in 1975. Melinda Hickman '88 has been on business school faculties at Lincoln Memorial University in Tennessee, Fort Hays State University, and Doane College in Nebraska. She had Fulbright scholarships to teach for two years at Belarusian State Economics University and for one year at Moldova State University. Lisa Ochs '95 is on the faculty of the Department of Psychology and Counseling at Arkansas State University. Mary Virginia (Ginny) Moore '96 is Professor of Business Law at Southeast Missouri State University in Cape Girardeau and was named the first Faculty Fellow for the Missouri Supreme Court. Ken Schallenkamp '02 is Assistant Professor in the College of Business and Technology at Black Hills State University in South Dakota and Andrew Warren '86 is at Western New Mexico University in the Criminal Justice Department. Ryan Pace '98 is Associate Professor and Director of graduate programs in accounting at Weber State University.

EPILOGUE

Researching this history of Washburn Law School confirmed for me that the school has core values that have guided it in times of achievement and sustained it during times of difficulty. So it was as the school began its second century. As Interim Dean during 2006–07, Bill Rich brought those core values that create loyal alums back to the forefront: respect for students; emphasis on student learning; faculty collegiality and comradery; and a caring atmosphere. The dean search conducted that year gave us an opportunity to identify the enduring strengths of the school and to describe them in a color brochure soliciting applications that deans and faculty members at other law schools were more likely to read than the marketing materials that so often go directly from mailbox to trash. The process reminded us of those enduring strengths too, and it boosted morale.

Thus, the start of the deanship of Thomas J. Romig in 2007 was greeted with much optimism and enthusiasm. He is a native Kansan and graduate of Kansas State University who is energetic and shares the school's core values. As the nation's thirty-sixth Judge Advocate General of the Army, he argued in a memorandum to Secretary of Defense Donald Rumsfeld that use of waterboarding and other extraordinary interrogation techniques at Guantanamo Bay and Abu Ghraib, Iraq, violated the Geneva Convention, international law, and the Uniform Code of Military Justice. He repeated that opinion during televised hearings before the Armed Services Committee of the United States Senate. Romig received the KBA's 2009 Courageous Attorney Award for his commitment to the rule of law that was reflected in those opinions. Romig retired from the Army in 2005 with the rank of Major General. Before coming to Washburn, he was deputy chief counsel for operations for the Federal Aviation Administration in Washington, D.C. Romig was selected for the Army's Fully

113. Thomas R. Romig, Dean 2007–present

Funded Law School Program while on active duty and graduated from Santa Clara University School of Law in 1980. He later taught for three years at the Army's ABA-accredited Judge Advocate General's School in Charlottesville, Virginia, specializing in International Law.

Norman Plass was right in 1902. Washburn was "the ideal place…for the establishment of a great Law School." Yet, he could not have envisioned how the school would grow or the influence its graduates would have. Washburn Law School's first century saw many innovations and significant contributions to the profession. It is well-positioned for the remainder of its second century and there is reason to believe its best days are ahead.

WASHBURN UNIVERSITY SCHOOL OF LAW
FULL-TIME FACULTY MEMBERS

*	Visiting Professor
**	Taught Substantially Full-Time While Practicing
***	Continued Teaching Part-Time After Retirement or Leaving Full–Time Teaching
****	Associate Dean for Student Affairs

1903–1907	Ernest B. Conant
1907–1913	Edward Delahay Osborn
1909–1915	William Reed Arthur
Fall 1911	Shelby L. Large
1913–1914	Clinton J. Evans**
1913–1914	Paul H. Dodge
Fall 1914	William Cullen Burns
Spring 1915–Fall 1915	Alfred Washburn Benson
1915–1928	Thomas W. Hughes
Spring 1916	Thomas Amory Lee**
1916–1917	William Chalmers Ralston**
1917–1919	Albert J. Harno
1920–1922	Charles E. Carpenter
1920–1926	James R. McBride
1922–Fall 1936	Harry K. Allen***
1926–1927	Norman F. Arterburn
1927–1950	Antrim M. Hambleton '14***
1928–1930	Howard Jones '28***
1930–Fall 1941	Edward Delahay Osborn
Fall 1932	Thomas A. Larremore
Spring 1933–1943	Kenneth Wagner '32
Spring 1937–Summer 1938	Rousseau A. Burch
1939–Fall 1940	Lester W. Feezer
Spring 1941–1942	Ralph Rice
1941–1943	James F. Price
1942–1943	Dorothy Davidson Tyner '41
Spring 1946–1947	Richard C. Donnelly '38

1946–1947	William Reed Arthur*
1946–1948	Frank Flaska
1946–1948	Earl Crawford
1947–1948	Glenn L. Archer '46
1947–1958	Schuyler W. Jackson
1948–1988	James R. Ahrens
1948–1951	Lloyd Hall***
1948–1959	Marvin Larson '40
1950–1951	Robert J. Fowks
1950–1959	Roy R. Bartlett '49
1951–1966	Melvin C. Poland '49
1953–Fall 1980	Robert J. Fowks***
1951–1953	Chester J. Antieau
1958–1959	Howard Jones '28**
1959–1978	John E. Howe
1959–1965	Walter D. Navin, Jr.
1959–1962	Richard C. Allen
1961–1968	William Harvey
1964–1971	Edward Robinson***
1963–1964	Keith Hey
1964–1965	Don Stimmel
1965–1968	Keith Hey
1965–2001	Raymond L. Spring '59
1966–1969	Larry Deemer
1966–1967	Virginia Creitz Martin '54
1966–1967	Maurice Michel
1967–1969	J. Scott Brown
1967–1984	Dorothea Warren '42
1968–2005	David L. Ryan '65
1968–1983	J. Elwood Slover
1969–1972	Ridgeley Scott
1969–1978	Otto Kratochvil
1970–Fall 1988	Donald F. Rowland '59
1970–1977	David Dale
1971–2000	Bruce Levine
1971–1979	William Treadway*

1972–1973	Dennis Stewart
1972–1982, Fall 1983	Mary M. Parr '47
1972–1975	W. Kurt Morgan
1973–present	James M. Concannon
1973–Fall 1982	Roy L. Bartlett '49
1973–1974	George E. Erickson, Jr. '66*
1974–present	Linda D. Elrod '72
1974–Fall 1998	John F. Kuether
1974–2010	Carl C. Monk (on leave to AALS 1988– 1990; 1992–2009)
1974–1979	Joel Meinecke '69
1974–1979	Randall Jones
1976–present	Gregory Pease
1976–Fall 1977	Colin K. Kaufman
1976–1977	Benjamin Farney
1977–present	Myrl L. Duncan
1977–present	William Rich
1978–2011	Ronald C. Griffin
1978–1992	Paul Rasor
Spring 1979	William Ward*
1979–80	Ted Frederickson* (Joint Appointment)
1979–Fall 1982	Randall Roth
1979–2004	Allen K. Easley
1979–Fall 2009	Sheila M. Reynolds
1979–Fall 2009	James W. Wadley
1979–present	John Christensen
1979–present	Nancy Maxwell
1979–present	Michael Kaye
Spring 1980–1985	John Lungren
1980–1981	Marjorie A. Wallace*
1980–1983, 1985–1991, Fall 1992, Fall 1993	Michael A. Barbara '53*** (on leave as Secretary of Corrections, 1983–85)
1980–1981	Eric C. Schneider*
Spring 1981	David Boeck*
Spring 1981	David E. Pierce '77*

1981–1982	Diane Acker*
1981–1983	Dixie Moss*
1982–1983	Warren Hill
1982–Fall 1994	Banks McDowell
1982–2003, 2007–2008	Charlene Smith
1983–2003	James W. Bayles
1983–present	L. Ali Khan
1983–1987	Robert W. Piatt, Jr.
1983–1984	Mark W. Dobson*
1984–1985	Laurence A. Benner*
1985–1991	Jean B. Reeves*
1986–1987	David Pierce '77*
1986–1990	Ellen Byers*
1987–1988	Emily Kofran '80*
1988–1989	Susana Valdovinos-Hall '88*
1988–1995	Nina W. Tarr
1988–1990	Arthur Chaykin*
1989–present	David Pierce '77
Fall 1989	John Wade (Ahrens Chair)*
1989–1991	Lisa Nathanson*
1989–1990	Thomas A. Rossi*
1990–2001	Jalen O'Neil '87
1990–1992	Shelley Ryan '87*
Fall 1990	Joel Meinecke '69**
1991–2005	Loretta W. Moore
1991–2003	Rogelio Lasso
Spring 1992	Taunya Lovell Banks (Ahrens Chair)*
1992–1994	Cathy Lesser Mansfield
1992–present	Lynette Petty '87
Spring 1994	Carl Hawkins (Ahrens Chair)*
Spring 1994–2001	Hon. Harold Herd '42 (Distinguished Jurist–in–Residence)
1994–2005	Ellen Byers
1994–1995	Ron Hersbergen*
1995–2006	Steve Ramirez
1995–1999	Michelle Rabouin

1995–1998	Julie Kunce Field
1998–2000	Bruce Plenk*
1999–present	Alex Glashausser
1999–present	John Francis
1999–2004	Peter Cotorceanu
1999–2000	Elizabeth Brandt*
2000–2001	Kim Dayton*
2000–2004	Megan Ballard
2000–2005	Carol Vizzier****
2000–2002	Richard Lavoie
2001–2006	Dennis R. Honabach
2001–2002	Deborah J. Challener*
2001–present	Mary Kreiner Ramirez
2002–2005	Stephanie Mathews
2003–2004	Suellen M. Wolfe*
2003–2004	Timothy R. Schnacke*
2003–2011	Lyn Goering '87
2003–present	Curtis J. Waugh '87*
2004–2005	Peter Linzer*
2004–present	Jeffrey Jackson '92
2004–2012	Aliza Organick
2004–2010	Brad Borden
2004–present	Janet Thompson Jackson
2004–2006	Nathan Webb*
2004–2007	Robert Rhee
2005–present	Aida Alaka
2005–2011	William Merkel
2005–2010	Kelly Lynn Anders****
2005–present	Joe McKinney '86*
2005–2006	Jack Preis*
2005–2006	Peter Reilly
Fall 2006	Joel Meinecke '69*
2006–present	Michael Hunter Schwartz
2006–present	Tonya Kowalski
2006–2007	Larry Putt*
2006–present	Randall Hodgkinson*

2006–2007	Fatina Williams*
2007–present	Thomas J. Romig
2007–present	Lori McMillan
2007–present	Rory Bahadur
2008–present	Jalen O'Neil Lowry '87* ****
2008–2009	Bruce Carolan*
2009–present	Amy L. Westbrook
2009–2010	Bert Westbrook*
2010–present	Reginald Robinson
2010–present	David Rubenstein
2010–present	Will Foster
2010–present	Ellen Byers*
Spring 2011	M. Christine Hutton '78*
2011–present	Craig Martin
2011–present	Patricia L. Judd
2011–present	Joseph Mastrosimone
2011–present	Emily Grant
2011–2012	Jeremiah Ho*

DEANS

1903–1907	Ernest B. Conant
1907–1909	Edward D. Osborn (Acting)
1909–1915	William R. Arthur
1915–1917	Thomas W. Hughes
1917–1919	Albert J. Harno
1919–1920	Thomas W. Hughes (Acting)
1920–1922	Charles E. Carpenter
1922–January, 1937	Harry K. Allen
February, 1937– October, 1938	Rousseau A. Burch
October, 1938–1939	Antrim M. Hambleton '14 (Acting)
1939–January, 1941	Lester W. Feezer
February, 1941–1943	James F. Price
1943–1947	Antrim M. Hambleton '14 (Acting 1943–February, 1947)
1947–1948	Glenn L. Archer '46
1948–April, 1958	Schuyler W. Jackson
April, 1958–1959	Howard A. Jones '28 (Acting)
1959–1970	John E. Howe
1970–1978	Raymond L. Spring '59 (Acting 1970–February, 1971)
1978–1988	Carl C. Monk (Acting 1978– February, 1979)
Fall, 1985	William J. Rich (Acting)
1988–2001	James M. Concannon
2001–2006	Dennis R. Honabach
2006–2007	William J. Rich (Interim)
2007–present	Thomas J. Romig

PROFESSOR OF THE YEAR AND
ADJUNCT PROFESSOR OF THE YEAR

	William O. Douglas Outstanding Professor of the Year	*Adjunct Professor of the Year*
1976	William E. Treadway	
1977	James M. Concannon	
1978	Otto Kratochvil	
1979	Linda Henry Elrod '72	
1980	Raymond L. Spring '59	
1981	Randall W. Roth	
1982	Paul B. Rasor	
1983	Gregory Pease	
1984	Allen K. Easley	
1985	John H. Lungren	
1986	Ronald C. Griffin	
1987	J. Wendell Bayles	
1988	Bruce Levine	
1989	Michael A. Barbara '53	
1990	John F. Kuether	
1991	David E. Pierce '77	Hon. Terry L. Bullock
1992	Gregory Pease	Marty Snyder
1993	Bruce Levine	Jane Lindhout '87
1994	David E. Pierce '77	Hon. Terry L. Bullock
1995	Ronald C. Griffin	Jane Lindhout '87
1996	Gregory Pease	Jane Lindhout '87
1997	J. Wendell Bayles Bruce Levine	Kirk Lowry '87
1998	Steven Ramirez Hon. Terry L. Bullock	Joseph M. Weiler '87
1999	Gregory Pease	Terri Savely Bezek '86
2000	Bruce Levine	John C. Fritz '87
2001	James B. Wadley	Terri Savely Bezek '86

2002	Richard Lavoie	Terri Savely Bezek '86
2003	Gregory Pease	Brian J. Moline '66
2004	Megan Ballard	John C. Fritz '87
2005	Alex Glashausser	Hon. Terry L. Bullock
2006	Gregory Pease	Ronald P. Pope '84
2007	David E. Pierce '77	C. William Ossmann '77
2008	William Merkel	John Wine
2009	John Francis	C. William Ossmann '77
2010	Rory Bahadur	Terri D. Thomas '88
2011	Reginald Robinson	C. William Ossmann '77
2012	Rory Bahadur	Terri D. Thomas '88

DIRECTORS OF THE LAW LIBRARY

   *   Taught one or more classes while serving as Librarian
  ** Served as Secretary of the Law School while serving as Librarian
*** Was Librarian while attending law classes

1922–1925	Ruth Inez Emch
1925–1926	Marie Russell '25
1931–1936	Clessie Jackson Gilmore '36***
1937–1939	Joy Whitney
1939–1941	Willette Price
Fall 1941	Dorothy Davidson Tyner '41
Spring 1942	Dorothea Grubbs '42***
1942–1943	Helen Loomis '42**
1943–1947	Christine Ash Johnson**
1947–1948	Charles M. Tansey, Jr.*
1948–1950	Elizabeth Bowers '48
1950–1951	Roy Bartlett '49*
1951–1952	John Bohannon '52 (Acting)***
1952–1958	Roy Bartlett '49*
1958–1959	Miles Mustain '58*
1959–1960	Eleanore Blue
1960–1966	Virginia Creitz Martin '54*
1966–1967	Maurice Michel
1967–1979	Dorothea Grubbs Warren '42*
1979–present	John E. Christensen

EDITORS-IN-CHIEF
WASHBURN LAW JOURNAL

Volume 0	Fall 1959	David Wheeler '60
Volume 0	Spring 1960	Robert L. Roberts '61
Volume 1	1960–61	Lowell Hahn '61
Volume 1	Fall 1961	Zerne P. Haning III '62
Volume 1	Spring 1962	Gerald J. Letourneau '62
Volume 2	1962–63	John E. Conway '63
Volume 3	Fall 1963	John E. Stumbo '64
Volume 3	Spring 1964	William J. Hunsaker '65
Volume 4	Fall 1964	William J. Hunsaker '65
Volume 4	Spring 1965	Stanley E. Antrim '65
Volume 5	1965–66	Donald R. Hill '66
Volume 6	1966–67	Larry K. Meeker '67
Volume 7	1967–68	Winton M. Hinkle '68
Volume 8	1968–69	Richard F. Hayse '69
Volume 9	1969–70	Mary A. Senner '70
Volume 10	1970–71	Darrell L. Warta '71
Volume 11	1971–72	Lawrence A. Stanton '72
Volume 12	1972–73	John E. Caton '73
Volume 13	1973–74	M. Kim Moore '74
Volume 14	1974–75	Harker E. Russell '75
Volume 15	1975–76	William A. Sidlinger '76
Volume 16	1976–77	Michael C. Manning '77
Volume 17	1977–78	Vivian W. Wiberg '78
Volume 18	1978–79	Robert Douglas Reagan '79
Volume 19	1979–80	Eugenia K. Godfrey '80
Volume 20	1980–81	Gary E. Knight '81
Volume 21	1981–82	William E. Bartholdt, Jr. '82
Volume 22	1982–83	Robert M. Barnes '83
Volume 23	1983–84	Michael L. Happe '84
Volume 24	1984–85	Marta Fisher Linenberger '85
Volume 25	1985–86	Terry L. Mann '86
Volume 26	1986–87	Lyn E. Goering '87

Volume 27	1987–88	Jay P. Golden '88
Volume 28	1988–89	Denise Anderson '89
Volume 29	1989–90	Dale Ward '90
Volume 30	1990–91	Mary Lynch Matthews '91
Volume 31	1991–92	Kristin Blomquist-Shinn '92
Volume 32	1992–93	Stacy L. Cook '93
Volume 33	1993–94	Jill M. Crumpacker '94
Volume 34	1994–95	Teresa J. Bowles '95
Volume 35	1995–96	Michael E. Callahan '96
Volume 36	1996–97	L. Christopher Wittman '97
Volume 37	1997–98	Peter J. Vanderwalker '98
Volume 38	1998–99	Sabrina Standifer '99
Volume 39	1999–2000	Brenda R. Mesker '00
Volume 40	2000–01	Lori A. Bolton '01
Volume 41	2001–02	Jodi M. Hoss '02
Volume 42	2002–03	Gregory C. Graffman '03
Volume 43	2003–04	Robin K. Carlson '04
Volume 44	2004–05	Sarah L. Shipman '05
Volume 45	2005–06	Joletta M. Friesen '06
Volume 46	2006–07	Michael J. Shultz '07
Volume 47	2007–08	Timothy R. Hurley '08
Volume 48	2008–09	Timothy M. Belsan '09
Volume 49	2009–10	Jonathan D. Stokes '10
Volume 50	2010–11	Eric Turner '11
Volume 51	2011–12	Jennifer Cocking '12

EDITORS-IN-CHIEF
WASHBURN EDITORIAL BOARD
JOURNAL OF THE KANSAS BAR ASSOCIATION

Spring, 1948	Derbert Scott '48
Fall, 1948	Leonard Milligan '49
Spring, 1949	Melvin R. Quinlan '49
Fall, 1949	Dean L. Gibson '50
Spring, 1950	Thomas C. Hurst '50
Summer, 1950	Keith Sanborn '50
Fall, 1950	Warren R. Southard '51
Spring, 1951	Boyd Adsit '51
Summer, 1951	Edgar M. Miner '51
Fall, 1951	James R. Groff '52
1952	James L. Berlin '53
Spring, 1953	Stanley E. Wisdom '53
Fall 1953	Thomas A. Wood '54
Spring, 1954	Gerald D. Lasswell '54
1954–1955	Gene A. Powell '55
Fall, 1955	William D. Bunten '56
Spring, 1956	Hugh L. Mauch '56
1956–1957	William L. Parker, Jr. '57
Fall, 1957	Daniel J. Stoops '58
Spring, 1958	Frank M. Rice '59
Fall, 1958	Daniel M. Dibble '59
Spring, 1959	Homer W. Fanning '59
Fall, 1959	David Wheeler '60
Spring, 1960	Robert L. Roberts '61

STUDENT EDITORS-IN-CHIEF
ABA FAMILY LAW QUARTERLY

1992–3	Rose Mulvany '93
1993–4	Laura Smithson-Corl '95
1994–5	Laura Smithson-Corl '95
1995–6	Michael R. Montero '96
1996–7	Lori Mays '97
1997–8	Rod Brown '98
1998–9	L. Travis Lamb '99
1999–2000	Tina Powers '00
2000–1	Elizabeth Sweeney-Reeder '01
2001–2	Andrew L. Kynaston '02
2002–3	Tiffany D. Tant '03
2003–4	Chris J. Kellogg '04
2004–5	Sarah Novascone '05
2005–6	David W. Barlow '06
2006–7	Amy C. Coppola '07
2007–8	Holly Fisher '08
2008–9	Anna Krstulic '09
2009–10	Ryan Eagleson '10
2010–1	Jennifer L. Lemus '11
2011–2	Letiffany Obozele '12

FOULSTON SIEFKIN LAW JOURNAL LECTURES

1978	Professor Vern Countryman, Harvard University
1979	Professor Arthur R. Miller, Harvard University
1980	Dean David G. Epstein, University of Arkansas–Fayetteville
1981	Dean John E. Murray, Jr., University of Pittsburgh (article only)
1982	Professor James J. White, University of Michigan
1983	The Honorable Monroe G. McKay, U.S. Court of Appeals, Tenth Circuit
1984	Professor Irving Younger, University of Minnesota
1985	Professor Willard Pedrick, Arizona State University
1986	Professor Stephen A. Saltzburg, University of Virginia
1987	Professor Arthur Kinoy, Rutgers University–Newark
1988	Professor Liu Gui-yun, Shanghai Institute of Foreign Trade
1989	Vincent T. Bugliosi, author *Helter Skelter: The True Story of the Manson Murders*
1990	William L. Webster, Attorney General of Missouri
1991	Professor Martha A. Field, Harvard University
1992	Professor John S. Lowe, Southern Methodist University
1993	Professor Jane E. Larson, Northwestern University
1994	Professor Timothy P. Terrell, Emory University
1995	Professor Cheryl L. Harris, Chicago-Kent College of Law
1996	Professor Derrick Bell, New York University
1997	Professor Burt Neuborne, New York University
1998	Hon. Alex Kozinski, United States Court of Appeals, Ninth Circuit
1999	Professor Edward J. Larson, University of Georgia
2000	Professor Akhil Reed Amar, Yale University
2001	Professor Joseph L. Sax, University of California–Berkeley
2002	Professor Rachel Moran, University of California–Berkeley
2003	Dean Mark A. Sargent, Villanova University
2004	Professor Mildred W. Robinson, University of Virginia
2005	Professor Erwin Chemerinsky, Duke University
2006	Professor Marc I. Steinberg, Southern Methodist University
2007	Professor Jeffrey Rosen, George Washington University

2008	Professor Karl Jorda, Franklin Pierce Law Center
2009	Professor Donald N. Zillman, University of Maine
2010	Professor William N. Eskridge, Jr., Yale University
2011	Professor Susan A. Bandes, DePaul University
2012	Professor Monroe H. Freedman, Hofstra University

GNIP GNOP AWARD RECIPIENTS

* Also Received Faculty Award

	Best Note	*Best Comment*
1977–8	Mark Buck '78*	
1978–9	Alice M. Fitzgerald '79*	
1979–80	Marla J. Luckert '80*	
1980–1	Linda L. Pfalzgraf '81	
1981–2	Kenneth Slowinski '82*	
1982–3	Derenda Mitchell '83*	
1983–4	Jana J. Deines '84 and Michael E. McMahon '84	Nancy Moritz Landis '85
1984–5	Evelyn E. Zabel '85	Information Not Available
1985–6	Tammie E. Mallory '86 and Katherine E. Rich '87*	Warren F. Frost '87
1986–7	Jalen O'Neil '87 and Curtis J. Waugh '87*	Michael W. Peters '88*
1987–8	Barbara M. Christensen '88 and Kristine A. Larscheid '88*	Gregory S. Brown '89
1988–9	Troy H. Gott '89 and William L. Townsley '89*	Lisa K. Hammer '90*
1989–90	Nancy Ogle '91	Douglas P. Witteman '91
1990–1	Laura Johnson '91*	Channel Townsley '92
1991–2	Jeffrey P. DeGraffenreid '92	Bruce Ney '92
1992–3	Charles C. Steincamp '93*	Patrick Hughes '94

1993–4	Troy A. Stremming '94	Clayton S. Skaggs '95
1994–5	Craig Edgar '95	Jennifer L. Ames '96
1995–6	Lisa Agrimonti '96*	Stephen Torline '97*
1996–7	John McBee '97	Lois Malin '97
1997–8	Boyd Isherwood '98	Jonathan Martin '99
1998–9	Michelle L. Brenwald '99 and Kay Redeker '99	Brenda R. Mesker '00
1999–00	Kristafer Ailslieger '00	Richard James '00
2000–1	William P. Nacy '01	Nathan D. Leadstrom '01
2001–2	Rebecca L. Farrell '02	Molly J. Staab '03
2002–3	John W. Broomes '03*	Robin K. Carlson '04
2003–4	Starla Borg '04	Lora M. Jennings '05
2004–5	Brian S. Sommer '05	Joletta Friesen '06
2005–6	Kristen D. Wheeler '06	Mike J. Wyatt '07*
2006–7	Mike J. Wyatt '07*	Tyler A. Darnell '08
2007–8	Justin W. Whinery '08	Brent M. Johnston '09
2008–9	Jeremy K. Schrag '09*	Jonathan D. Stokes '10
2009–10	Gage A. Rohlf '10*	Monique M. McElwee '11
2010–1	Jacob L. Porter '11	Andrew D. Holder '12

FACULTY LAW JOURNAL AWARD RECIPIENTS

* Also received GNIP GNOP Award

	Best Note	*Best Comment*
1966–7	John Frieden '67	Larry Luttjohann '68
1967–8	Jon Love '68	Terry L. Kramer '68
1969–70	Richard F. Hayse '69	Ronald W. Hill '70
1970–1	Roger L. Hiatt '71	Richard S. Hyter '71
1971–2	Robert A. Lewis '71	Thomas Haney '73 and James W. Parrish '73
1977–8	Mark Buck '78*	Victor W. Miller '79
1978–9	Alice M. Fitzgerald '79*	Information Not Available
1979–80	Marla J. Luckert '80*	Carol Gilliam Green '81
1980–1	(tie) Carolyn A. Adams '81 and Carol Gilliam Green '81	Information Not Available
1981–2	Kenneth Slowinski '82*	(tie) Janice Shaw Clothier and John D. Ensley '83
1982–3	Derenda Mitchell '83*	Information Not Available
1983–4	Catherine M. Foster '84	Mark J. Wagner '85
1984–5	Mark J. Wagner '85	Terry L. Mann '86
1985–6	Tammie E. Mallory '86 and Katherine E. Rich '87*	J. Lyn Entrikin Goering '87
1986–7	Jalen O'Neil '87 and Curtis J. Waugh '87*	Michael W. Peters '88*
1987–8	Barbara M. Christensen '88 and Kristine A. Larscheid '88*	Information Not Available
1988–9	Troy H. Gott '89 and William L. Townsley '89*	Lisa K. Hammer '90*

1989–90	Anne Hull '90	Anthony J. Powell '91
1990–1	Laura Johnson '91	Allen Olson '92
1991–2	Brent A. Mitchell '92	Stacey Cook '93
1992–3	Charles C. Steincamp '93*	Michael S. Ertz '94
1993–4	James P. Kenner '94	Peter A. Raith '95
1994–5	Clayton C. Skaggs '95	Lisa Agrimonti '96*
1995–6	Lisa Agrimonti '96*	Stephen Torline '97*
1996–7	(tie) Callie A. Marks '97 and James M. Morgan '97	Victoria Nilles '98
1997–8	Anthony M. Singer '98	Robert L. Shuck '98
1998–9	Scott Liljegren '99	(tie) Bryon L. Koepke '00 and Marti R. Paulsen '00
1999–00	Jennifer Koepke '00	Tony L. Atterbury '01
2000–1	Mary E. Christopher '01	(tie) Sarah McLean '02 and Luke A. Sobba '02
2001–2	Bach T. Hang '02	John W. Broomes '03
2002–3	John W. Broomes '03*	Donald H. Snook '04
2003–4	Luke R. Spellmeier '04	Andrea D. Walker '05
2004–5	Ryan S. Vincent '05	Melinda G. Young '06
2005–6	Amy L. Leisinger '06	Mike J. Wyatt '07*
2006–7	Mike J. Wyatt '07*	Dan E. Lawrence '08
2007–8	Dan E. Lawrence '08	Heather R. Klaassen '09
2008–9	Jeremy K. Schrag '09*	Ashley Hawkinson '10
2009–10	Gage A. Rohlf '10*	Chantz N. Martin '11
2010–1	Michael C. Duma '11	(tie) Andrew T. Newcomer '12 and Jacqueline Blaesi-Freed '12

ORDER OF BARRISTERS

1971

Michael G. Beckner
William Grimshaw
Philip A. Harley
William H. Nollkamaper III
Darrell Warta
Dean Raymond L. Spring–
   Honorary

1972

John Ambrosio
Jan Hamilton
Marcia L. H. Harley
Kenneth Havner
John C. Peterson

1973

Raymond L. Connell
Austin D. Cowan
Durward D. Dupre
Robert E. Keeshan
Rex Kenneth Linder
Ronald E. Wurtz
Prof. Edward Robinson–Honorary

1974

E. Eugene Clark
Randall E. Fisher
David H. Gray
Robert A. Prentice
Richard E. Samson

Van C. Stone
James R. Tanner
Prof. James R. Ahrens–Honorary

1975

Alan C. Goering
John J. Healzer
Stephen D. Hill
James P. Rankin
Alan L. Rupe
Prof. Otto Kratochvil–Honorary

1976

Dwight W. Duesing
Michael C. Germann
Michael L. Harris
Jeffrey C. Joy
Samuel D. Ogelby
Jay D. Thomas

1977

Roy Breedlove
David Dahl
Dennis Dow
Craig Shultz
Lloyd Swartz
Tim Troll

1978

Karl Dakin
Steve Garlow

Jan Montgomery
Steve Montgomery
David Seitter
Brian Vazquez

1979

Dick Blackwell
John Braun
Henry Cox
Kirk Nystrom
Mike Oliver
George Sowers
Hon. Harold Fatzer–Honorary

1980

Michael A. Childs
Kenneth Clark
Shannon S. Kyrsl
Margie J. Phelps
Gerald Poliquin, Jr.
George Robertson
Prof. James M. Concannon–
    Honorary

1981

Scott Averill
William Brewer
Kevin Fowler
Carla McBride
Thomas Shults
Donna Whiteman
Prof. Gregory Pease–Honorary

1982

Paul Amundson
Ricky Bailey
Caleb Boone
Neil Durrance
Bob Levy
Elizabeth Carson Plummer
William H. Kurtis–Honorary

1983

Martin Findley
John Jurcyk
Kyle Krull
Michael O'Hara
Michael Royle
Karen Wedel
Dean Carl C. Monk–Honorary

1984

Robert A. Anderson
Dan Church
Larry Gatenbein
Dennis Lacey
Michael Myers
Christine Tamburini
Dan Vokins
Hon. G. Thomas Van Bebber–
    Honorary

1985

John Banta
Alan Bransgrove
James Browne
Daniel D. Creitz

Cheryl Myers
Darla Orndorff
Deryl Wynn
Robert T. Stephan–Honorary

1986

John Gilliam
David R. Mitchell
Larry Pitts
Debra Vermillion
Joe Weiler
Hon. Richard D. Rogers–
   Honorary

1987

Greg Bachmann
Leonard Fisher
John Hakanson
Michael Lehr
Guy McCready
Cecelia T. Noble
Susan G. Stanley
Lindsey Topper
Brian Moline–Honorary

1988

Thomas Barnes
Kenton M. Hall
James Jarrow
Edward Kainen
Michael Montoya
Rick Scheuffler
John Smith
Prof. Ellen Byers–Honorary

1989

Marck Cobb
James A. Daringer
Timothy H. Henderson
Sam M. Herrera
Jose Hurlstone-Peggs
Carolyn P. Lanzillo
Brian Leininger
William Townsley
Hon. Jerry G Elliott–Honorary

1990

Mike Kuckelman
Charles Lawhorn
Brent Lonker
Brad Maudlin
Nina Miley
Rodney Murrow
Ken Robins
Ronald C. Small
Hon. Deanell R. Tacha–Honorary

1991

David Boman
Frederick D. Deay II
John Mazurek
N. Trey Pettlon
Anthony Powell
Douglas P. Witteman
Hon Harold S. Herd–Honorary

1992

Paul Ailslieger
D. Todd Arney

Alice Knetsch
Randall L. Rhodes
A. Michelle Roberts
Bryan W. Smith
Jacqueline Spradling
John Stehlik
C. William Ossmann–Honorary

1993

Brent Arnold Doane
William Jeff Kahrs
Michael Byron Lewis
Christian D. Marr
Tracie Lynn Murrell
Jacquelyn E. Ulrich
Michael Madison Walker
Prof. Jalen O'Neil–Honorary

1994

David R. Cooper
John Robert Doolittle, II
Michael Steven Ertz
Gary L. Foiles
Lynn S. McCreary
Douglas Todd Shima
Gary Carl West

1995

Matt M. Diaz
Rickie Emmanuel Ibe
Christopher McCurdy
Patrick G. Reavey
Patricia L. Steele
Michelle D. Yanchula
Danielle J. Zacher

1996

John Carpinelli
Rhonda Crowley
Taher Kameli
Christopher Todd Navrat
Stephanie Petrie
Amber St. Clair
Jeffrey Wicks
Elizabeth Rogers

1997

Chris Collins
David Hansen
Steven Heck
Judd McPherson
Jack C. Morgan
Brenda J. Parks
Joseph S. Passanise
Daniel Perez, Jr.
Patrice Petersen–Klein
Valerie Peterson

1998

Wade H. Bowie
James A. Crawford II
Jeffrey Winslow Deane
Lesley McFadden
Kyle J. Mead
Kristi Pettit
Todd D. Powell
Michael Allen Priddle
Kevin Todd Stamper
Patricia Voth

1999

Kris Ailslieger
Michelle Carter
Darrin Devinney
Mike Gayoso
Eric Kraft
Scott Liljegren
Justin Pulikkan
Kim Rogers
Rob Steffen
Michelle Wiedle

2000

Thomas E. Beall
Rex S. Chang
Robert A. Coulthard
Mark E. Curzydlo
Adam A. Edwards
Melissa A. Graf
Lynelle D. Homolka
Jeffrey S. Nourse
Kevin Shepherd
Kristi L. Simmons

2001

Angela D. Bloomer
Misty S. Crawford
Tracie R. England
Rebecca S. Jelinek
Francesca Montes-Williams
Therese M. Murphy
Carolyn S. Powell
Angela M. Sullivan
Elizabeth Sweeney-Reeder

2002

Teri Canfield-Eye
Jason R. Coody
Carlus L. Haynes
Jeff B. Heinrichs
Joseph N. Molina
Elpidio Pete Placencia
Jeremy D. Shull
Augustin G. Simmons

2003

Eric Bidwell
Gregory Graffman
Angelee Gregory
Karla Jones-Wilson
Benjamin Karpinski
Kelly Keane
Tad Layton
Tiffany Tant
James Thompson
Lawrence Williamson

2004

Amie Bauer
Jennifer Cross
Dollie LeAnna Cramer
Kevin Hancock
Jamie Karasek
William Peterson
Jennifer Rutherford
Judith Taylor

2005

Ann Kathleen Burns
William M. Burris
Brette Hart
Bradley Lane Hemsley
John Todd Hiatt
Cheryl A. Kessler
Paul M. Mzembe
Brian C. Perkins
Thomas E. Trunnell
Christina M. Waugh

2006

Jessica A. Bryson
Anthony T. Hunter
Ethan S. Kaplan
Jeffrey M. King
Brian Joseph Malone
Michelle Kristine Moe
Roy W. Mozingo II

2007

Matthew Clark Ballard
Zach Chaffee-McClure
Jason Covington
Shelby J. Grau
Jay Hall
Tracey D. Johnson
Kelly J. Kauffman
Kristen Clarke Kellems
Karen M. Quintelier
Melissa Marie Schoen

2008

Stephen Allred
Peter Andreone
Charles Ault-Duell
Holly Fisher
Scott Gordon
Shawn Jurgensen
Jason Landress
Amy Taylor
Tai Vokins
Jennifer Zook

2009

Adam Andersen
Kari Burks
Angela Carlon
Regan Duckworth
Allison English
Danielle Hall
Joseph Ledbetter
Kimberly Lynch
Vincent Rivera
Jayson Watkins

2010

Krystal L. Baer
Andrew Clark
Jeffrey Dazey
Kimberly Honeycutt
Jonathon Noble
Britain Stites
Alice Walker
Sarah Washburn

2011

Brian K. Carr
Laura N. Coughlin
Amanda Haas
Stephen P. Jones
Erilda L. Livingston
Benjamin E. Long
Michael D. Quinn
Sydney M. Snyder
Thomas J. Webb
Shawn P. Yancy

IRVINE UNGERMAN AWARD FOR
EXCELLENCE IN CLINICAL PRACTICE

1971–72	Frank Hummer	1998–99	Sandra Carr
1972–73	Unknown		Stephen Nicol
1973–74	Unknown	1999–2000	Karen Barry
1974–75	Unknown		April Rutter
1975–76	Unknown	2000–01	Tracie England
1976–77	C. William Ossmann		Ted Griffith
1977–78	Charley Laman	2001–02	Jeff Heinrichs
1978–79	Unknown		Amy Winterscheid
1979–80	C. David McDermott	2002–03	Jennifer Dahlstrom
1980–81	Unknown		Amy Jurgensmeier
1981–82	Jill Michaux		Kelly Keane
1982–83	Unknown	2003–04	Laura Lewis
1983–84	Steven Sublett		Kari Miller
1984–85	Brian Frost	2004–05	Wes Barnum
1985–86	Terra Morehead		Ryan Vincent
1986–87	Katherine E. Rich	2005–06	Steve Ellis
1987–88	Unknown		Nicole C. Edwards
1988–89	Kevin Loeffler		Brian J. Malone
1989–90	Casey Irwin	2006–07	Kana Lydick
1990–91	Linda Blackburn		Amy Coppola
1991–92	Sandra Lindell		Maria Nieto
1992–93	Chad Hooker	2007–08	Patrick A. Turner
1993–94	Tammy Dodson		Tai B. Vokins
	Conrad Doudin		Kelli Jackson
1994–95	Scott Snider		Lucas Thompson
	Peggy Fulks	2008–09	Jennifer Amyx
1995–96	Robert Drean		Larry Crow
	Todd Stramel		Erin Bruce
1996–97	Jack Morgan	2009–10	Danielle Sanger
1997–98	Michael Dunalewicz		Teresa Mata
	Dawn Hayes	2010–11	Samara L. Stemple
	Chris Vinduska		Charion L. Vaughn
			C. David Rouner

WASHBURN UNIVERSITY SCHOOL OF LAW*
ALUMNI ASSOCIATION PRESIDENTS

1953–1954	Irving W. Platt '14
1954–1955	Hon. Alex Hotchkiss '27
1955–1959	William Tinker, Sr. '37
1959–1960	Hon. Howard C. Kline '36
1960–1961	Clayton M. Davis '29
1961–1965	Lester E. Goodell '25
1965–1969	John E. Shamberg '37
1969–1971	J.C. Tillotson '32
1971–1973	Warren W. Shaw '31
1973–1975	Eugene Hackler '49
1975–1977	Ralph Foster '50
1978–1979	Gerald Goodell '58
1980–1981	Rae Batt '50
1982–1983	James Barnett '59
1984–1985	Hon. Bob Abbott '60
1986–1987	Hon. Mary Schowengerdt '57
1988–1989	D. Stewart Oswalt '51
1990–1992	Richard C. Hite '53
1992–1994	W. Terrence Kilroy '77
1994–1996	Lynn Johnson '70
1996–1998	Mark V. Heitz '77
1998–2000	Hon. Christel Marquardt '74
2000–2002	H. Allan Caldwell '73
2002–2004	Bernard A. Bianchino '74
2004–2006	D. Duke Dupre '73
2006–2008	Steven Cooper '73
2008–2010	Stephen W. Cavanaugh '80
2010–2012	Winton M. Hinkle '68

*Formerly Washburn Law School Association

WASHBURN UNIVERSITY SCHOOL OF LAW ALUMNI ASSOCIATION DISTINGUISHED SERVICE AWARD

1963	Marie Russell '25
1964	Hon. Delmas Hill '29
	Howard Jones '28
1965	Lester Goodell '25
1966	Phil Lewis '35
1967	Hon. Alex Hotchkiss '27
	Hon. George Templar '27
	Hon. Harold Fatzer '33
1968	Hon. Earl Hatcher '23
1969	Donald Moyers '34
	Stanley Garrity '27
1970	Duffie Hindman '27
	John Shamberg '49
1971	Roy Bartlett '49
1972	Jay Kyle '38
1973	Jack Wertz '47
1974	J.C. Tillotson '32
1975	Hon. Alex Fromme '39
1976	Meyer Ueoka '49
1977	Hon. Jerome Harmon '35
1978	Howard Harper '40
1979	Hon. Perry Owsley '38
1980	Warren Shaw '31
1981	Sen. Robert J. Dole '52
1982	Gerald L. Goodell '58
1983	Hon. Joe Morris '47
1984	Hon. Michael Barbara '53
1985	Jim Barnett '59
1986	Linda Elrod '71
1987	Raymond L. Spring '59
	Hon. Dale E. Saffels '49
1988	Hon. Bob Abbott '60

1989	Richard Hrdlicka '55
1990	No award given
1991	Herbert A. Marshall '43
	Hon. Patrick F. Kelly '53
1992	Ronald K. Richey '51
1993	Glenn Archer '46
1994	Richard Hite '53
1995	Hon. Harold Herd '42
1996	Wayne T. Stratton '58
1997	Hon. E. Newton Vickers '50
	Gerald L. Michaud '51
1998	W. Terrence Kilroy '77
1999	William Kurtis '66
2000	Hon. Sam A. Crow '52
2001	Lynn R. Johnson '70
2002	Hon. Christel Marquardt '74
2003	Delano E. Lewis '63
2004	David L. Ryan '65
2005	James R. Roth '66
2006	H. Allan Caldwell '73
2007	Bernard Bianchino '74
2008	D. Duke Dupre '73
2009	William D. Bunten '56
2010	Hon. Marla Luckert '80
2011	Paul R. Hoferer '75
2012	Carol Gilliam Green '81
	David E. Pierce '77

WASHBURN UNIVERSITY SCHOOL OF LAW
ALUMNI ASSOCIATION HONORARY LIFE MEMBERS

1963	Hon. Schuyler Jackson	1984	Dr. John Green
	Hon. Walter Huxman	1985	Hon. James MacNish
1964	William Treadway	1986	Professor David S. Dale
	Dr. Karl Menninger	1987	Jean B. Reeves
1965	Hon. David Prager	1988	Hon. Terry Bullock
1966	Professor Edward	1989	Robert E. Edmonds
	Robinson	1990	No award given
1967	Hon. Walter Thiele	1991	Dean James M.
1968	Oscar Stauffer		Concannon
1969	Gerald Barker	1992	Barbara King Wilson
	Dr. John Henderson	1993	Hon. Mary Briscoe
1970	Dean John Howe	1994	Professor Banks
	Hon. Hugh Wedell		McDowell
1971	Christine Johnson	1995	Charles Koch
	Hon. Robert Price	1996	No award given
1972	J. Richards Hunter	1997	Dean James M.
1973	Hon. Arthur Stanley		Concannon
1974	Hon. John Fontron	1998	Louis E. Mosiman
	Professor Robert W.	1999	Professor Bruce Levine
	Fowks	2000	Hon. Wesley E. Brown
	Professor James R.	2001	Martha M. "Marty"
	Ahrens		Snyder
1976	No award given	2002	Associate Dean Allen
1977	Hon. Spencer Gard		Easley
1978	Hon. Alfred G.	2003	Hon. Deanell Reece
	Schroeder		Tacha
1979	Hon. Frank Theis	2004	Professor Myrl L.
1980	Hon. Richard Foth		Duncan
1981	Dean Carl Monk	2005	Dr. Jerry Farley
1982	Congressman Keith	2006	Dean Dennis R.
	Sebelius		Honabach
1983	Hon. Richard D. Rogers	2007	Acting Dean William
			Rich

2008	Professor Nancy Maxwell
2009	Professor Sheila Reynolds
2010	Professor John Christensen
2011	Hon. Kathleen Sebelius
2012	Elizabeth A. Fischer

WASHBURN UNIVERSITY SCHOOL OF LAW ALUMNI ASSOCIATION LIFETIME ACHIEVEMENT AWARD

2005	Hon. Robert L. Gernon '69
2006	Hon. Kay McFarland '64
2007	Gov. Jack Campbell '40
	Hon. John Dawson '06
	Sen. Robert J. Dole '52
	Prof. Richard Donnelly '38
	Hon. Delmas C. Hill '29
	Richard C. Hite '53
	Cong. Clifford R. Hope, Sr. '17
	William H. Kurtis '66
	Amb. Delano E. Lewis '63
	Gerald L. Michaud '51
	Hon. Sherman A. Parks '55
	Marie Russell '25
2008	Elizabeth S. Bowers '48
	Hon. Paul L. Brady '56
	Hon. Harold R. Fatzer '33
	Mark Garlinghouse '39
	Edna Hopkins '18
	Hon. Patrick F. Kelly '53
	Hon. Joseph W. Morris '47
	Charles Scott, Sr. '48
	John Scott '47
	John E. Shamberg '37
	Dean Raymond L. Spring '59
	Hon. Dorothy Davidson Tyner '41
2009	Hon. James Buchele '66
	Philip L. Burton '48
	William A. Buzick '50
	Jack Focht '60
	Gerald L. Goodell '58
	Samuel C. Jackson '54

	Margaret McGurnaghan '27
	Richard D. McIntire '34
	Loren Miller '28
	Prof. Mary M. (Billie) Parr '47
	Cong. Bill Roy, Sr. '70
2010	Donald O. Concannon '52
	Hon. John E. Conway '63
	Hon. Homer Hoch '09
	Hon Raymond Reynolds '29
2011	Samuel E. Cary '10
	Hon. Sam A. Crow '52
	Brian Moline '66
	Martha Stewart Yerkes-Robinson '40
2012	Hon. J. Patrick Brazil '62
	Hon. Dale E. Saffels '49
	Hon. Edward R. Sloan '06
	Hon. William A. Smith '14
	Hon. H. George Templar '27

WASHBURN UNIVERSITY ALUMNI FELLOWS

(By Department)

School of Law

1992	Kent P. Smith '66
1994	David F. Fisher '75
1996	Edward H. Sondker '73
1997	John D. Kemp '74
1998	Thomas J. Corcoran, Jr. '79
1999	Durward "Duke" Dupre '73
2000	Bernard A. Bianchino '74
2001	Paul H. Hulsey '76
2002	Michael C. Manning '77
2003	Donald W. Rupert '76
2004	Sue Jean White '80
2005	Hon. Kay McFarland '64
2006	David A. Fenley '79
2007	Michael J. Manning '69
2008	Richard C. Hite '53
2009	Paul Hoferer '75
2010	Lynn R. Johnson '70
2011	George A. Barton '77

College of Arts and Sciences

1992	Paul T. Maricle '79
1993	Hon. Marla Luckert '80
2001	James C. Slattery '75

School of Applied Studies

2003	Bart A. Chavez '85
2007	Paul J. Morrison '80

School of Business

1994	Thomas F. Puckett '77
2009	John B. Wood '78

School of Nursing

1999	Theresa "Terri" Roberts '82

WASHBURN COLLEGE AND WASHBURN UNIVERSITY HONORARY DOCTOR OF LAWS

1888	Hon. David J. Brewer
1891	Hon. Solon O. Thacher
1902	John C. McClintock
1904	Hon. William A. Johnston
	William H. Rossington
1905	Archibald McCullough
1914	Jacob C. Mohler
1915	Harry Olson
	Washburn President Frank Knight Sanders
1916	Washburn Dean Duncan Lendrum McEachron
1917	Harry B. Wilson
1921	Governor Henry J. Allen
	Edward G. Buckland
1922	Ozora S. Davis
1923	Arthur E. Hertzler
1925	Senator Charles Curtis
	Oscar A. Kropf
	Richard E. Kropf
1926	Robert Stone
1927	Hon. John S. Dawson '06
1928	Sardius Mason Brewster
	Stephen S. Estey
1929	Hon. George H. Whitcomb
1930	Washburn President Parley Paul Womer
1931	Arthur Capper
	Lee Eldas Phillips
1933	Governor Alfred Mossman Landon
	Frank Martin Mohler
1935	Dean Harry K. Allen
	Thomas Allen McNeal
1936	A.A. Godard

1937	Frank A. Quail '29
1939	Ernest H. Lindley
	Herbert George Titt
1940	Governor John E. Erickson
	George Enfield Frazer
	William A. Irwin '34
	Anthony E. Karnes
	Secretary of War and former Governor Harry H. Woodring
1941	Washburn President Phillip C. King
1942	Rees H. Hughes
	Dean W. Mallott
1943	Francis D. Farrell
1951	William Addison Neiswanger
	Congressman Clifford R. Hope '50
1954	Gladden Whetstone Baker
	Hon. Edward Ray Sloan '06
	James Stanley Twyford '06
1955	Bruce W. Trull
1956	Hon. William A. Smith '14
1957	Annie B. Sweet
	Herbert Bernard Loper
	David M. Neiswanger
1958	Ray Hugh Garvey '15
	Donald Read Heath
	Hon. Delmas C. Hill '29
1959	Dale Elbert Sharp
	Alfred Bixby Quinton, Jr.
1960	Norman F. Ramsey
1962	Robert Mason Clark '34
1963	John R. Emens
1965	Paul Joseph Lovewell
	Verner J. Dunton '14
1967	Senator Frank Carlson
	General Howard S. Searle '16
1968	Senator Harry Darby
	President Dwight David Eisenhower

1969	Hon. Earl H. Hatcher '23
	Senator Robert J. Dole '52
	Hon. Byron R. White
1970	Richard James Farrell
1971	Hon. Harold R. Fatzer '33
	Hon. H. George Templar '27
1972	Leon Jaworski
1974	Governor Robert B. Docking
1976	Hon. Tom C. Clark
1977	Hon. Albert B. Fletcher, Jr. '51
	Donald P. Moyers '34
1978	F. Mark Garlinghouse '39
1979	Robert L. Brock
	Edwin R. Linquist '50
1980	William E. Treadway
1981	Hon. Joseph W. Morris '47
	Philip H. Lewis '35
1983	Meyer M. Ueoka '49
1984	John E. Shamberg '37
1985	Senator Robert J. Dole '52 (Doctor of Civil Laws)
1986	Gerald L. Michaud '51
1987	Philip H. Lewis '35 (Doctor of Juridical Studies)
1988	Senator Nancy Landon Kassebaum
1989	Malcolm S. Forbes
1990	Hon. D. Jerome Harman '35
	Hon. Sherman A. Parks '55
1991	Hon. Richard Holmes '53
2000	Delano E. Lewis '63
2001	Mark V. Heitz '77
2002	Gerald L. Goodell '58
2003	John D. Kemp '74
2004	Hon. Paul Brady '56
2006	Hon. Sam A. Crow '52
2007	Michael C. Manning '77
2009	Hon. Kay McFarland '64
2010	Durward (Duke) Dupre '73
2011	Richard C. Hite '53

COMMENCEMENT SPEAKERS

1971	Alfred Conard, AALS President, Professor, University of Michigan
1972	Leon Jaworsky, ABA President
1973	Governor Robert B. Docking
1974	William Pincus, President CLEPR
1975	Justin Stanley, ABA President-Elect
1976	Hon. Tom C. Clark, Justice–Retired, U.S. Supreme Court
1977	Hon. Albert B. Fletcher '51, Chief Judge, U.S. Court of Military Appeals
1978	F. Mark Garlinghouse '39, General Counsel, AT&T
1979	William L. "Bill" Taylor, Director, Center for National Policy Review
1980	Hon. Jean Dubofsky, Justice, Colorado Supreme Court
1981	Joseph W. Morris '47, General Counsel, Shell Oil Company
1982	Hon. Sherman Finesilver, Chief Judge, U.S. District Court of Colorado
1983	David Vernon, AALS President, Professor, University of Iowa
1984	Jim Marquez, '72, General Counsel, U.S. Department of Transportation
1985	Fred Graham, CBS News
1986	Hon. Harry Blackmun, Justice, U.S. Supreme Court
1987	Burt Neuborne, Professor, New York University
1988	Eugene C. Thomas, Past President, ABA
1989	Malcolm Forbes, Publisher, Forbes Magazine
1990	Kerry Kennedy, Founder, Robert F. Kennedy Memorial Center for Human Rights
1991	Sarah Weddington, counsel in Roe v. Wade
1992	Michael C. Manning '77, Partner, Morrison & Hecker
1993	B. Dan Pinick '52, Vice President, Boeing Corporation
1994	John Stumbo '64. President, Bristol House LTD
1995	Ron Wurtz '73, Chief Public Defender. Shawnee County
1996	Kellis E. Parker, Professor, Columbia University
1997	Hon. Christel E. Marquardt '74, Kansas Court of Appeals

1998	Senator Robert J. Dole '52
1999	Delano Lewis '64, President–Retired, National Public Radio
2000	Bill Kurtis '66, President, Kurtis Productions, Inc.
2001	Robert E. Hirshon, ABA President-Elect
2002	Carla J. Stovall, Attorney General of Kansas
2003	John Kemp '74, Partner, Pyles Sutter & Verville PC and former CEO, National Cerebral Palsy Association
2004	Hon. Paul Brady '56, U.S. Administrative Law Judge-Retired
2005	Bill Kurtis '66, President, Kurtis Productions, Inc.
2006	James Slattery '75, Partner, Wiley, Rein & Fielding LLP, and former Congressman
2007	Michael C. Manning '77, Partner, Stinson, Morrison & Hecker
2008	Congressman Dennis W. Moore '70
2009	Hon. Kay McFarland '64, Chief Justice, Kansas Supreme Court–Retired
2010	Durward D. (Duke) Dupre '73, General Counsel-Retired, Southwestern Bell, Inc.
2011	Richard C. Hite '53, Partner, Hite, Fanning & Honeyman L.L.P.

INDEX

women; students, tradition of public
service, Kansas Court of Appeals
Judges
Capper, Arthur, 33, 677
Card, Michael, 492, 493
Carlin, John, 319, 331, 332, 341
   See also governors, Kansas
Carlon, Angela, 666
Carlson, Frank, 130, 143, 678
   See also governors, Kansas
Carlson, John, 139
Carlson, Robin K., 652, 658
Carnegie, Andrew, 1
   See also Carnegie Foundation
Carnegie, Dale, 233
Carnegie Foundation, 53, 74
Carnegie Hall, 154, 156–157, 179–180, 403,
   619
   central air conditioning, 191
   donated courthouse items, 191
   photo, 154, 201, 202
   tornado, 196, 198, 199, 200, 205,
   209–211
      See also 1966 Tornado
   See also law school buildings
Carnegie Library, 1, 108, 153, 155
   photo, 155
Carolan, Bruce, 646
Carpenter, Charles E., 62–66, 76, 641, 647
   photo, 62, 64
   See also Washburn Law School deans
Carpinelli, John, 424, 664
   See also moot court
Carr, Brian K., 667
Carr, Sandra, 668
Carruth Hall, 255
Carter, Jimmy, 625
Carter, Michelle, 665
Carter, Robert, 600
Cary, Samuel E., 26–27, 589, 675
   photo, 590

Samuel Cary Bar Association, 590
   See also students, minority, African
   American
Case and Cane, 187, 233, 236, 272, 303, 382
   mimeographed format, 217
   publishing start, 179
   See also students; Washburn Law
   Digest
Case and Comment, 31
Caton, John E., 651
Cavanaugh, Stephen W., 669
Cecil, Joe, 453
   See also Ahrens Chair in Torts, Sym-
   posium
Celtic Fox, 9, 562
centennial celebration, 562–565
   See also anniversaries; Dole, Robert
   J., centennial celebration keynote
   speaker; Elrod, Linda Henry, centen-
   nial celebration master of ceremo-
   nies; Farley, Jerry; Honabach, Dennis
   R., centennial kickoff reception
   speaker
Chaffee-McClure, Zach, 666
Challener, Deborah J., 645
Chamber of Commerce, 25, 83
Chang, Rex S., 665
Chapman, Edward B., 618
   See also students, tradition of public
   service, Executive Branch
Chavez, Bart A., 676
Chaykin, Arthur, 420, 644
   See also faculty, visiting professors
Chemerinsky, Erwin, 655
Chesbro, Kenneth, 453
   See also Ahrens Chair in Torts, Sym-
   posium
Cheney, Duke, 87
Childs, Michael A., 662
Christensen, Barbara M., 657, 659
Christensen, John E., 322, 425, 636

Hoskinson, Gladys, 575
  See also students, minority, women
Hoss, Jodi M., 652
Hotchkiss, Alex, 179, 180, 581, 669, 670
Hotchkiss, Bruce, 179
Howe, John E., 220, 225, 238, 240, 249,
  250, 312
  30th Anniversary of the Tornado reunion, 515
  1966 tornado destruction, 196, 200,
  202–205, 209
  adding faculty positions, 182–184, 186
  background, 164
  building addition concerns, 258–259
  deanship, 160, 166, 538, 577, 647
  end of open enrollment, 180–181
  fundraising for new building, 210,
  214, 216
  improving Carnegie Hall, 191
  Honorary Life Member, 672
  making changes to the law school,
  168–169, 172–174
  merger between two law schools,
  193–195
  mobile units, 217
  new building dedication, 228–229
  photo, 165, 167
  resignation, 223
  retirement, 230, 280
  salary supplement recipient, 242
  scholarship program, 175–176
  teaching, 243, 584, 642
  Vernon's Kansas Statutes Annotated,
  277
  Washburn Law School Association
  Executive Secretary, 278
  See also faculty, growth; Washburn
  Law School deans
Howe, Marggy, 168, 205, 225
Howells, Geraint, 455
  See also Ahrens Chair in Torts, dis-

tance education
Hoyano, Laura, 455
  See also Ahrens Chair in Torts, dis-
tance education
Hrdlicka, Richard, 671
Huber, Richard, 297, 298, 368, 387
  See also in-house teaching
Hughes, C. Harold, 106
Hughes, Leonard, 603
  See also students, minority, African
American
Hughes, Patrick, 657
Hughes, Rees H., 678
Hughes, Thomas Welburn, 59, 61, 64, 70
  chapel exercises, 56
  deanship, 43, 45–47, 647
  full-time faculty member, 641
  increased credit hour requirements,
  75
  new building talk, 54
  photo, 44, 62
  raising admission requirements, 49
  retirement, 89
  teaching, 58, 59, 62, 63, 88
  See also Washburn Law School deans
Hull, Anne, 660
Hulsey, Paul H., 676
Hummer, Frank, 668
Hungate, Otis, 48
  See also faculty, first lecturers
Hunsaker, William J., 651
Hunter, Anthony T., 666
Hunter, J. Richards, 672
Huntsberger, John W., 22
  See also students, first students
Hurd, E. Bernard, 605
  See also students, minority, African
American
Hurley, Timothy R., 652
Hurlstone-Peggs, Jose, 663
Hurst, Thomas, 138, 653

tives, visitors
Robb, Clair, 598, 621
   See also students, tradition of public
   service, Kansas Supreme Court Jus-
   tices
Roberts, A. Michelle, 664
Roberts, Robert L., 169, 651, 653
Roberts, Theresa (Terri), 676
Robertson, George, 662
Robins, Ken, 663
Robinson Courtroom, 227, 262
   30th anniversary of *Brown v. Board of*
   Education panel discussion, 304
   Ahrens Chair in Tort Law celebra-
   tion, 371
   Bianchino Technology Center, 545
   Bob Dole's Disabilities and the Law
   lecture, 544
   Cooperation Agreement signing, 450
   legal proceedings, 266
   National Moot Court Competition
   host, 228
   remodeling, 509–512
      See also Gas Service Com-
      pany; Kansas Commission of
      Civil Rights; Kansas Corporation
      Commission; National Labor
      Relations Board; Senate Judiciary
      Subcommittee
   symposium on desegregation, 602
   United States Court of Appeals for
   the Tenth Circuit panel, 264, 403
   See also new building
Robinson, Edward, 222, 226, 229, 352
   Emeritus, 240
   full-time faculty member, 188, 642
   Honorary Life Member, 672
   Order of Barristers, 661
   processional march composer, 227,
   533
   "Tornado Twister" party, 219

   See also faculty, new hires
Robinson, Mildred W., 655
Robinson, Reginald, 646, 649
Robrhan, Reese, 610
   See also students, minority, disabled
Robson, Ruthann, 522
Rock, Darci, 583
   See also students, minority, women
Rock, Richard, 338, 431
Roe v. Wade, 374
   See also Blackmun, Harry A.
Rogers, Elizabeth, 664
Rogers, Kim, 665
Rogers, Richard, 275–276, 342, 663, 672
Rohlf, Gage A., 658, 660
Romig, Thomas J., 639, 646, 647
   photo, 640
   See also Washburn Law School deans
Rooney, Ed, 33, 134, 572
Roosevelt, Franklin D., 129
Rose, Lonnie, 362
Rosen, Eric, 622
   See also students, tradition of public
   service, Kansas Supreme Court Jus-
   tices
Rosen, Jeffery, 655
Rosen, John, 25
   See also faculty, first lecturers
Rossi, Thomas A., 644
Rossington, William H., 6–7, 12, 677
   See also faculty, first lecturers
Roth, Jim, 199, 291, 671
Roth, Julie, 587
Roth, Kent, 291
Roth, Randall, 321
   achievements, 291
   Continuing Legal Education (CLE)
   program, 362
   faculty scholarship, 300
   full-time faculty member, 643
   Professor of the Year, 648